"This is a large, complex, strongly argued book, which I found insightful and challenging. It is thorough and powerful and deserves a wide readership."
– Francis Elliott, in the *Canberra Times*

"Original ⸺ghout, Linden w anti-Semi ith the presence is clear that the has enormous sympathy for the Jewish people and their history."
– Robert C. Grogin, in *Canadian Journal of History*

"Lindemann's comparative study of the rise of modern antisemitism in Europe and the United States in the period 1870 to 1939 is impressive in terms of both breadth and depth of coverage. He presents a nuanced survey of the sheer variety and impact of antisemitism, which neither seeks to explain everything in terms of monocausal factors, nor adopts a teleological approach which views nineteenth century antisemitism wholly in terms of Auschwitz."
– Tim Cole, in *Economic History Review*

"Most open-minded readers . . . will find *Esau's Tears* a well-balanced and very readable history of antisemitism prior to the Holocaust."
– Bruce F. Pauley, in *Journal of Modern History*

"The two unorthodox but original and often brilliant works by Albert S. Lindemann [*The Jew Accused* and *Esau's Tears*] . . . received the full treatment of hysterical abuse in *Commentary* and elsewhere."
– William Rubinstein, in *History Today*

"*Esau's Tears* merits an important place in any historical assessment of modern antisemitism, while the author deserves a medal for bravery in writing the book."
– William Rubinstein, in *History*, the journal of the British History Association

Esau's Tears explores the remarkable and revealing variety of modern anti-Semitism, from its emergence in the 1870s in a racial–political form to the eve of the Nazi takeover, in the major countries of Europe and in the United States. Previous histories have generally been more concerned with description than analysis, and most of the interpretations in those histories have been lacking in balance. The evidence presented in this book suggests that anti-Semitism in these years was more ambiguous than usually presented, less pervasive and central to the lives of both Jews and non-Jews, and by no means clearly pointed to a rising hatred of Jews everywhere, even less to the likelihood of mass murder. Similarly, Jew-hatred was not as mysterious or incomprehensible as often presented; its strength in some countries and weakness in others may be related to the fluctuating and sometimes quite different perceptions in those countries of the meaning of the rise of the Jews in the late nineteenth and early twentieth centuries.

Esau's Tears

Esau's Tears

Modern Anti-Semitism and the Rise of the Jews

ALBERT S. LINDEMANN
University of California, Santa Barbara

CAMBRIDGE
UNIVERSITY PRESS

PUBLISHED BY THE PRESS SYNDICATE OF THE UNIVERSITY OF CAMBRIDGE
The Pitt Building, Trumpington Street, Cambridge CB2 1RP, United Kingdom

CAMBRIDGE UNIVERSITY PRESS
The Edinburgh Building, Cambridge CB2 2RU, UK   http://www.cup.cam.ac.uk
40 West 20th Street, New York, NY 10011-4211, USA   http://www.cup.org
10 Stamford Road, Oakleigh, Melbourne 3166, Australia
Ruiz de Alarcón 13, 28014 Madrid, Spain

First published 1997
First paperback edition 2000

Printed in the United States of America

Typeset in ITC New Baskerville

Library of Congress Cataloging-in-Publication Data

Lindemann, Albert S.
     Esau's tears : modern anti-semitism and the rise of the Jews.
1870–1933 / Albert S. Lindemann.
          p.   cm.
     Includes bibliographical references.
     1. Antisemitism – History.   2. Jews – History – 1789–1945.
     3. Europe – Intellectual life – 19th century.   4. Europe – Intellectual
life – 20th century.   I. Title.
     DS145.L594   1997
909'.04924 – dc21   97-5882
                                                                                   CIP
                                                                                   r97

*A catalog record for this book is available from
the British Library.*

ISBN 0 521 59369 7 hardback
ISBN 0 521 79538 9 paperback

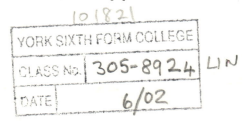

Contents

Preface	*ix*
Acknowledgments	*xxiii*

PART ONE: THE LONG-RANGE BACKGROUND   **1**

Chapter 1. Anti-Semitism before the Modern Period:
Overview and Definition   *3*

Esau's Tears: The Deepest Roots of Anti-Semitism	3
The Rise of the Jews	20
The Origins, Evolution, and Ambiguities of the Term Anti-Semitism	23
"Classical Anti-Semitism"	26
Christian Anti-Semitism	29
The Church Triumphant; John Chrysostom	33
The Charge of Deicide; Jewish Survival	35

Chapter 2. Modern Times (1700 to the 1870s)   *40*

The Enlightenment	40
The French Revolution and the Jews	44
Napoleon and the Assembly of Jewish Notables	48
Contrasts between East and West	50
Trends within Judaism	53
Secularism and Divided Fidelities	55
The Liberal Years of Midcentury	56
Backward Russia and the Ostjuden	57
The Pale of Settlement	61
Russia's "Liberal" Experiment	64
Revolutionary Agitation and Tsarist Reaction	67
The Concept of Race	70
Blood Imagery	74
Racism and Anti-Semitism	78
The Evolution of the Vocabulary of Race	84

Racist Ideas among Jews   90
The Ambiguities of Non-Jewish Racism   92

PART TWO: THE APPEARANCE
OF MODERN ANTI-SEMITISM (1870–1890)   97

Chapter 3. Germans and Jews (1870–1890)   *103*

The German Problem; the Sonderweg   104
German Liberalism and the New German State   107
Junker Hegemony and the Jews   110
The Rise of the Jews in Germany   114
The Mittlestand and Modernism in Germany   116
The "Founding Years" and the Crash of 1873   118
The Press Campaign against the Jews   120
The Kulturkampf and the Jews   122
Bismarck's Move to the Right   124

*Chapter 4. Anti-Semitic Ideology and Movement
in Germany (1879 to the 1890s)*   *126*

Anti-Semitic Ideology: Wilhelm Marr   127
Anti-Semitic Ideology: Heinrich von Treitschke   131
Treitschke and Graetz   139
Anti-Semitic Ideology: Adolf Stoecker   142
Anti-Semitic Movement and Countermovement   147
Anti-Semitic Movement: The Peasants and Otto Böckel   152
Precursors to Nazism?   155

Chapter 5. Socialists, Jews, and Anti-Semites   *158*

Socialist Movement and Ideology   158
The Enlightened Tradition of Socialism   160
Marxian Socialism and the Jews   162
French Socialism and the Jews   166
Jewish Attitudes to Socialism   168
Social–Democratic Attitudes to Jews   171
Socialist Interpretations of Anti-Semitism   174
Jewish Socialists and Assimilation   180

Chapter 6. Austria–Hungary: Radical Radicalism and Schlamperei   *182*

The Polyglot Empire   182
Austria-Hungary: Between Germany and Russia   185
Liberalism and the Rise of the Jews   187
German Nationalism and Ethnic Insecurity   190
The Jewish Press and the Crash of 1873   193
Anti-Semitic Ideology   194
Catholic Antimodernism and Anti-Semitism   197

Anti-Semitism and Humanitarian Idealism: von Schönerer 200

The Disintegration of Democratic Radicalism 202

Chapter 7. France: Liberty, Equality, and Fraternity **206**

The Evolution of French Jewry in the Nineteenth Century 206

The Third Republic and the Jews 211

The Rise of the Jews and the Dilemmas of Modernism 212

The Political Crises and Scandals of the 1880s 213

Nascent Political Anti-Semitism: The Boulangists 215

The Assumptionists 219

Anti-Semitic Ideology and Movement: Toussenel, Barrès, Drumont 221

A Gathering Storm of Anti-Semitism? 227

The Dreyfus Affair 230

A Dreyfusian Revolution? 234

Chapter 8. A Sweet Exile? **238**

Jews in Nineteenth-Century Great Britain 239

Jews in America: The Issue of Exceptionalism 251

Racism and Social Conflict in the United States 261

The Jews in Hungary 263

PART THREE: THE BELLE EPOQUE (1890–1914) **273**

Chapter 9: The Failures: Russia and Romania **279**

Worsening Jewish–Gentile Relations in Russia 279

The Paradoxes of Modernization in Russia; the Kushinev Pogrom 290

Modern Anti-Semitism in Russia 300

Nicholas II and the Power of International Jewry 301

The Beilis Affair 305

Romanian Anti-Semitism: "The Worst in Europe?" 306

Chapter 10. The Ambiguities of "Failure" in the Belle Epoque:
Germany and Austria **319**

The Appearance of Zionism 320

Anti-Semitism and German Traditions 330

The "Dormant Period" of Anti-Semitism in Germany 334

Anti-Semitic Agitation in Austria: Karl Lueger 337

The "Unpolitical" Germans: Langbehn, Lagarde, Chamberlain 347

Chapter 11. The Ambiguous Successes:
Great Britain and the United States **355**

Jews in Great Britain in the Edwardian Period 355

The United States: Still "Exceptional"? 371

The Leo Frank Affair 381

PART FOUR: A DECADE OF WAR AND REVOLUTION
(1914–1924)   387

Chapter 12. World War I   *391*

The Mood of August 1914   391
The Expansion of Germany into Russia   395
The Beginning of Disillusionment in the West   398
The Peace Settlement   406
The Balfour Declaration and the Palestinian Mandate   413

Chapter 13. Jews and Revolution (1917–1934)   *423*

The Jew as Revolutionary: Fantasy and Reality   424
Russian Jews in Revolution: From March to November   436
The Red Terror – A Jewish Terror?   440
Stalin and Trotsky   448

PART FIVE: THE FASCIST ERA:
EUROPE BETWEEN THE WARS   457

Chapter 14. Fascism and Anti-Semitism   *461*

Defining Fascism   462
The Origins of Fascism: Mussolini, from Socialist Revolutionary to Il Duce   464
The Jews of Italy   471
The Italian Model of Fascism   477
The Establishment of the Weimar Republic   481
Hitler's Early Career; the Genesis of His Anti-Semitism   483
Hitler and the Nazi Party   498

Epilogue and Conclusions   *505*
Index   *547*

Preface

The Jewish problem is one of the greatest problems
in the world, and no man, be he writer, politician or
diplomatist, can be considered mature until he has
striven to face it squarely on its merits. (Henry Wickham Steed)

The Messiah will not come until the tears of Esau
have been exhausted. [from the *Zohar,* a central
work of the mystical *Kabbalah*]

The number of books devoted to the murder of Europe's Jews during
World War II has expanded enormously in recent years, as have articles
devoted to that topic in the popular and scholarly press. Novels, movies, plays,
and television docudramas dealing with the Holocaust have also attracted
unprecedented audiences and widespread discussion. Trying to understand
why Jews have been so hated has obviously been a central issue in this outpouring, and many books, movies, and television programs have explored the
nature and history of anti-Semitism – perhaps too many, especially since a large
proportion of these explorations have been characterized by disappointing
intellectual standards and doubtful conclusions. Many are little more than potted, encyclopedia-style narratives, whereas others, more sophisticated in some
regards, still lack penetration in striking ways. A large number might best be
described as cries of pain or expressions of indignation rather than efforts to
understand.

An obvious and important example, from a somewhat earlier period but
still widely read and influential, is Lucy Dawidowicz's *The War Against the Jews,*[1]
which, whatever its overall merits, must be faulted for the dubious tenor and
simplistic nature of its background chapters: As an impassioned recitation of

---

[1] Lucy S. Dawidowicz, *The War Against the Jews, 1933–1945* (New York, 1975; 10th anniversary ed.,
1986, with new introduction).

the evils of anti-Semitism before the Nazi period, those chapters may be considered effective, but as scholarship, where balance and insight are the ideals, they fall short. Dawidowicz's curtness and disdainful tone in dealing with the work of other historians – revealing an imperfect grasp of some of the issues, especially notable in her Special New Introduction to the Tenth Edition – is further cause for concern, given the very large audience she has reached and the esteem her book continues to enjoy, at least with the general public and outside the historical profession.[2] A recent and even more impassioned work, also widely read and acclaimed outside the historical profession, Daniel J. Goldhagen's *Hitler's Willing Executioners* (New York, 1996), is far more questionable and simplistic; he typically ignores, or is ignorant of, evidence that contradicts his by no means original reading of German history (that "eliminationist" anti-Semitism was embraced by most Germans and was the fundamental cause of the Holocaust, against which other explanations have little significance). Goldhagen's work might be described as a case for the prosecution, but a major problem is that few serious historians would want to present a case for the defense, with all that implies about one-sided marshaling of evidence; history should not to be written in the same way that cases are presented to a jury.

Scholarly works dealing with the history of anti-Semitism as such, not simply as introductions to the Holocaust, have also appeared recently in large numbers. Obviously, volumes of serious history can never aspire to the audiences drawn to more popular media, but some of those that have reached a wide audience, for example, Robert Wistrich's *Antisemitism: The Longest Hatred*,[3] have suffered from defects similar to those in Dawidowicz's work, prominent among them a tendency to a colorful and indignant narrative, accompanied by weak, sometimes tendentious analysis. In Wistrich's case part of the problem is ostensibly that *The Longest Hatred* was first conceived as the background narrative to a television series – almost always fatal to nuance and complexity. He has published a number of other works of distinctly higher scholarly and interpretive standards. Dawidowicz, too, has accomplishments to her credit that I would be the last to denigrate, especially when they deal with the Jews rather than the enemies of the Jews. Nonetheless both of these widely read works are symptomatic of important problems, ones that may be less promi-

---

[2] The overall and recently much enhanced sophistication of the field of Holocaust studies is not the issue here; see Michael Marrus, "'Good History' and Teaching the Holocaust," *Perspectives: American Historical Association Newsletter*, vol. 31, no. 5, May/June 1993, 1–12. His own *The Holocaust in History* (Toronto, Canada, 1987) is a model of scholarship, and even such efforts at reaching a popular audience as Ronnie S. Landau's *The Nazi Holocaust* (Chicago, 1992) strike a distinctly different tone – more balanced, thoughtful, and less polemical – than Dawidowicz's book.

[3] Robert S. Wistrich, *Antisemitism: The Longest Hatred* (New York, 1991).

nent now than when Dawidowicz's work first appeared but that nonetheless remain – the enthusiastic popular reception of Goldhagen's work suggests that they may even be reemerging.[4]

A large yet delicate issue is at stake, in that efforts to assess Jew-hatred carefully, as distinguished from impassioned descriptions and denunciations of it, are sometimes dismissed as dubious, even dangerous: Does such careful attention imply a degree of "sympathetic understanding" for anti-Semites, tending toward excuses rather than condemnations of them? As Robert Jay Lifton, who published a work on Nazi doctors, has commented, "Psychological study in particular [runs . . .] the risk of replacing condemnation with 'insights,'"[5] at least, so he was warned by friends as he began his study.

The issue comes down in part to the purpose history is believed to serve. For many history is supposed to commemorate a glorious past, to honor their ancestors, or to rectify a previously unjust portrayal of those ancestors. On the Fourth of July, orators are not likely to dwell upon the defects of the Founding Fathers, and the goals of Black History Month are to honor famous or previously unrecognized African–Americans; balance and penetration are not the main concerns, except in the sense that polemical corrections of earlier bigoted accounts point to a more accurate and equitable kind of history. Much writing on the Holocaust, and on anti-Semitism, is characterized by a kindred tone and similar goals, prominent among them to denounce anti-Semites and to assure that the sufferings of past generations not be forgotten – or that the lessons of the past not be lost.

Most people recognize that one group's vision of "what actually happened" in the past is not the same as another's. One group's unassailable facts are another's slippery interpretations; one group's official narrative is another's erroneous rendition. Veterans of the front who claim a special understanding of war – beyond what scholars can achieve – must be listened to respectfully, as must the accounts of Holocaust survivors. Jews who have experienced anti-Semitism have an understanding of it that must be taken seriously by those who have not experienced it personally. But in none of these cases does direct experience translate into a monopoly on truth. Indeed, such experience sometimes is an obstacle to clear or fruitful thinking. Sacrosanct official narratives can lead and often have led to new tragedies for the groups that stubbornly insist that their vision of the truth remain untouchable.

There are certainly few topics more obdurate and tangled than the history

---

[4] Again, I must emphasize that there are a few highly praiseworthy studies of modern anti-Semitism. Subsequent footnotes will amply illustrate my debt to them. At the most general level, Richard S. Levy's *Antisemitism in the Modern World: An Anthology of Texts* (Lexington, Mass., 1991) deserves mention not only for making available in English many previously unavailable texts but also for its unusually penetrating interpretive introduction.

[5] Cf. Robert Jay Lifton, *The Nazi Doctors* (New York, 1986), xi.

of anti-Semitism, few in which emotions and rationality seem to push so powerfully in opposite directions, few where insiders' experience and outsiders' ratiocination so agonizingly clash. Gavin Langmuir, in an erudite meditation on the nature and history of anti-Semitism as it emerged out of the Middle Ages, has remarked that "So long as memories of the 'Final Solution' remain vivid, the use of that special term of dark origin implies that there is something unusually and uniquely evil about any serious hostility toward all Jews."[6] Jews have survived over the centuries in part by a tenacious sense of the justifying themes of their history and their separate identity; any questioning of those themes is likely to encounter an angry, indignant rejection. At the same time, negative perceptions of Jews are deeply imbedded in the culture of non-Jews, and for many of them that separate identity is often puzzling if not offensive. For either group, what has been termed the noble dream of historical objectivity may seem endlessly elusive.

The title of this volume, the many-sided implications of which will be more amply explored in the next chapter, hints at just such questioning, particularly in terms of how the relations of Jews and non-Jews are to be understood in history – and how realistic it is to hope that suspicion and hatred of Jews may be entirely banished if a separate Jewish identity is cultivated. A number of recently influential theoreticians have questioned the possibility of any historian's escaping the blinders of ethnicity, class, or gender. The ways that the older ideal of objectivity has been recently put into question have had a wide-ranging effect upon the way that history is currently written. This new variety of history, with its often crabbed and inelegant jargon (discourse, deconstruction, decentering), has reemphasized the familiar truth already alluded to, that objectivity, which as a matter of liberal faith should be within the grasp of all educated observers, easily escapes even the most sophisticated and carefully trained. Indeed, in the case of such observers the problem is in some regards greater because of their unjustified claims to being free of bias.

While I accept many of the points made by those who question whether it is possible to produce historical accounts untainted by ethnicity, class, gender, or many other blinding factors, I believe that there is still some point to writing a book like this – beyond simply offering one more opinion, as a kind of game. I retain an old-fashioned hope, in other words, that historical accounts can be so composed that differing groups will recognize them as at least partly valid and, more important, as contributing to a gradual process of mutual understanding, however laborious and disappointing in the short run. It is no doubt sometimes difficult to identify areas in which legitimate and productive debate may occur (as in exploring how much an especially virulent form of anti-Semitism led to mass murder in Germany), as distinguished from debate that is unproductive, even morally offensive (as in whether or not there was a mass

---

[6] Gavin Langmuir, *Toward a Definition of Antisemitism* (Berkeley, Calif., 1990), 314.

murder of Jews during World War II). Such issues arise in other areas, as for example, in the "creationist" challenge to the theory of evolution. However difficult, such choices must be made.

Several years ago, in a study of three famous anti-Semitic affairs in the generation before World War I, I set forth a number of theories about the nature of anti-Semitism.[7] These were in no strict sense original; most built upon monographs and theoretical perspectives developed by a number of scholars, although I tried to synthesize materials from diverse sources and present them in a fashion that would reach a larger audience than works of scholarship usually do. In the next several years, in a number of articles and public lectures, I offered a range of related interpretations. The positive reception of those efforts, both in the scholarly world and among a more general educated audience, including students in the courses I have taught at the University of California at Santa Barbara, has encouraged me to expand upon them, although a few of the following chapters necessarily overlap chapters of that book.

My efforts have also met with criticism, which I hope I will be able to address productively here, too. I face that task with some optimism since most of that criticism has been constructive and useful to me. My main concern is to offer a more penetrating and sophisticated analysis of the emergence of anti-Semitism in modern times. I avoid the presumptuous term "objective analysis," for I do not claim to be impartial and uniquely judicious in areas in which others have failed to be, but I do hope that readers will recognize in these pages a different tone – and a more productive one – than is to be found in many if not most previous studies.

The importance of Jew-hatred in the last hundred years is undeniable, the repercussions appalling. That I have devoted many years of study to anti-Semitism underlines how important I think it has been and is. Still, assertions about the significance of Jew-hatred in modern history have sometimes been exaggerated or crudely simplified, in ways that finally hinder rather than enhance our efforts to understand it. Similarly, the tendency to dismiss anti-Semitism as a bizarre hallucination, a fantasy of diseased minds, is undoubtedly justified in some instances but has also often been overdone and has thus hindered understanding, for Jews have been disliked for many reasons by a very wide variety of normal people, many of whom were neither emotionally unstable nor intellectually unsophisticated, and a few of whom were men and women of great ability (Wagner, Barrès, or T. S. Eliot, for example). It is far too easy, indeed, too reassuring, to describe anti-Semites as mentally deranged or morally flawed in all regards. The extent to which anti-Semitism was "normal" requires, in my opinion, a more serious and open-minded investigation, whether by scholars or the lay public.

---

[7] Albert S. Lindemann, *The Jew Accused: Three Anti-Semitic Affairs, Dreyfus, Beilis, Frank, 1894–1915* (New York, 1991, ppr. 1993).

The rapidly gathering interest in the Holocaust that has characterized the 1980s and 1990s, an interest that certainly must be considered positive in comparison to the relative silence about it in the first decades after World War II, has not always had a healthy influence on historical understanding in a broader and more rigorous sense. In particular the temptation to see all of European history as somehow building inexorably toward that terrifying climax has produced some oddly skewed visions of the past. Carelessly expressed and poorly thought-through claims that the Holocaust, and by extension anti-Semitism, are utterly beyond understanding have further muddied the waters.

Even in dealing with the history of the United States, where it is widely recognized by scholars and the general public that hostility to Jews has been less significant than in Europe, the legitimate concern to point out how Jew-hatred has been ignored or downplayed by some historians has led to overstatements, to elaborate and detailed attention to anti-Semitic figures with few followers, or to events with relatively little significance.[8] There has been, similarly, a tendency to evaluate pre-twentieth-century realities with late twentieth-century standards – indeed, to hold up utopian visions of perfect toleration and mutual respect against which all flesh-and-blood human beings, in whatever historical period, are easily shown to have failed. How we interpret history is always powerfully influenced by the concerns and values of our own age, but it is finally misleading and unjust to single out and indignantly describe, for example, the racism of nineteenth-century Germans ("proto-Nazis") without recognizing how much beliefs in ethnic or racial determinism were the norm in most countries and were to be found among oppressed minorities, Jews included, as much as oppressive majorities – were, in short, part of a shared intellectual world, a *Zeitgeist* – but did not lead to mass murder in every country.

Similarly, expressing irritation with Jews, as a number of prominent Germans did – and so did prominent figures, including Jews themselves, in nearly every country – is one thing; calling for their systematic murder is quite another. In many accounts (Goldhagen's is the latest in a long series) such distinctions are blurred; some writers go so far as to condemn the distinctions as morally dubious, thus making any irritation with Jews or criticism of them "anti-Semitic," a conclusion that takes on extraordinary dimensions when linked to such assertions as "all anti-Semitism is essentially the same" or "a little bit of anti-Semitism is as dangerous as a little bit of cancer." In some studies it is argued that expressions of irritation or distaste, by contributing to the general temper of hostility to Jews, finally made mass murder possible and therefore must carry a major responsibility for it.

---

[8] The most recent and scholarly of these, offering many qualifications, but still insisting, as is implicit in the title, on the point that anti-Semitism in America was stronger than previously realized is Frederick Cople Jaher, *A Scapegoat in the Wilderness: The Origins and Rise of Anti-Semitism in America* (Cambridge, Mass., 1994). His introduction discusses some of the other, less cautious works of the genre.

I cannot accept such reasoning, which seems to me facile, especially insofar as it implies that Jews, unlike other human groups, cannot provoke legitimate irritation or that anyone expressing irritation about Jews, or criticism of them as a group, inexorably enters the moral realm of the Nazis. I most emphatically do recognize, on the other hand, that hatred of Jews was more dangerous in some countries than in others; the German case undoubtedly is one that requires special attention. And irritation with Jews, because of its potential to connect with myths of unusually malignant potential, may be appropriately considered more dangerous than many other kinds of irritation. Similarly, the status of Jews as a minority, often a very small minority, in all countries of Europe and America, has tended to make their situation especially perilous.

This volume offers a considerably broader canvas than my previous book, both in years and in nations covered. In examining some ten different countries I have tried to demonstrate the benefits of comparative history, since anti-Semitism has appeared in many different environments and has differed in striking and revealing ways. I made this point for a more limited number of countries and a briefer span of time (primarily France, Russia, and the United States in the generation before 1914) in *The Jew Accused;* my hope is that the comparative perspectives I present here for a larger number of nations and broader period, with Germany as a central concern, will lead to a deeper and more nuanced understanding of anti-Semitism in general. Again, I must emphasize my conviction that hatred of Jews is best understood in terms of a range of actual human examples in history, not some absolute, never-attained ideal, and that theories about the nature of Jew-hatred must be painstakingly checked in the historical record, rather than letting one country or a brief period serve as definitive evidence.

In this work, I try, to a more extensive degree than in my previous book, to evaluate how much "fantastic" images of Jews, especially those derived from Christian doctrine but also from racist and other political ideologies, explain anti-Semitism, as distinguished from factors that have to do with the kinds of normal frictions and tensions that nearly all groups experience when encountering one another. In a related way, this volume tries to analyze whether it is appropriate to consider anti-Semitism as somehow unique (an exceedingly slippery concept). Has hatred of Jews differed in some essential way from hatred of other groups? Most groups, after all, have experienced hatred for both fantastic and "real" reasons. And most hatred may be considered in some sense unlike other varieties of it. I find strained, unpersuasive, and finally counterproductive the arguments that hostility to Jews lacks revealing parallels. I am persuaded, to the contrary, that hatred of Jews helps us to understand other hatreds, and those hatreds help us to understand anti-Semitism.

Negative fantasies about Jews, now and in the past several thousand years, unquestionably connect with images generated from the nether realms of religion, although the nature of that connection and the meaning of "religion" in this context are anything but clear, especially if the term refers to Christian religion, since hostility to Jews predates Christianity and is not and never has been limited to Christians. Similarly, many of the recurring themes of that hostility (for example, the Jews' alleged secret power, their arrogance and sense of superiority to others, and their repellent customs and rituals) also appeared before the advent of Christianity and have been picked up, into modern times, by those who have rejected Christianity or who were never Christians (the Japanese, for example, or much of the Muslim world, and, indeed, increasingly large numbers of the inhabitants of the world outside of Europe and the United States). Many of those themes, at any rate, hardly qualify as unambiguously religious, as the term is commonly understood; they might just as well be termed secular. The dividing line between what is religious and what is secular is anything but clear, and that blurred division has contributed to much confusion and muddled thinking. Most observers would not consider Shakespeare's *Merchant of Venice* or Dickens's *Oliver Twist* to be religious works, yet the image of the Jew in them has been undoubtedly influential, as indeed is the case for the novels and other writings of Benjamin Disraeli. Religion and secular culture blend in ways that are difficult if not impossible to untangle.

Since religious imagery is so many-sided and elusive, and since both positive and negative images of Jews emerge from Christian religion and the culture associated with it, tracing the influence of religion in given situations has been done mostly by those who in some sense knew what they were going to prove before they started their research. Without that emotional, preexisting "knowledge," the case for the role of Christianity lacks cogency and precision. One can unquestionably pinpoint Christian tendencies toward demonizing Jews, but such tendencies are balanced by others. The evidence is hardly persuasive that within Christian belief is contained a strongly determined predisposition, drawing in all Christians, to violent hatred of Jews. In modern times Christian peoples have differed enormously in their reactions to Jews, from mild philo-Semitism to murderous loathing. This range of sentiment cannot be convincingly connected to various traits within varieties of Christianity, whether Catholic, Protestant, or Greek Orthodox, sincere or lax, popular or elite. Catholic Poland tended toward hostility, Catholic Italy toward tolerance; Protestant Germany toward hostility, Protestant Holland toward tolerance; the relatively sincere Christians of the United States toward tolerance, the relatively insincere Christians in France toward intolerance.

These points will be amply explored in the main text; the point I wish to emphasize here is that religion, put forth in a large number of studies as the ultimate or fundamental source of anti-Semitism, is too elastic and ambiguous a category to offer much more than conjectural, ahistorical, and woolly explanations, in which the preconceptions and emotional agendas of the authors play a decisive role. Each of these countries was religious, but their reactions to Jews were so different that one obviously needs to look to other factors than religion in explaining those reactions. Moreover, nonreligious explanations for Jew-hatred are frequently more plausible and certainly more measurable. It is my contention that those other explanations are distinctly more satisfactory than religion, although I am also persuaded that some of them, for example, racial stereotyping, have also not exercised the powerful determinism often attributed to them.

That said, I hasten to note that the next chapter begins with an exploration of the undeniable power of mythic imagery based in religion, and the next two chapters explore the related modern "myths" of race and nation. My position, then, is hardly that such imagery has no or even little power. Rather, I am objecting to the incautious and tendentious use of such imagery as an explanatory device. At any rate, this book is not primarily about mythic imagery; the realms of theology, literature, and the fine arts are not its main concerns. I do not ignore or denigrate them, but I am more inclined to believe that truth is in the details, as it were, with the more measurable particulars of historical development. Politics, the economy, social change, and the way with which they blend and alter mythic imagery will be my main concerns.

My position is that whatever the power of myth, not all hostility to Jews, individually or collectively, has been based on fantastic or chimerical visions of them, or on projections unrelated to any palpable reality. As human beings, Jews have been as capable as any other group of provoking hostility in the everyday secular world. This remark, which some will consider a platitude, is nonetheless forcefully, even indignantly, rejected by others. One often encounters pronouncements such as the following: "We all know that anti-Semitism really has nothing to do with Jews; it can flourish even in places where no Jews live."[9] Or, "the psychic needs of Christians – and not the actual character of Jewish life – give anti-Semitism its power and appeal."[10] "Jew-hatred is one-sided . . . [and] functions independent of its object."[11] "Anti-Semitism is oblivious to Jewish conduct; it is independent of the very presence of Jews."[12]

However, that purported unanimous agreement – what "we all know" – does not exist, and never has. Indeed, the opposite position, that Jewish conduct is the main cause for hatred of Jews, has been described by Edward Alexander [disapprovingly] as "an argument of wide and enduring popularity,"[13] which it certainly is. It was even more popular in the nineteenth century

[9] Susannah Heschel, "Anti-Semites against Anti-Semitism," *Tikkun*, Nov./Dec. 1993, 52.

[10] Todd Endelman, *The Jews of Georgian England, 1714–1830* (Philadelphia, 1979), 95.

[11] Ruth Wisse, "The Twentieth Century's Most Successful Ideology," *Commentary*, vol. 91, no. 2, Feb. 1991, 33.

[12] "A Futile Fight" [editorial in] *The Jerusalem Post*, week ending Sept. 15, 1990, 24.

[13] Edward Alexander, *The Holocaust and the War of Ideas* (New Brunswick, N.J., 1994), 50.

when it was almost universally assumed, by both Jews and non-Jews, that Jewish behavior was the all-too-obvious cause of the appearance of modern anti-Semitism. To look only at the opinions of Jews themselves, many Zionists have considered Jews in the Diaspora ("in Exile") to be "objectively detestable"; their obnoxious characters, deformed by their powerless and precarious existence among Gentiles, are the reason they have been hated – indeed the reason they have so often hated other Jews and even themselves. As the following chapters will amply illustrate, it became a very widely accepted axiom of the nineteenth century, robustly enduring into the twentieth, that if Jews would "reform," abandon their offensive habits, then anti-Semitism would vanish. The Zionist position was unique mostly in its insistence that anti-Semitism would not go away, although again "unique" may be a misleading term, since right-wing traditionalists, both in the Jewish and the Christian camps, also believed Jewish reform to be either impossible or undesirable.

I hasten to observe that I do not accept these positions, Zionist or otherwise, although I will try to show how the partial truth in them is cause for reflection. Undoubtedly, the intransigence, the overkill of the previously quoted pronouncements about Jews' having absolutely nothing to do with the hatred directed at them derives in part from the understandable exasperation of Jews who believe they are being unjustly blamed, who cite their own experience that, time and again, Jewish conduct has no effect on anti-Semitic conviction. The naiveté of nineteenth-century reformers – and the terrible price Jews eventually paid for the illusions they harbored about the eventual disappearance of anti-Semitism in Europe – is another reason that "blaming the Jews" is so emotionally and categorically rejected by many today. And yet another reason is their belief that Jews, even in Israel, are a people uniquely afflicted by a drive to destructive self-criticism.[14] (The charge that Jews are uniquely inclined to destructive criticism of non-Jews rather than of Jews themselves is, however, and rather contradictorily, dismissed as an anti-Semitic fantasy.)

The following chapters will develop my own understanding of the peculiar and elusive interplay of fantasy and reality in anti-Semitism as well as my own firm rejection of the notion that exile has rendered Jews objectively detestable and invariably hated by any people among whom they live. At any rate, there is an important part of the truth in the assertion that autonomous psychic processes in non-Jews, ones that exaggerate reality or ignore it entirely, play a key role in anti-Semitism, as indeed they do in most hatreds, including those of Jews for non-Jews. Quite aside from strictly religious considerations, the position of Jews as long-term outsiders and dissidents in most societies has made them suspect and vulnerable in a myriad of ways, no matter what the actions or beliefs of individual Jews. But pushed very far, the position that

---

[14] Alexander, *Holocaust*, esp. 95–106.

hatred of Jews arises without their presence or activity approaches absurdity – anti-Semitism among the Jivaros, the Hottentots, or the Chumash?

Obviously we cannot expect to find Jew-hatred among peoples who historically have had absolutely no contact with Jews or Judaism, who have no idea who Jews are or what they represent. Similarly, if it is the psychic needs of Christians that give anti-Semitism its power and appeal, it would appear logical to expect the worst kind of anti-Semitic hatred among the most sincere Christians, but much evidence indicates that in modern times it was very often insincere, partial, or lapsed Christians, and even more those who mocked the ideals of Christianity, who manifested particularly virulent and violent forms of Jew-hatred. Similarly, can one seriously argue that Jew-hatred among Palestinians has *nothing* to do with the actions or attitudes of real Jews, whether Israelis or their Jewish supporters in the rest of the world, and is *entirely* one-sided, a Palestinian fantasy operating independent of its object? Is there evidence that Christian Palestinians hate Jews more than Moslem Palestinians? And if not, how is Christian religion to be considered a decisive factor?

In modern times, in particular the years examined most closely in the following pages (that is, the 1870s to the eve of the Holocaust), the sources of real as opposed to fantastic tensions between Jews and non-Jews were not quite so obvious as those in the Arab–Israeli conflict, but they were nonetheless palpable. Jews experienced remarkable changes in many regards during those years, in numbers, wealth, social position, and even political power. Such rapid changes typically produce tensions and problems for any group, and the Jews were no exception. A few of the critics of my book and articles have warned that pointing to a Jewish "rise" threatens to lend support to the old anti-Semitic charges that Jews are bent on taking over the world or, again, that they were alone responsible for the hatred directed at them. I do not find the warnings persuasive, since, to begin with, the evidence for the rise of the Jews is compelling, but also because I cannot accept that one should avoid any observations, even if accurate, that anti-Semites might misuse. It is a sad state of affairs when such purveyors of hatred are able to condition the terms in which one writes history, forcing it into black-and-white categories.

Similarly, my efforts to give a more nuanced treatment of certain anti-Semites have encountered the objection that I have thereby offered excuses for them. Again, I believe these objections miss a crucial point: The danger is not that anti-Semites will be exonerated by a nonpolemical analysis of them; far more dangerous is to offer representations that make no effort at a rounded treatment, for that provides ammunition to those who maintain that Jews and their supporters twist history to their advantage, that they are critical of all except Jews, and that they exaggerate the flaws of their critics while covering up Jewish misdeeds. (It is again simply astonishing, and revealing, how some Jewish observers believe that Jews are uniquely destructive in their self-criticism, whereas anti-Semites assert that Jews smother all criticism of themselves.)

The recent charge by prominent spokesmen for African–Americans that Jews were major beneficiaries of the slave trade, or indeed, primarily responsible for it, underlines the problem. The accusation is exaggerated; only a small number of Jews was involved – the Jewish population in a position to be slave traders was small – but it is nonetheless true that there were a number of Jewish slave traders and slave owners. It is also the case that prominent historians of the Jews, such as Oscar Handlin in his *Three Hundred Years of Jewish Life in America* (first published in 1954), ignored the issue, in Handlin's history even while mentioning by name the "great Jewish merchants," who made fortunes in the slave trade.

At any rate, I do not believe that the rise of the Jews was a negative phenomenon. Far from it. The evidence, as I see it, is that changes in the conditions of Jews benefited – indeed were in many regards central to the definition of – western society as a whole and furthermore generated both positive and negative reactions, as any great success is likely to do. Just as Christian belief could engender either hostility or sympathy (and more likely a voluble, contradictory mix of each, finding exaggerated expression in times of crisis), so "rising" Jews were feared and hated by some but welcomed and applauded by others. A systematically comparative perspective helps to make it clear, for example, that material success might generate jealousy and fear in some areas, as for example in tsarist Russia or Romania, but guarded admiration in others, notably in the United States, Italy, Hungary, or Great Britain. Within each of these examples, there were many complicating factors, among them the shifting economic situation, wars and revolutions, social class, regionalism, gender, and, yes, religion – to say nothing of the irreducible personal idiosyncrasies of key historical actors.

In my previous book I devoted careful attention to those idiosyncrasies in individual anti-Semitic affairs and concluded that the personal traits of Alfred Dreyfus, Mendel Beilis, and Leo Frank were absolutely crucial to the development of the affairs that grew up after their arrests. The personalities of key anti-Semites also played unpredictable and often unrecognized roles in those anti-Semitic affairs. I carry that argument further here. Evidence for the importance of personality, the role of the unpredictable and often surprising decisions of great historical personalities, is simply too abundant to be ignored. I am not one of those who believe that if Hitler had somehow been killed at the front in World War I or that if Stalin had perished in one of his early robberies, "history" would have somehow produced another Hitler or another Stalin, and developments in Germany and Russia would have been much the same. While historians do well to integrate into their narratives the insights and interpretations offered by the generalizing social sciences – as I have done with the notion of the rise of the Jews – at some point the irreducible uniqueness of history needs also to be recognized, and that uniqueness often has much to do with the peculiarities of personality. Hitler's actions would not have been possible without the rise of modern anti-Semitism in Germany and Europe as a whole, but that rise did not make the Holocaust inevitable; it was rather Hitler's peculiar personality that was the absolutely decisive factor.[15] And in Hitler's case it is extremely difficult to believe that sincere Christian convictions on his part were responsible for the particular virulence of his hatred of Jews, at least unless one stretches to intolerable limits what is meant by Christian convictions. The same holds for nearly all major Nazis, Himmler, Streicher, Goebbels, Goering, and Heydrich among them. Similarly, the Christian convictions of the German population, although no doubt responsible in part for the lack of effective opposition to Nazi persecution of Jews, were not primarily responsible for initiating that persecution or for the eventual murder of Jews.

On the other hand, Nazism and the Holocaust undeniably emerged out of Christian civilization; negative images of Jews had been nurtured and propagated by the Christian churches for centuries, and the secular societies that emerged in modern times were of course only partially secular and by no means unequivocally separated themselves from that tradition of Jew-hatred. Recognizing these truisms is possible without jumping to the simplistic conclusions that most ordinary Christians or former Christians, whether in Germany or elsewhere, actively desired the murder of all Jews and were willing to participate in it. Nazism and the Holocaust also emerged out of Germany and German culture; evidence for a German tradition of Jew-hatred is overwhelming. Yet, even that evidence does not justify crudely deterministic visions of what occurred in Germany between 1933 and 1945. Emotional attachments to such visions on the part of those who experienced Nazi tyranny, whether directly or from afar, although certainly understandable, do not serve the cause of historical understanding. Sadly, those attachments often serve to obstruct efforts to understand and to remedy the blight of anti-Semitism.

[15] Milton Himmelfarb, "No Hitler, No Holocaust," *Commentary*, vol. 77, no. 3, March 1984.

Acknowledgments

In preparing this paperback edition, I had valuable help from a number of scholarly readers, several of whom also earlier helped with the hardback edition. First and foremost, Richard S. Levy, Professor of History at the University of Illinois at Chicago, gave the prepublication manuscript of the hardback edition a particularly thorough and useful reading. He has since then been a source of unfailing wisdom and good humor, one of the closest approximations to the ideal of a gentleman and scholar that I have encountered.

Heartfelt thanks are also due to my colleagues at the University of California, Santa Barbara, who read various drafts over a number of years, saving me from many errors of fact and interpretation: professors Alexander DeConde, Harold Drake, Tibor Frank (as visiting professor from Hungary), Joshua Fogel, Richard Hecht, Stephen Humphreys, Sears McGee, and Jeffrey Burton Russell. Since the publication of the hardback edition, a number of scholarly experts, people of often very different backgrounds and convictions, have contacted me directly with words of support, as well as suggestions for improvement. Among the most important of them are Steven Beller, John Murray Cuddihy, William Goldstein, Jonathan Morse, Kevin MacDonald, Amy Nelson, Patrick O'Brien, Norman Ravitch, and Robert Skloot. I only regret that the limited adjustments possible for this paperback edition have not allowed me to expand more fully upon the many interesting issues they have brought up, but they have helped me avoid error and appreciate all the more nuances and intricacies of this topic.

I have also been contacted by a large number of readers, in that marvelous category of "intelligent laymen," who have offered astute commentary and support of a sort that has been particularly meaningful to me. It is not feasible to list all their names, but I want here to acknowledge that comments made by several of them have deeply moved and sustained me. A now retired professor who escaped Nazi Germany in one of the last Kindertransports (although his mother and other relatives perished in the Holocaust) wrote me that *Esau's Tears* "is by far the best book I have ever read on this sad subject," adding that "all of us who are of Jewish origin are permanently in your debt." Similar words from a number of others who escaped Nazi tyranny have confirmed me in my initial conviction that a work like this, for all its difficulties and pitfalls, was needed and worthwhile.

Most of these readers, as indeed many of the authors of the published reviews of *Esau's Tears*, have warned that I would be denounced, indeed slandered, by those who have an emotional and professional investment in different interpretations and who – more importantly – are determined to preserve an environment of dogmatism and intimidation rather than open inquiry in this area. I was of course aware of such possibilities, although I had not quite realized the extremes to which passion, partisanship, and sanctimony could drive otherwise decent and reasonable people. I have indeed been subjected to unfair and unkind abuse, but I hasten to add that the overwhelming majority of published reviews have been favorable, and, when expressing criticism, have done so in honest and productive ways. Somewhat amazingly, all the personal correspondence I received has been respectful and supportive.

In having Frank Smith as my editor at Cambridge University Press, I have been extremely lucky; he represents what most authors hope for but fewer and fewer actually find, that is, an editor who is a source of unfailingly good advice (if not always easy to accept!) both as to style and content, and who is able to mix warm friendship with professional expertise and rigor.

My most important and influential editor has been my wife, Barbara, who has for nearly four decades carefully read draft after draft of what by now numbers some thousands of pages of published books, articles, papers, and reviews. My debt to her, in this as in so many other regards, is beyond measure.

Albert S. Lindemann
Santa Barbara, California
March 2000

PART ONE

THE LONG-RANGE
BACKGROUND

= 1

Anti-Semitism before the Modern Period: Overview and Definition

And the Lord said unto [Rebecca], "Two nations are in thy womb, and two manner of people shall be separated from thy bowels; and the one people shall be stronger than the other people; and the elder shall serve the younger." And when her days to be delivered were fulfilled . . . the first came out all red, all over like a hairy garment; and they called his name Esau. And after that came his brother out, and his hand took ahold of Esau's heel; and his name was called Jacob. (Gen. 25.23–26)

Why did God create Jews and non-Jews? . . . And why in the world should they be separated from one another, not be able to stand the sight of one another, as if one were created by God and the other not? (Tevye the milkman, after his daughter, Khave, had married a Gentile).[1]

Esau always hates Jacob. (J. Taitlbaum)

Dictionary-style definitions of anti-Semitism ("hostility to Jews") are usually not much help, in part because their brevity and abstractness are inadequate to this particular protean phenomenon. Similarly, any effort to provide a brief overview of Jew-hatred throughout history must be highly selective and abandon any notion of a connected narrative. Yet a theoretical stance must obviously be made; these pages are based on the axiom that history informs theory.

Esau's Tears: The Deepest Roots of Anti-Semitism

The peculiar forms of hatred for Jews that emerged in the 1870s, although in some regards novel, also had substantial connections with a history

---

[1] Sholem Aleichem, *Gants Tevye der Milkhiger* (New York, 1920), 138. (ASL translation; transliteration according to Standardized Yiddish Romanization.)

3

of Jew-hatred that dates back thousands of years. Indeed, the division between Jew and Gentile goes to the very origins and structures of western civilization. It predates the advent of Christianity and may be found in the earliest texts of the Old Testament, or Hebrew Bible. Modern anti-Semitism cannot be productively studied without an appreciation of that much longer history. Some awareness is also necessary of a number of now little-known aspects of Jewish identity as it evolved, and in fundamental ways changed, over the centuries and millennia.

In those texts of the Hebrew Bible the mythical origins of the division between Jews and others are described, and a thought-provoking explanation for the antagonism of the two groups is offered. The account in Genesis of Esau and Jacob, twin brothers born to Rebecca and Isaac, has evoked a seemingly endless cycle of interpretations. Already in the earliest Jewish commentaries on the text in Genesis one encounters not only the rich layers of meaning but also the elusiveness, the profound ambiguity in the relationship between Jew (in archetype, Jacob) and Gentile (in archetype, Esau).[2]

Commentaries of the most diverse sort have continued well into the twentieth century. Adolf Hitler spoke of how "the Jew is the exact opposite of the German in every single respect, yet is as closely akin to him as a blood brother."[3] An African–American woman described the relationship of blacks and whites as "like the biblical Esau and Jacob. It's a love-hate relationship. . . ."[4] In the biblical account, Jacob conspired with his mother, Rebecca, to trick Esau out of receiving the blessing of their aged and blind father, Isaac. Esau, the firstborn, had already foolishly given over his birthright to Jacob in exchange for a bowl of lentils. But Esau remained Isaac's favorite, and Esau confidently expected his father's blessing after returning with the wild game that Isaac had instructed him to catch. Esau was outraged when he discovered that he and his father had been duped, that Jacob had posed as his older brother and had gained Isaac's blessing. Esau's rage prompted Jacob to flee into Mesopotamia.

Contrary to the apparent logic of the story (that the brothers would live in ever-lasting enmity), after the passage of twenty-two years, Esau, in meeting a now penitent Jacob, put aside his resentment, and the two were reconciled. Thereafter, however, Esau's descendants, the Edomites, recurringly came into conflict with Jacob's descendants; each butchered the other in various clashes. Rome was later identified in Jewish commentary with the Edomites, and after

---

[2] For a provocative suggestion of how the Esau–Jacob story reflects contrasting viewpoints of the biblical authors ("J" and "E") from the southern and northern kingdoms, Judah and Israel, in the ninth century, b.c.e. (before the common era), see Richard Elliott Friedman, *Who Wrote the Bible?* (New York, 1987), 68–9.

[3] Hermann Rauschning, *The Voices of Destruction* (New York, 1940), 238.

[4] Studs Turkel, *Race: How Blacks and Whites Think and Feel about the American Obsession* (New York, 1992), 357.

the fall of the Roman Empire, the Gentile rulers of Jews in Europe generally became classified as "Esau."

The Esau–Jacob imagery continued to appear frequently in both popular and learned speech until at least the early twentieth century. Even in the 1990s the notion of a somehow unbridgeable gap between Esau and Jacob, Gentile and Jew, remains central to traditional Jewish perspectives ("Esau always hates Jacob," "The Messiah will not come until the tears of Esau have been exhausted."). A comparable sense of the insurmountable obstacles to harmony finds expression among Jews who are less strongly tied to tradition (Raphael Patai: "The hands [are] still Esau's, and even while trying to help they inflict pain."[5]). Jews, whether religious or secular, have long retained negative, apprehensive feelings about Esau, the non-Jew – if not actual aversion or contempt then the kind of pity that one feels for an uncomprehending, potentially dangerous animal. Esau is hirsute, coarse, and brutal; he is the hunter, warrior, the untamed "natural man," while Jacob is smooth-skinned, delicate, and contemplative, if also wily and capable of ruthless deception in advancing his interests. He is also the "incorrigible overachiever" and forever getting into trouble because of that trait.[6] The title "Till Esau's Tears Are Dried" alludes to these traditional perspectives, with the implication that anti-Semitism will not disappear easily; the two identities are too different, and Esau will always feel aggrieved about Jacob's ingrained traits.

In his autobiography the Yiddish-language author Sholem Aleichem reported how as a child in Russia he once watched a rough and dirty ferryman laboriously pulling a boat across the Dnieper River. He wrote, "Esau! Only a Goy could do work like that, not a Jew. The Bible says of Esau, 'And thou shalt serve thy brother.' It is good that I am a descendent of Jacob, and not of Esau."[7] In old age the eminent Jewish–American intellectual Sidney Hook remembered how, as a boy, he had asked his religious teacher about the injustice of what Jacob did to Esau. The teacher responded, "What kind of a question is that? Esau was an animal."[8]

Anti-Semites of various stripes have drawn upon the Jacob–Esau tale as proof of the incorrigible cunning and moral corruption of the Jews throughout history: The tale reveals the reasons, reversing the traditional Jewish formula, that Jacob will always hurt Esau. As one such anti-Semite writing in the early nineteenth century put it, "where [else] is there such a people . . . that has such vile sacred tales, lacking any poetical sense, interwoven with glorified

[5] Raphael Patai, *The Jewish Mind* (New York, 1977), 234.

[6] Cf. Fernanda Eberstadt, "Responding to the Bible," *Commentary*, vol. 85, no. 1, Jan. 1988, 28.

[7] Sholem Aleichem, *Funem Yarid* (New York, 1937), 225; cf. Curt Levant, ed. and translator, *From the Fair: The Autobiography of Sholem Aleichem* (New York, 1985), 112–13. [ASL: the translation of the above phrase differs somewhat from that provided in Levant's volume.]

[8] Sidney Hook, "On Being a Jew," *Commentary*, vol. 88, no. 4, Oct. 1989, 29.

acts of thievery?" Jacob deceives his aged and blind father, tricks and steals from his brother. His mother, Rebecca – "Mother of Israel" – not only encourages such deeds but also had stolen from her own father.[9]

By the closing decades of the nineteenth century, enemies of the Jews had begun to use new terms, "Semite" and "Aryan," that reworked the biblical imagery surrounding Jacob and Esau to make the Semite detestable and the Aryan chosen and admirable. This reversal itself is related to the transposition that Christians originally had made in claiming that *they* had become "Jacob," God's chosen, while He now turned His face from His formerly chosen people, since they had rejected His Son, the Messiah or the Christ. The earliest and most influential Christians, such as Paul, Augustine, and Gregory, thus proclaimed a reversal in which "the elder" (the Jews) would serve "the younger" (the Christians). These Christian writers took up, in short, a central theme of the Hebrew Bible and refashioned it to Christian purposes to make Christians superior to Jews, rather than Jews superior to non-Jews.

The power of such biblical imagery over the centuries is impossible to deny but difficult to assess with any precision because of its profound ambiguity and the endlessly divergent interpretations to which it has been subjected. But it seems obvious that the negative representations of Esau, the non-Jew, in Jewish thought have no more rigidly determined that all Jews will hate all Gentiles than has the negative representations of the Jew in Christian texts rigidly determined that all Christians (or Gentiles descended from Christians) will hate all Jews. "Religion," again, is an endlessly elastic concept, not permitting firm conclusions about such causality.

The Esau–Jacob story and Jewish commentary on it do, however, suggest a number of provocative points in conceptualizing the nature of anti-Semitism. In a central passage of the Hebrew Bible, Esau's angry tears were presented as perfectly understandable; they were not the result of some mysterious fantasy about a wholly innocent Jacob. Aside from the suggestion that Jacob-Israel's sometimes improper actions had something quite tangible to do with Esau's enmity, and thus with the enmity of the Gentile world, the story touches on a tangled theme that is central to interpreting the interplay of Jew and Gentile throughout history.

It was long an axiom of Jewish history and Jewish consciousness that Jews in Galut (Exile), after the destruction of the Temple in Jerusalem, were necessarily a powerless and passive people, subject to the will of their Gentile overlords. It was natural for Jews to describe the sufferings they endured throughout history as caused by "the hands of Esau."[10] Jewish troubles and

[9] Jakob Friedrich Fries, *Ueber die Gefährdung des Wohlstandes und Character der Deutschen durch die Juden* (Heidelberg, 1816), 14–15. 22; quoted in Jacob Katz, *From Prejudice to Destruction: Anti-Semitism, 1700–1933* (Cambridge, Mass., 1980), 82.

[10] Cf. the recent use of this imagery in Stephen J. Whitfield, *Voices of Jacob, Hands of Esau* (Hamden, Conn., 1984).

even Jewish vices were considered the result of a hostile Gentile environment. In 1908 Max Nordau, an early Zionist leader, wrote a friend concerning the unsavory activities of certain Jews in Vienna. "These fellows [*Buben*] . . . have grown up in a Christian–Social atmosphere and, as is so often our Jewish way, have absorbed all the mannerisms and methods of the antisemites in the suburbs, just as many of our Russian brothers have adopted the style of the Black Hundreds."[11]

There have certainly been other opinions about Esau's responsibility for Jacob's troubles and vices. In the most radically opposing view, the "Other Nations" (the Goyim or Gentiles) have been described by Jewish spokesmen, from the Prophets onward, as merely agents of God's punishment for an evil that repeatedly comes from *within* Israel. Jewish defects and suffering are not, in a deeper sense, the result of Gentile oppression. As any reader of the Hebrew Bible must recognize, brutality was hardly an invention of the Other Nations; the biblical Jews committed, and their spokesmen afterwards glorified, unspeakably bestial acts, such as the massacre of "idolaters" – among them captives, women, children, old and sick people, and even pets and livestock.

An underlying issue in these contrasting views has to do with the responsibility of the Jews in history for their destiny and their being: Have they been wholly helpless and passive *objects,* without responsibility for their misfortunes, or have their actions and decisions in some substantial sense been their own, as active, conscious *subjects* in history, entailing some degree of responsibility? The inclination to picture Jews as perennially helpless victims, in no sense responsible for the ills that have afflicted them, has often been part of an unsophisticated and transparently defensive reflex. The popular writer Howard Fast concludes his book *The Jews, The Story of a People,* with this remark: "Such despair and agony as the Jewish people had to endure over the past thousand years is the result, not of what they are, but of what the Christian world has inflicted upon them."[12] This is by no means an isolated or unusual comment.

Jewish observers of widely differing sophistication have been inclined to accept the notion of Jewish passivity or "quietism" since the biblical period. Some have seen it as basic to Jewish identity: The centuries of powerlessness have provided, they believe, the ultimate foundation for Jewish ethics and sense of transcendent purpose as a separate people.[13] Attaining political and national power, Jews will be inevitably corrupted by it, as the Other Nations have all been. Such, then, is believed by some to be the danger in modern Zionism, with disturbing implications for the state of Israel in the last decades

---

[11] Quoted in Walter R. Weitzmann, "Politics of the Viennese Jewish Community," in Ivar Oxaal et al., eds., *Jews, Antisemitism and Culture in Vienna* (New York and London, 1987), 142.

[12] Howard Fast, *The Jews, The Story of a People* (New York, 1968), 370–1.

[13] Cf. Michael Selzer, *Zionism Reconsidered* (New York, 1970); and *The Wineskin and the Wizard* (New York, 1970).

of the twentieth century. Nobel Prize winner Isaac Bashevis Singer once wrote, "it . . . became clear to me that only in exile did the Jews grow up spiritually."[14]

There are related if more strictly religious and mystical ramifications to this line of thought. Some Jewish spokesmen have described anti-Semitism as God's device to purify and uplift the Jews. He had scattered them among the Other Nations, but it was not His will that they become fully part of those nations; anti-Semitism, in its eternally recurring cycles, is then to be understood most fundamentally not as a Gentile phobia but rather as a divinely supplied device to prevent Jews from disappearing. In a potent and mystical dialectic, the ultimate inability of Jews to forget their Jewishness has ensured Gentile hostility, once Gentiles realize the sometimes slumbering but ultimately ineradicable differentness of Jews, based on their biblically based sense of superiority and favored destiny. Eternal Jewishness and eternal anti-Semitism can be relied upon to reemerge, as part of God's plan. Human efforts against it, however apparently effective in the short run, must then be seen as ultimately futile. "Esau's Tears" are an aspect of a divinely ordered universe.

Modern Zionists, predominantly secular in perspective, although believing in a valuable and irreducible Jewish differentness, one that renders living among Gentiles dangerous, have arrived at other conclusions about the merits of Jewish suffering. They have identified powerlessness and marginality as the very things that they wish to shake off, the source of what they view as the many unattractive traits of Jews in modern times – and thus a fundamental cause of anti-Semitism. The mystical delights of being the suffering servant of the Lord do not much tempt such Zionists. Other modern Jewish activists, for example the socialists of the Jewish Bund, viewed Exile more positively, not as inevitably tragic; they believed in a fruitful interplay of Jew and non-Jew. Bund socialists urged that Jews begin to consider themselves active, responsible agents inside Gentile society, rather than passive, helpless victims.[15] Indeed, throughout Europe, from the 1880s onward, new forms of Jewish assertiveness in the secular arena can be observed, as well as a guarded optimism about the future of Jewish–Gentile relations, in spite of anti-Semitic flare-ups – a major theme of the following chapters.

The elusive question of Jewish power and responsibility goes to the heart of Jewish self-awareness in modern times as well as to conceptualizations of anti-Semitism. It evokes the enduring sense among many Jews of vulnerability, fearfulness, and physical ineptitude, of the need for quiet calculation and for accommodation to the physically more powerful. From that question others arise: Have Jews been hated because of their power (or Gentile fantasies about

---

[14] Isaac Bashevis Singer, "Yiddish: The Language of Exile," in Douglas Villiers, ed., *Next Year in Jerusalem* (London, 1976), 56.

[15] These issues have been explored most penetratingly by David Biale in *Power and Powerlessness in Jewish History* (New York, 1986).

Jewish power) or rather because of their powerlessness (which has rendered them contemptible)? Does anti-Semitism, even if conceptualized as entirely a product of the Gentile mind and having nothing to do with Jewish action, come primarily out of fear of or out of contempt for Jews?

The issue has been much envenomed by the passionate exchanges among Jews themselves over Jewish reactions to Nazi tyranny. Many Jewish leaders cooperated with the Nazis. Was that cooperation the result of foolishness, corruption, or understandable miscalculation? Is it true that most Jews went to their deaths passively, unresisting, "like sheep to the slaughter," as many, especially in Israel, put it?[16] An even more explosive assertion has been put forth by both anti-Semites and some Zionists: Europe's Jews, foreigners in Europe, actually deserved the hatred directed at them because they were a parasitic and psychologically perverse group, understandably inclined to self-hatred, indeed "objectively detestable."

Such issues are not unique to a study of the Jewish past. Large numbers of historians have directed their attention to the study of the downtrodden in history, to the defeated, the outsiders, the subordinate classes, the oppressed and powerless, and in each case have crept in notions much like those of "the suffering servant of the Lord," the mystical ennoblement of suffering, and the redeeming mission of the sufferer.[17] Professional scholars among them have not been immune to the temptations of writing thin, tendentious, or apologetic accounts about such victims. Yet blistering critiques have also been delivered against those historians whose works implicitly deny, for example, that women, workers, minorities, or even nation-states are to be conceptualized as active subjects, making conscious and rational choices that inevitably entail a degree of responsibility. Critics have charged that women, workers, or minorities have been portrayed one-dimensionally by some historians, as utterly helpless, uncomprehending, and pitiful victims in history, in no way responsible for their misfortunes (and to assert that they were responsible would be to commit the cardinal sin of blaming the victim).[18]

---

[16] Cf. Michael Marrus, *The Holocaust in History* (Toronto, Canada, 1987), 108–9. For a more recent treatment of the issue, by the historian most identified with the charge of Jewish cooperation, see Raul Hilberg, *The Politics of Memory: The Journey of a Holocaust Historian* (Chicago, 1996).

[17] Cf. Hannes Heer and Volker Ulrich, eds., *Geschichte entdecken: Erfahrungen und Projekte der neuen Geschichtsbewegung* (Reinbeck bei Hamburg, 1985); Gerhard Paul and Bernhard Schossig, eds., *Die Andere Geschichte* (Cologne, 1986); Roger Fletcher, "History from Below Comes to Germany: The New History Movement in the Federal Republic of Germany," *Journal of Modern History*, vol. 60, no. 3, Sept. 1988, 557–68.

[18] Cf. Tony Judt, "A Clown in Regal Purple: Social History and the Historians," *History Workshop*, vol. 7, Spring, 1979, 66–94; Wolfgang J. Mommsen, "Domestic Factors in German Foreign Policy before World War I," *Central European History*, vol. 6, March 1973, 3–43; Walter A. McDougall, "'Mais ce n'est pas l'histoire!': Some Thoughts on Toynbee, McNeill, and the Rest of Us," *Journal of Modern History*, vol. 58, no. 1, March 1986, 19–42.

Deciding who deserves the status of victim poses a large problem: Might Germans, too, be considered victims, since they were unwillingly or unwittingly "pulled into" World War I and then unfairly blamed for something for which others were equally culpable? Indeed, that same logic could lead to the conclusion that most Germans were uncomprehendingly drawn into the Nazi web, only realizing its evil when it was too late to oppose it, and thus the German people were also victims of the Nazis, by no means "willing executioners." Similarly, industrialization allegedly "overwhelmed" workers, corrupting and brutalizing them. Women's psyches were "enslaved" by sexism and male domination. Blacks were rendered childish, servile, and incompetent by the experience of slavery.

In each of these examples the concept of collective historical responsibility, beyond its obvious intellectual slipperiness, poses awkward and debilitating obstacles to the present political agendas of the groups in question, since placing blame squarely on the shoulders of others is central to their mind-set, whereas gaining recognition of victimhood is perceived as a means to open doors that have been long and unfairly shut. The logic of some feminists' position seems to attribute women's difficulties and dilemmas entirely to the influence of male domination; that femininity itself may generate its own kinds of contradictions is a much less attractive proposition – and far less studied – especially since there is little question that male domination *has* been the source of a large part of the difficulties that women have faced. Yet is it reasonable to assume that femininity is the source only of virtues, never vices, that female identity, "correctly" conceptualized (that is, free of corruption by male influence), is not burdened with existential dilemmas and imponderables? And might similar questions be posed about an African heritage, even when granting the undeniably large role of slavery and racism?

The sheer horror of the Holocaust has made it understandably suspect or even unconscionable in the opinion of some observers to suggest that Jews themselves may have had a degree of responsibility for that catastrophe. Similarly, to emphasize the positive aspects of Jewish–Gentile interplay in modern history repels some of those for whom the fruits of that interplay seem to be all too clear: mass murder. Even before the Holocaust anti-Semitism assumed a key position in many histories of the Jews. Gentile–Jewish interplay was presented in such accounts as primarily one of oppression, hatred, and bloodshed, punctuated by dramatic events. Yet an instructive case can be made that openly expressed aversion to Jews by Gentiles, Germans included, particularly one that espoused violence, has not been the predominant, most widespread, or most significant attitude in their long mutual history. Great numbers of non-Jews, in all stations of life, have tolerated and lived beside Jews, have admired and even loved them, but in most cases have simply found them useful, or of no major concern. Long stretches of peaceful cohabitation and

mutually beneficial intercourse have characterized Jewish–Gentile relationships. History conceived primarily as a narrative of dramatic *événements*
("events") – the pogroms, expulsions, and massacres – can easily blind us to
this deeper reality.

Although hatred by both Gentiles and Jews of one another was nearly
always present in past centuries, openly proclaimed enemies of Jews, especially
those calling for violence, have nearly always been a minority, although sometimes a powerful one. More relevant to the immediate concerns of this volume, until 1933 modern anti-Semites in western and central Europe were
mostly outsiders, generally denigrated if also sometimes cynically manipulated
by those in power. Even in eastern Europe, where anti-Semites more often
wielded political power, the situation was by no means always so consistently or
outrageously anti-Semitic as often believed.

Jewish survival cannot be satisfactorily explained if the peaceful and productive aspect of Jewish–Gentile relationships is ignored. Furthermore, Jewish
history *à la longue durée*, over the centuries and not blinded by short-term, dramatic events, will be ill-understood if Jewish existence is seen only in terms of
oppression and suffering. Jewish history is more satisfactorily conceptualized
in positive ways. The dean of modern historians of the Jews, Salo Wittmayer
Baron, has written that "it is quite likely . . . that even the average medieval
Jew, compared to his average Christian contemporary . . . was the less unhappy
and destitute creature – less unhappy and destitute not only by his own consciousness, but even if measured by such objective criteria as standards of living, cultural amenities, and protection against individual starvation and disease."[19] As the following chapters will amply show, similar remarks can also be
made about modern times, contrary to widespread belief.

Not only is Jewish survival ill-explained by such one-dimensional
approaches, but anti-Semitism also will remain incomprehensible if study of it
does not shake off some of the attitudes already described. Revealingly, a few
observers have indeed suggested that anti-Semitism is inherently and fundamentally incomprehensible. The popular American writer and humorist
Harry Golden has written, "dear reader, let's face it – anti-Semitism can't possibly be explained; it can merely be recounted."[20] Louis Namier, the noted
British historian, once wrote: "Understand and explain the problem [of anti-
Semitism] as much as you may, there remains a hard, insoluble core, incomprehensible and inexplicable."[21] These commonly encountered remarks
reflect not so much a coherent intellectual position as what might be termed
an instinct, one that can be sensed even in some relatively sophisticated

---

[19] Salo Wittmayer Baron, *A Social and Religious History of the Jews* (New York, 1952), vol. 1, 24.
[20] Harry Golden, *The Golden Book of Jewish Humor* (New York, 1972), 122.
[21] Quoted by Walter Laqueur in *Commentary*, vol. 44, no. 1, July 1967, 84.

accounts of the hatred of Jews.[22] But especially in popular history, a strong tendency exists to favor an emotionally laden description and narrative, especially of colorful, dramatic, or violent episodes, over explanation that employs calm analysis or a searching attention to historical context. Pogroms, famous anti-Semitic affairs, and description of the ideas of anti-Semitic authors and agitators are described with moral fervor, rhetorical flair, and considerable attention to the details of murder, arson, and rape. Background, context, and motives are often slighted or dealt with in a remarkably thin and tendentious fashion.

In such histories the antagonists of the Jews emerge as stick figures, devoid of the contradictions and ambiguities that are involved in membership in the human family. Violent episodes against Jews burst forth like natural calamities or acts of God, incomprehensible disasters, having nothing to do with Jewish action or developments within the Jewish world but only with the corrupt characters or societies of the enemies of the Jews. Even Jewish victims themselves in these accounts are implicitly denied their full humanity and often appear one-dimensional, passive and blameless, or heroic in a way that lacks a sense of human frailty and corruptibility under stress. Rather than tragedies, with often confused, inscrutable mixtures of motivations, conflicts between Jew and non-Jew emerge as simple stories of good and evil, innocence and guilt, powerless and powerful, heroes and villains.

To be sure, such black-and-white representations often appear perfectly plausible: Many if not most anti-Semites, certainly a heavy majority of the famous ones in modern history, were morally corrupt to a degree that renders efforts at sympathetic understanding highly problematic. The kind of hatred that such people expressed for Jews in general can hardly be considered justified, and it typically had little direct correlation to their experiences with Jews or to anything like a disinterested investigation of Jewish action. Considerations of background and context, too, often appear unhelpful, irrelevant, or misleading: How much does it help to learn that Hitler had an unfulfilled adolescence? Many others with similar backgrounds did not come to hate Jews. And even if we can demonstrate that Voltaire hated Jews because he was cheated by some of them or that Hitler hated them because he observed revolutionary Jews undermining his beloved Fatherland, what does that tell us about Jews in general?

---

[22] Examples will be provided throughout the following chapters, but perhaps two of the most prominent in this regard are George Mosse's *Toward the Final Solution* (New York, 1980) and Jacob Katz's *From Prejudice to Destruction* (Cambridge, Mass., 1981). Both Mosse and Katz are accomplished and distinguished historians, whose contributions I would be the last to denigrate and from whom I have learned much. Yet these two works bury their readers in lengthy descriptions of often minor and obscure anti-Semites and racists while offering disappointingly little in terms of explaining or situating them in a historical context, although certainly those matters are not ignored.

Remaining alert to such objections is essential, but there is nonetheless more to the story. The following pages will provide evidence that anti-Semites were frequently less simple and occasionally less morally corrupt than they have been generally presented. In few areas have hearsay and half-truths gone so unchallenged and blended into kitsch: the Nazi murderer who cites Goethe and plays the violin, the anti-Semite who never knew any Jews, the Jews who could not own land and exploited no one. Similarly, a profound aversion to conceptualizing Jews as flawed or ordinary ("human") individuals, distinguishable from their oppressors particularly by their lack of power, is widespread.

These tendencies have roots deep in Jewish history, religion, and culture. So too does the parallel instinct to view surrounding Gentile society as pervasively flawed, polluted, or sick. The belief of Jews in premodern times that they, God's chosen people, had been condemned by their god, because of their own sins, to live in subjugation in the polluted lands of the uncircumcised, the brutal, the unclean, the eaters of filth – of the reviled Children of Esau – took on new forms in a modern context. Jews in late ancient times and in the Middle Ages found it easy to harbor a sense of superiority to the non-Jews among whom they lived, since Jews were a literate people of ancient civilization residing among peoples often only half-civilized. But that comfortable and sustaining assumption of superiority became ever more tenuous with the advances of European civilization in the modern period, from the eighteenth to twentieth centuries. Increasingly, informed, sensitive Jewish observers began to feel that Jews were being left behind, that somehow Jewish culture had frozen at the premodern stage, while Gentiles were moving ahead to a higher stage of civilization. And for the large numbers of Jews who came to modern European civilization by way of the eastern European *shtetl* ("little town") the anxiety-filled transition from a sense of superiority to the Goyim to a sense of inferiority occurred with great abruptness, resulting in sometimes extravagant responses.

This anguished awareness, which typically was torn and uncertain and which at first affected only a small number of Jews in restricted areas of western Europe, involved thus a doubly pained or wounded Jewish consciousness: Not only had Jews been separated from their promised land, condemned to live as humiliated foreigners under the subjection of the unclean and ungodly Other Nations, but the older consolations that emerged from a sense of cultural and spiritual superiority were also slipping away.

It is not surprising, then, that many Jews have been, since the early nineteenth century, powerfully attracted to those modern secular ideologies that managed to reaffirm indirectly, with a new language, an older sense of the tainted qualities of prevailing Gentile life. Indeed, those ideologies carried a potent double message: The Other Nations were responsible not only for Jewish suffering (by their unjust laws and unprovoked attacks on innocent Jews) but also for Jewish backwardness. In the familiar words of Moses Mendelssohn at the end of the eighteenth century, "They bind our hands and complain that we do not make use of them."

To reason that Jews were themselves primarily, or even in more tenuous, remote ways, to blame for their backwardness eventually became as unacceptable to many Jews as it was to reason that Jews were to blame for the hatred directed at them. Here a fundamental shift from premodern Orthodox religious perspectives was accomplished, since prior to modern times Jews had seen their sufferings as imposed by a righteous god in response to their own failings. Now it became the perverse Gentiles who were oppressing wholly innocent Jews – and those Other Nations were no longer seen as mere tools of God.

Such modern ideologies as socialism (both Marxist and anarchist), Zionism, and various forms of the psychiatric worldview (Freudian psychoanalysis and related schools) all emphasize the tainted or sick qualities of modern Gentile existence, be it in exploitative capitalism, decadent bourgeois society, aggressive nationalism, or repressive Victorian prudery. Jewish frustration, anxiety, and rage at being considered inferior, and in some partial and tormented sense agreeing with that evaluation, found an alluring outlet in these ideologies – and a hope for eventual redemption.

Obviously, these ideologies cannot be described as simply or explicitly Jewish condemnations of the Gentile world; non-Jews in great numbers were also attracted to them. Marxism, for example, offered a widely persuasive analysis of capitalism. Even Zionism found a remarkable range of Gentile admirers (by no means all of them friends of the Jews). But by the end of the nineteenth century Jews were attracted to socialism and, after 1917, communism in significantly greater proportions than were non-Jews. It is instructive that it was Jewish intellectuals, Marx and Freud are the two most obvious examples, who became the most brilliant and preeminent exponents of these modern theories.

The attractions of what we might term "ideologies of revenge" that "get back" at oppressors are familiar in many other contexts. In many of the nations of the non–European world, western imperialism was denounced not only as emerging from a western sickness but was also blamed for the continuing ills and inadequacies of non–European countries – the West "bound their hands," to borrow Mendelssohn's words. That their own histories and traditions might offer a better explanation of their difficulties was, to say the least, not a popular hypothesis among many of their leaders. Interestingly, in spite of the purported crippling exploitation experienced by the non–European world, many of its spokesmen have insisted upon a sense of superiority, usually cultural or moral, to the West.

In an ironic way the rise of another important modern ideology can be seen in the same light: Anti-Semitism has been transparently an ideology of revenge, one that has blamed the ills of modern times on Jews who have infected modern nations, not on factors that emerged from European civilization itself. Modern anti-Semites found a new, "scientific," racist vocabulary to substitute for an earlier Christian charge of Jewish perversity. Anti-Semites were not impressed that large numbers of Jews joined those modern movements that stressed human equality, for Jews in those movements still seemed to such observers negative and mocking of their surroundings, subtly asserting their abiding if transformed sense of superiority, and concerned more with personal advancement, power, and "jewification" of those surroundings than with general human welfare. Since the 1960s Jewish and other neoconservatives have echoed, sometimes with considerable sophistication, some of that very same negative imagery in regard to left-wing Jewish intellectuals.[23]

Baron, the already-noted dean of modern Jewish historians, devoted much of his considerable energy, over more than half a century, to combating what he termed *Leidensgeschichte* (suffering-history, or the tendency to write Jewish history largely in terms of the suffering endured by the Jews at the hands of Gentiles). He sought to provide a richer, more multidimensional picture, and the ablest practitioners of Jewish history have followed his lead. Although Leidensgeschichte was most notably expressed by certain nineteenth-century historians, it had roots in the premodern, or what might be termed a fundamentalist-orthodox view of Jewish existence in the Diaspora (an angry God scattered His sinful people from the land of Israel). Contemplation of that history of suffering is thus a contemplation of the hand of God in history. Such history, as the reflection of the unknowable will of God, can, to recall Harry Golden's words, only be recounted, not really explained or understood in a modern sense.

Modern, nontraditional Jewish consciousness is less likely to accept the notion of an unknowable divine purpose. Such was the case even before the Holocaust, but since then to describe the methodical murder of millions of Jews by Nazis as part of God's plan is wholly unacceptable to most Jews, except for a few sects among the ultra-Orthodox. Study of the sufferings of Jews is now advocated mostly as a way of preventing suffering in the future, largely by exposing the sinful or corrupt nature of Gentile society and its responsibility for Jewish suffering and almost never as a means by which Jews could become aware of their own sins, except insofar as an error in judgment, a naive misperception of Gentile malevolence, is considered a sin. Anything else, again, would be blaming the victim. It would at any rate be difficult to imagine a Jewish sin large enough to merit the punishment of mass murder. (Some of the ultra-Orthodox believe that sin was the abandoning of Jewish tradition, a puzzling conclusion, even within traditional religious discourse, since the Orthodox Jews of eastern Europe died in higher proportions and much larger numbers than the non-Orthodox of western and central Europe.)

---

[23] Stephen A. Schucker, "Origins of the 'Jewish Problem' in the Later Third Republic," in Frances Malino and Bernard Wasserstein, eds., *The Jews in Modern France* (Hanover and London, 1985), 135–80. For a similar tack, by a non-Jewish neoconservative, see Paul Johnson, *History of the Jews* (New York, 1987), passim, and his *Intellectuals* (New York, 1988).

Yet, the older taste for Leidensgeschichte has continued to reassert itself in subtle ways. Whatever the explicitly proclaimed reasons for studying Jewish suffering, a detailed description of that suffering appears to have a much broader appeal for many Jewish audiences than a calm and balanced analysis of it. At times attention to causality seems to be resented, or rejected as wholly and utterly inadequate, sacrilegious even, a tendency that is especially strong and explicit in the literature of the Holocaust. Quite aside from the vast descriptive literature of the massacre of Jews by Nazis, of which perhaps Martin Gilbert's lengthy and remarkably unanalytical *Holocaust* is the most striking example,[24] many accounts of pre-twentieth-century Jewish history move from one pogrom to the next, from expulsions to plunders, from hostile legislation to anti-Semitic manifestos – providing "just the facts," yet ignoring so many other facts and finally providing accounts that seriously lack depth and balance.

The more mysterious certain aspects of the past remain and the more certain kinds of human actions and motivations appear irrational, the more one is able to perceive certain detested actors in history as wholly alien. Similarly, it becomes easier to maintain – and relish – a narrowly moralistic and judgmental stance. If a historical account, in contrast, by its texture, coherence, and accessibility, encourages its readers to project themselves into the mental world of the past, then figures or societies may emerge as less alien. This effort of sympathetic imagination is a central part of what was long meant by historical sophistication and "understanding," even if it also beckons one into the quicksands of moral relativism.

If history is read, or written, under the impelling rush of psychological need, emotional release, perceived need for group cohesion, or related judgmental agendas, the very idea of an open and exploratory approach to the records of the past may be experienced as unappealing, even threatening, and its possible conclusions may appear morally offensive. Philip Roth has provocatively observed that imaginative literature entails a "moral fantasy" that should not "seek to guarantee us of the appropriateness of our feelings."[25] Historical inquiry has something in common with fiction in this regard, for while the historian cannot create characters and situations that did not exist, the variety of what has existed is so great that a kindred experience may emerge. History lets us see what men and women have been, lets us understand how much more remarkable they have been than our untutored imaginations could possibly realize. At least such may happen if we are open to such experiences – if we have not already firmly made up our minds about what we will "discover."

---

[24] See the discussion of these tendencies in Saul Friedländer's introduction to Yehuda Bauer and Nathan Rotenstreich, eds, *The Holocaust As Historical Experience* (New York, 1981); also, Marrus, *Holocaust in History;* Martin Gilbert, *The Holocaust: The Jewish Tragedy* (New York, 1986).

[25] Philip Roth, "Writing about Jews," *Commentary*, vol. 36, no. 6, December 1963, 446–52.

Baron has put the issue of Leidensgeschichte, and the related one of Jewish passivity versus responsibility, in revealing historical perspective by showing how the modern desire by Jews to believe that they fought back against their oppressors is starkly opposed to earlier Jewish consciousness, in which passive acceptance of martyrdom was esteemed and writ large in various histories.[26] Accounts of fighting back, so precious to modern Jews, many of whom angrily reject the notion of Jewish passivity primarily because of its associated charge of cowardice,[27] were for earlier generations of slight interest, or even embarrassing. Still, one can find little of a genuine or broad consistency in these exchanges; a coherent rejection of the notion of Jewish passivity pulls one in the direction of Jewish activism – and responsibility, which many of the "we fought back school" also implicitly reject.

Jewish powerlessness is obviously a key theme of modern Jewish history, yet the term requires scrutiny. Jews for most of their history have exercised power in many areas, for example, in the regulation of their family life or in the preservation of cultural and moral values. Even in the political arena, Jews in exile have typically used their relatively limited power in highly skillful and effective ways.[28] That the twentieth century has witnessed a spectacular and tragic failure of time-tested uses of limited power by Jews has tended to blind us to this important truth.

Although the case is more problematic, choices by Jews as conscious subjects also played an important role in the organization of their economic activities. They were not moneylenders or merchants simply because they were forced to by the dominant non-Jewish powers; since ancient times they preferred those roles to others, for example, that were tied to the land or that required heavy manual labor. Jews often chose to live in ghettoes for reasons of their own (dietary and other ritual observances, for example), not simply because Gentiles required them to. Nor were Jews impoverished merely because of oppressive legal restrictions; Jewish tradition and conscious, responsible choices by Jews played a role as well. At any rate, more important, especially from a long-range perspective, than conscious choices by either Jews or their Gentile overlords were impersonal forces, such as population increases, rates of economic development, and disease and natural catastrophes, that neither Jews nor Gentiles controlled or even understood. Jews were poor in eastern Europe primarily because the overwhelming majority of the population in that region was poor.

---

[26] Salo Wittmayer Baron, *History and Jewish Historians* (Philadelphia, 1964), 94 ff.

[27] For one of the less sophisticated versions of this see Yuri Suhl, ed., *We Fought Back!* (London, 1968). The issue touches on Israeli charges of the "cowardice" of Diaspora Jews in a broader sense.

[28] Biale, *Power and Powerlessness,* ably develops this theme.

The issue of Jewish power might best be considered in terms of the obvious or axiomatic: Jewish action, whether evil or good, was effectively conditioned by Jewish values or Jewish character. Obviously that action, and even those values, encountered obstacles and incentives in terms of the Gentile presence, the restrictions imposed upon Jews by their Gentile overlords, and the more subtle influences of the non-Jewish majority. But that presence was not usually an overwhelming consideration in a long-range and more searching sense. A complex interplay resulted, and over the centuries changes in Jewish life occurred, but not because of an utterly lopsided influence of one force or the other. The values and mores of Jews have changed in striking ways over the centuries and millennia. In this light what is inherently Jewish and what has been picked up by Jews from surrounding civilizations and integrated into Judaism and Jewishness becomes a subtle matter indeed. Jews ranging from Arthur Koestler to Jacob Neusner have denied that much inherently and generically Jewish has survived, but many others have argued that an original, essential Jewish quality has persisted.[29]

A large body of work by historians concerned with history from below has stressed the autonomy and vitality of what might be termed "subordinate cultures," encompassing blacks, workers, and women.[30] The most instructive views of oppressed blacks, for example, portray them not merely as passive victims but as active agents, combating white oppression in often subtle but pervasive ways, with tools that they have fashioned out of a preexisting African identity. The same kinds of points hold for Jews, and more strongly so.

It is no doubt true that Jews were characteristically observers rather than movers and shakers in western civilization. The Jewish people or nation had no land, no state, no armies, no titled nobility, no Napoleons, and no Hitlers. Such considerations were a fundamental starting point for Leidensgeschichte, which concluded that the physically powerless, stateless, and landless Jewish people could not possibly experience the same kind of history that Gentiles did. Therefore, aside from describing the sufferings inflicted by the Gentile powerful on the Jewish powerless, Jewish historians were almost by necessity concerned with the history of Jewish intellectual life – Gelehrtengeschichte: the scholars, sages, and literary men, of which the Jewish nation had so many.

Since the most influential nineteenth-century Gentile historians believed that the political state and land-based nation were what historians should write about, Jewish historians of that time felt with poignancy the limitations of their own historical material. The tendency to concentrate on intellectual history, to

---

[29] Arthur Koestler, *The Thirteenth Tribe: The Khazar Empire and Its Heritage* (New York, 1976), 224–5; Rafael Patai, *The Jewish Mind* (New York, 1977), 8–12.

[30] Cf. T. Jackson Lears, "The Concept of Cultural Hegemony: Problems and Possibilities," *American Historical Review*, vol. 90, no. 3, June 1985, 576–93.

the neglect of other factors, has long remained a prominent trait of popular and influential works of Jewish history by Jewish historians even by the late twentieth century, when such concerns had become far less fashionable in the profession.[31]

The interplay of Jew and Gentile has been, and remains, almost inexpressably rich; a study of Jewish history takes us far beyond provincial concerns. Most of the greatest and most famous Jews in history were influenced in decisive ways by their contacts with surrounding non-Jewish culture and society. It is of no little symbolic significance that the most famous of Jews (at least before Jesus), Moses, had an Egyptian name; his ideas, insofar as we have reliable knowledge about them – which is, admittedly, not very far – seem to have derived from Egyptian sources. Without a constant interplay, century after century, with the Gentile world Jews simply would not be Jews in the sense now understood.

The issue is yet more intricate, since many if not most famous and influential Jews in the last 2000 years were deeply torn in their identities, often to the extent that their relations with other Jews and with Jewish religion were contentious, to say the least. (Some obvious examples through the ages are Josephus, Maimonides, Spinoza, Marx, Disraeli, Trotsky, Rathenau, Freud, and Einstein.) Similarly, western civilization, especially in the last 250 years, has been pervasively influenced and deeply enriched – if also sometimes bedeviled – by the activities and contributions of Jews, so much so that it is scarcely possible to conceive of what that civilization might have been like, for good or for ill, without them. An even more sweeping statement along these lines might be made about Jewish contributions to American culture in the twentieth century. Western civilization is undeniably a "jewified" civilization, however offensive the word may be to our ears because of the ugly use made of it by anti-Semites; it might well be used proudly.

These remarks hold above and beyond the obvious influence of Judaism, the Jew, Jesus Christ, and his Jewish disciple, Paul. They hold equally above and beyond the also obvious contributions of Jewish scientists, scholars, politicians, and social theorists. Jews were deeply and peculiarly involved in the emergence of modernity or modernism in Europe and America. In elaborating the many "isms" that emerged in response to modern times (industrialism, liberalism, socialism, conservatism) Jews were important far beyond their relative numbers in society. In a related way, anti-Semitism, hatred of Jews in their many roles, is an "ism" of central if elusive significance in modern western civilization. Anti-Semites believed that Jews were everywhere, and in a sense they

---

[31] As noted, in the previously cited works of Mosse, Katz; Léon Poliakov, *History of Anti-Semitism,* 4 vols. The more recent work of Paul Lawrence Rose, for example, *German Question/Jewish Question: Revolutionary Antisemitism from Kant to Wagner* (Princeton, N.J., 1992) represents a sophisticated expression of this tradition.

were almost everywhere that counted in modern society, in significantly greater numbers than strict proportionality would have assured.

The Rise of the Jews

The argument that anti-Semitism is an entirely baseless hatred, having nothing to do with Jewish reality or Jewish action in the real world, is contradicted not only by elements of Jewish tradition and by Zionist perspectives but also by many other sources. There is, for example, the assertion of the extremely influential seventeenth-century philosopher Baruch Spinoza, recognized as one of the most profound thinkers of early modern Europe, that Jewish separatism and sense of superiority, linked to Jewish religious rituals that insult, denigrate, and threaten other religions, have been the fundamental factors in evoking hatred for Jews throughout the ages. In the twentieth century, the noted author Arthur Koestler has stated the matter with characteristic bluntness: "The Jewish religion, unlike any other, is racially discriminatory, nationally segregative, and socially tension-creating."[32]

Spinoza and Koestler have been dismissed by some as "self-hating" Jews. But other Jewish observers, about whom that charge has not been made, have also argued that accurate perceptions of Jews and Judaism have something directly to do with the hatred directed at them. For example, the authors of a popular volume entitled *Why the Jews?* argue that it has been just such perceptions, having to do ultimately with the religious values of Jews, that have caused anti-Semitism: Gentile hatred springs from the rigor and high morality of those values, which threaten those who cannot or will not maintain them.[33] But one need not turn to such expressions of Jewish self-flattery to discover a more plausible and palpable explanation of the nature of specifically modern anti-Semitism.

"The rise of the Jews" had many dimensions, some of which are more problematic and uncertain than others. There certainly was a very widespread *impression,* by the mid–nineteenth century of a Jewish rise, whether in the minds of Jews themselves or of non-Jews. A perfectly palpable change in Jewish status, widely believed to be an improvement, was Jewish emancipation, the granting of equal civil rights to Jews in most of Europe, beginning in the late eighteenth century. The rise was also unmistakable in demographic terms, though here further research would certainly be valuable: The Jewish population of Europe and America, from around the middle of the eighteenth century until the Holocaust, increased at a greater rate than that of

---

[32] Arthur Koestler, "Judah at the Crossroads," in *The Trail of the Dinosaur and Other Essays* (New York, 1955), 111.

[33] Joseph Telushkin and Denis Prager, *Why the Jews? The Reason for Anti-Semitism* (New York, 1983). More sophisticated statements of similar ideas can be found in George Steiner, *In Bluebeard's Castle* (New York, 1974), and Maurice Samuel, *You Gentiles* (New York, 1924).

most non-Jews, and in certain cities and regions of eastern and central Europe the rate was strikingly greater. Jews were generally more mobile, moving into urban areas in greater numbers than most non-Jews (another general sign of relative improvement, whatever the horrors of the modern urban slum). The wealth of Jews on the average also increased more rapidly than that of non-Jews, again, in some areas spectacularly more, as did related factors such as health and longevity. Even where the Jewish common people were known to be desperately poor, as in Austrian Galicia or parts of the Jewish Pale of Settlement in tsarist Russia, their overall per capita wealth still seems to have been greater than that of the non-Jews, mostly peasants, among whom they lived.

The rise of the Jews had to do as well with a new prominence and visibility of Jews in key areas of modern urban life – journalism, medicine, the law, for example – in which certain intellectual proclivities were of special importance but which also connected with obvious aspects of Jewish tradition and culture. The strikingly disproportionate numbers of Jews who won Nobel prizes after 1905 is one of many signs of success. The same Ruth Wisse who was earlier quoted as describing anti-Semitism as functioning "independent of its object" observes at the same time, without apparently sensing any contradiction, that "the dynamism of the Jews in the nineteenth and twentieth centuries is almost unparalleled."[34] The rise of the Jews, notes Paul Johnson, was above all a rise of the Jewish intellectual, whose "shattering importance to modern history" can hardly be exaggerated[35] in nearly all realms but perhaps most strikingly in that of left-wing and revolutionary politics. In more mundane ways, when Jews and Gentiles were allowed to compete freely, as increasingly was the case in the modern world, much evidence indicates that the Jews often outdid the Gentiles, and where they did, especially but not infallibly where their numbers were large, hatred was the most intense.

Again what is least doubtful is the *impression* throughout Europe, among Jews as well as non-Jews, of Jewish success, and that impression, even when inaccurate in some regards, had profound implications: A once despised and legally set-apart group seemed to be prospering more than others, and, more to the point, it seemed to be assuming power over non-Jews. A few scandals or frauds involving Jews, Jewish braggarts, or strutters – and there was no lack of them – set off poisonous spirals of anger, indignation, and envy.

Without this fundamental factor, this ever more impressive rise, there would not have been a specifically modern anti-Semitism, although premodern forms might well have persisted, and at any rate they continued to be mixed with modern forms. (An obvious but often puzzlingly neglected point:

[34] Ruth Wisse, "The Twentieth Century's Most Successful Ideology," *Commentary*, vol. 91, no. 2, February 1991, 33.

[35] Paul Johnson, *A History of the Jews* (New York, 1987), 341.

The rise of the Jews did not create a sense of Jewish difference, or hostility to Jews, ex nihilo; that sense of difference, and mutual hostility, preexisted and would have continued without the precipitous rise of the Jews. But Jews had previously accepted a subordinate, deferential position and had been less numerous, less visible, and less threatening.)

The goal of modern anti-Semites was to undo the rise of the Jews and the perceived threat of Jewish power and "jewification" implicit in that rise. For some that meant merely revoking civil equality, returning Jews to their traditionally subservient position, outside civil society and the national community. Other anti-Semites spoke more vaguely of "controlling" Jews who were now out of control, somehow limiting their numbers, wealth, and influence, without actually undoing their civil emancipation. Anti-Semites of a more extreme persuasion wanted to "remove" Jews from their countries, and a few of them alluded to a removal that might be violent, even genocidal.

Hitler was the most fanatical and successful of those extremists. But however appalling his efforts, he finally failed in his goal of eliminating Jews and their values. In purely numerical terms, what he accomplished was to reduce the Jewish population to something like what it had been, proportionately, before the mid–eighteenth century when the rise of the Jews began. The issue is, of course, more than numerical: He inflicted on the Jews what may be termed their greatest tragedy, in a history marked by tragedies, but in spite of the millions killed he did not halt the rise of the Jews in modern times, above all in the United States, the most important country of the twentieth century.

To describe modern anti-Semitism as a response to the rise of the Jews in modern times does not of course address a more fundamental question: What was the nature of anti-Semitism before modern times, before the modern rise of the Jews? That question is not the main concern of this volume, but earlier outbreaks of Jew-hatred seem to have been related to earlier, roughly comparable kinds of perceived and real threats by "rising" Jews. Jewish commentators throughout the ages have repeatedly warned against provoking the Other Nations by "competing too ostentatiously" with them. The Satmar Rebbe, the leader of a major hasidic sect, described the Holocaust as the result of the Jews' willful rise, thus breaking their promise to God and freeing the Gentiles from their own promise not to oppress the Jews "too much." It is a recurring theme. Solomon ben Varga, in the Renaissance, explained the expulsion of the Jews from Spain in 1492 by the extraordinary success of the Jews there – and, even more, their tendency to brag about that success.[36] Thus, although

---

[36] Cf. Biale, *Power and Powerlessness,* 113; Amos Funkenstein, "Theological Interpretations of the Holocaust," in François Furet, ed., *Unanswered Questions: Nazi Germany and the Genocide of the Jews* (New York, 1989), 286.

the rise of the Jews may have been most remarkable in modern times, it was by no means a unique phenomenon in history.

The Origins, Evolution, and Ambiguities of the Term Anti-Semitism

Arriving at a fruitful conceptualization of modern anti-Semitism has also been much impeded by the remarkably chaotic use of the term over the past century. It originally appeared in the 1870s in the guise of what was claimed to be a scientifically based, racial antipathy to Jews, as distinguished from a more traditional or long-standing religious antipathy (the first "real," the second a "fantasy"). But from the beginning it was not used consistently, in part because "Semite" corresponded at best vaguely to a racial category (and "Semitism," referring to a set of Jewish racial–cultural traits, was even more diffuse and dubious, given the diversity of Jews in Europe). The word did have a reasonably precise application as a generic term for a group of languages (including Arabic, Aramaic, and Hebrew); less precisely, it referred to Middle-Eastern cultural patterns – a usage, it should be noted, that has been promoted well into the twentieth century by influential Zionists in modern Israel.[37] However, as a racial term, one that could be used to describe fixed physical and mental traits among people who had lived for millennia in far-flung and profoundly different areas of Europe, North Africa, and the Middle East, Semite lacked the degree of precision or palpability that other racial terms, such as Negroid, clearly had.

Newly coined words catch on, however, for significant reasons, even if we judge them to be bad reasons. There is little question that the very ambiguities and subtle associations of the term contributed to its popularity and durability. At first "anti-Semite" had a secular and scientific aura to it, which bolstered the self-image of certain kinds of Jew-haters and served the purpose of presenting their hatred as free of religious bigotry. As the term acquired ever more obnoxious connotations and lost respectability in the decades after it first appeared, many Jews themselves found it a useful term in denouncing their enemies. Its very vagueness and ability to evoke negative emotion were central to this usefulness.

But the use of the term undoubtedly meshed with the perception of rising Jews. Many observers, Jews perhaps more than non-Jews, were firmly convinced that the new, racial anti-Semitism of the 1870s and 1880s was entirely justified, given the arrogance and immorality of large numbers of newly successful, highly placed, and all-too-visible Jews. Indeed, a surprising number of thoughtful Jewish observers actually welcomed the expression of Gentile

[37] Biale, *Power and Powerlessness*, 146.

outrage, hoping that it might persuade certain notorious Jews to moderate their style, to choose a path of greater modesty and probity. This peculiar welcoming of anti-Semitism may be seen as a kind of reformulation, in new, secular guise, of the traditional Orthodox interpretation of Gentile attacks on Jews as deserved, as a form of warning from God. Jews have always been, whether in ancient or modern times, among the harshest and most unforgiving of critics of Jews.

The existence of such intra-Jewish hatred raises one of many fundamental questions concerning how much hatred of Jews as such can be described as the product of a specifically Gentile or Christian mind-set. A 1986 poll in Israel showed that fully a quarter of secular Israelis viewed their [ultra] Orthodox fellow citizens as "opportunists, liars, and charlatans,"[38] an attitude that has ample parallels in secular Jewish attitudes during the nineteenth century in central and eastern Europe. The breath-taking hostility between various elements of the Israeli population demonstrates in yet another way that these hatreds among Jews for other Jews are by no means a thing of the past or confined to Diaspora Jews.[39] Can one seriously maintain that it is primarily Christianity, or the Gentile world, that produces these intra-Jewish hostilities?

Michael Marrus has suggested a useful way of categorizing degrees or types of anti-Semitism. He proposes a set of concentric circles, into which qualitatively different kinds of Jew-haters are placed.[40] In the outermost circle are to be found anti-Semitic tendencies that are mild and unreflective, not strongly locked into an embrace by emotional needs. Such "outer-circle" anti-Semites occasionally express distaste for Jews but are not particularly preoccupied by the subject. More significant, they are open to education; they are capable of concluding that their negative generalizations may have been unfair, their reasoning faulty.

Anti-Semites who grow up in milieux or in cultures where distaste for Jews is unquestioned, where it is part of a general worldview, can often be placed in this outer circle. They might be sane and decent but still prone to mouthing anti-Semitic canards. H. Stuart Hughes, a distinguished American scholar of New England Brahmin background, remembers this "conventional anti-Semitism" of his youth. Once such people leave that surrounding culture, either physically or in the sense that they come to have an outsider's understanding of it, they experience relatively little difficulty in forming friendships with Jews and establishing otherwise normal relationships with them. Hughes refers to

[38] Yosef Goell, "The Secular Backlash," *The Jerusalem Post, International Edition,* week ending March 1, 1986, 15.

[39] Cf. Amos Oz, *In the Land of Israel* (New York, 1983).

[40] Michael Marrus, "The Theory and Practice of Anti-Semitism," *Commentary,* vol. 74, no. 2, Aug. 1982, 38–42.

"a long process of disentanglement,"[41] a process not unknown to Jews, after leaving their ghetto communities to live among those whom their forefathers regarded as incorrigible brutes.[42]

In seeking to establish a more rigorous definition of anti-Semitism, it is morally justifiable and intellectually useful to exclude this outer circle of casual and unreflective thought. Some people whose ideas may be placed in this outer circle are simply too lazy, busy, or unsophisticated to work out consistent ideas to match their immediate perceptions, crotchets, and quirks. Such people probably constitute the majority of the populations of Europe and America. Others may not have yet devoted much time or attention to the issues, failing to perceive how potentially offensive or dangerous their ideas might be. Yet others may find that close contact with Jews, or a reordering of their daily habits in order to make Jews feel more comfortable, is inconsistent with or threatening to their *own* identity, which of course parallels the feelings of some Jews regarding close contact with Gentiles and the reordering of Jewish life that such contact entails.

The famous German–Jewish social democrat Eduard Bernstein accepted as justified the charges made against Jews in the 1870s and 1880s in Germany. Bernstein was not an emotionally disturbed person, living in a world of fantasy, nor was he someone with an abiding need to hate. But his case brings up another important point: He gradually came to the conclusion that the charges against Jews, although certainly not imaginary, were in a deeper sense unjust, exaggerated, and potentially pernicious, particularly because of the kinds of people who were attracted to the anti-Semitic banners. He then began to move away from his initial tacit approval of the anti-Semitic agitation. The great French socialist leader Jean Jaurès was a man of reason and profound humanity who was nevertheless initially persuaded of Alfred Dreyfus's guilt and who feared that since Dreyfus was a rich Jew, his friends and family would be able to free him by means of bribery or other illicit influence. New evidence, however, brought Jaurès to believe in Dreyfus's innocence and to work for his liberation. This ability to change one's mind, to react to evidence and reason, is a significant indication of the difference between genuine anti-Semites – serious, consistent, dangerous ones – and others who express what has often been termed anti-Semitism.

Marrus suggests that a second, concentric circle is occupied by more single-minded, dedicated types, anti-Semites who are able in times of crisis to mobilize or intensify the low-key, unfocused feelings characteristic of the outer circle. These middle-ring anti-Semites are more conscious and consistent and become more involved; they may vote for anti-Semitic politicians or join an

---

[41] H. Stuart Hughes, *Prisoners of Hope: The Silver Age of the Italian Jews, 1924–1974* (Cambridge, Mass., 1983), vii.

[42] Cf. Gregor von Rezzori, *Memoirs of an Anti-Semite* (New York, 1981), 194, 204.

anti-Semitic organization. Here we may appropriately speak of anti-Semitic ideology, of sincerity, of people who gain both intellectual and psychological satisfaction through some sort of mythic construct directed against Jews.

Middle-ring anti-Semites do not support radical solutions, certainly not murdering Jews. They are inclined to see Jews as opponents, even possibly worthy opponents – not devils. They typically grant that there are "exceptional" Jews. Many such anti-Semites will even honestly maintain that they wish Jews no harm. They, too, may have friends who are Jewish, but they simply believe that at least certain numbers of Jews must be subjected to special controls. Some of these middle-ring anti-Semites might be termed Gentile Zionists, believing in a separate existence of mutual respect, which of course is also the attitude of many Orthodox Jews.

In the inner circle Marrus places the fanatical anti-Semite, the monomaniac on the Jewish question. In the eyes of such people the Jew loses any semblance of common humanity, any right to fair treatment. Inner-circle fanatics make no bones about their desire to chase Jews from their midst, even to destroy them. Such fanatical anti-Semites are not inclined to compromise, for one does not compromise with absolute evil, with the devil. In this case it is no longer adequate to speak simply of an ideology that satisfies certain subconscious desires; inner-circle anti-Semites are characterized by hatreds that dominate and seriously corrupt their personalities. In this inner circle are to be found Adolf Hitler, Edouard Drumont, Georg von Schönerer, and Pavolachi Krushevan. If we are to accept a language of pathology, here is where it seems most appropriate.

In normal times the inner-circle fanatic is likely to be considered strange and unbalanced by those around him. Indeed, even in times of trouble, the monomania and otherwise disturbed personal relationships of the inner-circle anti-Semite may well prevent him from being an effective proponent of his beliefs. But when anti-Semitic fanaticism is linked to real abilities and political savvy, the inner-circle fanatic may be capable of galvanizing members of the middle and even outer circle when they are deeply alarmed over economic, social, or political matters, so that an entire society can be pulled into the twisted world of the inner-circle fanatic.

Marrus's model is not without its limitations. The boundaries of each circle are hard to delineate, and many anti-Semitic figures appear to span them in awkward ways. But the model does allow for a sense of texture, for a relatively systematic and coherent way of dealing with degrees of anti-Semitism, and for rejecting the simplistic and ultimately dangerous reductionism of the stance that all anti-Semitism is essentially the same.

"Classical Anti-Semitism"

Premodern religious anti-Semitism and modern racist anti-Semitism, especially in their extreme forms, share a significant ideological–fantasy element. In both is to be found a belief in an unchangeable Jewish essence, an eternal Jewish character that is deeply threatening to those among whom Jews live. In both, the Jew is perceived as an arrogant, power-hungry outsider, scheming to undermine the beliefs, society, and culture of non-Jews. Jews are believed to possess mysterious qualities, in premodern times often linked to satanic connections, but even in modern times "race," for all its alleged scientific status, has had connotations of mysterious and malevolent potency, frequently having to do with sex.

However, it is a fair question whether pre-Christian hostility to Jews was characterized by the range and intensity of Jew-hatred in the Christian era. That is a large topic, but a few words about pre-Christian hatred may be useful, for certain aspects of it offer suggestive comparisons to modern anti-Semitism. All ancient sources are in agreement that hostility to Jews was particularly intense in Egypt, especially in Alexandria, a major economic and cultural center of the ancient world. In the third century, b.c.e. (before the common era), Ptolemaic leaders, heirs to Alexander the Great's empire, had settled large numbers of Jews in the city to serve as middlemen and had awarded them special privileges. In subsequent years Jews flocked to the city. Alexandria also attracted large Greek and Syrian populations as well as native Egyptians, but Jews eventually constituted something like forty percent of Alexandria's total population.[43]

That the numerous and privileged Jews were resented by the other peoples of the city is not surprising, but the special antipathy of the Egyptians was probably intensified by factors that may be termed uniquely religious. Egyptians were portrayed as opponents of the Jewish people in key passages of Jewish scripture; the god of the Jews proclaims, in Gen. 8.23, "I will put a division between my people [the Jews] and your people [the Egyptians]." The Jews at the time of Moses similarly recognized that "we . . . sacrifice to the Lord our God offerings abominable to the Egyptians." (Gen. 8.25). Thereafter, Egyptian humiliation provided occasion for annual Jewish rejoicing in Passover celebrations. Judaic prohibitions against intermarriage or other contacts with non-Jews were particularly stringent in the case of Egyptians. Central to Jewish identity, then, was a religious belief and a key ritual that commemorated the misery and death of thousands of Egyptians, rejoicing that the god of the Jews had shown his power, not only by thwarting Pharaoh's will but by repeatedly visiting the land with plague and disaster.

Obviously, such an account was not easy for Egyptians, themselves a proud and ancient people, to accept. In response, a leading Egyptian intellectual offered his own account – "discourse" would be the more fashionable term – of the Egyptian captivity, one that contrasted revealingly with that in the Book of Exodus.[44] The high priest, Manetho, in the third century, b.c.e., declared

---

[43] Baron, *History*, vol. 1, 171.

[44] Rosemary Ruether, *Faith and Fratricide: The Theological Roots of Anti-Semitism* (New York, 1974), 25 ff.

that the Jews had been driven out of Egypt because they, a band of destitute and undesirable immigrants who had intermarried with the slave population, were afflicted with various contagious diseases. The pharaonic authorities, therefore, expelled the Jews for reasons of public hygiene. Subsequent Jewish clannishness, Manetho maintained, was a result of the earlier identity of the Jews as lepers, diseased pariahs; the account in Exodus was an absurd falsification of actual events, an attempt to cover up the embarrassing and ignoble origins of the Jews.[45]

This Egyptian recasting of the Passover story found its way into the writings of anti-Semitic authors across the centuries. Nearly all ancient pagan anti-Jewish writers borrowed from it, and the charge that Jews were originally lepers seems to have been bandied about as much as the later charge that the Jews killed Christ. Even modern secular tracts against the Jews show traces of influence from this ancient source. Hitler and his mentor, Dietrich Eckart, for example, interpreted the exodus from Egypt as the result of revolutionary terrorism by Jews against the Egyptian ruling classes.[46]

We have little reliable outside evidence that would indicate how much truth there was in the Egyptian counterhistory or, indeed, even how widely it was embraced by the Egyptian masses of Alexandria, as distinguished from intellectuals like Manetho. To the modern historian, Manetho's account does have the advantage of plausibility (Egypt certainly did have an undesirable immigrant problem) and a lack of miracles. But whatever relationship either account may have to actual historical events, it is the psychological appeal of Manetho's account for Egyptians, and for those who later borrowed from it, that is of particular interest, since it is not necessarily what is verifiably true that has historical significance; it is rather what people want or need to believe.

Native Egyptians in Alexandria encountered great numbers of Jews in their midst who not only categorized them as "others" (Goyim), idolaters mired in uncleanness, but who also considered the Egyptian nation to be an especially reviled sort of Other Nation. Moreover, these foreign Jews enjoyed special privileges from the Greek authorities and were generally better off than native Egyptians. Imagine, then, the psychological satisfactions for Egyptians of an account that put the pretentious Jews in their place, that exposed their ignoble and diseased origins.

Tensions between the Jews and the Greeks of Alexandria were also important, and the two communities rose against one another in violent conflict on

---

[45] Further references in Samuel Sandmel, *Anti-Semitism in the New Testament* (Philadelphia, 1978), 2–3.

[46] Dietrich Eckart, *Der Bolschevismus von Moses bis Lenin. Zwiegespräch zwischen Adolf Hitler und mir* (Munich, 1924), 6–7; cf. Robert Wistrich, *Hitler's Apocalypse: Jews and the Nazi Legacy* (New York, 1985), 143.

a number of occasions. Yet the quality of Jew-hatred among the Greeks seems to have been different from that of the Egyptians, since the Greeks were the founders of the city and for many years constituted its ruling order. Greeks were the very people, in other words, who granted privileges to the Jews – and to whom the Jews constantly appealed for yet broader privileges – while the Egyptians in the city were a subject people, more often at the bottom of the social, economic, and political scale.

The Egyptian tales, and Egyptian hatred of Jews, may be considered a very early and in an important sense "classic" form of anti-Semitism. Egyptians derived profound psychological satisfaction from an ideology, or myth, that denigrated Jews. Of course others, such as the ruling Greeks, could also find satisfaction in the Egyptian tales or variations on them, just as ruling elites in modern times could denigrate Jews without sharing the raging resentments of the lower orders. The Egyptian ideology was not formulated, it should be noted, in the absence of real Jews or even on the basis of a wholly imaginary aspect of Judaism. Real Jews and real problems, economic, social, political, and religious, were involved. These real, palpable factors provided the context, the appeal, the driving force for the "fantastic" beliefs of Egyptians about Jews. And whether Jews and their religious beliefs were to be considered responsible in any sense for the hatred directed at them is by no means easy to answer.[47]

Christian Anti-Semitism

Much scholarly discussion has been devoted to the issue of whether Christian anti-Semitism grew directly out of pagan attitudes to Jews and, in a related way, of whether modern secular anti-Semitism, particularly Nazism, grew out of Christianity or is more accurately to be considered a rejection of Christian values and a reversion to paganism. There were undoubtedly fundamental differences between attitudes toward Jews on the part of the Graeco–Roman authorities, on the one hand, and of the Christian Church on the other. But ancient pagan and early Christian attitudes to Jews were sprawling, not internally consistent or unified; elements of overlap and of historical continuity are also obvious. Pagan and Christian anti-Jewish attitudes were mixtures, often strikingly inconsistent mixtures, of benevolent and malevolent elements. Christian hostility to Jews, similarly, cannot be seen as a single entity but rather as something that notably evolved in history; significant differences may be traced from the ancient times up through the Reformation. So, too,

---

[47] For a revealing exploration of the extent to which anti-Jewish sentiment during the Middle Ages had to do with charges based on reality (for example, it was certainly true that Jews did not accept Christ as the Messiah) as distinguished from those based on fantasy (the charge that Jews engaged in ritual murder), see Gavin Langmuir, *Towards a Definition of Antisemitism* (Berkeley, 1990), 11 ff.

with paganism over the years: The pagan beliefs of the Nazis cannot be plausibly linked with the paganism of Plato, Aristotle, Seneca, or Marcus Aurelius.

Undoubtedly, evolving Christian doctrine added potent and original elements to the negative imagery of the ancients. Most important in this regard was the Christian charge that the Jews had killed the Christ (Greek: *khristos*, the anointed one) and thus had been abandoned by God, or at least were being punished by Him. A common theme in ancient, Christian, and modern anti-Semitism may again be detected: Jews are charged with an unjustified pride, a desire to destroy, and an outrageous blindness. Christian identity was initially hammered out in an early, often fierce struggle against Jews – or, more precisely, between Christian Jews and Jewish Jews. Jewish followers of the Christ began as underdogs, with feelings of inferiority and persecution in regard to Jewish religious authorities, feelings that had few parallels among the Greeks and Romans, especially their upper classes.

In considering the original expressions of Christian Jew-hatred, we arrive at an obvious yet seemingly paradoxical conclusion: In the beginning Jews themselves conceptualized and propagated that hatred, since the Christ and the first Christians were Jews. Furthermore, the specific kind of anger and resentment they expressed, even once Christianity began to spread widely outside of Jewish circles, derived from a Jewish style and tradition of righteous, monotheistic intolerance rather than from the more tolerant, polytheistic attitudes of the Graeco–Romans.

Christian anti-Semitism in that sense comes from within Judaism, whereas the anti-Semitism of the pagans in the ancient world came from outside it. As Norman Ravitch has commented, "conflict is always keener when antagonists recognize their common ancestry and their close relations."[48] Christians claimed to be the "true Jews," or God's new chosen people, and in so doing they became as intolerant of the Jews as the Jews were of them. At the same time, key aspects of Christian belief, as it evolved, came from non-Jewish, largely hellenistic sources, above all through the works of St. Paul, himself a hellenized Jew, who blended Greek and Jewish elements in dizzyingly esoteric ways. In Paul's hands, and even more in the hands of the writers of the four Gospel accounts of Christ's life, Christianity became anti-Jewish, or at least profoundly hostile to the ruling elites of the religion at the time, angrily mocking and aggressively rejecting key elements of contemporary Judaism.

Paul rejected Jewish ritualism and legalism, proclaiming the freedom of Christians from the "curse of the Law."[49] The writers of the synoptic Gospels (Mark, Matthew, and Luke) ostensibly hoped to mask those elements of Jewish nationalism and subversion against Roman authority that may have been in

---

[48] Norman Ravitch, "The Problem of Christian Anti-Semitism," *Commentary*, vol. 73, no. 4, 1983, 45.

[49] Michael Grant, *The Jews in the Ancient World* (New York, 1984), 157.

Christ's original message. (It is generally accepted that the authors of the synoptic Gospels wrote in the late 60s and early 70s, that is, at the time of the anti-Roman rebellion in Palestine, although the earliest of them, Mark, may date from the 40s.) They sought similarly to blame the Jews rather than the Romans for Christ's crucifixion.

Both Paul and the writers of the Gospels radically redefined the traditional Jewish notion of messiah, from that of a secular ruler carrying out a divine mission but himself still fully human and acting in the natural world to that of a supernatural figure much resembling the dying and reviving salvation gods that were common to many pagan mystery cults of the day. There were certainly many overlaps between those cults and early Christianity. Mithraism, for example, which was widespread in the area of Paul's birth, also practiced baptism and Eucharist-like common meals. The Christian concept of the messiah was, similarly, linked to the notion of the suffering servant of God in ways that differed from the Jewish understanding of it.

The desperate, millenarian tendencies within Judaism at the time of Christ's birth, moreover, went beyond the prevalent Judaic intolerance of the day and tended to demonize their opponents. Such Jews, often influenced by radically dualistic tendencies of Babylonian origin, were inclined to describe fellow Jews who differed from them in belief and ritual practice not merely as mistaken but as active agents of the Evil One, enemies of the one true god, no better than the Other Nations, indeed worse.[50]

Another important factor gave a particular flavor to the pronouncements of early Christians. In Palestine they recruited primarily from the *ame ha'aretz,* or people of the land (roughly "peasants"), who did not keep ritual commandments so scrupulously as the educated and more affluent city dwellers.[51] As far as the learned rabbis and other members of the Jewish elite were concerned, Jesus was a mere manual laborer, wholly lacking in credentials – simply not qualified by background and training to be a Jewish religious leader.

As a Galilean, Jesus was even further suspect by Jewish leaders in Jerusalem, since residents of Galilee had much the same unsavory reputation that southern rustics have for educated city dwellers in twentieth-century America. That is, they were considered ignorant, gullible, and prone to violence. Galilee was a strong center of nationalist opposition to the Roman Empire and of social revolution. In the eyes of the Pharisees, scribes, and Sadducees, Jesus attracted around him nothing more than a filthy and dangerous rabble, comparable in a modern American context to a southern lynch mob.

This distinct social and intellectual inferiority meant that the attitude of most early Christians in regard to Jews, especially Jews in authority, may have

---

[50] Ruether, *Faith,* 49.

[51] Ibid., 77; John G. Gager, *The Origins of Anti-Semitism: Attitudes toward Judaism in Pagan and Christian Antiquity* (Oxford, 1985), 113–14.

had something in common with the previously described attitudes of the Egyptians in Alexandria. That is, they experienced a powerful psychological need, as denigrated inferiors, to demolish the pretensions of those in a superior position. Even when Christians began to recruit successfully among other classes and to assume more important or prestigious positions in society, their origins as inferiors to the Jews – and their lingering anxiety about Jewish pretensions and even more about the persistence and survival of the Jews – indelibly marked the relationship.

Early Christian hatred of the Jewish establishment was still further intensified by the persecutions that Christians, like other dissident Jewish sects, experienced at the hands of Jews in authority. Christian attacks on Jews were often seen as counterattacks, or acts of revenge. Paul, the former Jewish Saul, had himself been an ardent persecutor of Christians before he so suddenly embraced Christianity. Once a Christian, he suffered whippings at the hands of Jewish authorities for his proselytizing. In his works, then, he lashed back angrily at the Jewish authorities, above all at the Pharisees with whom he had formerly been associated.

Jewish authorities in turn struck back, especially in the period when Jewish patriots were fighting the Romans and when Christians were seen not only as idolaters and apostates but also as renegades and traitors.[52] Perhaps the greatest blasphemy conceivable from the Jewish standpoint was for a mere man to claim to be the one true god. And that was precisely what the Christians proclaimed their messiah to be.[53]

Once Christianity began to spread outside of Palestine and became a predominantly non-Jewish belief, especially after the Roman–Jewish wars of the first and second centuries, Jewish persecution of Christians began to subside. But the two faiths remained in sometimes fierce competition throughout the empire. In the Diaspora, Christian successes were particularly significant among the "half-Jews," those who admired certain aspects of Judaism but who were unwilling to take the steps to full conversion. Paul's Christianity offered them the possibility of becoming "Jews," God's chosen people, without the need, for example, of circumcision.

Antipathy between Christians and Jews unquestionably spread in the second and third centuries, but among the disparate ranks of the half-Jews who became Christians not all were inclined to hate Jews or even to conclude that the Jews had been rejected by God. Some modern biblical scholars doubt whether Paul himself believed that God had unequivocally abandoned the Jews; rather, he concluded that the Jews had "stumbled but not fallen."[54] A few other scholars have gone so far as to assert that in Paul's eyes

---

[52] Ruether, *Faith*, 168.

[53] Edward H. Flannery, *The Anguish of the Jews: Twenty-three Centuries of Anti-Semitism* (New York, 1965), 27–8; Baron, *History*, vol. 2, 129–36.

[54] Flannery, *Anguish;* Gager, *Origins*, 263.

Christ's mission was specifically to the Gentiles, without entailing an abandonment of the Jews.[55]

Judaism was at any rate not the weak and desiccated affair, dramatically pushed aside by a triumphant Church, that Christian polemics and apologetics in subsequent centuries tried to make it appear. It retained, well into the fourth century, c.e. (common era), widespread respect from non-Jews and the unusual privileges accorded it by the Roman Empire. It remained a more vigorous, vital, and attractive faith than Christian polemicists recognized, although it certainly became less of a proselytizing one.[56]

The so-called Pharisaic revolution, which was to a large extent the voice of the future in Judaism, stressed good will, concern for fellow beings, and even a proselytizing universalism, as opposed to the Temple sacrifices and the more tribalistic preoccupations of the Sadducees. In short, Christians and Pharisees may be seen as part of a larger "left wing" of Judaism, even if, as is so often the case among leftist factions, they were bitterly hostile to one another. In the nineteenth century a number of liberal Jewish scholars would affirm that they saw no significant difference between the Judaism of Hillel (a leading Pharisee) and Jesus, except for what was later unjustifiably added by non-Jews to Christ's original words. Recent scholarship has generally concurred that the teachings of Christ and those of the Pharisees were in many points close.

The Church Triumphant; John Chrysostom

The notion of a triumphant Church, natural enough to those who can see, with the advantage of historical hindsight, that the Church did indeed come to dominate much of the western world, was by no means so obvious in the first four centuries of what is now termed the Christian era. Christians perceived religious threats from many quarters, and principal among them, from Judaism. The Church Fathers, in their efforts to work out a coherent Christian doctrine, lashed out at many heresies, not the least of which were the "judaizing" heresies (those that denied the divinity of Christ and implicitly the unity of the god-head). Almost all of the church fathers and the major popes in the first 500 years of Christianity delivered lengthy attacks on the Jews, often as part of general campaigns against pagans, heretics, and other enemies. It is instructive for our purposes to look briefly at the church father who has generally been considered the most virulently anti-Semitic of them all, John Chrysostom, who lived in Antioch, in Asia Minor, in the fourth century. The unrelenting fury of John's anti-Jewish charges, his seemingly wild anger

---

[55] See the discussion in Gager, *Origins*, especially pp. 174–264.

[56] Cf. Baron, *History*, vol. 2, 129; Robert L. Wilken, *John Chrysostom and the Jews* (Berkeley, Calif., 1983), 65–6.

against the Jews, are at once shocking and puzzling to the modern reader. What explains the virulence of John's attacks? Was it something mysterious in his character, or were there significant "real" factors that help to explain his anger? The fourth century had begun with the Emperor Constantine's elevation of Christianity from a persecuted sect to a state-sponsored religion. However, by the time of John's mature years confidence in the triumph of the church had experienced a number of rude shocks. The Emperor Julian (361–363, "Julian the Apostate" in Christian histories) had abandoned Christianity. Following him, Valentinian, though a Christian, was unsupportive of many Christian concerns. Valentinian's brother, Emperor Valens, was an Arian (that is, the follower of a major Christian heresy).

Judaizing, then, remained a genuine and pervasive threat to Christians, not only because of developments at the pinnacle of power but because large numbers of Jews refused to accept Christianity's triumphalist claims. (Arian Christianity may be loosely termed a judaizing heresy – the term became a catchall, much like "red" in modern times – although it did not actually deny the divinity of Christ; Arian treatment of Christ's nature defies easy summary.) Many Christian leaders found the persistence of Judaism both threatening and infuriating. John put the matter revealingly to his listeners in a famous sermon in Antioch: "If you admire the Jewish way of life, what do you have in common with us? If the Jewish rites are holy and venerable, our way of life must be false."[57] In denouncing the Jewish threat, John, who was a highly schooled Greek orator, or *rhetor*, used the many rhetorical devices that were so esteemed by his contemporaries but that are little appreciated and poorly understood today. His sermons are filled with the stock phrases and familiar metaphors of the time. In describing the Jews as "drunken" and "diseased" or as "wolves" who would devour the Christian flock, he was using a language that was perfectly familiar to his listeners and that was also employed against other perceived threats, including the Arians.

Such graphic, abusive language was itself an integral part of a stylized rhetorical convention, the *psogos* ("tirade"), which might be described as the opposite of a similarly stylized rhetorical form that is more familiar today, the funeral eulogy. We all recognize and accept that at a funeral the deceased's faults will be little if at all mentioned. It is considered appropriate to dwell upon his or her virtues, even if all present know that they were minimal. So with the psogos; it was understood that no effort at a balanced treatment of an opponent would be forthcoming. Unqualified invective was expected – indeed relished – and the degree of a rhetor's inventiveness within the stock phrases and conventions, the richness and color of his language, was highly esteemed.

The accomplished rhetor was a cultural hero of the time, roughly comparable to modern movie stars or athletes, and his speeches were as much popular

---

[57] Wilken, *Chrysostom*, 68.

centuries – often the justification for violence against Jews – are to be found in John's sermons. He added doctrinal substance to the charge of deicide, and by the fourth century this charge had entered broadly into Christian rhetoric, not only in the limited sense of asserting that Jewish leaders in Jerusalem had demanded Jesus's crucifixion but also in a general sense that Jews were responsible for it – and, more to the point, that they *continued to rejoice in it*. Thus John added his voice to the rising chorus of Christian theologians who developed an elaborate theology of hate for Jews and Judaism, a demonizing theology in which the subtleties of the Pauline doctrine took second place or were simply ignored.

From the charge that the Jews killed the Christ, the emergence of the broader charge that Jews ineradicably or "essentially" hated Christians and wished to kill them was a logical step. Because the medieval mind, Christian or Jewish, was not sensitive to historical context, such talmudic injunctions as "the best among the Gentiles should be slain"[59] led Christians to conclude – since they certainly believed themselves to be the best among the Gentiles – that the Talmud enjoined Jews to kill Christians. The subtleties of the interpretations of such injunctions by Jews were simply lost.[60]

From the belief that Jews by their very essence hated Christians and were enjoined by the Talmud to destroy them, the further charge emerged, so bizarre to the modern mind but consonant with medieval essentialist thinking, that Jews *continually* tried to "kill Christ" by desecrating communion wafers (the mystically transformed body of Christ). That charge was the pretext time and again for violent attacks: Jews, it was averred, stole communion wafers and tortured them – the living body of the Christ! – with pins or befouled them with urine and spittle.

Equally bizarre but of even greater historical importance, reaching up into the twentieth century, was the charge that Jews regularly committed ritual murders of Christians, especially of virgins and children, since Jews required "pure" Christian blood for their various rituals and ceremonies to be mixed, for example, into their matzos for Passover. The Passover season, then, which is always close in time to Easter, became an occasion of great danger for Jews. While Christians were commemorating the death and resurrection of the Christ, charges that Jews had killed Christians for their blood often set off violent episodes.

Yet one must again resist exaggeration, for throughout the first millennium, c.e., before the actual charges of Desecration of the Host or of Blood Libel emerged, Jews continued to enjoy what can only be considered a privi-

[59] Cf. Jacob Katz, *Exclusiveness and Tolerance: Studies in Jewish-Gentile Relations in Medieval and Modern Times* (Oxford, 1961), 108.

[60] See also Jacob Katz, *From Prejudice to Destruction: Anti-Semitism, 1700–1933* (Cambridge, Mass., 1980), 13–22.

leged position. In Carolingian times, five centuries after Chrysostom delivered his sermons, most church leaders still looked upon Jews, in the words of one scholar, "not as despised pariahs but as dangerous competitors."[61] Both the church and emperors continued, for the most part, to protect the Jews and denounce violence against them.

A number of the Church Fathers, most notably St. Jerome, in trying to account for the unseemly survival of the Jews, theorized that they were being preserved for some divine purpose, and this general position was frequently supported by the popes and other church authorities. One of the most influential of popes, Gregory the Great, in the beginning of the seventh century ruled that the church should not only tolerate the Jews but also protect them. He similarly opposed forced conversions.[62]

The pronouncements of popes and high church officials did not by any means determine what lower officials or the general population actually did. During the times of the most notorious attacks on Jews, such as the crusades of the twelfth and thirteenth centuries, the episodes of Black Death in the fourteenth, and the religious wars of the sixteenth and seventeenth centuries, the attackers were generally the lawless and desperate elements of the population, over whom the church – or any other authorities – had little control. Such men, significantly, killed not only Jews but nearly everyone in their path. Jews were sometimes easier targets because they were typically unarmed, and they were tempting because they were often relatively wealthy.

Insofar as the church in these years consistently encouraged physical violence it was not against Jews but against Moslems and heretics – and in such cases often with an appalling ruthlessness, as when the heretical Cathari were systematically exterminated in the south of France in the thirteenth century. Jews were also at times physically attacked or forced to convert at the instigation of the church, most famously in sixteenth-century Spain, but these were not systematic campaigns to put Jews to death. By the late Middle Ages many of the rulers in western Europe, under the influence of the Church, had prohibited Jews from residing in their realms or had even driven them out. Yet the larger generalization holds, in spite of important exceptions: Church authorities protected Jews when they could, even while condemning them for the murder of Christ.[63]

The Middle Ages saw a gradual change in the attitude of Jews to the non-

---

[61] Arthur J. Zuckerman, "The Political Uses of Theology: The Conflict of Agobard and the Jews of Lyon," *Western Michigan Studies of Medieval Culture*, vol. 3, 1970, pp. 23–51, cited in Joseph B. Maier, et al., *German Jewry, Its History and Sociology: Selected Essays by Werner Cahnman* (New Brunswick, N.J., 1989), 20.

[62] Alan Edelstein, *An Unacknowledged Harmony: Philosemitism and the Survival of European Jewry* (Westport, Conn., 1982), 29–34.

[63] Cf. Kenneth R. Stow, "Hatred of the Jews or Love of the Church: Papal Policy toward the Jews in the Middle Age," in Shmuel Almog, ed., *Antisemitism through the Ages* (New York, 1988), 71–89.

Jews among whom they lived. The self-imposed separation of Jews from "idola-trous" non-Jews set down in the Talmud and more or less the norm in the ancient world gradually became more difficult in practical terms. Simply to survive, to find food and protection from the elements, Jews were required to mix with Gentiles, Christian and Moslem, more than they had before and to find powerful protectors among the non-Jewish population. Such compromises were made easier by the reasoning that the Christians and Moslems worshipped the same god as the Jews and in other ways were not to be equated religiously with the loathsome idolaters of the ancient world. Much ambiguity remained, however, particularly concerning how rigorously separation should be retained in religious ceremonies. (Into modern times the presence of a Gentile in a Jewish home on Passover was widely considered to pollute it, for example, and wine made by Gentiles could not be used by observant Jews.) Jews still lived typically as a separate nation and corporate body in the medieval scheme of things.

The Reformation and the religious wars that grew out of it in the seventeenth century were again perilous times for Jews, who were often caught in the crossfire of warring Christian sects. Nearly all accounts of the history of anti-Semitism mention Martin Luther's attacks on Jews, after his initial friendly overtures to them. Most accounts of the origins of Nazi anti-Semitism point to poisoned German roots, as it were, in Lutheran belief. Yet on closer inspection, Luther's role in this regard is less clear-cut than usually assumed, and again one must question or qualify the role that religion has played in fomenting Jew-hatred.

The importance of Lutheran beliefs in Germany, or at least northern Germany, makes plausible the assertion that there is a connection between Lutheranism and German anti-Semitism, yet some of the least anti-Semitic nations of Europe (Denmark, Norway, and Sweden) are also predominantly Lutheran – how rigidly deterministic, then, can we consider Luther's attitudes to the Jews on his followers? Moreover, Luther's diatribes against the Jews were not accepted by most Lutheran leaders and not taught to Lutheran followers, during his own lifetime and well into the nineteenth and twentieth centuries. Indeed, few rank-and-file Lutherans in modern times were much aware of Luther's anti-Semitic writings. One might then doubt how much those particular writings served to prepare the minds of Germans for Nazi racism.[64]

It is true on the other hand that modern anti-Semites, the Nazis most prominently, ransacked German history to prove how figures from Luther to Goethe were anti-Semitic. In that sense Luther's writings no doubt served to provide retrospective legitimacy to modern anti-Semitism, but it is more prob-

[64] Carter Lindberg, "Tainted Greatness: Luther's Attitudes toward Judaism and Their Historical Reception," in Nancy A. Harrowitz, ed., *Tainted Greatness: Antisemitism and Cultural Heroes* (Philadelphia, 1994), 23–5. For an honest wrestling with the problem from a Lutheran standpoint, see Robert M. Bigler, *The Politics of German Protestantism* (Berkeley, Calif., 1972).

lematic to consider Luther's writings as part of an unchallenged chain of unusually vicious, or "eliminationist," anti-Semitism in Germany. Luther's contribution to the tendency of Germans to accept political authority unquestioningly is also important in understanding how the Nazis were able to get away with their crimes, but an important point in that regard is easily overlooked: The German tendency to respect political authority worked, until the 1930s, mostly to the benefit of the Jews and was generally applauded by them.

The paradoxes of the Lutheran tradition are not unusual; many famous premodern anti-Semites and the traditions associated with them are more elusive in nature than usually appreciated. Goldhagen's case for eliminationist anti-Semitism in Germany might be termed a twentieth-century psogos, a tirade that is motivated by goals other than the impartial search for the truth. The words not only of Luther but also of Manetho, St. Paul, Chrysostom, and many other major figures before the advent of modern times, may be selectively pasted together to present what appears to be a monomaniacal concern to "eliminate" the Jews, but a paste-job is not history worth the name. This is of course not to suggest that a careful historical analysis will not in some instances indeed provide evidence of hatred that is very close to monomaniacal.

Dramatizing anti-Semitic pronouncements, and avoiding all that diminishes the drama, is understandable but finally counterproductive. Similarly, to describe anti-Semitic ideas in a polemical spirit easily leads to a skewed vision of them, especially when the polemic entails the assertion that anti-Semites were all utterly blind, possessed by fantastic visions, and reacting to nothing actually done or believed by Jews. Manetho, St. Paul, and Chrysostom, whatever their misperception and exaggerations, were facing real Jews and addressing genuine Jewish ideas. Indeed, they were facing Jews who enjoyed power and established position; the notion of the anti-Semite as underdog is one that needs to be given serious analysis. Even the Nazis began as a mocked and widely dismissed fringe element.

2

Modern Times
(1700 to the 1870s)

Never has any other religion been so fecund in
crime as Christianity. . . . There is not a line of its history that has not been bloody. . . . The abominable
cross has caused blood to flow on every side. (Dennis
Diderot)

Many a sober Christian would rather admit that a
wafer is God than that God is a cruel and capricious
tyrant. (Edward Gibbon)

The Enlightenment

Many historians consider the late seventeenth through the eighteenth
centuries the beginning of modern times in western Europe. European modern times are of special significance because they began to set the pace for the
rest of the world. Those years represent as well a period of renewed esteem for
the values and accomplishments of the pre-Christian Greeks and Romans.
This renewed esteem reflected a growing confidence in human reason and
human powers, what Peter Gay has suggestively termed a "recovery of nerve."[1]
The recovery had obvious roots in the Renaissance and even in the Middle
Ages, but it reached a high point in the mid-to-late eighteenth century. During
the Enlightenment, significant numbers of Europe's intellectual elites turned
away from revealed religion, and especially away from the intolerant attitudes
they associated with institutionalized religion, in large part because those attitudes were widely blamed for the horrifying death and destruction in the religious wars of the previous century. Even many of those who retained their religious faith emphasized the need for toleration.

An ever more bold reexamination of Christian theology and of the Bible was
undertaken in those years. Already by the early decades of the eighteenth century various authors had openly argued for the superiority of Graeco–Roman

[1] Peter Gay, *The Enlightenment* (New York, 1966).

thought over that of Moses and the Jews and what they had brought to humankind. Such authors particularly admired the ancient Greeks and Stoic philosophy, from which Christian theology and especially Christian ethics had in fact heavily borrowed. Other thinkers denounced what they considered the bigotry, superstition, and barbarity of the biblical Jews and looked to a natural religion of reason and tolerance. The English Deists were particularly harsh in their evaluation of the biblical Jews, arriving at what one author has problematically termed "secularized anti-Semitism."[2]

The work of a Jewish philosopher, Baruch Spinoza, had a significant impact on such thinkers. In the last decades of the seventeenth century he had provoked "serious debate about the trustworthiness of the Bible as history and about the importance of the ancient Jews."[3] This fundamental reorientation had far-reaching implications for the relationships of contemporary Jews and non-Jews, for inevitably much of the religious imagery that had governed their attitudes to one another was put into question.

A key interpretive issue arises: Was the Enlightenment a time when hatred of Jews began to diminish, or did its leaders merely refashion the hatred of the ancients into new but eventually even more malignant forms?[4] An equally tangled interpretive issue arises in considering the eighteenth and nineteenth centuries as a period of bourgeois–liberal triumph. Was the growing middle class, due to its attachment to ideas of individual freedom and equality under the law, naturally less hostile to Jews than the older, aristocratic elites, or the broad masses below? And since the great majority of Jews were neither aristocrats nor manual laborers, were they not natural allies for the non-Jewish middle class in its struggles against those two classes?

Many of the most important thinkers of the Enlightenment rejected not only the truth of Revelation, but they also believed that revealed religion had exercised a pervasively negative influence on the human spirit. The world would have been a better place, they concluded, without Judeo–Christian religion. Such thinkers dismissed the idea of a personal god, one who had favorites among the world's peoples, or who listened to their prayers. The Judeo–Christian tradition had awakened much that was hateful, it was believed; it had encouraged superstition, intolerance, and fratricide. Religion turned people against one another, perverted their reason; religious passion blinded them to a sense of their natural powers and of their common humanity. Since Christians recognized some sort of transcendental purpose to the survival of the Jews, although the most influential thinkers of the Enlightenment did not, it

---

[2] Todd Endelman, *The Jews of Georgian England, 1714–1830* (Philadelphia, 1979), 96–7.

[3] Arthur Hertzberg, *The French Enlightenment and the Jews* (New York, 1968), 30.

[4] Cf. Jacob Katz, *From Prejudice to Destruction* (Cambridge Mass., 1980), passim. See also Uriel Tal, *Christians and Jews in Germany: Religion, Politics, and Ideology in Germany, 1870–1914* (Ithaca, N.Y., 1975), 16 ff.

might be said that there was at least in potential a more destructive element in such secular attitudes to Jews.

On the surface, Enlightened thought seemed to echo what many ancient thinkers had said about both the Jews and the Christians, but the ancients were inclined to a sense of the inevitable tragedy of life, to a belief in degeneration from an earlier golden age, whereas Jews and Christians believed in a coming messianic age, a bright future. In this sense the most influential thinkers of the Enlightenment may have been more under the sway of the Judeo–Christian worldview than they realized. Many of them viewed their age as even greater than the most illustrious of ancient times, and they believed that it would continue to improve.

The ancients' irritated puzzlement or bemused contempt regarding the Jews became a more militant hatred in the works of key eighteenth-century writers, especially in France. Voltaire, often seen as a symbol of the Enlightenment, waged a lifelong battle against the church and organized religion more generally. *Écrasez l'infâme!* (crush the infamous thing!), he urged. The infamous thing was dogmatic religion, and men like Voltaire seemed to consider Judaism one of the worst forms of it, having infected Christianity with its intolerance and credulity.

The growing enthusiasm for what science and unaided reason could offer humankind was related to the growing conviction, much bolstered by Spinoza's writings, that much of the Bible was little more than the childish tales of primitive minds. Judaism in its eighteenth-century forms was even more widely condemned; the life of Jews was wrapped in an absurd and unnatural ritualism. The Talmud was even more cluttered and preposterous than the products of Christian scholasticism. As many Enlightened observers saw the matter, the Jews were not only the originators of intolerance, infecting the Christians and Moslems, but they also carried it to even greater extremes than did Christians. Equally damning, Jews denied human solidarity and fraternity by separating themselves from others, considering themselves a race apart, superior and specially selected.

In the course of the eighteenth century these charges took on a new and significant twist: Jewish separatism meant that Europe's Jews had lost contact with the unparalleled advances of western civilization. Jews had remained medieval, backward, sterile, and resistant to modern science. In their self-imposed isolation, their age-old rudeness had intensified, so that now more than ever they lacked the social graces and the gentle manners of civilized people.

However, critics of the Jews came to recognize a tendency among at least a part of the Jewish population to distance itself from the detested medieval past. The Jewish Enlightenment (Hebrew: *Haskala*) did not in all ways parallel trends in the Christian world; it spread later, with different rhythms and textures among the general Jewish population, and its center was more in Germany than in France. But in the Haskala was the same sense of emerging into light, of shaking off superstition, bigotry, and repression.

Most *maskilim* ("enlightened ones" in Hebrew) did not reject the Hebrew Bible or traditional Jewish learning with quite the same vehemence that characterized the rejection by the *philosophes* ("philosophers" in French) of Revelation and scholasticism. Nevertheless, many maskilim offered harsh criticism of Jewish tradition. Isaac d'Israeli (the father of Benjamin Disraeli) lamented that the rabbis of ancient Judaism had "cast their people into a bondage of ridiculous customs." Talmudic learning had led to a "degeneration" of the Jews; because of their absurd devotion to the study of it, they had become physically small and cowardly.[5] For their part, traditional Jews did indeed derisively turn their back on modern science and learning; the suggestion that non-Jewish learning might at least be equal to that of the Jews was considered heretical by many of the more traditional Jews of the period.[6]

Some philosophes expressed a degree of sympathy for the Jews but almost always because of the persecution they faced from Christian bigots and not for any positive qualities Jews may have had. Very few Enlightened observers, Gentiles or Jews, had anything sympathetic to say about the rabbis of the age. Nearly all Enlightened observers similarly expressed dismay at the cultural level and general moral tone of ordinary Jews, apart from a few exceptional individuals.

Enlightenment and Haskala were primarily concerns of intellectual elites, not the great mass of the population. However, the virtue those elites made of toleration and their hostility to traditional patterns of behavior found abundant if less strictly intellectual forms of support among the general population. Many who were abandoning the ways of their fathers did so without recourse to biblical criticism or philosophical reasoning. In the words of historian Todd Endelman, Jews

slipped into new patterns of behavior without much thought or serious pangs of guilt. To focus too exclusively on conscious perceptions of shifting values is to ignore these mundane adjustments in human behavior that constitute the stuff of reality. . . . Apathy and carelessness promoted the acculturation of European Jews as much as did the Haskala.[7]

Before the French Revolution rapidly and totally transformed the legal status of Jews in France, a number of measures had been passed under Louis XVI in the direction of liberalization and toleration. Elsewhere in Europe, most notably in Austria, under the Enlightened despot Joseph II, similar changes were being discussed and introduced, and earlier, in 1753, a much-debated

---

[5] Endelman, *Jews of Georgian England,* 152–3.

[6] Michael Stanislawski, *Tsar Nicholas I and the Jews* (Philadelphia, 1983), 49 ff.

[7] Endelman, *Jews of Georgian England,* 8.

Jewish Naturalization Bill had been introduced to the English parliament.[8] By the 1780s the issue of the civil status of Jews was being widely discussed among the educated elites in the German-speaking states. It was in those states that Moses Mendelssohn (1729–1786), the most famous and influential of the Jewish spokesmen in favor of Jewish civil equality, resided. It was he, perhaps more than any other individual in the eighteenth century, who effectively combated – by argument and by personal example – the charge of an unchangeably evil Jewish essence. Similarly, he argued, against general opinion, that Judaism and Enlightened principles could be reconciled. He translated the Pentateuch into High German (though using Hebrew characters), with an accompanying commentary that studiously ignored much of traditional talmudic learning.[9]

Mendelssohn was widely admired, but he by no means persuaded his contemporaries that most Jews could or would change. Even those favorably inclined to him expressed doubts whether most Jews, because of such practices as Sabbath observance and kashrut, could become soldiers or farmers. And if they could not, they could not then shoulder the burdens of citizenship – and should not be granted the rights of full and equal citizens. To be a citizen, at any rate, did not at this time entail, as it would later, becoming part of the German nation; even Mendelssohn believed that Jews were and would remain a separate people, or nation, inside Germany, with substantially different laws, customs, and beliefs. Still, many were ready to recognize that Gentile oppression may have made Jews even worse than they might otherwise have been. Mendelssohn's phrase "they bind our hands and then complain that we do not make use of them" was repeatedly quoted by Enlightened defenders of Jewish emancipation.[10]

The French Revolution and the Jews

Once revolutionaries had taken over in France after 1789 and had committed themselves to destroy the institutions of feudalism, replacing them with an Enlightened constitution, the question of what should be done about the Jews was unavoidable. As in Germany, Jews in France were considered, and considered themselves, a separate nation, a corporate body with special privileges granted by the king and with special obligations to him personally. They were not Frenchmen but rather Jews, a foreign people of Asian or Oriental origin (the terms were used by both Jews and non-Jews), living in France. Such a sense of separateness was distinctly stronger among Jews than it was among

---

[8] Endelman, *Jews of Georgian England*, 59–60 and passim.

[9] Jacob Katz, *Out of the Ghetto: The Social Background of Jewish Emancipation, 1770–1870* (Cambridge, Mass., 1973), 130.

[10] Ibid., 61.

other non-French but still Christian groups living in France. But it was hardly unique: Provincial and municipal fidelities among many residents of France also limited their sense of being part of the French nation. Basques, Alsatians, or residents of Brittany, for example, spoke different languages and had a strong sense of cultural distinctness from the French. Patriotism in the modern sense began to spread during the French Revolution but matured only gradually in the course of the nineteenth century, affecting the peasantry only in the early twentieth century.

When the revolutionaries of the new National Assembly proposed to make all residents of France into French citizens, equal under the law, sharp disagreement emerged concerning what should be done in the case of the Jews. Should they be recognized in the new constitution as resident aliens, and as such subject to special legislation, or should they be allowed to become French citizens, equal under the law to all other French citizens?

Many Jewish leaders, especially the rabbis, were at first hostile to the idea of French citizenship. French Jews had struggled, in the decades before the revolution, to gain greater freedom from discriminatory taxation, but most still favored legal and cultural separation from non-Jews. The rabbis had recently attempted to tighten up the bonds of corporate control and separateness to gain greater authority over the general Jewish population, in order to "control unruly Jews," as they put it.[11] The last thing most of them wanted was a systematic liberalization, giving Jews wider individual rights under laws that applied to Jews and non-Jews alike. The rabbis understood that such a liberalization would loosen their authority in favor of the authority of the French state. Indeed, in eastern Europe the idea of civil equality would soon be roundly denounced by Jewish leaders as a cynical device to disrupt the Jewish community – which in truth it often was. The assumption was widespread that "Jewish emancipation would have to be carried out against the desires of Jewish representatives."[12]

The Ashkenazic Jews of France, residing largely in Alsace, differed in profound ways from the small and scattered numbers of Sephardic Jews in the country. The Sephardim were generally French speaking, richer, more highly educated, and more thoroughly integrated into French society. The Ashkenazim were Yiddish speaking, more often poor and traditional in religion. Sephardic spokesmen often emphatically agreed with non-Jews concerning the general unsuitability of the Ashkenazim for French citizenship, due to their low moral character.

Even spokesmen for the Ashkenazim were inclined to agree with these pervasively negative evaluations, although most were quick to add that the unfortunate character of the Ashkenazim was the result of centuries of oppression.

[11] Hertzberg, *Enlightenment*, 317.

[12] Hannah Arendt, *The Origins of Totalitarianism* (New York, 1963), 33.

In a typically Enlightened fashion they asserted that a hostile environment had made them immoral and economically parasitic. Near unanimity among Jews and non-Jews apparently existed that the great majority of Jews in France needed "reform." A decade before the Revolution, the Metz Society of Arts and Sciences had offered a prize for the best essay on the question, "Are there means for making the Jews happy and more useful in France?" One essay described the Jews as a physically weak and ugly people, "disgraced by nature." It suggested removing them to the interior and putting them to work on the land in order to reform them. Another, written by an Enlightened Jew and generally eloquent in its defense of Jews, granted that "persecution throughout the centuries had indeed made the Jews a cultural backwater. . . . It accounts for the deplorable materialism and cowardliness of the Jewish character."[13]

That Jews were degenerate and physically unattractive seemed to pass as unchallenged assumptions in discussions among the Enlightened at midcentury.[14] Another Enlightened Jew, who was one of the prize winners of the Metz competition, emphasized the evil of Jewish tradition itself, at least in the form that tradition had assumed by the eighteenth century. His essay argued that the wickedness of contemporary Jews was not only the result of Gentile oppression; the Talmud, the rabbis, the teachings of Judaism were also to blame.[15] Thus, Jewish essence and an unfavorable environment were neatly joined. The implications of that argument were far-reaching: Could Jews remain Jews, preserving their traditions, and yet reform enough to become French citizens?

The debates in the revolutionary National Assembly, between 1789 and 1791, echoed the debates in salons and academies in the decades before the Revolution. No one offered a defense of the Jews as they were. Those considered friendly to the Jews merely argued that they at least should be given a chance to reform themselves; it would be inconsistent to abolish feudalism and retain the Jews in feudal isolation. Opponents of the idea insisted that Jews would never change – indeed, did not *want* to change. Therefore, they should simply be designated as resident foreigners, subject to the same limitations as any other noncitizens who took up residence in France.

Those defending the notion of civil equality for Jews also reasoned that anti-Jewish attitudes were a form of religious prejudice, and a growing consensus among the liberally minded was that religious conviction should be considered a private matter, one that need not get in the way of good citizenship. Opponents of Jewish emancipation retorted that Judaism was not a universalistic religion in the sense that the various Christian religions were. Judaic belief, they maintained, included the belief that Jews were a separate nation. It was

[13] Ibid., 329, 321.
[14] Endelman, *Jews of Georgian England*, 41.
[15] Hertzberg, *Enlightenment*, 335.

not then merely a private affair. Jews could not serve in the army because they would not eat the food that other soldiers ate. They would not drink wine produced by Gentiles. They would not wear the same clothes as other soldiers. They would not work or fight on the Sabbath. They could not be depended upon to defend the French nation because they were members of another nation, one that existed in other countries, potential enemies of France. A left-wing delegate from Alsace, while emphatically agreeing that most people living in France should not be excluded from citizenship because of religion, insisted that Judaism was a total way of life in which religious, civil, economic, and political principles were inextricably intertwined. He concluded, "It is not I that exclude the Jews; they exclude themselves."[16] There is little question that many traditional Jews in France and elsewhere agreed with him.

The delegates from Alsace, both right and left wing, were among the most vociferous opponents of giving citizenship to the Jews. Since Alsace was where the largest concentration of Jews in France was to be found, those delegates were the ones as well who had had the most extensive firsthand contact with them, and in the words of one historian, "there can be no doubt that . . . prejudice was fed by the actual appearance and behavior of the average Jew."[17] The delegates from Alsace bitterly and repeatedly complained about the activities of Jews in their province.[18] They no doubt harbored fantasies about Jews, but it would seem an odd conclusion that those fantasies were entirely responsible for their hostility to the notion of Jewish emancipation.

Opposition to the idea of civil equality for Jews from areas where the Sephardim were most numerous was distinctly less adamant,[19] and the Sephardim were granted civil equality first and separately (again, a development that is difficult to explain if Jewishness alone, or fantasies about Jewishness, were the only explanation for hostility to Jews at this time). Finally, in late 1791 after rancorous debate and a very close vote, the Ashkenazic Jews were also included. The record of the debate makes clear that this vote was made less out of sympathy for them than for the simple reasoning that it would not have been consistent with revolutionary principles to leave them out. In addition, the Revolution had awakened an intoxicating optimism in its first years, a sense that anything was possible for the Revolution – even reforming the Jews.[20]

Revolutionary armies carried the reforms of the Revolution to large parts of central and southern Europe in the following two decades. On the whole, Jews

[16] Hertzberg, *Enlightenment*, 335.

[17] Katz, *Ghetto*, 80.

[18] Hertzberg, *Enlightenment*, 335.

[19] Ibid.

[20] William H. Sewell, Jr., instructively explores the role of revolutionary ideology in this decision in "Ideologies and Social Revolutions: Reflections on the French Case," *Journal of Modern History*, vol. 57, no. 1, March 1985, 69–70.

in western German-speaking areas and in northern Italy greeted French armies as liberators. Ghetto walls were torn down, and Jews were encouraged to participate actively in the revolutionary governments that were established under French auspices, which many did. Even many of the rabbis who at first had been opposed to civil emancipation gradually came to favor it.

Napoleon and the Assembly of Jewish Notables

In the early years of the nineteenth century growing numbers of Jews in France responded positively and productively to emancipation, justifying the predictions of their defenders in the debates of the National Assembly. However, hesitations and suspicions remained. Many Alsatians insisted that Jewish vices, far from disappearing under the new laws, had actually gotten worse in their province. Jews had not taken the opportunity to assume honest physical labor but had pursued with even greater success their old ways of usury and exploitation.

The growing chorus of charges about Jews in Alsace finally reached the ear of Napoleon Bonaparte, who had gradually taken over leadership of the Revolution, becoming in 1804 Emperor of France and of the many territories conquered by France's armies. Napoleon had earlier entertained the idea of restoring the Jewish nation to Palestine, and he was widely regarded by Jews in western and central Europe as their liberator and protector. He nonetheless continued to think of them as a peculiarly troublesome national group with a number of tenacious vices that would require special legislation to remedy.[21]

In 1806 he expressed dissatisfaction with the "metaphysical" approach that had earlier led to the awarding of equal rights to Jews on the basis of abstract assumptions about a common humanity. He now insisted on "facts" and suggested that an assembly of the Jewish nation, like the French Estates General of 1789, be called. The Assembly of 111 Jewish Notables from France and Italy that met in 1806 contained rabbis of various persuasions, including some moderately Orthodox as well as laymen.[22] They were presented with a series of pointed questions that touched on the areas of continued suspicion and friction: the possibility of genuine patriotic and fraternal feeling for other French citizens by Jews; Jewish double standards in money lending and in other relations with Gentiles; and whether Jewish law forbade Jews to do certain kinds of work or to mix with Gentiles as equals. The answers provided by the Notables were transparently designed to put to rest any lingering suspicions. Jewish law, the Notables insisted, did not preclude full French citizenship for Jews, obedience to the French state, or fraternal feelings for non-Jews. As individuals, the

---

[21] Franz Kolber, *Napoleon and the Jews* (New York, 1975), 12, 55–62.

[22] Cf. in addition to Kolber, Jacob Katz, *Exclusiveness and Tolerance: Studies in Jewish–Gentile Relations in Medieval and Modern Times* (Oxford, 1961), 182 ff.

Notables favorably impressed government observers, one of whom termed them "highly admirable" men, whereas previously, in the various complaints about the Jews, "only the dregs . . . had come under notice."[23]

The Notables had been selected by French prefects, not elected by the Jewish rank-and-file. They thus did not speak for all or even most Jews in Europe, certainly not most of those in central and eastern Europe, where the overwhelming majority lived. How genuinely representative they were of Jewish opinion of the time even in western Europe is uncertain. Their answers were, moreover, hedged and evasive, as for example when they argued that Jewish law did not prohibit intermarriage with non-Jews (except, they recognized, for Egyptians and the Seven Canaanite Nations) or when they asserted that French Jews regarded Jews of other nations as "foreigners," just as much as non-Jewish French did.

Napoleon's advisers did not apparently raise the question of whether the Jews, in excluding Egyptians and members of the Seven Canaanite Nations, were also rejecting the *principle* of civil and human equality (Canaanites and Egyptians being presumably human in Jewish eyes), a principle that was central to the French Revolution. The more obvious question does not seem to have been posed explicitly: Could *halakha,* traditional Jewish law, and Enlightened–secular political principles be reconciled without doing violence to the essence of that law?

Napoleon thereafter arranged for a Great Sanhedrin, a central judicial body, to emerge from the Assembly of Notables. In the ensuing pronouncements of this body were to be seen, even more clearly than those of the Assembly, the assertion that Jews did not, at least not any longer, constitute a separate nation. "The Sanhedrin officially inaugurated the practice of the Emancipation era to make Israel appear a religious community . . . rather than as a separate people."[24] One observer has quipped: "Such majestic irony: the Sanhedrin, the supreme judicial institution of the Jewish community during five centuries of Roman rule in Palestine, now was summoned to abrogate Jewish legal authority."[25]

Many Orthodox representatives expressed vehement hostility to the Sanhedrin as a "radical assembly" led by Jewish heretics.[26] A key consideration for these Orthodox was whether the Gentiles with whom Jews were to deal were followers of the Noachide Laws (the commandments given to Noah, according to Jewish tradition, which included prohibitions against blasphemy, idolatry, sexual immorality, cruelty to animals, murder, and robbery). In other

---

[23] Kolber, *Napoleon*, 148.

[24] Ibid., 161.

[25] Jerold S. Auerbach, *Rabbis and Lawyers: The Journey from Torah to Constitution* (Bloomington, Ind., 1991), 73.

[26] Cf. Katz, *Ghetto*, 203–8.

words, they insisted on considering the issue in strictly halakhic terms. These were terms that were alien to French revolutionaries and that would certainly seem to eliminate many of them, especially the ruthless, blasphemous, and sexually immoral Napoleon himself. Even sympathetic non-Jews considered the Sanhedrin's assertions concerning Jewish national identity to be a goal rather than present reality.[27] Those assertions nonetheless did represent the voice of the future in western Europe. Yet the ambiguities would return to plague both sides. Before long some Jews, and not only the Orthodox, would come to wonder about the long-range implications of this bargain: Did it leave them with self-respect and the essence of their Jewishness intact?

Napoleon and his advisors were themselves less than completely persuaded by the answers of the Assembly of Notables, as became clear in 1808, with the introduction of what the Jews would term the "Infamous Decrees," which declared many debts owed to Jews null and void. Further, under these new laws no Jew was allowed to engage in trade without the specific approval of the municipality involved, and Jewish conscripts were prohibited from offering paid substitutes to take their places in the army. Napoleon's subsequent statements made it clear that he still believed Jewish law encouraged usurious exploitation of non-Jews and that special legislation would be necessary to induce Jews to abandon their centuries-old antisocial practices.

His viewpoint had wide support: Jews still had a lot of reforming to do; such seemed the consensus. And Jews themselves, whatever their religious position, might well retain certain reservations about the moral qualities of the Goyim with whom they were to enter into a new epoch of humanity and fraternity. But many observers on both sides were initially inclined to believe that the effect of an impatiently awaited freedom would solve all remaining difficulties.

Contrasts between East and West

The civil emancipation of Jews was retained in various degrees by most of the states that were subject to French rule, in spite of setbacks and backlashes in the reactionary decades after Napoleon's downfall in 1815. By midcentury a significant part of the Jewish population of western and central Europe, especially in the advanced urban areas, had accepted the fundamental break with the Judaism of the past. They had undertaken, in short, to "improve" themselves. Concurrently, growing numbers of Gentiles came to accept the idea of Jewish civil equality. Even where Jews faced continuing limitations on their exercise of citizenship, many if not most shared the optimism of the time and believed that as enlightenment spread among Gentiles and as Jews continued to improve themselves, those limitations would soon fall, as indeed they did to a large degree by the 1860s.

[27] Kolber, *Napoleon*, 165.

The situation in eastern Europe in the nineteenth century was distinctly different. The *Ostjuden,* or eastern Jews, most of whom lived in areas under the control of the recently much-expanded Russian Empire, still typically lived in premodern conditions. And from the standpoint of most ordinary Jews in eastern Europe – not just the rabbis – modern ideas originating in western Europe were a snare of the Evil One. Cultural assimilation and civil equality held few attractions for most eastern Jews. Even the small but growing minority of self-consciously modernizing among them generally retained a strong sense of themselves as a permanently separate people, with no interest in becoming Poles, Russians, or Romanians.

This division within Ashkenazic Jewry between western and eastern Jew evolved into a condition even more striking and important than the previously discussed division between Sephardim and Ashkenazim. Jews who had resided for a generation or more in modern cities like Paris or Berlin generally had a low regard for those Jews in the backward, scattered "townlets," or market towns (*shtetlekh* in Yiddish, *mestechki* in Russian), in which millions of Ostjuden lived.[28] Jews in the West were inclined to view Jews of the shtetl (pl., shtetlekh), in eastern Europe as rude, dirty, and superstitious. The Ostjuden, small numbers of whom continued to move into western Europe in the middle years of the century, were for western Jews painfully embarrassing reminders of a distasteful Jewish past; they were what western Jews had been before they had begun to improve themselves.

Western Jews viewed the Jews of eastern Europe not only as embarrassingly backward, ragged, and filthy; the imagery they employed paralleled that of the anti-Semites. Western Jews often described Ostjuden as parasitic and filled with hatred for non-Jews, those specifically Jewish qualities that were the source of the most insistent and hostile remarks by anti-Semites about Jews generally. And since those embarrassing "eastern cousins" continued to filter into western areas, the process of Gentile–Jewish reconciliation and adjustment, western Jews lamented, was being constantly disrupted.[29]

The problem was aggravated in that the economic and cultural distance between western and eastern Jews tended to widen in the course of the century. In the West (including France, Switzerland, the German and Italian states, the Netherlands, Belgium, Great Britain, Scandinavia, and the western parts of the Habsburg Empire) the high hopes of the Enlightenment for unceasing progress found ample fulfillment. The standard of living of all classes improved markedly, especially by the 1850s and 1860s, and Jews did especially well, most of them gradually entering the prosperous middle and upper-middle class, or

---

[28] Cf. Peter Gay, *Freud, Jews, and Other Germans* (Oxford, 1978), 152–3; Steven E. Aschheim, *Brothers and Strangers: The East European Jew in German–Jewish Consciousness* (Madison, Wisc., 1982).

[29] Aschheim, *Brothers,* 62.

bourgeoisie, in an age that was widely proclaimed to belong to the middle classes.[30]

The improvement was not only material. Jews who had been peddlers and dealers in secondhand clothing, with all that such activities implied in low social standing and coarseness of manner, gradually assumed the gentility and deportment of the educated western bourgeoisie. Away went the cassock, earlocks, and *sheytl* (the wig covering the shaved head of the married Jewish woman). The German sense of *Bildung*, of rational self-control and aesthetic refinement, became a potent model for the largest population of Jews in the West, those in German-speaking lands.[31]

In the first six decades of the nineteenth century, the Gentile bourgeoisie in most western countries was engaged in a protracted struggle for political rights, for the introduction of liberal political and economic institutions. The Jewish bourgeoisie was generally welcomed as an ally in this struggle, and Gentile liberal reformers were among the most consistent proponents of full civil equality for Jews. Among some of them a kind of philo-Semitism evolved; warm friendships between an elite of cultured Gentiles and Jews were common.[32] Just as during the years of revolution in France, when the Third Estate, led by the bourgeoisie, was termed the only useful estate, so in Germany the *Bürgertum*, Jewish and Gentile, was described by its defenders as the general or universal order *(Allgemeiner Stand)*, in which political virtue and social utility were to be found, as contrasted to the idle uselessness of the nobility and even parasitic harmfulness of the priests and rabbis.

In France and England, where there were significantly fewer Jews than in German-speaking central Europe, the Jewish population was even more overwhelmingly inclined to take up the manners and liberal political beliefs of the educated gentleman, whether bourgeois or noble. The classical education of such gentlemen increasingly became also the education of the Jewish bourgeoisie, for whom the ancient pagan authors Homer, Aristotle, and Cicero now vied with the books of Moses and utterly vanquished the talmudic commentary on those books. German, French, and English classics replaced the works traditionally read by learned Jews; Kant and Goethe, Diderot and Voltaire, Shakespeare and Dickens took precedence over Rashi and Maimonides. In Vienna, by midcentury, Jewish students in the *Gymnasium* (the elite secondary school) openly mocked the rabbis who were sent to teach them traditional Judaism. As a historian of Viennese Jewry has concluded, "For many, Judaism paled by comparison to Plato, Sophocles, or Julius Caesar, the real heroes of the Gymnasium world."[33]

---

[30] Cf. Robert S. Wistrich, *Socialism and the Jews: The Dialectics of Emancipation in Germany and Austria-Hungary* (East Brunswick, N.J., 1984), 55, for bibliography; also, Marsha L. Rosenblit, *The Jews of Vienna, 1867–1914: Assimilation and Identity* (New York, 1984).

[31] Cf. George L. Mosse, *German Jews Beyond Judaism* (Bloomington, Ind., 1985), 3 ff.

[32] Cf. Alfred D. Low, *Jews in the Eyes of Germans: From the Enlightenment to Imperial Germany* (Philadelphia, 1979), 167 ff.

[33] Rosenblit, *Vienna*, 123.

Eastern Europe did not enjoy a comparable rise in material welfare; desperate poverty among Jews as among other peoples remained widespread, as did disease, superstition, and illiteracy (contrary to common belief, illiteracy did exist among the poorest of Jews). Moreover, while political liberalization in the West was being refined and extended to ever-widening strata of the population, a heavy-handed, erratic, and often corrupt despotism prevailed in eastern Europe. Although Jews suffered from various legal restrictions, they were nowhere actually enserfed or enslaved, as was a major part of the non-Jewish lower classes. In that and a number of other important respects Jews remained privileged, usually better off materially than the peasant masses.

Another difference in eastern Europe was that Jews did not – could not – ally with the Gentile bourgeoisie in favor of a liberal program, since the eastern European non-Jewish urban middle class was minuscule. Even in those urban areas where there was a numerically significant non-Jewish bourgeoisie, it was also often foreign, typically German in the North, Greek in the South. Moreover, the eastern Jewish bourgeoisie was a westernizing bourgeoisie; even when it took up Polish or Russian as its language of communication, it retained a cosmopolitanism that was not typical of other groups.

Trends within Judaism

Rather than being affected by Enlightenment, refinement of manners, or Bildung, the great mass of Jews in eastern Europe had followed a contrary path, toward hasidic Judaism, which was pietistic, mystical, and plebeian – as well as aggressively anti-rationalist. The hasid could be positively disdainful of fine manners and of traditional Jewish learning, to say nothing of the intellectual and cultural products of the Goyim. All were seen as obstacles to godliness.

The hasidic masses had little use or emotional predilection for bourgeois virtues; they had scant understanding of or appreciation for liberal beliefs in individualism, self-reliance, rationality, and critical acumen. The overall style of the hasidim, to say nothing of their standards of hygiene, was shocking to the cultivated middle and upper classes, Jews and non-Jews. The Jews of the Austrian province of Galicia were notorious in these regards. Sigmund Freud's mother, Amalia, was described by her grandson as a member of a "peculiar race . . . absolutely different from Jews who had lived in the West for some generations. . . . These Galician Jews had little grace and no manners; and their women were certainly not what we should call 'ladies.'"[34]

To the western Jew the hasid appeared boorish, malodorous, and fanatical; to the hasid the western Jew was cold, formal, and vain – fair game for the most damning of epithets in Yiddish: *apikoyros* (free-thinker) or *meshumed*

---

[34] Martin Freud, *Sigmund Freud: Man and Father* (New York, 1958), 11; cf. John Murray Cuddihy, *The Ordeal of Civility: Freud, Marx, Lévy-Strauss, and the Jewish Struggle with Modernity* (New York, 1974), 100–1.

(convert, apostate). As far as the western Jew was concerned, the hasid had perversely turned his face against modern times and had locked himself into a culture of poverty, backwardness, and intellectual slavery. For the hasid the western Jew had abandoned God and piety for money and material welfare or for other, even less worthy forms of "Gentile pleasures" *(goyim nakhes)*.

These contrasts were less simple than a mere East–West division, however. Within eastern European Jewry, the so-called *mitnagdim* ("opponents") were fierce enemies of the hasidim, maintaining a more traditional taste for sober study and restrained religious expression, as opposed to the swaying prayers, vociferous singing, and sweaty religious exultation of the hasidim. For the mitnagdim the hasidim were the radicals, those who were breaking with a long-established Jewish tradition. Both mitnagdim and maskilim in eastern Europe were typically among the more affluent and educated of eastern Jews, and they were often favored by the authorities, further intensifying the suspicion and hatred for them by the hasidim, whom officials were more likely to distrust and mistreat. Thus, religious differences had important economic, social, and political dimensions.

Jews in German-speaking lands took up *Hochdeutsch,* or High German, and caustically belittled the traditional Ashkenazic tongue, Yiddish, itself mostly German in vocabulary and grammar. They spoke the noble and dignified language of Kant and Goethe, while the Ostjuden retained a "jargon" – a nasal, whining, and crippled ghetto tongue. The reactions of the overwhelming majority of western-educated German Jews to Yiddish paralleled and indeed epitomized their attitudes to the Ostjuden. Yiddish was, as one assimilated Jew typically put it, a "barbarous mishmash." It was "an insult against all languages, which it wrenches and distorts, monstrous in form and shocking in tone."[35] The anti-Semites would put it no more strongly, and the Zionists of the late nineteenth century, as well as Israelis of the twentieth, would add their voices to the abundant abuse of Yiddish as a proper language for self-respecting Jews.

The assimilation of Jews in the West entailed not only the enjoyment of an unparalleled prosperity, political freedom, and cultural refinement; a related alteration of Jewish religion was introduced, basing itself on the thought of Mendelssohn and other maskilim. This alteration subjected traditional Judaism to an often withering scrutiny. Many long-standing criticisms of Judaism by Gentiles were accepted as valid. Western Judaism became "spiritualized," emphasizing the more universalistic elements of traditional Judaism and deemphasizing the tribalistic and ritualistic.

The specific institutional forms that this alteration assumed were different from country to country, but in a general way they all sought to make Jewish religion not only more spiritual but more private. Jews became less publicly visible, whether in speech, gesture, dress, facial hair, or eating habits. And just

---

[35] Wistrich, *Socialism,* 142.

as this more spiritual Judaism emphasized points of common belief with Christianity, especially Protestant Christianity, so within their places of worship reforming Jews borrowed extensively from Christian practices: They introduced greater brevity, simplicity, and decorum in the services; they played music, allowed the sexes to sit together, and listened to sermons in modern languages. Many, similarly, no longer observed kashrut or the laws of niddah (the elaborate regulations concerning contact with menstruating women). Some Jews even advocated an end to circumcision; the kissing and sucking up of the blood of the infant's just-circumcised penis, in the traditional *bris* ceremony, was a source of shock or derision for Gentiles who heard of it and further embarrassed western Jews who considered the entire ceremony cruel or primitive.

Followers of Orthodox Judaism, who gradually became a small minority in the West, often considered this break with the Jewish past to be as significant as the schism within Christianity between Protestantism and Catholicism. Bitter conflicts of authority developed between Reform and Orthodox rabbis. But the latter were on the losing side, and they represented the more rural, less educated, and poorer Jews. Many Jews in the West became extremely lax in observing Jewish rituals, typically identifying themselves in a vague way with ethical monotheism, just as many Christians rejected much traditional dogmatic belief and ritual. Many Christians and Jews expressed profound relief in escaping what was for them the suffocating confinements of the faith of their forefathers.

As many of them viewed the matter, some sort of convergence of Christian and Judaic belief appeared possible around common ethical and metaphysical beliefs of a rationalistic and spiritualized nature. For both Christians and Jews, their identity as members of a modern nation began to take precedence over their religious identity. German Jews, for example, were careful to insist on the distinction that they were "Germans of Jewish faith," rather than Jews residing in Germany or members of the Jewish nation in Germany, as Jews had considered themselves only a few decades before.

Secularism and Divided Fidelities

During the middle years of the nineteenth century, growing numbers of Christians and Jews found a new purpose and a new fellowship in the secular ideologies and movements of the day, particularly in political liberalism. German Jews played an important role in the National Liberal (right–liberal) and Progressive (left–liberal) parties in the German Reich, and Jewish voters in Germany overwhelmingly chose one or the other of those parties. Similarly, in the Habsburg Empire liberal parties won the overwhelming fidelity of middle-class Jews, especially in the major cities Vienna, Prague, and Budapest.

Anticlericalism on the part of former Christians became a major force in a number of western countries. A Jewish equivalent, that is, a systematic hostility by western Jews to rabbinical authorities, certainly existed but was less prominent, mostly because Judaism, or the rabbis who led it, exercised nothing like the nationwide secular authority of the Christian churches. But general attacks by Jews on religious superstition, bigotry, and ignorance – both Christian and Judaic – were widespread.

Nearly all western Jews harbored a special detestation for what they ironically dubbed the *Wunderrabbiner* (wonder rabbis), the leaders of the hasidic masses, supposed miracle-workers, who ruled with a sometimes corrupt hand over their often gullible followers. Of course most western Jews had little sustained contact with the hasidic leaders, but knowledge of them filtered westward with the movement of Jews out of eastern Europe. Even inside eastern Europe, progressive Jews were inclined to blame hasidic leaders for much of the hostility that Jews experienced.

The inroads that non-Jewish ways made among Jews in the nineteenth century had few parallels in Jewish history. Even the hellenistic, Arabic, or Spanish influences of the past, which certainly exercised powerful attractions for Jews, do not seem to have so utterly overwhelmed such large numbers of them in their sense of independent worth as Jews. This potent cultural hegemony was part of a much wider triumph of western civilization, one that gathered force into the early twentieth century and that continues, if diminished, to this day. Just as non-Europeans throughout the world have wrestled with the dilemma of how to retain a sense of their own unique identity while incorporating certain elements of western civilization – elements that they find difficult to ignore – so European Jews wrestled with the dilemmas and ineffable complexities of acculturation and assimilation.

The Liberal Years of Midcentury

In the West, the years of the midcentury, especially the 1850s and 1860s, active and visible opposition to the notion of Jewish civil equality declined, though hardly disappeared, confirming the general optimism of the period concerning what freedom and equality would gradually bring in terms of human enlightenment. Most of the remaining legal restrictions concerning Jews were lifted, and many Jews became prominent politicians, respected businessmen, successful artists, and influential writers. In Russia, the 1840s and 1850s were dominated by the policies of Nicholas I, the most repressive and paranoiac of modern monarchs in Russia. Jews in the West looked eastward in horror – and in thankfulness for their own relatively favored situation.

Racist ideas gained wide popularity in western Europe in these same decades, yet racism did not yet translate into focused expressions of hatred for Jews as a race or even into effective opposition to Jewish emancipation. It is obviously true that hostility to Jews in a more general sense continued to live what Jacob Katz has termed an "underground existence" or what Jackson Lears has more suggestively termed a "counter-hegemony,"[36] just as many, perhaps most, Jews retained in the inner reaches of their psyches reservations or anxieties about what full membership in modern European societies might entail. But in these middle years of the century political parties did not denounce Jews in their programs; laws were not constantly proposed to "control" Jews.

All of these things would come later, in the more troubled last quarter of the century, but much of the population of western and central Europe either had more pressing concerns (these are years of national unification for Germany and Italy, for example) or were willing to grant that the experiment in Jewish emancipation might be·working. Gratification concerning material prosperity, optimism about the future, and exhilaration over national triumphs all smoothed over possible friction. This period of liberal triumph has been referred to as the "honeymoon years" of Jewish–Gentile relations. In truth, these relations were not much like romantic love, but even if the honeymoon imagery is accepted as appropriate, these years have been given, retrospectively, rosy hues that cannot bear rigorous scrutiny. And honeymoons always end, sometimes with bitter reflections concerning the flawed beliefs and naive expectations upon which the union was initially conceived.

Backward Russia and the Ostjuden

The great advances in the West left Russia behind, and her leaders became steadily more anxious concerning how progress in western Europe, especially in terms of increased military power, might threaten Russia. Yet, an imitation of western models promised to open a Pandora's box. Already in the early part of the century, European modernization had delivered a shock to the countries involved. For many Russians, a similar prospect for their country was wholly unacceptable. Russian institutions and traditions and objective conditions in Russia all seemed less adaptable. And in no arena did the issue of liberalization and modernization appear more threatening than that of Russia's Jews.

In Russia's western territories was concentrated by far the largest population of Jews in Europe, indeed in the world, and that population grew rapidly in the nineteenth century, more rapidly than most of the surrounding populations. Jews in the Russian Empire were approximately four times more numerous

---

[36] Jacob Katz, "Misreadings of Anti-Semitism," *Commentary,* vol. 76, no. 1, July 1983, 43; T. Jackson Lears, "The Concept of Cultural Hegemony: Problems and Possibilities," *American Historical Review,* vol. 90, no. 3, June 1985, 567 ff.

than in the Habsburg Empire, ten times more numerous than in Germany, and a hundred times more numerous than in France (5 million in Russia, 1.3 million in Austria-Hungary, 500,000 in Germany, 40,000 in France toward the end of the century). Jews were only one of a large number of conquered peoples or nations in the Russian Empire. Thus, the French model of an integral nation would have been incomparably more difficult to introduce into Russia and was not seriously entertained. At times brutal efforts were made by tsarist authorities to russify their various minorities, but the goal of russification was not to create an integral nation on the French model but rather to enhance the power of the central state and assure fidelity to the autocratic tsar.

In this regard the contrast with France is especially revealing, for the unbending demand by French authorities that French Jews speak French, attend French schools, follow French laws, and in pervasive ways adopt French culture was willingly accepted by most Jews in France. In Germany as well, Jews willingly became German in pervasive ways. But in Russia the populations to be russified, both Jews and other non-Russians, were significantly larger, more heterogeneous, and resistant. Moreover, to assimilate Russian culture was a less attractive prospect for them than to become French was for minority groups in France. The distinguished economist and sociologist Franz Oppenheimer, himself a German Jew, wrote,

Jewish culture, as it has been preserved from the Middle Ages in the ghettoes of the East, stands infinitely lower than modern [western] culture. . . . But it would be impossible for the Eastern Jews to be Russian or Rumanian. . . . For medieval Jewish culture stands as far above Eastern European barbarism as it is beneath the culture of Western Europe.[37]

Many regions in Russia's western and southern provinces were a quilt-work of nationalities, whose members lived side-by-side within towns, townlets, and villages, yet retained distinct identities and living standards. Leon Trotsky remembered how, during his childhood years in southwestern Russia, "in the German section the houses were neat . . . the horses large, the cows sleek. In the Jewish section the cabins were dilapidated, the roofs scattered, the cattle scrawny." The Ukrainian and Romanian peasants in the area were even lower in the economic and social scale.[38]

Russian Jews throughout the nineteenth century remained a nation most emphatically apart from the dominant Great Russians and from the other nationalities among whom they lived (Poles, Ukrainians, Byelo-Russians). Jewish national distinctness was obvious in many regards: religion, lan-

---

[37] Aschheim, *Brothers,* 97.

[38] Leon Trotsky, *My Life* (London, 1975), 38; cf. Robert Wistrich, *Trotsky: Fate of a Revolutionary* (New York, 1982), 15.

guage, dress, diet, and even civil law. Russia's political institutions, reigning religion (Russian Orthodoxy), customs, and history all seemed particularly unfavorable to the prospect of a harmonious compromise between Jews and non-Jews. Stringent prohibitions against Jews settling in Russian lands had been in force up to the late eighteenth century. The various Judeophobic strains to be found in other forms of Christianity were especially strong in Russian Orthodoxy; judaizing heresies had long been viewed with special aversion. The countervailing tendencies of toleration and philo-Semitism, seen especially in certain varieties of Protestantism, were weak in Russian Orthodoxy. Thus trouble was to be expected when Russia expanded into eastern Europe from the 1780s to 1815, suddenly bringing millions of Jews into its jurisdiction.

In the preceding three to four centuries Jews in great numbers had moved from central and western Europe into Poland and the surrounding lands dominated by the Poles (Lithuania, the Ukraine, Byelo-Russia). Polish kings and nobles had welcomed Jews, and Jewish settlers in Poland thrived.[39] The Jews were promised protection, autonomy, and corporate privileges, as were other foreign national groups in these years, most importantly, Germans. Thus, although Jews and Germans had settled in these lands centuries before the Russian occupation, their foreign origin was never in question, whereas Poles or Ukrainians were considered indigenous peoples. Indeed, Jewish and German settlers were both firmly intent on maintaining their separate identity. However, an elite of German settlers did gradually russify and merge into the ruling orders of the Russian Empire. Such was not the case with the Jews.

Jews in Poland occupied a peculiar economic and social stratum. They often took up the role of commercial middlemen, serving the Polish royalty and nobility as agents, stewards, and overseers, helping the upper classes to manage their lands. A proverb spoke of Poland as "paradise" for Jews and nobles, but "hell" for peasants.[40] For centuries Jews in Poland enjoyed more protection by kings and nobles, more civil autonomy and religious freedom than anywhere else in Europe.[41]

Jewish life in Poland was hardly uninterrupted bliss. In the mid–seventeenth century, a time of ferocious religious warfare throughout Europe, the Ukrainian leader Bogdan Chmielnicki rose up against Polish domination, exacting a bloody and wanton retribution on Polish overlords, Catholic clergy,

---

[39] Cf. Salo W. Baron, *A Social and Religious History of the Jews* (New York, 1965), vol. 10, 31 ff.; also Alan Edelstein, *An Unacknowledged Harmony: Philosemitism and the Survival of European Jewry* (Westport, Conn., 1982), 84 ff.

[40] William Hagen, *Germans, Poles, and Jews: The Nationality Conflict in East Prussia, 1772–1914* (Chicago, 1980), 13.

[41] Ibid., 17–21.

and Jews. In the course of the next century the arrival and increasing power of the Jesuits in Poland heightened insecurity for Jews but did so even more for the Protestant German settlers.

Recent research has suggested that the misfortunes of Jews in Poland were not quite so widespread or crippling as they have been portrayed in Jewish Leidensgeschichte. Historians now doubt that hundreds of thousands of Jews were killed by Chmielnicki's forces, as earlier accounts stated. In Poland as in much of the rest of Europe in these chaotic years, stomach-turning atrocities were committed, but it is open to serious question if Jews suffered in substantially larger numbers than others caught up in the raging battles. A recent painstaking historian has concluded that in fact most Jews avoided violence at this time and that the ravages of Chmielnicki's forces must be seen as a "brutal but relatively short interruption in the steady growth and expansion" of Polish Jewry.[42] By the end of the century Jews had sufficiently recovered economically and demographically that they represented ten percent of Poland's population. The figure is revealing in that such a percentage is impossible to account for had the destruction been as great or had the Jews died in anything like the numbers claimed by seventeenth-century Jewish chroniclers.[43] The modern rise of the Jews, then, had substantial roots in seventeenth and eighteenth century Poland.

The various partitions of Poland in the late eighteenth century and the final settlements agreed to at the Congress of Vienna in 1815 gave Russia the largest part of a no longer independent Poland. The Russian tsar became the king of what was called Congress Poland, encompassing a much smaller area than prepartition Poland. Prussia took the relatively small western Polish province of Posen, and Austria, the somewhat larger southwestern Polish province of Galicia. Thus, Prussia and Austria also suddenly acquired Jewish populations that were much larger and more concentrated than had been the case before.

By the middle years of the century, the Jews of Posen and Galicia were awarded Prussian and Austrian citizenship, including the right of free movement. They took advantage of it to an impressive degree. For example, in 1817 forty-one percent of Prussia's Jews lived in recently acquired Posen; by 1910 that figure had dropped to six percent. Hundreds of thousands of Jews also left Galicia in the same period for the opportunities of modern city life in the Empire, in Prague, Vienna, and Budapest, and of course in the New World. Jews in Russia's newly conquered provinces, however, were mostly required to remain in the so-called Pale of Settlement. As non-Christians they were generally forbidden to migrate to the big cities of Holy Russia's interior,

---

[42] Jonathan I. Israel, *European Jewry in the Age of Mercantilism* (Oxford, 1985), 121.

[43] Hagen, *Germans,* 22.

St. Petersburg and Moscow, or indeed even to Kiev, also considered a city holy to Christians, which was squarely within the Pale.

The Pale of Settlement

"Pale" in this unfamiliar sense meant "fence" or "boundary," and the Pale of Settlement generally enclosed those territories in which large Jewish populations were to be found. Technically, Congress Poland was not part of the Pale (a point not often understood), but most of the extensive territories to the east and south of Congress Poland, once ruled by Poland (Lithuania, Byelo-Russia, the Ukraine), were included in it. The tsarist state did not willingly recognize corporate rights, feudal heritage, or even Roman law,[44] and thus Russia's takeover of formerly Polish territories, where such recognition had existed, seemed to promise an end to the "paradise" of protection, autonomy, and privilege enjoyed by the Jews. But in fact Catherine the Great, the ruler at the time of the partitions, "treated her new subjects with even-handed liberality,"[45] and the extensive privileges the Jews had enjoyed under Polish rule were guaranteed.

Catherine was no friend of the Jews, but she hoped to encourage trade and industry in Russia. She gave her new Jewish subjects an equal footing with Christians in municipal governments, and she granted them admission to the urban estates of "townsmen" *(meshchane)* and members of the merchant guilds.[46] However, a large contradiction was contained in this recognition of Jewish urban privileges, for many Jews at this time lived not in towns or cities but in villages and market townlets (the previously mentioned shtetlekh). In principle they were required by the new laws to move to areas officially defined as urban, but in practice they usually did not, since their livelihood depended upon contact with the peasants. In the course of the following century, this contradiction would be the cause of much grief to the Jews of the Pale. An overriding concern of many tsarist ministers was to separate the peasants and the Jews, because it was believed that the Jews not only exploited the peasants but corrupted them, especially through the sale of alcohol, leading to drunkenness, indigence, and unrest.

Still, tsarist oppression was less fearsome and less omnipresent than many accounts maintain. Even under the arch-reactionary Nicholas I (1825–1855), Jews retained most of their privileges, and they were by no means the only nationality or religious group that faced official suspicion and mistreatment.

---

[44] Cf. Michael Stanislawski, *Nicholas I and the Jews* (Philadelphia, 1983), xi–xii.

[45] Hans Rogger, *Russia in the Age of Modernization and Revolution, 1881–1917* (New York, 1983), 200.

[46] *Meshchane* is roughly synonymous with "burgher" or "bourgeois," and even more strongly than the latter of those implies in Russian "Philistine" and narrow money grubbing.

The Catholic Poles, more numerous and far more inclined to violent resistance, were viewed as a larger problem by tsarist authorities, who often resorted to the strategy of divide-and-rule, playing upon the antipathies of Catholic Poles, Jews, Protestant Germans, Uniate Ruthenians, and Greek Orthodox Ukrainians.

The notorious drafting of Jews into the army for terms of up to twenty-five years under Nicholas I, a familiar theme of Leidensgeschichte, was part of an effort to rationalize the government, making Jews, like others, responsible for military service; it was not primarily designed to persecute them, although given the privileged status of Jews up to this point, they tended to perceive it as persecution, a sharp and cruel break with the special consideration they had long enjoyed under the Poles, which included not serving in the military.

In the course of the century large numbers of Jews from Prussian Posen and Austrian Galicia eventually prospered and entered the middle and upper-middle classes. Tsarist authorities, in introducing the Pale of Settlement, were determined to avoid exacerbating their own potentially far greater Jewish problem. They were intent on keeping large numbers of Jews out of Holy Mother Russia, on "fencing" them into the newly incorporated non-Russian lands. Still, the notorious inefficiencies and inconsistencies of tsarist policies often undermined such goals.

The Pale of Settlement covered a vast area. Its legal confinements, and the corruption of those who enforced them, could be stifling, but the geographical space was not. Jews were no more territorially confined in the new Russian holdings than they had been when those same territories were under the "paradise" of Polish rule. The Pale enclosed in fact a larger area than France or Spain; it stretched from the Baltic to the Black Sea, an area of approximately 1 million square kilometers, forty times as large as the modern state of Israel.

Descriptions of the quality of life within the shtetl communities have undergone remarkable shifts. The venomous denigration of the culture of the shtetl that was typical in western Europe for most of the nineteenth century stands in sharp contrast to the tendency, especially in late twentieth-century America, to romanticize and celebrate it. The romantic "cult of the Ostjuden" went through a number of stages, from the often highly intellectualized efforts to discover Jewish authenticity in eastern Jewish communities by thinkers like Martin Buber, around the turn of the century, to the banalities and anachronistic accounts offered by American television, popular novels, and Hollywood.

What is most often overlooked in most recent accounts is that life in the shtetl was not only materially poor but often cruel and benighted. Trotsky wrote of a scene from his childhood, "engraved in my memory forever": The Jews of the shtetl were dragging a woman through the street, kicking her, screaming at her, and spitting on her, since she had violated the sexual mores of the community.[47] Trotsky was a hostile observer, like millions of other Jews happy to have put that world behind him, but the point remains that few modern citizens could tolerate the cramped and intolerant life of the shtetl for even the briefest period.

A large part of the problem in arriving at a balanced view of tsarist rule and the quality of shtetl life is that the profound transformations in the Pale in the nineteenth century are easily misunderstood. Similarly, the Pale was diverse in geography, nationalities, and administrative regulations. Rather than being consistently and uniformly bad, the legal situation of the Jews varied from region to region and fluctuated significantly under different tsars, provincial governors, and local authorities. Nicholas I was the most repressive. Alexander II (1855–1881), the "tsar liberator," was relatively liberal, especially in his first years. Alexander III (1881–1894), taking over after his father had been assassinated, was once again repressive.

Jews could move about, own land (surely the belief that Jews could not own land ranks as one of the most often heard oversimplifications about their status, both in Russia and elsewhere in Europe[48]), engage in commerce, and attend universities. To be sure, each of these activities was regulated with a heavier hand and more erratic and corrupt management than in most western states. Jews may have experienced these regulations as more burdensome than others did because of the rapidly expanding numbers of Jews and their tendency to concentrate in certain occupations; few peasants were concerned about whether they got into the university, while many Jews were.

As the century progressed, increasing numbers of Russian and Polish Jews were obliged to take up manual labor. There had long been a fairly large class of Jewish artisans, and there were even some Jews, around one percent of the total Jewish population, who worked the land with their own hands, as opposed to hiring Christian peasants to do it, the more common situation. But Jewish agriculturists were never legally tied to the land, as were large numbers of Russian peasants until the 1860s.

In the Pale of Settlement as a whole, ten to fifteen percent of the population was Jewish (the only comparable concentration outside of Russia was in Galicia, at eleven percent), but Jews were concentrated in much higher numbers in

---

[47] Trotsky, *My Life*, 39.

[48] The matter entails complexities that cannot be entered into here, but the Jews' right to own land in Russia was guaranteed in statute as early as 1804, under Alexander I. The real issue became not whether Jews could own land, if they would work it with their own hands, but whether they could own land that allowed them to exploit the labor of the peasants. Cf. the relevant documents in Paul R. Mendes-Flohr and Jehuda Reinharz, *The Jew in the Modern World: A Documentary History* (Oxford, 1980), 304. In most of the rest of Europe, Jewish ownership of land was firmly recognized by the nineteenth century, if not before.

some areas. Bialystok's population in the 1860s was approximately seventy-five percent Jewish, Moghilev's, around ninety percent, and the population of Lodz was also overwhelmingly Jewish. By 1900 over half of the urban population of Lithuania and Byelo-Russia was Jewish. In Bessarabia (the province bordering on Romania, touching the Black Sea) and in Congress Poland the rate of growth of the Jewish population appears to have been about three times as fast as that of the non-Jewish population. The southern cities of Kishinev and Odessa, which would see major pogroms in the early twentieth century, had populations that were fifty percent Jewish. Commonly, Jews made up over ninety percent of the business class in Russia's cities. During the liberal or reforming period of Alexander II, large numbers of permits to leave the Pale were issued to certain categories of Jews who were deemed especially useful to the state. These included Merchants of the First Guild, doctors, skilled artisans, and prostitutes. Illegal passage out of the Pale was commonplace if risky; Russia had something like 500,000 illegal Jewish residents by the latter part of the century.[49]

Russia's "Liberal" Experiment

The twenty-two year reign of Alexander II (1859–1881) was devoted to catching up with western Europe. Alexander's goal was to bring to Russia the industrial productivity, institutional efficiency, and the military strength that came through western-style modernization. However, he sought to introduce and shape those reforms from above, without the broad participation of the people. Alexander oversaw far-reaching changes in the state bureaucracy, the judiciary, and the military; he opened up trade and communication; and he liberalized the press laws and freed Russia's serfs.

The loosening of the existing restrictions on Jews was part of a general program. They were encouraged to buy land and to become farmers (a few did, some successfully, in dairy and sugar production, for example). They were encouraged to attend universities, to hold public office, and to enter the free professions, and they did so in unprecedented numbers. To be sure, the great mass of impoverished Jews benefited relatively little from such changes, and anti-Jewish feelings were by no means effectively curbed. Still, Jews in Russia thrived materially in the 1860s and 1870s. Fortunes were made by an elite of Jewish merchants and industrialists, especially in textiles, liquor, tobacco, sugar, and railroad construction. These decades in Russia were thus not unlike the liberal 1850s and 1860s in western Europe in terms of Jewish upward mobility, the growing social differentiation of the Jewish population, and the tendency of a growing number of Jews to break with tradition.

---

[49] Martin Gilbert, *Atlas of the Holocaust* (Oxford, 1988), 74; Hans Rogger, "Government, Jews, and land in post-emancipation Russia," *Cahiers du monde russe et soviétique*, vol. 17, no. 1, Jan.–Mar., 181.

However, the absolute and relative number of Jews inside Russia was significantly greater, just as the poverty of the Jewish masses was more extensive and seemingly intractable. Jews in Russia became rich entrepreneurs by the hundreds, perhaps thousands, comfortable professionals by the tens of thousands, but the great majority of Jews – hundreds of thousands and millions – remained poor, some of them probably poorer than before because of the rapid increase in their numbers, the inability of traditional occupations to absorb them, and the inescapable disruptions of rapid economic and social change.

Industrialization produces winners and losers: Some Jews became rich, but increasing numbers of them entered the ranks of a pauperized proletariat. It was a development with parallels in the experience of the lower orders in western countries, but there were important differences. The Jewish proletariat in Russia only rarely entered into areas of primary production; there were few if any Jewish miners or steel workers, for example. Relatively few Jews were employed in the most modern factories, on the docks, or on the railroads. Employers in the primary industries would often not hire Jews, and non-Jewish workers at times refused to work beside them. Strenuous manual labor was widely regarded as inappropriate for Jews, and observance of Jewish ritual requirements undoubtedly did make it more difficult for observant Jews than for non-Jews to enter most areas of primary production. Such considerations explain in part the tendency of Jews to enter the clothing and needle trades, where a degree of independence was possible, and where the labor, although arduous, did not require great physical strength.

There was a further religious factor at work, in that the Judaic ordinance known as *sha'atnez* forbids wearing clothing made of more than one fabric, and thus Jews tended to produce their own, properly woven clothing. Similar considerations, deriving from the ordinances of kashrut, explain the large number of Jews engaged in preparing food. In short, factors coming from Jewish tradition, from within the Jewish community, had a palpable influence, in this and in other regards, upon the economic decisions and fortunes of Russia's Jews.

In the West the creation of a proletariat, under the stresses and strains of industrialization linked to rapid population growth, had been a fundamental cause of much popular unrest. Such stresses and strains were perhaps even greater in Russia, and the implications for Jews still graver, for mixed into the social and economic tensions were religious and ethnic tensions that although hardly absent in the West, were more severe in Russia. In the sprawling industrial centers, like Lodz and Bialystok, thousands of Jews from the shtetlekh, often desperately poor, were put into competitive relationships with thousands of Christians, former peasants and artisans, no less poor. By the 1880s relations between Jews and non-Jews in many urban areas were often tense, as were relations between many other ethnic groups as well as between social classes.

Although great numbers of Jews remained in the ranks of a propertyless working class, many were able to develop managerial skills, the special know-how necessary to succeed in a modern economy. Jews became prosperous industrialists, merchants, bankers, doctors, and lawyers in proportionately much larger numbers than did Great Russians, Byelo-Russians, Poles, or Ukrainians. Jews also entered white-collar employment in sharply dispropor-tionate numbers, while the Slavic nationalities tended to remain in unskilled, manual labor. Opportunities for upward advancement on a limited scale existed for the Slavic nationalities in the military and the civil service, although such posts were mostly reserved for Great Russians and for those of privileged birth. Jews were largely excluded from the government, especially its upper echelons, and from the ranks of the officer class unless they con-verted to Christianity or had medical degrees.

Even when the upper classes of the Slavic nationalities entered into areas of modern urban production, they frequently engaged Jewish managers or agents. In the countryside aristocratic landlords typically used Jewish lessees (the arondators, a combination of innkeeper and agricultural agent) to do the work of collecting rents and taxes, hiring and firing, and keeping accounts, as well as introducing measures of economic innovation. Exploited peasants often dealt most directly with Jews and found it easy to blame them for their miseries. On the other hand, there is much evidence of normal, harmonious relationships between Jewish managers and peasants. Nonetheless, peasants and workers often fell deeply in debt to Jewish innkeepers. Eastern European Jews were also infamous in the nineteenth century for involvement in activities associated with the saloon, as pimps, or in the language of the time, in "white slavery,"[50] but also in other illegal activities. A substantial Jewish subculture of criminality thrived in cities like Odessa and Bucharest.

Anti-Semitic conclusions were frequently drawn from the prominent partic-ipation of Jews in the liquor trade, saloons, usury, prostitution, smuggling, and racketeering. Such conclusions were drawn in the West as well as in eastern Europe and were part of the reason that western Jews often tended to con-sider Jews from eastern Europe to be social deviants, parasites, and criminals. Jewish reformers did not deny the existence or extent of Jewish criminality but rather emphasized how much the environment in eastern Europe encouraged criminality. They expressed concern about what they termed the "unnatural" situation of Jews in eastern Europe and the unhealthy Jewish character that resulted from it. Western Jewish leaders campaigned with special vigor to root out the large participation of Jews in prostitution.

Even the extraordinary success of Jews, as the century progressed, in busi-ness, medicine, law, and white-collar professions was also seen as unnatural and worrisome, begging for some sort of governmental control, some mea-

---

[50] Cf. Edward J. Bristow, *Prostitution and Prejudice: The Jewish Fight Against White Slavery, 1870–1939* (New York, 1983).

sures that would allow non-Jews to enter into those areas in greater numbers, more in proportion to their numbers in the population at large. Leaders of the awakening nationalities in central and eastern Europe – Ukrainians, Czechs, Slovaks, Romanians – typically reasoned that a vital first task for them was to nurture their own business and middle classes, which meant pushing Jews, and sometimes Germans or Greeks, out of their overwhelmingly dominant position in those classes.

But Jewish business and professional success was only part of the story. Large numbers of Jews were also sinking into degrading poverty, driving them and others who were outraged by their condition in desperate directions. One such direction was that of revolutionary activity, which became increasingly characteristic of a minority of young, idealistic Jews in the late nineteenth century. Anti-Semites in Russia were inclined to perceive yet another area of Jewish vice, one that emerged from the destructiveness of Jewish character, in the unusual proclivities of Jews to engage in subversive activity.

Revolutionary Agitation and Tsarist Reaction

The early to mid-1870s had seen much reformist and revolutionary fervor in Russia by the narodniks, or populists, culminating in the famous "Going to the People" in the summer of 1874, a bitterly disillusioning experience for the young idealists who encountered an uncomprehending and suspicious peasantry. Arrests and repression followed, and thereafter activists took a more violent and terroristic direction. When Alexander II was assassinated by revolutionary conspirators in 1881, much attention was drawn to the Jews involved in the conspiracy, especially since a number of Jewish revolutionaries and terrorists had gained notoriety in the immediately preceding years. Following the assassination, popular rioting against the Jews, or pogroms (the word originated in Russia), broke out in many areas.

In some areas, the authorities did suspiciously little to stop the rioters, and in a few instances in the south of Russia police officials apparently condoned the riots, or at least were unenthusiastic and inefficient in repressing them. In northern Russia more conscientious police action nipped mob violence off at the bud. The charge that the tsarist authorities actually engaged in a concerted plan, or plot, to foment the riots, believed by many Jews at the time and supported since then by many historians,[51] finds little support in

---

[51] This was the position of Simon Dubnov, *History of the Jews: From the Congress of Vienna to the Emergence of Hitler*, 4th rev. ed. (New York, 1971), 516–17; many authors thereafter followed his lead, most recently David Vital, *The Origins of Zionism* (Oxford, 1975), 20. Jean-Denis Bredin, *The Affair: The Case of Alfred Dreyfus* (New York, 1986), 25, goes so far as to say the tsar "ordered" the riots. Both Vital and Bredin, it should be noted, are otherwise first-rate, well-informed historians.

the documents or even in what might be termed a plausible explanation of developments at the time.[52] The new tsar and his highest officials were taken aback by the mass violence and feared at first that the assassination and riots were part of a planned revolution. Only later did it emerge clearly that the riots were largely spontaneous and that revolutionaries had little to do with instigating them, though a few did applaud them afterwards, considering them a sign that the Russian masses were awakening and attacking their exploiters.

The charge of conspiracy in one sense gives the tsarist authorities too much credit, since they were not sufficiently in control of the country to plan such a mass uprising. Indeed, they were often haunted by a sense that powerful forces inside Russia and outside it – forces that many of them identified with the Jews – were threatening the Russian way of life. At any rate, instigating mass violence was not the kind of thing that most tsarist officials were temperamentally inclined to do. They were above all concerned with control, law, and order. Many of them no doubt sincerely believed that their job was to care for the peasant masses, but at the same time they were convinced that those "dark" and ignorant masses required a strong hand. The last thing in their minds was to encourage the common people to riot and rampage.

The year 1881 marked a distinct end to the cautious liberal experiments of the 1860s and 1870s. Alexander's violent death seems as well to have acted as a catalyst for the mounting social and ethnic tensions of the time. Revealingly, the riots were all urban in origin, though they then sometimes spread to the surrounding countryside, and they seem to have been primarily the work of recent arrivals in the towns and cities of the south and southeast, many of them Great Russians who had lost their jobs in St. Petersburg and elsewhere in the industrial crisis and depression of 1880 and 1881.

These jobless, rootless, and alienated men had already been the cause of a sharp rise in urban crime in the South; some had even tried to get arrested so that they would at least have food and shelter in jail. Anti-Semitism may not have been primary for such men; Jewish shops and homes were simply natural and easy targets. There is some evidence, however, that local non-Jewish businessmen, artisans, and professionals, resentful about Jewish competition, encouraged the roving bands to attack the Jews.[53] A rumor spread that the new tsar, Alexander III, would soon issue an *ukaz* (imperial decree) to "beat the Jews" in punishment for the assassination of his father, and this rumor, combined with the news of the violence in the towns, may have provoked peasant actions against Jews. On the other hand, much testimony speaks for good relations between peasants and Jews in the countryside; many peasants pro-

---

[52] Cf. Michael Aronson, "Geographical and socio-economic factors in the 1881 pogroms in Russia," *The Russian Review*, vol. 39, no. 1, Jan. 1980, 18–31.

[53] Ibid., 23.

tected their Jewish neighbors, and some of the looters were contrite after-wards, returning their plunder.[54]

Alexander III set up a commission to investigate the causes of the pogroms, and the commission presented him with a report that emphasized the exploitative activities of Jews as the principal cause. Citing the need to "respond to popular indignation," officials under the new tsar introduced the May Laws of 1882. (These were sometimes called the Temporary Laws, since they were described as mere temporary measures to respond to pressing needs; they were supposed to be replaced later by more definitive measures, but they were in fact not formally repealed until 1917.)[55]

The May Laws may be seen as one of many reflections of a long-building disillusionment in Russia's ruling circles with the reforms of the previous two decades. The Laws were designed to bring Russia's Jews under control, since they had, in the eyes of the authorities and many other Russians, so gotten out of control in the previous "liberal" governing environment. Movement of Jews out of the Pale of Settlement was made more difficult. Restrictions on Jews' holding mortgages or leases on land outside of cities and townships were introduced to control what was considered the increasingly unscrupulous exploitation by Jews of peasants. Quotas on the number of Jews allowed in higher education were established to reduce and stabilize the numbers of Jews in the universities. The new goal was around ten percent, since by the 1870s the percentage of Jewish university students had grown much beyond that fig-ure in many areas, although total numbers were still quite small.

The 1880s marked the beginning of a massive Jewish emigration out of the Russian Empire, one of the most extensive movements of people in modern times. The effect of the growing social and ethnic tensions, the pogroms, the new legal disabilities, and the efforts of tsarist officials to exploit resentments against Jews was intensified by the economic depression of the 1880s. In bal-ance, economic factors were almost certainly more important than political ones; even without Alexander's assassination the Jewish flight from eastern Europe would have occurred, and indeed had begun to rise markedly before he was shot. Movement out of Austrian Galicia in the 1880s, where there was no comparable political repression but where Jews were also poor and rapidly expanding in numbers, was as important as movement out of Russia. Ethnic hostility mixed with economic pressures. In both western Galicia, with its Pol-ish Catholic majority, and eastern Galicia, where Greek Orthodox Ukrainians were the majority, rising nationalist feelings turned against the Jews in the form of boycotts of Jewish merchants and middlemen or of marketing cooper-atives designed to avoid dealing with Jewish businesses.

Throughout the middle years of the century, in Russia as well as in Germany

[54] Ibid., 29.
[55] Salo W. Baron, *The Russian Jew Under Tsars and Soviets* (New York, 1976), 45 ff.

and Austria, Jews had been moving into urban areas if and when they could. Now opportunities to get out of Russia opened up as never before, especially for those willing to go to the New World. Railroads and steamships could now carry the emigrants, employers were ready to hire them, and vital connections and contacts in the receiving countries and along the way were available as never before. Previously, one could speak only of a trickle or at most a steady flow of immigrants; now, Jews from eastern Europe arrived in floods – when relations between Jew and non-Jew had already begun to worsen in western countries for reasons largely indigenous to those countries. The arrivals of impoverished Jews from the East, long considered a problem, now acted as a radical intensifier, providing support for the parallel charge in the West that something had to be done to "control" Jews and to address a growing "Jewish problem."

Alexander III, while moving to curtail the liberal reforms of his father, still believed it vital to support Russia's industrial growth, and Russia in the 1890s made giant strides in industrialization, aided by large-scale investments from western Europe, especially from Russia's new diplomatic ally, France. But in sponsoring growth in the new industrial cities, Alexander also encouraged the continued expansion of those new social classes within Russian society that were already causing so much tension. Political parties would soon form, above all liberal parties, but revolutionary socialist parties as well. Workers began to organize, to grope for ways to protect their interests. In such efforts Jews and Jewish workers particularly distinguished themselves, confirming the belief among the authorities that Jews were a disruptive, destructive force.

But before pursuing that theme further, it is necessary to look at a related charge, then maturing in western Europe: that Jews were a destructive race.

The Concept of Race

By the middle years of the nineteenth century, the term "race" came to be commonly and unapologetically used by nearly everyone in western Europe, Jew and non-Jew, educated and ignorant, rich and poor, conservative and socialist, French and German. Much imprecision was associated with the term; in origin its meaning was close to the words "sort" or "kind," and this usage lingered, as for example in the term "the human race." But a more focused usage was also taking shape; consensus was emerging that race entailed an unchangeable, inherent physical type. Most observers also concluded that there was a link between body type and psyche; the common use, again by Jews and non-Jews, of the term the "Jewish race" is a prime example. In stark and revealing contrast to the situation by the mid–twentieth century, few questioned that there *was* a Jewish race. Many spoke of it as an unusually clear example of a pure race.

For us to appreciate the singular appeal of the notion of race in the nineteenth century requires a large effort of historical imagination, especially because a comparable use of racial categories today is so universally condemned on moral grounds and because the very concept of race, especially a "pure" race among humans, has been mostly abandoned by anthropologists and biologists. But in the nineteenth century racist terminology was employed not only by leading scientists of the day but also by other observers to support a wide range of intellectual trends. Racist terminology even crept into the writings and speeches of many of those on the liberal and socialist left, self-proclaimed universalists who believed character was the product of environment and who opposed tribalistic identities. In a related fashion, almost all of what have been seen as the major forces for change in the nineteenth century, however conceptualized (industrialization, the emergence of new social classes and economic structures, the progress of science and technology, nationalism, imperialism), had important racist implications and were often interpreted in a racist fashion.

Why was racism so appealing? Part of the explanation is simple enough, for attitudes that might be termed racist have existed and continue to exist in all societies. Most peoples view themselves as both different and in some sense better than "the others." The ancient Israelites were, to offer an obvious example, no exception. Modern educated parlance tends to term such attitudes "tribalistic" or "ethnocentric." A number of twentieth-century anthropologists have observed that primitive tribes typically do not recognize the humanity of others; indeed the very concept of a universal humanity is alien to the thought patterns of primitive peoples. They do have terms for themselves that are superficially akin to the English words "the people" or "human beings," but those terms do not apply to individuals from other tribes. What is forbidden among the people – murder, theft, or rape – is permitted, sometimes even encouraged, in regard to outsiders. The notion of human rights means nothing outside of the tribe.

Even after universalistic concepts, whether religious or secular, became widespread in Europe, racism or tribalism persisted. However, it would be facile to categorize such thought patterns as merely reversions to more primitive ways of thinking, since it is often difficult to extricate what can be properly denounced as racist from what is "identity," or a sense of cultural distinctness and unique value. These are matters that often lie at the heart of what is most impressive and attractive in various civilizations. Radical universalism leads in the direction of sameness and lack of distinct character, a danger that can be just as unattractive as that offered by radical particularism, or tribalism. The notion of Jewish identity, and the aversion to losing it through Gentile-dominated universalism, constitutes again an obvious example.

It is instructive to review briefly just how pervasive racism has been even among the most refined civilizations of the West and the world. The ancient Greeks had a low regard for the non-Greek barbarians; the very word "barbarian" apparently derives from the Greek sense of the crude sounds ("ba-ba") of non-Greek languages. Aristotle believed that the peoples of northern Europe, those future self-styled superior Aryans, lacked intelligence and skill. The ancient Greeks were inclined to believe that some peoples, or races, were inferior, suited only for slavery. The Romans entertained similar ideas. Cicero advised against buying slaves from Britain, since the natives of that area were "too stupid and incapable of being taught." The Chinese and Japanese, from ancient times to the present century, spoke disdainfully of yellow-haired and green-eyed people, who looked like monkeys and were probably descended from them. Even the more racially similar Vietnamese were considered by the Chinese to be irremediably or "racially" inferior.[56] An Arab sage of the eleventh century wrote that the people living north of the Pyrenees are "of cold temperament and never reach maturity. . . . They lack all sharpness of wit and penetration of intellect." In the fourteenth century another illustrious Arab, Ibn Khaldun, wrote about the black Africans' "low degree of humanity and their proximity to the animal stage."[57]

In the European Middle Ages the various tribes or "nations" (Franks, Saxons, Goths, Normans) were widely assumed to have inherent traits, physical and psychological, many of them remarkably like nineteenth- and twentieth-century racial stereotypes. In the Hebrew Bible and Judeo–Christian traditions derived from it, a similar tendency can be seen. The sons of Noah were supposed to have fathered the major races of the world: Japheth was the father of the Europeans; Shem of the "Orientals" (which included the Jews); and Ham of the Africans (Gen. 9.21–27). The Book of Deuteronomy has been described as providing a religious source for modern racism,[58] and its various exhortations concerning the extermination of the indigenous peoples of Canaan (e.g., Deut. 19, 20) offer justification, for those who seek it, for policies of racial extermination.

In talmudic commentary, protoracist elements are common. The rabbis increase the racist potential of the story of Ham beyond the bare biblical text, for example, by making the sons of Ham "ugly and dark-skinned."[59] Thus, religious exclusiveness meshed with "racial" exclusiveness, for in traditional Judaism lineage or ancestry (*yikhus*) – indeed, hereditary or "racial" sinfulness,

---

[56] Keith W. Taylor, "An Evaluation of the Chinese Period in Vietnamese History," *Journal of Asiatic Studies*, vol. 23, no. 1, 1980, 151 [thanks to my colleague Alexander De Conde for this reference].

[57] Cf. Henry Bamford Parkes, *Gods and Men: The Origins of Western Culture* (New York, 1964), 199–200. Ibn Khaldun, *An Arab Philosophy of History: Selections from the Prolegomena of Ibn Khaldun of Tunis (1332–1406)* (London, 1955), 98. Quoted in William McKee Evans, "From the Land of Canaan to the Land of Guinea: The Strange Odyssey of the Sons of Ham," *American Historical Review*, vol. 85, no. 1, Feb. 1980, 32.

[58] Parkes, *Gods and Men*, 115.

[59] *Bereshith Rabbah*, 36.1 (H. Freedoman and Maurice Simon, trans. and eds.), *Mishnah Rabbah*, 10 vols. (London, 1959), 1:293. Quoted in Evans, "Land of Canaan," 26.

as in the case of the descendants of Ham – remained categories of central importance, even if they were elusively mixed with categories of belief or conviction. Traditional Jews conceive of themselves as the "seed of Jacob," the lineal descendants of the Patriarchs, the chosen of God. In the opinion of later influential Jewish thinkers, such as the Maharal, inborn racial qualities were to be found in every nation; he considered it impossible that a member of one nation could become part of another.[60]

That judgment may be linked to what a modern Jewish observer has termed "the central myth of Judaism: Every generation of Jews – past, present, and future – was present at Mount Sinai when the covenant between God and the Jewish people was established."[61] From this perspective converts to Judaism are considered lost souls, Jews who were spiritually there for the covenant but for mysterious reasons were later born in Gentile bodies. They are thus not really converting to Judaism but discovering their true, essential identity. There is in this sense a predetermined quality even to the Jewishness of a convert.

Judaism, or at least major and deep-rooted traditional interpretations of it, must be considered only uncertainly a community of belief; mixed into the belief system of the religion as traditionally defined are "essentialist" (or "racist") notions in that one is born a Jew, rather than choosing to become one, and it is not possible to stop being a Jew by a change of persuasion or an act of will. As we have seen in the response of the Jewish delegates to Napoleon, even Jews of the early nineteenth century who wished to become part of the French nation did not try to deny traditional Judaism's categorical, antiuniversalistic prohibitions concerning intermarriage with certain races, such as the Egyptians or the Seven Canaanite Nations.

Those traditional prohibitions are only slightly less categorical in regard to other Goyim. The Jewish priestly caste *(kohanim)* is ruled by especially stringent regulations. Its members may not, for example, marry a convert to Judaism, who by definition lacks the necessary ancestry. A Gentile child, adopted by Jews at birth and brought up according to the faith, must still at a later point undergo a formal, individual conversion ceremony, according to halakha. Such a child can *never* qualify for priestly status, even if the ancestry of his adoptive parents would permit it for their natural children. A *mamzer* (roughly, a bastard, the product of adultery between Jews) may *never* marry a "full" or "real" Jew (that is, one born of a properly married Jewish mother), however faultless his practice of Judaism. Unions between *mamzerim* and Gentile converts are permitted, since both qualify as inferior types of Jews, insofar as their ancestry is concerned. Again, their moral probity or fidelity to the beliefs and rituals of Judaism, no matter how perfect, cannot alter their lower status.[62]

---

[60] Katz, *Exclusiveness*, 147–8.

[61] Charles E. Silberman, *A Certain People: American Jews and Their Lives Today* (New York, 1985), 70.

[62] Katz, *Exclusiveness*, 110.

These protoracist notions differ in important ways from the "science of race" that emerged in the nineteenth century, to say nothing of the crude and vicious applications of it under Nazi rule. (Nazis, too, said that one is born a Jew and Jewishness could never be relinquished.) But just as Christianity may be said to offer support only in vague, often contradictory ways to modern anti-Semitism, so these broader Judaic sources, partly incorporated into Christianity but in part uniquely Jewish, contributed in vague, often contradictory ways to modern racism, especially to its concern with racial exclusiveness and purity.

Blood Imagery

Imagery, rituals, and taboos having to do with blood, another protoracist concept, have taken on potent forms in both Judaism and Christianity. "Blood," "seed," and "soul" have been used by Jews in defining Jewishness, and according to such definitions Jewish qualities have been seen as both permanent and mysteriously latent or immanent, springing from inner, invisible, or otherwise obscure determinants – an unchanging and unchangeable Jewish essence. Even a modern Jew like Freud, who had broken entirely with traditional Jewish belief, spoke of a mysterious "inner identity of Jews," since they have, he asserted, a similar "psychic structure," "a miraculous thing in common, which [is] inaccessible to any analysis so far."[63] Eugene Borowitz has recently written that Jews have a mystical bond with one another, which allows them to "know how to find" one another.[64]

The belief that blood in some way determines character was held long before the advent of Christianity in Europe and lies deep in European culture. Blood imagery of this sort is not only premodern or prescientific; it is prehistoric, an aspect of the beliefs of Indo–European tribes before the dawn of written history. The ancient Greeks Galen and Hippocrates provided a systematic and long influential treatment, related to the notion that blood determines character, in their theories concerning the four humors or fluids in the body. The prevalence of one of the humors, they asserted, determined temperament (thus a "sanguine" as distinguished from a "phlegmatic" person). Such language was much used in Renaissance and Elizabethan literature, and in a vaguer sense it survives in figurative language (the hot-blooded Spaniard). It is related to other bodily derived and prescientific imagery, such as the "heart" that gives courage or sympathy. From at least the Middle Ages on, it was assumed that the "blue" blood of noblemen gave them certain qualities.

Jewish blood, then, was widely believed, by non-Jews and Jews alike, to be

---

[63] Sigmund Freud, Letters, 1873–1933 (London, 1961), 376–8; from Joseph Nedava, Trotsky and the Jews (Philadelphia, 1971), 10.

[64] Quoted in Silberman, Certain People, 76.

responsible for Jewish character. Indeed, the argument in favor of an unmixed strain of blood was assumed to be especially strong in the Jewish case, because of the Jews' non-European origin and their own stringent prohibitions against intermarriage. Even after conversion to Christianity, a Jew in the Middle Ages was believed to retain certain traits that revealed the potent influence of Jewish blood. Traditional Jewish commentators designated the *meshumad* (convert to Christianity) as a sinning Jew, but still a Jew. His baptism did not result in a loss of Jewish identity or even an exemption from any obligation that was his by virtue of his birth, lineage, or race.[65] Thus, by Jewish tradition, no less than by anti-Semitic assertion, an individual could not shake off his Jewish essence.

Yiddish-speaking Jews distinguished between Gentile *koyekh* (brutish, physical power) and Jewish *moyekh* (brains, guile, mental subtlety), a distinction related to those identified with Esau and Jacob. Non-Jews throughout most of recorded European history seem to have been impressed with a peculiar Jewish sharpness of intellect, a cleverness and cunning that baptism did not alter. In the Spanish Inquisition, these various perceptions of an unchanging Jewish essence, even after conversion, found expression in the concept of *limpieza de sangre* (cleanness or purity of blood). Jews who converted were still suspect; they retained impure blood that put their conversion into question.

For centuries afterwards, the Jesuit order established restrictions against candidates with Jewish ancestry, or impure blood. The Jesuits thus came up with a Christian equivalent of the prohibitions among Jews that sought to preserve the untainted lineage of the *kohanim*. However, the Jesuits' preoccupations with racial purity were not quite so categorical as those of the Jews; exceptions were frequently granted by Catholic authorities in a way simply not permitted by halakha.

The concept of cleanness of blood derived from and blended into concerns that were not religious in the familiar sense. The cultural preoccupation among Spaniards with lineage assumed almost fetishistic dimensions, and that Spanish pride, in the words of Raphael Patai, "was internalized in toto by Sephardi Jews." Their own preoccupation with "purity of blood" meant that they refused, well into the eighteenth century, to intermarry with non-Sephardic Jews – or, indeed, in some instances, even to touch the same dishes that Ashkenazic Jews, with their "impure blood," had touched.[66] Like non-Jewish Spaniards, they firmly believed that their nobility of character and overall superiority was a product of their blood.

In the nineteenth century, the word race began to replace blood, although the two long coexisted and were often used synonymously, as they continue to be in the twentieth century. Race was considered to be a more palpable, measurable

---

[65] Ibid., 68.
[66] Raphael Patai, *The Jewish Mind* (New York, 1977), 380–2.

term, based on scientific inquiry. Yet the claims to greater objectivity notwithstanding, there remained throughout the nineteenth century a certain mysticism associated with the concept of race. That is, the actual mechanisms of racial determinism were not explained with anything like scientific rigor. Why it was, for example, that blond hair and blue eyes went with a cold temperament, whereas dark hair and brown eyes were associated with a hot one, remained scientifically unexplained – and was in truth no more scientific than generalizations about the potency of blood. Much of the potent mysteriousness long associated with the Jews was retained in "scientific" racism.

We may sense, then, some of the reasons for the peculiar attractiveness of the concept of race in its nineteenth-century form for Jews themselves. Secular Jews who wished to be considered French or German patriots could conveniently identify themselves as "Jews by race, not religion,"[67] finding a formula that dealt with the awkwardness of being a modern Jew in a predominantly Christian nation. They could distinguish what they recognized was permanent about them (ancestry, body type, certain psychological traits) from what could be changed by an act of will (national identity). Jews, remaining Jews by race, could abandon certain aspects of traditional Jewish religious belief and ritual, could choose to consider themselves no longer a part of the Jewish nation, and could thus join one of the modern European nations.

A number of well-known Jews took yet further steps in embracing and embellishing the concept of race. Probably the best known and influential of them was the English politician and writer Benjamin Disraeli (prime minister, 1868, 1874–1880).[68] In spite of his having converted to Christianity as a child, he emphatically insisted that he remained a member of the Jewish race. He believed, moreover, that the Jewish race had been extremely influential in the course of European civilization. That influence was to be explained, he said, by the inherent genius of the Jewish race and because of the way that Jews stuck together, assiduously keeping their race pure and disregarding national borders in pursuit of common interests as Jews.[69] He asserted, in other words, what the Assembly of Notables in France had been at such pains to deny.

In his novel *Coningsby,* Disraeli depicted a vast and secret power of Jews, bent on dominating the world.[70] His noble Jewish character, Sidonia (whom

---

[67] Michael Marrus, *The Politics of Assimilation: A Study of the French Jewish Community at the Time of the Dreyfus Affair* (Oxford, 1971), 25.

[68] A recent contributor to the voluminous literature on this issue is Todd M. Endelmann, "Disraeli's Jewishness Reconsidered," *Modern Judaism,* vol. 5, no. 2, May 1985, 109–23, who uses most of the sources cited below.

[69] Cf. R. Blake, *Disraeli* (London, 1967), 201–5, 258–9.

[70] Benjamin Disraeli, *Coningsby* (1844), 302–3; cf. Fritz Stern, *Gold and Iron: Bismarck, Bleichröder, and the Building of the German Empire* (New York, 1979), 516.

Disraeli let it be known was based on Lionel Rothschild),[71] describes race as a supremely important determinant ("all is race; there is no other truth"). Race, he argued, had always been a central factor in the rise of civilization, and western civilization could not have flourished without the Jewish race.[72]

It is unlikely that many of Disraeli's English contemporaries took his grandiose claims concerning the power of the Jewish race seriously; such boasts were seen as one of his many idiosyncrasies. He was widely considered a strange person, yet he still won the affections and trust of much of the English establishment, including Queen Victoria. Such was apparently the case even when they agreed with Lord Derby, a close friend of Disraeli's, that his mental processes were not really English and remained those of a foreigner.[73]

Hannah Arendt has quipped that Disraeli "had an admiration for all things Jewish that was matched only by his ignorance of them."[74] Nevertheless, his novels and other writings would be very widely cited by influential anti-Semites throughout the nineteenth and twentieth centuries. Disraeli's works undoubtedly exercised a major influence on the perception of the Jew by his contemporaries. Houston Stewart Chamberlain, the influential anti-Semitic writer of the turn of century, urged his readers, "in days when so much nonsense is talked concerning this question, let Disraeli teach us that the whole significance of Judaism lies in its purity of race, that this alone gives it power and duration."[75]

Disraeli's very personality, the "potent wizard" of British politics, reinforced the popular imagery of Jews, again ambiguously mixed with negative and positive elements. He may have been, both as a writer and even more as a personal symbol, the most influential propagator of the concept of race in the nineteenth century,[76] particularly publicizing the Jews' alleged taste for power, their sense of superiority, their mysteriousness, their clandestine international connections, and their arrogant pride in being a pure race.

---

[71] The claim is questioned by Richard Davis, *The English Rothschilds* (Chapel Hill, 1983), 87, since Disraeli and Lionel at this point were not yet intimate; moreover, Lionel's personality differed substantially from that of Sidonia. But at least as powerful, mysterious financiers they resembled one another.

[72] Cf. Leon Poliakov, *The History of Anti-Semitism* (New York, 1967), 3:232.

[73] Colin Holmes, *Anti-Semitism in British Society, 1876–1939* (New York, 1979), 11–12. Holmes documents anti-Semitic attacks on Disraeli by the radical John Bright and several Oxford professors.

[74] Arendt, *Origins*, 70.

[75] Houston Stewart Chamberlain, *Foundations of the Nineteenth Century* (New York, 1914). Quoted in Paul R. Mendes-Flohr and Jehuda Reinharz, *The Jew in the Modern World, A Documentary History* (Oxford, 1980), 290.

[76] Oddly, George L. Mosse, *Toward the Final Solution: A History of European Racism* (New York, 1980), devotes only a few lines in a single paragraph to Disraeli, yet he devotes pages of dense description and analysis to scores of anti-Semitic writers and theorists, many of whom attracted a limited readership and obviously exercised little influence on their contemporaries.

It might be more accurate to say that he joined the chorus of racist commentary of the age rather than influencing others to accept racist ideas. In his attitudes toward blacks, to provide another example, Disraeli was typical of the age rather than propagating novel ideas: Consistent with the belief that if a race became impure, it would weaken and decline, he wrote that if the "great Anglo-Saxon republic" [the United States] allowed its white population "to mingle with [its] negro and coloured populations" it would be the beginning of the end for the new country.[77] It is indicative of the pervasiveness of nineteenth-century notions of blood and race that even spokesmen for blacks used it: W. E. B. DuBois wrote that "the Negro blood which flowed in the veins of many of the mightiest pharaohs had a powerful impact on Egyptian civilization." Blacks, he believed, as a race have a stronger inherent sense of beauty than whites, especially in sight and sound.[78]

Racism and Anti-Semitism

The diffuseness, variety, and omnipresence of racist notions suggests that rather than being causes they were merely reflections or enhancers of deeper determinants. Whatever role other abstract ideas may have played in history, the nineteenth-century idea of race is a poor candidate for the role of fundamental cause of nineteenth and twentieth century developments. In the first place, could any set of ideas so imprecise, so shifting, so malleable be said to "cause" anything, or at least anything that can be isolated and coherently described? Would it not be more appropriate to speak of racist ideas as being "used"?[79]

It is significant that racism in its nineteenth-century form had no single theorist whom most racists recognized, in the way that Marx was recognized by socialists or J. S. Mill was recognized by liberals. Racism did not become a movement in the way that socialism and liberalism did, nor did racists – even specific kinds of racists, such as anti-Semites – form coherent, durable parties comparable to socialist and liberal parties. Yet, many popular and scholarly accounts of nineteenth-century racism assume that racist ideas were fundamental causes, or powerful determinants, of anti-Semitism – and thus of the eventual mass murder of Jews.[80] Intellectual history conceived in this fashion

---

[77] Isaiah Berlin, *Against the Current: Essays in the History of Ideas* (London, 1979), 275.

[78] Carl N. Degler, *In Search of Human Nature: The Decline and Revival of Darwinism in American Social Thought* (Oxford and New York, 1991), 16.

[79] This issue must be separated from the larger, more carefully formulated one of whether cultural – ethnic attachments may be considered fundamental forces – for which much more persuasive evidence can be produced. I am referring here only to the idea of race in its "scientific," nineteenth-century form.

[80] Cf. Mosse, *Final Solution;* Poliakov, *History of Anti-Semitism,* vol. 3; Katz, *Prejudice;* Jehuda Reinharz, *Fatherland or Promised Land: The Dilemma of the German Jew, 1893–1914* (Ann Arbor, Mich., 1975).

tends to lapse into an elaborate description and analysis of racist ideas as such, with relatively little effort to explain how those ideas spread, or why they had an appeal, or even to distinguish which particular ideas had broad appeal and which of them spoke only to a small audience.

Whether or not one considers science, or the progress of science and technology, to be a fundamental historical force, there seems little question that increasingly systematic observations about various human societies had important implications for the growth of racism in the nineteenth century. The expanding contact with non-European peoples since the voyages of discovery helped to stimulate the speculative and analytic instincts of Europeans. The increasingly confident sense that Europeans acquired concerning their superiority to non-Europeans led naturally to the question of why Europeans were superior. By the mid–nineteenth century one simple and widely attractive explanation was that some as yet ill-understood racial genius in Europeans had facilitated their unprecedented achievements in the arts and sciences. More subtle explanations, having to do, for example, with the peculiarities of European historical evolution, were also being elaborated and were also of considerable importance in nineteenth-century thought, but racist explanations had a powerful attraction in terms of simplicity and self-flattery.

It was the ever more extensive contact with sub-Saharan Africa that seems to have most reinforced racist interpretations of European superiority. Black Africans had already been subject to enslavement for some centuries at the hands of Arabs, and Arab writers had also developed a rich vocabulary attesting to their belief in the racial inferiority of blacks, which in turn helped to reinforce the racial denigration of Africans that were generated from within European civilization,[81] in particular those that equated white with good and black with evil.[82] Contact with Asia or even with North Africa did not work in quite the same way, since the ancient civilizations of those areas hardly spoke for an unchanging racial inferiority in the way that the relatively unknown, divided, technologically undeveloped, and militarily weak tribes of sub-Saharan Africa were believed to.

It was not merely the superiority of European science that was decisive, however; Africans appeared physically more primitive to European observers, more animal-like. Pushkin, the great Russian poet, who had an African grandparent, revealingly spoke of his own "Negro ugliness" and referred to himself as "an ugly offspring of Negroes."[83] His European contemporaries did not seem to disagree with him on that point. Arab slave traders had earlier set the

---

[81] Cf. Evans, "Land of Canaan," 32 ff.

[82] On the issue of the moral connotations of white and black in European and American civilization, see Winthrop Jordan, *White over Black: American Attitudes to the Negro, 1550–1812* (Chapel Hill, N.C., 1968).

[83] David Magarshak, *Pushkin* (New York, 1967), 39.

tone: A popular work on slave buying described black Africans as "fickle and careless. Dancing and beating time are engrained in their nature." Another Arab source noted with disgust that Africans were "the most stinking of mankind in the armpits and sweat."[84]

Europeans in the nineteenth century were under the influence of what has been termed a "cult of Graeco–Roman antiquity," which entailed an identification with what the Greeks and Romans considered to be beautiful, noble, or godlike in the human face and body. Africans appeared far removed from such ideals, closer to the apes than to the gods. Jews, too, suffered from invidious comparisons, although not because of any supposed resemblance to animals but because of their "unnaturalness," their bizarre, "Oriental," and ungraceful appearance.

To accept that one human race was inferior went against the humanistic universalism of the time, and indeed against most of Christian universalism. Yet a belief in the inferiority of black Africans was very widespread in the eighteenth and nineteenth centuries, even among those Enlightened people whose general ideas inclined them to resist such beliefs. And once it was recognized that some sort of natural hierarchy among races existed – once the *principle* of human equality was put into serious or widespread doubt – it was easier to introduce various other refinements within that hierarchy, drawing from notions having to do with lineage, for example, or from biblically based racist categories.

Believing as they did in unlimited progress in the future, many thinkers of the eighteenth century turned to the question of how malleable the races of mankind were. The reflections of Immanuel Kant on this issue may be seen as an important signpost, although he was only one of many important thinkers who wrote about race. His conclusions by no means settled the debate, but in his typically penetrating way he examined the evidence available to educated men in his day and came up with what was regarded as a higher synthesis. In *The Different Races of Mankind* (1775) he concluded that race was both distinctive and immutable. Climate would not make blacks out of Scandinavians transplanted to central Africa, nor would African blacks become blond and white-skinned if moved to northern Europe.

Kant's conclusions about the fixity of race were not racist in the sense usually understood in the twentieth century. Indeed, they were, in the points just mentioned, perfectly compatible with modern scientific understanding. But what was of particular interest in his essay was the assertion that all human races were part of the same species; they were all human beings, members of the human race. On the other hand, he still implicitly accepted that there were distinctly different *and permanent* spiritual qualities, as there were physical, among the various races of mankind. In this, of course, there was a racist implication, at least to the extent that his ideas differ from prevailing twenti-

---

[84] Quoted in Evans, "Land of Canaan," 32.

eth-century liberal opinion, which denies that race and inherent spiritual qualities have any connection whatsoever.

Kant's assertion that all human races were equal did not come from empirical observation or from objective evidence rationally weighed; it came from metaphysical sources, themselves obviously related to both classical and Christian humanism (the equality of the human soul, equality before God). That is, Kant's humanistic universalism, which pervades the rest of his thought, could not possibly be proved by empirical evidence; equality in his sense was as much a matter of faith as was Christian universalism – or, for that matter, the Trinity. Thus, his position still left open the door, especially to those who rejected Christian or classical humanism, to the notion of superior and inferior races, if they could claim scientific evidence.

Kant's reasoning, while helping to strengthen the belief among the intellectual classes in the fixity of races, could do little to counter the increasingly pervasive belief in African racial inferiority. The late eighteenth and early nineteenth century witnessed a considerable expansion in the slave trade, and it seems plausible that the consciences of many Europeans and Americans were assuaged by a belief in the fixity of human races and the natural inferiority of some – above all African blacks, who were "natural slaves" to whites. The notion of natural slavery had of course a long ancestry, from the ancient Greeks to the Arabs of the Middle Ages, to say nothing of the Hebrew Bible.

Not all nineteenth-century racists came to such conclusions. Not even slave traders and slaveholders did so consistently. Some of the most famous theorists of race explicitly condemned slavery. Still, it seems a safe conclusion that the attractions of the slave trade, the economic needs it satisfied, and the money to be made from it and from slavery, also increased the attractions of racist thought for a significant part of the white population of Europe and America. And for those who did not benefit directly from slavery a belief in inferiority of black Africans could assuage whatever pangs of conscience some of them may have felt about that brutal institution.

The concept of race also meshed nicely with the kind of nationalism that began to gain strength in the course of the nineteenth century, since one aspect of that nationalism was a belief that certain groups, or races, properly belonged within the confines of certain nation-states. The French race, the German race, the Italian race, so the reasoning went, deserved a nation-state composed uniquely of the appropriate race. Such ideas were not easily reconciled with the abundant evidence that even in areas of common language and culture, physical types varied considerably in most areas of Europe; many nationalists were thus inclined rather to stress language, history, and culture rather than physical appearance. Still, this kind of racist component in nineteenth-century nationalism is usually apparent, if not consistently expressed or universally accepted.

The unification of Germany and Italy in the nineteenth century, and the consolidation of other states, was part of an ever more intense national rivalry in nineteenth- and early twentieth-century Europe. Thus nationalism not only awakened what might be termed tribalistic sentiments but also gave birth to anxieties concerning the progress of neighboring nations. Germany's neighbors after 1870 in particular felt threatened by the young, vigorous, and expansionist Prusso–German state.

The dynamism of nineteenth-century power politics may well have had much to do with the dynamism and creativity of European civilization generally, but it also undoubtedly led to insecurity within nations. It heightened demands for self-sacrifice from citizens, as well as for purity of national feeling, a sentiment that some concluded could only come naturally from those of a pure racial background, people whose fidelities were not weakened or put into question by racial or religious counterfidelities.

The far-reaching implications of such intensifying nationalism for the relations of Jews and non-Jews in the latter part of the nineteenth century will be a central concern of later chapters. But insofar as Jews were considered to be a race in the nineteenth century, they were to an important degree unique in having no natural European homeland (Gypsies were another example). They were recognized as a foreign race everywhere. Even those Jews who came to identify themselves as Germans, French, or English did not deny that their origins were non-European.

Racist thinking by the middle of the nineteenth century, as the case of Disraeli illustrates, was hardly unanimous in asserting that Jews could not somehow blend into or cooperate with other races. Indeed, there were a few who looked to a kind of hybrid vigor from that process. However, the movement of Jews out of the ghettos and, even more, the migration of large numbers of Ostjuden into western Europe obviously affected many Europeans, especially in German-speaking central Europe, much as the experience with sub-Saharan Africans affected the French and the English imperialists. That is, Jews were perceived as peculiarly alien at a time when European particularism, in the form of nationalism, was becoming stronger.

A further attraction of nineteenth-century racist ideas sprang from the nature of modern economic development. The advocates of a free-market economy stressed the importance of competition in allowing superior economic units to prevail over inferior ones – yet another example of the notion of dynamic interplay, with the attendant potential for insecurity, so typical of the nineteenth century. Indeed, in pervasive ways Europeans and Americans of European origin in the nineteenth century were fascinated by notions of struggle and strife. Marxism emphasized class struggle, with a final redemptive victory of the proletariat. Darwin's theories of natural selection were translated into social Darwinism, the assertion that in society as in nature, the superior rose to the top and the inferior sank to the bottom.

To conclude that superiority in economic terms had ultimately to do with racial determinants was an obvious and tempting step. Just as racism could offer a convenient rationalization for slavery, it could also be used to vindicate the large and apparently growing differences in social class and income that characterized nineteenth-century society. Those who were prospering could attribute their success to their superior racial stock; the poor, the proletarian masses, were racially inferior. Nationalist and imperialist ideas could similarly blend into social Darwinist and racist ideas by arguing that certain nations prevailed over others inside Europe because of race.

Social Darwinism of this sort tended to support the idea of Jewish superiority rather than inferiority – again Disraeli's point, since Jews were so successful economically in the nineteenth century. It was this very sense of Jewish economic superiority that fed at least one important source of anti-Semitism and that made hatred of Jews significantly different from antiblack racism. There were overlaps, to be sure, particularly in the description of the Ostjuden as racially primitive, but on the whole fear and envy, as distinguished from contempt and condescension, played a key role in European hostility to Jews, especially its more serious varieties.

The early nineteenth century witnessed a "romantic" reaction to the prevalent Enlightened conceptions of the previous century. Romanticism is a sprawling concept, but several significant shifts from Enlightened thought can be noted in it. The Enlightenment enthroned reason and distrusted emotion or believed that irrational impulses had to be rationally channeled. The Romantics expressed a new regard for the nonrational, for intuition, emotion, and mystical religious feeling. Thus, the inner person, or inner voice, speaking in mystical ways, gained a new importance.

Fascination with the nonrational had certainly existed in the eighteenth century, too, among both Christians and Jews, but not typically among the tone-setting intellectuals. In the early nineteenth century leading intellectuals became highly critical of the cold rationality of the Enlightenment, its formalism and artificiality. Emotional impulses were now believed to be more genuine, more expressive of the true person, the unique inner person. Again, such notions linked up comfortably to racism, since racism, with its belief in unseen inner determinants, had an element of mysticism in it. Rationalism, with its obvious origins in hellenistic esteem for a godlike reason, emphasized a universal human faculty, reason, which permits mutual understanding. Romanticism emphasized individual internal experience, one that by its very nature cannot be clearly or rationally communicated to others – unless those others happened to be of the same inner nature.

Such feelings are typical of religious experience, as for example in the mystical belief in being a Chosen People or in being mystically predestined as an individual for salvation. The very particularism of romanticism pointed in the direction of the particularism of race, toward an identification of the inner person with the inner, mystical determinants of race. These were by no means necessary connections; romantics did not all become racists. Mystics, emphasizing truths internally realized, sometimes come to universalistic, antiracist conclusions. But an inclination for romantics and mystics to become racists seems obvious enough. Indeed, the more vicious, emotional, and hate-filled forms of racism were often found among mystical racists and less so among those who were trained in scientific inquiry.

Romanticism had a particular appeal in German lands, where Enlightened ideas were often seen as imposed French ideas. Many German thinkers dismissed Enlightened universalism as a mask for French hegemony or even for the exploitation of other nations by France – not a far-fetched conclusion during the time of Napoleon's Empire, when his armies and bureaucrats plundered other lands. Once Napoleon had been brought down, German thinkers and artists experienced a sense of intellectual liberation, and they gave new, enthusiastic attention to things uniquely or essentially German, to German language, culture, customs, art, poetry, and song.

The Evolution of the Vocabulary of Race

A romantic thinker of considerable influence in the expression of German specialness was Johann Gottfried von Herder (1744–1803), whose most important works appeared in the late eighteenth century. He is best known for developing the concept of *Volksgeist,* or spirit of the people, the particular qualities and genius of each individual people. Herder's inspiration was anti-French, but his perspective had nonetheless a universalistic quality to it. That is, he emphasized that all the world's peoples should develop their own unique genius and should not be subjected to externally imposed universalistic molds. In the context of the early nineteenth century, such urgings meant shaking off French intellectual and cultural domination, but Herder's message could be applied in many contexts.

Volksgeist was not strictly speaking a racist notion. It did not stress body type, although some of Herder's writings were not free of ambiguities in that regard (he identified Germans, for example, as typically having fair complexions and blue eyes). Still, *Geist* refers to "spirit," not material or physical attributes. Even on a cultural level, while attacking French superficiality, Herder generally had supportive things to say about other peoples and cultures. He did not emphasize German superiority to all of them. Slavic nationalists borrowed enthusiastically from his work, as indeed did such Jewish nationalists as Ahad Ha'am, at the end of the century.

Herder was an admirer of Hebrew literature, but he saw a deep-seated corruption in the Jews of his day, deriving from their long-standing status as peddlers, merchants, and moneylenders. As these opposing evaluations suggest, his attitude toward the Jews around him was, as was the case with nearly all German thinkers of the time, an often subtle and shifting one, easily misrepresented or simply the cause of honest puzzlement.[85] He, like nearly all of his contemporaries, including Mendelssohn, did not believe that Jews were or could become Germans. Jews were a "strange people of Asia driven into our regions."[86] He presented himself as their outspoken friend, yet he rejected Jewish emancipation in Germany, at least in the near future, and termed Jews "parasites."[87] He emphasized Jewish strangeness but also the unity of humankind. He wrote that Jews "belong to Palestine and not Europe. Since Israel and its prayers despise all other peoples from which it is set apart, how can it be otherwise than that it is itself despised by other nations?"[88]

Whatever the ambiguities of Herder's notion of Volksgeist, it undoubtedly lent itself to racist uses. It was a natural enough step to assert that the special genius of a people was a product of race and, even more, to assert that one people possessed a superior genius to others – exactly the conclusion reached by Disraeli. Herder's writings did have, at any rate, a wide-ranging effect on early nineteenth-century thought and ultimately on thinkers who formulated the distinctions that would have a long and notorious history, that is, "Aryan" and "Semite."[89]

Herder's work was not scientific in the English sense of the word but rather philosophic and belletristic. Yet his concern with language as a key expression of a people's genius had a profound effect upon the growth of the new science of language study. Friedrich von Schlegel (1772–1829), who was one of the leading figures of German Romanticism, published in 1808 a pioneering work on the Sanskrit language and the civilization of ancient India. He pointed out structural similarities in Sanskrit, Greek, Latin, and German, which he termed "Aryan" languages. (The term derived from the Sanskrit word for "noble"; "Iran" is another modern derivative of it.) Aryan was more than a linguistic category for Schlegel; it had much in common with Herder's Volksgeist. He believed the Aryan languages to be part of a larger cultural whole, one brought to Europe by the ancient Aryan tribes.

Modern linguists largely accept the linguistic kinships that Schlegel pointed out, although the term Indo–European is now preferred over Aryan. Schlegel's flights of mysticism concerning Aryan cultural traits, however, now appear all too Romantic. He spoke in vague terms of the inner identities or

[85] Cf. the contrasting treatments in Arendt, *Origins*, 57; Katz, *Prejudice*, 60; Mosse, *Final Solution*, 36–9; Paul Lawrence Rose, *German Question/Jewish Question: Revolutionary Antisemitism from Kant to Wagner* (Princeton, N.J., 1992 [paperback, with new title and new afterward]), 97–109.

[86] J. G. Herder, "Über die politische Bekehrung der Juden," in *Adrastea und das 18. Jahrhundert*. Quoted in Arendt, *Origins*, 57.

[87] Katz, *Prejudice*, 60.

[88] Quoted in Rose, *Revolutionary Antisemitism*, 103.

[89] Cf. Bernard Lewis, *Semites and Anti-Semites* (New York, 1986), 42–57.

affinities of Sanskrit, Greek, and German, even of the "inner character" of the alphabets they used.[90] Aryan languages, he asserted, were "organic," meaning vital and capable of creative change, while other languages, such as those of the American Indians or the peoples of the Orient, were static, atomized, lacking in creative power.

Thus was established a modern, "scientific" basis for the notion of Aryan superiority. More generally, that notion supplied an answer to the question of how Europeans had advanced so far beyond the rest of the world's peoples. The idea had a wide and potent appeal, both to intellectuals and, eventually, to the common people. Schlegel also laid the pseudoscientific foundations for the assertion of Semitic inferiority, since the languages spoken by the ancient Hebrews could be allocated to the non-Aryan, "inorganic" category.

Schlegel's pupil and finally successor as professor at the University of Bonn, Christian Lassen, made precisely such connections in a four-volume work published in midcentury. It gained considerable popularity in racist circles. Lassen described the Semites, including both Jews and Arabs, as people without self-control or social discipline, prone to an unbridled egoism. They had no epic poetry, no sense of balance and harmony, no taste for the beauties of the natural world. This theme of the noble, creative Aryan and the ignoble, destructive Semite was picked up and elaborately developed by nineteenth-century scholars, theorists, novelists, and propagandists. In most cases, the two terms were blended into and supplemented by the already long-established imagery of Gentile and Jew, often in ways that had nothing to do with objectively observed linguistic or literary evidence. Some linguists complained about such misuse of their craft,[91] but the attractions of the terms easily overwhelmed such complaints.

The linguistic basis of Aryan and Semitic differences, as postulated by Schlegel, Lassen, and others, seems to have been bolstered by negative imagery concerning the Semitic Arabs that was spreading at the time, when Europeans were beginning to conquer territories inhabited by Arabs.[92] Reports of Arab religious fanaticism and ritual oddities, lack of self-control, cultural sterility, and backwardness easily meshed with a larger sense of Semitic traits that European observers claimed to see in the Jews who were moving out of the ghettos and the Pale of Settlement.

There were a number of cultural and religious similarities between European Jews and Middle-Eastern Arabs. And among those similarities were many that were deemed odd, primitive, Oriental, or African by nineteenth-century

---

[90] Mosse, *Final Solution,* 40.

[91] Lewis, *Semites,* 45–6.

[92] There is little literature on this subject. Many authors state categorically that anti-Semites in the late nineteenth century meant Jews and only Jews when they used the term "Semite." While it is certainly true that their hatred for Jews, whom they knew, had no real equivalent in their attitudes to Arabs, whom they knew scarcely at all, Jew and Arab seem often mixed together as "Semites."

Europeans (a few examples: the elaborate dietary taboos, ritual washings, isolation of menstruating women, circumcision, prohibitions against the use of natural images, tonalities of prayer, and sense of religion as ritual and form rather than inner conviction). Such peculiarities spoke to some Europeans for an underlying Semitic racial essence. A number of influential European anti-Semites drew attention to Arab and Jewish similarities and thus arrived at Zionist conclusions: The Jewish problem in Europe could be solved if the Jews would go to Palestine, among their fellow Semites, where they belonged.[93]

One of the most widely read authors of the mid– to late nineteenth century was the French scholar Ernest Renan. He brought to a wide public the findings of linguists and philologists. His *Life of Jesus* (1863) has been described as the most widely read work in France at the time, next to the Bible itself.[94] Renan had lost his Christian faith, and his book, like so many others at the time that were examining Holy Writ with profane eyes, outraged many of his contemporaries. But one of its central messages was "religious" in a way that paradoxically gave support to traditional Christian attitudes toward Jews. That message also echoed points made by Kant and the German liberal Protestant theologians whom Renan had studied: Christ had founded a genuinely universal religion, "the eternal religion of humanity, the religion of the spirit liberated from all priesthood, from all cult, from all observance, accessible to all races, superior to castes, in one word absolute." Judaism, on the other hand, remained tribalistic; it "contained the principle of a narrow formalism, of exclusive fanaticism, disdainful of strangers."[95]

Renan used the word "race" copiously, if in bewilderingly diverse senses, from a synonym for "type," to a social and economic group, to a physical category. Jacob Katz describes Renan as "the first writer to give it [race] free currency as an explanatory concept of historical phenomena,"[96] but there were others: By the 1840s and 1850s Disraeli and Robert Knox had made extensive use of race to explain the rise and fall of civilizations, as did Heinrich Heine in somewhat different ways. Katz's assertion is problematic as well because it is difficult to judge how much the term "race" actually explained in Renan's work, due to the looseness and inconsistency with which he used it. In some of his writings, Semitic inferiority in a cultural sense is a pervasive theme (particularly because of Semitic tribalism and intolerance), but he also considered the Semites and the Aryans to be part of the same "white race" (while of a different "physical type").[97] He described modern Jews as being perfectly capable

---

[93] Moshe Zimmermann, *Wilhelm Marr, the Patriarch of Anti-Semitism* (Oxford, 1986), 87; Andrew Handler, *Blood Libel at Tiszaeszlár* (New York, 1980), 29.

[94] Michael Marrus, *The Politics of Assimilation: A Study of the French Jewish Community at the Time of the Dreyfus Affair* (Oxford, 1971), 11.

[95] Katz, *Prejudice*, 133.

[96] Ibid., 134.

[97] Marrus, *Assimilation*, 12.

of becoming modern citizens with other enlightened, modern men.[98] In other passages, however, he laid historical responsibility on the Jews for the destructive intolerance introduced into the world through Christianity and Islam; even the death of Christ was a byproduct of Jewish intolerance. (Mosaic law called for the death of apostates, and Jews, by constantly rejecting Christ's universal message therefore perennially "wished for" his death.)[99] But Renan also praised the Semitic contributions to civilization. The very idea of human solidarity, of equality before one god, was, he wrote, "the fundamental doctrine of the Semites, and their most precious legacy to mankind," even if paradoxically contradicted by the Jewish notion of a Chosen People. He further spoke of both the modern European Aryans and Semites as noble, in contrast to the inferior races outside of Europe.[100]

Count Arthur de Gobineau (1816–1882) has often been called the "father of modern racism," but like Renan the precise nature and actual influence of his ideas are difficult to assess. Gobineau was a learned man, and his ideas were generally accepted by his contemporaries as serious contributions to scholarly inquiry. No less than Renan, he expressed shifting and ambiguous opinions about Jews, and those opinions were used by others in ways that he did not intend. His famous, multivolume *Essay on the Inequality of Races* (1853–1855) also used linguistic tools in a sophisticated fashion and sought to demonstrate Aryan superiority. His thought, however, rather than tapping Christian and Enlightened themes, made connection with an older aristocratic line of thinking, one that conceived of the upper orders of society as somehow inherently superior to the lower. Earlier, unsystematic efforts to explain what was the basis of that superiority spoke of blood or lineage; Gobineau identified it as being based on Aryan racial origins: The Aryan invaders had established themselves over the indigenous populations of Europe, becoming over the centuries the European aristocracy.

Gobineau linked to his thought an essentialist position on human races. He dismissed environmentalist theories of the rise and fall of civilizations, noting that civilizations rose, failed to rise, or declined in the same kind of environment. The real cause for the periods of decadence in earlier civilizations, he asserted, was the mixing of races, the corruption of aristocratic blood by that of the inferior masses. The lowest of all human races, he believed, was the Negro, and the lower classes in countries like France had qualities like those of Negroes: low intelligence and self-discipline, an inability to organize socially, and an overdeveloped sensuality and an inclination to destructive rampages.

---

[98] Mosse, *Final Solution*, 130.

[99] Cf. Katz, "Misreadings of Anti-Semitism," 42.

[100] Quoted in Stephen Wilson, *Ideology and Experience: Anti-Semitism in France at the Time of the Dreyfus Affair* (East Brunswick, N.J., 1982), 470–1.

Gobineau believed that race mixing, and thus degeneration, was almost unavoidable. And it was undermining Europe as it had undermined previous civilizations. The rise of the masses, of democracy, a large issue by midcentury – and of particular concern to Gobineau because of the forms it was assuming in Napoleon III's Second Empire – would eventually result, he believed, in the end of European civilization and its peculiar genius for freedom and creativity.

Not surprisingly, such ideas did not have a wide appeal in France, the land of revolution and *humanité*. Even among French Catholics and the political right Gobineau was strongly criticized.[101] He found a wider circle of admirers in Germany, however.[102] His later work, *Renaissance* (1877), won special acclaim there. He and the great German composer Richard Wagner became friends.[103]

Wagner (1813–1883) became one of the most famous German anti-Semites of the nineteenth century, and there is little question that he was influential in legitimizing anti-Semitic opinions among educated Germans. His *Das Judentum in der Musik* (Jewry in Music) first published anonymously in 1850 but then under his own name in 1869, offered a sweeping indictment of the Jewish spirit and its influence in Germany. Jews, he wrote, were interested in art only in order to sell it; the Jew worked to change the realm of artistic creation into a market place.

Wagner also questioned whether most Jews were capable of a genuine sense of unity with the German people. Jewish historical experiences and emotional roots remained alien to those of the Germans. He granted that Jews could produce great intellects, such as Spinoza or Moses Mendelssohn, but he denied that they could become specifically German poets, artists, and musicians, since creative activity required a sense of historical roots in a community. He lamented that alien Jews were, by midcentury, playing such an important role in Germany's intellectual life, especially in music and the theater, where they were their most destructive as critics.

Wagner did not absolutely exclude the possibility for some highly unusual Jews to become real Germans, but he believed the process would be at best extremely difficult. In his words, "in common with us [the destructive Jewish element], shall ripen toward a higher evolution of our nobler human qualities." At the end of *Das Judentum in der Musik*, he called upon Germany's Jews to achieve salvation, by casting off their destructive and commercial Jewish nature.[104] It was a call that more than a few Jews took seriously, as we will see.

---

[101] Mosse, *Final Solution*, 57.

[102] Poliakov, *History*, 3:380.

[103] Mosse, *Final Solution*, 56.

[104] Jacob Katz, *The Darker Side of Genius: Richard Wagner's Anti-Semitism* (Hanover, N.H., 1986), 69, 88.

Racist Ideas among Jews

The term "racist" in regard to Jews is problematic, especially since racism was eventually so appallingly turned against them. Nonetheless, insofar as the term suggests a belief in racial determinism, there were many Jewish racists in the nineteenth century. As noted, Disraeli was probably more influential in spreading certain general notions about the Jewish race than any of the theorists of race described in the preceding sections. Interestingly, he too considered the Arabs to be part of the same Semitic racial stock as Jews: "Arabs are only Jews on horseback," he once quipped.[105] Before Gobineau, Disraeli asserted that civilizations declined because of race mixing, and like Gobineau, he believed in superior and inferior races. He despised what he termed "that pernicious doctrine of modern times, the natural equality of man."[106]

In this kind of racism, Disraeli might also be termed typically English, since the nineteenth-century English were scarcely less than Germans attracted to racist conceptions. However, the racist vocabulary they used was different from that on the continent. They preferred the term "Anglo–Saxon" to Aryan, a preference that held in the United States as well. "Caucasian" was another term that gave Aryan some competition,[107] but all three referred in an imprecise way to the racially superior stock from which many English believed they originated.

Racism on the part of Jews in the nineteenth century has been much less studied than racism on the part of Gentiles, and obviously Jews who believed in Jewish racial supremacy had to be more circumspect about expressing their ideas. Still, Disraeli's claims were not an isolated phenomenon. His thoughts on the superiority of the Jewish race found rough but substantial counterparts in such writers as the popular German–Jewish historian of the Jews, Heinrich Graetz, who dismissed the accomplishments of prominent German thinkers and artists as largely derived from Jews. The celebrated German–Jewish poet Heinrich Heine, too playful perhaps to be taken seriously or literally on the issue, trumpeted the unparalleled triumph of the Jewish race in modern European history. He also grouped Jew and Arab together as Semitic kin.[108]

More obvious examples are Zionist, or proto-Zionist thinkers, such as Moses Hess (1812–1875), who already by midcentury had abandoned his earlier radical cosmopolitanism and had emphasized the primary importance of race, the distinct and immutable traits, both physical and cultural, of the races of humankind.[109] Hess, who had worked closely for a time with Karl Marx, later

---

[105] Robert Blake, *Disraeli* (New York, 1967), 204.

[106] Quoted in Paul Johnson, *A History of the Jews* (New York, 1987), 323.

[107] Cf. Mosse, *Final Solution*, 44.

[108] Cf. S. S. Prawer, *Heine's Jewish Comedy: A Study of His Portraits of Jews and Judaism* (Oxford, 1983).

[109] On Hess, see Shlomo Avineri, *Moses Hess, Prophet of Community and Zionism* (New York, 1985); Robert Wistrich, *Socialism and the Jews* (New Brunswick, N.J., 1982), 24, 40 ff.; Jonathan Frankel, *Prophesy and Politics: Socialism, Nationalism, and the Russian Jews, 1862–1917* (Cambridge, 1981), 6–27; Rose, *Revolutionary Antisemitism*, 306–37.

affirmed that the "race struggle is primary, the class struggle secondary." He believed that the Jews as a race would survive, triumph even, for the Jewish race was, in his words, one of the superior "primary races of mankind, and it has retained its integrity despite the influence of changing climatic environments." Similarly, Judaism would become the spiritual guide of humankind, whereas Christianity, "a religion of death," would wither.[110] He was a good friend of Graetz, who wrote him of his delight in "scourging" Germans. Graetz added that "we must above all work to shatter Christianity."[111]

Jewish racism, and of course Zionism, could build upon the tribalistic–nationalistic elements within Judaism, but no doubt equally important in the nineteenth century was the simple fact that nearly everyone believed in racial determinism. The extravagant claims of the sort expressed by Disraeli, Graetz, or Hess may also be seen as a defense mechanism against negative imagery concerning Jews and Semites. By this time in the West, Jewish self-hatred may have been more common than ideas like those of Disraeli, although the two were inextricably and paradoxically bound together in many cases, most famously in that of Heine.[112]

By the middle to late years of the nineteenth century the most common Jewish public stance among prominent western European Jews was universalistic. Yet, even within those universalistic convictions were nuances with racist undertones. The French–Jewish man of letters Julien Benda reported that among his Jewish acquaintances at the end of the century "were certain magnates, financiers rather than literary men, with whom the belief in the superiority of their race and in the natural subjection of those who did not belong to it, was visibly sovereign."[113] Similarly, a number of Jewish politicians on the left in France harbored a sense of their special merit or destiny as Jews to be political leaders, what they considered their "right to rule."

It would be a mistake, at any rate, to attribute to Disraeli, or other prominent Jewish racists of the nineteenth century, the aggressive and hate-filled racism that is to be found in some non-Jewish racists. Indeed, even to mention the occasional examples of the kind of racism cited by Benda or to pay attention to the boasting of Disraeli risks appearing to give credence to the exaggerated charges of nineteenth-century anti-Semites. But the point should not be lost that anti-Semitic beliefs about Jews fed upon the kind of observations made by Benda and Disraeli, not simply upon fantasies alone.

Some observers have dismissed Disraeli's exaggerated praise for all things

---

[110] From Moses Hess's *Rome and Jerusalem* in Arthur Hertzberg, ed., *The Zionist Idea, A Historical Analysis and Reader* (New York, 1969), 121, 122.

[111] Reuven Michael, ed., *Heinrich Graetz, Tagebuch und Briefe* (Tübingen, 1977), 287. Quoted in Michael Meyer, "Heinrich Graetz and Heinrich von Treitschke," *Modern Judaism*, vol. 6, no. 1, Feb. 1986, 11.

[112] Cf. the provocative treatment in Johnson, *History*, 341–7.

[113] Julien Benda, *La jeunesse d'un clerc* (Paris, 1936), 210. Quoted in Stephen Wilson, *Ideology and Experience: Anti-Semitism in France at the Time of the Dreyfus Affair* (New York, 1982), 410.

Jewish as lacking in seriousness; his noble Jewish characters have been seen as a specific response, or rebuttal, to the loathsome Jew Fagin in Charles Dickens's novel *Oliver Twist*. Certainly Disraeli's racism did not entail aggressive hatred of the non-Jew or any seriously conceived program for Jewish world mastery. Even if some Jews felt such hatred, they could not openly express it in the way that non-Jews expressed their hatred, given the numerical weakness and vulnerability of Jews in Europe.

The Ambiguities of Non-Jewish Racism

However, this recognition that Jewish feelings of racial superiority were rarely aggressive or violent in intent must be balanced by a similar recognition that aggressive hatred of Jews, with a concrete agenda of violence, was also not characteristic of the non-Jewish racists so far described. That is, in spite of the negative imagery concerning Semites that comes across in many theoretical or scientific works of the mid– to late nineteenth century, the overwhelming majority of them did not advocate violence against Jews. Most did not even advocate civil disabilities for them. Renan lived to witness the crude, populist anti-Semitism of the last quarter of the nineteenth century, and he was repelled by it. He then backed away from a number of his seemingly anti-Semitic pronouncements of the 1860s. He had never thought of himself as an enemy of Jewish contemporaries, and indeed he was himself attacked by the anti-Semites of the 1880s and 1890s. He joined with Victor Hugo in the early 1880s in organizing a relief committee for eastern European Jews, and he consistently defended the notion of civil equality for Jews.[114]

Jews in western Europe also began to move away from their earlier acceptance of racial categories, especially once they had come to appreciate how much mischief the idea of race was creating for them. And other racists also regretted the use that was made of their ideas. Gobineau, for all his vilification of Negroes, did not support their enslavement.[115] Even in England, for all the popularity of racist notions, J. C. Pritchard, a respected and influential English anthropologist, was known to argue that mixed races, rather than pure ones, were superior.[116]

Anti-Jewish imagery did not go unopposed among non-Jews, particularly the social Darwinists among them. The very survival of Jews over the centuries was frequently cited by various non-Jewish observers as a sign of biological or racial superiority.[117] The work of Sir Francis Galton, *Hereditary Genius* (1869), listed

---

[114] Cf. Shmuel Almog, "The Racial Motif in Renan's Attitude to Jews and Judaism," in Shmuel Almog, ed., *Antisemitism through the Ages* (New York, 1988), 257–8.

[115] Mosse, *Final Solution*, 54.

[116] Ibid., 70.

[117] Ibid., 80.

Jews as one of the groups that should be encouraged to reproduce, because of their racial superiority. Alphonse de Candolle, perhaps the most influential theoretician of race inside France, considered Jews to be a crowning culmination of the white race.[118] Similarly, in literature, Sir Walter Scott's noble and beautiful Rebecca in *Ivanhoe* can be seen as a powerful counterimage to Dickens's Fagin. Few if any works attempted to counter the racist denigration of African blacks.

Dickens, revealingly, was both astonished and appalled to see that he was considered an anti-Semite merely because he had created a particular unattractive Jewish character. Fagin was but one of many scoundrels in the novel, and certainly not intended, Dickens complained, to stand as a symbol of the Jewish people. It is nonetheless true that in many passages of the book, the portrayal of "the Jew," Fagin, does appear to borrow from crude, hostile stereotypes of Jews in general in ways that Dickens himself may not have fully appreciated. He subsequently wrote a novel, *Our Mutual Friend,* with an admirable Jewish character, Solomon Riah. Dickens remarked that he had made Fagin a Jew simply because Jews in London at midcentury were commonly associated with pickpocketing rings like that portrayed in *Oliver Twist.* Fagin was modeled after a notorious Jewish figure in London, Ikey Solomons, who in the 1820s headed a criminal network that included a chain of brothels.[119]

A further example from the literary realm that underlines the need to look carefully at those dismissed as anti-Semites in the mid–nineteenth century is the writer Gustave Freytag (1816–1895). The repellent Jewish characters in his extremely popular novel *Soll und Haben* (1855) certainly helped to propagate or reinforce negative images of Jews, yet there were also positive Jewish figures in the novel. Moreover, Freytag himself married a Jew, befriended many Jews, and publicly denounced racial and political anti-Semitism.[120]

Even Richard Wagner, whose anti-Semitism was blatant, nevertheless harbored ambiguous attitudes. His words about some Jews being able to become Germans were not entirely hollow. What is often not recognized about him – and certainly needs to be considered by those who maintain that anti-Semites typically have no experience with real Jews – is that throughout his life he worked with Jews, often closely. In his memoirs he called his friendship with the Jew Samuel Lehrs "one of the most beautiful . . . of my life."[121] Indeed, before the publication of his pamphlet in 1850 he might have passed as a philo-Semite.

---

[118] Ibid., 58.

[119] Edward J. Bristow, *Prostitution and Prejudice: The Jewish Fight against White Slavery* (Oxford, 1982), 18.

[120] Cf. Henry Wasserman, "The Fliegender Bläter as a Source for the Social History of the Jews," *Leo Baeck Institute Yearbook*, vol. 28, 1983, 95.

[121] Katz, *Darker Side*, 24.

Even after he had been acclaimed by Germany's anti-Semites as their hero, he continued to have intimate contacts with many Jews. Hermann Levi, the son of a rabbi, remained his favorite conductor, and "friend Rubinstein," a talented young Jewish musician who idolized Wagner, lived with the Wagners for extended periods.[122] Wagner was often unspeakably cruel to his Jewish "friends," and it is admittedly difficult to know what to make of these strange relationships, both from the standpoint of the Jews in question and from that of Wagner. The point here is simply to underline how the label "anti-Semite," no less than "racist," can mask some unfamiliar and elusive realities.

The least anti-Semitic of all of those in the nineteenth century who trafficked in concepts of racial determinism were the physical scientists, that is, those who were concerned with physical measurement in nature, with "good, hard facts" rather than the elusive abstractions of the more literary types like Renan and Gobineau. And the prestige of physical scientists was great and growing in the nineteenth century. Charles Darwin's *On the Origin of Species* was one of the three or four most influential works in that century. Although Darwin's theories of natural selection were refashioned by others into forms that assumed a racist character, he was himself not a racist in any notable sense, and certainly not an anti-Semite.

Darwin was merely the most famous of a growing corps of natural scientists who took pride in careful procedures, exact measurements, and theories based on solid facts. Darwin's illustrious contemporary, Paul Broca, the founder of the Anthropological Society of Paris in 1859, focused his attention on a meticulous measuring of human bodies. He devoted particular attention to an obvious human organ, the brain. Did a larger one mean greater intelligence? And did different races have different-sized brains? Broca arrived at a positive answer to both of those questions, based on careful measurement. Negroes have smaller brains than Europeans, just as women have smaller brains than men. And, he concluded, both Negroes and women were less intelligent, on the average, than whites or males.

Broca's studies confirmed a common-sense racist conclusion, one popularly made without the benefit of careful scientific measurement: that cultural differences and physical differences were related. In racist terms, skin color and hair type were in some way related to intelligence and psychological tendency. Broca was a man of the left, and what is particularly interesting in his case is that he did not ostensibly *want* to believe in human inequality, but he felt driven in the direction of believing in the inequality of races, and sexes, by what he deemed overwhelming evidence. By the standards of the day he was a careful scientist, even if today we can see the flaws in his research.[123] He stated that it was necessary for scientists to put aside their ethical hopes for human equal-

---

[122] Ibid., 99 ff.

[123] Stephen Jay Gould, *The Mismeasure of Man* (New York, 1981), 73–112.

ity: Truth was truth, even if unpleasant, and the truth was that races were unequal.

Purity of race in Gobineau's sense, the idea that so excited a number of German and Jewish observers, was not desirable in Broca's eyes. He believed that most great civilizations were based upon mixed races.[124] Broca was not an anti-Semite, and he denounced the enslavement of Negroes. Interestingly, a Jewish observer in France, Jules Carvallo, following Broca, concluded that since Jews had a larger cranial capacity than other races, they were particularly suited to survive in the social Darwinistic struggle for existence. Another Frenchman, Alfred Legoyt, emphasized the lower death rate among Jews as further scientific or objective evidence of their biological superiority.[125]

Broca's interest in brains was paralleled by other efforts to measure the human body (eyes, noses, head shapes, length of limbs) in order to establish rigorously scientific definitions of race.[126] The brilliant and famous Scottish anatomist Robert Knox in his book *The Races of Mankind* (1850) emphasized facial angle (in a line from forehead to chin) as a sign of racial superiority, although in truth many of his judgments about race were as willful and subjective as anything to be found in Renan and Gobineau. For Knox it was the "Saxons" and the "Slavonic" peoples who constituted the superior races. The black races of the world lacked the "grand qualities which distinguish man from animal."[127] In words strikingly like those of Disraeli, Knox proclaimed, "race is everything; civilization depends upon it." However, in a strong dissent from Disraeli, Knox considered the Jews to be lacking in creativity; they were parasites – without craftsmen, farmers, or productive members, and physically ugly. The Jews, like the Gypsies, lived by cunning, by cheating or exploiting others.[128]

Racist thought in the nineteenth century was bewildering in its diversity and apparent contradictions; the preceding remarks are suggestive, hardly exhaustive. What should emerge from them, however, is that while racist ideas in the nineteenth century were widespread, they were by no means of a piece, leading to unanimous conclusions, especially in regard to the Jews. The most hostile, categorical, and vicious imagery concerning Jews came mostly from the fringes of respectability, or from the so-called mystics of race,[129] who had relatively little influence upon their nineteenth-century contemporaries.

We are brought finally to conclusions about the influence of nineteenth-century racist thought on anti-Semitism that are similar to the conclusions already reached concerning the influence of Christianity and Enlightened

---

[124] Mosse, *Final Solution*, 89.

[125] Marrus, *Assimilation*, 18–19.

[126] Cf. Gould, *Mismeasure*, 113–45.

[127] Mosse, *Final Solution*, 68.

[128] Ibid., 69.

[129] Ibid., 96.

ideas: In each of them one may discover obvious anti-Semitic themes, but they are mixed with other themes that if not unequivocally philo-Semitic, nonetheless tend to counterbalance, mitigate, or neutralize hatred of Jews. More subtly, Jewish inferiority was less often identified with physical and intellectual traits than was the case with other denigrated races, especially African blacks. There was no clear consensus about Jews. Moreover, that Jews were seen in racially negative terms did not necessarily mean that they were considered inferior; indeed, many of those hostile to Jews were hostile because they were afraid of the power and ambitions of the Jews, linked to their undeniable abilities. Insofar as anti-Semites dwelt on Jewish inferiority it was often not physical or intellectual but moral.

We cannot conclude that racist ideas as such were the root cause of hatred of Jews in the nineteenth century. Many racists, perhaps most, were not anti-Semitic. And, as will be more fully explored in later chapters, a number who rejected racism were violently hostile to Jews.[130] Anti-Semitism was more than racism, much more. And racism was also much more than anti-Semitism.

[130] Cf. Katz, "Misreadings," 39–44.

THE APPEARANCE
OF MODERN ANTI-SEMITISM
(1870–1890)

A S USED BY SCHOLARS the concept "modern anti-Semitism" has come to entail significantly more than the contrast between premodern religious hatred and modern racial–secular hatred. "Modern" in these pages has so far been used in one of its more familiar forms, close to the generic notion of liberalism, deriving from the Enlightenment and, more distantly, from the Protestant Reformation and having to do with the establishment of personal liberty (of conscience, of political and economic activity), a belief in the powers of unaided reason, in progress, and in secular values. Such modernism was explicitly condemned by the pope in 1864 in his *Syllabus of Errors,* and it stands in sharp contrast to the premodern world of faith, corporate communities, ecclesiastical authority, and tradition.

Modern times also entailed the application of new techniques of production, which led to an unprecedented expansion of material wealth in the course of the nineteenth century. Parallel to this expansion was a rapid population increase, moving primarily into the cities of Europe and America. Finally, modern times saw the ever more extensive application of the principle of maximum efficiency to economic, social, and political life, often destroying the traditional and inefficient. A pervasive sense of loss, a yearning for the communal closeness of premodern life, as contrasted to the impersonal, atomistic striving and cosmopolitanism of modern society, was central to much of the thought and artistic expression of the nineteenth century – and to modern anti-Semitism, since Jews were so widely associated with these dynamic and destructive modern trends.

When scholars refer to the kind of modern anti-Semitism that flared up in the last decades of the nineteenth century, they are referring to something related but more precise and less obvious. Modern anti-Semitism was characterized by a call to action, a move into the modern political realm; anti-Semites are then new because they have a program of action in regard to the Jews, not simply harsh words or thoughts in their regard. Modern politics in this sense has to do with new democratic–populist or democratic–radical forms of organization, mobilization, and participation, as distinguished from the more elitist or "classic" liberalism of the preceding decades. In the last quarter of the nineteenth century broad masses of the population, previously not actively or consistently involved in political activity, began to assert themselves in new ways – not, to be sure, taking over but still constituting a presence, showing new energy, and appearing to be the voice of the future. The term "modern political anti-Semitism," then, refers to such phenomena. Anti-Semitic political activists, when they first appeared in the 1870s and 1880s, insisted on their difference from liberal leaders, and their call for specific political action against the Jews differed from earlier literary attacks on Jews, or from mere social snobbery.

The contrasts between nineteenth-century liberals of the classical variety and their emerging democratic–populist opponents were several. Liberals were not democrats in the sense of believing in the direct rule of the people; they operated according to more bourgeois–elitist methods than did the various emerging "democrats." (A range of more precise terms might be used for them: populist democrats, radical democrats, social democrats, or Christian democrats – but not liberal democrats.) Typically, liberal parties of the 1860s and 1870s had been run by committees of wealthy notables, often from business and professional circles. It was they who worked out political strategies and programs. They also nominated candidates for parliamentary office without feeling any particular need to elicit advice from or active participation of the electorate in general. Liberals characteristically considered the lower orders, who were just beginning to get the vote in many countries, a danger to political liberty – indeed, to civilization itself. Insofar as liberals were inclined to share power it was with the older ruling elites, to whom liberal notables still often deferred. There was a tendency in most countries in these years, partly in response to the agitation of the lower orders, for liberals to edge toward the right, establishing various kinds of alliances with the older elites, which often entailed a split in the liberal camp into right and left wings. Jewish liberals did not differ markedly from Gentile liberals in these regards. In some areas, notably Vienna, liberal Jews were particularly elitist.

Anti-Semites of the 1870s and 1880s were thus modern in ways that are not usually understood by the term, ways that seemed to go against the modern notion of the progress of reason and freedom. In this sense they presaged twentieth-century political realities more than liberalism did. Anti-Semites began to address, recruit, and mobilize the lower orders in new, antiliberal ways. These modern enemies of the Jews often used the language of race, but there was both more and less to modern anti-Semitism than racial hatred as such; anti-Semitism became a modern movement in the context of the constitutional nation-state, a movement that involved an active and positive kind of participation by the broad masses of people around a cluster of ideas, symbols, and motifs constituting an "ideology," again a term with characteristically modern implications.

For much of the nineteenth century anti-Jewish sentiment had remained primarily within the confines of traditional forms and institutions, reflecting Christian values, premodern derision, and social snobbery. Public agitation against Jews, and violence against them, had been disorganized, limited in scale, and in fact uncommon. The Russian pogroms of 1881–1882, occurring in a backward country, were only a partial exception; they engaged violent mobs and unquestionably reflected the growing pains of modernization in Russia, but they were short-lived outbreaks without coherent leadership, organization, or ideological motivation.

In comparison, after the mid-1870s, theorists, agitators, organizers, and broad masses in western Europe began to come together around new ideologies. Anti-Semites began to acquire offices and cadres, newspapers and presses; they formed parties and pressure groups; they organized regular meetings, collected dues, planned tours and campaigns, and joined local groups together with national centers. Funds devoted to electoral campaigns grew appreciably, as did the participation rates of voters and the energies devoted to elections. Rallies, parades, and demonstrations were organized by these new anti-Semitic parties and pressure groups. Like other ideologically oriented movements of the day, the anti-Semites produced formal programs that they sought to introduce through parliament and local representative bodies.

Many of those who have been described as anti-Semites in the 1870s and 1880s were not racists, and some were even firmly antiracist. Contrary to simplistic accounts, explicitly religious, not primarily racial, motifs played a central role in many attacks on Jews in these years. Those who denounced Jews and Jewish influence came from the ranks of Catholics and Protestants, believers and nonbelievers, reactionaries and progressives, and many who were rather confused about their identity and fidelities, including a number of prominent Jews themselves.

A key unifying trait of these diverse anti-Jewish groups was anxiety about the economic changes of the time and more broadly about the meaning of a wide range of modern trends, many of which seemed to benefit Jews. Yet, "antimodernism" can be a misleading label for these groups, for within them were figures who prided themselves on their modern, progressive ideas. Insofar as the anti-Semites of the time were motivated by religious concepts, they used religion in new ways, consistent with the idea of an ideologically based modern movement.

Premodern religious anti-Semitism might also be termed "ideological" in that the presence of Jews, and the problems their presence presented, had been integrated into Christian theology. But modern religious anti-Semites attempted to adjust to the new realities of an industrial economy, impersonal society, and nation-state. To be sure, many religious anti-Semites agitated in favor of a return to premodern controls and norms insofar as the Jews were concerned, but anti-Semites used modern methods in their agitation in favor of those premodern norms. Moreover, those supposed premodern norms were typically romanticized, misrepresented, or misunderstood by anti-Semitic spokesmen – also in modern ways.

Tensions between Jews and non-Jews in the 1870s and 1880s flared up where modern trends were having a pronounced impact, particularly where Jews were conspicuous: the new commercial and industrial cities; the stock market, the financing of railroads, and the retail trade; and journalism and other publicly prominent professions, such as law and medicine. These flare-ups varied in timing and intensity from country to country, but they were everywhere cause for surprise and even shock in those quarters where it had been assumed that Jew-hatred was one of the medieval prejudices that was being steadily overcome by Europeans in this age of science, religious tolera-tion, and inexorable progress. To such observers, Jew-hatred was anachronistic and irrational; it just did not make sense.

Such observers had other shocks to deal with. The surprise at the appear-ance of anti-Semitism seems to have been intimately connected with the feel-ing of shock that came with the unexpected economic depression in Europe that began in 1873. For the economy to falter suddenly put many other things into question. The optimism and the belief in unending progress had them-selves been intimately linked to a faith in steady economic growth, to confi-dence in the free-market system. An interlocking structure of beliefs, among which was the supportive Gentile–liberal attitude to Jewish emancipation, was put to the test after 1873.

We cannot accurately speak of the "end" or "collapse" of liberalism during the depression of the following two decades; it was more a matter of the older, conservative elites, which had by no means been wholly vanquished in the 1850s and 1860s, reasserting themselves and in many cases seeking popular support against the liberals. The wealth of these elites was based to an impor-tant degree on land and agriculture; the drop in agricultural prices in the depression alarmed them. They thus "discovered or rediscovered the cardinal importance of politics"[1] and effectively worked for the introduction of legisla-tion that protected their interests, most notably in tariffs.

The depression of the mid-to-late 1870s, 1880s, and early 1890s, known for years afterward as the Great Depression, was a minor affair by later standards.[2] Present-day economic historians describe it as a leveling off of productivity, fol-

---

[1] Arno J. Mayer, *The Persistence of the Old Regime: Europe to the Great War* (New York, 1981), 32.

[2] Cf. Hans Rosenberg, *Grosse Depression und Bismarckzeit* (Berlin, 1967); Hans-Ulrich Wehler, *Bis-marck und der Imperialismus* (Berlin, 1969), 39 ff.; J. H. Clapman, *The Economic Development of France and Germany, 1815–1914* (Cambridge, 1961).

lowed by a recovery in the 1890s and generally impressive growth until 1914. In short, the shock associated with it appears in historical perspective to have been an overreaction. The anti-Semitic "explosion" of those years needs to be viewed in a similar light, for it was also mild by post-1914 standards. In the decade or two immediately before the war, when the economy regained its vitality, a renewed, if also chastened confidence in the future of Gentile–Jewish relationships emerged, one that saw a distinctly greater degree of Jewish assertiveness than had been the case in midcentury.

Part Two of this book examines developments in Germany in the 1870s and 1880s with special care because of the influence the new Reich came to have in those years. Subsequent chapters of Part Two explore the revealing variations of Jewish–Gentile relations in Austria–Hungary, France, Great Britain, and the United States.

3

Germans and Jews
(1870–1890)

To have a declining economic class [the Junkers]
hold political authority in its hands is dangerous
and, in the long run, not compatible with the
national interest. (Max Weber)

As for anti-Semitic feelings, the Jews themselves are
to blame, and the present agitation must be ascribed
to their arrogance, vanity, and unspeakable inso-
lence. (Meyer Carl Rothschild in a letter to Gerson
Bleichröder)[1]

No longer can we suffer to see the Jews push themselves everywhere to the front, everywhere seize leadership and dominate public opinion. They are
always pushing us aside. They take our breath and
air away. (Otto Glagau)

This remarkable people, yielding yet tenacious, was
in the ancient world as in the modern world everywhere and nowhere at home, and everywhere and
nowhere powerful. . . . Even in the ancient world
Judaism was an effective leaven of cosmopolitan and
national decomposition. (Theodor Mommsen)[2]

---

[1] Quoted in Fritz Stern, *The Politics of Cultural Despair: A Study of Germanic Ideology* (New York, 1965), 94.

[2] Theodor Mommsen, *History of Rome* (Glencoe, 1957), 5:417–19.

The German Problem; the Sonderweg

The German problem is central to modern European history and is in revealing ways linked to the Jewish problem. The relationship of Germans and Jews has been the subject of innumerable studies; it might be termed a major subfield of German history, with its own journals, specialized monographs, and works for the general reader. The nature of German–Jewish interplay is still bitterly debated – in particular the extent to which one can properly speak of mutual benefit and respect – but there is little doubt that nowhere else have Jacob and Esau had a more intricate, fecund, and yet finally tragic relationship.[3] Nowhere was the rise of the Jews more notable, and nowhere was it more searchingly debated whether the nature of Jews was unchangeably foreign, undermining those among whom they resided, or adaptable and beneficial to the host people. Similarly, the possible ramifications of the notion of chosenness are nowhere more clearly revealed than in the history of modern Germany, for growing numbers of Germans came to believe that they were somehow chosen by history for a special destiny.[4]

It is a common assumption, and a position expressed in much of the literature dealing with both the German and Jewish problems, that the relations of Jews and non-Jews in Germany, dating back into the Middle Ages, were peculiar, ominously different from those in other nations. A related assertion has been that the unusual, often disastrous historical experiences of Germany between 1870 and 1933 exacerbated those differences. The broader issue of Germany's *Sonderweg*, or "special path," has spawned a contentious scholarly literature, centering on the degree to which modern Germans were more authoritarian, militaristic, xenophobic, and racist than other Europeans. One school of historians has argued that Germany's ruling elites manipulated large sectors of the German population, mobilizing mass support against the threat of further liberal-modernizing political reform. Those same elites, the argument continues, managed to provide special protection to the privileged, premodern sectors of Germany's society and economy, resulting in a strange – or "special" – mix of premodern and modern, one that contained ultimately incompatible elements and that produced dangerous tensions.[5]

---

[3] For a recent discussion, with references to most of the literature, of an old controversy see Enzo Traverso, *The Jews and Germany: From the 'Judeo–German Symbiosis' to the Memory of Auschwitz* (Lincoln, Nebr., 1995; original French edition, Paris, 1992). Among the more recent overviews of German anti-Semitism, see Helmut Berding, *Moderner Antisemitismus in Deutschland* (Frankfurt am Main, 1988). A series of articles, again with ample bibliographical references, treats the role of religion in German anti-Semitism: "Symposium: Christian Religion and Anti-Semitism in Modern German History," *Central European History*, vol. 27, no. 3, 1994.

[4] Cf. Hartmut Lehmann, "The Germans as a Chosen People: Old Testament Themes in German Nationalism," *German Studies Review*, vol. 14, no. 2, May 1991, 261–73; the footnotes in this article provide a fairly extensive literature on the topic.

[5] These issues are explored and the Sonderweg thesis critically scrutinized in David Blackbourn and Geoff Eley, *The Peculiarities of German History* (Oxford, 1984). See also the introduction to Marilyn Coetzee, *The German Army League* (Oxford, 1990).

One of the most portentous aspects of this manipulation, historians has argued, was that Jews, long outsiders but r wealthy and influential, were now blamed for Germany's accusations were made, on the one hand, by those who sincerely beⁿᵉ. the baneful influence of Jews and on the other by cynics who were perfectly aware that those ills had many causes, most of them little or only remotely related to the presence of Jews in Germany. Blaming the Jews had the advantage of diverting attention from the genuine causes of distress.

Other scholars have argued that the rise of anti-Semitism in Germany must be understood as much more complicated than a matter of cynical manipulators and gullible masses. The ruling elite could not simply call modern anti-Semitism into being ex nihilo, and the efforts of that elite to control expressions of Jew-hatred once they burst forth were anything but smooth, confident, or successful. Real issues were involved, issues that emerged from the concentration of Jews in certain occupations, from their related extraordinary economic and social success, and from a range of cultural traits that distinguished them from non-Jewish Germans.[6] These real issues engaged large numbers of Germans in a spontaneous way, independent of the efforts of cynical manipulators.

To speak of German citizens engaged in a spontaneous, independent way brushes upon another much debated aspect of Germany's peculiar condition: the putative political passivity of the educated, middle-class citizenry, the reticence of the educated bourgeoisie – "supine and star-struck"[7] – to challenge the established authorities. Those who believe in the importance of that political passivity have seen it as central to the later victory of Nazism. The anti-Semitic movement in the 1880s thus appears in a paradoxical light: Insofar as anti-Semites were agitating in favor of popular power against the authorities, they were demonstrating an un-German and "healthy" activism, one that may be seen as part of a necessary if painful process of political maturation.

Those historians who have argued that the political passivity of Germans has been overstated or carelessly conceptualized have had to deal with yet another sign of "disease": From the Middle Ages to the beginning of the modern period Jews in Germany had been often associated with the authorities and frequently protected by them. Thus, popular activism against the authorities, in premodern as in modern times, often blended into attacks on Jews.[8] Anti-Semitism can therefore be interpreted as an aspect of "wholesome" trends, of popular activism against autocratic leaders.

---

[6] Cf. Blackbourn and Eley, *Peculiarities;* also the useful discussion in W. E. Mosse, *Jews in the German Economy: The German–Jewish Elite, 1820–1935* (Oxford, 1987), esp. 381–405.

[7] Blackbourn and Eley, *Peculiarities,* 13. (The authors are using these words, it should be made clear, ironically and critically, to describe the views of other historians.)

[8] Cf. Christopher R. Friedrichs, "Politics or Pogrom? The Fettmilch Uprising in German and Jewish History," *Central European History,* vol. 19, no. 2, June 1986, 186–228.

There were other paradoxes in the situation by the mid–nineteenth century: The German problem had much in common with the Jewish problem in that both Germans and Jews were expanding in various ways – numbers, wealth, power, prestige – at a rate that alarmed those around them, that challenged older elites and traditional relationships, and that evoked defensive reactions. Both Germans and Jews, especially German Jews, were admired – and feared – in ways that are difficult to sort out. Both had traits that were widely esteemed, yet both were in other ways perceived as troublesome, overbearing, and threatening to cherished values.

One peculiarity of Germany's development in the late nineteenth century seems beyond dispute: The shock of the Great Depression was particularly severe. German-speaking Jews were the largest and economically most successful population of assimilated Jews in Europe, and because of their important positions in the German economy, they were almost unavoidably identified with the Depression. Germany's economy, or the economies of the various German states before unification, had been growing with remarkable, even breakneck speed in the 1860s, and it grew even faster in the early 1870s. Jews seemed to benefit disproportionately from that growth, and they were widely and plausibly (which is not to say justifiably) blamed for its sudden collapse. The expression of both antiliberal and anti-Jewish feelings in Germany was subsequently more widespread and assumed richer, at times more sophisticated forms than elsewhere in Europe. For much of the 1880s and 1890s the first modern anti-Semitic movement found its most impressive and influential form in Germany.

Given the growing prestige of Germany and things German, the nascent German anti-Semitic movement took on a special significance. The final steps of German territorial unification came with brilliant, Prussian-led military victories over the Habsburg Empire (1866) and then over Napoleon III's Second Empire (1870–1871). Especially after 1871 it seemed to many observers that the new German Reich was replacing France as the leading nation on the continent, not only in the obvious military and diplomatic realms but also economically. Germans stood out in science, technology, and scholarship (here most strikingly of all, since German universities became models for the world); and in the arts, music, and literature – indeed, in nearly every realm. Germany seemed simply more dynamic than France; the relative growth of the two countries' populations suggested that dynamism perhaps more than anything else: From 1871 to 1914 the population of the German Reich rose fifty-eight percent (from 41 to 65 million) while France's population, in the eighteenth century the largest in Europe, grew relatively little, settling at 39 million by 1914.

Germans were gaining a new respect among nations; admiration for things German and imitation of German models spread throughout Europe. ("German," it should be noted, can refer to the new, Prussian-led Reich but also to the extensive areas of central Europe where millions of Germans lived and where German culture and language prevailed – the *deutscher Kulturbereich*, the German cultural realm. German-speaking scientists and artists in Vienna or Prague, although not residing in the newly unified German Reich, nevertheless both enhanced and enjoyed the general prestige of things German.) As noted, many Germans were inclined to see world historical significance in the establishment of the German Reich; it represented a turning point in modern history. Even more grandiosely, some German nationalists believed the new Reich was the expression of divine purpose, an affirmation of the mission of the German spirit in the modern world. How unique or "special" such beliefs actually were is debatable. We will see that Jews in many countries, not only Germany, were inclined to see the rise of the Jews in modern times as expressing a divine purpose or a Jewish mission. Citizens of the United States, too, with their notions of Manifest Destiny, expressed a belief that they and the new American nation were agents of God's will.

No one was especially surprised to hear that Jews were being persecuted in retrograde Russia or Romania. But the new German Reich was widely respected as a land of cultured, disciplined, and law-abiding citizens. Its government was considered unusually efficient and responsible. And the assimilation of Jews in the German lands that would constitute the new Reich had progressed much beyond what was the norm in eastern Europe. That degree of assimilation had, indeed, few equivalents in other areas of Europe with a large Jewish population, except for the western, largely German-speaking territories of Austria and the Magyar-dominated areas of Hungary. For such reasons the wave of anti-Jewish indignation and outrage that passed over Germany, and the efforts to give to that wave the form of a modern mass movement, caught the attention of the civilized western world.

German Liberalism and the New German State

The liberal middle years of the century had seen the final steps in granting civil emancipation to Jews in most German-speaking lands, not without mean-tempered dissent from various quarters. Even German liberals were not unanimously persuaded that Germany's Jews were ready for full emancipation. The German model of emancipation, unlike that of the French, was characterized by wary gradualism; the German defenders of Jewish emancipation in the early part of the century had spoken of a process that would take three or four generations. They also insisted that assiduous attention by the political authorities to educate Jews to the responsibilities of citizenship would be necessary.[9] But those steps were generally accepted as part of the reforms necessary if newly unified Germany was to become a land of free and independent citizens and if

---

[9] Reinhard Rürup, *Emanzipation und Antisemitismus* (Göttingen, 1975), 74 ff.

the country was to enter into the ranks of Europe's most modern nations, France and England. Being counted among the most modern, most highly civilized nations was important to Germany's elites; discriminatory laws against the Jews characterized the backward nations, such as Russia and Romania.

By the late 1860s liberal principles were given fuller application in many arenas besides those touching the condition of the Jews. Indeed, those general principles were the primary consideration; the emancipation of the Jews was seen as a necessary aspect of them, much as was the case in the debates of the French National Assembly from 1789 to 1791. Freedom of movement for goods and individuals was firmly established in law, which meant a loosening of the earlier economic controls and a weakening of the privileges of corporate bodies like the guilds. Limited liability joint-stock companies were legalized, and regulations concerning the stock market were significantly relaxed. Similarly, to express one's opinions freely and to form political organizations became easier, less tied down by legal restrictions.

These were liberal rights that had been in place for some time in France and Great Britain. However, modern Anglo–French ideas and practices had received a mixed reception in Germany; they were identified with the hated French invaders and the untrustworthy, materialistic "nation of shopkeepers." Already early in the century some of Germany's best minds had subjected liberal tenets to a penetrating critique. As the century progressed German liberals remained relatively uncertain of themselves and politically unassertive when compared with their counterparts in England or France, especially at the national, as contrasted with the local level. Even the liberal belief in human rights, and in particular the rights of Jews as human beings, expressed itself cautiously in Germany. Jews were expected to show themselves, by a steady and prudent improvement of their habits, worthy of German citizenship. They could not claim it as an abstract right, on the French model.[10]

This caution was an aspect of the political reticence of Germany's educated classes. Since the Protestant Reformation, Germans were known to consider internal or spiritual freedom as particularly important, while external or political liberty was of a lower priority or, really, of a different order. The German historian Gerhart Ritter has written of an "essentially Lutheran" distaste on the part of the educated classes in Germany for the messy confusions of politics, for the divisiveness of political parties, and the compromises and corruptions of parliamentary activity.[11] These traits were often associated with the anarchic French temper or the crass materialism of the Anglo–Americans. Lack of self-restraint in material terms and more generally an attention to the external, nonspiritual world were also widely believed to be Jewish characteristics, as also those of the Latin peoples.

---

[10] Ibid., 82.
[11] Gerhart Ritter, *Das Deutsche Problem* (Munich, 1962).

Related to that Lutheran distaste was a deep-seated tendency to believe in the political wisdom of properly constituted rulers. Germans characteristically were willing to sacrifice a degree of justice in the secular realm for order and tranquillity or, indeed, to see a higher justice in such a sacrifice. In a deeper and also Lutheran sense, Germans were inclined to believe that "right belief," a proper spiritual state, necessarily preceded "right action." In contrast, the teachings of Judaism were known to stress the importance of right action, without straining over issues of right belief (a tendency found in some Christian denominations as well, most notably the Church of England). The identity of Germans as a spiritual people, and their inclination to portray the Jews as lacking in true spirituality, borrowed much from these dichotomies and no doubt fed anti-Semitic convictions.

Although the enemies of Jews in Germany denigrated them as pushy, divisive, and "un-German," there seems little question that the great majority of German middle-class Jews finally came to resemble German Christians more than they did Jews in other countries, both in terms of public manners and in their attitudes to secular authority. Indeed, Jewish liberals of midcentury were berated by following generations of Jews for their "Germanic" political passivity *as Jews*. That is, German Jews allegedly allowed civil equality to be given to them, rather than winning it in open political struggle. Similarly, and perhaps more importantly as far as their retrospective critics have been concerned, they hesitated to combat political anti-Semitism openly and actively as Jews, rather than respectfully waiting for the properly constituted authorities to deal with it. The language of these critiques broadly resembles the language with which German bourgeois liberals have been criticized: for insufficient boldness in pursuing their own interests, for failing to take up the "historic claims" of their class to rule Germany by replacing the Junker aristocracy.

There was much soul searching among Germans concerning the kind of national unity achieved under Bismarck's leadership. The new state remained, in spite of the exhilaration that accompanied the dramatic final stages of unification, "a very imperfect expression of the national community."[12] Especially in its first two decades, the 1870s and 1880s, that community remained deeply divided and uncertain of its future, and that uncertainty played a role in demands in some quarters for "pure" German feeling, with obvious implications for Jews, very recent claimants to membership in that community.

Among the many contentious issues was the exact nature of the state: Was it to be explicitly Christian (the conservative ideal) or secular (the liberal ideal)? If Christian, was it to be unequivocally Lutheran–Protestant (and thus anti-Catholic)? Did its more liberal–democratic aspects, in particular universal manhood suffrage and the free movement of goods and people, not threaten

---

[12] James J. Sheehan, "German Politics, 1871–1933," in Charles Burdick et al., eds., *Contemporary Germany: Politics and Culture* (Boulder, Colo., 1984), 3–4.

to degenerate eventually into a crass and materialistic mass democracy, as in the United States? These questions hid intricate nuances, some of direct relevance to the relations of Jews and non-Jews.

Many Germans were not comfortable with the way that western-style freedom and modernity were given to them in the 1850s and 1860s. These things were "given" because the German people, and their presumed liberal leaders, had failed to "take" them and thus control or shape them thereafter. The efforts of liberals, in other words, to unify all German-speaking lands around liberal principles in the revolutionary upheavals of 1848 had ended in a series of humiliating failures. Bismarck was not a liberal or, strictly speaking, even a German nationalist; at midcentury he was known as a reactionary, a devoted servant of the Prussian monarchy, and opposed to the liberal nationalists. The subsequent unification, under Bismarck's and Prussia's leadership, of a more restricted number of German-speaking peoples (purposely excluding the German Catholics in lands held by Austria), entailed as well a distinctly more restricted liberalism than was to be found in the French and English models. Unification was more a Prussian triumph than a triumph of broad German nationalism or liberalism.

In 1871 a number of important liberal principles were incorporated into the constitution of the new German Empire, such as free trade, the rule of law, representative institutions, and guarantees of free speech. Religious freedom and Jewish equality under the law were also a part of the constitution. However, there were other less liberal, more authoritarian elements: The Reichstag, Germany's parliament, while elected by universal manhood suffrage, lacked certain key powers that were exercised by England's or France's parliaments. It could not, for example, dismiss the prime minister, or chancellor, who remained responsible only to the emperor, the king of Prussia. Still, Bismarck as chancellor, after initially attempting to ignore the claims of the Reichstag, did strive to maintain a majority in it, and the Reichstag's control of the budget gave it indirect and potential power over him.

To the intransigent liberal the compromise with authoritarianism contained in the constitution of the new Reich was unacceptable. On the other hand, many traditionalists were outraged by the new constitution, since in it the privileges of the old aristocracy were curtailed, as were those of organized religion, and some old dynasties were abolished. Bismarck nimbly fended off resentments from left and right, but it was a tightrope act, and perhaps only a man of his extraordinary abilities could have succeeded in it – if "success" is finally the appropriate term for his accomplishments.

Junker Hegemony and the Jews

Whatever their reservations about the immediate impact of the new constitution, conservatives were for the most part protected by it, and they were certainly its long-range beneficiaries, which was Bismarck's intent. Such was especially true of the Prussian Junkers (landed nobility), Bismarck's own class. Their power and prestige remained distinctly greater than that of nobles in France and England. In those countries the privileged upper classes had historically faced a more determined and numerous bourgeoisie, and while the French and English bourgeoisie had by no means wholly destroyed the power of the older ruling elites, there were significant differences in the relations of bourgeoisie and nobility in Germany as compared with England and France. In the new German Reich the emperor was the Prussian king, a Hohenzollern (a Junker dynasty). In practice the Reich chancellor was always a Prussian. Junkers dominated the military and the upper ranks of state offices, and they jealously guarded their positions in spite of liberal-inspired constitutional provisions that in principle opened military and governmental offices to all qualified applicants.

In short, the liberal forms that were officially incorporated into the new state were often unofficially interpreted in less than liberal ways by those in power. Such was especially the case in those areas where it was believed that pure German feeling was essential (for example, in primary education, the military, and the judiciary). For many Reich officials the all-too recent entry of the "foreign" Jewish nation into the German national community cast into doubt the ability of Jews to function reliably in positions of high authority. In a more practical sense, many such officials reasoned that Jews as judges, military officers, and primary school teachers would simply not be respected or accepted by most ordinary Germans and thus could not function effectively.

The long-debated issue of how much Jews could, or would, abandon the age-old nationalistic elements of their religious identity and transform themselves into real Germans became an increasingly hot one in the decades immediately following unification. The term *Reichsfeinde* (enemies of the Reich), which carried much emotional bite in the last decades of the nineteenth century, was applied at first to Catholics, social democrats, Poles, and others who were less than enthusiastic about the shape of the new Reich. Unlike most of them, German Jews in the 1860s and 1870s were predominantly middle-class, liberal, and Prussophile. German Jews undoubtedly saw themselves as benefiting from the Reich's founding. Many were inclined to applaud whatever measures Bismarck considered necessary to firm up national unity, even if Jews were also prominent among his critics. A few extremely rich Jews entered into the narrow ranks of the establishment of the Reich, or at least were on its fringes.

In sometimes subtle but also pervasive ways, the Lutheran–Christian, authoritarian, and militaristic values of the Junkers penetrated German society, even as an opposing modern commercialism and industrialism also spread. Elsewhere in Europe and America, the diffusion of such modern economic tendencies was closely associated with more open, middle-class or bourgeois values, which in turn were conducive to the rise of the Jews. Junker hegemony in certain ways "unnaturally" perpetuated the historic weakness of the German bourgeoisie and the related weakness of modern, liberal values.[13]

The negative implications for Jews of Junker hegemony are obvious. German Jews were overwhelmingly middle-class and liberal. Junkers were known to be suspicious of intellectuals, especially liberal ones; Jews held intellectuals in esteem. Junker wealth was based in the land; Jewish wealth lay in commerce, banking, and industry. Junker social prestige derived from lineage and ancestry; Jews gained social prestige in German society through personal accomplishment, usually in professional excellence or through wealth accumulated in business. Jewish style was lively, verbal; Junkers were reserved, taciturn. The value system of Junkers was based on such notions as *Treue, Obrigkeit, Gehorsam* (loyalty, authority, obedience); the value system of assimilated Jews centered around the more modern notions of liberty, justice, and reform. (Each of these meshed with the central Jewish value of *tsedaka*, "justice–charity.")

Junker cultural values emerged from preindustrial, militaristic society, and Junkers were often narrowly Prussian, faithful to the Hohenzollern dynasty and to Prussian traditions, not to the German people or the German nation. Populism and nationalism were notions that Prussian conservatives considered dangerously radical. Many Junkers not only considered Bismarck a revolutionary but also a traitor to his class because of his alliance, in the 1860s and 1870s, with German liberal nationalists in the Reichstag. His numerous personal contacts with Jews, his defense of Jewish emancipation, to say nothing of his curtailment of some Junker privileges, did not improve his image in the eyes of such Junkers. In the long run, however, he won many of them over by offering them economic protection, new opportunities, and continued, indeed enhanced, prestige.

As far as many Junkers were concerned, a liberal constitution and a free-market economy were Jewish ideas; the English and Jews, two commercial peoples, were kindred. Thus the romantic, anti-Enlightened tendencies that had a special appeal in Germany could be blended with Prussian, anticommercial tendencies, and sometimes synthesized into more all-embracing, modern racist notions, into a sense of an organic, disciplined, Aryan community *(Gemeinschaft),* as opposed to a cosmopolitan, quarrelsome, egoistic, Semitic "society" *(Gesellschaft).*

Anti-English and anti-French xenophobia was often linked to a sense of Germanic superiority to Slavic peoples, who often constituted the peasant class in the East-Prussian lands owned by Junkers. Thus the Jews who came from pre-

---

[13] Cf. David Blackbourn, *Class, Religion and Local Politics in Wilhelmine Germany: The Center Party in Württemburg Before 1914* (New Haven, Conn., 1980); Geoff Eley, *Reshaping the German Right: Radical Nationalism and Political Change After Bismarck* (New Haven, Conn., 1980); and in an entirely different direction, Arno J. Mayer, *The Persistence of the Old Regime* (New York, 1981). It should be noted that Eley rejects any close or automatic association of the bourgeoisie with liberal values.

dominantly Slavic areas were further associated with what was considered an inferior culture. Most of those from the Slavic lower orders were Catholic Poles, and so there was also an element of Protestant feelings of superiority.

However, the image of the Junker as militaristic, antiliberal, and racist in tendency (and thus anti-Semitic) requires qualification. Further, to portray the Prussian-led state merely as a narrow defender of the values and interests of Junker reactionaries – or as a linear precursor of the Nazi state – can be especially misleading. In this period Junkers were not much attracted to race theory to buttress their belief in privilege and hierarchy. Since the eighteenth century, Prussia had been considered one of the more rationally organized and *progressive* states in Europe; its unusual efficiency, its hardworking and relatively incorruptible officials, the impartiality with which it protected law and order, all were widely admired long before Bismarck's time. A sense of order as necessary to genuine freedom – and, if necessary, a sacrifice of justice for order – was thus even more typically Prussian than German. Again a tempting if easily overdone contrast presents itself, for Jews, by their own understanding of themselves, have historically harbored a special passion for justice, often entailing a sacrifice of order and respect for authority.

Prussia had long been a *Rechtsstaat,* a state of laws. The German term implies much more than the English translation: The Rechtsstaat was conceived as something that transcended the Anglo–French secular–liberal state. The latter was a practical convenience, a mere regulator of human relations, best restrained to a minimal role; the former had a deeper ethical purpose, a more positive role in providing order and justice to human society. The Prussian Rechtsstaat had existed when many other German states were petty tyrannies, subject to the will of erratic rulers, and for many Jews life under such leaders was insecure. Partly for such reasons, Jews were long among the front rank of Prussia's admirers.

Whatever their failings, Junkers were not all shallow, pompous xenophobes any more than Jews were all pushy, materialistic Philistines. Within the ranks of the Junkers were some admirable and capable individuals, who personified the higher ideals of Europe's aristocracy – a point of some interest in that Junkers were relatively little attracted to the radical anti-Semitism of the generation before World War I and, later, to Nazism. However, Junkers undoubtedly had reservations about many liberal tenets, and those reservations played a role once liberalism in the 1870s was further put into question by unfavorable economic developments.

Jews favored the Prussian Rechtsstaat for another very important reason: It was associated with liberal–progressive economic ideas (free trade, wide markets, competition, the factory system). Even when Prussian Jews faced social disdain and discriminatory legislation, they could still rely upon relatively honest and predictable treatment from the officials with whom they had to deal, in contrast to the often highly corrupt officialdom in the rest of central and eastern Europe. Jews could also rely upon the Prussian state to protect their property, to encourage their economic enterprise, and to keep the lower orders in check, again in sometimes sharp contrast to the surrounding areas.

The Rise of the Jews in Germany

With the unification of Germany, Jewish wealth began to expand even more rapidly than before, and Jews also began to move into a number of prominent positions in politics. However, until 1914 they remained almost completely excluded from the very highest and most prestigious positions of the state, as did most non-Jews without the proper pedigrees. Nonetheless, throughout the late nineteenth century Jews continued to nurse hopes for an eventual change in such exclusionary practices; they persuaded themselves that much steady progress had been made and that the future was bright.

Not all or even a clear majority of Germans aped the Junker ruling class. Many continued to derive a sense of identity in opposition to the rule of Prussia. Residents of the states *(Länder)* in southern and western Germany, or the proud burghers in the independent cities of Frankfurt and Hamburg, for example, self-consciously resisted Junker hegemony, and perhaps no part of the German population did so more obviously than the often irreverent residents of the new capital, Berlin.

Junkers, too, differed among themselves, from the arch-reactionary *Krautjunker*, overlords of small, inefficient estates, to the more enterprising, modernizing individuals who managed extensive lands that produced for sale on the international market. Modernizing Junkers of this sort made social, economic, and political contacts with the industrial magnates of western Germany. Among those magnates were a number of Jews, the so-called *Kaiserjuden,* who had connections with the glittering world of the imperial court (the Bleichröders, Rothschilds, Warburgs, Rathenaus, and Ballins). These contacts were visible enough that some populist anti-Semites could entertain the belief that Prussian–Junker domination of the rest of Germany was subtly manipulated by Jews.

The extraordinary upward mobility of German Jews in the nineteenth century is to a certain degree easily explained. Ironically, the very tendency of the traditional sectors of the economy to block entry to Jews encouraged them to strike out in new directions. A liberal system tends to favor those who are mobile, open to new ways of doing things, not strongly tied to traditional patterns. Many Jews benefited from long experience in Europe with economic enterprise and financial acumen.[14] Gentile peasants, artisans in traditional

---

[14] Cf. Werner Sombart, *The Jews and Modern Capitalism* (Glencoe, Ill., 1951) [original German edition, Leipzig, 1911], who often carries the argument concerning the special proclivities of Jews in capitalism beyond what the evidence will support but still makes some thought-provoking points.

handicrafts, shopkeepers, and land-holding aristocrats were generally less flexible, less likely to prosper, and indeed more likely to find their way of life undermined by the relentless dynamism of modern capitalism. Thus, while German Jews on the whole prospered many non-Jews did not, or prospered less abundantly, an experience that often seemed to provoke more antipathy than not prospering at all.

The specific economic conditions of the late 1870s and the 1880s, especially the fall of agricultural prices, intensified these general tendencies. Quite aside from the aversion of the haughty aristocrat to the newly rich, it was often profoundly troubling for many ordinary people to find that their arduous labor brought them so little, while those who manipulated money and other intangibles, never bringing sweat to their brows, prospered. Such troubled feelings were all the greater when the newly rich were perceived as alien. The traditional idea of a just return for honest labor seemed to have been abandoned in the emerging economic scene. Resentments of this sort were felt throughout Europe and America, and they fed into various reformist or socialist movements. While these movements by no means all blamed the Jews, the temptation to do so was strong.

The visibility of Jewish success in certain areas had far-reaching implications. New retail outlets, large department stores, were largely in the hands of Jews, and such stores were often bitterly resented by small shopkeepers who could not compete with the reduced prices and variety of goods offered in the new stores. Banks, although less exclusively Jewish in Germany than elsewhere in central and eastern Europe, were still often owned and operated by Jews (estimates range from forty to fifty percent,[15] whereas Jews were one percent of the total population). The man reputed to be the richest in Germany was the Jewish banker Gerson Bleichröder, who was also Bismarck's personal banker. The wealth of the Rothschilds, financiers who had made their start in Frankfurt, was already legendary in Germany and in the rest of Europe.

Jews in Germany moved rapidly into the professions. Upwardly mobile Gentiles, or those who hoped for upward mobility in their children, encountered a most unwelcome competition to get into medical school or law school; Jews in those schools became overrepresented, often by ten, twenty, even thirty times their numbers in German society. In Prussia, for every 100,000 Jewish males, 519 went through higher education; for a similar number of Catholic males, the figure was 33; for Protestants, 58.[16]

The liberal press was overwhelmingly in the hands of Jews. The German-language liberal press enjoyed prestige and influence inside Germany, in Austria–Hungary, and in many neighboring countries. Most of the dailies in

---

[15] Sombart put the figure at forty-five percent; cf. Norman Stone, *Europe Transformed, 1878–1919* (Cambridge, Mass., 1984), 164.

[16] Ibid., 181.

Frankfurt, Berlin, and Hamburg were Jewish owned and employed large numbers of Jewish journalists. The Jewish liberal press was the "most widely read, best written, and best edited" press in Germany; it was an arena "in which Jewish intellectuals could be active in an unhampered way."[17]

Toward the end of the century, a popular press began to appear – often racy and vulgar – also to an important degree perfected by Jewish journalists. The Jewish-owned *Berliner Tageblatt* introduced the then shocking device of selling large numbers of papers through sensational stories and gaining revenue primarily through advertising rather than purchase price. Non-Jews often believed that Jewish employers, in journalism as elsewhere, hired exclusively from the ranks of their religious or racial brethren when managerial or well-paid positions were in question.

Jewish presence in the more modern segments of the economy was, however, not nearly so overwhelming in Germany as it was in Austria–Hungary and Russia. Gentile Germans in large numbers were also successful professionals, bankers, industrialists, merchants, and journalists. Social contacts between middle-class Jews and Gentiles were more extensive in Germany than in the rest of central and eastern Europe. A significant number of Junkers found it economically advantageous or otherwise attractive to marry into wealthy, cultured bourgeois families, Jewish families included. This trend may have worked to mitigate Junker disdain for Jews, at least for a small minority of extremely rich and cultivated Jews, who themselves were often notorious in their own contempt for "low" Jews.

Much evidence suggests that the most vehement, all-embracing kind of anti-Semitism was not typical of Junkers, especially not those who adjusted reasonably well to the new conditions of the Reich. Rather, such hatred more typically came from those who felt threatened by the incursions of modern, liberal society. Such people seem to have been particularly numerous in the ranks of the lower-middle class, the artisans, shopkeepers, and small businessowners, although that is yet another familiar generalization that has recently been subjected to qualification by scholars.[18]

The Mittelstand and Modernism in Germany

Jews themselves in nineteenth-century Germany were predominantly of lower-middle-class origin, but their rapid upward mobility had only weak parallels in the Gentile lower-middle class, a development that threatened the self-image of many of its members. Also threatening were the widespread predic-

---

[17] Werner Becker, "Die Rolle der Liberalen Presse," in Werner E. Mosse, *Deutsches Judentum in Krieg und Revolution* (Tübingen, 1971), 67.

[18] Cf. Richard F. Hamilton, *Who Voted For Hitler?* (Princeton, N.J., 1982); Michael H. Kater, *The Nazi Party: A Social Profile of Members and Leaders, 1919–1945* (Cambridge, Mass., 1982). Although these works deal with a later period, the issues are similar.

tions that the petty bourgeoisie, or *Mittelstand* (middle estate), as they preferred to call themselves, would inexorably be pushed into the working class
by the forces of modern industrialism. Marxists were the most systematic and
dogmatic in their assertion that the Mittelstand would inevitably disappear,
but a number of non-Marxist university scholars forwarded similar analyses.[19]
Some of these predictions were clearly overdrawn, but the perception of the
threat, the fear of social decline, was at least as important as the reality. Here,
as with anti-Semitic belief, fantasy and reality interacted powerfully.

Members of the Mittelstand were inclined to picture themselves as the
backbone of the nation, much as the American middle class has historically
fancied itself.[20] But one of the many differences between Germany and the
United States at the end of the century is revealed in this comparison, for this
German "backbone" was more insecure about its own standing and its future
than was its American counterpart. The Mittelstand was similarly more
inclined to find solace in ideologies that romanticized the preindustrial past,
when Jews had been legally restricted.

Just as the *Bürgertum*, or bourgeoisie, the class positioned above the Mittelstand and below the nobility, was relatively timid and prone to being junkerized, so the Mittelstand in Germany was inclined to exaggerated efforts to ape
its superiors. This inclination assumed a number of forms: vehement opposition to the organized, socialist working class (the threat from below); xenophobic patriotism and militarism (with the cherished dream of becoming an
officer of the reserves); demands for legal measures to limit the incursions of a
destructive industrialism; paranoiac fears about the activities of the political
establishment; and an attraction to political anti-Semitism.

In literature and many of the other arts Jews were prominent in modernist
trends, not only in Germany but in most other countries. Modernism was
characterized by a contempt for traditional aesthetic norms; modern art
became ever more divorced from what ordinary people could appreciate, ever
more disdainful of popular tastes, ever more "difficult." In these elitist aspects
modern art was radically different from modern mass politics, although both
were breaking from established norms. Those arguing for an "organic" Aryan
art, one that had roots in the traditional peasant communities of Germany,
could see modern art as inorganic, market-driven, cosmopolitan – and
Semitic. Jews did not have deep and genuine roots in German culture, did
not and could not share aesthetic experience with Germans who had
been part of a traditional Christian culture for centuries. Kindred arguments,
obviously connecting with Herder's notion of *Volksgeist*, stressing the importance of deep historical roots in popular feelings were also made by spokesmen of other nationalities. Yiddish artists, for example, stressed qualities of

[19] Cf. Heinrich A Winkler, *Mittelstand, Demokratie und Nationalsozialismus* (Cologne, 1972), 25–6.
[20] Ibid., 21ff.

yiddishkayt, concerning which Gentiles could have little understanding, since they lacked those roots and traditions.

Still, by no means all German–Jewish artists, or all German–Jewish audiences, preferred modern art. Jews were also well represented in more traditional artistic activities, and indeed they were among the greatest admirers of classical German culture, especially music. A number of observers have spoken of a "love affair" between German culture and German Jews. Jews in Germany were outstanding consumers of high culture, of whatever sort.

Yet the image of modernist Jews as "culture destroyers" reflected an undeniable reality, however much exaggerated by anti-Semites. The disproportionate numbers, visibility, and volubility of Jews in modern art roughly corresponded to the disproportionate numbers of Jews in journalism, medicine, law, banking, and revolutionary parties. These were all arenas that saw attacks on the traditional status quo, that were restlessly innovative and often destructively dissatisfied with the past – a past with which Jews had every reason to be dissatisfied.

The "Founding Years" and the Crash of 1873

Wherever it appears, modern urban–industrial life tends to strike those from the countryside as restless, impersonal, and cruel. The shock and disgust expressed by those from small towns and villages concerning the crowded streets, the pushing and shoving, the single-minded search for profit, has been an aspect of urban existence in every country that has experienced it. In Germany, where modern urbanization and industrialization came with unusual rapidity in the late 1860s and early 1870s, laments concerning the reckless scramble for profit, the boisterous, Philistine quality of city life, were heard from many sensitive observers, whether right wing or left wing, philo-Semitic or anti-Semitic, non-Jew, or Jew.[21]

By the end of the century revulsion against such aspects of modern German existence became a central theme of German intellectual life, in part because of the unusual degree to which Germans felt an emotional attachment to a past of small towns and rural living, during which, in the epoch of Goethe, Schiller, and Kant, Germany's greatest cultural efflorescence occurred. Many of the country's best minds, especially among its academic "mandarins," were deeply troubled by what they perceived as an emerging urban–industrial society of social irresponsibility and class conflict, where a wider community of shared values and ideals ceased to exist.[22]

Jews in Germany were heavily concentrated in the large cities, and often

---

[21] The shock experienced by shtetl Jews in the big cities of Europe and America is a common theme in Jewish literature of the late nineteenth and early twentieth century. Sholem Aleichem's novels and short stories abound with examples. Perhaps the best known example in America of the genre, from a somewhat later period, is Michael Gold's *Jews Without Money.*

[22] Fritz Ringer, "Inflation, Anti-Semitism, and the German Academic Community of the Weimar Period," *Leo Baeck Institute Yearbook,* vol. 28, 1983, 3–9.

they were involved in the get-rich-quick enterprises of those "founding years" *(Gründerjahre)*. Many highly visible Jews made fortunes in dubious ways, as did many non-Jews. Probably the most notorious of these newly rich speculators was Hirsch Strousberg, a Jew involved in Romanian railroad stocks. He was hardly unique in his exploits, but as Peter Pulzer has written, "the . . . difference between his and other men's frauds was that his was more impudent and involved more money."[23] His name was much in the newspapers of the day.

Nouveaux riches of whatever origin have rarely been known for gracious manners. Those Jewish newly rich in Germany who had recent origins in the eastern European shtetlekh, where standards of civility or public manners were markedly different from those of Germany, were widely regarded as especially offensive. It was often believed as well that because of their impoverished background, they were unusually ruthless in their quest for monetary gain. Franz Mehring, a sharp-tongued opponent of what he termed "the repulsive spectacle of anti-Semitism," noted nonetheless that Jewish pushiness and brashness in Berlin in the early 1870s provoked widespread animosity. He added, "whoever denies this has . . . not spent the last ten years in Berlin. . . ."[24]

Similar remarks concerning the public manners of Jews in large cities, New York being an obvious example, were commonplace in following decades, but the issue was broader. Early capitalism in England generated the same remarkable profits and elicited similar protests against the coarseness and immorality of those making them. In England, Jews, far less numerous than in Germany, played a negligible role in the new industries, and the new industrialists were not denounced as "Semites." In Germany during the early seventies, the contrasts between rich and poor, successful and unsuccessful, were perhaps even more striking than in the opening stages of England's industrialization. The 5 billion francs levied on France as war reparations in 1871 pumped money into the German economy in a way that added all the more to the frenetic temper of the time. Whatever the exaggerations of the anti-Semites, Jews were hardly immune to the temptations of the Gründerjahre, and many of them were especially well placed to take advantage of the peculiar opportunities of the time.

In the summer of 1873 the stock markets in New York and Vienna collapsed. By the autumn of that year Germany's industrial overexpansion and the reckless proliferation of stock companies came to a halt. Jews were closely associated in the popular mind with the stock exchange. Widely accepted images of them as sharp and dishonest businessmen made it all but inevitable that public indignation over the stock market crash would be directed at them. Many small investors, themselves drawn to the prospect of easy gain, lost their savings through fraudulent stocks or questionable business practices in which Jews were frequently involved.

Certain anti-Semitic themes took on particularly sharp expression by the

[23] P. G. J. Pulzer, *The Rise of Political Anti-Semitism in Germany and Austria* (New York, 1964), 20.

[24] Quoted in Paul Massing, *Rehearsal for Destruction* (New York, 1967; 1st ed., 1949), 184, 314.

late 1870s. A more intense anxiety about Jews was widely expressed, one that a number of historians have seen as qualitatively stronger,[25] as compared with the tone of minor irritation and cultural derision that had prevailed earlier in the century. And this anxiety began to find potent focus in newspaper articles, pamphlets, and public speeches. Organizations began to spring up; a new movement seemed to be forming.

Now it was declared that Jews, constituting a mere one percent of the population, were more than "too influential"; they were taking over the new German nation, its economy, its political institutions, its art and music. Jewish or Semitic traits were undermining and corrupting German traits. The new rules of the game, introduced in the liberal 1850s and 1860s, had allowed them to advance with startling and unforeseen rapidity. The new society was "too free"; it operated as a milling crowd, in which those who swindled, who pushed and shoved, elbowed and shouted, came to the front.

The Press Campaign against the Jews

The popular (circulation ca. 350,000) and generally liberal magazine *Die Gartenlaube* published a series of articles in December 1874 by Otto Glagau exposing the role of various shady entrepreneurs in the stock market crash. This paper was up to this time known to be friendly to Jews, as part of a general editorial policy directed at providing a positive image of the middle-class citizen as industrious, honest, and thrifty. It was a leading example of the probourgeois, antiaristocratic voice in Germany, and its editors seemed to accept Jews as natural allies, upholders of bourgeois values.[26]

Glagau at first attacked both non-Jewish and Jewish swindlers, offering ample detail in each case. But as the articles continued, the tone became more heated and more explicitly anti-Jewish. He lamented the "invasion" of Ostjuden from Posen into Berlin and their making quick fortunes on slim talent. He maintained that ninety percent of brokers and stock promoters in the capital were Jews, which may have been true (reliable figures are not available). It was a conclusion, at any rate, that even many Jews accepted as plausible and that most non-Jews apparently considered axiomatic.[27]

Whatever his claims to impartiality, there is little question that Glagau's pre-

---

[25] Cf. Fritz Stern, *Gold and Iron: Bismarck, Bleichröder, and the Building of the German Empire* (New York, 1979), 494 ff.

[26] Cf. Henry Wasserman, "Jews and Judaism in the *Gartenlaube*," *Leo Baeck Institute Yearbook*, vol. 23, 1978, 47–60.

[27] Cf. Jacob Katz, *From Prejudice to Destruction* (Cambridge, Mass., 1981), 248–9. It is interesting that Stephen Birmingham's *The Rest of Us: The Rise of America's Eastern European Jews* (New York, 1984), argues, on the basis of anecdotal evidence, that there was a distinct difference in the United States between the Gentile robber baron types and the Jewish nouveaux riches, in that the Jews were much more honest.

existing distaste for Jews, especially eastern Jews, made him prone to exaggerate the actual extent of Jewish malfeasance, but revealingly Franz Mehring, who had no use for Glagau or anti-Semites in general, commented that "the more mischievous elements among Berlin's Jews participated, in an abnormally high proportion, in bogus stock and stock-company swindles."[28] Eduard Bernstein, a Jew himself, dismissed as shallow the assertions that Jews and non-Jews had the same shortcomings: "Certain unpleasant characteristics may indeed be encountered more often in Jews than in non-Jews, although not to the extent the anti-Semites claim to be true."[29]

A century later, when it became clear that the stock market scandals of the mid-to-late 1980s in the United States saw an overwhelming preponderance of Jews – at least ninety percent was a widely accepted figure – that clear correlation seemed to interest the broad American public scarcely at all, or at least it elicited few public expressions of anti-Semitic indignation, and overwhelmingly non-Jewish journalists and politicians skirted the issue. But in Germany in the 1870s popular interest and indignation were intense; demands for new controls over the stock market (the laws concerning which had been liberalized only a few years before) blended into demands for greater controls over the free market generally. Such controls were especially necessary, it was believed, since Jews, now equal under the law, were so much inclined to go out of control in a liberal environment, to take an unfair and destructive advantage of the new system.

By no means all Germans agreed with Glagau. He was publicly attacked and privately reprimanded by influential non-Jews for "reviving medieval prejudices" and "spreading intolerance." But these criticisms seemed only to inflame him. He responded that

No longer should false tolerance and sentimentality – cursed weakness and fear! – prevent us Christians from moving against the excesses . . . and presumption of Jewry. No longer can we suffer to see the Jews push themselves everywhere to the front, . . . everywhere seize leadership and dominate public opinion. They are always pushing us aside, . . . they take our breath and air away. . . . The Jews cultivate the greatest pretense and the greatest luxury, far greater than the aristocracy or the Court.[30]

Two years later, Glagau collected what he had written for the *Gartenlaube* into a book about the financial scandals. In it he intoned, "the whole history of the world knows no other example of a homeless, physically and psychically degenerate people ruling over the orbit of the world, simply through fraud and cunning, through usury and jobbing."[31]

[28] Massing, *Rehearsal*, 314.

[29] Ibid., 256.

[30] Stern, *Gold and Iron*, 501–2.

[31] Katz, *Prejudice*, 252.

The *Kreuzzeitung*, generally seen as the voice of Junker conservatism, followed Glagau's lead and launched an all-out attack on the liberal policies that had, it insisted, led to the present sad state of affairs. The editors made much of the activities of Bleichröder, whom they described as a "mastermind" behind the scenes. He and other Jewish bankers had joined hands with the Jewish liberal press to exercise a malignant, self-interested control over Germany.[32]

The Kulturkampf and the Jews

Bismarck's achievements on the battlefield and in the diplomatic arena had resulted in a new German nation, but he soon turned his attention to those forces and institutions inside the country that he considered insufficiently "state preserving," or even hostile to the new Prussian-led Reich. Popular indignation concerning how Jews allegedly went out of control in a liberal environment found another revealing focus in the charge that Jews played a major and unseemly role in support of Bismarck's anti-Catholic *Kulturkampf* (roughly, "struggle for modern civilization").

In southern Germany, Catholics were a majority and their church strong; the Catholic hierarchy and the pope had been recently aggressive in defending what they saw as the rights of the church in public education and in resisting the encroachments of the modern nation-state upon the fidelities of Catholic citizens. In Posen and West Prussia, Polish nationalism was linked to Catholicism. German nationalists were inclined to see the Lutheran Church as the proper German national church, and liberal nationalists believed the Catholic Church was both hostile to genuine German national feeling and a potent force for preserving the bigotry of the past.

Like liberals in other countries, German liberals favored a limitation of the influence of religion, especially that of the Catholic Church, in public life. Historically, Jews had ample reasons to fear Catholic influence. Most recently, church spokesmen had been among those in Germany who opposed Jewish emancipation. Liberals, non-Jews and Jews, saw the struggle as primarily defensive in nature, "forced upon us" by the militancy of Catholic Church, as one of them put it.[33]

The Kulturkampf was waged at many levels. It included the proscription of the Jesuit order, a measure that found especially warm support among Jews, given the long-standing reputation of the order as hostile to them.[34] But Bismarck's anti-Catholic measures found their sharpest focus in the arena of public education. On all levels, the Kulturkampf was presented by Bismarck's sup-

---

[32] Ibid.

[33] Uriel Tal, *Christians and Jews in Germany: Religion, Politics and Ideology in the Second Reich, 1870–1914* (Ithaca, N.Y., 1975), 98.

[34] Ibid., 93.

porters as a struggle between progressive modern civilization, represented by the new German Reich, and the demands of the backward-looking, obscurantist, and particularistic Catholic Church. A number of liberal Jewish journalists, writing in support of Bismarck, gained notoriety for the virulence of their attacks on the church, to the point that even some Jewish liberal leaders urged them to moderate their language. Bismarck's choice of the lieutenant to carry out the decrees of the Kulturkampf, Heinrich von Friedberg, was of Jewish origin. His brother, Emil, became Bismarck's minister of justice in 1879.[35]

Orthodox rabbis expressed alarm when a prominent national organization of Jewish citizens denounced the Catholic Church as "the internal enemy" of the new German nation. (Orthodox Jews in Germany, it should be noted, by this time lived predominantly in small towns with Catholic majorities, and they resented what they considered inflammatory and short-sighted attacks on the church by big-city Reform Jews. Such attacks, they believed, endangered the welfare of Jews living in rural areas, where by the mid–nineteenth century they had often established reasonably cordial, if limited and traditional, relations with church authorities.[36])

By the 1870s German Catholics held a wide range of political opinions, some fairly left wing, but many of them reacted with alarm against the harsh attacks on their church by liberals – and especially liberal Jews – backed up by the power of the German state. The Catholic newspaper *Germania* launched a series of hard-hitting attacks on Jewish liberals. They were accused of suffering from a special Prussian malady, that of the "bicycle rider" *(Fahrradler)*, head bent down to those in authority but legs flailing away at those below – servility to those in power, arrogance to those perceived as vulnerable.

However, in the long run German Catholics, themselves a minority and thus inclined to be at least somewhat more sensitive than Protestants to the issue of minority rights in the Reich, never became as hostile to Jews as were Catholics in countries where Catholicism was the majority religion, such as France, Austria, or Poland. Ludwig Windthorst, the leader of the Catholic Center Party, maintained reasonably cordial relations with a number of Jewish leaders in Germany (though it would be too much to describe him as friendly to Jews in general); he urged his followers not to blame all Jews for the arrogance and intolerance of what he dismissed as a few Jewish loudmouths. However, there were certainly those in the Center Party who were ready to exploit political anti-Semitism; for a short period Windthorst was obliged to struggle desperately to prevent his party from taking an openly anti-Semitic stance.[37]

[35] James Parkes, *Anti-Semitism*, (Chicago, 1964), 28.

[36] Ismar Schorsch, *Jewish Reactions to German Anti-Semitism* (New York, 1972), 33.

[37] Pulzer, *Anti-Semitism*, 272–3; David Blackbourn, "Roman Catholics, the Centre Party, and Anti-Semitism in Imperial Germany," in Paul Kennedy and Anthony Nicholls, eds., *Nationalist and Racialist Movements in Britain and Germany Before 1914* (London, 1981), 106–29.

Bismarck's Move to the Right

After a few years Bismarck backed away from this confrontation with German Catholics, partly because he began to envisage a new right–center parliamentary coalition that would require the support of the Catholic Center Party. Bismarck's move to the right at this time (the late 1870s) represented a victory for Germany's Catholics; it also represented the beginnings of a long-range rightward drift in German politics until World War I. That drift meant that liberals were no longer an indispensable element of his parliamentary support, as they had been in the 1860s and early 1870s. Indeed, his new right-wing stance entailed the introduction of measures that may be considered distinctly illiberal, including new tariffs (violating the liberal belief in free trade), social–welfare legislation (violating the liberal belief in self-help and individual responsibility), concessions to guilds and small retailers (violating the liberal belief in open competition),[38] and an outlawing of the Social Democratic Party (violating the liberal belief in free political activity).

It must be said, touching upon the previous remarks about the weaknesses of German liberalism, that the National Liberal Party was itself "illiberal," at least insofar as it did not consistently oppose tariffs, welfare legislation, and measures against the Social Democrats (the left liberals, or progressives, were more consistent in these regards). Jewish liberals, who could previously feel that Bismarck was in some sense an ally, if a problematic and worrisome one, sensed a new vulnerability. They were also increasingly divided among themselves. Some of them were content to move to the right with Bismarck or, perhaps more accurately, to continue moving right with Bismarck, since a significant part of the Jewish bourgeoisie had already moved to the right in embracing the terms of German unification and the constitution of 1871. Many Jewish leaders enthusiastically joined in his attacks on the socialists, just as others had joined in his attacks on the Catholics.

The more prescient of Jewish observers, however, warned their coreligionists that for Jews to attack other minorities in this way was short-sighted; no group should be more sensitive to the principle of toleration for minority rights than Jews.[39] There is little doubt that enemies of the Jews were both relieved and encouraged by the indications that Bismarck was no longer so distinctly, as they saw it, "in the Jewish camp" and might even give support to anti-Semitic initiatives.

Bismarck, ever the consummate politician, played these various perceptions and expectations for all they were worth, but he also continued to maintain

---

[38] Cf. Winkler, *Mittelstand*, 44–6.

[39] Robert S. Wistrich, *Socialism and the Jews: The Dialectics of Emancipation in Germany and Austria-Hungary* (East Brunswick, N.J., 1984), 75–6. The parallels in this exchange with the exchange between neo-Conservative and liberal Jews in the United States a century later are striking: Cf. Earl Shorris, *Jews Without Mercy* (New York, 1982).

close relations with a number of Jews. In this as in so many other regards, Bismarck's own convictions are not easily surmised, but it would certainly be inaccurate to term him an anti-Semite in a strictly racial sense. His attitudes were impenetrably pro- and anti-Jewish. They seem also to have altered over the years, away from the more open hostility of his youth. By the 1870s rich and conservative Jews, the so-called *Geldjuden* (money-Jews), generally won his respect and occasionally his friendship, whether or not they were converts to Christianity (Bleichröder was not, for example). He retained a Jewish doctor and lawyer as well as a Jewish banker, and he asked Karl Rudolf Friedental, a Jewish convert to Christianity, to help frame the imperial constitution. The intellectual founder of the Conservative Party was another Jewish convert, Friedrich Julius Stahl. But Jews on the left, the *Reformjuden*, once Bismarck's allies, evoked in him an increasingly ferocious antipathy, since they became his most vocal opponents after the late 1870s, particularly in the left–liberal Progressive Party.

Some of Bismarck's advisers were certainly unfriendly to the Jews, and expressions of irritation with Jews popped up frequently in official circles. A common attitude at the time, seen in figures as different as the Emperor Wilhelm I and the social democrat Eduard Bernstein, was that flare-ups of anti-Semitic feeling could even serve a useful purpose. In Wilhelm's own words, "the hubbub is useful to make the Jews a little more modest."[40] Words in that vein became close to a cliché in following years. Theodor Herzl typically remarked, a decade later, that anti-Semitism served to "inhibit the ostentatious flaunting of conspicuous wealth, curb the unscrupulous behavior of Jewish financiers, and contribute in many ways to the education of the Jews."[41] There were at any rate few if any at this time who argued that the rising hostility to Jews had absolutely nothing to do with actual Jewish behavior or with real issues. That would have been seen as a most curious point of view, as would the notion that anti-Semitism was entirely or even mostly the result of Gentile fantasy, of unfounded preconceptions about Jews.

[40] Stern, *Gold and Iron*, 522.
[41] Ernst Pawel, *The Labyrinth of Exile: A Life of Theodor Herzl* (New York, 1989), 76.

4

Anti-Semitic Ideology and Movement in Germany (1879 to the 1890s)

If I ever again write about the Jews, I would say that there is no reason to object to them. The only problem is that they came to us Germans too soon. We were not strong enough to absorb this element. (Richard Wagner)

The Semitic race is stronger and tougher than the German. (Wilhelm Marr)

The Jews are our misfortune! (Heinrich von Treitschke)

The image of the peasant robbed by the Jew drives me onward. (Otto Böckel, the "Peasant King")

By the late 1870s, as the overall political climate became more conservative in Germany, the National Liberal and Progressive parties lost the narrow majority they had enjoyed in the Reichstag of 1874–1877, and Bismarck began to construct coalitions with the parties to their right. Attacks on liberal, and Jewish, influence in the Empire became ever bolder. Most accounts of the rise of political anti-Semitism in Germany have focused on a number of prominent spokesmen for the anti-Jewish sentiment of this period. This chapter is devoted in large part to a reconsideration of them, questioning in particular if they, as "anti-Semitic ideologists," may be appropriately presented as part of an unbroken chain or logical development in German history leading to Nazism. This chapter is also influenced by the belief that even scoundrels have the right to a fair trial, and that these men – many of whom were undoubtedly scoundrels – were more sophisticated and ambiguous in their beliefs than many accounts would lead one to believe.

Anti-Semitic Ideology: Wilhelm Marr

One of the best known of those ideologists was Wilhelm Marr (1819–1904), whom a recent biographer has termed "the patriarch of anti-Semitism."[1] Marr has been given credit for coining the term "anti-Semitism" and for giving wide currency to the distinction between premodern, religious hostility toward Jews and modern, secular–racial hostility to them. He undoubtedly helped to popularize what were becoming central themes of modern anti-Semitism – the "jewification" of Germany and the unwillingness of Jews to become real Germans. His pamphlet *Der Sieg des Judenthums über das Germanenthum* (roughly, The Victory of Jewry over the Germans) has been described as the first anti-Semitic best-seller (still small by twentieth-century standards: twelve editions, 20,000 copies in 1879). He became a symbol for younger anti-Semites, a pioneering hero of their movement.[2]

But he was a strange hero, and his hatred for Jews even stranger, as his admirers eventually came to realize. Indeed, the often startling contradictions of his thought and action, his physical and spiritual wanderings in a remarkably long life spanning the nineteenth century, defy efforts at a concise summary. He presents major problems – especially as the symbolic "patriarch" of modern anti-Semitism – for those who assert that anti-Semites typically do not know or have no real contact with Jews. He was married four times, the first three times to Jewish women. To the end of his days he spoke tenderly of his love for his second wife, who died tragically in childbirth. He had intimate Jewish friends, business partners, and political allies; in the 1840s he was closely associated with a number of Jewish radicals and was attacked for his supposed philo-Semitism. He was a lifelong admirer of the Jewish artists and writers Heinrich Heine and Ludwig Boerne.[3] In the final decade of his life, in the 1890s, he broke with the anti-Semitic movement of the day, describing the anti-Semites as worse than the Jews and requesting the pardon of the Jews for what he had earlier written. He declared that it was in reality problems of industrialization and modernization that had provoked him, not the Jews as such.[4]

How did such a man come to be known, even into the twentieth century, as the patriarch of modern anti-Semitism? Given the remarkably mixed signals he gave off, can we confidently conclude that he played a major role in the growth of anti-Semitic ideology? Such paradoxes are hardly unfamiliar, for as we have seen, Richard Wagner also had left-wing associations in the 1840s, and the great composer had many intimate Jewish friends and co-workers.

[1] Moshe Zimmermann, *Wilhelm Marr, The Patriarch of Anti-Semitism* (Oxford, 1986).

[2] Cf. Moishe Zimmermann, "Two Generations in the History of German Anti-Semitism: The Letters of Theodor Fritsch to Wilhelm Marr," *Leo Baeck Institute Year Book*, vol. 23, 1978, 89–106.

[3] Zimmermann, *Patriarch*, 19.

[4] Ibid., 109.

Wagner, too, lamented as early as 1850 that Jews were taking over Germany. Both Wagner and Marr emphasized inherent and tenacious Jewish racial traits, ones that were destructive to Germans. Both men saw the Jews as materialistic and commercial outsiders to genuine German feeling. Wagner believed Jewish interest in German art was mostly to sell it; Marr denounced the commercial aggressiveness of Jews and left no doubt concerning his low regard for a religion that lacked idealism – that was ultimately based, as he put it, upon a "business deal" with God.[5]

Did Marr construct pure fantasies about Jews, drawn from Christian religion and based on no experience with them? In his pamphlet and in his other writings he referred extensively to Jewish acquaintances (although he said nothing about his wives), and he went to some length to distance himself from religious imagery about Jews; his attitude, he emphasized, was a modern, objective, and reasonable one, based on a scientific concept, race, not religion. He described it as ridiculous to blame the Jews for Christ's crucifixion. He similarly ridiculed charges that Jews require Christian blood for Passover or that they desecrate communion wafers, and he expressed sympathy for Jews who had been persecuted for such superstitious reasons.[6]

His reasons – and the legitimate reasons – for disliking Jews, he stated, rather than being religious, had to do with Jewish "abhorrence of real work" and their inclination to exploit the labor of others. That abhorrence was linked to the Jews' "animosity established in law" for non-Jews.[7] Even when Jews appear outwardly courteous, inwardly they seethe with derision for the Goyim, and they scheme relentlessly to find ways to subjugate them, to undermine their society. Wherever they go, Jews try to dominate and jewify the surrounding society. To do so is in their racial nature, their essence; it is part of the destructive mission of Jewry in history.[8]

Marr's pamphlet was certainly not an original or important work of literature or science, in the way that the works of Renan and Gobineau might be considered. Similarly, Marr spoke to a different audience than did Wagner. Marr's work is better seen as a condensation, simplification, and vulgarization – evidence of a filtering down – of the thought of more serious theorists of race in the nineteenth century. Marr spoke to a growing audience of the newly and partially literate.

One must wonder, further, how much those who cheered Marr actually paid attention to the contents of his writings. His pamphlet, above all its title, seems to have become more of a vague symbol than a handbook that elicited careful reading or that inspired a consistent program. No doubt certain of the

---

[5] Wilhelm Marr, *Der Sieg des Judenthums über das Germanthum* (Bern, 1879), 16.

[6] Ibid.

[7] Ibid., 6.

[8] Ibid., 42.

points made in the pamphlet became part of the rallying cries of the anti-Semites of the following decades. But there are many passages in the work that decidedly do not fit into the anti-Semitic canon. It has often been noted, in regard to more serious thinkers of the nineteenth century, that the great majority of their readers misunderstood them (Nietzsche and Marx are two obvious examples); even in the case of this short and plebeian pamphlet, those who hailed it often ignored significant parts of it and "saw" only those parts that were satisfying or otherwise bolstered existing beliefs.

Part of the German public was ready by late 1879 to acclaim a hard-hitting pamphlet entitled the *Victory of the Jews over the Germans,* one that emphasized racial rather than religious factors. Marr himself had written much the same kind of thing in the 1860s, in his *Judenspiegel* (Jewish Mirror), but had attracted relatively little attention, most of it in the form of ridicule and condemnation.[9] The popular success his work now enjoyed reflected a different climate, one in which political initiatives to counter the "victory" of the Jews seemed promising. Context, in short, was more important than content.

But even the content of this pamphlet was odd, not quite what one might expect from the title. Marr's reasoning was often clumsy, his points repetitive, his arguments thin, his tone exasperatingly ambiguous. As in his earlier writings, he insisted that he "harbored no hatred against any Jews, for all the world knows I have intimate friends among them." Throughout the pamphlet he mixed praise for Jews, recognition of what he saw as their many admirable qualities, with angry outbursts against them. Since the 1840s, Marr had detested German bourgeois liberals – the "fat Jew" Gabriel Riesser, a leading liberal politician, in particular – and now, when liberalism was in retreat, his antiliberal tirades received a new hearing. Of particular interest was his rejection of one of the central beliefs of the liberal assimilationists, that a "blending" of Jew and non-Jew was both possible and desirable. His having a son by a Jewish woman, and thus a Jewish son by Jewish law, would certainly seem to add a complicating element to this argument. He later wrote in his memoirs that "I . . . came to know the Semitic race in a thorough manner, in its most intimate details, and I *warn* against the mingling of Aryan and Semitic blood."[10]

But this pamphlet provided few details of his various intimacies with Jews. Hopes for Gentile–Jewish "blending," of compromises on both sides, were now dead, he affirmed; it was a matter of victory or defeat – Jacob and Esau must fight to the finish, not work out ways in which they could live together. He noted that other peoples had indeed blended, had become German: the

[9] On his earlier works, see Uriel Tal, *Christians and Jews in Germany: Religion, Politics and Ideology in the Second Reich, 1870–1914* (Ithaca, N.Y., 1975), 262; Zimmermann, "Two Generations," 89–91; and Zimmermann, *Patriarch,* 53 ff.

[10] Ibid., 73.

French Huguenots, the Wends, various Slavic peoples. But not the Jews. Marr concluded that the Jews are "stronger and tougher" *(stärker und zäher)* than non-Jews.[11] It was naive of him, he now recognized, to have hoped for a reconciliation, since the Jews are finally interested only in domination, and they pursue it with relentless tenacity.

This cluster of beliefs is monotonously repeated in the pamphlet; at times they intrude into his arguments almost incoherently, in ways that suggest an overpowering surge of emotion and that would seem to point to anti-Semitism of a serious dimension. Yet the tone is not exactly or consistently one of bigotry or intolerance, at least as those terms are normally understood. In an earlier work, published in the mid-1870s, he had explained that he found both Christianity and its parent, Judaism, "detestable" because they instilled in their followers "the zeal to persecute and kill one's fellow man."[12] Similarly, the Judeo–Christian worldview made unrealistic, "inhuman" demands on human beings, filling them with guilt, morbid anxieties, and absurd superstitions. The religious impulse itself was "diseased," in his view.

In earlier years Marr had both employed Jews and worked for them. But his fortunes were in decline by the 1870s, and he claimed that Jews now blocked his way, preventing his success as a journalist. Any Jew, he wrote, regardless of ability, could find work with other Jews, whereas only the most talented – or the most obsequious – Gentiles could hope to find work with them. Jews were ruthless against anyone they perceived as inadequately submissive. They blackballed anyone in the theater, in the arts, in music, in journalism, who met with their disfavor. Marr cited as further evidence of Jewish intolerance the attacks on Catholics during the Kulturkampf. Jews themselves, however, remained supersensitive to criticism: "We cannot expect delicate feelings in dealing with Jews – although they demand of us Germans that we handle them like the thinnest glass."[13]

Marr blended into these familiar charges against Jews some significant uses of the racist and social Darwinist language of the day, implying that Jews were physically and intellectually superior, while morally inferior. But since social Darwinism considered victory to be the ultimate test – and according to Marr the Jews were winning – even moral condemnations do not emerge unequivocally in his pamphlet. In one passage, after lamenting what Christians had done to Jews in the past, Marr remarked, "perhaps your [Jewish] realistic view of life is the right one."[14]

The tone of resignation he assumed, even if not sincere, is revealing. Undoubtedly it spoke to the growing anxieties concerning decadence and

---

[11] Ibid., 23.

[12] Wilhelm, Marr, *Religiöse Streifzüge eines philosophischen Touristen* (1876); quoted in Tal, *Christians and Jews,* 262–3.

[13] Marr, *Sieg,* 27.

[14] Ibid., 48.

decline in Germany by the late 1870s, especially among those classes of Germans who feared that modern Germany, becoming soulless and materialistic, would no longer have a place for them. However, the extent to which Marr genuinely felt this pessimism is difficult to gauge. He may have used it merely as a provocative device, to rouse his listeners. He may well have been of two minds himself about the future of Germany; his muddled sentences strongly suggest that. His biographer believes that his pessimism was genuine, that it reflected his belief that the Germany he loved was doomed. His health was failing – although he lived many more years – and his material fortunes were at a low ebb.[15]

Marr was familiar with Disraeli's boasts about Jewish blood and the ability of Jews to work behind the scenes. Without weapons, he noted, Jews had become the masters of Germany. "If I were a Jew, this would be a point of great pride for me."[16] There had in fact been a war since 1800, a war pitting two races, and the Jews had won it. Germans could no longer do anything against the Jews, although perhaps the Slavs would be able to. Even the "brutal anti-Jewish explosion" that was inevitably coming would not effectively dislodge the Jews from their domination in Germany.[17]

Whether or not these were genuine words of despair for Marr, for others they became a rallying cry, a challenge to fight back against the Jewish menace. His own next pamphlet revealed a far more activist perspective: Its title was *Elect No Jews! The Way to Victory of Germans over Jewry.*

Anti-Semitic Ideology: Heinrich von Treitschke

The complaints and laments of Glagau and Marr did not immediately alarm most Jewish observers, since these two could be easily dismissed as lowbrow, demagogic, and lacking in respectability. Many influential Jewish observers considered Marr and his following not only beneath contempt but laughable. However, late in the same year and early in the next (1879–1880), Heinrich von Treitschke, the celebrated historian of Germany and popular university professor,[18] published a series of articles critical of the role of Jews in Germany. Treitschke used the new term "anti-Semitism," giving it a legitimacy that Marr could not. (Treitschke had used *Semitentum* [Semitism] as early as the 1860s.)[19] These articles were much more seriously discussed than were the writings of Glagau and Marr, particularly among Germany's educated classes.

---

[15] Zimmermann, *Patriarch,* 22, 75 ff.

[16] Marr, *Sieg,* 23.

[17] Ibid., 46.

[18] The standard biography of Treitschke in English is Andreas Dorpalen's *Heinrich von Treitschke* (New Haven, Conn., 1957).

[19] Walter Boehlich, ed., *Antisemitismusstreit Der Berliner* (Frankfurt am Main, 1965), 244.

Entitled "A word about our Jewry," Treitskche's articles appeared in the prestigious academic journal, *Preussische Jahrbücher*, which he edited. A noted liberal–nationalist intellectual and a leading figure in Germany's academic elite, among a people that revered university professors, Treitschke expressed derision for plebeian pamphleteers of Marr's ilk, for their "dirt and crudity." Treitschke's articles seemed to indicate that the issue of the rapid rise of Jews in German life was posing problems that now concerned not just insecure petits bourgeois and demagogues but also serious thinkers and respectable people.

Most of the points he brought up in 1879–1880 had already been widely discussed by liberal intellectuals in the 1860s, but the context then was different; there was no economic crisis, no stock market scandals, and no best-selling anti-Semitic broadsides. Liberal intellectuals in the 1860s, like Treitschke in 1879, had made known their concern that many of Germany's Jews seemed unwilling to sacrifice enough of their sense of separateness, their historical particularism, to be able to blend into the German national community as other formerly particularistic inhabitants of German lands had done or were now doing.[20] Much of what Treitschke said was merely a reformulation of these questions in a more forceful language – and in a much more emotion-filled context.

As with Marr, many of Treitschke's positions seem strange ones for a man who has often been described as a proto-Nazi. He expressed dismay over the persecution of Jews in history. He did not believe in an unchangeable Semitic racial essence. He rejected condemnations of Jews that failed to recognize their many internal differences; he wrote that "there is no German commercial city that does not count many honorable and respectable Jewish firms." His own historical writings sharply criticized early nineteenth-century attacks on Jews in Germany (what he termed "the hollow and baseless . . . Teutonic Jew-bating of 1819"). His articles spoke of the Jews' "old and sacred past, which all of us hold in reverence." He also wrote that "it would be a sin to forget that a great number of Jews, baptized and unbaptized, Felix Mendelssohn, Veit, Riesser [the 'fat Jew' so detested by Marr], and others, not to mention the ones now living, were Germans in the best sense of the word, men in whom we revere the noble and fine traits of the German spirit." Nor did he demand that Jews wholly abandon their separate identity: "The matter can never be fully resolved . . . There will . . . always be a specifically Jewish culture *(Bildung);* and, as a cosmopolitan power, it has a historical right to exist. But the conflict will soften when the Jews, who speak so much of tolerance, really become tolerant and show respect for the faith, customs, and feeling of the German people, who have atoned for the old injustices and bestowed upon [the Jews] their rights as human beings and as citizens."[21]

---

[20] Cf. Tal, *Christians and Jews*, 40 ff.

Treitschke was politically liberal in the junkerized sense of the time. He had earlier opposed Bismarck but had, like so many other liberals, come around to an acceptance of the Reich constitution and the new Prussian-dominated German nation. He served between 1871 and 1884 as a National Liberal Reichstag deputy. As a liberal, he insisted that "there can be no talk among the intelligent of an abolition or even a limitation of the [Jewish] Emancipation. That would be an open injustice, a betrayal of the fine traditions of our state, and would accentuate rather than mitigate the national contrasts." Although he used the term anti-Semite, he explicitly rejected it as accurately describing him or his position; he would have little to do with the anti-Semitic movements that began to form in the early 1880s, refusing to sign their petitions. He clearly would have been appalled by any suggestion that violence against the Jews was justified (an attitude, it should be noted, that was shared by Wagner and Marr).

How, then, has Treitschke earned such an evil reputation in many influential accounts of the origins of Nazism? It seems that many of those histories have judged him in a facile manner. One author of a well-researched and respected study of anti-Semitism in France writes that Treitschke "constitutes one of the most open and influential sources of dictatorship in modern times, and both openly and indirectly he helped to bring anti-Semitism into the world."[22] Few popular accounts of the intellectual origins of Nazism fail to single him out as a major influence.[23] Even some of the otherwise most penetrating and balanced histories of these years are inclined to facile judgments in his regard, particularly in terms of blaming him for the growth of anti-Semitism in the following years.[24]

Treitschke's case, like so much else in nineteenth-century Germany, has been refracted through the distorting mirror of the Nazi years. It is revealing

---

[21] The entire drift of Tal's *Christians and Jews* is to deny that these words accurately reflect Treitschke's deepest beliefs, or the beliefs of most liberal intellectuals. [All quotations of Treitschke below may be found in Paul Mendes-Flohr and Yehuda Reinharz, eds, *The Jew in the Modern World* (New York, 1980), 280–3. The original German text and replies to Treitschke at the time have been reproduced in Boehlich, *Antisemitismusstreit*. I have occasionally altered the translations in Mendes-Flohr and Reinharz when they seemed misleading or doubtful.]

[22] Robert F. Byrnes, *Anti-Semitism in Modern France* (New Brunswick, N.J., 1950), 16.

[23] A sampling of well-known and influential works that treat Treitschke in a one-dimensional way (Although merely brief, passing references, they have helped to perpetuate facile, unqualified condemnation of him and of others like him as proto-Nazis.): Lucy Dawidowicz, *The War Against the Jews* (New York, 1975), 36; H. H. Ben-Sasson, ed., *A History of the Jewish People* (Cambridge, Mass., 1976), 875, 1079. Alfred D. Low, *Jews in the Eyes of Germans* (Philadelphia, 1979), commendably offers balanced treatments of other Germans who have simplistically been termed anti-Semites, but he makes little effort to treat Treitschke similarly (375).

[24] Cf. Robert S. Wistrich, *Socialism and the Jews: The Dialectics of Emancipation in Germany and Austria-Hungary* (New Brunswick, N.J., 1984), 120; Fritz Stern, *Gold and Iron: Bismarck, Bleichröder, and the Building of the German Empire* (New York, 1979) refers to the "evil that Treitschke had let loose" (512–3).

how often he is described, in a way that inaccurately represents the German scene, simply as a "conservative."[25] More to the point, many mistakenly present Treitschke's criticisms as a mysterious, unfounded, and irrational outburst by a man who had lost his moral bearings and who knew little or nothing about Jews.

The new German Reich was in some ways in a more precarious state by the late 1870s than immediately after unification, since some of the strongest supporters of a united Germany led by Prussia were now beginning to express misgivings. The much longed-for unity of Germans seemed to be slipping away. Southern and western Germans, Catholics in particular, were increasingly uncomfortable with Prussian domination. Germany's working class was rallying by the hundreds of thousands to the banners of the outlawed (after 1878) Social Democrats, whom the future Emperor Wilhelm II would denounce as *vaterlandlose Gesellen,* that is, unpatriotic or "fatherlandless" fellows. "Enemies of the Reich" *(Reichsfeinde)* were everywhere. Treitschke was a strong, even truculent defender of that Reich – there is no believer like a convert.

Liberals were by definition concerned with issues of personal freedom. That the nation-state not become too powerful, not pose too much of a threat to personal liberty, to the autonomy of the individual, naturally preoccupied them. Yet they also believed that the nation-state, the *Rechtsstaat,* served important practical, historical, and moral purposes. Most of them, Treitschke included, were torn between the demands of personal liberty and those of state power and were perhaps even more uncertain about the proper historical role of the German nation-state in modern times.

In just these areas, Jews posed awkward problems. Liberals were, on the one hand, concerned that the personal freedom, autonomy, and property of Jews be protected, yet, on the other, liberals had to recognize that Jewish freedom and autonomy could and did mean significant degrees of Jewish separatism. Already in the 1860s and early 1870s liberal intellectuals, men who would later firmly oppose political and racial anti-Semitism, often expressed annoyance with what one of them termed "a primitive and narrow-minded urge for separatism" on the part of the leaders of Germany's various Jewish communities; Jews, although enthusiastic for German unification, showed an "unwillingness . . . to identify completely with the German national will."[26] Theodor Mommsen, the distinguished historian and colleague of Treitschke's – but opposed to the form of Treitschke's attacks on Jews – went so far as to describe Jewish organizations, when not strictly religious, as "positively harmful," because they legitimized particularistic or (non-German) nationalistic fideli-

---

[25] For example, Jehuda Reinharz, *Fatherland or Promised Land: The Dilemma of the German Jew, 1893–1914* (Ann Arbor, Mich., 1975), 17. Byrnes, *France,* 15, terms him an "anti-liberal."

[26] Tal, *Christians and Jews,* 44.

ties at a time when other Germans were modifying their local, provincial, or otherwise particularistic attachments.[27] This annoyance was linked to a deeper, less frequently expressed belief of many liberals: There was no good reason, at least not any more, for modern Jews to retain their separate identity. One liberal described the insistence by some nonreligious Jews that they still had a special mission in the modern world as "tasteless verbiage" *(geschmackloses Gequatsch),* and he asked his Jewish friends to stop talking in such terms.[28]

Still, many Jewish spokesmen firmly insisted upon the right, the duty even, of Jews to remain "separate" (the exact meaning was highly elusive) in a modern state. To do so was indeed part of their mission, as newly defined in modern times, and was a reflection of their superiority, for example, to those non-Jews who allowed themselves to be overcome with state worship and xenophobia. The principal organ of German Jewry, the *Allgemeine Zeitung des Judenthums,* went so far as to urge its readers to abandon liberal nationalism if it threatened Jewish particularism, which the article strongly implied it soon might.[29]

Many liberal nationalists considered national unity still fragile and shared Treitschke's fears concerning the new nation-state's survival: fears about the socialists, about the reactionaries, about mass society, about war clouds, about Catholics – and about Jews. Treitschke's concerns were not unique or simply due to a hyperactive imagination. However, the more difficult question remains: To what degree were his expressed concerns about the destructive influence of Jews in the new Reich exaggerated? Why was he unable – or at least no longer able – to accept the notion of a Jewish "irritant" in Germany that would actually be *beneficial* to the nation in the long run? (Such was the much misunderstood position of Mommsen, whose phrase "ferment of decomposition" in regard to the Jews was twisted by anti-Semites, particularly by Nazis;[30] Mommsen considered the Jewish contribution to a new German identity, although necessarily destructive of the old to some degree, as nonetheless an essential part of a new German amalgam. Many Jews accepted the validity of Mommsen's concept, and roughly similar language was commonly used by other non-Jewish observers: Jews were described as "leaven" [*Sauerteig*], for example,[31] in the "bread" of a vibrant, modern society.)

That the presence of newly emancipated Jews in Germany could present a genuine problem, not a fantasy, was freely recognized by a number of

[27] Ibid., 49.

[28] Ibid., 40.

[29] Ibid., 43.

[30] Ibid., 52.

[31] In Hugo Bettauer's novel *Stadt Ohne Juden* (Vienna, 1922) his main character declaims that Jews, like leaven, "in too large quantities [are] destructive *(schädlich),* but in the proper mixture necessary for our daily bread" (162).

thoughtful Jewish observers at this time, as in years past; Jews did indeed have significantly different cultural traditions from the rest of the population.[32] That would of course be a central assertion of a later generation of Zionists, often in starker terms than those used by Treitschke. Real problems need to be addressed honestly, not ignored or emotionally brushed aside as unworthy of discussion. And among the numerous ranks of those who have been called anti-Semitic, Treitschke discussed the problem in a relatively sober and intelligent way. The issue here is not whether Treitschke was in all ways admirable or generous – he clearly was not – but rather whether he has been judged too harshly.

Mehring, a man of the socialist left who often expressed sympathy for Jews,[33] nevertheless considered Treitschke's articles to be "dignified" and "high-minded" – indeed, "great and unforgettable." Mehring did not agree with Treitschke on all points; he considered the rebuttal to Treitschke by the respected Jewish academic and neo-Kantian philosopher Hermann Cohen also to have been "serious and high-minded." Significantly, however, Mehring complained that many other Jewish opponents of Treitschke engaged in "intellectual terrorism," attempting as they did to smear as anti-Semitic anyone who expressed whatever critical reservations about the actions of Jews.[34]

Conceivably, if men of the caliber of Treitschke, Cohen, and Mehring had set the tone of the debate in the ensuing generation, some happier resolution or at least diminution of the tensions between Jews and non-Jews in Germany at this time might have emerged. Treitschke explicitly recognized, in terms that uncannily underline his differences from the Nazis, that a "final solution" was not possible,[35] and he did not ask for a total submission or disappearance of Jews. He urged Jews, as representing a tiny minority, to become "simply and justly . . . Germans, without prejudice to their [religious] faith. . . ."[36] For him it was Germany, the German spirit and its agent, the Prussian state, that had a special mission in modern history, not the Jews. His claims may be seen as supporting state worship (the other main and more widely recognized charge

---

[32] For a general discussion of this issue, see Ismar Schorsch, *Jewish Reactions to Anti-Semitism* (New York, 1972). Also, the discussion in Richard S. Levy, *The Downfall of the Anti-Semitic Parties in Imperial Germany* (New Haven, Conn., 1975).

[33] Mehring's attitudes defy easy categorization; the "anti-Jewish strand" in his thought is given penetrating and disapproving attention by Wistrich, *Socialism*, 116–26. Mehring unquestionably had a penchant for astringent commentary, perhaps more in regard to Jews than others, but by no means exclusively in regard to them.

[34] Franz Mehring, *Herr Hofprediger Stoecker der Sozialpolitiker* (Bremen, 1882), 64–5; pages excerpted and translated in Paul W. Massing, *Rehearsal for Destruction* (New York, 1949), 314.

[35] He did not in fact use the term later made notorious by the Nazis, *Endlösung*, although some translations have used that phrase: his words: *Die Aufgabe kann niemals ganz gelöst werden* (cf. Boehlich, *Antisemitismusstreit*, 18).

[36] Cf. Schorsch, *Jewish Reactions*, 62–3; Wistrich, *Socialism*, 61, 78.

against him), but in kind they were little different from those made by many nationalists of the day.

Treitschke's consternation about Jewish influence also reflected his rising distaste for modern mass culture. He, like most educated Germans, felt an abhorrence for what he perceived as the shallow *Mischkultur* (mongrel-culture) that was coming to characterize the United States in these years. They did not believe that the German spirit, in its barely achieved unity, could survive the kind of cultural pluralism – a chaotic and debilitating mongrelization in their eyes – that seemed to be growing up in the New World. That threat blended with the wider dangers of mass society – yellow journalism, corrupt political machines, narrow interest groups, pervasive materialism, and the unprincipled scramble for profits.[37] Treitschke had before his eyes as well what he considered the corrupt and jewified German culture of the Austro–Hungarian Empire.

Treitschke's explicit assurances that he could accept a degree of Jewish separatism and that Jewish differences had even been beneficial in the past are difficult to reconcile with his concern about retaining the purity of the German spirit and protecting German unity. These ideas are inherently imprecise, and it is often difficult to determine exactly what he had in mind, what acceptable German–Jewish personality he envisaged. But in Treitschke's opinion a certain class of Jews had recently come to the fore that was too critical, too cosmopolitan, too self-assured – and simply destructive. Above all, the corrosive, mocking, verbally clever style of alienated Jewish intellectuals, small in numbers but often enormously influential because of their prominence in journalism, the arts (especially as critics), law, and other such tone-setting positions in society, threatened the Germans, a people of a very different temper, who had long suffered from a sense of cultural inferiority in regard to the French and English. Treitschke remarked, in words that help explain what appears hypersensitivity to observers a century later: "Ours is a young nation. Our country still lacks national style, instinctive pride, a firmly developed individuality; that is the reason we were defenseless against alien manners for so long."

The Jewish population of other western countries, such as France, Great Britain, and Italy, Treitschke observed, was insignificant in numbers as compared with that in Germany, and those Jews were to a significant degree Sephardic, more cultured and more western. In their great majority they "became good Frenchmen, Englishmen, Italians, as far as can be expected from a people of such pure blood and such distinct peculiarity." France and England could look back to centuries of national unity. Absorbing a few, long-resident Jews presented no major problems for them. But the young German nation, long divided and still unsure of itself, was being flooded "from the

---

[37] Cf. Peter Gay, *Freud, Jews, and Other Germans* (Oxford, 1978), 184.

inexhaustible cradle of Poland," its next-door neighbor, by a Jewish population that was "incomparably more alien," more imbued with a specifically Jewish nationalist spirit, than was Sephardic Jewry, and was thus "especially
[threatening] in regard to the German national character." At any rate, the
steady stream of insults and withering, destructive criticism now being directed
at Germans by the Jews in their midst would never have been accepted by the
English, French, or Americans, however secure their national identity.

Precisely which Jews or which statements by Jews Treitschke had in mind is
difficult to determine, but German Jews themselves, in seeking to limit the
influx of Ostjuden in Germany, had often made points similar to those of
Treitschke, especially that Jews from eastern Europe were too much attached
to the idea of Jewish nationhood to be absorbed into German national
feeling.[38] Treitschke argued further that the materialism of the early 1870s, so
threatening again to the moral tone of the young German nation, was significantly reinforced by Jews. Treitschke added his voice to a common observation
of the day, one that Marr had also made: Jews lacked the instinctive reserve of
Germans, their inclination to discipline and respect for authority, their distaste for external display. Jews were wonderful with words, using them with little sense of responsibility or awareness of how wounding they could be to people unused to such a cultural style.

Again, Mehring was inclined to support Treitschke's evaluations: "In Berlin,
particularly, the Jewish voice *(Vermauschlung)* in public life reached such a
pitch as to make even the most intrepid admirers of the wise Nathan [Less-
ing's Jewish hero] feel ill at ease."[39] Eça de Queiroz, a prominent Portuguese
novelist residing in Berlin and also an enemy of the anti-Semites, similarly
observed, "if the Jew's wealth irritates [the German], the show the Jews make
of their riches absolutely maddens him. [The Jews] always talk loud as if tread-
ing a conquered land. . . . They cover themselves with jewels . . . and they love
vulgar and showy luxury."[40] Testimonies of this sort from people who were not
generally hostile to Jews and who had no use for the political anti-Semites of
the day were common. Certain prominent Jewish observers, Karl Kraus and
Maximilian Harden, for example, were even harsher.[41]

Treitschke complained that Jewish journalists had introduced an element
of petty quarrelsomeness and intolerance, of a wholly one-sided sort: "About
the shortcomings of the Germans [or] French, everybody could freely say the
worst things; but if somebody dared to speak in just and moderate terms about
some undeniable weakness of the Jewish character, he was immediately

---

[38] Cf. Steven E. Aschheim, *Brothers and Strangers: The East European Jew in German and German Jewish Consciousness, 1890–1923* (Madison, Wisc., 1982), 53.

[39] Massing, *Rehearsal*, 188 [from Mehring]. "*Vermauschlung*," it should be noted, referred deroga-
torily to specifically Yiddish intonations and vocabulary.

[40] Stern, *Gold and Iron*, 519.

[41] Wistrich, *Socialism*, 121.

branded as a barbarian and religious persecutor by nearly all of the newspapers." "What Jewish journalists write in mockery and satirical remarks against Christianity is downright revolting, and such blasphemies are offered to our people as the newest acquisitions of 'German' Enlightenment!" Mehring, too, was offended by the intolerance of much of the Jewish-owned and edited Berlin press and also remarked on the stark contrast between that intolerance and the hypersensitivity whenever issues involving Jews were brought up.

Again, these concerns were not unique to the late 1870s. But a key point for Treitschke, what prompted him to speak up as he had, was his belief that matters were worsening, that a "recently . . . dangerous spirit of arrogance has arisen in Jewish circles." This judgment has found considerable support, even among scholars who are highly critical of Treitschke. Uriel Tal, for example, notes that the Jewish press was often "aggressive and provocative" and that such tendencies indeed did seem to be growing in the 1870s.[42] Treitschke warned that "the influence of Jewry upon our national life, which in former times was often beneficial, has recently often been harmful." Mehring also recognized a new temper, which he saw as an expression of a formerly oppressed people – "a gifted, shrewd, tough-fibred race," "intoxicated" with its new freedoms, and "anything but modest and sensible, thoughtful and cautious." Jews in Berlin had developed into "an expansive and explosive force which is hard to imagine for anyone who has not seen it with his own eyes."[43] On this point, again, Mehring found much agreement from German Jews themselves.[44]

Treitschke and Graetz

Treitschke's ire in these regards was especially directed at another scholar, the noted historian of the Jews, Heinrich Graetz. Indeed, it is likely that reading Graetz's work acted as a catalyst for Treitschke, prompting him to add his voice to the chorus of complaints about Jews in Germany.[45] In the conflict between Treitschke and Graetz some revealing issues arose, often neglected or ignored in accounts of the period. Graetz's work had become popular among the German–Jewish reading public and had gained a great deal of attention, partly because he tried to present a modern history of the Jews using the most advanced historical techniques of the day, but also because it "breathed a partisan commitment to Jewish revival within the modern world."[46] Although his *History of the Jews* is still lauded by twentieth-century Jewish historians as one of the great nineteenth-century histories of the Jews,

---

[42] Tal, *Christians and Jews,* 208–9.

[43] Massing, *Rehearsal,* 314 [from Mehring].

[44] Cf. Wistrich, *Socialism,* 47. Wistrich disapproves of this "self-accusing assumption."

[45] Meyer, "Graetz and Treitschke," 8.

[46] Ibid., 2.

there is little question that the sense of Jewish superiority expressed in it, especially in the eleventh volume, which had first appeared in 1868, was at times narrow and excessive. Indeed, compared with it, Treitschke's history of the Germans may be described as generous in spirit, especially in its treatment of the relationships of Jews and non-Jews, their relative merits and defects.

Graetz conceived Jewish history as the unfolding of an immanent idea and was inclined to minimize the notion of productive interplay between Jew and Gentile, especially if that interplay entailed Jews learning from or borrowing from the civilizations in which they had existed over the centuries. Even the reconciliation of traditional Judaism with modern culture, as he presented it, was primarily a matter of Jewish self-realization rather than being influenced by Gentile culture. He harbored a deep contempt for the ancient Greeks and a special derision for Christians in the Middle Ages. Even certain tendencies within Judaism, hasidism, for example, he dismissed summarily – they were not, in his eyes, truly Jewish. He denigrated the culture of the Jews in eastern Europe and considered Yiddish an "ugly mongrel tongue." For such reasons, though even more because of questions raised about the trustworthiness of his scholarship, his history was widely attacked by both Jewish and non-Jewish historians in the 1870s.[47] Before Treitschke had read Graetz and responded with such fury, Mommsen had dismissed Graetz's work as "talmudic"; its intellectual level was similar to that of Catholic defenders of the church, with all their "historical falsifications."[48]

Since Graetz, borrowing from Herder, believed in a Jewish *Volkseele* ("folk soul" or a Jewish essence) that was unfolding in history, and since he was hostile to the idea of Jewish assimilation, he naturally rejected Reform Judaism, which Treitschke favored. Graetz considered contemporary European civilization to be "morally and physically sick," thereby further offending not only Treitschke but a number of liberal Jews in Germany.[49] The distinguished philosopher Hermann Cohen, who had written a rebuttal of Treitschke's articles, nevertheless spoke of Graetz's "perverse, emotional judgments." Ludwig Bamberger, a leading Jewish liberal politician of the day, called him a "zealot and fanatic."[50]

Other Jewish observers regretfully commented upon the bad blood created not only by Graetz but also by other Jewish historians.[51] Indeed, in the subsequent polemical exchange of articles between Graetz and Treitschke, Graetz himself backed down somewhat. He emphasized that his by now notorious eleventh volume was composed before the "glorious victory of Germany" over

---

[47] Cf. Michael A. Meyer, *Ideas of Jewish History* (New York, 1974), 32.

[48] Tal, *Christians and Jews*, 53.

[49] Ibid.

[50] Cf. Reinharz, *Fatherland*, 21; Schorsch, *Jewish Reactions*, 232.

[51] Schorsch, *Jewish Reactions*, 45–6.

as our fellow citizens and honor Judaism as the lower stage of divine revelation."[59] Such words may not conform to late twentieth-century notions of religious toleration, but they were remote from Nazism.

Like a number of thoughtful German conservatives in the late nineteenth century, such as Max Weber and Friedrich Naumann,[60] Stoecker was troubled by the "social question," the poverty, unemployment, and general disruption of German life spawned by industrialization. Such conservatives could not accept Marxist socialism as an answer, but their consciences also rebelled against what seemed the rotten fruits of liberalism and the free market. As Stoecker devoted more and more attention to these problems, he gradually came to believe that Jewish influence was helping to destroy the foundations of the German–Christian nation and state. He repeated a phrase that Glagau had earlier propagated, "the social question is the Jewish question"; the modern Jew epitomized everything that endangered the traditional Christian classes and the sense of Christian responsibility and community.

Neither Stoecker nor Glagau seem to have been particularly impressed by the obvious fact that other countries, most notably Great Britain and the United States, also suffered from the social question, yet had a much smaller and less influential Jewish population than did Germany. Still, Stoecker emphatically distanced himself from what he termed the "rabble-rousers"; he believed that efforts to counter Jewish influence must remain sober and moderate, under conservative Christian direction, and he explicitly rejected as a distortion the charge that he had blamed all of Germany's woes on the Jews.[61] Similarly, he considered the secular left, above all the Social Democrats, to be a more fundamental danger to German–Christian society than were the Jews, as such, although of course Jews were prominent on that secular left.

In 1878, before his anti-Semitic activity, Stoecker had founded the Christian Social Workers' Party, with the specific intent of drawing workers away from the ranks of the Social Democrats. Bismarck launched his attack on the Social Democratic Party in the same year, persuading the Reichstag in late 1878 to pass the so-called Anti-Socialist Laws, a body of legislation that made it impossible for the Social Democrats to carry on normal political activity. Stoecker conceived of his activities to gain the fidelity of the working class to existing society and state as complementary to Bismarck's own efforts.

Stoecker was especially indignant over the attacks by Jews on Christianity, attacks that he, too, believed had grown in scope and intensity during the 1870s. Interestingly, he was aware that at least part of the reason for the rising

[59] Ibid., 251.

[60] Cf. the stimulating discussion in James T. Kloppenberg, *Uncertain Victory: Social Democracy and Progressivism in European and American Thought, 1870–1920* (Oxford, 1986), passim, but especially 322 ff.

[61] Levy, *Antisemitism*, 59.

attacks on Christianity by spokesmen for the organized Jewish community was defensive: Those spokesmen had themselves become alarmed about the incursions of liberal Christianity into the ranks of the Jewish community. In a speech entitled "What we demand of modern Jewry," delivered in September of 1879, Stoecker denounced the Jewish press for its "poisonous" attacks on practicing Christians; Jewish journalists, he noted, gather up information from sermons in which Christians engage in self-criticism, but those same journalists "hush up the Jewish question and do everything to prevent its readers from hearing . . . unpleasant voices" concerning Jewish vices.[62]

Stoecker mocked Jewish claims, whether Orthodox or Reform, to be bearers of lofty moral and religious ideals for mankind as a whole. Judaism of whatever variety was, he said, "dead at its very core," having long since abandoned God for Mammon. If Jews have a modern mission, he asked, "where are your missionaries? Perhaps at the stock exchanges of Berlin, Vienna, and Paris?" Which Jews "preach, praise, and honor the living God?" Perhaps the legions of writers for the Jewish gutter press?

Stoecker's message, while religious, was nevertheless modern and much concerned with the secular world. He, too, did not call for the persecution of Jews or for the re-establishment of ghettos, and certainly not for violence against them. But he did believe that some form of state control over German Jewry was necessary as part of a general reorientation of the state away from those liberal secular measures that had led to such mischief and toward measures of state interventionist social welfare. Such a reorientation was already under way, in that Bismarck had begun to introduce measures to protect the Mittelstand from competition, the farmers from cheap grains, and the workers against economic insecurity. "The social abuses which are caused by Jewry," Stoecker intoned, "must be eradicated by wise legislation. It will not be easy to curb Jewish capital. Only thoroughgoing legislation can bring it about."

Stoecker called for new regulations to limit Jewish predation in the stock exchange and the credit system. He proposed making certain kinds of real estate inalienable and unmortgageable, and he favored a limitation in the appointments of Jewish judges to conform to their percentage of the population. He believed that Jewish teachers should be removed entirely from primary schools. But he did not call for a complete revocation of the principle of Jewish civil equality. He termed Jewish emancipation "a fact, not only amongst us but amongst all civilized nations."[63]

Stoecker's criticisms of the free market resembled in some ways the socialist criticism, above all in his attacks on the rich and in his suggestion that they be

---

[62] All quotations following from Stoecker are from Reinharz and Mendes-Flohr, *Jew in Modern World*, 278–80.

[63] Peter Pulzer, *The Rise of Political Anti-Semitism in Germany and Austria* (London, 1964), 10.

Semitic agitation of the day, but at the same time fairness requires a recognition that those defects were more limited than often assumed.

Anti-Semitic Movement and Countermovement

There is little question that a number of more radical, more hate-filled anti-Semites either took inspiration from Treitschke and Stoecker or gained a sense of legitimacy from their statements. The so-called Berlin Movement of the early 1880s, which sought to challenge the predominance of the left–liberals in Berlin politics, had in its leading positions a number of fervently anti-Semitic university students, young men who recognized fewer moral limits and who were inclined to demonize Jews in ways that Treitschke resisted, to harbor fantasies about them that remained only distantly related to real social, economic, or cultural conflict. The Berlin Movement was one of many attempts to fashion new political alignments, to bring together previously antipathetic parties and social groups around anti-Semitism, to make of it what the Germans term an *Integrationsideologie*. Marr and others had already made an effort to establish anti-Semitic "leagues." Other agitators circulated the Anti-Semites' Petition, which by October 1880 had gathered some 265,000 signatures, 12,000 in Berlin.

The Petition, which was presented to Bismarck in the following year, established what might be termed a basic or minimal program for the myriad of anti-Semitic parties that would emerge in the following two decades. It charged that an "alien tribe" in Germany had gained domination over the "Aryan race." In order to combat the incursions of that tribe a number of measures were needed: (1) the limitation of Jewish immigration into Germany, (2) the exclusion of Jews from positions of high governmental authority, (3) a special census to keep track of Jews, and (4) the prohibition of Jews as teachers in elementary schools.

This minimal program was moderate in that it looked to orderly action through the Reichstag, not to popular violence, not to chasing Jews out of Germany, and certainly not to an overthrow of the existing Reich. Few Germans of any political persuasion openly demanded that all Jewish citizens should be chased from Germany, that their wealth should be taken from them, or that they should be put into a ghetto. The moderate program of the Berlin Movement, its emphasis on legal action, reflected a political climate that was substantially different from that following World War I. It reflected in turn the greater prestige enjoyed by the Bismarckian Reich than by the Weimar Republic.

Right-wing revolutionaries comparable to the Nazis were not common at this time and found only sporadic support among the masses. Left-wing radicals, that is, Social Democrats, certainly did have more extensive support from the working masses, but, as will be explored further in the next chapter, Social

ɔught the anti-Semites. The German anti-Semitic activists of the 890s were mostly law abiding and respectful of the constitution.

ḥat shaky consensus, those activists disagreed in many ways, often conṭṭṭ ₅sly. They were generally conservative, but some were emphatically not. Some spoke for Junker interests, others for the Mittelstand, yet others for the peasants. Since the interests of such social groups diverged, at times sharply, a common anti-Semitic program for them proved impossible to agree upon. Conservatives were repelled by the demagoguery of some anti-Semites. A few anti-Semites were racists in a dogmatic, cultish sense; others were more practical and limited in goals. Some were sincere in their anti-Semitic belief; others approached anti-Semitism more cynically, as a mere device with which to manipulate the masses, to gain popular support for conservative programs, without themselves feeling an intense, emotionally driven hatred for Jews.

These and many other differences within the movement led to schism after schism in the 1880s and 1890s. Moreover, the actual popular support for the new political anti-Semites, their ability to attract voters to their banners – as distinguished from their undeniable ability to make noise and attract notoriety – was from the very beginning in doubt. In the elections of 1881, the left–liberals in Berlin, led to an important degree by Jews, totally overwhelmed Stoecker's party. The Progressive Party gained thirty-three new seats in the country at large, based on a nearly seventy percent increase in popular votes.[66] After these electoral returns were in, Bismarck evidently concluded that not much political mileage was to be had from even covert identification with the anti-Semites, and he let it be known that "I most decidedly disapprove of this fight against the Jews."[67]

At the height of its popularity in the 1880s political anti-Semitism in Germany won scarcely five percent of the popular vote, and a large part of that vote probably reflected inchoate protest rather than systematic anti-Semitic convictions. On the other hand, there were certainly many who felt hostility to Jews but who did not vote for the anti-Semitic parties. Some of the more idealistic or intelligent of the young people who were initially attracted to political anti-Semitism were eventually repelled by the low moral and intellectual tone of many of its leaders. The young Junker Helmut von Gerlach was initially attracted to the Stoecker movement and sincerely hoped to be able to remedy the social question through Christian socialism. But before long he observed that aside from the many decent Jews he met, it was the anti-Semites themselves who cured him of anti-Semitism.[68] Houston Stewart Chamberlain, the famous "evangelist of race" and Wagnerian anti-Semite, impishly remarked that attendance at the meetings of the political anti-Semites of these years left

[66] Massing, *Rehearsal,* 21 ff.

[67] Stern, *Gold and Iron,* 527.

[68] Cf. Massing, *Rehearsal,* 309; Pulzer, *Political Anti-Semitism,* 106.

young man. His victory over the Conservative deputy, whose political methods were typical of the older *Honoratiorenpolitik* (that is, political activity dominated by small groups of notables), carried a potent symbolism of new forces at work in the German political scene, what one scholar has termed "anti-plutocratic populism."[77]

Böckel had made frequent excursions into the countryside of Hesse or *Hessenland* (the term refers to a cultural area in central Germany, with a number of political and administrative subdivisions) and was much moved by the plight of the peasants he encountered. As he recorded in his pamphlet *Die Juden, die Könige unserer Zeit* (The Jews, Kings of our Time), "the image of the peasant robbed by the Jew drives me onward."[78] The pamphlet went through a hundred editions by the end of the century.

Hessian peasants, like farmers elsewhere in Germany, had seen golden years between 1850 and the mid-1870s. The growth of cities had increased the demand for agricultural products, and agricultural prices had generally risen. The depression that struck in the mid-1870s marked the beginning of a long-range reversal of that trend. German farmers in general were threatened by the cheaper grains that began arriving from abroad, principally from the Americas. (In the Hessian case, however, most were livestock farmers who actually benefited from cheaper grains insofar as they provided cheaper fodder; tariffs to protect Junker grain farmers thus harmed them, but they had many other problems, among them hoof-and-mouth disease and the competition offered by cheaper meat shipped in refrigerated ships.) Peasant indebtedness in Hessenland sharply increased, as did bankruptcies.

Such trends, which touched peasants everywhere in Germany without prompting such pronounced peasant anti-Semitism, were probably not decisive in Böckel's success. It is tempting to conclude that it was simply his personal genius as demagogue and organizer that made the difference. He used pomp and fanfare, mass meetings, torchlight rallies, songfests, and sloganeering with great creativity. He was able to link peasant festivals and rituals with new political devices and goals. He established a newspaper that reached thousands of peasants who had never before read newspapers. He established credit cooperatives, offered inexpensive insurance, set up centers for legal information, and advertised "Jew-free" markets. Idealistic university students, also concerned by the plight of the peasants, flocked to his banners. Some called him a "second Luther," and many peasants did indeed look upon him as a savior.

Yet, without minimizing the importance of Böckel's personality, conditions

---

[77] Cf. Geoff Eley, *Reshaping the German Right* (New Haven, Conn., 1980), 19–40; T. Nipperdey, *Die Organisation der deutschen Parteien vor 1918* (Düsseldorf, 1961).

[78] Otto Böckel, *Die Juden, Könige unserer Zeit*, 15th ed. (Marburg, 1887). Quoted in Richard S. Levy, *The Downfall of the Anti-Semitic Parties in Imperial Germany* (New Haven, Conn., 1975), 43.

peculiar to Hessenland were also important, not only for what they reveal about the nature of peasant Jew-hatred but also for what they reveal about the situation of Jews in Germany more generally. Jews in Hessenland were in a number of ways exceptional. They were more rural and more often Orthodox than elsewhere in Germany. They were also long-time residents, not significantly reinforced by immigrants from eastern Europe. They were less rich than other German Jews, and they lived more traditionally than Jews in the major urban centers. Their economic activities were only partly modern: They acted as middlemen, cattle dealers in particular, in a situation in which market opportunities were opening up. They were also moneylenders, often providing peasants in the 1850s and 1860s with the funds to buy land, to take advantage of new market opportunities. When those opportunities diminished after the mid-1870s, many peasants found themselves hopelessly in debt to Jewish moneylenders, finally losing not only newly acquired properties but also their ancestral lands. One of Böckel's galvanizing experiences was attending a trial of a peasant who had murdered a Jew who had taken over his farm.

These economic foundations for tension between Jews and Hessian peasants were only part of a larger picture. There was also the perception by the particularistic peasants, deeply suspicious of outsiders and "city-slickers," that Jews were the agents of Prussian intrusion, that Jews were benefiting unfairly from measures brought to Hessenland under Prussian aegis: new liberal laws, new institutions and officials, railroads, and cheaper meats and grains – again, "modern times," but in "foreign," Prussian garb.

In 1866 Hessian Jews had been openly jubilant when Prussia directly annexed Electoral Hesse, since for them the Prussian Rechtsstaat appeared enlightened, efficient, and fair-minded when compared with the arbitrary and erratic rule that they had endured up to that time. And these expectations were not disappointed, for within a decade what has been called the "stimulating presence" of Prussia in former Electoral Hesse had resulted in a marked improvement in Jewish fortunes, reflected in per capita income, access to higher education, and entrance into the liberal professions. It was precisely in those areas of Hessenland where Prussian presence was the most "stimulating" that anti-Semitism was the most intense.[79]

Thus, the situation, while in some ways unique, was also familiar: Jews under progressive rule prospered, while non-Jews believed themselves threatened with ruin, especially during an economic downturn. One can even see echoes of the older syndrome, one familiar in eastern Europe, where Jews were blamed for the exploitation that they undertook in the name of the nobility. In this case, to focus anger away from mighty Prussia and widely popular Bismarck to the Jewish population of Hessenland proved a brilliantly suc-

---

[79] Ibid., 53.

cessful political stratagem for Böckel,[80] and one that certainly did more than play upon religious prejudice or ignorant fantasies about Jews.

Böckel's speeches and writings resembled those of the leaders of the Berlin Movement but were applied to a substantially different context. He offered the same warnings, that a "stubborn, old, and thoroughly alien race" was taking over; that modern capitalism was weakening the very backbone of Germany. Böckel avoided using such terms as "Aryan" and "Semite" in addressing his peasant audiences, who would not have understood them, but the virtues he believed to be found in the German peasant much resembled what was elsewhere termed "Aryan," and the evils of the commercial city much resembled what was elsewhere termed "Semitic."

Another revealing aspect of Böckel's appeal is that his greatest success was with previously unorganized, Protestant peasants; Catholic peasants in contiguous areas seemed largely immune to him or any other anti-Semitic agitators. These Protestant peasants had reason to feel abandoned by national and regional leaders, in ways that was not true for the Catholics, and Böckel undoubtedly offered them an all-important emotional support as well as organization and ideology.[81] These differences in peasant response underline once again how simplistic it can be to isolate Christian belief, as such, as the factor that leads to anti-Semitic action.

Böckel was also distinctly more of a left-wing reformer than the leaders of the Berlin Movement. He vigorously opposed military expenditures, since they were paid for by higher taxes on the peasants, and he repeatedly attacked the Junkers, who indeed had contrary interests – and far more power to protect them. One of his key slogans was "against Jews and Junkers."

For such reasons and others having to do with his personal traits, Böckel quarreled endlessly with other anti-Semitic leaders. His movement, too, became involved in scandal and corruption, without, however, undermining the fidelity of his peasant followers to him personally. Nevertheless, his movement finally disintegrated. He simply did not have a long-range or realistic program; his was a movement of slogans and pyrotechnics, emotional catharsis for his followers, not long-range political realism. Even his cooperative movement, which was quite successful at first, was finally outdone by cooperatives that eschewed politics and avoided anti-Semitism.

Precursors to Nazism?

Böckel was one of the more appealing and colorful of the anti-Semitic figures of the time, but his inadequacies as a leader suggest an important question: Would it have been possible for a leader of greater abilities to have

---

[80] Ibid., 54.
[81] Ibid.

united these various factions and to have accomplished something more substantial? Hitler also faced a myriad of rival factions and mutually hostile personalities; the Nazi movement, too, was full of contradictions. Could a man of Hitler's abilities have united the anti-Semites of the late nineteenth century in Germany as Hitler united them in the late 1920s and 1930s? This question overlaps with one posed earlier: To what extent or in which sense may the expressions of anti-Semitism of the 1880s and 1890s be considered precursors of the Nazi movement? More definitive answers to these questions are best left for subsequent chapters, but a few points can be profitably noted here.

The sufferings, disappointments, and anxieties that emerged from the Great Depression of 1873 to 1896 can hardly be compared with those experienced by Germans in the years from the First World War to the Great Depression of the 1930s. Similarly, the Bismarckian Reich enjoyed wide popular support, and by the mid-1890s it began once again to experience economic expansion. Revolutionary opposition to the German state continued to exist, but it was mostly confined to the left, which was opposed to political anti-Semitism.

The moderation of late nineteenth-century German anti-Semites reflected the substantially different conditions of the time. There was much in the speeches and pamphlets of anti-Semites at this time that large numbers of Jews recognized, both privately and publicly, as justified, if also expressed in a mean-spirited way. Criticism of Jews could be accepted as having some element of truth without arriving at the conclusion that violence should be done to them, or even that they should be deprived of their civil rights.

On the other hand, it is easily overlooked by those whose attention is focused on prewar anti-Semitism that Hitler's movement, although beginning in the early twenties as a fringe party dedicated to violent revolution, increasingly took on moderate, respectable airs in the late 1920s in an effort to gain both popular support and acceptance by influential elites. Hitler persuaded many observers, well into the mid-1930s, that he was a moderate on the Jewish question. He did not publicly advocate murder of Jews, at least not in any clear or consistent fashion (he made threats and dropped hints in both radical and conciliatory directions). Mostly, he suggested that Jews needed to be "controlled" through political measures, in a way that could easily be seen as similar to what the anti-Semites of the 1880s had called for. He spoke of an "anti-Semitism of reason" in contrast to the kind of irrational violence against Jews that was typical in eastern Europe.

Thus, it appears justified to question the distinction that late nineteenth-century anti-Semites had limited goals, while Nazism had unlimited ones, since Nazi goals were not clear and may not have been worked out with any precision until the Second World War provided a radically altered situation – and vast new opportunities. At any rate, the image of a steadily rising tide of anti-Semitism in Germany in the years before 1914 is a problematic one. If anti-Semitism grew in Germany, it was in subtle ways, ones that are frustratingly difficult to plumb or measure confidently; that growth was not in terms of political anti-Semitism, or of an anti-Semitism that reflected a coherent ideology of violent destruction or that attracted and effectively integrated masses of followers. Perhaps it is best to choose other imagery, to speak not of a rising tide of anti-Semitism but of resentments that assumed obscure shapes and shadows, ones that easily deceived contemporaries concerning their meaning and importance.

At this point, two dangers might be recognized in these efforts to understand German anti-Semitism. On the one hand, one must recognize that Nazism grew up in Germany and obviously had some sort of connection with German history and traditions. But one must at the same time be careful not to brandish the notion of proto-Nazism incautiously, to oversimplify the nature of the connections. Too often it has been assumed that German history before 1914 or 1933 pointed to some sort of inexorable tragedy, that German attitudes toward Jews were uniquely poisonous. In truth, expressions of anti-Semitism in Germany before 1914 had strong parallels in most other countries, including the democratic models, France and Great Britain. Indeed, anti-Semitism appeared much stronger elsewhere, especially in eastern Europe. At any rate, figures like Marr, Stoecker, von Treitschke, or Böckel held beliefs that were incompatible in many regards with later Nazi beliefs.

= 5

Socialists, Jews, and Anti-Semites

The Jewish race, concentrated and clever, always devoured by the drive to make a profit, manipulates the capitalist system with great skill. (Jean Jaurès)[1]

Marxism is not a scientific theory at all, but a piece of clever Jewish superstition. (Paul Johnson)[2]

Jews from Moses to Marx and Lassalle have inspired all the revolutions. (G. B. Shaw).[3]

Socialist Movement and Ideology

In the last three decades of the nineteenth century, when modern anti-Semitic movements made their first appearance, the socialist movement grew with great rapidity, above all in Germany after the turn of the century, when support for anti-Semitism waned. The socialist movement, or, as it was called in Germany, the social–democratic movement, may be seen as a successful model of a modern mass movement in a way that the anti-Semitic movement was not. The two ostensibly grew in response to many of the same developments and had a similar anti-liberal complexion. They were often bunched together by liberals, especially by Jewish liberals – falsely but not implausibly.

Socialist ideology grew up in the early nineteenth century as part of a broader protest against capitalism, irresponsible individualism, and an increasingly triumphant liberal ideology. Partly because Jews were widely identified with each of those, early socialist thinkers often attacked Jews, individually and collectively. However, as socialist ideology evolved and became more sophisti-

---

[1] Quoted in Stephen Wilson, *Ideology and Experience: Anti-Semitism in France at the Time of the Dreyfus Affair* (East Brunswick, N.J., 1982), 68.

[2] Paul Johnson, *A History of the Jews* (New York, 1989), 348.

[3] George Bernard Shaw, "The Sanity of Art," *The Complete Prefaces of Bernard Shaw* (London, 1965), 800–1.

cated, particularly once Marxism became the leading ideology of socialists, Jews were less often singled out by socialists and blamed for the ills of modern capitalism. Marxian socialists identified social class, not race, as the key category of analysis. Similarly, they came to accept modern industrialization as promising a bright and harmonious future, once its capitalist stage was over and socialism had triumphed.

Marxist ideology and the working-class movement that grew up around it were characterized by a more confident, hopeful tone, rather than the fear and resentment of the anti-Semites. Indeed, there were elements of philo-Semitism in socialist movements by the turn of the century, with the important qualifier that few socialists saw much value in the notion of the survival of Jews as a separate people or in the mission of Judaism as understood by Jews themselves.

Friedrich Engels wrote in a personal letter in 1890,

We owe a great deal to the Jews. Not to mention Heine and Börne, Marx was of purely Jewish origin; Lassalle was a Jew. Many of our best people are Jews. My friend, Victor Adler, who is now paying in a prison in Vienna for his devotion to the cause of the proletariat; Eduard Bernstein, the editor of the London *Sozialdemokrat;* Paul Singer, one of our best men in the Reichstag – people of whose friendship I am proud, and all of them Jews![4]

Bernstein, writing years later for a Yiddish journal, said of Singer, "no one achieved such popularity among the Berlin masses as Paul Singer. . . . Singer's funeral was the most impressive that Berlin had ever seen."[5] And Bernstein added, "I have belonged to the Social Democratic Party for almost fifty years, and I know of no instance when a person was not chosen as a candidate for office or defeated [as a candidate] for a party post because he was a Jew."[6] By the 1890s, Jews had almost entirely disappeared from leading posts in the National Liberal and even the left–liberal or progressive parties.

Franz Mehring, the socialist biographer of Marx, observed that "side by side with a good many defects in modern Jewry, it is perhaps its highest glory that there is today not one person of culture in Germany who is not linked in intimate relations of heart and intellect with one or more Jews."[7] (The ambiguity of this praise it typical; Mehring had a penchant for nasty comments about Jews, as is partly evident from his remarks, quoted in the previous chapter, in defense of von Treitschke. His was, at any rate, a prickly and acerbic personality, with a string of short-lived friendships and little time for customary courtesies.)

---

[4] Paul Massing, *Rehearsal for Destruction* (New York, 1967), 312; Robert S. Wistrich, *Socialism and the Jews: The Dialectics of Emancipation in Germany and Austria-Hungary* (East Brunswick, N.J., 1984), 35.

[5] Massing, *Rehearsal*, 424.

[6] Ibid., 329.

[7] Ibid., 316.

These quotations offer some sense of the tone of Gentile–Jewish relations in the socialist movement in Germany. In most countries, but especially in western Europe and the United States, it was much the same. Even in Russia at the end of the century Jews and non-Jews in the socialist movement bridged to a degree unequaled in other political movements the chasm that separated their two communities. The non-Jew Lenin and the Jew Trotsky forged a powerful partnership in 1917. Lenin worked closely with many Jews, both before and after taking power, and to his death he retained the highest personal affection for his Jewish factional opponent, the Menshevik leader Julius Martov. And of considerable symbolic importance was the famous partnership of the Jew, Marx, and the Gentile, Engels.

The Enlightened Tradition of Socialism

Nineteenth-century socialists were self-consciously heirs of the Enlightenment and through it of pagan antiquity. They were thus universalistic, humanitarian, and egalitarian. Their identity with the underdog, the oppressed, the exploited manual laborers was central. They believed that it was a bad economic and social system that made bad human beings. Racist theories were logically incompatible with socialism, especially insofar as those theories asserted that some human beings were unchangeably inferior to others. The logic of the socialist position worked particularly against theories like those of Gobineau that categorized the working class as inferior because of race. Similarly, socialists grew to realize that racist ideas in their various forms, including anti-Semitism, were being exploited by enemies of the working class and socialism.

The most widely read work of either Marx or Engels in the late nineteenth and early twentieth centuries was entitled *Anti-Dühring* (1876, with many subsequent editions), an attack on the racist, anticapitalist theoretician Eugen Dühring, whose anti-Semitic writings had attracted much attention and had even won praise at first from social–democratic leaders. Dühring was an economist and social theorist who presented a more sophisticated variety of antireligious anti-Semitism than did Wilhelm Marr. He called for a reformed capitalism through a strong labor movement. Reading him in 1882, Theodor Herzl observed that Dühring "should be read by every Jew. The slippery slope of Jewish morals and the lack of ethical seriousness that characterize so many (all, according to Dühring) activities of the Jews are being mercilessly exposed and stigmatized. One can learn from this!"[8]

Dühring was a fiercely belligerent man, at a period when academic contentiousness reached sometimes astonishing levels. He attacked with such ferocity and irresponsibility that he was expelled from his university position.

---

[8] Ernst Pawel, *The Labyrinth of Exile: A Life of Theodor Herzl* (New York, 1989), 76.

Hostility to him was further sharpened because he rejected the Judeo–Christian tradition as a whole; it represented, he wrote, a "hatred of life," a diseased, slave morality. He urged a return to healthier, more natural, Germanic beliefs. Much more unequivocally than Marr, he saw a cosmic evil in an unchanging, destructive Jewish race.

The popularity of Engels's *Anti-Dühring* derived not so much from its attack on Dühring as from its clear presentation of Marxist ideas, designed to show their superiority to those of Dühring. Engels certainly did not stress the Judeo–Christian foundations of socialism, yet it is possible to see in this work the influence of a central myth of the socialists that had much in common with Christianity: That is, their vision was of a future society of fraternity and solidarity; all peoples and races, Jews and Gentiles, German and French, would live in harmony and mutual sympathy. This universalism and the socialist concern for the poor and downtrodden was fundamentally different from Dühring's contempt for the Judeo–Christian "slave mentality" and his rejection of race mixing.

Socialists attacked not only racism but what they saw as related beliefs: militarism, nationalism, traditional religion, and local or ethnic particularism. All were illusions, and they were used by the ruling orders, and their servants, the priests and rabbis, to keep the people ignorant, obedient, and hostile to one another. Marx's famous phrase "religion is the opiate of the masses" epitomized the socialist position. For many, socialism served as a replacement for religion, supplying emotional, moral, and intellectual satisfaction as well as a new set of holidays, rituals, and heroes. It offered a cause or an ideal that transcended individual desires and tastes.

Socialist opposition to anti-Semitism did not entail sympathy for Jewish religion, nationalism, or ethnic particularism, each of which were viewed as divisive, as hostile to human solidarity. Judaism was, indeed, particularly guilty in the eyes of many socialists: As heirs to Enlightened paganism, they rejected the Jewish sense of enduring specialness, what socialists considered the stubbornly irrational attachment of Jews to absurd rituals and taboos. More to the point, socialists frowned at what they believed to be the refusal of Jews to accept equal membership in *humanitas,* the human family.

However, since Judaism was weak and persecuted, whereas organized Christianity was powerful and oppressive, it was the latter that elicited more plentiful denunciations from socialists, especially in western Europe. In eastern Europe, on the other hand, where rabbis exercised a potent authority over traditional Jewish communities, socialists – often themselves of Jewish origin – more typically expressed bitter denunciations of the role of organized Jewish religion.

Nineteenth-century socialist leaders identified with the cultural refinements of the Enlightenment, with *Bildung.* A central element of their sense of mission was not only to free the masses from poverty and exploitation but to make of them cultured, intellectually self-reliant citizens, people able to appreciate the higher products of western civilization. Anti-Semitism represented to such socialists much that was ugly, mean, and unrefined. The style of anti-Semitic leaders was typically vulgar and uncivilized; their moral tone was of the gutter, their hatred atavistic.

This distaste for the debased moral tone of anti-Semitism was of course not unique to the socialists; leading spokesmen of liberalism expressed similar concerns about it, as did indeed a number of conservatives. But by the early twentieth century the socialists proved to be more consistent and unshakable defenders than the liberals themselves of many values that have been vaguely termed liberal (free and reasoned discourse, toleration, defense of civil liberties, international harmony). Historians have often remarked that the socialists, after the turn of the century, tended to move away from revolutionary rhetoric to more moderate and reformist positions, tacitly taking up many of the causes that liberals, themselves concurrently moving to the right, were no longer willing to defend so energetically (including free trade, which socialists saw as providing cheaper food for the working class, whereas tariffs protected large landowners and privileged industries). More to the point, liberals and conservatives, especially the latter, were at times tempted to try to gain political advantage from anti-Semitism. Socialists prided themselves in rejecting such low temptations.

Marxian Socialism and the Jews

Karl Marx (1818–1883), the most influential socialist theoretician of the nineteenth century, was, as Engels noted, himself of "pure" Jewish origin. His father, Herschel, was a convert to Christianity, but like so many Jewish converts of the early nineteenth century, Marx's father apparently accepted Christianity more for practical reasons than heart-felt conviction. Herschel (or Heinrich, to use the Christian name he assumed) was at any rate indifferent to traditional Judaic ritual and belief. Again, like many Jews of his time and place, he had enthusiastically embraced the values of the Enlightenment; he was a perfect example of the kind of Jew who was enamored with German Bildung. When, after Napoleon's fall, he found himself obliged to embrace Christianity formally in order to retain his position in the Prussian judiciary, Herschel-Heinrich took the step with little apparent difficulty.

Young Karl, growing up in the 1830s, was therefore not raised as a Jew, certainly not in the sense of having a traditional Jewish education, although interestingly his mother refused for some time to join his father in formally converting. Marx attended a German–Gentile school under Prussian auspices, which at that time entailed a large exposure to Christianity as well as to the Graeco–Roman classics. He established few if any contacts with the Jewish community of the town in which he grew up, that is, Trier, along the Moselle

River. Young Marx moved in Gentile circles, married a Gentile, and did not raise his children as Jews (although interestingly they, in their adult lives, retained or regained a sense of Jewish identity, even though they, too, did not marry Jews and were not Jews by Jewish law, which their father was).[9]

Marx's mature theory emphasized the malleability of the human personality, its historical permutations under the influence of economic development and social class. He did not accept inherent or unchangeable human categories, beyond a basic human nature, or "species being" *(Gattungswesen)*. However, Marx's own attitudes to Jews and Judaism present the student of his thought with some apparently flagrant contradictions. His letters to Engels contain stunningly vicious remarks about Jews, Slavs, and blacks. To make sense of these and other writings is no easy task, and not surprisingly scholars remain divided concerning their meaning. Some lament that Marx has been "so frequently and unjustly accused of anti-Semitism," while others consider him to have been a closet racist.[10]

One of Marx's earliest essays (1844) was entitled "On the Jewish Question." In a manner typical of the Hegelians with whom he was associated at the time, he reveled in paradox, allusiveness, and arcane wordplay. He built elaborate logical and verbal structures based on doubtful axioms, arbitrary definitions, and nebulous abstractions. It is remarkable how much attention has been given to his crabbed, often hugely obscure first essays, which for many years remained mostly unread. However, "On the Jewish Question" was fairly often cited, both by socialists and anti-Semites in the late nineteenth century, and certain of its underlying ideas seem to have exercised some influence. A large problem remains – in this as in so much else of Marx's writings, early or late – in deciding "what Marx really meant."

Much of the essay seems simply to borrow from standard anti-Semitic fare: Judaism and capitalism are described as basically the same. The Jew of Marx's essay worships money, as does the capitalist. Marx argues that the Jew will have to cast off his "Jewishness" – that is, his mean and grasping ways – in order to become fully human. That development will be possible only with a total reorganization of society and the end of capitalism/Judaism.

But this essay is mild and abstract compared with what is to be found in a few of Marx's later writings, and these later statements force one to doubt the argument put forth by some apologists for Marx that the impression of anti-Semitic sentiment in this early essay is an incorrect or superficial one or that the more mature Marx disassociated himself from such expressions.

[9] Cf. Chushichi Tsuzuki, *The Life of Eleanor Marx, 1855–1898: A Socialist Tragedy* (Oxford, 1967); also [same author] *H. M. Hyndman and British Socialism* (Oxford, 1961).

[10] The quoted words are Hannah Arendt's, *The Origins of Totalitarianism* (New York, 1963), 34. For a hard-hitting critique, see Nathaniel Weyl, *Karl Marx, Racist* (New Rochelle, N.Y., 1979). A sophisticated defense of Marx can be found in David McLellan, *Karl Marx, His Life and Thought* (New York, 1963), and a sophisticated critique in Wistrich, *Socialism*.

Marx was a man of fierce personal antipathies, and he came to bear a particular grudge against Ferdinand Lassalle, the charismatic leader of the budding socialist movement in Germany in the early 1860s. Lassalle was himself of Jewish origin, and Marx called him "the Jewish nigger," "the little kike," and "the water-Pollack Jew." Marx wrote,

It is clear to me that, as both the shape of his head and his hair texture shows, he descends from the Negroes who joined Moses's flight from Egypt (unless his mother or grandmother on the paternal side hybridized with a nigger). Now, this combination of Germanness and Jewishness with a primarily Negro substance creates a strange product. The pushiness of the fellow is also nigger-like.[11]

Marx, in a way that was typical of German Jews of the time, harbored a towering contempt for eastern European Jews. He delighted in mocking the Yiddish accent and complained that the Ostjuden were "reproducing like lice." He commented that eastern Jews have not only dirty and smelly bodies but black souls, agreeing with Engels that Jews from Poland were "the dirtiest of all races."[12]

Marx consented to read a work of Lassalle, but only "if it doesn't smell of garlic." Engels, too, termed Lassalle a "greasy Jew," and he dismissed another Jewish acquaintance as "a real little Yid."[13] Lassalle's own writings are filled with similar remarks. In a celebrated quip – his sense of humor was certainly lighter than Marx's – he noted, "There are two classes of men I hate: journalists and Jews. Unfortunately, I belong to both."[14]

But Lassalle personally encountered little anti-Semitism among the German working masses. They were, on the contrary, inclined to idolize him. They never called him "king," as Böckel's followers called him twenty years later, but much of the adulation that workers showered on Lassalle resembled that of the peasants for Böckel. Even the Junker elite, with whom Lassalle occasionally hobnobbed, often treated him respectfully. Bismarck described him as one of the most intelligent men he had ever met, an impressive tribute in light of Bismarck's notorious hatred for socialists. It was Lassalle's fellow socialist and Jew, Marx, who, more than anyone else, seemed to hate him for being a Jew.

In attempting to gain some sense of balance and perspective in evaluating Marx's outbursts, one needs to remember that racist language of a sort that is wholly taboo in respectable circles today was fairly widespread in the nineteenth century, even on the part of people not usually considered to be racists. It is also difficult to sense accurately the emotional connotations in the mid-

---

[11] Weyl, *Marx*, 71 [Weyl does not give a source; it is from a letter of 1862]; Wistrich, *Socialism*, 31.

[12] Edmund Silberner, *Sozialisten zur Judenfrage* (Berlin, 1962), 128.

[13] Wistrich, *Socialism*, 32–3 [further references on page 357, nt. 72].

[14] Ibid., 46.

nineteenth century of words like "kike" and "nigger." Today they stun, but it is a fair guess that Jews of the 1860s and 1870s, when these above remarks were made, might have been more offended by "water-Pollack Jew" than by "kike." The first term has retained scarcely any emotional connotation or even any meaning today (it referred to an impoverished class of Jews in Poland, roughly like "cotton-picker"); "kike" was still a new word, thus still picking up some up of its present emotional power and was apparently often used in a casual way simply to refer to an uncultured or unpleasant Jew.

We must also keep in mind that these were private remarks, not intended for public consumption. Many were uttered when Marx and Engels were young, brash, or suffering from frustrations (among them intense jealousy of Lassalle and a belief that he was stealing Marx's ideas). Marx's public statements, especially his more mature ones, rarely if ever contained such scurrilously anti-Semitic language. On the contrary, he publicly opposed racism and ridiculed anti-Semites. He was himself attacked by anti-Semites, and his theories were denounced as typical products of the Jewish mind.

The tone of much of Marx's correspondence with Engels is indeed peculiar – familiar and swaggering; one can almost sense a lowering of the voice, a barroom tone, or the tone of adolescents behind the woodshed, telling dirty stories, uttering every obscene word they know, followed by giggles. In reading these letters, one feels at times a voyeur, witness to things that were not meant to be heard outside the family, and certainly not to be given general importance.

Revealingly, Marx's comments about members of his own family in his letters were not so very different from things he said about Lassalle and others. For example, Marx's daughter, Laura, married Paul Lafargue, who was of African, Indian, and French ancestry. Marx and the rest of the Marx family joked about the marriage in their letters. Marx was by all accounts a devoted and loving father, adored by his children, but he referred to Lafargue as "the gorilla" and observed that one of his daughters was helping solve "the color question by marrying a nigger." His daughter Jenny spoke of her sister's producing "ten little nigger boys."[15] That Marx's family and close friends referred to him, because of his dark complexion, as "the Moor" also suggests that his own ostensibly racist comments about blacks were not necessarily what they seem to later observers.

Still, it is difficult to deny that a strain of something akin to mean-spirited racism and anti-Semitism was to be found in Marx, even if inconsistent with his thought and action in other regards. This is true even taking into account Marx's pronounced distaste for the histrionics that often surrounded the Jewish question. He rarely expressed sympathy for Jews suffering from oppression. Particularly remarkable and revealing is how rarely he referred to his own Jewish ancestry. Such was true even when many of his opponents emphasized it,

---

[15] Weyl, *Marx*, 74.

and when it would thus have been natural to respond.[16] He could be classed as a near opposite in this regard of his contemporary Disraeli; Marx took little pride in his Jewishness. He must be considered a prime candidate for that problematic category, along with Lassalle and Heine, of the self-hating Jew.[17]

French Socialism and the Jews

Pierre-Joseph Proudhon (1809–1865) expressed a much more consistent and unambiguous hostility to Jews and Judaism. His socialist theories, more than Marx's, reflect the conflict within socialism between the attractions of modern freedom and premodern security, between atomistic liberalism and corporatist conservatism. Of rustic, petty-bourgeois background himself, Proudhon attacked Jews not only as typical representatives of a detestable modern capitalism but also as the supporters of the modern, bureaucratic centralized state. Proudhon's influence as a theoretician of socialism was less important than Marx's, especially in the long run (the two became bitter antagonists, with Marx as the generally recognized victor), but nevertheless his writings were widely read and appreciated, especially in southern and eastern Europe, in the areas that were less industrialized and more inclined to anarchism than to action through political parties or trade unions.

Proudhon's influence extended beyond the ranks of organized socialism. Tolstoy admired his writings; *War and Peace* was a title borrowed from Proudhon. But Proudhon was a simpler, less disciplined thinker than Marx, whereas his hatred of Jews was much more than a private and contradictory quirk. Anti-Jewish statements pervade his writing, early and late, private and public. Much of what Proudhon wrote of Jews, while making points that were antireligious and violently anticlerical, betrayed certain traditional religious perspectives, mixed with the newer pseudo-scientific racial vocabulary of the day.

The Jew is by temperament unproductive, neither agriculturist nor industrialist, not even a genuine trader. He is . . . always fraudulent and parasitic, in business as in philosophy. . . . He is the evil element, Satan, Ahriman, incarnated in the race of Shem.[18]

The list of Proudhon's hatreds and phobias is long and revealing. Not only Jews but also Protestants and nearly all foreigners were subjects of his vituperation. Women were, he believed, only half-formed human beings, and their efforts to achieve equality with men could result only in the collapse of civilized life.[19] His writings predate by several decades those of the German anti-

---

[16] Silberner, *Sozialisten*, 127–8.

[17] Cf. Wistrich, *Socialism*, 356–7, nts. 66, 67, for literature.

[18] Pierre-Joseph Proudhon, *Césarisme et Christianisme* (Paris, 1896), 1:139. Cited in Léon Poliakov, *History of Anti-Semitism: From Voltaire to Wagner* (New York, 1975), 3:374.

Semites discussed in the previous chapter, but he shared with
Jews, as distinguished from a condescension or contempt for th
he believed, destroying all that he cherished.

While Marx's writings, especially his early ones, are often ︹︹︹ and
obscure, Proudhon's are impossibly sprawling and poorly integrated. The tone
of both men, however, was similar: cocksure and mean-spirited in a way that
stuns the modern reader. Proudhon's private thoughts, even more than those
of Marx, are shocking in their omnipresent hatred:

> The Jews, unsociable, stubborn, infernal. . . . First authors of the malicious super-
> stition called Catholicism. . . . Make a provision against that race – which poisons
> everything by butting in everywhere without ever merging with any people – to
> demand its expulsion from France, except for individuals married to French-
> women. Abolish the synagogues. . . . The Jew is the enemy of mankind. That race
> must be sent back to Asia or exterminated.[20]

The seminal French socialist theoreticians of the early nineteenth century
were also often hostile to Jews. The works of Charles Fourier (1772–1839), for
example, are filled with fulminations against merchants and bankers – not
only Jews, but he considered the usury of Jews more dangerous, their egoism
and lack of concern for the rest of society more extreme than was the case
with non-Jews. The separatism and unsociability of Jews deeply offended
Fourier, especially their unwillingness to eat with non-Jews, since the delights
of human society, among them the pleasures of the table, were integral to
Fourier's socialist utopia.[21]

Yet, many other French socialists, especially by midcentury, such as Cabet,
Blanc, Pecqueur, and Blanqui, were either little concerned with Jews or not
notably anti-Semitic. Such being the case, one must again doubt the alleged
potency of the Enlightened anti-Semitic tradition. Jews numbered prominently among the followers of Saint-Simon (1760–1832) to such a degree that
Saint-Simonism was considered more or less a Jewish sect. However, it can easily be questioned whether Saint-Simonism, especially in the forms it assumed
that were most attractive to Jews, was really a form of socialism. It would better
be termed "technocratic modernism," for it glorified the emerging world of
modern industrialism and sought to enthrone bankers and financiers, along
with scientists and artists, at the head of society in the name of the general welfare rather than the profit motive. Saint-Simonians by midcentury were known

---

[19] Poliakov, *History*, 3:377–8.

[20] P. Haubtmann, ed., *Carnets de P.-J. Proudhon* (Paris, 1960–1961), 2:337. As cited in Poliakov, *History*, 3:376. [Translation slightly altered, ASL.]

[21] Poliakov, *History*, 3:369; Nicholas Riasanovsky, *The Teachings of Charles Fourier* (Berkeley, Calif., 1969); Jonathan Beecher and Richard Bienvenu, *The Utopian Vision of Charles Fourier* (Boston, 1971).

Empire came to play a prominent role as leaders and theoreticians even in those socialist movements that were composed in their overwhelming majority of non-Jews. And even in western Europe, Jews came to assume a leadership role in socialist movements that was entirely disproportionate to the Jewish percentage of the population.

Undoubtedly, one of the many reasons that a significant minority of Jews in western Europe were attracted to the rapidly growing socialist parties in the last decades of the nineteenth century was their sense that socialism was a solidly humanitarian and universalistic movement, opposed to anti-Semitism. Liberals and liberal movements, on the other hand, proved at times fainthearted on the issue of defending Jewish rights and were declining in popular support and overall political influence.

Far and away the most important socialist movement in Europe was that in Germany. It was approximately ten times as large as the French socialist movement, which held second place. And more than any other German party, the *Sozialdemokratische Partei Deutschlands* (Social Democratic Party of Germany, SPD) fought the anti-Semitic Berlin Movement of the 1880s. By the turn of the century, when the educated and propertied upper-middle class had begun to weaken in its earlier commitments to liberal principles of toleration and respect for minority rights, it was the SPD that became the most consistent defender of those principles. As noted, rank-and-file workers appeared little attracted to the blandishments of Stoecker and other demagogues, while their loyalty to the many Jewish leaders of the Social Democratic Party did not significantly waver.

However, the great majority of German Jews in the late nineteenth century certainly did not abandon liberalism for socialism. Most of them remained bourgeois in class identity, and that identity, deeply attached as it was to private ownership of property, a cultured bearing, and social respectability, counted more heavily than anything that socialism had to offer. By the turn of the century, economic trends may have pushed a small number of young German Jews in the direction of socialist activity. A new and numerous generation of Jewish lawyers, journalists, and other professionals began to enter a tight job market. Even under ideal conditions of toleration and receptivity to their talents, they would have found that Germany's economic and social structures could not have absorbed all of them. Needless to say, conditions were not ideal; young Jewish professionals faced rising social and political prejudice, resistance in many areas to what was perceived as a Jewish "invasion," and what was undeniably a rise in the numbers of young Jews looking for white-collar and professional employment.

A small number of such aspiring young Jewish professionals found that the expanding structures of the SPD and its associated organizations offered them employment consistent with their training. Meshed with these practical considerations were others, probably more important: The social–democratic movement extended opportunities to idealistic Jews alienated from both their own Jewish milieu and from respectable, bourgeois society as a whole. The social–democratic movement was strongest in Germany's large cities, where the Jewish population was also concentrated, and thus contact between Jew and urban worker was facilitated. The small towns and rural villages, where the SPD had few members, also counted small Jewish populations or had no Jews at all. Even Jewish capitalists and merchants in the urban industrial centers could in some instances present themselves as relatively friendly to workers. Jewish large-scale retail outlets in food and clothing, for example, offered lower prices to the urban lower classes (while at the same time angering small-scale retailers, who resented the "unfair" competition).

Jews in the SPD were accepted as comrades for obvious reasons, the same reasons that Jews themselves joined the movement: Socialists believed in human solidarity across religious and racial lines. That acceptance had other, less obvious foundations as well. One might say that ordinary workers not only accepted but even gratefully accepted Jews, since the Jews who joined the party were an energetic and talented lot who forcefully defended the workers' cause and who added much in terms of intellectual luster to a movement of unschooled manual laborers. The theoretical sophistication of the SPD, a source of international prestige and of pride to its rank-and-file members, was to an important degree attributable to Jewish theorists.

The SPD's most influential theorist, Karl Kautsky, was widely believed to be a Jew, a false perception enhanced by the fact that he had married a Jew and had a number of friends who were of Jewish origin. Party representatives, who had to be verbally nimble, capable of holding their own in debates with bourgeois intellectuals, were often university-educated Jews. In 1912 eleven out of the twelve Jews who were SPD deputies to the Reichstag had university educations, which was true of only twelve of the remaining ninety-eight non-Jewish SPD deputies.[24] The task of bringing enlightenment and Bildung to the masses was also frequently in the hands of Jewish social democrats. One of the more ambitious projects of the SPD, adult-education evening classes, was directed by the Jew Rosa Luxemburg, who was also prominent in other party activities.[25]

The luster brought to the party by this Jewish minority was more than intellectual or cultural; it was also "moral." There may have been some grumbling that Jews joined the party for careerist rather than idealist reasons, but for the most part the bourgeois origin of Jews in the party was a cause for openly expressed satisfaction, a sign of the moral superiority of the socialist movement in a rigidly hierarchical society and a state that treated manual laborers disdainfully – and socialists as pariahs. These bourgeois Jews had voluntarily

[24] Wistrich, *Socialism*, 81.

[25] Cf. J. P. Nettl, *Rosa Luxemburg*, abridged ed. (Oxford, 1969), 262–7.

abandoned their class in favor of the working class, although "abandoned" may be too strong a word, since bourgeois Jews typically continued to live in bourgeois material comfort and to perform tasks, as journalists or parliamentary deputies for the workers' movement, that were consistent with a bourgeois lifestyle. Workers recognized that Jews who openly identified with the social–democratic movement subjected themselves to hatred and social exclusion by their own Jewish fellow citizens, to say nothing of an even more pervasive or unyielding rejection by respectable Gentile society.

Such Jews became a valuable symbol of the moral superiority of the workers' movement, a matter of particularly great importance by the end of the century when Germany's educated classes seemed to be moving in the direction of brash militarism and tribalistic racism. Many Jews in Germany had distanced themselves from Judaism because they disliked what appeared to them as its backward and tribalistic tendencies; the world of the German nation seemed a broader, more cultivated and tolerant one. When such Jews then found that growing numbers of Germans were behaving in tribalistic ways, the attractions of a cosmopolitan faith like socialism became all the stronger, especially for a younger generation of Jews who were intent on disassociating themselves from the philistinism and self-satisfaction of their fathers' generation.

The extent to which Jewish religious identity of a more positive sort contributed to the remarkable predilection of a small but influential minority of Jews in western Europe for socialism, and later for communism, cannot be confidently estimated. But even among the most completely assimilated Jews in western Europe there were those who retained certain values or psychological traits that may be connected with Jewish tradition, "embodied by the Jew who does not feel comfortable unless the prophet's cloak is warming his shoulders, the living communicant of Judaism's greatest contribution to Western civilization."[26] The Jewish author Isaac Deutscher suggestively entitled the opening volume of his biographical trilogy of Leon Trotsky, modern history's most famous Jewish revolutionary, *The Prophet Armed.*

Social–Democratic Attitudes to Jews

Paul Singer, so admired by Engels and Bernstein, was not only a Jew but also a highly successful manufacturer – a capitalist; but it would be hard to imagine a man more beloved by the Berlin working masses, and their devotion to him was unmistakably wrapped up with their perception of him as a Jew. Attacks on him by anti-Semites seemed merely to increase the admiring ardor of the social–democratic masses for him. A Jewish observer at one of Singer's speeches in the 1880s, at the time of the Berlin Movement, described how the workers chanted,

[26] P. G. J. Pulzer, *The Rise of Political Anti-Semitism in Germany and Austria* (New York, 1964), 262.

"Jew Paul! Jew Paul!. . . Bravo Jew Paul!". . . Like a fire [the phrase] swept through the hall. Soon it swelled to a storm. The phrase was born completely out of the idiom of Berlin labor. At other occasions, it would simply have been a way of addressing a colleague of Jewish faith, with a playful characterization of his difference, without a trace of unfriendliness. Here, too, the epithet was meant without any mischief; it was nothing but an expression of great intimacy. Everyone understood this. . . . The workers would not calm down. They swarmed over the platform and carried Singer down . . . into the streets.[27]

Wilhelm Liebknecht, a revered non-Jewish leader and founding father of the SPD, revealingly observed in 1893, "we find that their humiliating situation has cultivated, in stronger and nobler Jewish individuals, a sense of freedom and justice, and fostered a revolutionary spirit. There is, in proportion to their numbers, a far greater stock of idealism among Jews than among non-Jews."[28] Kautsky remarked that the Jews "have given to the world more great thinkers . . . perhaps than any other nation, in proportion to their numbers." He lauded the Jews' "splendid power of abstraction and keen critical intellect."[29]

August Bebel, the cunning and forceful leader of the SPD until the eve of World War I, similarly often expressed admiring words for the Jews. Thus, the three men who could be classed as the three most influential leaders of the party, Bebel, Kautsky, and Wilhelm Liebknecht, were all friendly to Jews and opposed to anti-Semitism. (That all three leaders were non-Jews is worth noting: After Lassalle's death in 1864, Jews did not occupy many of the very highest positions in the party, in spite of a large Jewish presence in leadership positions of second rank; they were rare as leaders of whatever rank in the social–democratic trade union movement.) If one searches diligently enough in the middle and lower levels of the party, it is possible to find spotty evidence of mildly anti-Semitic incidents, at a time when they were commonplace in other parties and in society as a whole, but the party leaders usually disciplined sternly any such divergence from the official party position.

On the other hand, evidence of what would today be called anti-Semitism but that might better be termed insensitivity to Jewish feelings, or poor taste in reference to Jews, is plentiful. Jewish physical appearance was often slightingly or humorously mentioned in the party press and at party congresses. The Jewish nose was always good for a laugh, and Bebel, in his public speeches, showed a special taste for humor of that quality, shared by his working-class audiences.[30] Jews in the party seem to have made such jokes as often as non-Jews. The historian Peter Gay, referring to German Jews generally, not just

[27] Paul Massing, *Rehearsal for Destruction* (New York, 1967), 204.

[28] Ibid., 203.

[29] Wistrich, *Socialism*, 83–4.

[30] Cf. August Bebel, *Sozialdemokratie und Antisemitismus* (Berlin, 1906), 7, 10. Also, Karl Kautsky, *Rasse und Judentum* (Berlin, 1914), 1.

those in the social–democratic movement, has remarked that "both the jokes and the caricatures, indeed, seem to have amused its targets as much as its retailers."[31] A consensus apparently existed in Germany at the time that "Aryans" were physically more attractive than "Semites" (both terms, significantly, gained some currency in social–democratic circles). Phrases such as "he was of impeccable Aryan appearance" or "he was a handsome man, with little trace of his Semitic origin," were dropped by non-Jews and Jews alike.

Jokes about Jewish physical appearance seem to have been accepted much in the same temper as one might today joke about the red hair of the Irish or the blue eyes of the Swedes. As in so many other spheres, it is often intent rather than content that makes the difference, and for the most part hostility was apparently neither intended nor perceived in these phrases. Such remarks hold even for the not infrequent references by party leaders to Jews as pushy and lacking in manners, Jews as unscrupulous businessmen, or Jews as people who avoid honest physical labor. In addition to the admiring words that Bebel had for Jews, he also spoke of their "loud and brash character" *(vorlautes oder überlautes Wesen)*, their "desire to stand out and to push ahead," their "ostentation and vanity," and "lack of tact."[32]

Social democrats implicitly accepted the existence of a Jewish race and even, in an unsystematic way, did not question that Semites naturally had certain unpleasant traits. Bebel described these characteristics as "partly in-born" [*eingeborene*] and partly due to environmental influences, which, interestingly, he presented in vaguely social Darwinistic language.[33] Still, the tone of remarks by social democrats was distinctly different from that of the anti-Semites of the day. Jewish or Semitic virtues and vices were considered together, without particular heat or polemical edge, in the context of an underlying assumption that environment was more fundamental than race and that Jews and Gentiles could live in harmony, especially once socialism had triumphed. If it is accepted that anti-Semitism as a significant problem exists when powerful emotional needs are satisfied through negative imagery that blinds one to reality, then these remarks were not significantly anti-Semitic.

It would be too easy, however, to leave the matter at that, for when all allowances are made for context, nuance, and intent, one cannot ignore a more alarming undertone to some of the joking that went on. Jewish socialists were often cruelly hard on other Jews, harder than they were on other religious and ethnic groups. And that cruel harshness connected with a range of negative feelings about Jews and Jewishness, with an implicit conviction that it

---

[31] Peter Gay, *Freud, Jews, and Other Germans* (Oxford, 1978), 15.

[32] Silberner, *Sozialisten*, 204.

[33] Bebel, *Sozialdemokratie*, 8: "nach den darwinischen Anpassungs- und Vererbungsgetzen [ist es] nur natürlich, dass die eigentümlichen Charaktereigenschaften dieser Rasse sich im Laufe der Zeit immer mehr entwickeln und vervollkomnen müssen."

would be better if many Jewish traits would disappear, if not Jews themselves. No doubt few if any Jews had satisfactorily sorted out these ineffably complex feelings, and Gentiles seem rarely even to have made much of an effort in that direction. Some merely spoke of the necessity of eradicating Jewish "ghetto" traits – such as servility, deviousness, clannishness, and fearfulness – without explicitly denying some worth to a larger or broader sense of Jewishness. Others seemed to feel aversion for nearly everything that might be identified as Jewish. Such confused or inchoate feelings colored the positions taken by Jewish socialists concerning a wide range of key issues.

Socialist Interpretations of Anti-Semitism

Once the Berlin Movement had proved itself unable to attract a significant mass following, the social radicalism of other anti-Semites, in particular the "Peasant King," Böckel, posed revealing difficulties for social–democratic theorists. If anti-Semites merely functioned as a front for conservative interests, as many social–democratic theorists maintained, how could one explain the attacks on the Junkers and the capitalists by a number of the anti-Semites of the late 1880s and 1890s? Böckel, in a statement that was given much publicity in the social–democratic press, seemed to be reconsidering the blame he laid on the Jews for the problems of his peasant followers, shifting it instead to the capitalist system, a position, it will be recalled, that Marr, too, finally embraced.

Similar theoretical problems arose in attempting to explain anti-Semitic feelings against poor Jews. Marxist theory viewed hatred of Jews as deriving fundamentally from economic factors; Jews were hated by the lower orders as exploiters or by the Mittelstand as competitors. How, then, to explain the murderous hatred directed at Jews who were themselves poor and exploited, as many certainly were, especially in Russia and in Austrian Galicia? What was the explanation for the barbaric attacks made on the most miserable of Jewish proletarians following the assassination of the tsar in 1881? German social–democratic theorists grappled only feebly with these apparently large inadequacies of Marxist theory. They would come back to haunt socialists in the years that followed.

By the 1890s theoreticians in the SPD, and in other socialist parties as well, arrived at the firm conclusion that anti-Semitism was no threat to the workers' movement. On the contrary, those theoreticians maintained that the new political anti-Semites often did valuable work, since they awakened the more backward and traditionalist elements of the population to the evils of capitalism and, more importantly, to an awareness that those evils could be remedied by political action. Peasants, who at first thought of their economic plight as simply in the nature of things, like floods or drought, and who did not readily oppose established authority, were encouraged by anti-Semitic agitation to assume a more activist stance. Moreover, before long, so Marxist theoreticians reasoned, peasants would come to see that blaming the Jews was both superficial and unfair. Then those peasants would recognize their real enemies. It was not only socialists who reasoned in that way; many liberals and conservatives in Germany feared Böckel and his ilk precisely because he was "awakening" the peasants against the market economy and the unequal distribution of land.

Thus socialists arrived at a position that in retrospect seems both blindly doctrinaire and harmful: They described anti-Semitic agitation as "a source of satisfaction," since it was awakening the masses, doing the work of the social democrats among elements of the population that so far had been stubbornly resistant to socialist propaganda. The earlier sense of urgency and moral indignation in opposing the Berlin Movement subsided, and a more characteristic tone of confident derision came to the fore, one that meshed into the confident expectation by Marxists that capitalist development would ultimately bring socialist revolution. Time and again, socialists dismissed the anti-Semitic movement as "a bundle of contradictions" or "the socialism of fools" (*Sozialismus der dummen Kerls*). Political anti-Semitism had no future, they concluded, since it represented a hodgepodge, the incompatible interests of the Junkers, frightened liberals, Mittelstand, and peasantry. Many socialist leaders urged the party to direct its attentions to more important, more pressing problems; this one would take care of itself.

One can detect here traces of what would later be called the "worse-is-better syndrome" that emerged from Marxist theory. Marx's prediction of proletarian "immiseration" (*Verelendung*), for example, meant that growing misery for the working class was necessary – again, in some paradoxical sense a source of satisfaction – to provoke the revolution. The French Marxist leader Jules Guesde described the "corrosive influence" of Jewish finance as "good" because it was helping to destroy the French peasantry and petty bourgeoisie, both of which had to be undermined before socialism could triumph.[34]

Behind these theoretical ratiocinations lay factors of a more practical and opportunist nature. In most continental countries, certainly in Germany, France, and Austria, socialists viewed the liberal parties as their main enemies. The liberals represented the capitalist party, the party of the bourgeoisie, the party that in Germany had supported Bismarck's Anti-Socialist Laws. At the same time, liberals, especially left–liberals, posed to socialists the most serious immediate competition for the allegiance of the lower orders. Time and again Kautsky emphasized how supremely important it was for Marxists to instill in the minds of their working-class followers the crucial differences between liberalism and socialism, since workers might easily be fooled into accepting liberal ideas or liberal political leadership.

In this sense, too, the rise of political anti-Semitism could be welcomed by

[34] Silberner, *Sozialisten*, 83.

observers like Kautsky; it could be considered a cause for satisfaction, since it so disrupted the ranks of the liberal enemy. It appealed to those classes that liberals hoped to win over to their worldview and to vote for liberal programs. Peasants who once supported liberal candidates in Germany often turned to anti-Semites.[35] In Austria the rise of Karl Lueger's Christian Social Party profoundly undermined the already weakened forces of Austrian liberalism, and in Austria the newly formed social–democratic party naturally took satisfaction in that weakening.

There was an intriguing twist to the Austrian situation: Among the most aggressive and articulate antisocialists were Jews. Jewish liberals typically branded all antiliberalism as anti-Semitic in inspiration and thus lumped antiliberals of a Marxist persuasion with antiliberals of a Christian–social persuasion. There was more than simple opportunism in this stance, for it was a sometimes subtle matter, in a country such as Austria–Hungary, where Jews and liberalism were almost synonymous, to distinguish attacks on liberals from attacks on Jews. On the other hand, it was all too convenient for Jewish liberals to attempt to discredit any attacks on liberal principles and practices as motivated by racial or religious bigotry. Even in Germany, Marxian socialists and anti-Semites were sometimes lumped together by their opponents,[36] a tendency that was in part due to the belief held by the National Liberals that both social democrats and anti-Semites were undermining liberal constituencies, "overturning the comfortable certainties of local politics."[37] But in Austria the assertion that antiliberalism was fueled by anti-Semitism, or indistinguishable from it, was much more pervasive and plausible.

In Austria, however, Jews were very prominent not only in the liberal camp but also in the socialist camp, and Jewish socialist leaders, not surprisingly, deeply resented being denounced as enemies of the Jews. No doubt because it was a family quarrel of a sort, and one within a family that was prone to rhetorical excess, the war of words between Jewish liberals and Jewish socialists in Austria was bitterly abusive. Austrian social democrats often formulated their attacks on capitalism in terms of personal attacks on individual capitalists, and such attacks did at times seem to verge into anti-Semitism. Jewish social democrats in Austria urged their followers not to "discredit themselves" by overwrought opposition to the anti-Semites; the social–democratic movement must above all not be perceived as a tool of the Jews. Most Austrian social democrats of a Jewish background betrayed a notable lack of enthusiasm for public denunciations of anti-Semitism. Their distaste for actively defending

---

[35] Geoff Eley, *Reshaping the German Right: Radical Nationalism and Political Change After Bismarck* (New Haven, Conn., 1980), 19 ff.

[36] Cf. Hannah Arendt, *The Origins of Totalitarianism* (New York, 1963), 38, who mistakenly says that the anti-Semites and the SPD voted together on all major domestic issues.

[37] Eley, *Reshaping*, 24.

Jews – what many of them derisively termed "philo-Semitism" – was more frequently and caustically expressed; they were usually less willing to attack anti-
Semites, and more willing to attack Jews, than were Gentile social democrats.

At the Brussels congress of the Socialist International in 1890 Jewish socialists from the United States presented a resolution that condemned anti-Semitism as inconsistent with socialist convictions. The most stubborn and articulate
opposition to that resolution came from Jews, among whom were Paul Singer,
the popular Berlin Social Democrat, and Friedrich Adler, the leader of the Austrian Social Democratic Party. Adler had been known to remark that the large
number of Jews in the Austrian party was a "burden," one that made it more
difficult to recruit industrial workers, who were overwhelmingly non-Jewish.
The resolution that was finally passed, and the one that set the tone for official
Marxist pronouncements concerning anti-Semitism in following years, emphasized that socialists opposed racism in all forms but added that both "anti-
Semitic and philo-Semitic agitation . . . [represent] maneuvers by which the
capitalist class and reactionary governments try to . . . divide the workers."[38]

Those familiar with the subsequent socialist and communist reaction to the
Nazi movement will see in these prewar judgments and slogans a striking similarity to the argument made in the 1920s and early 1930s that the Nazi Party
represented contradictory interests, ones that could never constitute a successful movement in the long run. Nazism was dismissed as the "death rattle" of
capitalism – its growth, again, a source of satisfaction. Such attitudes to Hitler's
followers proved disastrously mistaken, but the weaknesses of such analyses
were not really evident before 1914. It was logical enough for the leaders of
the SPD to conclude that the anti-Semites posed no serious long-range threat,
since the anti-Semites eventually proved themselves, in measurable political
terms at least, utter failures. On the other hand, the optimism of the socialists
concerning their own future, their boast that "tomorrow is ours!" seemed
wholly justified, since they went from electoral success to success in the generation before World War I. Their enemies seemed to worry about that future as
much as socialists believed in it.

The success of the SPD was not, however, without some troubling aspects
from the standpoint of the future of the movement in general and of Jews
within the party in particular. To look forward for a moment at matters that will
be central to later chapters, tensions within the party grew, especially after the
turn of century. As the party and its associated trade unions expanded, they
became something like a state within the German state, an imposing structure
of newspapers, insurance funds, workers sporting clubs, offices and archives,
officers, and functionaries. The aura of idealism and self-sacrifice of the heroic
1870s and 1880s gave way to a more pragmatic tone, one that shied away
from revolutionary rhetoric and that concentrated on day-to-day reform. Angry

[38] James Joll, *The Second International, 1889–1914* (New York, 1955), 68.

critics on the left of the party denounced these trends as "bureaucratization," "bossism" *(Verbonzung)*, and even "bourgeoisification" *(Verbürgerlichung)*.

The ironies went deeper, for most of these left-wing critics were themselves of bourgeois origin and most of those condemned for bourgeoisification or bossism were of working-class background. Franz Mehring had early on fretted about the mediocrity and cocksure dogmatism of many worker functionaries, especially the leaders at the local level, who took on petty bourgeois airs and manners once they attained a modicum of upward mobility by becoming party bosses. Himself a man of refined aesthetic sensibility and intellectual audacity, Mehring at times experienced feelings of despair and even loathing when having to deal with such men. Their penchant for ill-digested phrases and their insensitivity to historical heritage and cultural nuance at first drove him away from the social–democratic movement.[39]

As Mehring's presence among the party radicals suggests, the confrontation between party bosses and revolutionary activists was not clearly related to Christian or Jewish background. The chief theoretician of reformism, or Revisionism (since it "revised" Marx's revolutionary theories), was the Jew Eduard Bernstein, who eventually found his strongest support among the overwhelmingly non-Jewish party and trade union bosses. Nevertheless, there were at times unmistakable undertones of a Gentile–Jewish conflict in the tensions between social–democratic reformists and revolutionaries, since the percentage of Jews among the latter was high – and remarked upon by many.

Nowhere was this conflict more notable than in the relations of the Jew Rosa Luxemburg, a fiery leader of the party's revolutionary left, and Karl Kautsky, the recognized leading theoretician of the party. At the turn of the century Kautsky and Luxemburg had worked together in combating the Revisionist heresy, but by the second decade of the new century, Kautsky was pushed to second thoughts about Luxemburg. Her ill-disguised sense of superiority and her intolerance irked him. He noted that she was "an extremely talented woman . . . but tact and a feeling of comradeship were completely foreign to her." She in turn found him "heavy, dull, unimaginative, and ponderous."[40]

These words may be considered an almost archetypal Gentile–Jewish confrontation. Kautsky might as well have said "pushy Jew" and Luxemburg "*a goyisher kop.*" To be sure, neither of them expressed their differences as ones based primarily on Jewish–Gentile differences. They would almost certainly have indignantly rejected such an interpretation. Nevertheless, these concerns with "tact" and "comradeship" are unmistakably akin to the concerns expressed by Marr or Treitschke, as well as many others who were not anti-Semites.

Most party and trade union functionaries considered Luxemburg a quarrelsome outsider, a sharp-tongued, disrespectful, impractical troublemaker –

---

[39] Massing, *Rehearsal*, 184–5.

[40] Cf. Gary P. Steenson, *Karl Kautsky, 1854–1938* (Pittsburgh, 1978), 134; Nettl, *Rosa Luxemburg*, 255.

and a foreign, eastern Jew to boot. (She came to the SPD from the Polish revolutionary movement and retained important contacts with it.) Victor Adler
considered her a "poisonous bitch," who was "too clever" (*blitzgescheit*); she
lacked in a sense of responsibility and was driven by "a perverse desire for
self-justification."[41]

It would be hard to deny that her opinions of them, whether privately or
openly expressed, were contemptuous and uncomradely. Similarly, many of
the bureaucrats perceived Luxemburg as a divisive force in the party – yet
another kind of perception that Jews were destructive, full of negative criticism. Of course, those bureaucrats would not have put the matter in that fashion, certainly not in public, nor did it apparently assume major proportions in
their minds. As irritated as Bebel became with "that wretched female's squirts
of poison," he still affirmed that "I wouldn't have the party without her."[42]

Luxemburg, though perceived as a Jewish presence in the SPD, by no
means spoke for most of the Jews in it. Indeed, her bitterest battles seem to
have been with other Jews. The language used against Kautsky and the party
bosses was mild compared with what she used against Karl Radek, for example. Luxemburg, too, was vulnerable to the charge of self-hatred. She had, in
the words of her generally admiring biographer, "no time for self-conscious
Jewishness, either as a pattern of behavior or as basis for personal identity.
One of the first things to annoy her, *chez* Kautsky, was the Jewish atmosphere of
pointless stories and too much food."[43]

Non-Jewish radicals in the party were often also abrasive – Mehring, to cite a
prominent example. But the charge of abrasiveness was more often made
about Jews. Even such an extremely popular and not particularly radical figure
as Paul Singer impressed some non-Jewish leaders as overbearing and strident
in personal contacts. Friedrich Austerlitz, in the Austrian party, was widely recognized as a man of refined literary tastes and impressive journalistic talent, yet
he too repeatedly offended those around him because of the "incredible ruthlessness in his intercourse with his fellows," his "coarse and even violent" manners.[44] The French socialists seem to have been particularly put off by the manners of the central and eastern European socialists of Jewish background.[45]

One must avoid paying too much attention to these reports. Socialists prided
themselves in keeping private preferences separate from public or party stances.
Refined manners and tact were less important in a party of self-consciously anti-
bourgeois socialists than they were in parties that styled themselves bourgeois or
aristocratic. The "end of the honeymoon" imagery used previously to describe
relations between Jews and liberalism does not really apply in the case of Jews

---

[41] Nettl, *Luxemburg*, 291.
[42] Ibid.
[43] Ibid., 860.
[44] Julius Braunthal, *In Search of the Millennium* (London, 1945); cf. Wistrich, *Socialism*, 395.
[45] Cf. Silberner, *Sozialisten*, 71 ff.

and socialism; Jewish and non-Jewish socialists stuck together through thick and thin for most of the twentieth century. There was no real end to their honeymoon, not at least until well after World War II (except of course under Stalin in the 1930s, but even that was not an open or explicit break).

Jewish Socialists and Assimilation

Rosa Luxemburg, like most of the radical revolutionaries in the social–democratic movement, stood well within the ranks of the assimilationists. She had no sympathy for Jewish nationalism or even for separate Jewish contingents within the socialist movement. Jews should participate, she believed, in the context of the major nationalities, as German, Pole, French, or English. Although of eastern European origin, she was nearly as contemptuous of traditionalist Ostjuden as any German–Jewish bourgeois.

The issue of nationalism within the socialist movement was a tangled one, especially when an effort was made to work out a position consistent with international socialist ideals, but it had considerable importance in the relations of Jews and non-Jews. Marx and Engels had not written much of importance or profundity on the matter. Both were inclined to dismiss the nascent nationalities of central and eastern Europe – Slovak, Yugoslav, or Romanian, for example – as "historyless" and thus properly absorbed into the superior "peoples of culture" (Kulturvölker) around them, which was Luxemburg's position. It was, moreover, an opinion widely expressed outside of the ranks of the socialists. John Stuart Mill expressed a common liberal position in observing that it was much more "beneficial" for a Basque or a Breton to become French than to remain a "half-savage relic of past times." A similar reasoning applied, he believed, for someone from Wales or a Scottish Highlander in becoming English. French Jacobins were even more intolerant of the idea that regionalisms or peasant dialects should be revered or preserved.[46]

The first socialist to work out a reasonably systematic treatment of the nationality question was Otto Bauer, a leading figure on the left of the Austrian party and also of Jewish background. His writings on the subject were both broader and deeper than Marx's and Engels's. He took into serious consideration, as they had not, the psychological and social roots of national consciousness. Bauer also stepped beyond the prevalent socialist position of his day, which had defined nationalism in terms of a people's common language, common territory, and diversified economic life. He defined a nation as a "community of character and fate." Unlike many socialists, he did not foresee the disappearance of national distinctiveness under socialism. Indeed, he believed that as the proletariat began to participate fully in a national culture, an even greater variety might result than was the case under bourgeois hegemony.[47]

[46] Norman Stone, *Europe Transformed* (Cambridge, Mass., 1984), 59.

[47] Wistrich, *Socialism*, 305.

Bauer's ideas were not appreciated by those who believed that both the "historyless" peoples of eastern Europe and the Jews should identify themselves with the superior surrounding cultures. The young Josef Stalin, who was a nationalities expert among the Bolsheviks at this time, condemned Bauer's ideas of nationalism as "something mystical, intangible, supernatural."[48] Lenin was concerned that Bauer's ideas would provide ideological support to the Jewish Bund, which had broken away from the Russian Social Democratic Workers' Party. Lenin believed that the Bund's emphasis on Yiddish language and Jewish national culture was divisive and posed a serious obstacle to the progress of the Russian proletariat as a whole. There were many Russian-speaking Jews in the Bolshevik Party, and Lenin welcomed them, but he warned that Jewish separatism served the interests of "the rabbis and the bourgeoisie . . . our enemies."[49]

Even Bauer concluded that Jewish nationalism was not viable – or desirable. Zionist aspirations, he believed, could not be considered fundamentally similar to the nationalism of other awakening national groups. He believed that if the Jewish proletariat (in this case he had primarily the impoverished masses in Galicia in mind) became nationalistic, it would merely encourage the power-hungry rabbis, with their retrograde perspectives. For Bauer, German language and culture represented the realm where Jews could best achieve liberation and progress. The only culture that Jews could call their own, the Yiddish culture of the Ostjuden, he considered vulgar and unoriginal – irremediably inferior. He advised Jewish workers to give up their annoying habits and special dress in order to be more easily accepted by Gentile workers, thus strengthening proletarian solidarity.[50]

Socialists in the late nineteenth century were a diverse group, but the lack of sympathy that most of them felt for Jewish particularism went beyond the assertion that Jewish religion had no role, no mission in modern life. Socialists, with the notable and obvious exception of the Jewish Bund, failed to see much cultural value even in more secular forms of Jewishness. They were inclined to believe that it would be better for all concerned if Judaism, Jews, and various associated phenomena simply disappeared, just as Christianity and bourgeois nationalism should eventually disappear in a world of reason and fraternity. And while they rejected anti-Semitism as well as other ethnic hostilities, they too would have been puzzled by the assertion that real Jews had nothing whatsoever to do with anti-Semitism.

[48] Quoted in Wistrich, *Socialism*, 305.
[49] Ibid., 306.
[50] Cf. Silberner, *Sozialisten*, 242–4.

= 6

Austria–Hungary: Racial Radicalism and Schlamperei

The [Jewish] Viennese press . . . pursued every word that anyone dared to utter against the Jews with the jealous hatred of their god Jehovah into the fourth generation. (Friedrich Austerlitz)

Christians in Austria are being robbed, dominated, and reduced to pariahs by the Jews. (Baron Karl von Vogelsang)

In this period [in Vienna] my eyes were opened to two menaces of which I had previously scarcely known the names, and whose terrible importance for the existence of the German people I certainly did not understand: Marxism and Jewry. (Adolf Hitler[1])

The Polyglot Empire

Adolf Hitler was born and spent his young adulthood in Austria–Hungary, not Germany. It has been argued that the main roots of Nazism are to be found in Austria, and especially in Vienna, rather than in specifically Prussian–German traditions. Political anti-Semitism was undeniably more successful in Austria prior to World War I than in Germany. The man who might be called Austria's most impressive politician in the years immediately before the war, the legendary mayor of Vienna, Karl Lueger, used anti-Semitism as a political device and was admiringly mentioned in *Mein Kampf.* Nevertheless, anti-Semitism in the Austro–Hungarian Empire was an even more sprawling and elusive phenomenon than it was in Germany, and facile conclusions have too often been reached about it.

The United States has been called a polyglot nation, a land of many nationalities, races, and religions, but there were revealing differences between the

---

[1] Adolf Hitler, *Mein Kampf* (Boston, 1971), 21.

United States and the Austro–Hungarian Empire in the late nineteenth century. The many nationalities that thronged into the United States understood that they were going to a foreign land, where they would be expected to learn English and become American. In the Austro–Hungarian Empire, in contrast, most national groups thought of themselves as "at home," and they increasingly fought to assert their independence and distinctiveness.

The empire encompassed a bewildering mosaic of nationalities and ethnic groups – Germans, Italians, Magyars, Poles, Czechs, Slovaks, Romanians, Slovenes, Serbs, Croats, Ukrainians, Ruthenians, and Macedonians – and many of these had problematic connections (Were the Slovenes, Serbs, and Croats really one nationality, the Yugoslavs?). Members of the same nationality did not necessarily speak the same language or follow the same religion. Jews, for example, if they are to be considered a nationality (they were not in Austria–Hungary, not officially at any rate), spoke Yiddish in one area, Magyar in another, German in another. Aggressive German nationalists sometimes had names of Slavic origin. People who felt themselves to be Poles nevertheless at times spoke German better than Polish, a situation that was actually common among Ruthenians (a Ukrainian group, differing from other Ukrainians primarily in their Uniate or Greek Catholic religion).

Various degrees of assimilation into surrounding groups were common. The "historic" peoples, the Germans, Poles, and Magyars, often stood in a position of domination and exploitation over the "historyless," who were typically illiterate peasant peoples (the Slovaks, Ukrainians, Romanians) with a weak or nonexistent aristocracy and bourgeoisie, no written language until modern times, and little consciousness of themselves as a people in the nineteenth-century sense.

How the Jews fit into these categories was the subject of endless discussion, since they had no landed aristocracy or peasantry of any significance, and the nature of their history was not like that of the other historic peoples. They were a majority in no large area, ruled over no state, and had no kings, no generals, no armies, no native land in Europe. Yet, they were also more literate than other peoples and had a highly developed if not quite modern sense of themselves as a separate people in history. Their integration with non-Jews, even in the western part of the empire, was generally less developed than in Germany. In Vienna, where long-time Jewish residents typically left behind all immediately visible or external evidence of their Jewishness, they lived in their own neighborhoods and retained Jewish friends and acquaintances almost exclusively.[2] The various Germanized Slavic minorities also retained cultural traits traceable to their non-German origins.

---

[2] Cf. Marsha L. Rosenblit, *The Jews of Vienna, 1867–1914: Assimilation and Identity* (New York, 1984), 7 ff.; George Clare, *The Last Waltz in Vienna: The Rise and Destruction of a Family, 1842–1942* (New York, 1981), passim.

In such a context, what it meant to be purely Magyar or German was often anything but clear. For Treitschke, speaking from his standpoint of threatened Germanism, Austrian Germans were "unspeakably corrupted by Semitism."[3] He found a growing number of German Austrians, facing as they did the largest population of Jews in Europe outside of the Russian Empire, who ardently agreed with him. (The name "Treitschke," interestingly, is of Slavic origin, as is "Nietzsche"; even in Germany "pure" Germanness was an elusive ideal.)

On the other hand, from the standpoint of Yiddish-speaking Jews, numerous in Galicia and as recent arrivals in Vienna and the other large cities of the empire, German-speaking Jews were *fardaitsht,* germanized – not a compliment, but usually a bitter reproach, relating to stuffy manners, loss of Jewish identity, and even apostasy (which is "death" in traditional terms). Indeed, the derision expressed by Ostjuden for germanized Jews resembled Treitschke's derision for Germans who were influenced by Jews, who were *verjudet,* jewified. Contempt in both cases was mixed with a sense of being threatened.

In this turbulent brew of national, ethnic, and linguistic identities there existed as well an array of religions. Catholics constituted a solid majority of 31 million, joined by 5 million Uniates, out of a total population of 46 million at the turn of the century.[4] There were important minorities of Protestants in Bohemia and in Hungary and of Greek Orthodox along the eastern borders. Explosive religious tensions existed within the ranks of the Christians, even within the ranks of the Catholics. Among Jews hostilities were perhaps the most bitter of all, and not only between the assimilated and traditional; the hasidic followers of various leaders (*rebbes*) quarreled incessantly, sometimes violently.[5]

Lines of political and administrative authority ran through these various national, linguistic, and religious divisions. The Austrian province, or crownland, of Galicia spread into eastern Europe, almost enveloping the Hungarian half of the Dual Monarchy. The Austrian, "western" half of the empire had a curious shape, roughly like a crescent, surrounding the "eastern" Hungarian lands on the north. The Galician cities of Brody and Tarnopol were 500 miles to the east of Vienna. They were also east of Budapest – even east of Warsaw.

Galicia contained the largest population of Jews in Europe outside of the Russian Empire (810,000 or 11 percent of the total population of the area by the turn of the century).[6] It was also the most economically backward, with the largest population of hasidic Jews, of any major area, including the Pale of Settlement. Although Galicia and the small adjoining Duchy of Bukovina

[3] Quoted in Geoffry Field, *Evangelist of Race: The Germanic Vision of Houston Stewart Chamberlain* (New York, 1980), 144.

[4] John W. Boyer, *Political Radicalism in Late Imperial Vienna* (Chicago, 1981), 56.

[5] Liz Harris, "Reporter at Large: the Lubovitcher Hasidim," *The New Yorker,* Sept. 16, 1985, 41–101; Sept. 23, 57–100; Sept. 30, 73–110.

[6] Rosenblit, *Vienna,* 32.

fed Jews in massive numbers into the other areas of the Dual Monarchy, and to the New World, their Jewish population continued to rise, nearly three times as rapidly as the surrounding mostly peasant population.

Galicia might be considered another "pale of settlement," with the difference that the "fence" in Galicia was not a legal one. It existed within the spirits of the Jews themselves. Indeed, the impoverished situation of Jews in Galicia underlines how inadequate it can be to credit tsarist oppression alone for the poverty of Jews inside Russia. Galician Jews, without a comparable political oppression, were at least as poor as the Jews in Russia, probably poorer. Similarly, the feuding among the hasidim, which many assumed to be an outgrowth of oppressive atmosphere of the Old World, continued unabated into the late twentieth century, not only in the United States but also in Israel.

The causes for the poverty of the Galician Jews were many, having to do with the general economic backwardness of the region, with their extraordinary population growth, and with the sometimes ruthless efforts of the various Slavic peoples to counter Jewish economic preeminence by boycotts, credit unions, cooperatives, and the prohibition of Jews in the liquor trade. Traditionalism itself of course presented economic problems for Jews in confronting modern times.

Austria–Hungary: Between Germany and Russia

The unified German Reich of the Hohenzollerns, whatever its insecurities, must be counted as successful – indeed its dynamism was the cause of many of its insecurities, as well as those of its neighbors. Austria–Hungary of the Habsburgs was engaged in a sometimes inept, seemingly hopeless struggle to survive. On the one hand, there were Prussian efficiency and incorruptibility, on the other, Austrian *Schlamperei* (roughly, "slovenliness") and *Protektion* (the often corrupt bureaucratic practice of "looking after" those who have the proper class and ethnic background or political credentials). Bismarck's efforts to make a more integrated nation-state of the Prussian-led Reich encountered much resistance, but the challenge of enhancing the unity of the far-flung lands and diverse peoples ruled by the Habsburgs was incomparably greater.

German national feeling under Bismarck was a source of strength for the new nation-state. Nationalism in the Habsburg lands was a cause of weakness, threatening to tear the multinational empire apart. Germany industrialized rapidly in the latter half of the nineteenth century; per capita income rose markedly. Austria–Hungary's record in those regards was uneven, its overall rate of industrialization much slower. Germans in Bismarck's Reich had trouble enough in shaking off their preindustrial past; Austrians remained more powerfully in the grips of that past, of a time that in Austria was termed *Biedermeier,* when the simplicities and moral certainties of small-town life prevailed.

Bismarck allied with German liberals in the 1860s and 1870s, and liberalism in Germany, even if it was an uncertain and decreasingly popular liberalism, shared with Bismarck the prestige of ruling a victorious, unified, proud Germany and of presiding over Germany's impressive economic growth. The liberal measures introduced in the Austrian Empire in 1860s, on the other hand, were largely a reaction to defeat and were thereby tarnished. German nationalists in Austria who had hoped for a national state of all German-speaking people found themselves excluded by Bismarck from the new German Reich after Austria's humiliating defeat by Prussia in 1866. At the same time the nationalism of the Magyars threatened to tear the Habsburg Monarchy apart. And thus a compromise, or *Ausgleich*, was reached in 1867, one that created a strange and unprecedented entity: the Dual Monarchy, two nation-states in one.

Both halves of the monarchy established liberal states of a sort, with separate constitutions, parliaments, and ministries, united by allegiance to the Habsburg Emperor and common ministries for finance, foreign affairs, and defense. But Germans and Magyars did not constitute a majority even in their respective states. Although German and Magyar were designated as the official languages in each half, numerous minorities existed in each. In a notorious quip, an Austrian leader commented that the Compromise of 1867 meant that the Germans and the Magyars were given the right to deal with "their own barbarians" in their own way, which helps explain why those "barbarians" were increasingly restive in the Dual Monarchy.

Universal male suffrage, introduced by Bismarck with the unification of Germany in 1871, did not come to Austria–Hungary until 1907. The Austrian Emperor personally interfered in the operations of the Reichsrat (the Austrian parliament) and in the Austrian courts of law to an extent that was almost unthinkable for the German Emperor. In other ways, press censorship, for example, Austrian authorities regularly offended liberal ideals. Austrian liberals were even more elitist, more reluctant than liberals in Germany to accept the notion of popular participation in government. Liberals in Austria came to power mainly because of the inadequacies of the old order, not by their own strength, and from the beginning of their period of political power they recognized the necessity of sharing that power in a major way with the imperial bureaucracy.[7]

The Dual Monarchy might suggestively be described as a political form existing, conceptually as well as geographically, between the Bismarckian Reich and the tsarist autocracy. It was incontestably a loser when compared with the most impressive winner in Europe at the time, Germany. On the other hand, it was not quite so terminally ill as many of its detractors imagined, destined to be picked apart like the Turkish Empire. Similarly, Austro–Hungarian autocracy and incompetence were by no means so pervasive as in tsarist Russia.

---

[7] Carl E. Schorske, *Fin-de-Siècle Vienna, Politics and Culture* (New York, 1981), 5 ff.

Austria and Hungary after 1848 enjoyed one large advantage over most countries: an extraordinarily long-lived emperor who, if not particularly intelligent, was conscientious and stable. Franz Joseph, who ruled from 1848 to 1916, was certainly a more effective leader than the four Russian tsars of the same period, in part simply because he was the head of state for such a long time and provided a valuable symbol of stability and of continuity. And whatever their many inadequacies, the institutions of the Habsburg Empire unquestionably served the interests of many of its inhabitants – and won their fidelity, however grudging and ambiguous; the empire has been dubbed "the healthy invalid."[8] The emperor's conviction that such a far-flung empire could never be run according to full-fledged liberal principles, that without a firm hand from above it would disintegrate into quarreling factions, was widely shared.

Liberalism and the Rise of the Jews

These remarks have a special meaning for the situation of Jews of the empire. Franz Joseph, although a stiff ruler who lorded over Europe's most exclusive court and who was firmly tied to the Catholic Church, nevertheless looked upon his Jewish subjects with benevolence, which most of them understood and appreciated. He made a firm decision to promote modernization, and Austria's Jews, or an important minority of them, proved useful in that regard. He considered them "state preserving"; Jews were a people who helped keep the empire together by their devotion to the emperor and by the vital role they played in the economic development of the empire in its struggle to survive in the world of European power politics.

Franz Joseph often expressed his appreciation for the loyalty of "his Jews," as he put it, a loyalty that was often less conspicuous or consistent among his other subjects, whether they were Magyars, Czechs, Poles, or even Germans. Austro–Hungarian Jews, especially the prosperous bourgeoisie, were without question *Kaisertreu* (faithful to the emperor).[9] He decorated prominent Jewish financiers, railway magnates, and press lords – the power elite of Austrian modernization – with many honors, including titles of nobility. Although Jews were only rarely considered *hoffähig* (that is, to be included among the narrow elite that was privileged to appear at court), some of them had his ear in matters of state, and a few even married into prominent noble families of the empire.

Such privileged Jews added their presence to that of the older and more prominent unifying or preserving elements of the Habsburg Empire, such as the nobility, the army, the bureaucracy, the Catholic Church, and of course the emperor himself. In favoring the Jews, Franz Joseph was building upon

[8] Joachim Remak, "The Healthy Invalid: How Doomed the Habsburg Empire?" *Journal of Modern History*, vol. 41, 1969, 127–43.

[9] Arno J. Mayer, *The Persistence of the Old Regime: Europe to the Great War* (New York, 1981), 114.

precedents established by Metternich, the reactionary prime minister of the pre-1848 period, who had invited the Rothschilds to Vienna and obtained titles of nobility for them, among many other honors and privileges.

Jews in Austria–Hungary received full and formal emancipation in 1867, and for important numbers of them the story of rags-to-riches was even more dramatic than in Germany. In Austria–Hungary, moreover, Jews faced fewer obstacles in the way of entry into the government and military than in Germany. By the eve of World War I there were over 3,000 Jewish military officers, out of a total of 27,000.[10] There were even a fair number of Jewish generals and high-ranking diplomats in Austria by 1914, an inconceivable state of affairs in Prussia, where by that time Jews had scarcely penetrated the lower ranks of the officer caste. Jews in Austria–Hungary still faced prejudice and unofficial barriers when entering government service, as did non-Jews who lacked the proper background or connections; the areas of the greatest Jewish success had to do with modern, urban, and industrial life, not government service.

Just as the reforms in Russia under Alexander II were introduced by tsarist decree, so Austrian liberalism was not initially an accomplishment of the bourgeoisie through hard-fought political battles. Liberal reform in Austria was rather ushered in by an element of the aristocracy, both high and low, preserving the heritage of the reforms of the Enlightened despot Joseph II at the end of the eighteenth century. And just as Tsar Alexander II's reforms found enthusiastic response on the part of Russia's Jews, so large numbers of Jews in Austria and in Hungary applauded the new liberal era.

The liberal honeymoon in western Europe had its Austrian and Hungarian versions. In fact, from the beginning of modern times, Austrian authorities did not view Jews with quite the same suspicion as did their counterparts in Russia. Joseph II, in the 1780s, was among the first of Europe's leaders to envisage the civil emancipation of Jews. Similarly, Metternich, in the 1820s and 1830s, although abhorring most of the initiatives taken by Joseph, remained friendly to a certain moneyed Jewish elite and hostile to ethnic and religious bigotry. Austrian aristocrats were even more willing than Junkers like Bismarck to have Jews manage their money, advise them on legal matters, attend to their health – and inevitably be identified with "Jewish" liberal ideas.

The rapid movement of Jews into Vienna, the capital and major city in the western half of the Dual Monarchy, and into Budapest, its counterpart in Hungary, was remarkable. In the latter half of the nineteenth century, Jews in Austria–Hungary did not face significant legal restrictions on their movement, and they streamed out of areas of former Polish rule. In 1860 there were some 6,000 Jews in Vienna; in 1870, 40,000; in 1910 there were over 175,000 – in about two generations an expansion of something like thirty times.[11]

---

[10] Norman Stone, *Europe Transformed, 1878–1919* (London, 1983), 55.

[11] Cf. Rosenblit, *Vienna,* 18; Alexander Whiteside, *The Socialism of Fools: Georg Ritter von Schönerer and Austrian Pan-Germanism* (Berkeley, 1975), 17.

The figures are even more striking for Budapest, which was called "Judapest" by the anti-Semites. In the same period the Jewish population rose to 204,000, which constituted 23 percent of the population, as compared to 9 percent in Vienna. The much-used term "Jewish invasion" was closer to reality in Vienna and Budapest than it was in Berlin, Frankfurt, or Hamburg. Similarly intensifying the sense of a sudden Jewish presence, most Austro–Hungarian Jews migrated to Vienna, Budapest, or Prague, whereas in Germany Jews lived in a number of German cities over a longer period, and the growth in their numbers was less dramatic.[12]

No other ethnic or religious group moved into the cities of the Dual Monarchy as rapidly as the Jews, and few religious minorities were as visible on the streets, because of the characteristic Jewish dress, facial hair, and mannerisms of the most recent immigrants. As elsewhere, Jews moved into certain professional groups to an entirely disproportionate degree. Non-Jews in some occupations were either driven out by competition from Jews or departed of their own volition. The rise of the Jews in Austria–Hungary may well have been the most sudden, impressive rise of Jews in modern history.

The school system was overhauled in the 1850s, and the curriculum emphasized secular science and learning. In that context Jewish students excelled: Many of the great names of science, literature, and scholarship by the end of the century obtained their education in these schools. Even the Catholic clergy among the instructors did not necessarily foster clericalism or feel the need to try to convert their numerous Jewish students. The Piarist fathers, members of a renowned teaching order, were much imbued with the Enlightened spirit of Joseph II's reforms, and Jewish parents with hopes of upward mobility for their children often preferred to send them to such Catholic elementary schools because of the high quality of the secular instruction in them.[13]

These Jewish successes were less widely shared by members of the Gentile lower and lower-middle classes. Similarly, Jews did not become, or long remain, artisans, factory proletarians, or other kinds of manual laborers. Urban Jews were in general upwardly mobile; non-Jews were more often proletarianized – overwhelmed by the forces of modern urban civilization. Tens of thousands of small shops in Vienna went bankrupt in the latter half of the nineteenth century, and thousands of peasant plots in the surrounding countryside were put up for auction. The benefactors of these Gentile misfortunes were frequently Jews.

By the turn of the century, a German–Jewish writer who had moved to Vienna from the German Reich was struck by how much

all public life was dominated by Jews. The banks, the press, the theater, literature, social organizations, all lay in the hands of the Jews. . . . The aristocracy would have

---

[12] Cf. Martin Gilbert, *Jewish History Atlas* (New York, 1976), 77.

[13] Boyer, *Political Radicalism*, 68.

nothing to do with such things. . . . The small number of untitled patrician families imitated the aristocracy; the original upper-middle class had disappeared. . . . The court, the lower-middle class and the Jews gave the city its stamp. And that the Jews, as the most mobile group, kept all the others in continuous motion is, on the whole, not surprising.[14]

Henry Wickham Steed, correspondent for *The Times* of London in Berlin, Rome, and Vienna from 1896 to 1914, and widely recognized as one of the best informed, most penetrating observers of the day, wrote that "among the peoples of Austria–Hungary the Jewish people stands first in importance. . . . Economically, politically, and in point of general influence they are . . . the most significant element in the Monarchy."[15]

The issue of Jewish identity had different nuances than in Germany. The cultural expressions of even the most acculturated of Austro–Hungarian Jews often retained distinctively Jewish qualities. As a recent historian of Viennese Jewry states, "in Vienna, and presumably elsewhere . . . Jews created new patterns of Jewish behavior, which differed from traditional ones but which were nevertheless distinctly Jewish." Moreover, embracing German language and culture by no means meant merging into German–Gentile society. Time and again assimilated Jews themselves referred to the Jews' "stubborn emphasis on racial solidarity." Overwhelmingly they preferred the company of other Jews, a preference that was both matched and reinforced by a Gentile reticence to mix with Jews socially.[16] These preferences were not simply a reflection of anti-Semitism, on the one hand, or Jewish contempt for Gentiles, on the other; there was in both a more positive aspect, centering around what today would be called identity.

It seems reasonable to conclude that any group, even one enjoying wide esteem, that rose as fast as the Jews in Austria–Hungary would have encountered some resentment and hostility. One must ask again, too, whether hostility to Jews was produced *entirely* by Gentile fantasies about Jews rather than by a mixture of accurate and distorted impressions.

German Nationalism and Ethnic Insecurity

Treitschke's charge that German culture had been "unspeakably corrupted by Semitism" in Vienna had some foundation, although an observer less affected by his xenophobic nationalism might have remarked that Viennese German culture was "marvelously stimulated by Semitism," if by "Semitism" one means simply Jewish influence. Although Jews and Gentiles did not

---

[14] Quoted in Robert S. Wistrich, *Socialism and the Jews: The Dialectics of Emancipation in Germany and Austria–Hungary* (East Brunswick, N.J., 1984), 204–5.

[15] Henry Wickham Steed, *The Habsburg Monarchy* (London, 1914), 145.

[16] Rosenblit, *Vienna*, 7–9.

mix socially to any great extent, in the realm of the intellect, in science and the arts, a mutually stimulating contact was made, no doubt one of the most productive in history.

If a man of Treitschke's intellectual sophistication could feel threatened in Berlin and in the German Reich, where the Jewish population was approximately one-fifth as great as that of Austria–Hungary, more widely dispersed geographically, slower in its growth, and distinctly less influential in public and political life, it is hardly surprising that the ethnic insecurity of German-speakers in Austria, especially in Vienna, was more serious. Moreover, German-speaking Austrians had other concerns that intensified their sense of insecurity. The threat from the Slavic nationalities, who were more numerous than the Jews and who were far more often hostile to Germans, was prominent among those concerns.

While Germans were the dominant group in the western part of the empire, they still constituted only around 36 percent of some 28 million inhabitants by the end of the century. They faced other, almost as numerous Slavic minorities (23 percent were Czech, 18 percent Poles, 12 percent Ukrainians and Ruthenians) whose birthrate generally exceeded their own.[17] The sense of separate identity among Austria–Hungary's various nationalities turned ugly as the century progressed. In many of the historically German cities and towns in the western part of the empire, the Czech population edged toward a majority, where there had previously been a secure German majority. The non-Germanic and non-Magyar peoples expressed growing discontent with the terms of the Ausgleich of 1867; they agitated for greater official recognition, wider legal privileges, more autonomy, even political independence. University students became embroiled in violent nationalistic conflicts.

Such agitation was cause for deep concern from Franz Joseph and officials loyal to the Habsburg monarchy, as well as from Germans who sought to preserve the German *Besitzstand,* a term roughly comparable to "status quo" that referred to their long-standing possession of leading positions in the bureaucracy and army and their established economic, political, and cultural strength.

The Jewish component of the above statistics cannot be easily determined, since Jews were not counted as a nationality in Austria–Hungary; they were recognized officially only as a religious community, which was the general practice in western Europe. The chief rabbi of Vienna favored a universalistic form of Judaism, one that adamantly distanced itself from Jewish nationalism. Yiddish was not recognized as an official language in the empire, even though a large percentage of the approximately 800,000 Yiddish-speaking Jews in Galicia could not adequately read, write, or speak any of the official languages, including German. Thus, Jews, whose total population in the Austrian half of the

[17] Wistrich, *Socialism,* 176.

empire was around 1.3 million, 4.7 percent of the population, were required to be counted as members of one of the officially recognized nationalities.

In a typical Austro–Hungarian paradox, most Galician Jews were officially counted as Poles, even though their identity as Polish was at best tenuous. The practice of counting Jews as Poles reflected a historical relationship of cooperation between the Polish nobility and Jewish leaders, but it was also a cynical fiction that helped bolster the control of the Polish nobility in the area. At the time of the Ausgleich, perhaps 10 percent of the Jews in Galicia could actually speak Polish with anything like fluency, and there were vast cultural differences between Jews and ethnic Poles, although toward the end of the century steadily increasing numbers of educated, urban Jews in Galicia did take up Polish language and culture. A small but also growing number of Jews in Bohemia and Moravia, where there was a large Czech population, identified themselves as Czechs. But in general when Jews were free to chose German as their stated nationality, they did so in heavy majorities. Thus, the 36 percent German element of the Austrian population contained an important Jewish contingent, perhaps as much as 500,000 German-speaking Jews out of a total German-speaking population of 10 million by the end of the century.

The reasons that Jews preferred to identify themselves as German were many. Yiddish and German are linguistically close, and thus German was easier for a Yiddish-speaking Jew to use than Polish or Czech. More important, German was the language of government and of commerce. For the ambitious and upwardly mobile, a knowledge of German was essential to respectable middle-class status, to business success, and to employment in government service. Perhaps most important, for Jews who had distanced themselves from traditional Jewish life, German was the language of modern culture, art, science, and literature. German civilization as a whole was perceived as more advanced, more attractive, and, as is often overlooked today, less anti-Semitic than the various forms of Slavic civilization (Czech, Slovak, Polish, Russian, Ukrainian, or South Slav).

Many Austrian Jews identified strongly with the sentiment, one that dated back to the eighteenth century, that German speakers in Austria had a cultural mission as a civilizing and integrating force in a heterogeneous and largely backward population. Just as bearers of French language and culture prided themselves, over the centuries, in bringing a higher civilization to France's provinces and colonies, so German language and culture would accomplish something similar in Austria. The unifying effects of French political institutions, with the blessing of French law, also offered appealing models. After Bismarck's formation of a separate *kleindeutsch* state, significant numbers of German-speakers in Austrian lands concluded that a unified nation-state of all Germans would never be established, and they were inclined to reaffirm their sense of a special German civilizing mission within Austria.

Such notions were of special significance for German-speaking Jews. As Germans, culturally but not racially, they seemed ideally suited to the idea of a multinational empire with a dominant and civilizing German element. And there is no question that in the latter half of the century German-speaking Jews immeasurably increased the prestige of German culture and strengthened the hand of the German-speaking authorities. Jews were generally welcomed by the political establishment, then, not only as contributors to the economic health of the empire but also as allies against the rising tide of Slavic demands. Large and growing numbers of Jews in both Austria and Hungary were educated, articulate, and energetic. Mehring's remarks about Jews in Berlin being an awe-inspiring force held even more truth in Vienna and Budapest.[18]

The Jewish Press and the Crash of 1873

No area of Jewish influence in Austria–Hungary was more important than journalism in terms of spreading German language and culture – with a Jewish nuance. Jewish-owned and -operated newspapers in the empire were even more important than in Germany. The *Neue Freie Presse,* owned by the strongly Germanophile Jew Moritz Benedikt, became an enormously influential journal of international news and liberal opinion. Herzl and Schnitzler were but two of many distinguished authors who wrote for it. Benedikt had contacts in court circles and enjoyed extensive links with Austria's Jewish leaders of finance and industry. "After Moritz Benedikt, the most important man in the realm is Franz Joseph"[19] was a popular witticism. He and his paper were admired by some, feared or detested by others. Nearly all observers regarded him as a man of fierce ambition and easy morals.[20]

Resentment about journalists has characterized most modern societies, and other countries where Jews were less prominent in the press, such as France, Great Britain, and the United States, also saw at times violent resentments concerning modern journalism. The complaints in Austria about Jewish journalists were often quite similar in nature to those in Germany, and, as in Germany, some legitimate basis for those complaints was recognized by those friendly to the Jews as well as by many Jews themselves. The complaint that Jewish journalists were vituperatively critical while remaining hypersensitive to criticism themselves was often expressed in Austria. The social–democratic leader Friedrich Austerlitz, himself an editor and a Jew, complained about "the callow intolerance of the Viennese [Jewish] press."[21] Wickham Steed

---

[18] Wistrich, *Socialism,* 182.

[19] Ernst Pawel, *The Labyrinth of Exile: A Life of Theodore Herzl* (New York, 1989), 115.

[20] Wistrich, *Socialism,* 182.

[21] Ibid., 276.

described the *Neue Freie Presse* as a "journal that embodies in concentrated form and, at times, with demonic force, the least laudable characteristics of Austro–German Jewry." He further observed that

It is owned, edited, and written by Jews, and appeals in the first instance to a distinctly Jewish community of readers, many of whom, like the bulk of its non-Jewish readers, suspect it of aiming constantly at influencing the Stock Exchange. [They] profess disgust at its chronic unfairness . . . and persistent advocacy of its particular conception of Jewish interests.[22]

The stock market crash in 1873, which catalyzed political anti-Semitism in Germany, affected Austria in similar ways, although with some differences: Less than upright practices were more familiar in the Austrian scene and constituted less of a cultural shock. As a recent historian of Austria has commented, "The Viennese press wallowed in venality. Officials played favorites, leaking stories or planting false ones. The 'revolver press' blackmailed prominent persons and businesses by threatening revelations unless compensated."[23] Thus, although the Austrian stock market crash actually preceded the German one, popular indignation in Austria was slower to gather. In both cases Jews were obvious culprits, even more so in Vienna than in Berlin, since Jews in the stock market in Vienna were even more prominent than in Berlin. Glagau could at least recognize that some non-Jews were involved in corrupt schemes; in Vienna, Jews appeared more plausibly to be major culprits. In Austria the capitalist robber barons, to borrow a phrase from the American scene, the railroad-building and factory-owning plunderers of the countryside, the nouveaux riches, those ostensibly responsible for the bankruptcies of artisans and small retailers, the deceivers of the small investor were overwhelmingly made up of Jews, if only because Jews constituted a heavy majority of those involved in such modern economic activities.

Anti-Semitic Ideology

The antiliberal offensive of the years following the market crash found broader and more sustained popular support in Austria than it did in Germany. It also became more thoroughly identified with anti-Semitism. In other countries the new capitalist bourgeoisie was widely criticized for hypocrisy; capitalists everywhere were denounced for hiding greed and corruption behind a mask of moral rectitude. In Austria it was easier and more plausible for critics to categorize such qualities as specifically Jewish because the capitalists and the bourgeoisie were so predominantly Jewish.

[22] Wistrich, *Socialism*, 182–3.
[23] Boyer *Political Radicalism*, 48–49.

As noted in the previous chapter, socialists in Austria regularly encountered accusations in the liberal–Jewish press that they represented the barbarism of the mob, a mortal danger to modern civilization. Such accusations pushed many socialists to furious counterattacks. Members of the Gentile lower-middle class similarly encountered malicious caricatures of themselves in the liberal Jewish press, mockery of the traditional, petty-bourgeois values they cherished, often accompanied by a complete lack of sympathy for their dilemmas and insecurities. Catholic leaders encountered articles by liberal Jews that encouraged anticlerical students, that indeed even incited them to violence.[24]

The famous Viennese journalist Karl Kraus saw in Benedikt's *Neue Freie Presse* the embodiment of unprincipled commercialism, the unscrupulous efforts to manipulate popular opinion, that so troubled many public-spirited observers. It says much about the Austrian scene that Kraus, himself Jewish, was one of the most persistent critics of Jews in Austria. Revealingly, his own style – intransigent, mocking, sophisticated, and supremely witty – was precisely the kind of style that anti-Semites considered typically Jewish. He would at any rate have considered the charge that hostility to Jews was based entirely on Gentile fantasy either ludicrous or incomprehensible. As far as he was concerned, Viennese anti-Semitism was without a doubt the result of justified resentment by Gentiles concerning the outrageous antics of Jewish journalists.

He was by no means alone in that opinion. Friedrich Austerlitz further asserted that the Jewish-owned liberal press was concerned to serve Jewish interests, to cover up misdeeds by Jewish capitalists, and to shower with abuse anyone who criticized Jews. Jewish press supremacy, he later observed, "was a conspiracy in favor of the Jews; the legend of the solidarity of all members of the people of Israel was at that time a reality." Austerlitz granted that in the earlier part of the century, when Jews had been oppressed, criticism of their "eccentricities" was inappropriate, but by the latter half of the nineteenth century, when they dominated so much of public life in Austria and when their activities were so often corrupt, criticism was not only appropriate but the duty of all honest observers, Jews and non-Jews.[25]

The souring of relations in the 1880s between Gentile Germans and German-speaking Jews was paradoxical, in that Jewish–German nationalists often earned a special hatred from the Slavic minorities for being "too German." Such Jews represented the most articulate advocates of German hegemony in the empire; they were known for a particularly contemptuous dismissal of Czech or South Slav claims to cultural equality.[26] Now the leaders of this loud "advance guard" of German supremacy discovered that they had become unacceptable to many Germans as partners in a common struggle against the

---

[24] Wistrich, *Socialism*, 248; Boyer, *Political Radicalism*, 60.

[25] Wistrich, *Socialism*, 276–7.

[26] Cf. Oszkar Jaszi, *The Dissolution of the Habsburg Empire* (Chicago, 1961), 174

Slavs. The notion of racial purity, of Aryan superiority, gained an even stronger hold on parts of the Austrian German-speaking Gentile population than it did in Germany itself. Similarly, in Austria fears about the "destructive mission" of Jews, their alleged tendencies to take over, dominate, and jewify, were even more pervasive.

The notion of a German–Jewish synthesis, advocated by men like Hermann Cohen and favorably viewed by Mommsen in Germany, took on a different appearance in Austria, where Jews were numerically and culturally more powerful. Any synthesis of German and Jewish culture implied a distinctly larger Jewish component, an unacceptable result to many *völkisch* Germans, who seem to have been driven, ostensibly *because* of the elusiveness of what it meant to be a German in the Austrian context, to an almost panicked assertion of the need to preserve the mystical "purity" of their race. They dreaded a loss of identity, a so-major dilution of what it meant to be a German that the word would lose its appeal for them. Feelings of German nationalism in Austria came increasingly to include a call for liberation from Jewish influence, a freeing of the Aryan–German spirit from the destructive inroads of "Semitism."

Radical anti-Semites in Germany, as we have seen, had little success in recruiting among a general population that increasingly supported the existing form of the state and that revered its creator, Bismarck. The Austro–Hungarian state and its principal politicians had fewer admirers in the general population. And the empire lost rather than gained in popularity in the course of the century. Hatred of Jews in Austria–Hungary, much more than in Germany, could link itself to popular movements of reforming zeal and to radical opposition to the form of the state. Anti-Semitism could more plausibly appear in the guise of a noble cause, a movement of humanitarian and progressive concern, against a corrupt and discredited form of government. It was a guise that Böckel had assumed fairly successfully but that had eluded most other anti-Semites in the German Reich. In 1884 Karl Kautsky observed that in Austria "the anti-Semites are now our [the social–democratic movement's] most dangerous opponents, much more dangerous than in Germany, because their appearance is oppositional and democratic, thus appealing to the workers' instincts."[27]

Anti-Semitism in Austria–Hungary also gained wide support among Catholics in ways that did not correspond to the situation in Germany. Austrian Catholics did not share the German Catholic awareness of being a vulnerable minority, with the attendant concern to defend the principle of minority rights. The attitude of Austrian Catholics, especially those in the church hierarchy, was rather one more typical of a group that has long enjoyed power but is losing it and thus exhibits anxious or paranoiac tendencies.

[27] Wistrich, *Socialism*, 227.

For such reasons the underlying issues of the Kulturkampf assumed a different expression in Austria–Hungary. Those in Germany who defended Bismarck's attack on the church did so by stressing the claims of modern civilization against the reactionary designs of the Catholic Church. However exaggerated such claims may have been in Germany, there is little question that in Austria the Catholic Church hierarchy was a defender of reaction, a determined and aggressive opponent of modern secularism. In short, non-Catholics – Jews, Protestants, the nonreligious – faced an active and determined opponent, hardly a figment of their imaginations.

The fears worked both ways, since Catholics feared a takeover of their society by the forces of liberal, secular humanism – also for good reason. In the eyes of many Catholics such a takeover had already begun with the Ausgleich, with the revocation of the preexisting Concordat with Rome, and with the new, liberal constitution, burdened as it was with secular humanist and religiously tolerant aspects, including civil equality for Jews.

The perception by Catholics of a Jewish takeover was accurate in the limited sense that Jews were among the leading proponents and the most visible beneficiaries of liberalism in Austria–Hungary. Jews in Austria–Hungary as elsewhere powerfully forwarded the ideals of secularism. In some countries, such as France and the United States, Jews constituted only a minor contingent of the secularizing forces, but in Austria–Hungary they were unquestionably a major if not the dominant element, only weakly seconded by people of Christian backgrounds.

Above all in Vienna and Budapest, assimilated, secular Jews were for traditional Catholics a formidable and alarming enemy. Jews were very rapidly increasing in numbers, and some were becoming spectacularly rich. They were articulate in ways that made many of their opponents feel the rage of impotence. As far as many Catholics were concerned, Jews were not only taking over modern economic life; they were also taking over the cultural life of the empire.

Catholic Antimodernism and Anti-Semitism

Efforts by Catholic leaders to criticize modern society from a Catholic standpoint assumed many forms, but all of them found in liberal ideology a number of unacceptable tenets. Perhaps most inadmissible was the liberal position concerning individual freedom in the moral arena, the notion that individuals could reject the moral authority of the church and rely on individual reason. Catholic spokesmen similarly found it difficult to accept the liberal ideal of a state that interfered as little as possible in the lives of its citizens, that regulated only minimally their economic relationship, and that left them freedom of choice in religious matters.

Catholic social philosophy retained the sense of state, economy, and society as necessarily dominated by precepts of corporate responsibility and moral injunction. Christian charity could not accept the implications of the liberal assertion that the poor were poor because of their own failings or that the rich were rich because of their moral and intellectual superiority. For such Catholic observers, the liberal conception of the individual and of personal freedom appeared not only contrary to reality but also potentially pernicious. Too much freedom offered grave dangers. It was in fact a position that traditional Jews shared with traditional Catholics.

Stoecker had expressed similar ideas, but his Lutheran form of Christian socialism differed in some regards from the Austrian Catholic form. Both considered the influence of modern, secular Jews to be destructive of Christian values of charity and social responsibility, but Stoecker's ideas were more compatible with German nationalism, whereas in Austria the existence of large numbers of Catholics who were Italians, Poles, Czechs, Magyars, and Germans inevitably reduced the degree to which Catholicism and xenophobic German nationalism could comfortably ally. In this sense the Catholic Church complemented the Habsburg Monarchy; both were universalistic and multinational. The linkage of racism, xenophobic nationalism, and Lutheranism in Germany was also accomplished more easily than a linkage of Catholicism, racism, and xenophobia in Austria. The Catholic Church took a strong stand against racist theories – they were yet another form of threatening modernism – and the most extreme racists in Austria were inclined to be hostile to the Catholic Church.

One might expect, then, that the "state-preserving" Jews and the universalistic Catholic Church would have found at least some sense of common purpose. But for large numbers of Austrian Catholics, Jews became "the enemy," to be vigorously combated, and large numbers of Jews felt similarly about the church. The sophisticated, cosmopolitan, atomistic, and materialistic life of the modern city symbolized a world of evil and moral anarchy – prostitution, corruption, drunkenness, social and economic irresponsibility – for the Church, whereas for secular Jews the church was a repository of bigotry and unreasoning fear of the modern world.

Austrian Catholic antiliberalism flourished under the militant antiliberalism of the papacy in the 1860s. In 1864 Pope Pius IX, who had been initially friendly to liberal principles but who turned bitterly against them after 1848, presented a long list of modern ideas (modern rationalism, science, belief in progress) for condemnation in his *Syllabus of Errors*. In 1870 the doctrine of papal infallibility was proclaimed, further evidence of the church's determined rejection of modern, liberal–rationalist tendencies.

In taking these steps, the pope was evidently influenced by one of the most penetrating Catholic social theorists of the time, Baron Karl von Vogelsang, who was a Prussian-born convert to Catholicism from Protestantism. Vogelsang was born in the same year (1818) as another penetrating and influential social theorist, Karl Marx, but they held revealingly different views about the meaning of modern times. Vogelsang hoped for a return to an idealized past, whereas Marx confidently predicted a transformed, if no less idealized, future. In their descriptions of liberal capitalism, however, they were in agreement: It was a system of unbridled egotism, and they were both inclined to derive anti-Semitic conclusions from that judgment.

Vogelsang was a man of aristocratic tastes and intellectual sophistication who felt genuine sympathy for the poor in modern society. He dreamed of a return to something resembling medieval corporatism, where Christian ideals of justice, love, and solidarity would form the basis of a Christian community. He was not simply a reactionary, however; his Christian socialism sought to address in a realistic fashion those modern trends that he viewed as unalterable.

Vogelsang, like Marx, dismissed as absurd the claims of liberals that laissez-faire capitalism and liberal political institutions were "natural" or somehow eternal in validity. For him they were made by humans and could be changed by them; there were no iron laws of economic development. To this extent, Vogelsang's reasoning was commonplace among conservatives, akin to the more familiar ideas of Disraeli and the Tory Democrats in Great Britain. But Vogelsang further concluded that liberal rules favored Jews, allowing them to prosper extraordinarily and unjustly. Jewish prosperity, he observed, was paralleled by growing misery for the Christian lower orders. And that could hardly be accepted by a Christian as natural to the proper order of things.

Vogelsang lamented that Austria had lost its Christian bearing, had lost sight of the basis in Christian morality for social harmony. The country's indigenous Christian population was being "robbed, dominated, and reduced to pariahs by the Jews." The problem was not only exploitative Jewish capitalists; the "incredibly insolent Jewish press" worked constantly to undermine the moral fabric of society, as did the atheistic Jews at the head of the revolutionary parties.[28]

Vogelsang was not a racist; he welcomed Jewish converts. He believed, however, that unconverted Jews could infect and undermine an entire society if they were allowed to get out of control. And he was persuaded that just such an infected society had come into existence: "If by some miracle," he wrote, "all our 1,400,000 Jews were to be taken from us, it would help us very little, for we ourselves have been infected with the Jewish spirit." The taste for pushing and shoving, the mocking of sacred tradition, the sardonic wit and intellectual arrogance, the sensuality and sexual immorality – these many "Jewish" traits had infected Catholics in Austria and were fatally undermining Christian society.[29]

[28] Ibid., 191.
[29] Ibid.

Vogelsang was willing to grant that capitalism and its associated modern industrial techniques could increase material wealth, but the price paid in moral terms, he believed, was too high. It meant the breakdown of the family, alcoholism, and urban crime; the replacement of quality production by the cheap and shoddy; the swelling ranks of the chronically unemployed; and the bars, cabarets, and prostitutes. Capitalism and liberalism atomized society, destroyed valuable social and economic ties. Vogelsang thus looked to controls over profit making; to laws against usury; to the establishment of compulsory guilds, producers' cooperatives; and to measures that would assure quality control of products, even at the expense of a slower rate of economic growth.

To an instructive degree, the issues that Vogelsang brought up regarding the impact of capitalism in Austria resemble the issues involved in the so-called standard-of-living debate that long preoccupied modern economic historians. One school maintained that the initial stages of industrialization in England saw a decline in the material living standards of workers. An opposing school drew attention to evidence of rising wages, lower death rates, and improved diet. Yet others granted that a certain material improvement occurred, but it exacted a terrible psychological and moral price, destroying traditional family life, encouraging criminality and alcoholism, undermining social solidarity, and generally cheapening the quality if not the material aspects of lower-class life.

The nature of this debate, its emphasis on the ambiguities of modernization, points as well to the profound ambiguity of the suddenly important position of Jews in the public life of Austria–Hungary and indeed in many other countries. Modern secular Jews could be credited with bringing progress, new industrial techniques, scientific discoveries, cultural sophistication, and a new intensity and richness to life in cities like Vienna. They could also be credited with exploitation, corruption, crime, prostitution, alcoholism, social disintegration, and cultural nihilism. Both views had some basis in reality: "Progress" and "corruption" went hand-in-hand in nearly every country, whether or not Jews were present. But which aspect of this reality was "seen" depended upon such matters as the social situation, religious background, and psychological predisposition of the observer.

Anti-Semitism and Humanitarian Idealism: von Schönerer

In spite of much transparently manipulative and insincere rhetoric on the part of anti-Semites in Austria–Hungary, their reformist and humanitarian concerns, like those of Böckel for the Hessian peasants, were often more than mere window dressing. Even the most radically racist of the major anti-Semitic leaders in Austria, Georg Ritter von Schönerer, was apparently sincere, at least insofar as human motives can be measured. Hannah Arendt terms him "sincere beyond doubt" in his concern to protect the German peasants, artisans, and shopkeepers who were threatened by the advent of modern industrialism in Austria.[30] And there is similarly little question that he introduced legislation that helped them.

In the 1870s and early 1880s when von Schönerer began to attract a national following, his determination to defend the underprivileged and exploited generally paralleled those of Vogelsang. However, von Schönerer's humanitarianism was democratic–radical and forward looking rather than reactionary. His political activity was modern in much the same way that Böckel's was. He used new devices and a new language to mobilize a part of the Austrian population against liberalism. The political servility, the respect for established authority that has been described as a principal failing of the educated middle classes in Germany did not characterize von Schönerer and his followers. However, for von Schönerer there was a problem with the radical–democratic notion of "one man, one vote," since his idealized common man was an ordinary member of the German *Volk*, not a Czech or Pole, Italian or Slovene. In order to be consistent as a democratic radical he should have supported universal manhood suffrage; as a German nationalist that path was unattractive for the simple reason that Germans in Austria were not a majority. (Von Schönerer also suffered from a defect common among others on the left: a tendency to idealize the people in the abstract but distrust them in practice.)

One of his preoccupations, and characteristically democratic–radical, was to abolish privilege (aristocratic, monarchical, clerical, or capitalistic). That preoccupation was itself related to the democratic–radical idealization of the small producer, the independent farmer, the artisan, and the shopkeeper – the "solid middle class," or the Mittelstand. From such values emerged as well a suspicion of large concentrations of power or wealth, which in the Austrian context implied not only aristocrats but Jews, most notoriously the Rothschilds. It is revealing, however, that in the initial stages of his intellectual and political development, von Schönerer worked in close association with radical–democratic Jews, most notably Victor Adler and Heinrich Friedjung, both of whom later became social democrats. Hatred of Jews, in other words, does not appear to have been what initially awakened him to political activism. Anti-Semitism came later, but it is again hardly the case that his anti-Semitism was based on little direct familiarity with Jews.

Extreme nationalism, verging into xenophobia, characterized other democratic radicals in the nineteenth century. The Jacobins, not the conservative right, in France were the bellicose and extreme nationalist party until the turn of the century. A narrow and suspicious nationalism characterized Jacksonian democrats as well as the followers of William Cobbett in England, and Cobbett was himself a venomous anti-Semite. Obviously, extreme nationalism verging

---

[30] Hannah Arendt, *The Origins of Totalitarianism* (New York, 1963), 43.

into xenophobia in an area of extensive national mix posed larger problems than had to be faced in England or France. Who were the "foreigners" in Austria – the Czechs, the Poles, the Italians, the Slovenes, the Jews? For von Schönerer and the Pan-German movement that rallied around him the answer was "all are – and especially the Jews." In the beginning of his public activity, in the 1870s, von Schönerer's humanitarian concerns, his struggle against privilege, and his ardent German nationalism found broad support on the extreme left. Jews on the left were also enemies of the Rothschilds, those internationalist supporters of the old aristocracy. Even when von Schönerer attacked liberals in Austria as "power-hungry, obsequious, and jewified," many Jews committed to radical social reform did not object.[31]

In the early 1880s, particularly in the year 1882, the Austro–Hungarian Empire experienced an upsurge of popular hostility to Jews, much exceeding that in Germany, although not as physically violent as in pogrom-afflicted Russia. The so-called *Reformvereine* (reform organizations) brought together rowdy artisans whose economic and social antipathies found expression in a particularly vulgar anti-Semitism: Posters, figurines, and jingles portrayed thick-lipped, large-nosed Jews in various undignified guises, often hanging from gallows. "By the end of 1882, virtually the entire handicraft-worker class had been converted to the idea that anti-Semitism was the answer to its problems."[32]

In some regards von Schönerer was a surprising figure to give leadership to this upsurge. He was a man of respectable background; the "Ritter" in his name was a noble title won by his father for service to the state, as an engineer for the railroads, where, ironically, he had worked closely with the Rothschilds. But the younger von Schönerer, in what might be interpreted as a rebellion against the world of his father, began to use language in attacking the Jews that went much beyond anything so far heard in respectable circles. He spoke in coarse and brutal tones, with violent threats and violent actions.

The Disintegration of Democratic Radicalism

In 1882 German-speaking democratic radicals in Austria met to approve the so-called Linz Program. It expressed a strong attack on privilege and demanded measures from the state to help the poor and vulnerable. It called for democratic suffrage, a progressive income tax, nationalization of the railroads, and old-age pensions. The program offered to the Slavic nationalities the option of accepting German identity or suffering the consequences of being classified as aliens. Considerable debate surrounded the issue of an "Aryan Paragraph," but finally the question of whether Jews could aspire to true German nationality was left undecided.[33]

---

[31] Cf. Whiteside, *Socialism of Fools,* 84.

[32] Ibid., 87.

[33] Ibid., 91–2.

The year 1882 also saw a ritual murder trial in Hungary, followed by brawls and riots when the Jews in question were found innocent by the courts. Von Schönerer gave leadership to efforts to hound Jews out of democratic–radical caucuses, student fraternities, and various other political and social institutions. Jews who had been active in those areas were shocked and incredulous. It required some time for many of them to comprehend that their "Semitic race" disqualified them irremediably in the eyes of people like von Schönerer from becoming "real" Germans. They were informed that no matter how perfectly they spoke German, they remained Jews; their fundamentally Jewish–Semitic character, or essence, forever separated them from German–Aryans.

The various strands of what promised for a short time to be a powerful radical–democratic movement in Austria began to unravel after 1882. The Pan-German movement, led by von Schönerer, assumed an ever more aggressively racist stance. The Austrian Social Democratic Party, officially founded in 1889, rejected that stance and embraced secular universalism. A third major strand moved in the direction of Christian socialism, achieving great success in Vienna under Karl Lueger. The Pan-Germans thus found overriding meaning in race, the social democrats in social class, and the Christian socials in religion. They all continued the democratic–radical practice of denouncing privilege in the various forms it assumed under the Habsburgs, and they retained a concern for the downtrodden, although they each reformulated their definition of what "downtrodden" meant, or where it was most significant.

For a time in the early 1880s von Schönerer captured the attention of the nation, although his movement remained quite small in relation to the major political groupings; even the *Neue Freie Press* described him as the "man of the hour." He established broad and intimate contacts with artisans, peasants, and university students, obviously giving them a message they wanted to hear. It is interesting, however, that von Schönerer had little familiarity with the racist literature of the nineteenth century. His ideas seem, as his biographer puts it, to have been "acquired by the mysterious osmosis through which intellectual abstractions are diffused throughout the non-reading population and become a 'climate of opinion.'"[34]

But it would be facile to describe von Schönerer as infecting the Austrian masses with racist ideas. At most he played upon, intensified, and gave political focus to ideas and feelings that were emerging spontaneously in his own mind as well as in the minds of his followers. He conceivably gave to those ideas a more aggressive leadership than they might otherwise have found. Just as Stoecker in Germany discovered that anti-Semitic speeches were more enthusiastically attended than speeches devoted to Christian charity, so in Vienna von Schönerer was greeted by crowds chanting "it's the Jews' fault!" University students had obviously been formulating racist and anti-Semitic opinions before hearing von Schönerer's speeches. Rather than being seen as

[34] Ibid., 75–6.

causing anti-Semitism, von Schönerer, like Stoecker, Marr, or Treitschke, can be more properly described as responding to it. Similar remarks also hold for von Schönerer's political style and organizational techniques. If, under his leadership, "politics in a new key" had emerged only in Austria, then perhaps he could be credited with a greater personal role. But mass politics, with all its reforming zeal, resentments, vulgarity, and new organizational devices was to be observed throughout western Europe and the United States in this period.

Von Schönerer was nonetheless more intransigently racist than the great mass of people in Austria; his hate-filled paranoia was more extreme, more deeply rooted. Indeed, his dead seriousness in matters having to do with race put him in a problematic relationship with what might be termed a more authentic Austrian character. In that regard, von Schönerer's unbounded admiration for Prussia and Prussian values is revealing, since the great mass of ordinary Austrians certainly did not share that admiration. Similar remarks hold concerning his hatred for the church, an institution that the Austrian masses never rejected in a similarly intransigent or fundamental way, nor were they anywhere near as hostile to the Habsburg dynasty as he was. He could "infect" the Austrian masses only in restricted ways; they did not really become like him however much some of them may have acclaimed him.

It will also not do to describe von Schönerer as more Prussian in spirit than Austrian, for although he made much of his admiration of Prussian traditions, of Bismarck and the Junkers, his own style markedly differed from that of the Prussian elites, with their taste for law and order, for prudent and reserved behavior. By the early 1880s von Schönerer was emphatically shedding many of the beliefs that were part of the cluster of ideas associated with the European left, but he was also distancing himself from certain characteristic beliefs of the traditionalist European right. For him race became a fundamental criterion for all civil rights. His taste for violent language and action, his anti-Catholic paganism, and his fanatical nationalism and anti-Semitism were similarly unacceptable to conservatives, especially Austrian ones. As Carl Schorske has commented, von Schönerer "might have succeeded as a Prussian Junker, but never as an Austrian cavalier. For the Austrian nobiliar tradition demanded a grace, a plasticity, and, one might add, a tolerance for the wrongs and ills of this world that were wholly foreign to von Schönerer's make-up."[35]

In short, von Schönerer's position "no longer fit neatly anywhere into the conventional Austrian political spectrum."[36] If one is to speak of proto-Nazis at this time, von Schönerer is a far more tenable example than Treitschke or Stoecker. Von Schönerer's speeches grew in their wild intemperance. He threatened, intimidated, bullied. He resembled a raging bull, not a traditional European political leader of almost any variety.

---

[35] Schorske, *Vienna*, 1980), 132.

[36] Whiteside, *Socialism of Fools*, 106.

For such reasons, experienced political leaders believed he offered no great threat to those who kept their head. And von Schönerer's fanatical rage *was* self-destructive: It provoked endless factionalism, and his taste for violence soon landed him in trouble. He was repeatedly challenged to duels, and in 1888 after he broke into the editorial offices of an offending Jewish-owned newspaper, he was stripped of his parliamentary immunity and then sentenced to serve a jail term. The Jew in question, who had himself earlier been sentenced to jail for libel against von Schönerer – and had fought a duel with him – happened to be a close friend of Crown Prince Rudolf.[37] With his arrest, von Schönerer also lost his title of nobility. At approximately the same time, he and the Pan-German movement were subject to much ridicule when it became known that Frau von Schönerer had a Jewish great-grandfather.

Von Schönerer's greatest if transient political success was achieved in the debate over whether the Nordbahn railway lines should be nationalized. The stockholders of the Nordbahn were mostly Jews, prominently the Rothschilds. Von Schönerer and his followers attacked the liberals for their support of a renewal of the Nordbahn government contract, asserting that the "Jew newspapers" had sold out to Jewish financial interests. In the parliamentary debates, ardent Schönerites chanted "Down with parliament, down with the Nordbahn Jews, *heil* Schönerer!" In the final compromise settlement, von Schönerer was widely viewed as a victor. The *Neue Freie Press* gave him credit for achieving the "first victory for the [common] people in the history of constitutional Austria."[38]

Such victories, however, were not typical or long-lived. The Pan-Germans were thrown into disarray in the late 1880s and early 1890s, as the authorities arrested many of their leaders. The League to Combat Anti-Semitism, founded in 1891 by the noted pacifist and subsequent (1905) recipient of the Nobel Peace Prize, Bertha von Suttner, attracted a broad Gentile membership, mostly among members of the educated upper bourgeoisie, such as Professor Hermann Nothnagel, but also among nationalist aristocrats who were put off by the vulgarity of the Pan-Germans, the "narrow beer-hall politics of the unshaven," as one of them put it.[39] A number of prominent clergymen and Catholic intellectuals, too, joined the League.[40] These efforts by no means meant the end of political anti-Semitism in Austria, but its beginnings were hardly an unqualifiedly success.

---

[37] Schorske, *Vienna*, 131.

[38] Whiteside, *Socialism of Fools*, 111.

[39] Ibid., 143.

[40] Jacques Kornberg, "Vienna, the 1890s: Jews in the Eyes of their Defenders (The Verein zur Abwehr des Antisemitismus)," *Central European History*, vol. 28, no. 2, 1995, 153–73.

7

France:
Liberty, Equality,
and Fraternity

Jews, vomited from the ghettoes of Europe, are now installed as the masters of the historic houses that evoke the most glorious memories of ancient France. . . . Jews are the most powerful agents of disorder the world has ever seen. (Edouard Drumont)

The Republic has governed in the interest of the Jews. . . . It is . . . the Republic, which by raising Jewish power to new heights . . . has stirred up wishes for revenge. (Arthur Mayer)

Jews are possessed by millenarian dreams inherited from the depths of Asia. . . . In whatever sphere he works the Jew carries with him the taste for destruction, the thirst to dominate, the need to pursue an ideal, whether precise or confused. (Joseph Caillaux)

Behind every fortune lies a crime. (Honoré de Balzac)

The Evolution of French Jewry
in the Nineteenth Century

Just as many readers believe that Hitler picked up his anti-Semitism in Austria, so many will have read that in France occurred the most dramatic and influential outburst of anti-Semitism in a western country in the nineteenth century, in the famous Dreyfus Affair. Yet a comparison of the condition of Jews in the two countries offers some stark contrasts. France had long been unified and after the revolution was the model of a modern nation-state. Whatever the country's many differences of political persuasion, what it meant to be truly French was far clearer than what an Austrian identity entailed, let alone a "pure Austrian" identity. Similarly, France had long been a great nation – *la Grande Nation* – "the" Great Nation, a source of pride for the French, whether monarchists or republicans, capitalists or socialists. Nationalist insecurity, of the sort experienced by Germans, whether in Austria or Germany, was not typical in France.

The French state was unified and highly centralized. There remained many regional differences, from the Bretons in the northwest to the Provençals of the southeast, but these differences were not institutionally part of the state. The language of instruction in all schools was French; it was also used in the law courts, in the army, and in all official proclamations. Less palpably, French national identity was emphatically "unitary," the opposite of the polyglot, multinational identity of Austrians and Hungarians. Jewish identity, which in Austria was forced into awkward choices between Yiddish, German, or Magyar, in France had only one choice. Similarly, what it was to be French in a cultural sense was abundantly clear, and French Jews chose that model overwhelmingly and with relatively little indecision. The residual Jewishness characteristic of German Jews in Austria, their tendency to live in separate social spheres, was far less to be seen in France.

France had been the first European country to award civil equality to Jews, more than seventy years before it was granted to them in Germany and Austria–Hungary. Throughout the early nineteenth century the legal position of Jews in France was widely envied by Jews in other countries. And not only the legal position: In much of central and eastern Europe, the common expression "to live like God in France" summed it up; France was idealized as a secular paradise of polished manners, fine food, intellectual sophistication, and *joie de vivre.*

In the early 1880s the waves of popular hostility that Jews faced in central and eastern Europe had only weak counterparts in France. Throughout the century France was no stranger to popular uprisings or to harsh social and economic conflict. The country experienced a number of bloody episodes, most notably in the revolutionary upheavals of 1848 and again in 1871, but in none of these were Jews prominently attacked as being responsible for France's troubles. Similarly, the Great Depression of the mid-1870s and 1880s had a smaller and less dramatic impact in France than in most of the rest of Europe, and its less serious effects were less often blamed on Jews.

These remarks are not meant to suggest that French Jews faced no hostility in the early and middle years of the century. There was no shortage of French theorists of anti-Semitism and other forms of racism.[1] But scientific racism in these years remained a theory that attracted isolated intellectuals; it did not become part of French political life to the same degree that it did in German-speaking Europe of the 1880s.

---

[1] Cf. Jacob Katz, *From Prejudice to Destruction: Anti-Semitism, 1700–1933* (Cambridge, Mass., 1980), 107–44; Léon Poliakov, *The History of Anti-Semitism,* vol. 3 (New York, 1975).

The transformation of Jews in France into a prosperous bourgeoisie paralleled that in central Europe, but France's significantly smaller Jewish population made the rise of the Jews less noticeable and less threatening. The total population of French Jews, approximately 75,000 toward the end of the century and concentrated largely in Paris and the northeastern departments, grew at a rate that was about the same as the French population as a whole, which stood at 39 million in the 1890s. The percentage of Jews in France toward the end of the century ranged from 0.1 to 0.2 percent of the total population.[2]

France's Jewish population was about one-tenth that of Germany, one-fiftieth that of Austria–Hungary. In Russia's western regions Jews were about one hundred times more numerous in relation to the Gentile population than in France. Had France's Jews by the late nineteenth century wanted to maintain a strictly separate identity – which most certainly did not – such an identity would have been far more difficult than in central and eastern Europe simply because Jews in France were overwhelmed by the sheer numbers of Gentiles.[3]

The allures of assimilation in France and the pressures to conform culturally were greater not only because of the prestige and hospitality of French civilization, as compared with many of the cultures of central and eastern Europe, but also because French cultural style was highly "integral." That is, in France cultural pluralism was firmly discouraged; there was only one "permissible" cultural model. Paris stood as the unquestioned center of French life, not only politically and administratively but in nearly every other sense, and its spirit massively dominated France's cultural life. The belief expounded by influential Americans by the early twentieth century that each immigrant group had a special gift or contribution to make to American culture found few parallels in France. There was similarly almost no talk of cultural synthesis between Jews and the French, comparable to the remarks of Mommsen or Cohen in Germany. Claims such as those made by Graetz that German philosophy and literature owed an overwhelming debt to Jews were simply unthinkable in regard to France.

Insofar as a separate Jewish identity remained for French Jews, it was a most elusive matter. Their internal divisions, along lines of class and political fidelity, appeared to most French Jews to be more significant than divisions they felt in relation to non-Jews. Many contended that there was no Jewish "community" in the way that one could speak of such a community in Germany, Austria–Hungary, or Russia. Similarly, the "solidarity of the Jewish race,"

---

[2] Patrick Gérard, *Les Juifs de France de 1789 à 1860* (Paris, 1976), 105–14; Katz, *Prejudice*, 120.

[3] Cf. Michael Marrus, *The Politics of Assimilation: The French Community at the Time of the Dreyfus Affair* (Oxford, 1970), 29, for further statistics.

emphasized by some Jews and by anti-Semites, was hard to discern in France. One French Jew remarked that although he and his family belonged to Jewish organizations of various sorts, his uncle was "incapable of reciting Kaddish by his father's coffin, as I was myself incapable of reciting it by his. My father, who would have thought it dishonorable to have had me baptized, would have thought it stupid to have me fast at Yom Kippur."[4]

By the fifth and sixth decades of the century French Jews began to enter the liberal professions in impressive numbers. They also began to reach the middle and upper echelons of the government, in smaller absolute numbers than in Austria–Hungary but still disproportionately large in relation to the Jewish population of France. By the 1880s French Jews began to make a widely noted appearance in fashionable circles. One contemporary wrote, "today [1885], the barons of Israel represent luxury . . . charity . . . the arts . . . the smart set . . . fashion's latest style."[5]

Even the military in France enrolled a surprisingly large number of Jewish officers (the figure of 300 was often mentioned by the early 1890s, of whom ten were generals).[6] Indeed, in spite of the reputation of the French army as a haven for right-wing nationalists and monarchists, the Jewish percentage among regular officers was consistently at around 3 percent from the 1860s to the eve of World War I.[7] Jews no doubt encountered prejudice in the ranks of the French military, but such figures suggest that those Jews who desired a career in the French military did not face overwhelming obstacles.

Jews came from eastern Europe to France in small numbers during the 1870s and 1880s. There was a more significant influx of Jews, around 10,000, out of Alsace and Lorraine, mostly to Paris, after those provinces were annexed to Germany in 1871. Resentments were directed at these new arrivals by parts of the Parisian population, but these were Jews who had grown up as French citizens and who were, after all, leaving the newly expanded German Empire in order to remain in France and were less likely to incur resentment than those of foreign origin.

In the early 1890s rising numbers of Jews from eastern Europe began to arrive in Paris, settling in a number of immigrant neighborhoods,[8] but their

---

[4] Quoted in Stephen Wilson, *Ideology and Experience: Anti-Semitism in France at the Time of the Dreyfus Affair* (New Brunswick, N.J., 1982), 695.

[5] Alexandre Hepp, *Paris tout nu* (Paris, 1885), 169; quoted in Eugen Weber, *France: Fin de Siècle* (Cambridge, Mass., 1986), 131.

[6] Jean-Denis Bredin, *The Affair: The Case of Alfred Dreyfus* (New York, 1986), 21.

[7] Doris Bensimon-Donath, *Sociodémographie des Juifs de France et d'Algérie* (Paris, 1976), 166 ff.; Rabi, *Anatomie du Judaisme français* (Paris, 1962), 67; David Cohen, *La Promotion des Juifs en France à l'époque du Second Empire*, vol. II (Aix, 1980), 420; Weber, *France: Fin de Siècle*, 133.

[8] Cf. Nancy L. Green, *The Pletzl of Paris: Jewish Immigrant Workers in the "Belle Epoque"* (New York, 1986).

numbers, not much more than 10,000, were insignificant compared with those arriving in other capitals at the same time. Predictably, most French Jews, those who had been citizens since the revolution, were at least as contemptuous of these "primitive" eastern Europeans as were acculturated Hungarian or German Jews. Charles Péguy, a Catholic man of letters who had many cordial contacts with Jews, commented that anti-Semitic feelings were to be found among three-quarters of the French Jewish upper bourgeoisie, among half of the Jewish middle bourgeoisie, and among one-third of the Jewish petty bourgeoisie.[9]

Julien Benda, a prominent French intellectual of Jewish background, described the eastern Jews as "blind preservers of a set of customs that have lost their meaning." Bernard Lazare, also of Jewish (Sephardic) background, earlier made a distinction between "Jews" (the Ostjuden) and "Israelites" (western, assimilated Jews). He felt nothing in common with the former; they were "predatory Tartars, coarse and dirty. . . . Everywhere, up to the present time, the Jew has been an unsociable being. . . . The Jewish nation is small and miserable . . . demoralized and corrupted by an unjustifiable pride."[10]

Prominent and highly successful French Jews, such as the eminent sociologist Emile Durkheim or the man of letters Daniel Halévy, spoke of the "defects" and "tainted idiosyncrasies" of their "race."[11] When newspapers associated with Jewish organizations began to publish articles that openly celebrated the successes of French Jews, a number of those Jews objected. They wanted recognition as successful French citizens, not specifically as Jews.[12]

In the early part of the nineteenth century, conversions by Jews to Christianity were fairly common in France, as they were in central Europe.[13] But even those French Jews who did not convert to Christianity still typically expressed a sense of relief at being free of the confinements of traditional belief. Halévy wrote, "how happy I am to have left that hell, to have escaped from Judaism."[14] Solomon Reinach similarly complained that "at a time when the progress of science and consciousness has done everything to bring men together, the ritualism of the Jews isolates them. . . . It gives credit to the deceitful idea that the Jews are strangers among nations."[15]

French Jews excelled in the realm of the intellect, a matter of no little significance in a country where intellectuals enjoyed a peculiar prestige. At the

[9] Wilson, *Ideology*, 707.

[10] Quoted in Lazare Prajs, *Péguy et Israël* (Paris, 1970), 48–9; cf. Marrus, *Assimilation*, 61, 170.

[11] Wilson, *Ideology*, 707.

[12] Marrus, *Assimilation*, 122 ff.

[13] Katz, *Prejudice*, 406.

[14] Marrus, *Assimilation*, 40.

[15] Ibid., 60.

lycées (the French elite secondary schools), Jewish students were represented well beyond their relative numbers. One alumnus of the lycées recalled that

the Jewish boys topped the list. They understood all the problems, handed in the best compositions, and collected most of the prizes at the end of the year. There was no vying with them; they were far ahead of us, and even offered to coach us during recreation hours. Math, languages, literature, everything seemed their forte.[16]

The Third Republic and the Jews

From the ruins of the Second Empire the Third Republic emerged uncertainly in the early 1870s. A republican constitution was accepted by the national assembly in 1875, but the republican form of government was at first not popular, especially in the countryside, where monarchist sympathies prevailed. A republic with a conservative constitution was finally acceptable as the form of government that divided the French least. Most monarchists continued to consider the republic a temporary expedient, until the monarchy could be reestablished.

The political struggles of 1871 to 1875 worked themselves out with little reference to the Jews, whose civil equality was not at issue in the debates concerning the new constitution. The upward mobility of French Jews in the 1870s and 1880s continued at a rapid pace, whereas the tendency of Jews in France to identify with what a noted French scholar has termed the "party of movement," as distinguished from the "party of order," became ever more pronounced.[17] In the 1870s and 1880s many French Jews supported the so-called Opportunist party, headed by Léon Gambetta. This support was mostly as advisers and as behind-the-scene financial supporters, not as elected political leaders. As voters their numbers were too small and too scattered to be of real significance, even in Paris, where the largest concentration of Jews in France was to be found (ca. 40,000 of the 70,000 in France as a whole).

Gambetta had been a fiery radical and intransigent nationalist, but in the years following the war he moved toward the political center (thus the term Opportunist). In so doing he earned the gratitude of those who yearned for an end to the unrest of the preceding years. Those Jews who rallied to Gambetta's banners were mostly of the propertied bourgeoisie; they found him attractive in large part because he was an effective opponent of the extreme left, yet he was no reactionary. The French right, traditionalist, monarchist, and Catholic, was perceived by most French Jews as unfriendly to their aspirations, although

---

[16] Quoted in Wilson, *Ideology*, 406.

[17] François Goguel, *La Politique des partis sous la IIIe République* (Paris, 1958).

a few extremely rich Jews, such as the French branch of Rothschilds, moved in monarchist circles, as did a few Jewish artists and intellectuals.

To the dismay of the monarchists, the Third Republic, a mere temporary expedient in their minds, slowly began to win wider popular support. Similarly, republicans gradually displaced the older monarchist and bonapartist cadres in the civil service and government bureaucracy. This displacement entailed a change in social class as well, from aristocrats to bourgeoisie, and in religion, from Catholic to Protestant or nonbeliever – or Jew. Many monarchists in the French civil service retired to their country estates in disgust or disgruntlement.

The Rise of the Jews
and the Dilemmas of Modernism

The growing importance of Jews in the new republican establishment was different in nature from the older connections that Jewish financiers had established with kings and emperors in the earlier part of the century, but as the republic grew in popular support in the late 1870s and early 1880s, its enemies professed to see a connection between the long-standing power of the Rothschilds and that of the newly important Jews among the Opportunists. Anti-Semites warned about the "Jewish Syndicate," a purported clandestine organization that worked behind the cover of the Alliance Israélite Universelle, which had been formed in 1860 to protect and educate Jews outside of France. Enemies of the republic were similarly inclined to see rising Jewish power in terms of a growing foreign influence inside France. Jewish immigrants from Germany were particularly resented, at a time when the new German Reich loomed as a continuing major threat to France.

Fantasies aside, the Rothschilds had undeniably built up an imposing financial empire in France, Germany, Austria, and Great Britain, an empire that was widely discussed by the general public, non-Jewish and Jewish. The spectacular ascent of the French branch and their unmistakable German origin made them a perfect symbol for those who harbored visions of a foreign threat.

The Rothschilds made a near fetish of privacy and secrecy and of keeping their power within the family. But they also eagerly sought out public honors and titles of nobility, much as did Bleichröder in Germany. Their purchase of the Hôtel Talleyrand, overlooking the Place de la Concorde in Paris, was for some French citizens an unbearable symbol of foreign, Jewish money, pushing aside the older, genuinely French elites. The Alliance Israélite Universelle also operated clandestinely at times. The belief of anti-Semites in France about Jewish secretiveness was based on a real secretiveness of some highly placed and influential Jews. What anti-Semites suspected was not so much pure fantasy as a malicious if plausible exaggeration, since solid facts were hard to come by.

The belief by older elites in the rise of the newly moneyed classes was also exaggerated. France's rate of economic growth was more gradual and less disruptive of traditional society than was the case in Germany or the United States. However, this gradual rate of growth entailed another kind of concern. The French began to worry that lacking the economic dynamism of other leading countries, they were being left behind. From its position as the second industrial power in Europe early in the century, France dropped to fourth place, passed by both Germany and Russia on the eve of World War I. Moreover, the deceleration of France's economy in the 1880s (from a 1.6 percent growth rate in the previous decade to 0.6 percent) was due in large part to the ravages of foreign competition, German and American prominently.[18] French population growth also lagged behind nearly all other European countries, finally an even greater source of anxiety than industrial stagnation.

France was rich in natural resources and enjoyed an unusually well-balanced economy, but much of its population continued to live in the countryside and in small towns, remaining attached to premodern, small-scale production, with an emphasis on handicrafts, not factory production. The French typically took pride in quality production – high fashion, perfumes, fine wines, objets d'art – in contrast to the mass-produced goods that were ever more typical of America or Germany. Small towns and villages, independent peasants and artisans rather than industrial cities and proletarianized masses characterized France: The survival of the Third Republic from 1875 to 1914 clearly had something to do with these persisting social and economic realities, for the "little man" in France increasingly supported the republic.

But this was an age in which the little man was everywhere under attack, and the middle and lower-middle classes in France saw many dangers on the horizon. France's defeat by Prussia in 1870–1871 supported the potent symbolism of a rising Germany and a declining France. France's centuries-old antagonist, England, was also outstripping the country in material wealth and military power. Across the seas, the United States represented another kind of vague threat; "americanization" became a dirty word for the French right, and indeed for many cultured Frenchmen.

The Political Crises and Scandals of the 1880s

Those on the right did not believe that the republic could lead France effectively in these threatening times, a belief that was buttressed by a series of scandals in the 1880s. France seemed, in historian Eugen Weber's words, in a state of "endless crisis."[19] One such crisis involved Jews only indirectly but

---

[18] François Caron, *An Economic History of Modern France* (New York, 1979), 105–12.

[19] Weber, *France: Fin de Siècle*, 105 ff.

powerfully nonetheless. From 1879 to 1886 a highly controversial body of leg-islation, known as the Ferry Laws, was introduced. These laws sought to estab-lish secular control over primary education and to expand the scope of that education, consistent with liberal–secularist goals. In removing primary educa-tion from the control of the Catholic Church, the Ferry Laws were designed to help modernize the countryside, liberating the minds of the peasants, so to speak, by providing them with a secular–republican education. Although the excitement over these laws did not quite assume the dimensions of Bismarck's *Kulturkampf,* the issues and political forces involved were broadly similar.

French Jews, like German Jews, generally joined the ranks of those who wanted to remove public education from the control of the Catholic Church. French Catholics were not particularly concerned about the principle of minority rights in education; being Catholic was in their minds an integral part of French identity. In Germany the issue of modernizing education and putting it under state control took on a Lutheran and still a Christian aura, whereas in France the supporters of the Ferry Laws were often vehemently anticlerical. Since many French Jews supported these enemies of organized religion, they could be presented more plausibly as anti-Christian and antireli-gious – again, "destroyers."

French Catholics began to feel besieged under the Third Republic. It was, they believed, increasingly dominated by atheists, secularists, and Jews, all of whom had set out to de-Christianize France. There were elements of exaggera-tion in that belief, but in truth many of the leaders of the Third Republic had explicitly set out to undermine the Catholic Church, which they considered an enemy of progress – which it was. Many traditional Catholics, for their part, regarded the republic as corrupt, quarrelsome, and venal, led by often reck-lessly ambitious politicians – which it was.[20] More disputable, although also cor-responding to reality in a number of documented cases, was the belief of many traditional Catholics that the republic's leaders were in the pay of Jews. A story circulated, of doubtful authenticity but still indicative of what some French Catholics feared, that at a banquet given by the Rothschilds, Gambetta, "heated by wine," had said that "the priest is the past, the Jew is the future."[21] The distin-guished historian of France, D. W. Brogan, has written that by the 1880s

In certain parts of the administration, it was rare to find a practising Catholic in a position of power. A Jewish prefect could, with impunity, observe Passover, but a pre-fect who was openly zealous in the observation of Easter might find himself under violent attack from a paper like the *Lanterne,* whose main stock in trade was anti-cler-ical scurrility and whose editor was a Jew, the great "priest-eater," Eugène Mayer.[22]

[20] Theodore Zeldin, *France, 1848–1945,* vol. I (Oxford, 1973), especially chapter 19, "The Politi-cians of the Third Republic."

[21] Wilson, *Ideology,* 396.

[22] Denis W. Brogan, *The Development of Modern France, 1870–1939,* vol. 1 (New York, 1966), 276.

Jewish testimony of these years speaks of how some French Jews believed the future belonged to them; as a superior people they had a "destiny" to rise, to assume greater power. Non-Jews like Emile Zola or André Gide reported much the same impressions in regard to many Jews they encountered.[23] Leaders of the Alliance Israélite Universelle warned its members against "arrogance," yet still implicitly accepted, often in the social Darwinian language current at the time, the notion of Jewish superiority.[24]

The financial scandals of the 1880s in France undeniably involved Jewish culprits. One of the most famous of those scandals involved the Union générale, a bank that Catholic financiers had established with the explicit goal of allowing Catholic investors to avoid Jewish and Protestant banks. After promising beginnings, the new enterprise collapsed in 1882, ruining many small Catholic investors. It was widely believed that the fledgling bank had been done in by the Rothschilds, with whom it was for a time in fierce competition.[25] Newspapers exploited the issue, and the directors of the bank were quick to blame the Jews in order to cover up their own mismanagement. Few doubted at any rate that the Rothschilds could be ruthless when challenged.[26]

Zola was France's most famous novelist at this time, an enemy of the traditional right. That such a man shared the apprehensions of the period about the rise of Jewish power suggests how much that sort of anti-Jewish suspicion cut across the political spectrum. Even Friedrich Engels was put off by the activities of Jewish financiers in France. He commented, "I begin to understand French anti-Semitism when I see how many Jews of Polish origin and German names intrude themselves everywhere."[27] Lucien Wolf, the Anglo–Jewish activist, famous for his efforts on behalf of Russian Jewry, similarly observed how the "obnoxiousness of [the] Jewish element" of the French bourgeoisie was accentuated by the German origin of a number of its prominent members.[28]

Nascent Political Anti-Semitism: The Boulangists

According to historian Zeev Sternhell, it was with the Boulangist movement of the late 1880s that the "mobilizing power and . . . revolutionary

---

[23] Wilson, *Ideology*, 410.

[24] Marrus, *Assimilation*, 16–17.

[25] Jeannine Verdès-Leroux, *Scandale financier et antisémitisme catholique: le krach de l'Union générale* (Paris, 1969); Brogan, *France*, vol. 1, 171.

[26] Robert Byrnes, *Anti-Semitism in Modern France* (New Brunswick, N.J., 1950), 102, 109.

[27] Quoted in Wistrich, *Socialism*, 34.

[28] Lucien Wolf, *Essays in Jewish History*, ed. Cecil Roth (London, 1934), 449.

force" of popular anti-Semitism in France began to be realized.[29] Undoubtedly, many of those Frenchmen who believed that the republic could never bring France back to unity and glory were inclined to look to a Man on Horseback. A strong-man could heal France's wounds and vanquish the state's enemies. After the revolutions of 1789 and 1848, just such men, Napoleon and then his nephew, Napoleon III, had overthrown the first and second republics and introduced authoritarian regimes. General Boulanger seemed to some to be a possible savior, a new Napoleon.

He had at first been a protégé of the Opportunists and had, as minister of war, introduced a number of well-conceived reforms, including better food, more comfortable barracks, and new weapons. He won a dazzling popularity with the common people through military parades and patriotic speeches that emphasized the need to stand up to the Germans. He attracted workers and shopkeepers who had been up to that point followers of the Radical Party (the republican left), yet he also won the support of wealthy conservatives. In many areas the notables of rural France, who represented an "old-fashioned political style of personal influence and aristocratic prestige,"[30] lost influence in competition with the Boulangists. Although he repeatedly proclaimed his attachment to republican principles, Boulanger secretly accepted funds from the monarchists and the bonapartists. He retained an American political adviser and used "American" methods, or what has been called, in the French terminology of the day, political "burlesque" – songs, poems, broadsheets, raucous demonstrations.[31] Most historians have since termed these methods simply "modern," but some have detected protofascist elements in them. Undoubtedly, in the way that General Boulanger was able, through public pageantry, to put together an improbable alliance of old elites and a volatile, resentful populace, he did resemble Mussolini or Hitler.

Historians have questioned, however, the importance of anti-Semitism in the Boulangist movement.[32] It was rumored that he had promised he would get rid of the many Jewish public officials who had been appointed by Gambetta, if he were to come to power. However, such rumors were almost certainly spread by the anti-Semites in Boulanger's entourage. He was not an anti-Semite and did not disguise his distaste for some of the more prominent French anti-Semites of the day, even though he was willing to accept their sup-

---

29 Zeev Sternhell, "The Roots of Popular Anti-Semitism in the Third Republic," in Frances Malino and Bernard Wasserman, eds., *The Jews in Modern France* (Hanover, N.H., 1985), 103.

30 Patrick H. Hutton, "Popular Boulangism and the Advent of Mass Politics in France," *The Journal of Contemporary History*, vol. 11, 1976, 92; as cited in Michael Burns, *Rural Society and French Politics: Boulangism and the Dreyfus Affair, 1886–1900* (Princeton, N.J., 1984), 59.

31 Ibid., 8.

32 Compare the accounts in Sternhell, "Roots"; Wilson, *Ideology*; Burns, *Rural Society*; and Philip G. Nord, *Paris Shopkeepers and the Politics of Resentment* (Princeton, N.J., 1986).

port.[33] Several Jews were prominent in the Boulangist movement and were the general's personal friends. He never used anti-Semitism as a political device in his campaigns.[34]

Still, there were a number of anti-Semites among leading Boulangists, and many of them would be active in the anti-Semitic movement that emerged out of the Dreyfus Affair a decade later. Their greatest successes, revealingly, both at the time of the Boulangist agitation in 1889–1890 and a decade later were in the Paris region, particularly among the shopkeepers and small merchants of the capital. It was in such strata that the encroachments of economic modernization were particularly apparent. There, too, the threat of modernism in a more general sense was the subject of open discussion and agitation.

From the 1860s on Parisians witnessed extensive changes. Many of the older *quartiers* were demolished in order to build the spacious *grands boulevards* and the new railway stations, themselves potent symbols of modernization. These changes not only forced many center-city residents to the suburbs but also transformed the patterns of economic activity within the city. Department stores (*grands magasins*) became prominent, offering an unwelcome competition to small merchants. Shopkeepers "watched once prosperous businesses wither as, not a hundred feet away, boulevard boutiques and department stores did a booming trade." They believed that "outsiders," non-Parisians, were bringing a ruinous competition to the city. "Foreigners, cosmopolitans and Jews were infiltrating the world of commerce from every side."[35]

The complaints ranged beyond charges of destructive competition. Organizations representing small business drew a picture of an invasion of mass-produced, shoddy merchandise; of a new architecture, inhuman in scale – of which the detested Eiffel Tower came to serve as a symbol – and of faceless crowds in the boulevards. Some even attributed the moral decline of the day to the frenzied atmosphere within the department stores, which encouraged kleptomania and an unhealthy mixing of the sexes. Quality merchandise, hand work, and artistry were being driven from Paris, they claimed. The charm and calm of the old quartiers, the very heart of Paris, could not survive.

Shopkeepers harbored hopes that Boulanger would come to their rescue by introducing legislation that would protect the little man. In the course of the 1880s owners of small businesses had come to feel neglected by the Radical Party, which they had until then supported. At the same time, they began to sense a new hostility to them on the part of the working class, increasingly

[33] Sternhell, "Roots," 104.
[34] Burns, *Rural Society*, 21, 114.
[35] Nord, *Shopkeepers*, 191.

organized into militant trade unions and socialist parties. The Opportunists, to the right of the Radicals, had dismissed the petite bourgeoisie as doomed to disappear from the modern scene. Members of that class thus felt threatened from large-scale production and from organized labor, from above and below.

Yet, it is not justified to dismiss the shopkeepers of Paris as people who were acting irrationally or who were willing to throw themselves into the hands of reactionary demagogues who offered anti-Semitic nostrums. Parisian shopkeepers were undoubtedly attracted to anti-Semitism, but they were not consumed by it. They had been up to this point among the staunchest supporters of the republic and believers in the ideals of the revolution, of liberty, equality, and fraternity. They were reticent to join the ranks of those on the right, whom they had heretofore considered their worst enemies. The Boulangist movement did not present itself to them as reactionary but rather as progressive in important ways. Shopkeepers attacked contemporary economic developments in the progressive language of Radical republicanism: The department stores represented a "new feudalism," a new and dangerous concentration of wealth and power. These monstrosities threatened to ruin the little man, the small property owner who was the mainstay of republican democracy and an egalitarian society. The new factories and the new collectivist organizations of the working class also posed a threat because of their concentration of power, because of the way that they undermined self-sufficiency and independence. Such ideals were as central to American democracy of the time as they were to the republican shopkeepers of Paris.

The old order of kings, nobles, and privileged orders did not much attract these shopkeepers, who continued to believe in an open society, upward mobility, equality before the law, and free, republican institutions. They were unquestionably afflicted by a xenophobic fear of menacing outsiders, but their hostility to Jews was fed not only from xenophobia but also from the Radical hatred of privilege and concentrated power. Jews represented to them the fabulously wealthy and privileged, or the newly rich owners of factories and department stores, ruinous to the little man and threatening to the future of the republic. The parallels with Vienna are remarkable, as are the broader parallels with the Mittelstand in German-speaking Europe as a whole. Still, there were important differences in France.

The völkisch racism of central Europe had relatively little popular appeal for the French. Nor did the charge, again common in central and eastern Europe, that Jews were the inspirers of collectivist socialism gain much credence in France at this time. Eastern European Jews in Paris had begun to make themselves felt as peddlers – unwelcome competitors, to be sure, vulnerable to charges of introducing cheap and shoddy merchandise – but their numbers were still too small to present a major problem. Much the same might be said about Jewish revolutionaries from Russia; they were the subject of suspicion but were not yet numerous enough to cause widespread alarm. All of these issues had potential, but as yet that potential in France was realized less than in central Europe. They had not been effectively tied together and widely propagated through a racist ideology that could make the Rothschilds, the Jewish department store or factory owner, the peddler, and the revolutionary socialist all part of a single threat, the threat of the destructive Jewish race.

These words are not meant to suggest that even in German-speaking central Europe such an ideology had reached a coherent and widely effective form, but the process was further advanced there. Boulangism at first appeared to have potential as such an ideology, but the movement collapsed ignominiously. The anti-Semitic organizations that began to form in the ranks of the Boulangists also fell apart. Boulanger, in exile, committed suicide at the grave of his mistress. The republican establishment, so suddenly threatened by the wave of Boulangist agitation in 1889–1890, breathed a sigh of relief.

Some have seen the Boulangist movement as a rehearsal for the anti-Semitic movement of the late 1890s in France,[36] but others have pointed to important differences between Boulangism and the anti-Dreyfusards, differences in leadership, in following, and in ideology.[37] While a number of Boulangists did become anti-Dreyfusards, a large number also became defenders of Dreyfus. The workers who voted in such surprising numbers for Boulanger in 1889 moved, after the movement collapsed, not to the right but to the left, into the ranks of the socialists. The Parisian shopkeepers, too, by no means moved directly into the camp of the reactionaries.

At any rate, from the standpoint of the Opportunists and their Jewish supporters, the republic had survived another storm. Jews could more confidently reaffirm their long-standing beliefs that anti-Semitism had no staying power in France. Non-Jewish republicans in France, as well, took pride that in their country the backward-looking bigotry of central European racists had failed to gain the support of the French masses.

The Assumptionists

Anti-Jewish, anti-modern feelings were building in other areas, outside Paris, and they found other champions. A rural counteroffensive against the secular republic was under way in these years, one self-consciously distinct from developments in Paris but part of the larger Catholic struggle against modern trends. Combating the Ferry Laws became a special concern of the recently created Assumptionist Order. In addition, its members took upon

---

[36] Zeev Sternhell, *La Droite révolutionnaire, 1885–1914: les Origines françaises du fascisme* (Paris, 1978).

[37] Cf. Nord, *Shopkeepers.*

themselves the special task of struggling against Jewish influence. In a statement that graphically reflected the order's viewpoint, one of its leaders declared that God had allowed the modern church to suffer like Christ himself, "to be betrayed, sold, jeered at, beaten, covered with spittle, and crucified by the Jews."[38]

The Assumptionists published a newspaper, *La Croix* (The Cross), that aggressively forwarded Catholic–traditionalist ideas but that was edited and marketed in a modern way, seeking to reach the Catholic peasant masses by new means.[39] *La Croix* was only one of many newspapers that appeared in France in the 1880s, and many of them propagated anti-Semitic imagery of one sort or another.[40] Particularly in the rural areas of France, Catholics who had not regularly read a newspaper now got their information from *La Croix* much as Hessian peasants began reading the newspapers published by Böckel. The Assumptionists contributed to the tendency of many devout French Catholics in these years to retreat into an intellectual and cultural ghetto. Such tendencies in turn meshed with a resurgent popular fundamentalism among French Catholics of the late nineteenth century. They showed a renewed interest in miracles, prophesies, and relics. This was a time, for example, when the Lourdes cult flourished.[41]

Most Jewish observers in the 1880s were not particularly alarmed over the activities of *La Croix* and the Catholic fundamentalists. French Jews tended to dismiss anti-Semitism, whether religious or racial, as alien to the modern French spirit. Jew-hatred seemed endemic in Russia, and still strong in central Europe, but in France anti-Semitism was harbored only by a few reactionaries, whose numbers and power were dwindling, by a fanatical wing of Catholicism, whose activities were being curbed by the state, or by the ignorant mob, which was gradually disappearing through education and a rising standard of living. Time was on the side of the Jews, and on the side of enlightenment, reason, and justice.

Peasant anti-Semitism had not yet much developed in France. The implication, found in many histories, that the agitation of the Assumptionists played an important role in the Dreyfus Affair, for example, is questionable. The Assumptionists represented a certain provincial mentality of the time, but in Paris they attracted almost no following. More broadly, anti-Semitism among peasants throughout Europe, whether in France or in Russia, remains a relatively ill-understood phenomenon. As a modern racist ideology it had little appeal, or meaning, to peasants.

[38] Quoted in Wilson, *Ideology*, 554.

[39] Pierre Sorlin, *"La Croix" et les juifs (1880–1899): Contribution à l'histoire de l'antisémitisme contemporaine* (Paris, 1967).

[40] Sternhell, *Droite révolutionnaire*, 217.

[41] Wilson, *Ideology*, 557.

Anti-Semitic Ideology and Movement:
Toussenel, Barrès, Drumont

Jew-hatred was relatively weak in France, but there is little question that the ideology of modern anti-Semitism was maturing and becoming attuned to special French sensibilities by the early nineties. The explosive popular appeal of anti-Semitism by the end of the decade, and even more the extent to which anti-Semitic imagery seems to have been accepted by a wide range of educated French citizens by that time, must be understood not only in terms of the economic, social, and religious developments so far mentioned but also in the productions of a number of theorists.

As early as the 1840s a flood of both theoretical and polemical works aimed at exposing the Rothschilds and denouncing all they symbolized had appeared in France. One of these, reprinted in the 1880s, is worth special attention, for it exercised an obvious influence on the most prominent anti-Semites of those years. Alphonse de Toussenel (1803–1855), a follower of Fourier, developed what might be termed an aristocratic and aesthetic – or even environmentalist – variety of socialism. His many books on nature and wildlife enjoyed a great popularity throughout the century; he was called the "Balzac of the natural world." He evoked with considerable power the fear that his beautiful homeland, *la belle France*, was being irreparably spoiled – ravaged by railroads, ugly smoking factories, and characterless industrial cities. Toussenel saw the destruction of pristine nature as primarily the work of foreigners, to a large degree Jews, capitalists and industrialists who had contempt for the common people, no feeling for the land, and no deep roots in the country, and who were consumed by the egoistic pursuit of profit.

In his book *The Jews, Kings of the Epoch* (first published in 1845), Toussenel lamented the role of Jews in France in terms that were based on long-standing or traditional perceptions of Jews, even on Jewish self-perception, dating back to ancient times. He described the Jews as a people who had lost a feeling for the beauties of nature. For thousands of years, he observed, Jews had not worked the land or hunted in the forests. Instead, they had cooped themselves up in dank, airless rooms, poring over talmudic tomes, and in those very works was to be found a fundamental suspicion of the natural world. The livelihood of Jews for thousands of years was similarly not one that involved the world of soil, open air, animals, forests, and mountains. Rather it was an urban world, of money, profit, calculation, and financial enterprise. In modern times Jewish capitalists were ravaging the countryside, polluting the natural world, ruining the honest, hardworking artisan and peasant, all in the service of capital accumulation, greed, and profit. Modern railways, financed by Jews, were violating the pristine fields and pastures; factories were fouling the air.

Toussenel's portrayal of Jews was not based on biological racism but rather on historical–cultural factors. He also bitterly attacked French Protestant capitalists, especially the "foreign" ones based in Geneva. As he put it, even the English and Dutch "who profess the same contempt as does the Jew for the laws of justice and the rights of the workers" were Jews without the name.[42] Similarly, Toussenel was talking about real issues, however questionable his presentation of them, not fantasies. His ideas meshed nicely with those that argued that Aryans were at home in nature, whereas the Semites were unnatural, locked into messianic visions and alien ideals designed to destroy the peoples among whom they lived. Moreover, in combining anticapitalist, antibourgeois themes with those of an aesthetic preference for traditional production of artisans and for the beauties of the precapitalist natural world, Toussenel's writings spoke to both right and left, and contributed to an emerging "new right," or "revolutionary right," in France at the end of the nineteenth century. This kind of aesthetic anti-Semitism would be a key characteristic of that new right.

Maurice Barrès (1862–1923), a novelist and poet, was a leading Boulangist and theorist of the new right. His graceful, lyrical prose earned almost universal admiration and a place in the Académie Française. Some indication of his stature may be gained from the comment in the memoirs of Léon Blum, a literary dandy in the 1890s who would serve as France's first Jewish prime minister in 1936. He wrote that "for me Barrès was not only the master but the guide; we formed a school around him, almost a court." Blum, significantly, approached Barrès at the beginning of the Dreyfus Affair, absolutely certain that his "master" would support Dreyfus. Barrès demurred, saying that the case was too uncertain, and when faced with such uncertainty he relied upon "the national instinct."[43]

Barrès, like Toussenel, is interesting not only because of the subtlety of his intellect but also because his anti-Semitism was focused on real issues and rarely, if ever, partook of the more fantastic ravings of the radical wings of the anti-Semitic movement. Even the racism that came to play an ever larger role in his thought was more cultural–historical than biological or genetic. He was able to have Jewish friends and admirers, like Blum, and even later to conclude, witnessing the patriotism of French Jews during World War I that the Jews could be considered part of the legitimate French family.

The Boulangist excitements helped to interest Barrès in anti-Semitism, which he openly described as attractive because it might bind together left and right, the oppressed lower classes and the privileged upper classes. In Boulangism, he reasoned, was hope for a national reconciliation of a much divided French people. But Barrès linked his sense of the unbridgeable foreignness of Jews with attention to real issues. In complaining, for example, that the numbers of Jews in the republican government "infinitely exceeded"

---

[42] Poliakov, *History of Anti-Semitism*, vol. 3, 371.

[43] Bredin, *Affair*, 197.

what they would have been if proportionate to the Jewish population of France, he was referring to a disproportion that both Jews and philo-Semites openly recognized – indeed, some took pride in it.

Such observers were naturally less willing to accept his claim that Jewish money was regularly used to obtain government appointments and other privileges, and of course they could only angrily reject his charge that the republic was "enslaved" by the "Semites."[44] But the point is not that Barrès's beliefs were free of exaggeration but rather that he was addressing real issues; his vision of Jews in France was not a total fantasy. His ability to speak to the concerns of traditional French citizens regarding the turn that modern French life was taking – how that turn benefited Jews, attached as they were to commerce and industry, but hurt French workers in traditional occupations – built upon undeniably real trends. Factories, railroads, and department stores were of course not uniquely "Semitic" in inspiration or ownership, and neither Toussenel or Barrès claimed that they were. But Jews were disproportionately involved in them and benefited from them more than French people of traditional backgrounds.

Toussenel and Barrès were joined by crude demagogues and men who discovered new careers in anti-Semitism after having failed repeatedly in others. The most famous of them was Edouard Drumont (1844–1917), who in 1886 published *La France juive* (Jewish France). It became a runaway best-seller, going through a hundred printings in one year, over 100,000 copies, and continued to sell well into the twentieth century.[45] It finally outsold Marr's pamphlet of 1879 by a wide margin. It constituted, indeed, one of the best-selling books in the history of French publishing before World War I.

The sudden and enormous popularity of this work, paralleling the rise of the Boulangist movement, would seem to cast doubt on the stubborn optimism of French Jews about their situation in France. It would also seem to indicate that tens of thousands of people in France were ready to move beyond the vague prejudices and disjointed imagery of the past to embrace a modern ideology of anti-Semitism. Yet the meaning of Drumont's success is more difficult to evaluate than might at first seem to be the case. It was a peculiarly French and even more a Parisian phenomenon. If the political anti-Semitism of Germany and Austria was a "socialism of fools," then Drumont's work was even more a product for fools.

In it was a scissors-and-paste anti-Semitism, assembled with almost comical defiance of consistency and judiciousness. *La France juive* was a two-volume work, with many of the trappings of scholarship and learning, but Drumont was not a serious scholar, nor could his scribblings be compared to those of Toussenel, from whom he borrowed amply, or other writers like Barrès and

44 Sternhell, "Roots," 108.
45 Ibid., 35.

Wagner. Drumont's volumes were an ill-digested, credulous, and journalistic compendium. Only one consideration seemed to interest him: to include anything and everything negative that might be said about the Jews, even if one account implicitly contradicted the next. Accounts of ritual murder out of the Middle Ages found their place next to factual examinations of Jewish political and economic power. Drumont borrowed from premodern and modern, right wing and left wing, Catholic and secular, the relatively serious and factual along with the ludicrous and absurd – a potpourri of anti-Semitic anecdotes, legends, rumors, and jokes. One theme was pervasive, almost monomaniacal: the operation of the Jewish Syndicate behind the scenes.

Some observers dismissed Drumont's anti-Semitic writings as lacking in seriousness. Without a doubt many thousands of readers in Paris and in France's major cities, where the overwhelming majority of copies were sold, viewed his pages as little more than light entertainment, a *jeu d'esprit* from which no coherent program in regard to Jews was to be derived. He was widely suspected of being interested in making money through light if outrageous entertainment, by pandering to popular prejudice and the voracious taste for scandal that characterized French journalism of the day. Even sophisticated readers – Jews themselves – seemed to find a curious private delight in this assortment of often bizarre diatribes against the Jews. Doubts about Drumont's sincerity were buttressed by his earlier employment by Jewish publishers: His praise of them, when he was in their pay, was as unbounded as was his vitriol now for Jews in general.[46] The man was a failed literary entrepreneur, many plausibly concluded, and he had at last found something that would sell.

Whatever the truth of these conclusions, it is again obvious that this anti-Semite had extensive contact with Jews. Getting Drumont's measure turns out to be an unexpectedly difficult task. He was a strangely emotional man, shy and lonesome on the one hand, brash and populist on the other, oddly credulous in many areas. He counted among his closest friends and admirers a remarkable range of characters, from semi-criminal brawlers to distinguished artists, writers, and political figures, such as Georges Bernanos (mildly anti-Semitic), Edgar Degas (increasingly inclined to vehement anti-Semitism),[47] Benoit Malon (a labor leader who retained a pre-Marxian hostility to Jews), and Victor Hugo (mildly philo-Semitic).[48] Jean Jaurès, the revered socialist leader and later prominent among the defenders of Alfred Dreyfus, admired Drumont for his uncovering of corruption in the government, and the two for

[46] Frederick Busi, *The Pope of Anti-Semitism: The Career and Legacy of Edouard-Adolphe Drumont* (Lanham, Md., 1986), 35.

[47] Cf. Linda Nochlin, "Degas and the Dreyfus Affair: Portrait of the Artist as an Anti-Semite," in Norman L. Kleeblatt, ed., *The Dreyfus Affair: Art, Truth, and Justice* (Berkeley, Calif., 1987), 96–116.

[48] Bredin, *The Affair,* 554. Cf. also Busi, *Pope of Anti-Semitism.*

a while exchanged compliments.[49] A representative for an organization of shopkeepers in Paris asked, [Who could doubt] "the indisputable good faith of this anti-Semitic polemicist?" His comment came as Drumont was being sued for libel, after he had accused a parliamentary deputy of taking a bribe from the Rothschilds.[50]

Drumont was much admired by the petite bourgeoisie of Paris. Before publishing *La France juive,* he had written *Mon vieux Paris* (My Old Paris). Although not the record-breaking success of the anti-Semitic work, it touched on many of the same points. Its central theme was a lamentation over the passing of the old Paris, its destruction through railroad stations and department stores, faceless crowds, iron and steel – terms that were nearly identical to those that appeared in the journals of the shopkeeper organizations.

For all his meandering and ranting in *La France juive,* Drumont was also concerned about real changes. In his subsequent political and journalistic career, he was quick to deny that he attacked Jews out of religious bigotry. He insisted that he was concerned with real economic and social issues, that it was the Semitic race, not Judaism, that he detested and blamed for France's misfortunes. Drumont intoned, "the dream of the Semite . . . his obsession, has always been to reduce the Aryan to servitude."[51]

If Drumont's writings may be seen both as a sign of the growth of modern anti-Semitism in France and as an important vehicle through which an anti-Semitic ideology was beginning to take roots in French society, one might expect that he would be able to turn his sudden literary success into more concrete directions, into an anti-Semitic movement with a political program. He certainly tried to do so. He became involved in the organization of an anti-Semitic league in 1890, associated with the Boulangists, but it collapsed within a year. When he ran for a parliamentary seat in 1890 he was overwhelmingly defeated.[52]

The cause of these defeats is not entirely clear, but part of the reason seems simply to have been that Drumont lacked talent as a speaker. Still, there were others associated with him whose talents in the street and at the tribune were more notable, without finally achieving much more success in the world of political action. Prominent among them was the Marquis de Morès, a man who rivals von Schönerer as the clearest example of a proto-Nazi in these years. De Morès worked diligently among working-class organizations. In a notorious episode, he accused a Jewish meat firm of selling rotten meat to the army. He was sued and found guilty of libel. Nevertheless, the butchers of la Villette

---

[49] Cf. Harvey Goldberg, *The Life of Jean Jaurès* (Madison, Wisc., 1962), 209 ff.

[50] Nord, *Shopkeepers,* 387.

[51] Wilson, *Ideology,* 509–10.

[52] Busi, *Pope of Anti-Semitism,* 93 ff.

slaughterhouse welcomed this embarrassment of a business competitor. The butchers claimed to be offended by the practice, increasingly present in Paris by the early 1890s, of kosher butchering (*shehita*). They denounced it as unnecessarily cruel. Efforts to get the city authorities to outlaw ritual slaughter did not succeed. In a number of cases the La Villette butchers were reported to have intervened to put animals that were dying according to Jewish ritual practices to a more speedy death.[53] De Morès, at any rate, became a hero to the butchers, and he gradually gathered around him an armed bodyguard of young toughs from La Villette, complete with uniforms and arm bands.

In spite of this devoted following among a part of the Parisian petty bourgeoisie – and it must be said that the La Villette butchers were a distinct subgroup, with their own peculiar traditions – de Morès was only slightly more successful in elections than Drumont. Both lost badly in 1890. However, Drumont's good fortune with *La France juive* encouraged him to establish the newspaper *La Libre parole* (Free Speech), to which de Morès was a frequent contributor. While not quite so lowbrow as the yellow journalism that was growing up throughout Europe and America in these years, Drumont's paper was full of recklessly sensational stories. One frequent charge that caused a particular sensation was that the army was filled with incompetent and even treasonous officers, often Jews.

Drumont showed undeniable talent as a muck-raking journalist, and *La Libre parole* had a field day with the Panama scandal of 1888–1892. Investigation into the activities of the Panama Company revealed widespread bribery of parliamentary officials to assure support of loans to continue work on the Panama Canal, work that had been slowed by endless technical and administrative difficulties. Here was a modern project that involved large sums of French capital and threatened national prestige. The intermediaries between the Panama Company and parliament were almost exclusively Jews, with German names and backgrounds, some of whom tried to blackmail one another. One of those being blackmailed then committed suicide, but not before providing Drumont with a list of members of parliament who had been bribed.[54]

Thousands of small investors lost their savings in the Panama fiasco. "The Panama scandal was a Republican debacle. Over a hundred deputies, senators, ministers, and ex-ministers were implicated in the company's dishonest and demeaning shenanigans."[55] A trial in 1893 was widely believed to be a whitewash. The accused escaped punishment through bribery and behind-the-

---

53 Nord, *Shopkeepers*, 381–2.

54 Byrnes, *Anti-Semitism*, 331; Lavaillant, "La Genèse de l'antisemitisme sous la troisième République," *Revue des études juive*, vol. 53, 1907, 97; cited in Hannah Arendt, *The Origins of Totalitarianism* (New York, 1963), 96.

55 Weber, *France: Fin de Siècle*, 113.

scenes machinations, or so it was widely believed. The Panama scandal seemed almost designed to confirm the long-standing charges of the French right that the republic was in the clutches of corrupt Jews who were bringing dishonor and disaster to France.

A Gathering Storm of Anti-Semitism?

The preceding account of the 1880s and early 1890s would seem to offer much concrete evidence for a gathering storm of anti-Semitic hatred in France on the eve of the Dreyfus Affair. The traditionalist right in France, as well as important elements of the population that had previously voted on the left, felt under attack, and Jews were perceived as prominent among their antagonists. On the other hand, anti-Semitism as a modern political movement was unable to get off the ground, even to the limited degree that it had in Germany and Austria in the same period. Foreign visitors to France, such as Herzl, were impressed with the differences between France and central Europe in terms of the Jewish integration in state and society. French Jews themselves constantly emphasized how little popular appeal anti-Semitism had in France and how much better off French Jews were than the Jews of nearly any other country of the world.

Some even claimed that a significant degree of philo-Semitism existed in France, and there is little question that philo-Semitism played a role in French life. Nineteenth-century admiration of Jews is a large and neglected topic, but mention might be made of such works as Theodore Vibert's *La Race Semitique*,[56] the writings of the already mentioned Péguy, and George Eliot's *Daniel Deronda,* completed in the late 1870s. One author has judged Eliot's work as "probably the most influential novel of the nineteenth century" in terms of its practical effects (in particular, in spreading sympathy for Jews among the British ruling elite).[57] Similarly, as noted, Ernst Renan began to make philo-Semitic pronouncements in the 1890s, partly to counter what he realized were the ugly uses being made of his earlier writings.

The "gathering storm" of anti-Semitic agitation in the late 1880s and early 1890s in France remained mostly moderate in tone, moderate in the sense that violence was condemned and the rights of Jews as citizens and human beings recognized. Nearly all French anti-Semites argued that immigration into France by Jews should be limited by law, hardly a radical proposal. The notion of somehow controlling those Jews already in France also found support. Léon Daudet, a prominent monarchist anti-Semite and friend of Drumont, stated the matter as follows:

---

[56] Wilson, *Ideology,* 464.
[57] Paul Johnson, *A History of the Jews* (New York, 1987), 378.

Kept under close surveillance by a power as clear-sighted as the monarchy, the Jews would be tolerable and almost acceptable. . . . To persecute Israel would be unwise and odious. But to lay down guidelines limiting Jewish activity, particularly in the political sphere, would be a good thing, and a benefit that the Jews themselves would quickly appreciate. . . . Many intelligent and prudent Jews are beginning themselves to feel the need for order, for an order which puts them cordially but firmly in their place.[58]

Writers for the Assumptionists called for a prohibition of Jews in the army, in the financial world, in education, and in the courts of law, areas where they would be "in command of Christians." But those same writers concluded that once such measures were in place, "let us leave the Jews alone and not persecute them as in the Middle Ages." Charles Maurras, along with Barrès one of France's leading right-wing intellectuals, wrote in 1898, at the height of the Dreyfus Affair, that "care should be taken not to pass a law against the Jews which persecutes them, that is to say, which injures them as human beings."[59]

The tone in these pronouncements was the prevalent one, as we have seen, nearly everywhere in Europe at this time. In Germany, Austria, and France proposals of a more radical nature were certainly made. On occasion Drumont launched into tirades that described Jews as vermin that should be exterminated,[60] but such outbursts were widely condemned. Inflated rhetoric, at any rate, was by no means the exclusive preserve of the anti-Semites; workers on strike in France referred to employers as "lice" and coined slogans that called for putting them to death.[61] People without power typically resort to verbal excess, to calls for violence that do not necessarily reflect genuinely violent intent.

Suggestions that violent action be taken against Jews found a much less general acceptance than the more moderate proposals already mentioned, and even they seem to have had distinctly limited appeal. Legislation to deprive Jews of civil equality had not the remotest chance of being passed in the French parliament. The idea of expelling the Jews was widely rejected as impractical, quite aside from humanitarian considerations. Suggestions that heavy taxation should be levied on large concentrations of Jewish wealth were often made but also consistently rejected, since they were seen as an attack on property, smacking of socialism.

There was nothing like a consensus about what should be done about the problem of French Jews, even among the small minority that believed there was a problem in need of political remedy. The political situation in France might be usefully presented in terms of two large, opposing clusters: one that

[58] Wilson, *Ideology,* 672–3.

[59] Ibid., 673, 679.

[60] Busi, *Pope of Anti-Semitism,* 97.

[61] Cf. Susanna Barrows, *Distorting Mirrors: Visions of the Crowd in Late Nineteenth-Century France* (New Haven, Conn., 1981), 193.

was republican, secular, left wing, modernist, and on balance friendly to modern Jews (the previously mentioned party of movement) and another that was monarchist, Catholic, right wing, antimodernist, and thus not friendly to Jews (the party of order). The word "cluster" is chosen because these were anything but clear and consistent positions. Individuals moved from one cluster to another or, more typically, felt themselves drawn in different directions simultaneously. One of the reasons that the Dreyfus Affair is of such interest is that it exerted powerful pressure on these clusters to shape up, to become internally more consistent and ideologically coherent. The French were obliged to decide where their most fundamental commitments lay. It was an arduous process, producing many surprises.

Before the outbreak of the Dreyfus Affair, a tragic event occurred that in retrospect underlines the indeterminacy of developments in France and that further puts into question the notion of a gathering storm of anti-Semitism. The articles in Drumont's *La Libre parole* about treasonous activities in the army, with direct accusations of Jewish officers, led to a number of duels. In 1892, the Marquis de Mores, who had written a number of the articles, was challenged by a Jewish officer, Captain Armand Mayer, and in the ensuing duel the young Jewish officer was mortally wounded.

By 1892 the anti-Semitic movement was in disarray, and Captain Mayer's death further discredited it. The French public reacted with revulsion. Denunciations poured out from nearly all quarters against Drumont, de Mores, *La Libre parole,* and the anti-Semitism they had cultivated. Commentator after commentator, of widely different persuasions, lamented that officers of the French army should be subjected to aspersions by low scandal mongers and thugs like Drumont and de Mores. Even Drumont and de Mores appeared contrite: Drumont openly regretted that "such an honorable man" was not able to shed his blood in defense of France, and de Mores joined in expressing his regret over the death of "this honorable man."[62]

A great funeral cortège was arranged for Captain Mayer, attended by the largest crowd that Paris had seen since the death of Gambetta, a decade before. The grand rabbi of France, Zadoc Kahn, eloquently addressed those assembled at the grave. It appeared that the whole French nation was being led in heartfelt mourning by a rabbi over the death of a Jewish officer of the French Army at the hands of a universally detested anti-Semite. It seemed a final nail in the coffin of a dying anti-Semitic movement in France.

French Jews felt, in this great outpouring of sympathy, yet further evidence in support of their trust in the decency of the average Frenchman, in what the grand rabbi termed "the unifying force of French opinion." Even more, French Jews were inclined to view the army, in whose ranks Captain Mayer had

---

[62] Ernst Pawel, *The Labyrinth of Exile: A Life of Theodor Herzl* (London, 1990), 169–70.

proudly served, as a "magnificent example of toleration." It was a "single family" of French, Jews and non-Jews, again in the widely applauded words of the grand rabbi.[63]

At this same period, that is, the early 1890s, Jews in Germany and Austria were finding themselves excluded from fraternities and social clubs; they were dropping away from leadership positions of the liberal parties; and they were encountering a rising racist fanaticism in the Pan-German movements. Of course, at no time, even in the earlier liberal period, had German Jews entered into the military, the judiciary, and other high government offices as had Jews in France. If someone had described the Prussian military establishment as a single family with the rest of the nation, or as magnificently tolerant, he would have been considered a lunatic. French Jews did indeed appear to be living in a significantly different world and one steadily, in spite of some unpleasant contretemps, changing in their favor.

That impression was further reinforced by the parliamentary elections of 1893, which were believed to register a final, definitive victory of the Opportunist republic over the antirepublican and anti-Semitic reactionaries. Only seventy-six candidates of the right were elected. Four years earlier, the conservatives and Boulangists had won 210 seats in the assembly. The governing coalition of prorepublican parties, after the elections of 1893, constituted approximately 280 deputies, a coalition that was becoming more anxious about the extreme left than the extreme right, since the 1893 elections had also seen a dramatic increase in votes for the socialists (from 90,000 in 1889 to 600,000). The socialists now counted 50 deputies, while the Radicals (immediately to the right of the socialists) counted 143.[64] The long-range leftward drift of French politics since the mid-1870s continued, while the drift in Germany, Austria–Hungary, and Russia from the 1870s to the 1890s seemed more to the right.

Whatever the contrasting potentials of the situation in France, toward greater hostility to Jews or away from it, we know that another historical accident, the arrest of Alfred Dreyfus, suddenly tapped the potential toward an increase in openly expressed anti-Semitic hatred. "What might have been" should not be ignored, but "what was" must draw our attention, for the events following Dreyfus's arrest seemed to change everything, to put all earlier confidence and optimism of French Jews into question.

The Dreyfus Affair

Few trials in modern history have evoked such passionate attention as the trial of Alfred Dreyfus, a French officer who was accused in the autumn of 1894 of passing military secrets to the Germans. The trial evolved over the

---

[63] Marrus, *Assimilation,* 197–201.

[64] Statistics from Bredin, *Affair,* 39.

course of around four years into an "affair," engaging a wide spectrum of French society. On one side were the Dreyfusards, who believed that Alfred had been framed by a reactionary clique in the army high command. On the other were the anti-Dreyfusards, who believed him guilty and who considered his defenders to be in the pay of the Jewish Syndicate. The issues finally ranged far beyond his innocence or guilt. His arrest and ensuing trial galvanized and altered the nature of the right and left in France. For the right, Dreyfus the traitor came to symbolize the dangers of allowing "aliens" to gain high position in the French state. For the left, he came to represent a victim of the intrigues of the church and military; his cause became synonymous with the cause of truth and justice. In retrospect, one can see how both sides tended to demonize the other and to assume things for which there was slim evidence.[65]

For the purposes of this study two of the more interesting aspects of the affair have to do with the role of anti-Semitism in Dreyfus's arrest and with how much the idiosyncrasies of his personality conditioned the extraordinary turn of events between the fall of 1894 and 1898–1899. Although the Dreyfus Affair has become strongly linked in most accounts with the rise of modern anti-Semitism, the evidence points persuasively to the conclusion that it was not his Jewish origin that explains his arrest or conviction. Anti-Semitism certainly flared up *as a result* of that arrest and conviction – and even more potently when it appeared that his conviction might be overturned – but those are separate issues. His arresting officers thought him guilty and were sure they had the proof. A few of the arresting officers, suspecting at some point that an error had been made, did not have the courage to recognize it publicly; trying then to conceal that error, they became entangled in a web of deception, concocting stories about how the security of the nation would be deeply threatened by further investigation of the case, and reinforcing the sense that a conspiracy had been there from the beginning.

Alfred Dreyfus was an awkward and distant man, with few friends or admirers in the military before his arrest. Most of those who worked with him dismissed him as a graceless and pretentious parvenu, forever bragging about his money and success with women. No doubt some of them were inclined to dislike him because of his Jewish origins, but again there is little evidence that such feelings were decisive. There were many Jews in the French military by the 1890s, and unfair treatment of them was not condoned. Indeed, as already suggested, French Jews in general were inclined to think that equality of opportunity and fair treatment characterized the military career in France more than they did in many other careers.

---

[65] For a more extensive examination of ambiguities of the Affair, see Albert S. Lindemann, *The Jew Accused: Three Anti-Semitic Affairs, Dreyfus, Beilis, Frank, 1894–1915* (Cambridge, U.K., and New York, 1991).

It seems entirely possible that a man of different qualities, more affable, less stiff, reclusive, and haughty, would not have been arrested or convicted, a conclusion Dreyfus himself eventually reached. The issue of the role of personality in this case resembles and may appear to contradict a point made in previous chapters, where doubt was expressed that individuals like von Treitschke or Stoecker can be considered primarily responsible for the upsurge in Jew-hatred by the late 1870s and early 1880s. The question of Dreyfus's personality, however, is fundamentally different. His intellectual influence is not the issue. Rather, it is that certain of his personal traits made it easier for others to reach false conclusions about his guilt, and those false conclusions eventually had enormous repercussions.

These unorthodox judgments about the case may be joined with a number of others, implicit above. The eventual outcome of the Dreyfus Affair – that is, Alfred's exoneration – has often been described as representing the triumph of truth and justice over lies and bigotry. That is too simple. Both sides in fact played fast and easy with the truth – even with the facts as they knew them. Emile Zola's famous manifesto, *J'accuse!*, denouncing the arrest and conviction of Dreyfus, which has been seen as one of the most courageous and dramatic political tracts of modern times, nonetheless contained a number of reckless and false accusations, which were guesses on Zola's part, and he knew he could not prove them. Moreover, Zola, who became famous among Jews as a virtuous Gentile, a man willing to stand up and defend the Jews, had earlier written vicious things about them in his novels. Like many French intellectuals, right and left, Zola was alarmed by the rapid rise of Jews in France. His main concern in composing *J'accuse!* was not to express sympathy for Jews, or even to fight for justice on their behalf; it was rather to counter what he believed were reactionary, Jesuit, and militarist conspiracies, concerning which he harbored fantasies that were strikingly akin to those harbored by Drumont in regard to the Jewish Syndicate. Others who rallied to Dreyfus's cause did so at least as much because of the political mileage they perceived as out of an attachment to justice.

As the Dreyfus case developed into a major affair by the fall of 1898, France – or, more accurately, significant parts of the country's intellectual and political elites – divided into warring camps. Drumont's newspaper, *La Libre parole*, fanned the fires from the beginning: He had been handed an opportunity to overcome his discredit over the duel between de Morès and Captain Mayer, and he jumped at the chance. He solemnly warned his readers that Dreyfus, rich Jew that he was, would finally escape punishment, even though he had "admitted everything." The Panama scandal was still fresh in the public's mind, and a large number of observers expressed concern that a rich man like Dreyfus might also escape justice. Long before Dreyfus's official trial, he was tried and convicted in the popular press, often on the basis of rumor, conjecture, and misinformation. Those few who urged that judgment should be suspended until adequate and reliable evidence could be obtained were drowned out by those who were vehemently convinced of Dreyfus's guilt.

Through its ineffably complex twists and turns, the Dreyfus Affair witnessed some interesting shifts of mood, opinion, and political alliance. Symptomatic was the change in Jaurès. He initially called for the death penalty, adding a number of anti-Semitic remarks and complaining that Dreyfus was getting special treatment because of his wealth. But as evidence of Dreyfus's innocence multiplied, Jaurès abandoned his earlier hostility. In a more general way, socialists in France began a transformation of attitude, believing Jews to be victims – in the same situation, then, as the proletariat – rather than capitalist exploiters. Similarly, Jews in France increasingly entertained the notion that the socialists, rather than being the voice of the mob, might prove to be among the most reliable defenders of Jewish and human rights. These were only trends, not sudden shifts, but they were significant nonetheless.

These larger political and social changes should not obscure the irreducible role of personality in the case, however. Perhaps even more decisive to the eventual outcome of the Affair than Dreyfus's personality was that of Georges Picquart, head of Military Intelligence. Although anti-Semitic himself and contemptuous of the entire Dreyfus family (including Alfred's brother, Mathieu, who worked tirelessly for Alfred's exoneration), Picquart uncovered evidence of Dreyfus's innocence and persisted, against pressure by his superiors, in seeing to it that the case was reconsidered. Picquart prevailed, eventually becoming minister of war – in the same year (1906) that saw an impressive electoral victory for the Dreyfusard left. The republican left, finding a rallying point in the Dreyfusard movement, proved after all to be much more powerful than the anti-Semitic, antirepublican, anti-Dreyfusard right.

What may be termed an ultimate sign of success was that the mob, that is, those members of society prone to violence and vandalism on the streets, which had rallied to the anti-Dreyfusards in 1898, had begun to attack and abuse those same anti-Dreyfusards in the latter stages of the Affair.[66] Another sign of "success" was that the Dreyfusards were willing to use the force of public opinion, now on their side, to exert improper pressure on judicial authorities.[67] In years to come that victory of the left in France, however flawed, would loom large. Anti-Semitism had raised its ugly head, yet it had been decisively defeated by a republican state and movement that enjoyed broad popular support. Indeed, Jews and non-Jews were brought closer together, so some argued, through a common fight for decency and toleration.

[66] Arendt, *Origins*, 108.

[67] Benjamin F. Martin, "The Dreyfus Affair and the Corruption of the French Legal System," in Kleeblatt, ed., *Dreyfus Affair*, 45.

A Dreyfusian Revolution?

Such conclusions have not found universal assent by subsequent generations, looking back from the perspective of the violent waves of anti-Semitism that broke out at the end of World War I, the widespread if more "cold" anti-Semitism of the 1930s, and, of course, the Holocaust. Many have questioned whether it is appropriate to speak of a dreyfusian revolution, in the sense of a decisive, long-term victory of the forces opposed to anti-Semitism. Others have suggested that anti-Semitism was not defeated but simply went underground.

These issues are not easily resolved. By 1906 anti-Semitic activists of the 1880s and 1890s in France recognized that they had lost another battle, if not the war. Some of them lost heart or restrained themselves in public. A number of their leaders died in the immediate prewar years and did not find successors. The church, the monarchists in the military, the anti-Semitic popular press, and the anti-Semitic leagues were all unmistakably chastened by the Affair. Public expressions of anti-Semitism visibly receded; no anti-Semitic riots, demonstrations, or boycotts occurred in France in the remaining years before the war, and the anti-Semitic press lost readership. However much anti-Semitism survived in a subterranean way, the disintegration of the anti-Semitic movement of 1898–1900 suggests that Jew-hatred, in itself and not pulled along by other issues, lacked a self-generating substance, or broad popular appeal.

Insofar as political anti-Semitism survived in France and in German-speaking central Europe it was mostly as part of larger conservative movements, not as self-standing anti-Semitic parties. In France, the new right's claims to speak for the nation were successfully contested by a new generation of establishment conservatives, such as Raymond Poincaré. As the historian of the shopkeeper movement in Paris has written, "extremist protest gave way to conservative reintegration."[68] Owners of big business and moderate liberals, who had earlier dismissed the distress of the small shopkeepers as unworthy of serious attention, now showed a new sympathy for them. Anti-Semitism undoubtedly remained in the ranks of such establishment conservatives, but it was a cooler sentiment, not a central concern of theirs. It was significantly different from the ardent, radical, populist variety of Drumont and de Morès.

Recent scholarship has also shown rather conclusively that the Dreyfus Affair has been overdramatized, its long-range significance exaggerated. Its immediate impact throughout France was less extensive than once believed. Captain Dreyfus's story has been too tempting, too appealing to the popular, vulgarizing kind of historian, and too appealing to various political agendas, particularly those Zionist interpretations of modern history that emphasize

[68] Nord, Shopkeepers, 477.

European decadence, ineradicable Jew-hatred, Jewish self-hatred, and the need for Jews to leave Europe. Intellectuals have been especially drawn to the story; it has been hard for them to accept that the majority of the French, who were not intellectuals, were not as strongly moved by the issues of the Affair as they. Recent studies have shown how little the peasantry and the population of small towns, still a heavy majority of the population of France, were touched by the Affair.[69]

It is revealing that Jewish immigration to France did not decline in response to the Affair. It actually increased in 1898,[70] although the numbers of Jews moving into France from the 1880s onward were far smaller than those moving into other countries. Parallel observations have been made about the continuing influx of Jews into Vienna during the years of Karl Lueger, the city's immensely popular anti-Semitic mayor.[71] In short, the sweep of political anti-Semitism appears to have been shallow in comparison to that of developments in the economy and society of Europe in these years.

The elections of 1893 had already registered what seemed a definitive victory of the Opportunist republicans over their enemies. One scholar has argued that those elections presaged the political and social alignments that came together as the Affair heated up. The elections of 1898 and 1906 did no more than establish beyond doubt an already overwhelming republican majority.[72] Again, one might easily doubt how much the Dreyfus Affair as such exercised a fundamental effect, one way or another, on these deeper shifts.

An important point should not be overlooked: The victory of the Dreyfusards, whether "revolutionary" or not, was a morally flawed one, for the republicans who came to power are best described as enemies of the anti-Semites rather than of anti-Semitism. Moreover, many Dreyfusards harbored what might easily be termed anti-Semitic doubts about the rise of the Jews, especially about how far it would go: What were the limits of Jewish success in a country like France, where they remained less than two-tenths of one percent of the total population? That such concerns existed in the ranks of the Dreyfusards again underlines the point that apprehension about the rise of the Jews was not limited to reactionaries, to people who were insecure or personal failures, to those threatened by modern trends or whose minds were overcome by fantasies about the Jews.

Bigotry was not decisively defeated by the Dreyfusards in part because in their own ranks were many bigots, Jewish and non-Jewish. Nor was a respect

[69] Cf. Burns, *Rural Society;* Nord, *Shopkeepers.*

[70] Cf. Green, *Pletzl,* 28–9.

[71] Cf. Richard S. Geehr, ed., *"I Decide Who Is a Jew!": The Papers of Dr. Karl Lueger* (Washington, D.C., 1982), 323.

[72] Rudolf Winnocker, *Papers of the Michigan Academy of Science, Arts, and Letters,* vol. 30, 1936, 465 ff.; Bredin, *Dreyfus,* 521.

for truth, come what may and unsullied by political calculation, particularly notable among leading Dreyfusards; many of them were quite willing to believe that the justice of their cause made it acceptable to bend the rules – an "end justifies the means" perspective that is finally difficult to distinguish from that forwarded by some anti-Dreyfusards.[73] Once in power the Dreyfusards proved themselves scarcely less prone to duplicity and illicit manipulation of the legal system than had the anti-Dreyfusards. Waldeck-Rousseau, the Dreyfusard premier during Dreyfus's retrial, secretly contacted the prefect in that district and instructed him to contact the military prosecutor, even the judges, with the purpose of influencing them to arrive at a not-guilty verdict.[74]

The ideals of truth and justice, claimed by the left, were not without their power among those who spoke of competing claims of discipline and authority. They could not ignore the dishonesty and cowardice of some of Dreyfus's accusers, but they did not find it easy to identify with Dreyfus's defenders, who were also dishonest and opportunistic.

The victory of the Dreyfusards was soured by quarreling within their ranks, of a personal but also a more ideological nature. The depth of hostility among those who worked to free Alfred Dreyfus was symbolized at the final hearing where he was fully exonerated: Mathieu Dreyfus offered Picquart his hand, and Picquart refused it. Picquart made no secret of his belief, even at this date, that the Dreyfus family was scheming and pusillanimous; all that he had been through had not much changed his anti-Semitic attitudes.[75]

Historically better known are the reflections on the Affair of Charles Péguy, the Catholic poet and man of letters who was among the earliest of the Dreyfusards. He was an interesting example of a philo-Semite in these years, one who received much Jewish financial support but who was anything but a pawn of the Jews.[76] He became bitterly disillusioned with the moral qualities of the Dreyfusard camp. His reflections on the Affair in *Notre Jeunesse* (Our Youth), published in 1910, eloquently bemoaned the move from *mystique*, the selfless idealism of the initial, lonely crusaders for truth and justice, to *politique*, the cynical calculations of politicians and careerists.

Péguy was also offended by the anti-Catholic demagogy of many in the Dreyfusard camp, especially in the Radical Party, and by the anti-Catholic legislation that accompanied the political victory of the Dreyfusards. Even Jaurès, who in moral terms stood head-and-shoulders above most parliamentary deputies of the day, earned Péguy's vitriolic contempt. When Jaurès was assassinated by a right-wing fanatic on the eve of World War I, Péguy was recorded

---

[73] Cf. Martin, "Corruption of the French Legal System," in Kleeblatt, ed., *Dreyfus Affair*, 43.

[74] Bredin, *Dreyfus*, 396.

[75] Ibid., 467–8, 476.

[76] Cf. Lazare Prajs, *Péguy et Israël* (Paris, 1970); Marjorie Villiers, *Charles Péguy, A Study in Integrity* (London, 1965); Hans A. Schmitt, *Charles Péguy, The Decline of an Idealist* (Baton Rouge, Louisiana, 1967).

to have let out a "shout of savage exultation."[77] Péguy's own psychic development after the Affair, before he would die in the opening battles of World War I, was feverish and often bizarre, marked by bitter quarrels with former friends and colleagues and growing, all-consuming patriotism.

What especially embittered men like Péguy and Picquart was the nature of the final amnesty granted by the government, since it entailed letting men like General Mercier go scot-free (he was minister of defense at the time of Dreyfus's arrest and deeply implicated in the irregularities of his arrest and conviction). Mercier's real crimes were thus implicitly equated with the "crimes" of Dreyfus and Picquart. All these crimes were to be equally "forgotten" in the general amnesty legislation that was overwhelmingly approved by both houses of the French legislature and was clearly supported by the population at large. Undoubtedly in terms of healing the wounds in French society, of calming political passions, such an amnesty was politically astute. The general population seemed rapidly to lose interest in the Affair, and in anti-Semitism, after the amnesty. But in terms of justice and truth, the legislation was a travesty.

The Affair marked certain changes in France rather than being a cause of them. Modern mass politics was more firmly established, and the political rule of notables was coming to an end. The older sway of committees of local notables and elected intermediaries began to give way to new pressure groups and organized interests: the press, various leagues (such as the League of the Rights of Man or the League of Patriots), trade unions, and professional and business organizations. These and many others now began to regard themselves as more active, central participants in public life and to exert powerful pressure on parliament and other institutions of state.[78]

[77] Goldberg, *Jaurès*, 566.
[78] Cf. Madeleine Rebérioux, *La République radicale* (Paris, 1975), 40 ff.

8

A Sweet Exile?

Two races headed the movement [of modernity],
though under vastly different conditions – the
British and the Jews; they were the pioneers of capitalism and its first, perhaps chief beneficiaries.
(Lewis Namier)[1]

Here [in America] individuals of all nations are
melted into a new race of men. (St-Jean de Crèvecoeur)[2]

America is our Palestine: here is our Jerusalem.
(Rabbi Max Lillienthal, 1867)

The optimism about the future of Jewish–Gentile relations, linked to a
liberal faith in progress, that was to be observed in France in the 1870s and
1880s found an even stronger expression in a number of other countries.
Such was the case even though in those countries economic depression, the
more general dislocations of modernization, and the mass immigration of
Jews were significantly more important than they were in France. In two of
these countries, Great Britain and the United States, modern racial–political
anti-Semitism was so weak in the 1870s and 1880s as to be considered of no
significance by many contemporaries. In Hungary, where modern political
anti-Semitism did make a flashy early appearance, it was dismissed by leaders
of the ruling liberal elite as not only ephemeral but ludicrous. Many Jewish
immigrants to these countries spoke of finding, at last, a secure resting place,
even a "new Jerusalem."

---

[1] Lewis Namier, *In the Margin of History* (London, 1939), 56; cf. Fritz Stern, *The Politics of Cultural Despair: A Study in the Rise of the Germanic Ideology* (New York, 1974), 84–5.

[2] Quoted in John Higham, *Send These to Me: Immigrants in Urban America*, rev. ed. (Baltimore, Md., 1984), 178.

These areas of "sweet exile" or "happy galut" (Hebrew: *galut metuka*) were all firmly Christian – certainly no less so than France, on the one hand, or Russia, on the other, underlining again the dubiousness of seeing "religion" as the decisive component of anti-Semitism in this period.

The countries of sweet exile had many political problems, but leading figures in them were not likely to blame the Jews for those problems. Again, an interesting question then arises: If Jews are always available to be blamed, no matter what their numbers, role, or moral quality, why were they so rarely blamed in these countries? The answer seems to be that only when a matrix of conditions comes together does anti-Semitism become important. The process is hardly inevitable and certainly not invariable. Indeed, rather than blaming Jews for national problems, an opposing tendency, that is, crediting Jews with helping nations to become stronger, was often cited by leading politicians in these countries, a tendency, of course, to be seen even in Germany and Austria.

Jews in Nineteenth-Century Great Britain

More will be said further on about the concept of "exceptionalism" as applied to American history, but the concept, if not the word, has also been applied to the history of the British Isles. In the eyes of many observers British history has been fundamentally different from that of the Continent. "Almost without exception [British historians] have assumed that Britain had a unique political culture, and they have analyzed its power struggles and social conflicts with scant reference to developments in contemporary Europe."[3] It is only natural to expect that the history of Jewish–Gentile relations in Great Britain should also be unique, substantially different from those on the Continent. Revealingly, such Continental critics of Jewish influence as von Treitschke, Wagner, or Drumont were all Anglophobes, since they believed that Jewishness and Englishness overlapped or were synonymous.

There is ample confirmation in the historical record of an "exceptional" relationship between the Jews and the British. Relations of Jews and non-Jews in all of the English-speaking world (the United States, Canada, Australia, New Zealand, Ireland, and even South Africa) have been notably more harmonious than most other areas in modern times. In the nineteenth century Jews preferred English-speaking lands for immigration, when they had a choice, and once arrived they typically enjoyed success, not only materially but also politically in being elected to high office – popularly elected, not

---

[3] Geoffrey Searle, "The 'Revolt from the Right' in Edwardian Britain," in Paul Kennedy and Anthony Nicholls, eds., *Nationalist and Racialist Movements in Britain and Germany before 1914* (Oxford, 1981), 21–2.

merely appointed or serving as advisers to powerful non-Jewish politicians, as in France, Germany, and Austria.[4]

One obvious aspect of the relative success of Jewish–Gentile relations in English-speaking countries is that liberal ideology was deeply rooted and robust in them, paralleled by an advanced commercial and industrial development (although the cases of Ireland and South Africa require qualification). British liberalism, moreover, was significantly different from that of the Continent; it developed as a "philosophy of prudence, born in anxiety and nurtured by dissatisfaction with the idea of human perfectibility." British liberalism was gradualistic and cautious in reform and much concerned with procedural niceties, respect for tradition, and privilege, what has been termed a Whig, or aristocratic version of liberalism. By contrast, French Jacobinism was a product of the aggressively confident, universalizing rationalism of the Enlightenment, much more prone to dogmatism, ideological intoxication, and revolutionary violence.[5] Liberalism in Great Britain, furthermore, did not become strongly associated with integral or völkisch nationalism, as in France and Austria, respectively.

Liberal ideas, particularly in the economic realm, encountered many critics in nineteenth-century Britain, but it is revealing that one of the most widely known of those critics was himself of Jewish origin, Benjamin Disraeli. Moreover, the "state worship" to be seen in the writings of Treitschke, where the Prussian state was viewed as a moral agent charged with the resolution of social conflict, was alien to British political culture.[6] These different conceptions of liberty and the nature of the state had important implications for Jews in Great Britain and, indirectly, other English-speaking areas.

When Jews moved into British colonies or former colonies, they encountered relatively few impediments. These were open societies, not only in an ideological sense, but also in the sense that there was much open space, geographical and social, for them to move into and relatively little resistance from traditional classes. The societies of the United States, Canada, Australia, New Zealand, and South Africa were not dominated by entrenched oligarchies or long-established political customs; their European populations were predominantly middle class. They were by no means free of the various anti-Jewish *mentalités* that were part of their European heritage, but on balance Jews encountered less fear and hostility in the nineteenth-century English-speaking world than they did in most of continental Europe. One student of immigration into Britain's colonies has written that "anti-Semitism

---

[4] Cf. Howard M. Sachar, *Diaspora: An Inquiry into the Contemporary Jewish World* (New York, 1985), passim.

[5] James T. Kloppenberg, *Uncertain Victory: Social Democracy and Progressivism in European and American Thought, 1870–1920* (Oxford, 1986), 174.

[6] Ibid., 178.

was not merely disreputable, but also possessed the same sort of reputation as witchcraft."[7]

Even when Jews confronted the more closed and status-conscious world of the mother country, relatively large numbers of them became wealthy and managed to gain admittance to its highest ranks. British Jews were never legally obliged to live in ghettoes, although they did tend to congregate in certain urban areas. More than their Continental counterparts, British landed elites had embraced modern commercial and industrial developments. Partly for such reasons they were less inclined to perceive Jews as symbols of a destructive modernism. On the religious level, too, Jews faced relatively little of the kind of suspicion that they did from Continental Christian denominations, whether Catholic, Lutheran, or Greek Orthodox. From the late seventeenth century on, the notion of toleration for both political and religious dissent and the related conviction that the state "had no legitimate interest in the religious beliefs of obedient citizens" gradually became accepted among the English-speaking peoples.[8] Toleration in this sense became recognized as a British national trait.

By the early nineteenth century, the so-called Anglo–Jewish Grand Dukes were not only opulently rich; many of them were also on intimate terms with the aristocracy, even the extended royal family. The *Kaiserjuden* of central Europe or the wealthy financiers who mixed with the old aristocracy in France never achieved quite the position of their British counterparts. Already by the early nineteenth century, Jews in Britain began to gain noble titles and to intermarry with prominent families. The Grand Dukes strived, when not forming marital alliances with old English families, to marry within their own ranks,[9] reproducing in this as in other ways the practices of the British aristocracy.

One mark of the success of this elite of British Jews was that its members constituted, in their heyday of the 1870s to the 1920s, nearly a quarter of Britain's non-landed millionaires. The population of Jews in Great Britain constituted, however, less than one-half of one percent of the total (60,000 in 1880, of a total population of 26 million).[10] Their wealth was concentrated in the City of London, in such families as the Rothschilds, Montefiores, Montegus, and Goldsmids.

Those social classes most inclined to anti-Semitism on the Continent were less likely to be anti-Semitic in Great Britain because they, like the aristocracy, did not feel threatened by Jews. The British lower-middle class did not, at least not by the middle years of the nineteenth century, notably yearn for an idealized

---

[7] J. A. Garrard, *The English and Immigration, 1880–1910* (London, 1971), 57.

[8] Todd Endelman, *The Jews of Georgian England, 1714–1830: Tradition and Change in a Liberal Society* (Philadelphia, 1979), 44.

[9] Sachar, *Diaspora*, 142.

[10] B. R. Mitchell, *European Statistics, 1750–1975* (New York, 1981), 34.

premodern community, since that community had already vanished, and for reasons that could not plausibly be blamed on the Jews. Similarly, a British peasantry in the Continental sense had mostly disappeared in the eighteenth century. A British Böckel would have found few peasants to recruit and, in contrast to the situation in Hessenland, no long-established Jewish cattle merchants or moneylenders.

The British middle class was proportionately and absolutely the largest of any in the world. British merchants and industrialists were confident and optimistic; they had relatively little cause to fear being overwhelmed or outdone in the business world by Jews. And British national identity was both more diffuse and more secure than many Continental varieties. That the British nation was recognized as being composed of four "races" (English, Scottish, Welsh, and Irish) may have made it somewhat less likely that those who sought to define British identity would argue that Jews could never become "real" members of that nation. Purity of national feeling, while certainly an issue, did not preoccupy British intellectuals to quite the same extent that it did those on the Continent, and many prominent politicians were of Scotch, Welsh, and Irish as well as English background.

Jewish emancipation came not only in a piecemeal, typically British way; it was also part of a general trend to recognize the rights of religious or other kinds of minorities, and not particularly much as part of a program to convert Jews into acceptable English citizens. Particularism rather than centralism was the recognized political principle in Great Britain, in sharp contrast to the situation in France. What was accepted as a tolerable national style, or of social comportment, was somewhat wider and more diverse in nineteenth-century Britain than in most countries. In such an environment, persistent Jewish peculiarities stood out less than elsewhere. Jews in Britain were no less concerned with becoming perfect Englishmen than were French Jews with being perfect Frenchmen; it was simply that "perfect" was a somewhat more diverse category in Britain.

Just as bad times in a material sense have repeatedly proved to be "bad for the Jews," so economic prosperity has been "good for the Jews." By the second half of the nineteenth century Great Britain had reached the acme of its economic power and international reputation. Its ruling elites were inclined to serene confidence. The long-established unity and independence of the country were not seriously threatened; Britain suffered no military defeats in the nineteenth century even remotely comparable to those of France in 1871, no invasions, lost provinces, or outraged national honor. (The most obvious and important exception, in South Africa at the turn of the century, will be covered in Chapter 11.)

Political struggle remained for the most part within parliamentary, constitutional limits, especially after 1832. The decisions of parliament were widely respected. Conservative and Liberal parties were closer to one another, sharing basic values, than were their counterparts on the Continent. The left in Britain after 1848 harbored relatively few fears of a military coup, and the right did not demonize the left to the extent that it did in France or Germany. Both Conservative and Liberal parties made efforts to win over the working classes and succeeded in doing so, at least more than their counterparts in Germany and France did, incomparably more than in Russia.

Great Britain had its share of political worries and excitements, to be sure, but its ruling class and monarchs experienced little to compare with the constant fundamental challenges to authority – and the assassinations – that characterized Russia. While the republic in France seemed to be tottering on the edge of disaster for much of the 1870s and 1880s, politics in Britain worked better than ever before; this was the era of the classic two-party system, the great duels in parliament between Gladstone and Disraeli, all within the boundaries of legality and constitutional precedents, of a "loyal opposition."

Preoccupation with social class was an important aspect of British life, yet the British state and ruling class were less often so violently hated by minorities as were the Russian or the Austro–Hungarian (the Irish minority is an important exception), while Queen Victoria enjoyed an even wider veneration by the common people than did Franz Joseph, and nearly as long a reign.

It says much about Great Britain's reputation for liberality and tolerance in the nineteenth century that modernizing Jews everywhere on the Continent tended to look to it as a model. An activist among the Yiddish-speaking workers of Russia in the late nineteenth century reported that in the evening classes he taught, the "life of the peoples" began with primitive tribes and ended with the pinnacle of contemporary civilization: "the English, their parliament and trade unions."[11] As a boy of eleven in a remote and isolated shtetl, Chaim Weizmann wrote in 1884, "Why should we look to the Kings of Europe for compassion? . . . In vain! All have decided *the Jews must die,* but England will nevertheless have mercy upon us." In 1911, having amply experienced how ferocious Gentile hostility could be, Weizmann still affirmed that "the English Gentiles are the best Gentiles in the world."[12]

The formulation of an anti-Semitic ideology in Germany, Austria, or France had no serious counterpart in Great Britain in the 1880s. There were no Marrs, Stoeckers, or Drumonts, no anti-Semitic best-sellers. The Jewish Question, while certainly of interest to educated Britons, did not preoccupy them in the same way it did parts of the educated classes of central and eastern Europe. Indeed, the interest of educated non-Jews in Britain in Jewish matters

---

[11] Ezra Mendelsohn, *Class Struggles in the Pale: The Formative Years of the Jewish Workers' Movement in Tsarist Russia* (Cambridge, U.K., 1970), 35.

[12] Jehuda Reinharz, *Chaim Weizmann: The Making of a Zionist Leader* (Oxford, 1985), 14, 528 (n. 7).

often had more to do with the implications of the Jewish Question in foreign affairs than in domestic policy.

The scholarly literature devoted to anti-Semitism in Great Britain has been relatively meager. Hatred of Jews, not being a major problem in Great Britain, has not been studied with anything like the same intensity as it has been in Germany or Russia. The *Jewish Encyclopedia* (1965) claimed that there simply was no anti-Semitism worth mention in Great Britain (or the United States) before 1914.

If German history in this period is to be considered an example of aberrant or somehow ominously retarded development, it was Great Britain that was long accepted as representing the healthy path of a modern nation. But the relatively small numbers of Jews in the British Isles for most of the nineteenth century undoubtedly had much to do with the relatively low level of anti-Semitism there. As the numbers of Jews rose rapidly in the last decades of the century, so did expressions of anti-Semitism. From perhaps 8,000 in the mid–eighteenth century, the numbers of Jews grew fairly slowly, to approximately 35,000 by the 1860s, 60,000 by 1880. Thereafter the growth rate was much more rapid, reaching approximately 250,000 in 1914, 350,000 on the eve of World War II.[13] (All such figures are necessarily approximate because the census did not ask for the religion of Britain's population.)

At 0.1 percent of the population at midcentury, British Jews constituted approximately the same proportion of the total population as French Jews did in their country at the same time. There were other instructive resemblances to the French scene, in that well over half of the Jews in Britain lived in the capital city, mostly in London's East End. But there was no rural area, comparable to areas in Alsace, where large numbers of Jews had lived since early modern times. England's Jews in the nineteenth century were overwhelmingly recent immigrants who moved directly to a modern urban environment. Some of the most notable early immigrants were of Sephardic background, such as Disraeli, but, especially from the early nineteenth century on, others who became prominent were Ashkenazim from central Europe. Jews of Polish or Russian origin did not come in large numbers until the 1880s and did not achieve prominence until after the turn of the century, Chaim Weizmann being perhaps the best known example.

The granting of civil emancipation to Jews in Great Britain was even more gradual and hedged with qualifications than in Germany. One historian has claimed that the issue of removing Jewish civil disabilities interested only a small, wealthy group of Jews; the rest of the Jewish population in Great Britain in early to midcentury was mostly indifferent to political matters. Henry Mayhew, a popular writer of the day, commented that "perhaps no men buy so few newspapers, and read them so little as the Jews generally."[14]

---

[13] Colin Holmes, *Anti-Semitism in British Society, 1876–1939* (London, 1979), 4.

[14] Geoffrey Alderman, *The Jewish Community in British Politics* (Oxford, 1983), 14.

On the Continent, too, only an elite of mostly wealthy Jews participated actively in issues of emancipation and defense of Jewish rights; the poor were more concerned with mere survival. Yet, in Great Britain it was easier to ignore politics because specifically anti-Jewish legislation, especially in the economic arena, was practically non-existent. Jews in very small numbers had been officially readmitted to England in 1656. They were excluded throughout the eighteenth century from Crown office and from other positions in parliament and in the municipalities because of the obligatory religious oaths for such offices, but they were not subject to any discriminatory economic legislation as Jews. The nature of debates about giving civil equality to Jews paralleled those on the Continent, although with seemingly less passion and proceeding in parliament without much engaging the attention of ordinary Jews.

Jews were increasingly accepted as one of several legitimate minorities in a country that had spent centuries gradually coming to grips, in legal but also in complex psychological and cultural ways, with its minorities, both religious and ethnic. Jews gained civil equality, step-by-step, in much the same way as Christian dissenting minorities did. When legal reform that benefited Jews was accomplished, it was widely greeted as removing vestiges of an anachronistic past. The burning hostilities between Christian denominations in Germany, in the Kulturkampf, and in France, with the passage of the Ferry Laws, moved the population of Great Britain less in these years. The British seemed to have gotten those passions out of their system, so to speak. Symptomatic of the tone of debate was Macaulay's quip that "the real difficulty in speaking in favor of the Jews . . . [is that] there are no valid arguments advanced against them"[15] – a comment that would have been unlikely in Germany, Russia, or even France.

British Jews were not easily identified with the secular left, certainly not to the degree that they were in the Kulturkampf and in the struggles over the Ferry Laws, and were less likely to be the object of attack by the religious right. Jews did tend to side with the dissenting churches, but they did so without the kind of animus so often seen on the Continent. In a country where both Conservatives and Liberals were in fundamental ways liberal, the right was not so distinctly perceived by Jews as unfriendly territory. Indeed, among the most virulent of those who denounced the "blaspheming Jew" in the early to middle years of the century was the enormously popular agitator on the left, William Cobbett. The Chartists, while occasionally condemning the persecution of Jews, showed little sympathy for or understanding of Jews as a people; for most Chartists, Jews were identified either with the rich or with the criminal class of London.

Gladstone at first opposed Jewish emancipation. Even after he had accepted it as consistent with the principles of his Liberal Party, his suspicion of Jews remained, an attitude that may have been influenced by his aversion to his political opponent, Disraeli. But that suspicion did not become a full-blown

---

[15] Quoted in Holmes, *Anti-Semitism in British Society*, 115.

prejudice, did not extend to Jews in a categorical way; Gladstone had excellent relations with Lionel Rothschild, in spite of the latter's closeness to Disraeli and other Tories. Gladstone was also close to Lionel's son, Nathan; he recommended both father and son to Queen Victoria to be raised to the peerage.[16] (Lionel, it should be noted, was very widely liked and admired, both among the upper classes and the common people. He was said to have transformed Lord Randolph Churchill [Winston's father] from a man who maligned Jewish "vested interests" to a notable friend of the Jews. Lionel's death in 1879 was marked by popular mourning in London, much like funeral of Paul Singer in Berlin but extending much beyond the working class; the costermongers put black crepe on their barrows, and the *Pall Mall Gazette* wrote that "it is owing to the life of Lord Rothschild that Great Britain has escaped those collections of race feeling . . . with which so many other countries have been embarrassed during the last generation. He was at once a Prince in Israel and an Englishman of whom all of England could be proud."[17])

Complete Jewish civil equality may have come more slowly in Great Britain also because of the divisions within the Jewish community over the issue. As on the Continent, some Jewish leaders in Great Britain openly worried that full emancipation would lead to a loss of identity and an eventual disappearance of Jews. But others argued – and here the differences with those on the Continent are to be seen most sharply – that so long as Jews were allowed to live their lives free of harassment by the state, to compete freely with non-Jews in the economic arena, and, especially, to own land, certain political rights, particularly the right to hold high office, were relatively unimportant. Some Conservatives used these differences within the Jewish community to bolster their own reservations about Jewish emancipation, but even among Whigs and Radicals there was little real enthusiasm for the cause of Jewish civil equality.[18]

Because of the gradualness of civil emancipation in Great Britain and, indeed, because of the very nature of the British Constitution, one cannot easily determine when full civil equality was achieved.[19] One might say that the process was formally concluded when Jews became eligible to serve in parliament (1858). Within a decade there were six Jewish members of parliament, all Liberals, "a figure already so disproportionate to the size of the Jewish population . . . that it was in itself a source of worry in some communal quarters."[20] One might mark the decisive point at the passage of the Promissory Oaths Act of 1871,

---

[16] Chaim Bermant, *The Cousinhood* (London, 1971), 99–100; Holmes, *Anti-Semitism in British Society*, 109.

[17] Paul Johnson, *A History of the Jews* (New York, 1987), 320.

[18] Alderman, *Jewish Community*, 18–19.

[19] Cf. U. R. Q. Henriques, "The Jewish Emancipation Controversy in Nineteenth Century Britain," *Past and Present*, no. 40, 1968.

[20] Alderman, *Jewish Community*, 31.

which admitted Jews to high office, or with the granting of a peerage to Nathan Rothschild in 1885. But all of these suggest a date for "emancipation" that is too late; English Jews had felt much freer in a practical, de facto sense than most Jews on the Continent since at least the late eighteenth century.[21]

Modern racist ideas were pervasive in Britain. Whether the British ruling class was racist in the "scientific" sense, it had few doubts about its inherent superiority to non-Europeans; "the white man's burden" in their eyes was to bring civilization to the lesser peoples of the world. Many European races, indeed, were considered inferior to the "Anglo–Saxons." Even Macaulay proudly wrote that the English were the most civilized race in the world, the universally "acknowledged leaders of the human race."[22]

This British sense of superiority did not much turn against Jews, especially not the native born; as we have seen, many prominent English citizens looked upon the Jews as one of the superior races. Disraeli consciously played upon and undoubtedly enhanced that perception. Lord Balfour, the Conservative politician who would eventually play a celebrated role in modern Jewish history, not only accepted Jews as equals but described them as "the most talented race since the Greeks of the fifth century."[23] Quite the opposite of fearing a weakening of English blood by race mixing, Balfour was disappointed that Jews refused to intermarry, since he believed Jewish blood would enhance that of the other races in Great Britain, adding to the power and glory of the nation. The prominent journalist Arnold White spoke of the desirability of infusing "Jewish mind and thrift" into the "racial common sense" of the Anglo–Saxons.[24] There were suggestions in such remarks of the argument made by Mommsen, that Jews – as a "ferment of decomposition" – would help to form a modern German identity.

It says much symbolically that at the time anti-Semitism was mushrooming in central Europe, a prime minister of Jewish origin, Disraeli, came to power in Great Britain. Moreover, he hardly corresponded to the anti-Semitic stereotypes about Jewish bankers, stock market swindlers, or revolutionaries. As leader of a party that stood for tradition and stability, he was of the same general political persuasion as most of those on the Continent who were inclined to point accusing fingers at the Jews.

That said, there is much about Disraeli's personality and appeal that is puzzling. Although a Conservative, native born and speaking English without an accent, he was not English in the sense that many right-wing leaders understood it. Similarly, as Isaiah Berlin has written, Disraeli cut a singular figure:

---

[21] Cf. M. Freedman, ed., *A Minority in Britain* (London, 1955), 39.

[22] Quoted in Petr Geyl, *Debates with Historians* (London, 1970), 37.

[23] L. Stein, *The Balfour Declaration* (London, 1961), 157. See also Raddock F. Mackay, *Balfour: Intellectual Statesman* (Oxford, 1985), 317.

[24] B. Gainer, *The Alien Invasion* (London, 1972), 124–5.

"Rings on his gloved fingers, elaborate ringlets of hair falling about his pale, exotic features . . . [he was] a Pied Piper leading a bemused collection of dukes, earls, solid country gentlemen and burly farmers, one of the oddest and most fantastic phenomena of the entire nineteenth century."[25]

Disraeli rejected much of the liberal–Enlightened heritage that so appealed to western Jews in the nineteenth century. He also disdained the world of commerce and industry that was so essential to the rise of the Jews. In certain regards his values were similar to those of Stoecker in Germany or Vogelsang in Austria–Hungary: He saw it as his political mission, as a Tory Democrat, to come to the rescue of the lower orders, oppressed by the business classes and the factory system, and he tried to orchestrate a coalition of the upper and lower classes against the middle class – again, not unlike what Bismarck or Napoleon III attempted in approximately the same years. For Disraeli, the English Utilitarians and the laissez-faire economists were dreary and vulgar. "He was passionately convinced that intuition and imagination were vastly superior to reason and method. He believed in temperament, blood, race, the unaccountable leaps of genius. He was antirationalist through and through."[26] Disraeli was, in short, the kind of man who might have been an anti-Semite, had he been a German or a Russian, especially given his nearly mystical belief in the role of conspiracies in history. It is not surprising that so many anti-Semites cited him to bolster their own beliefs about Jews.

As a political leader Disraeli was constantly in the center of controversy, and it was nearly inevitable that some of his many enemies would be tempted to use his Jewish origin against him. Gladstone, Disraeli's moralistic antagonist in the Liberal Party and the dominant figure in that party from 1868 to 1894, considered him a deadly enemy of all that was right and good, "a clever Levantine manipulator . . . without principles or ideals . . . a soulless leprechaun."[27] There was much anti-Semitic potential in these visions, but it is again instructive that Gladstone did not make political use of them to any significant degree; political anti-Semitism of the Continental variety simply did not mesh with the ideals of the Liberal Party. A left-wing critic revealingly wrote, on the occasion of a visit by Gladstone to Lord Rothschild, that

Nobody . . . could impute any impropriety to Mr. Gladstone. But it is not nice . . . when the foreign secretary [Rosebery] is closely connected by marriage with the same intriguing financial house, to see Mr. Gladstone hobnobbing with Lord Rothschild [Rosebery was married to a Rothschild]. We know what has come of this Rothschild influence in Vienna and Paris.[28]

---

[25] Isaiah Berlin, *Against the Current: Essays in the History of Ideas* (Oxford, 1961), 260.
[26] Ibid., 265.
[27] Berlin, *Against the Current*, 267–68.
[28] Holmes, *Anti-Semitism in British Society*, 83.

Gladstone's bitterest confrontations with Disraeli came in the area of foreign policy. Disraeli was a firm supporter of the so-called Eastern Policy of propping up the Ottoman Empire, a policy that dated to the early part of the century and that had as a central rationale the concern of Great Britain to contain tsarist Russia, to prevent Russia from moving into areas that the weakened Ottoman Empire was having difficulty ruling.

When the Turks massacred rebellious Bulgarian Christians in 1875, Gladstone's moral passions were galvanized, but Disraeli judged it in the interests of Great Britain to continue to support the Turks against the Russians. Gladstone had just relinquished the post of prime minister to the Conservatives under Disraeli in 1874, and this "immoral" foreign policy on the part of a nation that prided itself in being Christian was intolerable to him. He took up the cause of the Bulgarian Christians, making it a central issue of Liberal attacks on the Conservative government.[29]

Outside of parliament, indignation was expressed in some quarters over the Conservatives' toleration of Turkish anti-Christian violence, especially as it became clear that prominent Jews, because of their hatred of anti-Semitic Russia, were favorable to Disraeli's policies. Particularly revealing were the attacks on Disraeli by Goldwyn Smith, who had been Regius Professor of Modern History at Oxford from 1858 to 1866. He and Disraeli had been bitter opponents since the 1840s when Disraeli had publicly mocked him as one the "prigs and pedants" of the country, and in Disraeli's novel *Lothair* (1870), there was an Oxford professor, widely recognized as Smith, who was incompetent and parasitical.[30] Smith, who had so far avoided the issue of Disraeli's Jewish origins, began to deride him as a "Semite" whose "Oriental" craftiness and vindictiveness was leading the country astray.

Smith also broadened his attacks to other Jews, especially those of formerly Liberal fidelities who were now supporting Disraeli and his toleration of the atrocities in Bulgaria. Smith charged that aside from their fanatical hatred of Russia, British Jews were supporting Disraeli because of Jewish financial interests in Turkey.[31] Smith took yet another step in the direction of Continental anti-Semitism by questioning the wisdom of Jewish emancipation, since Jews, he argued, were too racially exclusive to become genuine British patriots or to put the interests of Britain above those of international Jewry. Smith did recognize that some Jews had genuinely embraced a British identity, but he maintained that they were exceptional and no longer really Jews.[32]

Smith's anti-Semitic articles appeared at about the same time (1878) as those

---

[29] Ibid., 10; R. Blake, *Disraeli* (London, 1966), 167.

[30] Holmes, *Anti-Semitism in British Society*, 11.

[31] Cf. D. C. Blaisdell, *European Financial Control in the Ottoman Empire* (New York, 1929), 37, 84; Holmes, *Anti-Semitism in British Society*, 11–12.

[32] Holmes, *Anti-Semitism in British Society*, 12, 238.

of another university professor, von Treitschke, and a number of parallels suggest themselves, particularly the extent to which Smith and von Treitschke were goaded to intemperate statements by prominent Jews (Disraeli and Graetz) – again, not by fantasies about Jews. But it is the differences rather than the parallels that are the most instructive. Smith's attacks attracted nothing like the following among university students and other respectable citizens that von Treitschke's did. Smith was also a man of academic prominence, yet his outbursts are incomparably less well remembered by subsequent generations, for the obvious reason that no important anti-Semitic movement in Great Britain developed, and there was no particular reason to look back to Smith to trace poisoned roots, as it were. One must again ask if anti-Semitic ideology exercises the mystical, self-generating power attributed to it by some, why it remained so feeble in Smith's hands and relatively strong in von Treitschke's.

Smith's anti-Semitism was not as isolated as might be assumed. Mention has been made of Cobbett's particularly vicious attacks on Jews; the Radical John Bright attacked Disraeli because of his Jewish background; and another Oxford historian, E. A. Freeman, joined Smith in attacking Disraeli for his alleged Jewish traits. Yet, these attacks and others simply did not find many in British society ready to be mobilized into political action by them.

Some historians have found in the Bulgarian crisis of the mid-1870s the beginnings of a transition of Jewish opinion in Great Britain toward an open support for the Conservative Party. But the growing wealth of native-born Jews and their rising acceptance by the upper classes probably had more to do with that move, which was at any rate quite gradual, hardly decisive. Another factor was the support of Gladstone's Liberals for Irish Home Rule in 1886. Jewish financiers and business interests shared the fears of their Gentile counterparts that the Liberal Party was moving too far to the left. The Liberal Unionist secession, which finally joined the Conservatives, was the result of Liberal support for Home Rule. By 1900, the Conservative Party, in 1850 a party of land and church, had become a party of big business as well.[33] It was natural for those Jews who were involved in finance and industry to be more attracted to it than they had been before.

The arrival of tens of thousands of Jews from eastern Europe also tended to push native-born Jews in a rightward direction. At first, there was relatively little alarm in British circles; prominent figures took special pride in their country's status as a haven for the persecuted. Calls for limitations on immigration were expressed mostly by the xenophobic right, though also by labor leaders who feared competition from the impoverished immigrants. At any rate, Great Britain served more as a transition point than as a final destination for the great majority of immigrating Jews, who headed for America.

[33] Alderman, *Jewish Community*, 38–50.

Nevertheless, many more eastern European Jews remained than was the case in Germany. From 1881 to 1914, the Jewish population increased about fourfold (from 81,000 to over 300,000), thus raising the population of Jews in Britain to well over twice that of France and about half that of Germany. The attitudes of native-born Jews to the Jews of eastern Europe were only too predictable. *The Jewish Chronicle,* the voice of assimilated Anglo–Jewry, devoted many articles to the issue of "improving" the Ostjuden, expressing confidence that once they had attended English schools and learned English ways, they would be accepted by the English.

Although the slogan "England for the English!" could be heard in certain anti-immigrant circles, opposition to the influx of Jews into Great Britain remained politically unfocused. Even in the economically hard-pressed 1880s and early 1890s, anti-alien leaders were often at great pains to deny that they were anti-Semitic; their concern, they averred, was to protect their compatriots from a major threat to their well-being, not to attack Jews as such. The problem was simply that most of the immigrants happened to be Jews.[34]

Some of these protests were transparently the expression of a mean-spirited xenophobia, especially those that dwelt upon the allegedly filthy habits and rude social demeanor of the new Jewish arrivals. *Justice,* the official organ of the small Marxist movement in Great Britain, argued that "the bestial behavior of rich Jews rouses a prejudice against the whole [Jewish] race." It continued that "we have no feeling against Jews as Jews; [we denounce them] as nefarious capitalists and poisoners of the wells of public information." It claimed that Jewish proletarians would gladly join in the attack on Jewish capitalists.[35] Yet even these qualified attacks on Jews were the expression of a fringe, one that did not speak for a significant number of English citizens and that went unnoticed by most of them.

Jews in America: The Issue of Exceptionalism

A widely accepted generalization about the situation of Jews in the United States is that it has always been "exceptional," distinctly less afflicted by anti-Semitism than anywhere else in the world in modern times. Only qualified dissents have been registered against that consensus, and they have been based primarily on a complaint that historians of America have not sufficiently recognized the importance of anti-Semitism in American history.[36] Rarely if

---

[34] Gisela Lebzelter, "Anti-Semitism, a Focal Point for the British Radical Right," in Kennedy and Nicholls, eds., *Nationalist and Racialist Movements,* 92.

[35] Ibid., 94.

[36] Cf. Leonard Dinnerstein, *Uneasy at Home* (New York, 1987); Michael Dobkowski, *The Tarnished Dream* (Westport, Conn., 1979), and Dobkowski, "American Anti-Semitism: A Reinterpretation," *American Quarterly,* vol. 29, 1977, 167–90.

ever has the claim been made that things have been worse for Jews in the United States than elsewhere. Jewish leaders have repeatedly described the United States as fundamentally different from the countries of Europe. In this New World democracy, Jews could at last feel at home – more than anywhere else here was a "happy Galut."

In historical perspective, the hyperbole of such descriptions is obvious. Jews in Great Britain but also in Hungary and France by mid–nineteenth century made similar claims. Indeed the Jews of many European countries, Italy perhaps most prominently, but also Bulgaria, Holland, and Scandinavia have claimed exceptional histories, largely free of the anti-Semitism of other European countries.[37]

Scholars have recently questioned how appropriate it is to term the American experience exceptional.[38] The issue of national exceptionalism became a staple of debate among historians in the 1970s and 1980s, especially in comparing American history with Germany's opposite kind of exceptionalism, its *Sonderweg*, as far as Jews are concerned. In reviewing this debate, one historian has revealingly concluded that "upon scrutiny every nation had its own exceptionalism."[39]

Historical perspective also suggests the need to correct another kind of retrospective romanticism: Most Jews did not come to the United States primarily in a search for religious freedom but rather for immediate, pressing reasons, hopes to escape poverty most of all. The majority certainly did not come because they perceived the country as a haven of cultural pluralism. Indeed, it is anachronistic to speak of cultural pluralism as an ideal for Jews coming from eastern Europe; such ideas were simply not part of their intellectual baggage. Similarly, long-resident Americans accepted immigrants, Jews included, because their labor was believed necessary to build the country, not because of any cultural contributions Jews might make. ("Immigrant gifts" is, again, a concept worked out by later generations.)

"Accepted" is not quite the appropriate word, at any rate, since native-born Americans were never asked to accept immigration. There was no national referendum, no searching for political consensus concerning whether millions of Jews and other immigrants should be invited to the United States. No one can state confidently what such a referendum might have produced, but it is a rea-

---

[37] Cf. Dan Antonio Segré, *Memoirs of a Fortunate Jew: An Italian Story* (Bethesda, Md., 1987).

[38] Cf. Daniel Bell, "The End of American Exceptionalism," *The Public Interest*, no. 41, Fall 1975, 205, in which he emphasizes that Americans "have not been immune to the corruptions of power. We have not been the exception." Also, Alexander Deconde, "Historians, the War of American Independence, and the Persistence of the Exceptionalist Ideal," *The International History Review*, vol. 5, no. 3, 1983, 399–430.

[39] Charles S. Maier, *The Unmasterable Past: History, Holocaust, and German National Identity* (Cambridge, Mass., 1988), 108.

sonable guess that there would have been a solid majority in opposition to large-scale immigration. Jews and other immigrants came by the millions not because they were in some sense invited by the American people but rather because of the "push" from Europe and the "pull" of the expanding labor market in the United States. The Founding Fathers had in fact been mostly hostile to the idea of large-scale immigration, and profound doubts about it continued to be expressed by leading Americans throughout the nineteenth and twentieth centuries.

But those doubts never found a powerful political focus. Historians of anti-Semitism in America have been concerned primarily with issues of lingering stereotypes, social exclusion, and obstacles to equality of opportunity, not anti-Semitism as a political device. During the nineteenth and early twentieth centuries, Jews found many occupations and neighborhoods closed to them by the forces of bigotry, but hostility to Jews in America remained mostly latent and ambiguous, not overt, militant, or violent. One historian has written that in America "no decisive event, no deep crisis, no powerful social movement, no great individual is associated primarily . . . with anti-Semitism."[40] Another has concluded that if the United States "has not been utter heaven for Jews, it has been as far from hell as Jews in the Diaspora have ever known."[41]

Prior to World War I in the United States as in Great Britain there were no significant American ideologists or popularizers of anti-Semitism comparable to Dühring, Marr, Barrès, or Drumont, with the minor exceptions of Ignatius Donnelly and Tom Watson, to be discussed in Chapter 11. Even the underlying expectation that Jews should "disappear" once they had been given civil equality was not so all-embracing; it was closer in nature to the British toleration of idiosyncrasies and lingering ethnic differences than, say, French integral nationalism. Still, prior to the mid–twentieth century, few if any non-Jewish Americans expressed much sympathy for Jewish separatism, and the insistence of American ruling elites that immigrants conform to Anglo–Saxon linguistic and cultural norms was typically unyielding. But that insistence gradually weakened as American identity grew less narrowly associated with notions of a single "truly American" race, religious tradition, and integral culture – a protracted process, to be sure, stretching well into the final years of the twentieth century.

What is perhaps most exceptional in American history has been the ongoing,

---

[40] There are few overall introductions to the subject; perhaps the best is Charles Hebert Stember, ed., *Jews in the Mind of America* (New York, 1966), especially the essay in it by John Higham, "American Anti-Semitism Historically Reconsidered," from which the preceding quotation is taken. The essay may be found also in Leonard Dinnerstein, ed., *Anti-Semitism in the United States* (New York, 1971), 63–77. See also, David Gerber, ed., *Anti-Semitism in American History* (Chicago and Urbana, Ill., 1986).

[41] Jonathan D. Sarna, "Anti-Semitism and American History," *Commentary*, March 1981, 47.

often tumultuous process of redefining what it means to be an American. There has been a slow but gathering consensus that American identity is properly pluralistic and open to all people. In that regard, developments in America may be said to have paralleled the nineteenth-century process in Great Britain of a gradual, prudent, yet ever-widening toleration of minorities, but in America the process was more influenced by Jews themselves, in both theoretical and practical ways.[42] That the Statue of Liberty, the symbol of America for much of the world by the early twentieth century, had placed at its base in 1903 a bronze plaque with a poem composed by a Jewish American, Emma Lazarus ("Give me your tired, your poor, your huddled masses, yearning to breathe free . . ."), suggests the importance of that role. (The poem, with its reference to the immigrants as "wretched refuse," is not without some awkward undertones. Lazarus, moreover, was at best an inconstant defender of the Yiddish-speaking element of those huddled masses; she embraced Anglo–Saxon cultural preeminence without much question.)

The rise of the Jews in modern times has been especially significant and lasting in the United States. As one author has stated the matter, "It is as if centuries of Jewish energies and ambitions . . . found here a sudden and stunning release. . . ."[43] Or another: "More than any other immigrant group, Jews have found their way into almost every interstice of American life, have taken just about every opportunity this nation has to offer, and have given back to America in enriching ways that are wondrous."[44] That rise has not provoked a non-Jewish backlash of anything like the dimensions in Europe. The nightmare of European nationalists, a jewification of their national identity, has been far less a concern of non-Jewish Americans. From at least the mid–nineteenth century, a Jewish contribution to American civilization has been tacitly and increasingly recognized, as have contributions of the Irish, Italians, or Germans. Even those who were most adamant in their insistence upon the identity of the United States as an Anglo–Saxon, Protestant nation, were often also warm defenders of the contributions of Jews to American civilization. They saw no major dangers in those contributions and no important contradictions between Jewish and American values.

In this there are certainly strong parallels with the situation in Great Britain, but also some important differences. Aristocratic values and the cultural hegemony of the upper classes have been more important in British history. In the more plebeian American scene, a blending of Jewish cultural traditions (notably humor), language (the numerous Yiddishisms that have become part of American speech), and other tastes (food, music) proceeded

---

[42] Stephen Steinberg, *The Ethnic Myth: Race, Ethnicity, and Class in America* (New York, 1981), 45 ff., 253.

[43] Leonard Fein, *Where Are We? The Inner Life of America's Jews* (New York, 1988), xvii.

[44] Howard Simons, *Jewish Times: Voices of the American Jewish Experience* (Boston, 1988), 7.

with greater ease into a modern American amalgam. That amalgam has been pointed to, particularly by the mid–twentieth century but still with origins going well into the nineteenth, as a good example of how in America cultures can blend and find strength in the blend, of how American identity remained relatively optimistic and lacking in the kind of paranoia and fear of the future so characteristic of many European countries. Similarly, American nationalism in the nineteenth and twentieth centuries remained extraordinarily self-confident. Citizens of the richest and most powerful country in the world were relatively unaffected by fears of invasion or subversion. The "People of Plenty," in historian David Potter's phrase,[45] lived in a different world from most Europeans, still insecure in their national identities, fearful of national survival, and haunted by visions of poverty and want.

The issue of fantasy versus reality in Jewish–Gentile relations takes on revealing forms in American history, for negative fantasy about Jews has played a relatively small role; normal social and economic frictions have been less influenced by ideological inflation than elsewhere. The more grotesque of the fantasies, such as the blood libel, have been almost entirely absent. Even the common perception of Jews as culturally destructive has not been used against them to the degree that it has elsewhere. Their large role in the American left, as a dissenting minority among other dissenting minorities, has been a source of both favorable comment and resentment by non-Jewish Americans. Mommsen's description of Jewish critical destructiveness as useful in the building of a new national character could hardly find a better example than in the role of left-wing Jews in the emerging, ever-changing American national character. Still, in the United States as in Great Britain, politically conservative Jews, and those close to the political establishment, have played an important role, so that the notion of Jews as invariably left wing, although certainly present, has been less widely embraced.

One important reason that the rhetoric in favor of American exceptionalism was once so unqualified and prone to myth making was that the Jews who came to America found comfort in an image of themselves as opponents of European tyranny and bigotry, as a courageous people pursuing freedom – in the American tradition – rather than being "wretched refuse" driven by poverty. They pictured themselves as resisting not only the tyranny of European Gentile leaders but also that of rabbinical authorities and the Jewish upper classes, both of whom typically cooperated with Gentile authorities. Jewish immigrants to America long retained simmering resentments against the European Jewish establishment, secular and religious[46] – another uncomfortable topic that has been almost entirely forgotten by the last decade of the twentieth century.

[45] David M. Potter, *People of Plenty: Economic Abundance and American Character* (Chicago, 1954).
[46] These resentments form a key theme in Arthur Hertzberg, *The Jews in America: Four Centuries of an Uneasy Encounter: A History* (New York, 1989).

Even when the American reality was bitterly disappointing, as it unquestionably was for many Jews, public statements by Jewish leaders were influenced by a sense of how much worse things were in Europe, above all in the Russian Empire, and it was of course from that troubled, despotic land that the great majority of American Jews by the first decades of the twentieth century had recently come. As some Jewish observers would later recognize, Jews were understandably tempted to exaggerate not only European sins but also American virtues.[47]

Earlier generations of Jewish scholars felt with particular force the need to stress how Jews had blended into American society, how they had become one hundred percent American. The most recent generation of Jewish–American historians, coming of age in the 1960s and 1970s, with a different, often explicitly contrasting consciousness from those earlier historians – and in particular not feeling the same need to prove their Americanness – have often felt freer to point out conflict and dissonance in America's past.[48]

At any rate, without some strong sense of the European reality, and its own important variations from country to country, descriptions of the dark side of American history in regard to its Jewish citizens may become mired in provincialism, in unbalanced and morally absolutist condemnations, or in sweeping statements that anti-Semitism was stronger than "previously thought." Yet "strong" and "weak," without the concrete reference points that comparative history provides, remain vague, prone to strongly subjective evaluations.

In the seventeenth and eighteenth centuries the Jewish population in the American colonies was extremely small and mainly Sephardic. Even more than the Sephardim in France and Great Britain, Jews in America by the mid-1700s were accepted by the surrounding society and desired acceptance by it, although many colonial legislatures passed measures limiting their rights in the earlier part of the century. Many of the Founding Fathers seem to have had friendly feelings toward the Jews, and only occasionally did they express disdain for them.[49] George Washington, the symbolic father of the nation, was well known for his welcoming "the children of the stock of Abraham." He expressed hope that they would "continue to merit and enjoy the good will of other inhabitants" under a government that "gives to bigotry no sanction."[50]

At the Constitutional Convention, the framers of the American Constitution did not even debate whether Jews should have civil equality. Article VI specifically prohibits a religious test for office in the United States, in this

---

[47] Cf. Steinberg, *Ethnic Myth,* 49–51.

[48] These issues are provocatively explored in John Patrick Diggins, "Comrades and Citizens: New Mythologies in American Historiography," *The American Historical Review,* vol. 90, no. 3, June 1985, 614–49.

[49] Morton Borden, *Jews, Turks, and Infidels* (Chapel Hill, N.C., 1984), 26 ff.

[50] Quoted in Jehuda Bauer and Paul Mendes-Flohr, eds., *The Jew in the Modern World* (Oxford, 1980), 363.

regard much in advance of the British Constitution. The First Amendment specifically prohibits any federal law that would establish a national church or limit the free practice of any religion. There was no comparable restriction on the states, however, and in a number of them religion and politics became deeply enmeshed. Naturalization of new citizens also became the subject of a prolonged and often rancorous debate.

America's leaders of the Enlightenment, such figures as Thomas Jefferson, Benjamin Franklin, and John Adams, did not harbor the enmity to Jews so typical of such European intellectuals as Voltaire and Diderot. In the 1760s Franklin did openly fret, in what would now be called an ethnocentric way, about the dangers of "germanization" in Pennsylvania, where there was a large and growing German population, but "jewification" was not an issue. His concerns to preserve the dominant position of English culture of the country were widely shared by the Founding Fathers and were reiterated by prominent Americans throughout the next two centuries. Similarly, the hostility of the Founding Fathers to large-scale immigration derived from their fear of its divisive potential.

The population of Jews was extremely small in the eighteenth and early nineteenth centuries, and there were not many Jews in America who hewed "stubbornly" to Orthodox practice or who seemed to non-Jewish Americans to exhibit the kind of social separatism or contempt for their neighbors that would prevent their becoming good citizens. Jews simply played a less visible role in the early stages of American life, both in a negative and a positive sense, than they did in any major country of Europe. While Jefferson, in a typically Enlightened way, seems to have accepted as valid the frequent deprecation of the Talmud and Jewish morality of his time,[51] he did not attack Jews with the ferocity and monomania of Voltaire. On the other hand, Americans did not have Jewish figures who could be compared with Mendelssohn, Heine, Marx, or Disraeli. The extremes are missing in the first centuries of American history, as is the richness that characterized the European scene.

American culture did not have the drawing power that the great cultures of Europe at the time had for Jewish secular intellectuals. Rather than being attracted, most Jewish intellectuals in Europe were repelled, especially by the late nineteenth and early twentieth centuries. Figures as diverse as Sholem Aleichem, Leon Trotsky, and Sigmund Freud held American culture in extremely low regard. Religious Jews were even more profoundly repelled by American life, but whether religious or secular, European Jewish intellectual elites were almost unanimous in rejecting American culture as raw, vulgar, and crassly materialistic.

Nevertheless, for ordinary Jews – and it was they, rather than the European Jewish elites, who came to America in great numbers – America remained, as a

---

[51] Lester J. Cappon, *The Adams–Jefferson Letters*, vol. II (Chapel Hill, N.C., 1959), 383.

variety of English culture, decidedly in the ranks of the higher civilizations of the time. Jews who were little attracted to the predominantly peasant and premodern cultures of eastern Europe could still feel pride in entering into the ranks of one of the world's highest civilizations by embracing Anglo–American culture. Jews who came to America were, if possible, even more concerned to assimilate culturally than were Jews in England, France, or Germany. Much the same may be said about religious adaptation, insofar as it can be distinguished from cultural assimilation: American Reform Judaism, even more than its German counterpart, took giant steps in the direction of becoming like Protestant Christianity.

The Christian churches in America, whether Protestant or Catholic, were less hostile to Jews than were their counterparts in continental Europe. America's predominant Christian traditions contained important tendencies toward philo-Semitism. The American Puritans fancied themselves modern versions of the ancient Hebrews; their religious beliefs owed relatively much to the Old Testament and relatively little to the New. The crucifixion and the Jews' responsibility for it were less central to their beliefs. Similar remarks hold for America's fundamentalist and anabaptist sects; they did not typically demonize or seek to oppress those that they often admiringly referred to as "the People of the Book." Jewish refusal to believe in Christ, while often mentioned by American Christians, does not seem to have evoked the same quality of resentment in America that it did in much of Europe.

Still, Christians in America as elsewhere could hardly ignore the potently anti-Judaic and anti-Jewish passages of the New Testament. Negative images of Jews were amply propagated in Sunday schools and pulpits in nineteenth-century America. Remarks about Jewish vengefulness and the unforgiving character of Jews are to be widely found in nineteenth-century sermons, speeches, novels, and editorials.[52] But again, such statements do not seem to have evoked the same quality of resentment as in continental Europe, no doubt in part because they were not backed up legally or institutionally to a major degree, nor did they mesh with deep-rooted historical traditions. Jews in America had never been part of a medieval-style corporate body, and they had not been legally isolated in ghettos. They never formed a distinct commercial caste, nor were they ever required to wear distinctive clothing.

Even Catholics in America, who in the eighteenth century were also small in numbers and without the kind of political power they exercised in many countries of continental Europe, eventually came to esteem toleration between religious communities, Jews included, no doubt to an important degree because Catholics themselves suffered from intolerance. The most serious religious hostility throughout much of the early history of the United

States was between various Protestant denominations, or between Catholics and Protestants, or even between Reform and Orthodox Jews, much less often between Jews and Christians. Over the long run, America's identity as a haven from religious persecution by the state became ever more central, and Jews inevitably benefited from that identity. Indeed, they helped powerfully to shape it.

Anglo–American political and cultural traditions, which blended with religious preferences, emphasized toleration and compromise. Jeffersonian distrust of centralized political power, linked to an insistence on personal freedoms, posed a powerful obstacle to national legislation hostile to Jews. The American frontier supported the Yankee's preference for putting distance between himself and the central government, and in a broader way permitted escape from the confinements of tradition. Jews, like other Americans who headed westward, had unparalleled opportunities to do and be what they wanted, without fear of central government, repressive rabbinical authority, or more subtle community pressures.

Yankee traits, like British ones, were easily identified as Jewish in nature. The noted German scholar Werner Sombart, in a widely discussed study published in the first years of the twentieth century, made much of the similarity of the Jews and the Anglo–Americans. He noted, for example, that both believed the acquisition of material wealth was a sign of divine favor.[53] German conservatives typically made a distinction between *Helden* and *Händler,* heroes and tradesmen, and they typically saw the Yankees as ignoble money-grubbers. The English themselves were often taken aback by the commercial scramble in the United States in the nineteenth century, by the "Jewish" souls of the Yankees. Frances Trollope, the mother of the famous novelist, wrote that one "never heard Americans conversing without the word DOLLAR being pronounced between them."[54] Nearly a century later, Sigmund Freud saw only one reason to have anything to do with Americans: to get their money; they were "useful for nothing else." Americans were "savages" and "swindlers."[55] His sneering attitude to the American *Dollaronkel* (dollar uncle) and the malevolent tone of his private remarks about Americans are remarkably like those of German aristocrats in regard to the *Geldjuden* (money Jews). Richard Hofstadter's *American Political Tradition* suggestively speaks of America as a "democracy of cupidity rather than a democracy of fraternity."[56] A democracy of fraternity, whatever its merits, is also likely to be more difficult for outsiders

---

[53] Werner Sombart, *The Jews and Modern Capitalism* (Berlin, 1911); cf. the discussion in Gerald Krefetz, *Jews and Money* (New Haven, Conn., 1982), 42; Marcus Arkin, *Aspects of Jewish History* (Philadelphia, 1975), 143–8.

[54] Nancy McPhee, *The Book of Insults* (New York, 1978), 96.

[55] Peter Gay, *Freud, A Life for Our Times* (New York, 1988), 563–4.

[56] Richard Hofstadter, *The American Political Tradition and the Men Who Made It* (New York, 1957), v–xi; cf. Diggins, "Comrades and Citizens," 615.

to enter, especially when linked to notions of integral nationalism or *völkisch* identities.

In the United States, Jews who showed a devotion to commercial gain were less likely to encounter hostility, particularly aristocratic, anticommercial snobbery, than in Europe. The Wagnerians maintained that the only interest Jews had in art was to sell it, whereas true art emerged mystically from the memory of shared experiences of a people over centuries. The linkage of art and commercial gain became more important in America than in any other country in history, and charges that Jews wanted to make money from art did not have the same sting.

Barrès complained that for Jews, rootless, eternal wanderers, France was merely a place "where their self-interest is best pursued." The patriotism of French Jews, he concluded, was opportunistic, shallow, and fleeting, whereas for the true French, the *patrie,* the fatherland, is the resting place of their ancestors beyond memory, and thus a source of a deep and selfless attachment.[57] Americans, an emigrant people, could not make such exalted claims and were less likely to denigrate Jews as recent arrivals. Compared to Europeans, Americans were nearly all rootless wanderers in a democracy of cupidity, commercialism, and narrow self-interest.

America's lack of a titled nobility similarly meant that Jews faced fewer obstacles to gaining social acceptance in the United States. European anti-Semites were nearly unanimous in seeing the United States as a land without a sense of honor, of history, of aristocratic virtue. A. J. Langbehn, an influential speaker for German anti-modernist, aesthetic anti-Semitism, remarked at the end of the nineteenth century that "the crude cult of money is a North American, and at the same time Jewish, trait. . . ."[58] Revealingly, influential Jewish leaders in the United States made many of the same points but found merit where Europeans found fault. Louis Brandeis, who would become a Supreme Court Justice, spoke glowingly of America as a land where Jews could remain Jews and be perfectly at home. He asserted that "the Jewish spirit . . . is essentially modern and essentially American." In the same period, Drumont equated "Americanism" and "Semitism," both soullessly modern and destructive of traditional values.[59]

Brandeis eventually became a Zionist, but of a peculiarly American sort. For most European Zionists anti-Semitism was not only an important cause for their joining the movement; it was also a bitter personal experience. For Brandeis it was neither. Like many other leading American Jews, Brandeis expressed

57 Paula Hyman, *From Dreyfus to Vichy: The Remaking of French Jewry, 1906–1939* (New York, 1979), 13.

58 P. G. J. Pulzer, *The Rise of Political Anti-Semitism in Germany and Austria* (New York, 1964), 240.

59 Drumont, *France Juive,* vol. II, 258–60; from Frederick Busi, *The Pope of Anti-Semitism: The Career and Legacy of Edouard-Adolphe Drumont* (Lanham, Md., 1986), 72.

faith in the goodwill of the non-Jewish majority, and he had few if any experiences of anti-Semitism that left him with bitter memories.[60] He did believe in a Jewish homeland in Palestine – for others, not American Jews.

Since the Jews who came to the United States were to an important extent those who cared relatively little for Jewish religious tradition, America was all the more attractive to them. Few of them could claim illustrious Jewish lineage (*yikhus*). Many yearned to escape from their Jewish identity, or at least from certain elements of it. Jewish self-made men were legion in America. If many of them lacked polish, it was not particularly important in this new land. The commonly criticized tactlessness of Jews, their loud and pushy ways, all were less an issue in a country where manners were generally coarse, where civility, genteel style, and patrician culture in the European sense were suspect – indeed, "un-American." Even American speech, considered by educated Europeans to be nasal, sloppy, and vulgar in form, corresponded to the views of assimilated European Jews concerning Yiddish; both were dismissed as whining, debased dialects, with the tonal qualities appropriate to hawkers and peddlers.

Racism and Social Conflict in the United States

The preoccupation with race in Europe in the late nineteenth century definitely had its counterparts in the United States but in ways that may have decreased rather than increased anti-Semitism. America's black population was believed by the majority of nineteenth-century white Americans to be racially inferior, and the findings of nineteenth-century "science" that confirmed black inferiority were welcomed as a modern justification of social separation and the political disenfranchisement of blacks. Jews were accepted as whites; potential hostility to them as different was minimized, since blacks were incomparably more different – and threatening, decidedly not "inoffensive." Just as religious hostility in the United States was significantly deflected from Jews, finding expression between Christian sects, so American racial hostilities, which were almost certainly more intense than religious hostilities by the middle of the nineteenth century, tended to be between blacks and whites, while Jews were accepted as whites by most non-Jews.

Insofar as the notion of racial inequality among whites was espoused in the middle years of the century, it was in regard to the newly arriving Irish. In these years, Jews themselves typically shared the Anglo–American negative evaluations of both blacks and Irish. Rabbi Isaac Mayer Wise, a prominent Jewish leader at midcentury active in Reform Judaism, energetically defended Negro slavery. He believed it just to buy and sell "savages," and to "place them under the protection of the law [securing for them], the benefit of civilized

[60] Peter Grose, *Israel in the Mind of America* (New York, 1984), 55–6.

society."[61] Wise was bitterly opposed to Abraham Lincoln, whom he described as an "imbecile."[62]

Wise did not speak for all Jews in America. Most northern Jews were supporters of Lincoln, and he became undoubtedly the most popular president among Jews until Franklin D. Roosevelt. It is nevertheless possible to recognize in Wise's words the same kind of language used by nationalistic, and racist, German Jews in denigrating the Slavic peasant peoples around them in the late nineteenth century. In America as in Europe the evidence suggests that prevailing Jewish attitudes to race, until the turn of the century, did not differ markedly from non-Jewish attitudes.

The German-speaking Jews from central Europe who began to arrive in increasing numbers after the failures of the revolutions in Europe in the late 1840s were perceived by native-born Americans primarily as Germans rather than as Jews. Germans were, after the English, the largest ethnic group in America and were widely considered an up-and-coming people. German-speaking Jews were on the whole more educated and less inclined to alcoholic abuse and violence than were the Catholic Irish. German Jews quickly rose in wealth and in social position by the latter part of the nineteenth century.

During the Civil War, Jews in some areas encountered an upsurge of hostility. They were accused by both sides of being unpatriotic, interested only in profiteering.[63] General Grant's infamous Order No. 11 charged Jews, "as a class," with "violating every regulation of trade" established by the authorities; they were given twenty-four hours to get out of the war zone. But Order No. 11 was reversed within a few weeks, as soon as President Lincoln heard of it. Wars are notorious for bringing out the worst, and the best, in people, or the worst and best potential in any given society. On balance, Grant's order appears to have been more of a contretemps than a symbol of a deep or serious problem.

The charges against Jews in the Civil War appear to have been for the most part exaggerated or simply false.[64] Although there were unscrupulous Jews who sought to profit from the war, such individuals were to be found from all religious backgrounds; there is little evidence to support the charge that Jews were war profiteers significantly more often than others. It is possible that Jews were noticed more because they looked different and also because their profiteering was small-scale and without powerful protectors, whereas Gentile profiteers operated on a larger scale and had friends in influential places. But however

---

[61] Quoted in Hertzberg, *Jews in America*, 125.

[62] Grose, *Israel*, 28.

[63] Cf. Bertram W. Korn, *American Jews and the Civil War* (Philadelphia, 1951); this study includes a chapter on the violent expressions of anti-Semitism in the South as well as in the North, part of which has been reprinted as "American Judaeophobia: Confederate version," in Leonard Dinnerstein and Mary Dale Palsson, eds., *Jews in the South* (Baton Rouge, 1973), 135–55.

[64] Cf. Korn, "American Judaeophobia."

important these negative impressions of Jews may have been, individual Jews on both sides of this American war served with bravery on the battlefield, and both sides honored them with abundant recognition. Many non-Jews stepped forward, in the South as in the North, to defend Jews against their accusers.

Even Grant had friends who were Jews, a number of whom he later appointed to high office.[65] Grant's wartime orders do not seem to have reflected any special hatred for Jews. Indeed, he regretted those orders for the rest of his life. As president, in response to appeals from Jews in the United States, he lent his support to protests against the persecutions of Jews in Romania, and he told Jewish representatives that "the sufferings of the Hebrews of Roumania profoundly touch every sensibility of our nature."[66]

The financial scandals that marked the end of the liberal era and the beginning of the economically troubled 1870s and 1880s in Europe had plentiful counterparts in the United States. Corruption in high places became even more of an issue in the United States than in Europe at that time. Yet Jews in America were not conspicuous in or blamed for difficulties in those years. The European anti-Semitic agitators of the 1870s and 1880s could plausibly identify Jews as having a major role in financial crashes, bribery, corruption in high places, and spoliation of the landscape. These matters were of concern in the United States as well, but Jews were rarely blamed for them.

The Jews in Hungary

Jews in Hungary in the second half of the nineteenth century encountered, on the whole, an even more hospitable environment than in western Europe. A persuasive case might be made that in Hungary there was a more remarkable success story than in the United States, remarkable because of the numbers of Jews in Hungary and the rapidity of their rise in other regards. From less than 1 percent of the population for most of the eighteenth century, the proportion of Jews in the country steadily rose: 2 percent in the first decades of the nineteenth century, 4 percent by midcentury, 5 percent at the turn of the century. By 1910 there were 911,000 Jews in Hungary out of a total population of 21 million.[67] Between 1787 and 1910 the overall population of Hungary grew 125 percent, whereas the number of Jews in the country grew 1,021 percent.[68]

---

[65] Alan Edelstein, *An Unacknowledged Harmony: Philosemitism and the Survival of European Jewry* (Westport, Conn., 1982), 24, n. 32.

[66] Gary Dean Best, *To Free a People: American Jewish Leaders and the Jewish Problem in Eastern Europe, 1890–1914* (Westport, Conn., 1982), 6–7.

[67] *Hungarian Jewry before and after the Persecutions* (Budapest, 1949), 25 ff.; cited in Randolph L. Braham, *The Politics of Genocide: The Holocaust in Hungary,* vol. 1 (New York, 1981), 2.

[68] Randolph L. Braham, ed., *Hungarian-Jewish Studies* (New York, 1966), 62.

There seems little question that Hungary experienced the largest relative increase in Jewish population through immigration of any major country in the world in the nineteenth and early twentieth centuries. The Jewish population in France for the same period increased only two or three times, slightly more than the rise of the non-Jewish population. Even the massive increase, absolute and relative, of Jews in the United States hovered between 1 and 2 percent of the population.

These figures still do not convey the entire story, in that a larger percentage of Jewish immigrants moved to the capital city in Hungary than into any other capital city. The Jewish population of Budapest toward the end of the century surged to over 200,000, close to a quarter of the population of the city and the largest population of Jews in any capital city of Europe. (Its rival in this regard, Warsaw, was not yet a capital city, since Poland was not yet independent.) In Paris, a city with a much larger total population than Budapest (Paris: 2.7 million in 1900; Budapest: 732,000), Jews numbered between 30,000 and 40,000, around 1 percent of the total.[69]

What might be termed the Jewish presence in Budapest overshadowed even that striking percentage. Jews flocked to the professions; by 1910 45 percent of the capital's lawyers were Jews, as were 43 percent of the journalists and 62 percent of the doctors.[70] Much more than in Vienna, Jews in Budapest could exercise a decisive influence in elections, since as an affluent population they constituted about half of those in the capital who were qualified to vote. Similarly, in national elections, in which only 5 percent of Hungary's population had the vote, Jews played a role wholly disproportionate to their own 5 percent of the total population, both as qualified voters and, more subtly but even more importantly, as those who provided money, advice, and organizational support to parliamentary candidates. As one scholar has remarked, "Hungarian liberals actually governed the state and used their power vigorously to defend Jewish emancipation."[71]

The rise of the Jews in Hungary was noteworthy not only in terms of easily measurable aspects – increasing population, per capital income, educational levels, representation in high political, military, and judicial positions – but also in terms of the generally favorable attitude of the older ruling orders to that rise. The experience of Jews in Hungary stands as an instructive counterexample for those who maintain that the absolute number of Jews, or the proportion of Jews to non-Jews in any given area, constitutes a decisive stimulus to anti-Semitism. The Hungarian experience suggests how much more tangled are the causes of Jew-hatred than mere numbers, however important that

---

[69] B. R. Mitchell, *European Historical Statistics, 1750–1975* (New York, 1980), 86–9.

[70] Richard S. Levy, *Antisemitism in the Modern World: An Anthology of Texts* (Lexington, Mass., 1991), 93.

[71] Ibid., 92–3.

factor may generally be. It similarly offers a revealing example of the intricate interplay of fantasy and reality.

Throughout the nineteenth century Hungary remained an attractive destination for Jews, and the ruling elite of the country welcomed large numbers of them as did no other. It was not that the ruling classes in Hungary were philo-Semitic, and it would be a mistake to describe the country as a haven for the oppressed and poverty-stricken Jews from eastern Europe, as the United States would later become. Indeed, the disdain that many of the Magyar nobility felt for the Ostjuden was scarcely distinguishable from the feelings of the ruling elites elsewhere in Europe. Even the willingness of the Magyar upper orders to work closely with Jews in specific areas, for example, to let Jews handle their economic affairs, was not significantly different from the attitudes of the upper orders in much of eastern Europe. The main difference was that the Magyar ruling class was inclined to accept Jews who embraced Magyar language and culture as "real" members of the nation, not as permanent outsiders whose race or religion precluded their ever becoming adequately Magyar. Such an inclination was not entirely absent but was less significant among the Polish, Russian, Romanian, and German elites in their respective countries.

A related point is that Magyar nationalism focused more on cultural, as distinguished from racial or religious, matters; those Jews who adopted Magyar culture were acceptable in ways that Jews who embraced German culture in Germany or German-speaking Austria ultimately were not, since the issue of race loomed larger in those areas. Similarly, since Catholic religion was so integrally a part of Polish national identity, it was difficult for Poles to accept non-Catholics as genuine Poles, whether they were German Protestants, followers of Russian Orthodoxy, or Jews. Religious and racial intolerance were present in Hungary also, but the ruling elites by the later half of the nineteenth century come across as subtly more tolerant in regard to acculturated Jews than were their counterparts in most other countries of Europe. It must be reemphasized that these were nuances, not stark contrasts; social barriers remained for Jews, even when political and economic barriers were lower. Still, the nuances of Magyar–Jewish relationships came to have long-range significance in the unusual ability of Hungary to assimilate large numbers of Jews, to accept them both as useful and genuine members of the Magyar nation.

Several factors played an obvious role in the evolution of this peculiar attitude on the part of the Magyar elite. One is that both Catholic and Protestant faiths were significantly represented among the ruling orders of Hungary, reducing the attractions of unitary nationalism based on religious identity. In this blurring of issues of nationalism and religion, Hungary had something in common with Great Britain and the United States. Probably more important in reducing potential Magyar hostility to Jews, however, was the status of the Magyars as a minority in the lands over which they ruled; they were especially concerned about their numerical weakness in an epoch of nascent nationalism in eastern Europe, and they were eager for allies. There was a fairly numerous Magyar peasantry, but much of the rural lower class in territories claimed by Hungary was Slavic and Romanian, whereas the urban middle class was predominantly German and Jewish. Magyar nationalists were haunted by the remark of Herder that Magyars might eventually disappear, swallowed up by the Slavic and Germanic peoples that surrounded them.[72]

This Magyar fear of disappearing through absorption by more rapidly reproducing peoples, which many contemporaries described as verging on an obsession, led government authorities in Hungary, particularly in the second half of the nineteenth century, to launch a concerted, sometimes brutal effort to magyarize the population.[73] Those authorities often encountered stubborn resistance from peoples who hung on tenaciously to their national–linguistic identity. Therefore, any non-Magyars who willingly took up Magyar language and culture were viewed as valuable allies.

Of the groups that did magyarize during the nineteenth century, the Jews were important in sheer numbers but even more because magyarized Jews contributed more powerfully than other groups to the modernization of the Magyar nation and to its economic development, scientific progress, and international stature. A significant proportion of the Jews of Hungary embraced a Magyar cultural identity with genuine enthusiasm. Such Jews accepted, often in a quite combative way, the prevalent nineteenth-century notion that there were "historic" peoples, such as the Germans, Poles, and Magyars, and "historyless" peoples, such as the Slovaks, Romanians, or Ukrainians – who should be absorbed by the historic peoples.

Jews came to be perceived as shock troops in the struggle for Magyar domination. In the process they sometimes earned for themselves a special enmity from the peoples who refused to disappear and who resented being dealt with as inferiors. Such resentments, as we have seen, assumed even larger dimensions in the relations of German-speaking Jews with "historyless" peoples elsewhere in the Dual monarchy, since German-speaking Jews were equally notorious as crusaders for the superiority of German culture. Jews in central Europe, who would later suffer so much at the hands of racists, were themselves often perceived, and not without reason, as racist defenders of Magyar and German superiority.

A surprising number of the major artists, poets, and authors in the Magyar language in the nineteenth and twentieth centuries were of Jewish background. The accomplishments of Jewish–Magyar scientists were possibly even more impressive.[74] Again we are speaking of a nuance, since in nearly every country of Europe, acculturated Jews made major contributions to the arts

---

[72] William L. Langer, *Political and Social Upheaval: 1832–1852* (New York, 1969), 271–2.

[73] Cf. R. W. Seton-Watson, *Racial Problems in Hungary* (New York, 1972; first published, 1908).

[74] William O. McCagg, Jr., *Jewish Nobles and Geniuses in Modern Hungary* (New York, 1972).

and sciences, but their contribution finally stands out in Hungary more than elsewhere.

Yet another aspect of the Hungarian scene that made for a warmer welcome to Jews was the nature of liberalism in the country. We have seen the considerable variety of liberalism in Germany, Austria, France, Russia, Great Britain, and the United States. Hungarian liberalism represents yet another variant. Whereas in most western countries liberal ideas were identified with the bourgeoisie or the middle classes, in Hungary those ideas were forwarded by intellectuals from the nobility, a class that was more numerous than in nearly any other country. (The noble to non-noble proportion was 1 to 820 in Bohemia–Moravia, 1 to 100 in France, and 1 to 12 in Hungary.)[75] Such intellectuals saw liberal, modernizing reform as necessary to the survival of their country and as a necessary element of a national assertion in the modern world. Their relatively large numbers also gave them a plausible claim to speak for the Hungarian nation. However, they were not themselves bourgeois in style and habits, and they did not normally engage in commerce and industry.

There were liberal, reforming nobles in France and Great Britain, but their numbers were small in relation to the French and British liberals of middle-class origin with whom they were allied. In Hungary the non-noble allies of the reforming nobility were overwhelmingly Jews who embraced the cultural style of the Magyar nobility and gentry. Again, an absorption by the upper classes of the bourgeoisie was a common enough phenomenon in other countries, as, for example, the much-discussed junkerization of the German bourgeoisie, but in Hungary it was particularly striking in the case of the Jews. The highest aspiration for many Jews in Hungary was to become like the haughty Magyar nobility and gentry, even if such Jews did retain certain bourgeois traits, having to do, for example, with financial discretion and regular work habits.

A final reason that might be mentioned for the relative weakness in Hungary of anti-Jewish sentiment was that Hungary's non-Jewish middle class was still small and tended to be German in origin, "native" only in that it had been in the country since the eighteenth century, when Empress Maria-Theresa had invited German settlers into Hungary to help remedy the ravages of Turkish occupation. Interestingly, Hungarian anti-Semites in the late 1870s were hurt to some degree by the accusation that they were introducing a foreign, Germanic–racist ideology into Hungary.

There were organized anti-Semites in Hungary by the mid-1870s, but they remained on the fringe of political life even more than was the case in Germany. With the vastly increased movement of Jews out of eastern Europe by the early 1880s, out of the lands bordering on Hungary, those anti-Semites began to attract a larger following. Although most of the Jews leaving Russia, Galicia, and Romania made their way to the New World, for some of them

[75] Ibid., 72.

Hungary, where Jews had been granted full civil equality in 1867 and where there were many economic opportunities, was an attractive destination. It was also close by, whereas the New World was distant and for many a frightening prospect. Jews had been moving into Hungary since the early part of the century. At first they came from the western, mostly German-speaking parts of the Habsburg Empire. But by the 1880s migration out of Russia and out of neighboring Galicia began to replace the earlier patterns.

The first waves of Jewish immigrants to Hungary in the early nineteenth century were relatively modern in their habits and were German speaking. They took up Magyar language and culture with relative ease. However, the next waves were more backward, poorer, religiously more Orthodox, and more resistant to acculturation. In Hungary there developed a replication of the tensions between Jews of German origin and Ostjuden that were so conspicuous in all the countries so far examined, with much the same sources, prominent among which was a fear that the backward Jews from eastern Europe would revive or intensify anti-Jewish feelings where they had been steadily dwindling, which would mean a loss of hard-gained status for the native born Jew.

As one historian has put it, "within a few decades, the Jews of Hungary achieved a formidable, if not commanding, position in the country's economic, financial, and cultural life."[76] Grumbling began to be heard on the part of non-Jewish Hungarians who had previously remained silent. When wealthy Jews began to buy up, at a rapid rate, land previously held by the gentry and aristocracy, the grumbling became more pronounced. When Jews from Russia threatened to pour into the country at an even greater rate, after the tsar's assassination in 1881 and the ensuing pogroms, even Hungarians who had defended a Jewish presence as beneficial to the country began to express reservations. Back in the 1840s, in the debates concerning Jewish emancipation, Count István Széchenyi, a prominent statesman and reforming, liberal aristocrat, had remarked that other, larger countries might be able to absorb large numbers of Jews, since such countries were "lakes" into which a bottle of Jewish "ink" could easily disappear, but the same amount of Jewish ink would spoil the Magyar "soup."[77] Although his arguments did not prevail, by the 1880s the metaphor of Jewish ink ruining the Magyar soup took on new meaning and appeal.

Széchenyi does not qualify as an anti-Semite as defined in previous chapters. His arguments were based on real factors, not fantasies, and his tone was calm – indeed, his concern with the Jewish question was not major. The first

---

[76] Braham, *Politics of Genocide*, 2.

[77] George Barany, "Magyar-Jew or Jewish-Magyar," *Canadian-American Slavic Studies*, vol. 8, 1974, 1; Jacob Katz, *From Prejudice to Destruction: Anti-Semitism, 1700–1933* (Cambridge, Mass., 1980), 234.

important anti-Semite in modern Hungarian history was Győző Istóczy, one of the more enigmatic agitators to appear in Europe in the 1870s. Istóczy's early life and personality hardly suggest the makings of a racist bigot. He was of Catholic background, a member of the landed gentry, well educated, widely traveled, an excellent athlete, a "friendly, well-mannered young man who moved with facility and grace in social circles,"[78] and successful in his career as a lawyer and public servant in the late 1860s and early 1870s. In these years his political views were liberal, which naturally entailed an acceptance of Jewish emancipation and a belief that Jews could be useful additions to the Hungarian nation.

What turned Istóczy so single-mindedly against the Jews is not clear. By his own account, which in some ways resembles Böckel's account of the experiences that impelled him to defend the Hessian peasantry, it was because of his experience with Jews in a complicated series of trials surrounding the auction of an estate, during which a large number of them conspired in false testimony against him.[79] He eventually won the case and was cleared of the charges that the Jews allegedly concocted against him, but that experience, he avowed, totally altered his attitude to Jews. He was subsequently elected to the Hungarian parliament, and in a debate about granting citizenship to foreign Jews living in Hungary, he broke into an anti-Semitic tirade. Revealingly, his words were greeted with surprise, catcalls, and laughter. The prime minister dismissed his remarks by stating that there was no Jewish problem in Hungary, in sharp contrast to the countries on her borders, both to the east and the west.

Istóczy's first outburst occurred in 1875. In the next few years, his attacks on Jews took on texture and scope, but he remained on the fringe of Hungarian politics. He began to seek out contacts with the anti-Semitic agitators in Austria and Germany, although unlike many of them, his hostility to Jews was expressed in cultural rather than explicitly racial terms. Also unlike German-speaking anti-Semites, he developed a program for solving the Jewish problem that had intriguing proto-Zionist elements to it. To some degree his argument was familiar: that it was unreasonable to believe that the Jews, who had resisted assimilation for millennia, could now, within the span of a few decades, become genuinely Hungarian. Their ultimate and strongest attachments would always be to the Jewish nation. What was less familiar were his conclusions: Jews should be actively encouraged to move to Palestine, where they would find kindred Semitic peoples in the Arabs and might, with their many talents, even be welcomed by the sultan.

Istóczy's attitude to the Jews, much like that of Marr, remained a disorienting brew of admiration and distaste, broad-mindedness and narrow resentment.

[78] Andrew Handler, *Dori: The Life and Times of Theodor Herzl in Budapest, 1860–1878* (Tuscaloosa, Ala., 1984), 108.

[79] Ibid., 109.

Even in attacking them, however, he did not describe them as vermin or call for their physical destruction. But he did try to mobilize political support for anti-Semitism, to use resentment against Jews as a political device.

His greatest opportunity came with the notorious Tiszaeszlár Affair in 1882. In a bizarre trial, one that attracted worldwide attention, Jews in the village of Tiszaeszlár were accused of ritually murdering a fourteen-year-old girl. One of the many unusual aspects of this trial was that the chief witnesses for the prosecution were the sons of the synagogue sexton. They testified that they had seen their father, aided by a *shohet* (ritual slaughterer), murder the girl in the synagogue and collect her blood. Their motives in testifying against their own father remained murky, and their testimony was discredited in the trial. Still, much confusion and rancor developed over the body in question, found in the river several months after the alleged murder. Anti-Semites charged that the badly decomposed body was not that of the girl but rather of a Jewish prostitute who resembled her. The substitute body was part of an elaborate conspiracy, in which the powerful Jews of Budapest had become involved, to cover up what had actually happened to the girl. The ambiguous verdict of "not proven" rather than "not guilty," linked to the prosecuting attorney's remarks that he did not himself believe the Jews guilty, fed anti-Semitic indignation and the charge that there had been no real trial, since the prosecution had not even tried to uncover evidence against the accused. Immediately following the trial, anti-Jewish rioting spread across Hungary, and the anti-Semitic press charged that Jews had achieved a stranglehold on the institutions of the Hungarian state and its legal system; Jews would go to any length to protect fellow Jews, including lies, bribery, and intimidation.

In October 1883 Istóczy founded the National Anti-Semitic Party, with a platform that called for major reforms: loosening and counterbalancing the powerful role of Jews in Hungary's political, economic, and cultural life; regulation of licenses to sell alcoholic beverages, designed to prevent Jews from owning taverns; a prohibition of civil marriages between Jews and Gentiles; and measures to stem the influx of Jews into Hungary.[80] In 1883 his party won thirteen seats to the Hungarian parliament.

Yet this flare-up of hostility to Jews in Hungary, which undoubtedly was serious, had no important sequel, at least not before World War I. In the long run, Istóczy was even less successful politically than the anti-Semites in Germany and Austria. His movement collapsed only a few years after it started. None of his proposals were passed in parliament or even had a remote chance of success. The authorities and other prominent non-Jewish leaders spoke up quickly and forthrightly against Jew-hatred. The minister of culture characteristically remarked that "anti-Semitism serves only as a pretext to undermine the foundations of the social order. . . . [Riots] begin with Herschko or Itzig

[80] Ibid., 178.

[characteristic Jewish names in Hungary] and lead to Prince Esterhazy."[81] In short, non-Jews had good reason to oppose anti-Semitism and to feel relieved that it failed to gain a significant following. That was by no means an unusual attitude throughout Europe.

Part Two, in surveying the appearance of modern anti-Semitism in seven countries, has provided ample evidence of how different from today were opinions in the 1870s and 1880s about the nature of Jew-hatred. Then nearly everyone believed that Jews were hated for real, palpable reasons, for things that they did – or at least that large numbers of them did – not for baseless fantasies about them. Jews themselves forwarded this position at least as often as non-Jews, although Jewish leaders typically insisted that all Jews should not be held responsible for the misdeeds of a minority of them. It was also widely believed that hatred of Jews would diminish as they continued to reform themselves.

This survey has also emphasized how many common beliefs and generalizations to be found in histories of anti-Semitism cannot survive close scrutiny. The move from religious hatred to racial hatred, for example, is often too simply conceived, since religion continued to play a central role in the activities of men like Stoecker or in organizations like the Assumptionists, whereas racism played a minor or negligible role in the proposals of many if not most considered to be modern anti-Semites – von Treitschke, Istóczy, Stoecker, and Vogelsang, for example. Moreover, many of the self-described modern, antireligious racists, such as Marr, described the Jewish race in ways that differed in a number of important ways from later Nazi racism. Indeed, the attitude to Jews seen in nearly all of these men was "moderate" compared with later Nazi attitudes. Treitschke and others saw Jews as posing a problem that needed a solution, whether political or simply in terms of changes in attitudes; he and others like him did not think of the Jews as demons who should be banished from their countries or murdered.

It is particularly inaccurate and misleading to insist that these anti-Jewish leaders were lashing out at targets they knew nothing about. Nearly all of the prominent anti-Semites of these years had regular, even intimate contacts with Jews. Marr is the most extreme example of an anti-Semite with extensive Jewish contacts, but Drumont worked closely with Jews in his early career, as did von Schönerer and Wagner – indeed, in Wagner's case they continued well into his mature years. Von Treitschke's ire at Graetz's writings was hardly the result of baseless fantasies, and Goldwyn Smith's anger at Disraeli was based on the fact that Disraeli had mocked him. Smith and others who attacked Disraeli in anti-Semitic language also simply differed with Disraeli on political and foreign policy issues.

The rise of the Jews in the nineteenth century – another form of "what the

---

[81] Quoted in Nathaniel Katzburg, *'Antisemiut Be-Hungaria, 1867–1964* (Tel Aviv, 1969), 171.

Jews actually did" – is a subject that has so far received inadequate attention or analysis in most accounts of anti-Semitism. Undoubtedly, Jews were perceived in all countries as "rising," and they *were* rising, though hardly to the extent that many believed. Anti-Semitism and rising Jews need to be studied together. Fear and hatred of them were by no means rigidly or infallibly linked to their rise, as the British, American, and Hungarian examples demonstrate, but on the other hand those examples do not prove that there was absolutely no relationship between a Jewish rise and a rise in anti-Semitism – or that hostility to Jews was based *entirely* on fantastic perceptions of them.

Many accounts of the Jews in the nineteenth century celebrate their remarkable accomplishments, but little effort has been made to relate or reconcile that story with the widespread belief that Jews faced terrible obstacles – crippling discrimination and pervasive hostility. Striking a proper balance is of course inherently elusive, but how credible is a story that, on the one hand, tells of Jews rising dramatically, to become a starkly disproportionate part of the extremely wealthy and of the professional classes in many countries, and, on the other, that emphasizes how Jewish aspirations were cruelly blocked wherever they turned? Indeed, there are implications to this disparity that are not often considered and that will be central to following chapters: If Jews were so remarkably successful in the face of pervasive and tenacious hostility, how much greater might their success have been if they had faced no hostility at all? Does their great success in spite of pervasive hostility not speak in favor finally of their superiority to the peoples among whom they lived? Might their supposed "right to rule" have been achieved if they had not been so unfairly held back? Would they have taken over leading positions in many of the countries in which they lived, even as a minority of 1 to 5 percent of the total population?

The paradoxes of the Dreyfus Affair – when anti-Semites like Picquart played a key role on Alfred Dreyfus's eventual exoneration – find echoes in every country. Similarly, although there were many crude and simple-minded anti-Semites, many other self-declared enemies of the Jews were of first-rate abilities and worldly success. Wagner and Barrès are among the more striking examples, but there are a large number of others, among them von Treitschke, Goldwyn Smith, Istóczy, and Vogelsang. Other examples, some even more striking, will be provided in subsequent chapters.

PART THREE

THE BELLE EPOQUE
(1890–1914)

Now that sixty years have passed, and only the disillusionment of reality remains, we look back . . . with a sad feeling of regret; we were happy then and did not know it. (Paolo Minelli)[1]

The decades immediately before World War I appear in retrospect to have a vague unity to them, one reflected in such terms as *belle époque*, Wilhelmian, or Edwardian. The temptation to see these years as a whole, in spite of a dazzling diversity in the intellectual and cultural arenas, derives in part from the simple facts that a new century began in 1900 and a world war erupted in 1914. But there were other markers, dating back to 1890. In that year Bismarck left office, the new chancellor, von Caprivi, spoke of a "new course," and the new emperor, Wilhelm II, began to put his peculiar stamp on German – and European – life. Queen Victoria's death in 1901 and the accession of the sybaritic Edward VII marked as well a distinct change of tone. The removal of those imposing older figures from the scene implied an end to confinements and restrictions – portentous, at least in retrospect.

The rosy hues of this beautiful epoch, of what has also been called the "Golden Age of Security,"[2] have been often overdrawn, but a persuasive case can be made that these years represented the pinnacle of modern European civilization, even if their reckless dynamism also brought insecurity and threatened self-destruction. Thus, intertwined with the sense of delight in some quarters were feelings of decadence and decay, of anxiety over social and political disintegration – inklings of coming disasters.

Other developments in the 1890s also struck contemporaries as epoch making. The German Social Democratic Party emerged from its outlawed status and began a process of rapid growth, promising to take power in Germany

---

[1] Eleonora Bairati et al., *La Belle Epoque: Fifteen Years of European History* (New York, 1978), 6.

[2] Stefan Zweig, *The World of Yesterday: An Autobiography* (New York, 1943); cf. Hannah Arendt, *The Origins of Totalitarianism* (New York, 1963), 50.

in the near future, a prospect that profoundly alarmed the ruling classes in Germany. France, Russia, and Great Britain entered into a gradual process of diplomatic rapprochement, resulting in what Germany's leaders had long-feared: encirclement. Germany's ruling orders believed that they faced growing threats, both inside and outside Germany, and their efforts to counter these perceived threats – and even their exaggeration of them in order to mobilize support for the status quo – set the tone to the twenty-odd years in Europe before the war. The continuing drift of Germany's already junkerized and "panicked" middle classes toward a more tribalistic nationalism seems to have been much influenced by anxiety about enemies on all sides. Yet Germany's neighbors in turn felt ever more menaced by what they perceived as an expansionist, saber-rattling Germany.

On a more hopeful note, the Great Depression of the 1870s and 1880s eased, after a final plunge in the early 1890s, and Europe's economies again showed considerable productivity, driven forward by what economic historians have termed a "second" industrial revolution, based on the chemical and electrical industries. In them a chain of scientific and technological discoveries helped to transform the material living conditions of millions of people, providing such innovations as electrical lights, more rapid and easily available transportation, and mass production of synthetic clothing. The situation in the rural sector shifted significantly also, with a rise in commodity prices and income from land, a rise that was largely the result of the rapidly growing demand for food and other agricultural commodities in the ever more populous urban industrial centers.

These changes found abundant if sometimes inscrutable expression in the shifting relations of Jews and non-Jews. Anti-Semitism assumed different dimensions. Politically, it weakened to insignificance in Germany, whereas in Austria the anti-Semitic Christian Social movement achieved unparalleled successes. As has already been described, a dramatic anti-Semitic affair erupted in France; similar eruptions occurred in Russia and the United States, shaking the population of those countries, too, and drawing worldwide attention to the issues of Jewish victimization as well as alleged Jewish power.

A puzzling contrast thus presents itself as a central theme of Part Three. In Germany, where political anti-Semitism first appeared as an influential movement in the 1880s, a relatively dormant period in terms of political attacks on Jews ensued from the 1890s to the eve of the war. On the other hand, in France, where anti-Semitism had been widely assumed to be weak, a major episode of anti-Semitism erupted around the Dreyfus Affair. These various developments contributed to, or were a part of, a fundamental shift in Jewish self-image and in a related faith in the possibility of Gentile–Jewish harmony. The intricate issues of modern Jewish identity, of pride and self-hatred, and of fighting back against anti-Semitism became increasingly important. So, too, did the issue of whether Jewish "reform" held any lasting hope for eradicating anti-Semitism.

The emerging industrial scene was different in tone from both the confident 1850s and 1860s and the anxious 1870s and 1880s, again with important if subtle implications for the relations of Jew and non-Jew. The liberal belief in individual enterprise and individual responsibility, already shaken by the 1880s, faced further assaults. Industrial concentration, large corporations and cartels seeking to control and plan production, became more important. So, too, did large trade and industrial unions; organized business and organized labor tended to stimulate one another. Laissez-faire was not abandoned, but tariffs and other measures of economic control became more prominent. Extraparliamentary interest groups, most notably those representing agriculture and traditional crafts, often succeeded in winning special consideration from the state, protecting them from the rigors of the free market.

The state sought to regulate the economic relations of its citizens through taxation and social welfare measures. Generally, the power of the state grew, the absolute and relative number of its employees increased, and the size of its armies expanded. These were new, mass armies, impressive military machines that inducted, trained, and attempted to regiment unprecedented numbers of the general population. In education, similar trends prevailed: an extension of primary instruction to previously untouched elements of the population. The popular press expanded from its modest beginnings in the preceding decades and sought to address the millions of recently literate readers in Europe, often in crude, sensationalistic ways, playing upon war scares, spies, colonial adventures, and government swindles.

Trends that put new kinds of power in the hands of political and economic elites inevitably increased the appeal and plausibility of long-standing charges, trumpeted by the popular press, that "money men" were working behind the scenes. It was widely believed, for example, that wealthy Jews were responsible for the Boer War (1899–1902). The Russo–Japanese War (1904–1905) was similarly believed to have been orchestrated by internationally powerful Jews to humiliate Russia, whereas the ensuing revolution in Russia in 1905 was considered to be the work of an unlikely alliance of Jewish capitalists, socialist agitators, and populist demagogues. The sensational anti-Semitic affairs of the period were based on beliefs in Jewish conspiracies of various sorts.

Contrary to facile assertion, clandestine Jewish involvement, or actions by Jewish power brokers, did exist in these various events. They were often part of Jewish self-defense, of "fighting back," although hardly in the far-reaching ways believed by the anti-Semites of the day. But the belief that powerful Jews were manipulating important events often excited the general public of Europe and America. To denounce Jewish conspiracies was a natural temptation for popular politicians and the gutter press, but established, respectable politicians made similar denunciations.

As we have seen, the 1870s and 1880s witnessed the often uncertain first steps of modern, antiliberal mass parties, the most important of which was the

German Social Democratic Party, but Christian Social, peasant–populist, and petty bourgeois stirrings were also evident. In the two decades before the war the rise of the masses in a political sense became a more solid reality. Many observers believed that a qualitative change in political life was irrevocably under way and that the bourgeois, elitist liberalism of the *notables* and *Honoratioren* was a thing of the past, that the antiliberal masses would inevitably take over. The so-called Arendt Thesis, that this was a period in which European governments became subject to the power of the mob – with ominous implications for the Jews – represents an early interpretation along these lines.[3]

The vote was extended to previously unrepresented parts of the population in many countries, and the growth of new, bureaucratically organized parties of the masses paralleled the concentration and organizational concerns of the industrial corporations and trade unions and, indeed, the growing ranks of the state bureaucracies. Extraparliamentary organizations, again focusing on a growing presence and assertiveness of the previously unorganized and inarticulate common people in European life, perfected new methods of propaganda and mobilization, of a piece with the new journalism, based upon appeals to emotion rather than reason – slogans, banners and symbols, demonstrations, and street music. There was constant talk of mass uprisings and general strikes, talk that found occasional bloody expression in most countries of Europe.

The intellectual and cultural life of Europe and America in the two decades before the war both reflected and intensified trends in the economic and political realms. Intellectual and cultural expressions, all with obvious roots in the 1870s and 1880s, which have been variously termed "neo-romantic," "decadent," "antiliberal," "anti-bourgeois," "irrationalist," and "antipositivist," thrived between 1890 and 1914; Fritz Stern has emphasized the "cultural despair" of the time in Germany;[4] Emile Durkheim spoke of a "renascent mysticism" in France.[5] It was a time "when the basic assumptions of eighteenth and nineteenth century social thought underwent a critical review from which there emerged the new assumptions of our own time."[6] Artists, literary figures, and scientists, of both Jewish and Gentile backgrounds, expressed often mean-tempered dissatisfaction with what they believed were the easy truths of the mid-nineteenth-century liberal perspective. Mixed into these expressions were elements of generational conflict, of youthful idealism against middle-aged stolidity. In Germany, youth groups, the *Wandervögel* (wandering birds), took

[3] Arendt, *Totalitarianism*, 11–53.

[4] Fritz Stern, *The Politics of Cultural Despair: A Study in the Rise of Germanic Ideology* (New York, 1965).

[5] Emile Durkheim, *The Rules of Sociological Method* (Chicago, 1938), xl; quoted in H. Stuart Hughes, *Consciousness and Society: The Reorientation of European Social Thought, 1890–1930* (New York, 1958), 35.

[6] Hughes, *Consciousness*, 33; Talcott Parsons, *The Structure of Social Action* (Glencoe, Ill., 1949), 5.

to the forests and mountains, seeking authenticity and expressing a profound aversion for modern urban industrial existence. And although young Jews themselves partook in these wanderings, the status of Jews as preeminently modern and urban could hardly avoid being subjected to hostile scrutiny by such developments.

It is natural enough to conclude that the new feelings for "deep consciousness" and "racial intuition" constituted a dark portent for the relations of Jews and non-Jews. The widely expressed disillusionment with the fruits of reason seemed to spell a definitive end to the already battered universalistic ideals of the liberal nineteenth century. But another key concern of Part Three is to explore how the "death of liberalism" in these years has been described with more drama and decisiveness than is justified. Liberalism was not as robust or self-confident as it had been in midcentury, but it was not yet dead by any means. The rise of the masses and the antibourgeois, antiliberal expressions of the time are most accurately seen as gropings by dissatisfied yet indecisive elements of the population. Those who claimed to speak for the lower orders were not ready to assume power, nor did the critics of the liberal era have clear-sighted alternatives in mind.

Liberalism was unquestionably being attacked from many quarters, and the twenty-odd years before World War I saw not only a rise of the masses but also the appearance of quirky, elitist "conservative revolutionaries,"[7] who were ambiguously connected to a reassertion of the older elites. Napoleon III, Bismarck, and Disraeli had all explored the potential of mass support for conservative ideas, but conservatives in the *belle époque* took further steps in mass mobilization, hoping to preserve vested interests. Nonetheless, the older elites were not simply antiliberal; they had absorbed or even generated themselves many values that have gone down in historical works as "liberal." The point has similarly often been made that the socialists by the turn of the century themselves fought for many liberal tenets. In "death" liberalism still had a wide if subtle influence over a diverse company.

Historical memory, particularly a knowledge of what was to follow in the 1930s and 1940s, has presented major problems to clear and dispassionate understanding in these regards. An optimism that cannot be dismissed as foolishly blind about the future of Jewish–Gentile relations persisted among most Jews and non-Jews in Europe. Such was especially true of the older generation of liberals, but even most of the younger "irrationalist" thinkers of the period immediately preceding World War I retained a deeper faith in the power of reason. Freud is an obvious example, since he believed in the use of reason to probe the irrational – and to bring it under rational control.[8]

Similarly, nineteenth-century faith in progress was by no means fatally

---

[7] Stern, *Despair*, 15.

[8] Cf. Hughes, *Consciousness*.

undermined before the war. The conditions of material existence, a more fundamental determinant in the lives of ordinary people than the productions of artists and intellectuals, continued to improve. Impressive feats of science and technology continued to bolster a belief in unending progress, especially among the great masses of unreflective citizens, who were now beginning to enjoy a hitherto unknown material security.

9

The Failures: Russia and Romania

[Russian Jews] never seem for an instant to lose the consciousness that they are a race apart. It is in their walk, in their sidelong glance, in the carriage of their sloping shoulders, in the curious gesture of the uplifted palm. (Harold Frederick, 1892).[1]

We felt joy and pride in our newness: we eat and rejoice, while all Jews fast and cry. (A member of the Jewish Bund, in Vilna on the Day of Atonement)[2]

The scribblers here try to persuade the reader that the shtetl was a paradise full of saints. So comes along someone from the very place and says "stuff and nonsense!" They'll excommunicate you. . . . (Isaac Bashevis Singer, from *Lost in America*)

Worsening Jewish–Gentile Relations in Russia

Tsarist Russia was the widely recognized opposite of a sweet exile. From 1890 to 1914 many of the already severe tensions between Jews and non-Jews worsened, breaking again into large-scale violence after the turn of the century. Suspicion of the Jews by tsars Alexander III and Nicholas II grew; they listened less to those who advocated reforms to make the Jews more "useful." More and more they concluded that the Jews were incorrigibly destructive, that they would have to be repressed or encouraged to leave the country.

Whether or not Russian Jews constituted a state within a state, more than a separate nationality faithful to the tsar, became an ever more explosive issue. In 1868 a Jewish convert to Christianity, Jacob Brafman, had charged that the

---

[1] Harold Frederick, *The New Exodus: Israel in Russia* (London, 1892), 79–80.

[2] Ezra Mendelsohn, *Class Struggles in the Pale: The Formative Years of the Jewish Workers' Movement in Tsarist Russia* (Cambridge, U.K., 1970), 153.

kahillot (roughly, Jewish parliaments, dating from the days of the Polish Commonwealth) continued to exist clandestinely, in spite of being abolished by Nicholas I in 1844. They had established firm contact, he claimed, with such Jewish organizations as the Alliance Israélite Universelle.[3] Brafman's charges were believed by many officials and blended into related beliefs about international Jewish political power. Such officials worried especially that the clandestine power of Jews was used by Jewish financiers to protect and advance the economic success of Jews in Russia. (In truth the kahillot did survive, though the extent of their connections with Jewish organizations in the West is much less certain.)

The rise of the Jews, and the parallel, seemingly contradictory pauperization of large numbers of them, had major implications in the Russian Empire, culminating after the turn of the century in a Jewish counteroffensive, inside and outside Russia, against the oppressive rule of the tsars. In spite of the movement of millions out of Russia from the 1870s onward, the population of Jews inside Russia continued to grow. Massive internal migrations, from the north to the less densely populated south, preceded and then paralleled emigration to other countries. The overall rate of population growth for Jews in Russia in the sixty-year period from 1820 to 1880 was about 150 percent, whereas the non-Jewish population increased only 87 percent. Even more remarkable was the Jewish increase in the southwest of Russia, where anti-Semitism made its most violent appearance in the late nineteenth and early twentieth centuries: From approximately 3 percent of the population in 1844, Jews made up around 9 percent of the population by the turn of the century. During the period from 1844 to the eve of the war, the Jewish population increase in the southern provinces was nearly 850 percent, the non-Jewish 265 percent.[4] Jewish population growth was especially notable in the newer urban areas, which were also the most turbulent in Russia.

Anti-Semitism in Russia, especially from the 1880s onward, was hardly a hatred without palpable or understandable cause; it had something quite directly to do with a fear that Jews threatened vital Russian interests and values. And this fear, although it connected with exaggerated, even preposterous fantasies about Jews, was related to real factors. Such fearfulness blended into a larger paranoiac Russian psyche, related to the existence of an array of by no means imaginary enemies surrounding Russia. For many Russians, their country's Jewish population appeared as a rapidly growing and increasingly hostile body, actively if secretly collaborating with those enemies. (Hatred or fear of Russia, to state the obvious, also was based on real factors, into which, perhaps inevitably, were mixed exaggerations and fantasies.)

---

[3] Steven J. Zipperstein, *The Jews of Odessa: A Cultural History, 1794–1881* (Stanford, Calif., 1985), 115.

[4] Salo W. Baron, *The Russian Jew Under Tsar and Soviets* (New York, 1987), 63–4.

For Slavophiles, men who believed in a special Russian nature and destiny, the traditional, religiously based antipathy to Jews was replaced with a secular one: Jews came to symbolize for them the threat of an alien and decadent West, of a destructive modernism, one that would undermine their hopes and dreams for Russia. Traditional Jews were objectionable enough to such Russian nationalists, but at least Jews of that sort were politically passive, respectful of authority. But as hundreds of thousands of Jews began to abandon their traditional ways and embrace western ideologies, they appeared ever more menacing – and were ever more menacing.

Anti-Jewish racism as such was relatively weak in Russia, as might be expected of a country only beginning to embrace modern science. Older religious charges were relatively common. Well into the twentieth century the accusation that Jews used Christian blood for their ceremonies was commonly made. Several Jewish converts became notorious for their cooperation with the tsarist regime in offering "expert" support for the charge of ritual murder.

Fears about the incursions of modernism afflicted a large part of Russia's ruling elite. The rise of the Jews in countries on Russia's western borders was seen as a warning by such men. A rise in Russia comparable to the rise of Jews in Hungary, for example, was a prospect that Russian nationalists regarded with horror, to be prevented at all costs, in part because those nationalists plausibly concluded that most Jews in the Russian Empire were not at all interested in blending, to become Russians, as Jews in Hungary had become Hungarians. And even if Jews in Russia might actually be inclined to compromise their long-standing separatism, their large numbers would almost necessarily entail a compromise with a much larger Jewish component than Russian nationalists were willing to entertain. There was no getting around the fact that Jews in Russia were twice as numerous in relation to the general population as in Hungary, ten times as large as in Germany, a hundred times as large as in France or Great Britain.

Since the charge of Jewish aspirations to power was one that was taken seriously by men as different as Drumont, Zola, and Gide, it is not surprising that Russian nationalists, facing a Jewish population a hundred times as large as the one in France in an economically backward, peasant country, were obsessed with it. They maintained that the peasants would fall under the rule of the Jews and would inevitably be undermined morally by their contact with them. In the eyes of such nationalists, the peasants, unsophisticated in money matters, borrowed money from Jews and eventually lost their lands to them. Jews offered the peasants both cheap credit and cheap vodka, encouraging and exploiting their tendencies to drunkenness and improvidence. Even when the role of Jews was not painted in such negative colors, many Russian nationalists believed that Russians, as other Slavs, were simply no match for Jews in a modern, liberal, and competitive society – thus "controlling" the Jews was absolutely necessary.

Arnold White, an English journalist and member of parliament, who had on occasion represented the Jewish philanthropist Baron de Hirsch and who had spent much time dealing with Russian officialdom, vividly communicated the extent of Russian nationalist fears: He predicted that if Russia were to "fling down the barriers to Jewish emancipation, not five years would pass before Russia would be Jewish. In ten years every place of importance in the empire would be filled by a Jew."[5] One conservative Russian nationalist warned that "the Jewish force is extraordinary, almost superhuman."[6] The reactionary minister and tutor of Tsar Nicholas II, Konstantin Pobedonostsev (1827–1907), with whom White had much contact, openly defended Russia's discriminatory policies by asserting that Jews were natively more intelligent, more aggressive, and more inclined to seek an education than was the mass of the Russian population.[7] For him, government control of Jewish activities had a quality of *noblesse oblige* to it. The peasants needed paternalistic protection by the state or else they would become in effect slaves of the Jews.

Such paranoiac views were not limited to the reactionary right. Among more moderate, liberally minded members of the ruling class there seemed to be a consensus that Jewish character was inherently alien to Russian national character and that Russians were not able to compete successfully with Jews. Even on the socialist and liberal left in Russia, where by the turn of the century anti-Semitism was denounced as a reactionary device, the notion that Russia's Jews were unchangeably foreign, economically threatening, and morally destructive to the non-Jewish population popped up with arresting frequency.[8]

The mid-to-late 1880s were relatively calm, marked by repression and vigilance by the government over popular agitation. These years saw the beginnings of what would develop into very rapid industrial growth in the 1890s, financed by investments from the West as well as by "squeezing" peasant savings inside Russia. That growth fed popular agitation of a sort that had only just begun to be felt in 1881. An industrial proletariat, most of it with one foot still in the village, concentrated in a few burgeoning industrial areas and increasingly rebellious, assumed a new importance. The peasantry, too, became once again restive.

The conditions in the new industrial centers were, as one historian has commented, "fantastically overcrowded, unhygienic, and squalid."[9] Revolu-

---

[5] Quoted in Isadore Singer, *Russia at the Bar of the American People: A Memorial of Kishinef* (New York, 1904), 153.

[6] Maurice Samuel, *Blood Accusation* (New York, 1966), 88.

[7] Baron, *Russian Jew*, 53.

[8] Cf. the article by Tugan-Baranowsky (Professor of Political Economy at St. Petersburg), "Anti-Semitism in Contemporary Russia," *Monthly Review*, Jan. 1904; in Singer, *Russia at the Bar*, 224 ff. Tugan-Baranowsky, typical of many liberals, emphasized that the peasants were in fact friendly to the Jews, seeing them as economically useful in the village economy; it was, rather, the middle and upper classes that felt threatened and that increasingly took up anti-Semitic agitation.

[9] Lionel Kochan and Richard Abraham, *The Making of Modern Russia* (New York, 1963), 229.

tionaries who had looked to an oppressed peasantry to overthrow tsarism and introduce a humane, rational regime now turned to the industrial proletariat to perform that redeeming mission for Russia, moving from Russian populist (narodnik) theories to those of western Marxists.

The more simplistic Marxists of the time were inclined to fit the growing industrial violence of the end of the century into a pattern of capitalist–proletarian class conflict and to see a redemptive mission in it. But in truth that violence was characterized by a random, unideological quality, turning in directions that are difficult to fit into preconceived Marxist patterns – or into preconceived notions about the anti-Semitic motives of those who engaged in violence. Some of the looting and vandalism no doubt served the purpose of challenging tsarist authority and of giving support to demands for a more humane and rational society, but violence by members of the lower class was by no means all so rationally directed as that. As Lenin would later formulate the issue, providing a more sophisticated Marxist perspective, the "spontaneity" (*stikhinost'*) of the proletariat, in rebelling against its condition, could be "purely destructive" if not properly guided by revolutionary leaders with "consciousness" (*soznanie*), by men who "knew better."[10]

Members of the ruling orders spoke in similar terms. Prince Mirsky commented, in a conversation with Empress Alexandra, that "it is the intellectual class that makes history everywhere, while the masses are merely an elemental power; today they massacre the revolutionary intellectuals, tomorrow they may loot the Czar's palaces."[11] Such opinions much resembled the long-standing belief of the tsars and their officials that the "dark" masses were forever prone to wild and brutal outbursts; constant vigilance by the authorities was absolutely necessary. A recent historian has graphically expressed a slightly different but still related perspective: She notes that oppressed workers could join socialist parties and fight for a world of justice and humanity, but they also could "loot, brawl, break machinery, beat up intellectuals and Jews, and rape women from the old upper classes."[12] Many Russian revolutionaries, from the 1870s on, accepted that "popular excesses" – often, they acknowledged, of a shocking brutality and irrationality – were an unavoidable aspect of a revolutionary uprising of the people.[13]

Whether it was a focused anti-tsarism, anticapitalism, or anti-Semitism that motivated such people, as distinguished from simple, undifferentiated anger, material distress, and brutal resentment, may certainly be questioned. Again,

[10] Cf. Alfred G. Meyer, *Leninism* (New York, 1963), 43.

[11] Abraham Yarmolinsky, ed. and trans., *The Memoirs of Count Witte* (Garden City, N.Y., 1921), 190.

[12] Sheila Fitzpatrick, *The Russian Revolution* (Oxford, 1982), 6.

[13] Jonathan Frankel, *Prophecy and Politics: Socialism, Nationalism, and the Russian Jews, 1862–1917* (Cambridge, Mass., 1981), 99–101.

even Jewish workers by the early 1880s were "beating up the industrialists, breaking looms, striking, struggling," as one of them proudly put it.[14] The Jewish Bund, proclaiming that Jews must fight back, must end their millennia-old passivity, was not always able to guide, in the Leninist sense, the anger and resentments of Jewish proletarians. This was the beginning of a process even more impressive among Jewish workers than among non-Jewish: Passivity and fatalism were being shaken off; Jewish suffering was no longer accepted as God's will but rather something that Jews could fight against and change. But such changes did not proceed smoothly, and working-class leaders, whether Jewish or non-Jewish, could not maintain a firm control over the turbulent working masses.

As in western Europe, the new techniques of production and distribution, linked to precipitous population growth, not only spawned a new proletariat but also undermined the position of traditional industries and handicrafts, resulting in sometimes explosive tension within both the working and the middle classes. Inevitably, ethnic differences were mixed into these tensions. Jewish employers at times used the more pliant and less class-conscious Christian workers as strike-breakers against their Jewish employees, even filling the Christian workers' heads with stories of how Jewish workers hated them. Jewish socialists found it necessary to implore Jewish workers to refrain from violent retaliation against Christian scabs. In Bielsk, Jewish workers organized special "terrorist squads," often composed of semicriminal elements, against both employers and strike-breakers.[15] Christian hoodlums were similarly organized by the so-called Black Hundreds to terrorize Jewish workers, finally achieving, from 1903 to 1906, a level of horror and bloodshed that exceeded anything even dreamed of by these earlier Jewish terrorist squads.

By the turn of the century, local officials and the secret police began to mix into these conflicts. The secret police at times collaborated with the Jewish underworld and with Jewish employers. At Dvinsk, the Jewish owners of Zaks's match works employed gangsters and pimps, with the support of the secret police, to attack striking workers. In Warsaw, in an episode that was widely reported in the European press of the day, followers of the Bund rioted for three days in 1905 in what was called a "pimp pogrom." Jewish pimps and the Jewish underworld in Warsaw had also engaged in strike-breaking and other antiworker activity; Jewish workers, in retaliation, broke into houses of prostitution, smashing windows and furniture, knifing both pimps and prostitutes, and throwing them out of the windows. The government did not intervene in any consistent or effective way in this pogrom as in so many others, and the rioting stopped only when the leadership of the Bund was able to regain control over

---

[14] Mendelsohn, *Class Struggles,* 28.

[15] Ibid., 99–104.

the rioters. Some eight dead and over a hundred injured were counted at the end of this pogrom by Jews.[16]

Most of the rapidly growing cities in European Russia, especially in the Pale of Settlement, were populated by ethnic groups that were different from the surrounding majority peasant populations, which were mostly Slavic. Germans and Jews were among the most successful of those urban minority groups in taking advantage of the new economic opportunities, and the Jews were not only the most numerous of such minorities but also the most vulnerable. As in western Europe, modern, racist anti-Semitism linked to nationalism seems to have been most pronounced in those urban areas where elements of the Jewish and Gentile middle classes found themselves in competition. Violence between Jew and peasant in the countryside seems to have been of a different quality, less systematic or ideological, more personal, and more sporadic.

Tsarist ministers repeatedly complained that the Jews were unusually prone to joining revolutionary socialist movements, a complaint made as well by Jewish employers. Several ministers also charged that the Jews were extraordinarily successful as capitalists. There was truth to both of these assertions. Not all Jews, or even anything like the majority of them, became revolutionaries, but Jews did join socialist organizations in disproportionately high numbers. Jewish activists at the time took pride in it while lamenting the major role of Jewish capitalists. Both trends have been amply affirmed by later historians.[17]

The proclivity of an important minority of Jews throughout Europe for revolutionary socialism had many roots, but in Russia one factor was that especially after the educational reforms of the 1860s and 1870s, there may have been more university-educated Jews than the Russian economy could absorb – certainly more than Russian society was ready for.[18] In 1889 the ministry of justice submitted a special report to the tsar, warning that the legal profession was being "flooded with Jews" and that their peculiar traits were tarnishing the reputation of the bar. The tsar approved measures to limit Jewish lawyers.[19]

The problem of a "Jewish flood" in certain occupations existed also in Germany, with a Jewish population one-tenth that of Russia's and with a larger job market for the university educated, whereas in Austria and Hungary the Jewish presence in all the professions often exceeded 50 percent. In Germany and Austria, too, many educated Jews, especially lawyers and journalists, found

[16] Edward J. Bristow, *Prostitution and Politics: The Jewish Fight Against White Slavery, 1870–1939* (Oxford, 1983), 58–62.

[17] Cf. Robert S. Wistrich, *Revolutionary Jews from Marx to Trotsky* (New York, 1976), and *Socialism and the Jews: The Dilemmas of Assimilation in Germany and Austria–Hungary* (East Brunswick, N.J., 1983).

[18] Mendelsohn, *Class Struggles*, 29.

[19] Cf. Samuel Kucherov, "Jews in the Russian Bar," in Jacob Frumkin et al., eds., *Russian Jewry* (New York, 1966), 220–2.

attractive careers in the social–democratic movement.[20] But Jews in Russia inevitably felt themselves, more than in any western or central European country, to be hated and hounded outsiders in a regime of incompetence and bigotry, and thus the attractions of radical revolutionary doctrines were all the greater.

Jews in Russia, as throughout eastern and central Europe, were even more disproportionately represented in certain kinds of commercial enterprise than in socialist activism. Many of the most successful Jewish capitalists remained loyal to tsarism and naturally hostile to socialism. They were encouraged by Russian authorities, with erratic swings from minister to minister, to play a "useful" role in Russia's effort to keep up with the West. However, the great mass of Russian Jews, while increasingly urbanized and not usually the poorest of the poor, were not strongly present in primary production or in the introduction of the most advanced techniques of production. "Almost invariably, the larger and more modernized the factory, the fewer the number of Jewish workers employed."[21] This fundamental economic reality worked in the long run against prosperity for a large part of the Jewish masses inside Russia, at a time when their aspirations began to climb. It was yet another structural factor, along with the absolute and relative increase in the Jewish population, that was finally more important than the anti-Semitism of individual tsars or their ministers in producing poverty and despair among Jews. But of course these factors cannot easily be disentangled, and oppression by the authorities and the legal disabilities were more visible than structural factors; they were something that could be fought. It was the combination of subjective factors (the actions of individual tsars and their ministers) and structural change unfavorable to millions of Jews, linked to rising expectations, that made Jewish life in Russia ever more intolerable and that led Jews themselves, with a rising sense of urgency, to search for solutions to the Jewish Question – emigration (to America, western Europe, or Palestine), assimilation and integration (an unrealistic or unappealing option to the great mass of Jews), or revolution.

Even Jews who were abandoning old ways usually held on to elements of their traditional culture, and many, perhaps most, Russian Jews before 1914 remained attached to the old ways and to religious orthodoxy. They continued to view their miseries, material and otherwise, as God given, certainly not to be changed by political activity. Orthodox rabbis were notorious for cooperating with the police in ferreting out Jewish socialist and union activists, a cooperation that may be seen as yet another aspect of the growing class conflict within Jewish communities.[22]

But in balance the liberal-to-socialist left exercised a powerful attraction for

[20] Wistrich, *Socialism*, 81; J. P. Nettl, *Rosa Luxemburg* (Oxford, 1969), 262–7.

[21] Mendelsohn, *Class Struggles*, 23.

[22] Ibid., 106–7.

those Jews who in one way or another had begun to enter the modern world, even if pushed unwillingly into it. As in western countries the left was friendly territory in comparison to the territory of the Russian conservatives. The program of the left in Russia promised civil equality for Jews and other minorities, and its leaders denounced anti-Semitism and other forms of religious and ethnic hostility. It was no accident that the authorities, and the Russian right more generally, were ever more inclined to bunch liberals, socialists, intellectuals, and Jews into one hated category.

Under Nicholas II (1894–1917), tsarist authorities grew ever more suspicious of their Jewish subjects. Nonetheless, certain classes of Jews (merchants of the first guild, university graduates, and skilled artisans, for example), continued to enjoy important privileges. Wealthy Jews usually enjoyed access to the tsar's ministers. Still, the legendarily wealthy Jewish magnates in Russia, the Brodskys, Ginzburgs, and Poliakovs, some of whom were honored by the government and who even acquired titles of nobility, did not mix with Nicholas and his court in the way that their counterparts in Germany did with Wilhelm II, or, to cite the more conspicuous example, the way wealthy English Jews did with Edward VII of England.

Nicholas and his ministers saw the hand of the Jews not only in revolutionary activity but also in Russia's foreign policy disasters. And increasingly Jews, both inside and outside Russia, were themselves inclined to view Nicholas II and most of his ministers as implacable enemies. The great Jewish historian Simon Dubnov, in describing this period, declared that "Russian Jewry has developed an irreconcilable hatred for the despotic regime. . . ."[23] An escalating underground "war" (the word was used on both sides) between Jews and tsarist authorities developed in the generation before World War I. It broke repeatedly into violence, in pogroms against the Jews, on the one hand, and in assassinations of government officials and revolutionary violence by Jews, on the other.

The 1882 May Laws had been passed with a special concern to prevent Jews from exploiting the peasantry. The laws decreed that Jews were not to settle in peasant villages, and they were forbidden to buy more land. The laws in one sense merely reinforced an existing demographic trend in both Russia and the West, and everywhere among Jews more than any others, to move from the countryside to the new, rapidly expanding urban centers. But those centers could not easily absorb the Jewish population moving into them. A study done in 1907 analyzing the Russian census of the same year concluded that approximately three-quarters of the Jews in Russia lived in urban areas by the end of the century.[24] Given the dimensions of the population increase among Jews,

---

[23] Quoted in Frankel, *Prophecy and Politics*, 137.

[24] Israel Rubinow, "The Economic Condition of Jews in Russia," *Bulletin of the Bureau of Labor*, no. 72 (Washington, D.C., 1907), 487–583; cited in Stephen Steinberg, *The Ethnic Myth: Race, Ethnicity, and Class in America* (Boston, 1981), 94.

May Laws or no May Laws, there would have been overcrowding in the urban centers of Russia. No such laws existed in the United States, yet nearly catastrophic urban overcrowding of Jews occurred there as well, especially in New York. Similar problems developed in London.

In any case, a full and consistent implementation of the May Laws was repeatedly postponed in the decade following their introduction. Moreover, they did not apply in Congress Poland, a large area of particularly dense Jewish settlement. As with the pogroms of 1881, too simply described as the reason for the emigration of Jews in the 1880s, so with the May Laws: They were less the source of urban ills than was the population increase of the time, linked to the disruptive effects of rapid economic development, trade, and unemployment cycles. But also like the pogroms, the May Laws were more palpable, satisfying targets for criticism than impersonal economic forces or demographic expansion. It would be wrong, however, to conclude that the May Laws were without major harmful effect. By the turn of the century they were deeply resented and widely denounced as ill-conceived by both Jews and non-Jews. The laws may be seen as a perfect symbol of the bungling and simple perplexity of the tsar's officials about what was to be done about Russia's Jewish population.

Even those Russian conservatives who believed in the need to keep the Jews under strict control came to recognize that the laws did not work. Jews succeeded in circumventing them on a massive scale by leasing land through proxies, by remaining in the villages "temporarily," by bribing officials, and by illegally moving out of the Pale of Settlement. An American diplomatic observer remarked in the early 1890s that the laws "have heretofore been so loosely and lightly observed as practically to be inoperative."[25]

Time after time recommendations were made by various committees and ministers to amend or revoke the laws, but they remained in effect until 1917, largely because Nicholas II himself repeatedly blocked any change of them, at times referring to an "inner voice" that guided him in resisting reform.[26] Bribery on the part of Jews seeking to evade the multitude of special laws concerning them became a way of life in many areas. The courts were crowded with Jewish criminals and litigants, quite aside from the large numbers arrested for revolutionary activity, incurring the ire of overworked officials. The governor of the province of Bessarabia, Prince Urussov, a liberal nobleman who was widely recognized as friendly to the Jews and who openly criticized the May Laws, commented in his memoirs, in words that strikingly recall those of Istóczy in Hungary, that the judges he encountered in the province in 1904

---

[25] Gary Dean Best, *To Free a People: American Jewish Leaders and the Jewish Problem in Eastern Europe, 1890–1914* (Westport, Conn., 1982), 27.

[26] H. H. Fischer, *Out of My Past: Memoirs of Count Kokovtsev* (Stanford, Calif., 1935), 164; Alexander B. Tager, *The Decay of Czarism: The Beilis Trial* (Philadelphia, 1935), 14; Baron, *Russian Jew*, 61.

unanimously declared that not a single lawsuit, criminal or civil, can be properly conducted if the interests of the Jews are involved. In civil suits . . . [the Jews arrange] fictitious deals and contracts, . . . concealment of property, and usury . . . hidden in legal guise. Criminal cases . . . afford the Jews a chance to fill the court with false witnesses set against one another.[27]

The conservative anti-Semitic editor V. V. Shulgin complained that the May Laws and other restrictions on Jews "are offensive to us and we strongly desire to get rid of them. They are full of nonsense and contradictions . . .; the Police of the Pale of Settlement live on Jewish bribery on account of Jewish restrictions."[28]

Jews were understandably inclined to evade laws that they considered unfair, indeed that in some cases made it nearly impossible for them to earn an honest living. Jews gained a reputation of being inveterate liars when dealing with the authorities. A Yiddish-language paper in the United States wrote that even after leaving Russia and dealing with American or German authorities, "Our Jews love to get tangled up with dishonest answers," or they get themselves into trouble by offering bribes to officials unaccustomed to receiving them.[29]

Thus the May Laws over the years contributed in a major way to corruption, ethnic tension, and other mischief in Russian life for both non-Jews and Jews. Urussov remarked how he "frequently observed that the hatred of the police officials toward the Jewish population is partly due to the worries, annoyances, complaints, explanations, mistakes, and responsibilities which constantly fall to the members of the police in consequence of the senseless and ineffective legislation concerning the Jews."[30]

Periodic and unpredictable crackdowns made the situation all the more unbearable. In 1891 thousands of Jews, many of whom had established a relatively comfortable existence, were abruptly ordered to leave Moscow and return to the Pale. Similar administrative edicts followed for the Jewish population of other major cities outside of the Pale, including St. Petersburg, causing much misery. In 1896 the state set up a liquor monopoly, depriving thousands of Jews of lucrative occupations, either as wholesale liquor merchants or as innkeepers. In many areas up to this time, the liquor trade had been important to Jewish economic survival. In the villages of Zhitomir province, for example, 73.7 percent of the Jews earned a living by leasing distilleries and selling the product at inns.[31] Not surprisingly, after the establishment of the state liquor monopoly, many Jews continued to produce and smuggle contraband alcohol,

[27] Prince Serge Dmitriyevich Urussov, *Memoirs of a Russian Governor: The Kishinev Pogrom* (New York, 1908; reprinted, 1970), 73–4.

[28] Samuel, *Blood Accusation,* 245.

[29] Ibid., 44.

[30] Urussov, *Memoirs,* 32.

[31] Mendelsohn, *Class Struggles,* 2.

further swelling the ranks of Jewish "criminals" who found it necessary to bribe local officials to survive.

After the turn of the century, the tide of terrorist acts again rose, and assassins succeeded in killing a remarkable number of Russian officials, both high and low. The role of Jews in these assassinations was unquestionably more extensive than it had been two decades before. "There was a procession of pale, thin, and often Jewish students to the gallows and to Siberia, after spectacular trials."[32] The much-discussed role of individual Jews in these assassinations deeply impressed the tsar and his officials. The assassins did not claim to speak for the Jewish population of Russia, and the Marxist organizations, including the Jewish Bund, explicitly rejected terrorism. But such distinctions little impressed those whose suspicion of Jews was already so much aroused. In any case, many Jews in Russia only feebly disguised their satisfaction at the violent deaths of notoriously anti-Semitic officials. On several occasions those deaths were cause for open celebration in the streets by Jews. In 1902 when Hirsh Lekert, a Jewish shoemaker who tried to assassinate Vilna's repressive governor general, was hanged, it was cause for Jewish mourning and the elevation of Lekert to the status of Jewish martyr.

The Paradoxes of Modernization in Russia; the Kishinev Pogrom

The diplomatic alliance with France that developed in the early 1890s was supplemented by the movement of investment capital from France into Russia. Investors, businessmen, and various technical experts from other western countries, prominently Germany, Great Britain, and Belgium, also took an interest in Russia. Foreign investment in Russia soared, from 98 million rubles in 1880 to 911 million by the turn of the century.[33] Unavoidably, Russia's leaders began to feel a new dependence on western good will, and in turn western governments exploited that feeling as a form of leverage in dealing with the Russian government.

Jews inside Russia, whether revolutionary socialists or legalistic liberals, were not slow to realize that this was a potentially powerful weapon to be used in their "war" with the tsars. They seized every opportunity – and there were many – to embarrass and expose Russian officialdom. Similarly, Jews outside of Russia, in attempting to aid Jews inside the country, did their best to publicize the malfeasance of Russian officials and to mobilize public opinion in their own countries against tsarist policies. This was the case especially in countries, such as Germany and Austria–Hungary, that considered Russia to be a poten-

---

[32] Norman Stone, *Europe Transformed, 1878–1919* (Cambridge, Mass., 1984), 214.

[33] Kochan and Abraham, *Making of Modern Russia*, 227.

tial enemy in war. Even in allied or more friendly countries the left was quick to denounce Russia's reactionary internal policies.[34]

The pogroms of the early twentieth century were the most notorious of the alleged misdeeds of the tsar and his ministers, and the most notorious of them occurred in April 1903 in the city of Kishinev, the capital of the province of Bessarabia. Indeed, this pogrom might be described as the most widely publicized act of anti-Semitic violence in Europe before 1914. It is now recognized as the first of ever-rising waves of pogroms in Russia, over 600 in all, that rolled over the country from 1903 to 1906. The Kishinev pogrom merits careful attention for what it came to symbolize. In bloodshed and destruction to property it exceeded any single previous pogrom in modern times: Forty-five Jews were reported killed, over 500 were "injured" (including rapes), and approximately 1,500 homes and shops were vandalized. The Kishinev pogrom was thus responsible for more deaths and injuries in a few days than the hundreds of riots in early 1881.

Jewish sources initially reported over 700 dead, but these figures were denounced by Russian officials as typical examples of Jewish exaggeration and falsification. Hyperbole and mendacity do seem to have been a problem, on both sides, since the initial official news releases denied that there had been any pogrom at all. But as even a friendly American reporter recognized, some of the atrocities initially reported simply did not occur, and some Jews made false claims in hopes of getting relief money from western Europe and America.[35] On the other hand, rapes were almost certainly underreported, since by traditional Jewish law a raped woman is no longer eligible for marriage by an observant Jew. The Jews of Kishinev and Odessa were known as the least observant in Russia, so it is uncertain how relevant traditional law was, but there is little question that rapes were held in special horror and underreported.

The Kishinev pogrom is revealingly understood not only as an expression of the rising tensions of the period but also as part of a public relations war: Exaggerations and indignant denials in the press were part of a battle to gain the favor of international public opinion. It may seem the height of paradox to describe a pogrom as marking a rising Jewish combativeness. Yet the Kishinev pogrom, in terms of what it symbolized and, especially, what Jews made of it, became just that.

Kishinev was prominent among the cities that had grown rapidly in the preceding decades. Some 50,000 Jews lived there by the eve of the pogrom, close to half of the population. Contemporary accounts of the relations of Jews and non-Jews in the city differ markedly. Some observers claimed that relations

---

[34] For a detailed account, see Best, *To Free a People.*

[35] Michael Davitt, *Within the Pale: The True Story of Anti-Semitic Persecution in Russia* (New York, 1903), 240–1.

were harmonious, that the majority population, made up of Moldavians (ethnically and linguistically close to the Romanians), was easygoing and tolerant. Part of the explanation for this harmony, so it was maintained, was that the social separatism and religious intolerance of the Jews themselves were less prominent here than in other parts of Russia. The contemporary Jewish historian Dubnov, however, dismissed the non-Jewish population as living in "gloom and crude superstition,"[36] harboring resentments against the Jews, who constituted a large proportion of the wealthy and professional classes of the city. The Moldavians of the city, numbering slightly more than 50,000, were described by some as especially prone to Jew-hatred and barbaric violence.[37] Neighboring Romania was reputed to be the most anti-Semitic nation in Europe. Ethnic Russians, who held most of the posts of authority in the city, numbered only around 10,000.

Such oddly contrasting perceptions characterized many contemporary descriptions of the relations of Jews and non-Jews in the rest of Russia. What various observers "saw" derived not only from the enormous variety of conditions in Russia but also from where those observers stood in the propaganda war between the Jews and the regime. Russian conservatives, who emphasized that the Jews were hated for good reason, pointed to the rapidly growing wealth of the Jews and their exploitation of the rest of the population. They rejected the assertion that the hatred was based on religious bigotry or on government manipulation of popular fantasies about Jews. Indeed, many Russian officials steadfastly maintained that without government protection, Jews faced a rising danger of violence by the resentful lower classes, whether urban or rural.

Other observers denied the importance of social and economic resentments against the Jews. Particularly in the countryside, so these observers maintained, the peasants lived mostly in harmony with their Jewish neighbors, even welcomed them as useful elements in the rural economy, since Jews marketed the peasants' produce and brought to the isolated peasant villages commodities they would otherwise lack. Attacks on Jews occurred only when the credulous peasants were misled by malevolent agitators, who were often aided by tsarist officials. Modern racist hostility, at any rate, did not reflect the mentality of the peasantry.

Kishinev had been relatively calm in 1881, during which anti-Jewish riots had broken out elsewhere in Russia. In the following two decades, the city underwent a transformation, as tens of thousands of new residents, Jews and non-Jews, arrived. Such sudden population changes are conducive to civil strife in almost any environment. Violent attacks on Jews had since ancient times been stimulated by a rapid increase in Jewish numbers or power.

---

[36] Simon Dubnov, *History of the Jews: From the Congress of Vienna to the Emergence of Hitler*, vol. 5 (New York, 1973 [first English edition, 1920]), p. 717.

[37] Davitt, *Pale*, 93.

However, it is far from clear in this instance whether the economic role of the Jews in the city was universally or even widely resented. The respected mayor of the city, Karl Schmidt, who had been in office since the 1880s, openly attributed the city's prosperity to its Jews. He noted that in the 1870s the city had been an isolated outpost, "on a level with the average Turkish town," but the Jews "built up its commerce, organized its banks, developed its general business, and made it the handsome, thriving city it is today."[38]

These accomplishments undoubtedly generated envy and resentment in some quarters. Moreover, Schmidt's favorable attitude to the Jews was not shared by others in authority. In the early 1890s there had been a notable incident involving one of the police chiefs in the city. When the Jews tried to resist his greed for bribes, he retaliated with fury, applying the May Laws in full severity, as was also being done at this time in a number of cities in the north.[39] The official directly above that police chief, the vice-governor, Ustrugov, let it be known that he considered the Jews of the region to be a "plague."[40]

It was at about this time (1894) that Pavolachi Krushevan, a virulently anti-Semitic journalist, arrived in Kishinev. He established a newspaper, the *Bessarebetz*, which began a scurrilous campaign against the Jews of the region, denouncing them as corrupt businessmen and as socialist agitators. Such charges were common enough in the Russian conservative press, but Krushevan's attacks were unusually venomous and unbridled.

It is tempting to conclude that Krushevan was taking cues from Drumont in France, who by 1894 was the object of comment throughout Europe. Dreyfus's arrest occurred in this year as well; it was an event that naturally concerned France's new ally, Russia. Krushevan, like Drumont, had previously written a popular work of local color,[41] and like Drumont he seemed obsessed by a belief that Jewish capitalists were destroying sacred local traditions. Krushevan was ostensibly following Drumont's lead as well in introducing both modern racist themes and a grab-bag of accusations against the Jews.

There were, on the other hand, some revealing differences in the situations of the two. Even at the height of his success, Drumont remained an outsider, a fringe agitator attacking the republican powers. Krushevan established friendly contacts with the officials of the area and received financial support from them. Some officials wrote columns for his newspaper. Drumont's journal was an example of the flourishing popular Parisian press of the time, but it was merely one of many. Krushevan's became the only paper of any significance in Kishinev, with a circulation of around 20,000. It was delivered to the

---

[38] Ibid., *Pale*, 93.

[39] Ibid., 96.

[40] Urussov, *Memoirs*, 12–17.

[41] Krushevan's work *Bessarabia* seems to have had something in common with Drumont's *Mon Vieux Paris;* cf. Urussov, *Memoirs*, 10.

offices and libraries of the educated, ruling elite, the police officials, army officers, and high church officials.

An American reporter marveled, in observing the quality of the anti-Semitic press in Russia, that "among educated and enlightened Russians one finds anti-Semites who are not one whit less rancorous than the ignorant and benighted mujik [peasant]."[42] Prince Urussov, who would become governor after the pogrom, also expressed dismay at the bigotry to be found among the educated classes, but he denied that the peasants of the region were hostile to the Jews. Indeed, in his tours of the countryside he found the peasantry either supportive or without decided opinions about the Jews.[43]

Much like Drumont, Krushevan tried to gain readers and followers among the middle and lower-middle classes. One of his first press campaigns focused on the many Jews who served as municipal employees, and he succeeded in having a number of them dismissed, to be replaced by Christians. Such efforts paralleled not only those of Drumont but also of Karl Lueger, the mayor of Vienna, again a possible model. Krushevan succeeded in attracting an especially ardent following among non-Jewish physicians in the city, who were up-in-arms over the large Jewish proportion of the medical profession.[44]

In the political arena, Krushevan's activities paralleled those of Drumont and de Morès. It is tempting to conclude that Krushevan studied the methods of the French Ligue antisémitique in the anti-Semitic riots of 1898. However, not having to worry about police intervention, he had a simpler task. Almost all observers credit Krushevan with actively organizing the rioters of 1903. He openly recruited them, to a large degree from the villages around the city. But he also brought in Macedonian and Albanian thugs from afar, armed them all with iron bars, and even provided them with addresses of Jews in the city.[45]

In one regard, Krushevan's organized efforts appear to have been substantially different from those of the Ligue antisémitique. De Morès made a genuine and substantial contact with a settled, productive element of the Parisian common people, the La Villette butchers, as did Drumont with other elements of the commercial lower-middle class. The Kishinev pogrom has not benefited from the kind of in-depth studies that have been devoted to the French riots of 1898, but the evidence suggests that Krushevan's contacts, aside from those with government officials, were rather with the rabble of Kishinev and surrounding villages, joined by professional criminals and a few seminary students. At any rate, he was not "rousing the masses" so much as organizing and arming outsiders and a marginal riffraff that did not number

---

[42] Davitt, *Pale,* 117.

[43] Urussov, *Memoirs,* 162.

[44] Davitt, *Pale,* 96 ff.; Singer, *Russia at the Bar,* 3 ff.

[45] Singer, *Russia at the Bar,* Davit, *Pale,* and Urussov, *Memoirs* – in many ways quite different in tone – agree on these details.

more than a couple of hundred. He spread rumors, similar to those of 1881, that a "punishment" of the Jews would be favored by the tsar and not opposed by the local authorities. Also similar to the events of 1881, others began opportunistically to join in, once the riots were under way, since the forces of order did not intervene forcefully and consistently.

Still, the participation of those opportunists did not constitute a popular uprising, and accounts by some Jews in Kishinev of massive popular approval of the violence remain dubious.[46] A few of these accounts paralleled, with striking and suspicious similarity in certain ghoulish details, stories handed down from the Chmielnicki massacres of Jews in the seventeenth century. No doubt the shock concerning what happened, which was horrifying enough, and the failure of significant numbers of non-Jews to come to the aid of the Jews further inclined Jewish observers to sweeping condemnations and sensationalism. But many of the more lurid accounts by Jewish witnesses were put into doubt by later investigations.

Krushevan exploited tensions in the city, but one must wonder if he could turn large numbers of established residents into the kinds of monsters who drove nails into people's eyes, disemboweled their pregnant victims, or forced fathers to watch the rape of their wives and daughters. It is plausible that the non-Jewish poor could be encouraged to envy and resent the Jewish rich, and it is likely that the Christian middle class in competition with the Jews also felt envy and resentment. All accounts emphasize that Christian merchants in Kishinev feared Jewish competition and that Jews were generally more successful in business. The purported rapacious business practices of Jews were widely denounced.[47] But it can be doubted if the drunken, rampaging mobs in Kishinev were in any fair sense representative of the city's population. Those mobs were made up overwhelmingly of young males, which was certainly the case for the 300 or so who were later arrested.[48] Their inhibitions were dissolved not only by drink and the urgings of Krushevan but also by their character as outsiders and by their sense that no legal authority would oppose them. In short, they were not "the people," nor was this a popular uprising.

The feeble response of the authorities was of decisive importance in this pogrom, as in those of 1881. The reasons for this inactivity remain unclear, but the police forces in Kishinev were woefully understaffed. Police recruits were insufficiently trained, poorly paid, and generally held in low regard by the populace.[49] The situation in the army was even worse; its officers disliked

---

[46] Cf. Singer, *Russia at the Bar,* 13 ff.

[47] Davitt, *Pale,* 116.

[48] Singer, *Russia at the Bar,* 273.

[49] Cf. Neil Wasserman, "Regular Police in Tsarist Russia, 1900–1914," *The Russian Review,* vol. 44, 1985, 45–68; Shlomo Lambroza, "The Tsarist Government and the Pogroms of 1903–06," *Modern Judaism,* vol. 7, no. 3, Oct. 1987, 292.

becoming involved in civil disorders, and its recruits were raw and unreliable. The initial failure to repress the disorders may have been the result of confusion, because of ambiguous orders, may have reflected covert sympathy by the police and army for the rioters, or may have been a mixture of these, since there was much variety in the response of the forces of order in various parts of the city. At any rate, when the mobs perceived that the authorities in some areas of the city were passive, the rumors about the tsar's desire to see the Jews "punished" seemed justified. The rioters became more brazen, and some bystanders began to join in. Once the police and army began to intervene energetically, the rioting ceased almost at once, suggesting that such a response initially might have prevented the entire tragedy.

Immediately following the pogrom, accusations were made that it had been instigated by the minister of interior, Viacheslav Plehve. These accusations have found their way into a number of the classic accounts of the period, and they were for many years uncritically accepted.[50] Even recently an otherwise well-informed writer identifies Plehve as the minister who "fomented the Kishinev pogrom," without providing documentation, presumably because Plehve's role is so well known as not to require it.[51] But as in 1881, the available evidence does not support charges of direct complicity by officials in St. Petersburg. Rather, one finds confusion, incompetence, and purely local complicity.[52]

It was no secret that Plehve by 1903 considered the Jews to be enemies of the regime. He angrily told a Jewish delegation from Odessa that "the Jews in southern Russia constitute ninety percent . . . of all revolutionaries."[53] But he did not directly foment the pogrom. (Plehve would be assassinated in the following year by a Jewish terrorist. Krushevan, too, would be shot down by a Jewish assassin in the same year, though he survived.[54]) Not all local officials supported Krushevan's efforts, and some, for example, Mayor Schmidt, were strongly opposed to them. Schmidt in particular insisted that the rioters were simply a criminal band brought in by Krushevan.[55] The provincial governor at the time of the riots, von Raaben, was not an anti-Semite, but he was lazy and pleasure seeking; he handed most of his duties over to subordinates, including the anti-Semitic vice-governor, Ustrugov. Von Raaben was dismissed in disgrace immediately after the pogrom, and his replacement as governor, Prince Urussov, was known as a moderate liberal, opposed to the persecution of the

---

[50] Cf. Wasserman, "Regular Police," and Lambroza, "Tsarist Government," for a discussion of the historiography of this issue.

[51] Bernard Avishai, *The Tragedy of Zionism* (New York, 1985), 63.

[52] One of the most amply documented studies is Lambroza, "Tsarist Government," 287–96.

[53] Baron, *Russian Jew,* 56.

[54] The case would be handled by Gruzenberg, who would later become one of Beilis's lawyers. Cf. Samuel, *Blood Accusation,* 177.

[55] Singer, *Russia at the Bar,* 254.

Jews. Urussov was familiar with the ruling circles in St. Petersburg and later commented that Plehve was "too shrewd and experienced to adopt such an expedient [that is, fomenting a pogrom]" in his fight against the Jews,[56] particularly because he was aware of the damage it might do to Russia's international standing.

Urussov, who had privileged access to governmental files, found no evidence of complicity in the riots on the part of any higher officials, although he suspected that the secret police, whose records were closed to him, may have played a role. Plehve often met western observers, and usually impressed them favorably. Even Lucien Wolf, the noted Anglo–Jewish journalist and militant critic of Russia's policies, after meeting Plehve in 1903 commented favorably on his personal geniality and openness. Plehve emphasized to Wolf that he considered himself a moderate conservative and opposed the extreme reactionary, anti-Semitic party in Russia.[57]

Those who have accused Plehve have not been entirely off the mark, however, even if his responsibility was not direct. He had one face for one audience, as his angry accusations in meeting the delegation of Odessa Jews demonstrate, another for visitors like Wolf or, more famously, Herzl, who would also confer with him after the Kishinev pogrom. Plehve's widely recognized shrewdness came close to tacit acceptance of anti-Jewish excesses. Certainly, he did little to discourage the climate in which fanatics like Krushevan flourished. Urussov's memoirs note how Plehve, in ministerial meetings, openly spoke of his "war" against the Jews. He reported that while Plehve was capable and rational on most issues of state, he would not listen to words defending the Jews.[58] Other observers expressed similar opinions about Plehve,[59] adding that whatever his personal beliefs may have been, he knew the tsar would not condone a more equitable policy in regard to the Jews.

Many Jewish contemporaries recorded the Kishinev pogrom as a turning point for them. The issue of fighting back was now posed in a brutal form. Some Jewish activists lamented what they considered the cowardice of the Jews themselves at Kishinev. How could it happen, they asked, that thousands of adult Jewish males, of a total Jewish population of 50,000, were unable or unwilling to fend off several hundred rioters? As one reporter put it, "ninety percent of them [Jewish males] hid themselves, or fled to safer parts of the city for refuge."[60] There were isolated acts of Jewish bravery, but they were even less notable than the few incidents in which Christians risked life and limb to protect the Jews. In the searing words of the Jewish poet Bialyk, Jews

---

[56] Urussov, *Memoirs,* 15.

[57] Cecil Roth, ed. *Essays in Jewish History by Lucien Wolf* (London, 1934), 68–9.

[58] Urussov, *Memoirs,* 9, 172–5.

[59] Yarmolinsky, *Memoirs of Count Witte,* 190.

[60] Davitt, *Pale,* 170–1.

in Kishinev reacted to their attackers "with trembling knees, concealed and cowering."[61]

It was even more outrageous in the eyes of many activists that the poor suffered the most from the ravages of the pogromists. A few rich Jews were attacked, but for the most part the richest of them, according to Dubnov, "bribed the police with substantial sums of money to gain protection" or left town.[62]

In earlier times, such passivity would have been elevated as martyrdom, not denounced as cowardice. But these were new times. Not long after the pogrom at Kishinev another broke out at the town of Gomel, which also had a large Jewish population (20,400 Jews in a population of 36,800), but there the Jews of the town organized and fought back against the pogromists.[63] The Gomel pogrom, which finally registered more victims than did Kishinev,[64] has not gone down in history, has not been the subject of searing poetry and indignant commentary. Kishinev was the first, the one around which world attention centered, and thus it became a powerful symbol.

A lesson was learned at Kishinev that young Jewish activists already knew by heart and had been reciting for some time: Jews must fight back; Jews must learn to rely on their own resources; Jews must stop being physical cowards. A writer at the time observed that "the Kishinev pogrom . . . met a new Jewish people, very sensitive to its human dignity, holding an enormous store of militant energy within itself. . . . In everybody, and before all else, there emerged the thirst for revenge."[65]

Approximately 300 of the rioters at Kishinev were tracked down and arrested. However, the ensuing trial was a disappointment. Although the governor and vice-governor were dismissed, they were not charged with responsibility for the pogrom. Even more outrageous, Krushevan escaped indictment. Only those members of the mob who were accused of violent acts were arrested, not the ringleaders. Moreover, the testimony of many of the Jewish victims was contradictory and filled with implausible details for which no proof could be found, so that the lawyers appointed to defend the rioters had an easy job discrediting Jewish witnesses – indeed, they exposed several of them to ridicule and laughter in the courtroom.

Jewish testimony suffered from low regard on the part of the legal officials of the area; Jews themselves joked about how they lied before officialdom, and it was widely believed that Jews conspired in false testimony. Even Urussov, who by the time of the trial was being denounced by the anti-Semites for his

---

[61] Paul R. Mendes-Flohr and Yehuda Reinharz, *The Jew in the Modern World* (Oxford, 1980), 330–1.

[62] Dubnov, *History*, 719.

[63] Baron, *Russian Jew*, 57; Frankel, *Prophecy and Politics*, 51–4.

[64] Frumkin, *Russian Jewry, 1860–1917*, 32.

[65] Frankel, *Prophecy and Politics*, 143.

"sentimental philo-Semitism," observed that Jewish testimony at this trial, as in others, was "often worthless. . . . The Jews, anxious to prove more than what really occurred, get extremely excited, fly into a passion, and exaggerate matters. . . ." Witnesses who first stated they remained in their cellar for the entire three days of the pogrom then provided graphic details of what they "saw" in other parts of the city; "witnesses identified different persons among the accused as the perpetrators of the murders they saw. . . . A bacchanalian orgy" of contradictory witnesses arose, "confounding the unhappy judges" and throwing the lawyers for the Jewish plaintiffs into dismay.[66]

Urussov was also disappointed that the lawyers representing the Jewish victims seemed to be interested in the trial as a political platform, a way of gaining political mileage by uncovering the responsibility of officials in St. Petersburg. Bringing the rioters to justice counted for little. The lawyers did not prepare the witnesses and did not check the reliability, consistency, or credibility of their stories.[67] The testimony of many of the rioters was scarcely less bizarre and incredible. They freely admitted to "sinning a little"; they had stolen and committed vandalism, but they had not killed anyone, God forbid. Many testified that the Jews were "nice people," with whom they wanted to live in peace, except that now Jewish witnesses were "vexing them with false evidence."[68]

It was a natural temptation for Jewish organizations, in their frantic efforts to elicit sympathy and funds for the victims and to discredit Russian authorities, to present the most sensational accounts possible. The unvarnished truth was at any rate difficult to obtain because of tsarist censorship. But in their indiscriminate attacks, in their single-minded determination to get the maximum of political mileage from the pogrom, some foreign Jewish publicists may have been unfair to individuals and to the general non-Jewish population of Kishinev. The presiding judge, Davydov, for example, was described not only as an anti-Semite (with the name "Davidovich") but as a man who himself had a part in planning the pogroms.[69] That account of him is difficult to reconcile with the account of Prince Urussov, who does not hesitate to condemn Krushevan, Ustrugov, and others, but who presents Davydov as a valued personal friend, a man of great personal honesty and judicial fairness, who was at any rate not even in the area at the time of the pogroms.[70]

That such inaccurate and distorted accounts were published in the West and that such ostensibly mendacious testimony was given by Jewish witnesses further envenomed Jewish–Gentile relations. Even Prince Urussov expressed frustration with accounts of the pogrom in the press, foreign and Russian. He

---

[66] Urussov, *Memoirs*, 75–6.

[67] Ibid., 74–6.

[68] Ibid., 44.

[69] Ibid., 3–4.

[70] Ibid., 74.

became finally exasperated with those Jews who "exaggerated their cases to such an extent, and who ornamented them with such extravagant details, that it was absolutely impossible to give full credence to them."[71] Urussov was also distressed by the tendency of Jewish leaders, who on other occasions expressed outrage that Jews were held collectively responsible for the acts of Jewish assassins, to hold the Christian residents of Kishinev collectively responsible for acts by non-Jewish criminals with whom they by no means identified.[72] However, by all accounts he was gradually able to soothe these various resentments and generally to reduce tensions in the city. It was impressive testimony to how the riots might have been avoided in the first place had competent and responsible authority been exercised.

Modern Anti-Semitism in Russia

The Kishinev pogrom and the reactions to it may be seen as a portentous sign of political awakening on both the left and the right, among Jews and among anti-Semites. However, as supporters of autocracy and as enemies of liberal democracy, right-wing activists who sought to organize the masses inevitably involved themselves in contradictory activities, since to mobilize the people was considered a western, un-Russian activity.[73] Political parties and agitation by independent groups violated fundamental precepts of tsarist autocracy. Nevertheless, such groups began to proliferate.

The most important of these right-wing organizations was the Union of the Russian People. It was the organization as well that went the farthest in terms of independent action, even of pressuring the authorities, albeit always under the guise of ardent support for the principle of tsarist autocracy. Those historians who have maintained that the tsar and his ministers actively conspired to provoke anti-Jewish pogroms have also accused those authorities of working hand-in-hand with the Union and similar organizations (all of which were often grouped under the imprecise designation of "Black Hundreds").

However, the coordination between government and organizations like the Union throughout Russia was both less extensive and less effective than many have supposed. The Union suffered not only from a confusion as to its goals but also from incompetent leadership and poor organization. It was torn by internal dissension and lacked staying power. For such reasons government officials were chary of dealing with it.

The Russian right as a whole was scarcely more impressive than such newer reactionary–populist organizations as the Union. The integration of tradi-

---

[71] Ibid., 24–5.

[72] Ibid., 12.

[73] Cf. Hans Rogger, *Jewish Policies and Right-Wing Politics in Imperial Russia* (Berkeley, Calif., 1986), 188 ff.

tional conservatism with newer forms of popular agitation was thus less developed in Russia than in countries like Austria or France. Partly because of its organizational and ideological weakness, the Russian right was tempted by terrorism and other forms of ruthless, disorganized violence.

Russian nationalist conservatives often come across as unsophisticated, frightened men with little vision. They were given to a kind of mystical pessimism in the face of powerful forces that they could not successfully resist or even understand. Of course the Russian right finally faced a much greater challenge than did the right in western and central Europe. The prospect of a socialist revolution in France, Austria, or Germany, however much it haunted the privileged and propertied, was in reality remote, whereas Russia exploded into revolution in 1905. Thus, it is not entirely appropriate to compare the relative moderation of anti-Semitic forces in western Europe with the desperate, often nihilistic violence of those forces in Russia.

The pogroms instigated or exploited by the Union, or the Black Hundreds more generally, cannot be termed a success for the reactionaries. The random, senseless violence finally disgusted nearly everyone, including many anti-Semitic spokesmen. In Kiev, where the Beilis Affair would take place six years later, the principal participants and beneficiaries appear to have been the criminal elements of the city, much as was the case in Kishinev. The general population was disgusted by the scenes of brutal pillage and rape.[74] The pogroms were intended to intimidate the left and to terrorize the Jews. Those goals may have been achieved, but it was at the price of discrediting the regime and the reactionary cause more generally.

Nicholas II and the Power of International Jewry

The Russian Empire's problems in the generation before World War I would have challenged the ablest of leaders. Hopes had initially arisen that Nicholas II would be another reforming tsar, and in his first years he succeeded in giving the impression that he was a gentler man than his father. He enjoyed a favorable treatment in the international press, in part because of his role in convening the International Peace Conference in The Hague in 1899. Rumors even spread that Nicholas was a friend of the Jews, that he would at last see to a general reform of the regulations that so oppressed them.

These hopes proved ill founded, for Nicholas soon surrounded himself with avowed Jew-haters. In conversations with his ministers, he habitually used the coarse and insulting Russian term *zhidy* (kikes) rather than the more polite *yevrei* (Hebrews). It gradually emerged that rather than sympathizing with the Jews, he believed they were to be held responsible for provoking pogroms.[75]

---

[74] Samuel, *Blood Accusation*, 18.

[75] Yarmolinsky, *Memoirs of Count Witte*, 190.

The full measure of Nicholas II's inadequacies became clear in Russia's war with Japan in 1904–1905. His habitual term for the Japanese was "monkeys." Many members of the ruling elite of Russia believed that a foreign war could resolve the country's internal problems by inducing Russia's subjects to rally around the flag, and Nicholas soon embraced those beliefs. However, the war with Japan proved a disaster for Russia, one that played a major role in provoking the revolution in 1905. Yet Nicholas showed little understanding of the wave of revolution that swept the country. He refused to believe that his "own people" could be ultimately responsible. It had to be "foreign" people, above all the Jews.

A parallel concern to Nicholas and his high officials was their belief that a number of powerful Jewish financiers outside of Russia were working ever more openly and effectively to deny the country the financial aid it sought. There was some foundation to that belief: A most tenacious enemy of tsarist Russia was Jacob H. Schiff, the American financier. Schiff played a crucial role not only in denying the Russians the bonds they sought in the international market to finance the war but also even more decisively in providing financial support for Japan, which then so humiliatingly defeated Russia.[76] In Great Britain, Lucien Wolf, joined by the English Rothschilds and, in central Europe, Paul Nathan, led the efforts to isolate Russia both economically and diplomatically.[77]

By this time American Jews had begun to claim a leading role in international Jewish affairs. Schiff delighted in the way that he and other Jews had been able to contribute to the humbling of the great Russian Empire. He boasted that after its humiliation in the Russo–Japanese War, Russia had come to understand that "international Jewry is a power after all."[78] When Count Witte arrived in the United States to negotiate the peace treaty with Japan, he was contacted by Simon Wolf, another American Jewish leader and long-time confidant of presidents, who told him that Russia needed two things, money and friends. He added,

The Jews of the world, as citizens of their respective countries, control much of the first . . . There is no use in disguising the fact that in the United States the Jews form an important factor in the formation of public opinion and in the control of finances. . . . By virtue of their mercantile and financial standing in this country they are exercising an all-potent and powerful influence.[79]

This boasting by Schiff and Wolf was transparently designed to impress the Russians, with the quite explicit goal of pressuring them to cease the persecu-

---

[76] Best, *To Free a People*, esp. 92 ff.; Eric Herschler, ed., *Jews from Germany in the United States* (New York, 1955), 62–4.

[77] Zosa Szajkowski, "Paul Nathan, Lucien Wolf, Jacob H. Schiff, and the Jewish Revolutionary Movements in Eastern Europe (1903–1917)," *Jewish Social Studies*, vol. 29, no. 1, Jan. 1967, 3–26.

[78] Best, *To Free a People*, 108.

[79] Ibid., 109.

tion of Jews inside Russia, but by 1905 such boasts were widely accepted as justified. Observers as different as Winston Churchill and Theodore Herzl firmly believed that international Jewry exercised enormous power in international relations. Arnold White, who praised Russia's Jews as the "most virtuous and prolific race" in the tsar's empire, wrote that the European press and international finance were in Jewish hands, and that "the Prime Minister and the Cabinet of England alter their policy and abandon an important bill in parliament at the frown of the Rothschilds." He concluded that Jews were making "monotonous progress toward the mastery of the world."[80]

Russia's minister of foreign affairs, Count Vladimir Nikolaevich Lamsdorf, informed the tsar that the Revolution of 1905 had been "actively supported and partly directed by the forces of universal Jewry," led by the Alliance Israélite Universelle, which had "gigantic pecuniary means" and an "enormous membership."[81] Lamsdorf had long opposed Russia's French alliance and hoped to break it up, to return to an alliance with Germany,[82] and his words partly reflected that agenda. But there is no question that Schiff was both supporting the Japanese and financing revolutionary socialist agitation among the Russian prisoners of war taken by Japan. His agent in that operation boasted that he had won over thousands of soldiers to revolutionary socialism.[83] In short, one of the more improbable fantasies of anti-Semites like Lamsdorf, that Jewish capitalists were supporting socialist revolutionaries, had at least that limited basis in fact.

Nicholas was an attentive listener to those who spoke of a worldwide Jewish conspiracy against him. Especially after 1905 he was haunted by a fear that the Jews, their non-Jewish agents, and a network of Jewish financiers who had intimate contacts in the corridors of power in the West were out to undermine tsarist Russia, destroy his empire, and even to kill him personally. Although his mind worked in confused ways, he was undoubtedly correct in believing that growing numbers of Jews, inside Russia and out, Marxist revolutionaries like Trotsky as well as sober financiers like Schiff, did want to destroy him and his empire.

Quite understandably, Jews of a wide variety of political persuasions and national origins were motivated by a determination to combat the policies of Nicholas, to put strong pressure on him to relent in his anti-Semitic stance. This was not a concerted, worldwide Jewish conspiracy of the sort supposed by men of Nicholas's mentality; it was rather a fairly wide international consensus among Jews and also among non-Jews of liberal to socialist persuasion. Still, it fed conspiratorial fantasies in Nicholas's mind and in the mind of many right-

---

[80] Singer, *Russia*, 148–9.

[81] Salo Wittmayer Baron, *Steeled by Adversity: Essays and Addresses on American Life* (Philadelphia, 1971), 331–2.

[82] Baron, *Russian Jew*, 62.

[83] Best, *To Free a People*, 107.

wing Russians. They were not wrong in believing that Jews were a power in the world, and a rising one, particularly because of the influence they could exercise in the up-and-coming United States.

The Duma, or parliament, that was elected in 1905 included twelve Jewish deputies, a remarkable figure in that Jews were a minority in all electoral districts, and it became clear that the Duma would abolish the discriminatory laws that Russian Jews faced.[84] These intentions were soon undermined by waves of counterrevolution at the end of the year and in 1906, waves that entailed anti-Jewish rioting on a scale that dwarfed the pogroms of 1903. This new violence was directed not only at Jews but also at all those who supported the revolution. By this time the authority of the tsar and his ministers was much diminished as compared with that in 1903, as was their ability to control events.

The anti-Semitic right naturally elicited both covert and more open support from tsarist officials. Prince Urussov, whose memoirs cast doubt on the role of Plehve in the Kishinev pogrom, made a famous speech in early 1906 on the floor of the Duma denouncing the role of tsarist officials in the pogroms of that year. Witte, the prime minister, was appalled to discover that the secret police had been active in instigating a new pogrom in the town of Gomel.[85]

Even at this point the support of the government for anti-Semitic counterrevolutionaries was not part of a coherent policy, and certainly not one that Nicholas's ministers had all agreed upon; again the government remained divided, confused, and incompetent. With the events of 1905 conservatives began to lose confidence in the government's ability to maintain order and to protect itself – and them. They were thus inclined, temporarily at least, to give support to organizations like the Union of the Russian People.

Unquestionably, the government gave financial support to the Union and to other right-wing organizations; Nicholas publicly praised the Union and met its delegations. Still, as one of the most careful historians of the subject has stated, "there were no concerted efforts on the part of the administration to create for itself a popular ally," to link autocracy to a modern mass movement of the anti-Semitic right. Peter Stolypin, who would become the prime minister, had no use whatsoever for Dubrovin, a prominent leader of the Union; the government fined his newspaper, and Stolypin had him prosecuted for the murder of a liberal deputy.[86]

Many conservatives "began to recoil with distaste or even horror" from the methods of anti-Semitic mobs.[87] As the threat from the left receded and public

---

[84] Frumkin, *Russian Jewry*, 47.

[85] Urussov's speech and other related documents may found in E. Séménoff, *The Russian Government and Massacres* (Westport, Conn., 1972; first published in 1907), 149–60.

[86] Rogger, *Jewish Policies*, 215, 217.

[87] Ibid., 219.

order was restored, there emerged a wobbly consensus that such methods should not be used again, that the thugs and murderers of the anti-Semitic mass organizations were as much a threat to conservative principles as were the revolutionaries of the left.

The Beilis Affair

In September 1911 when the revolutionary threat had been well contained, Nicholas visited Kiev to dedicate a statue to his assassinated grandfather, Alexander II. His prime minister, Stolypin, standing a few feet from the tsar in the ceremonies, was shot down by a Jewish anarchist who was also a police spy and double agent. This would have been the ideal time for pogroms to break out in Kiev, if indeed such had been what the tsar and his ministers desired. No pogroms occurred. The calm was all the more remarkable since the city was unnerved: Earlier in that year in Kiev, the Jew Mendel Beilis had been arrested and charged with the ritual murder of a young Russian boy.

The Beilis Affair, lasting from Beilis's arrest in 1911 until the trial in 1913, has been seen by many observers as the ultimate symbol of the decadence of tsarism by the eve of World War I. It was widely trumpeted as a Russian version of the Dreyfus Affair, but although it gained for a while a comparable publicity, it was a weak imitation of the French affair. Few actually believed poor Mendel Beilis guilty, and the identity of the criminal band who killed the young boy became clear early on. Similarly, the manner in which the government sought to frame Beilis was exposed both by minor government officials and by the press – including some of the anti-Semitic press, whose editors simply could not accept such a blatant miscarriage of injustice.

Typically, the intentions of the government in the Beilis Affair were confused and inconsistent, but insofar as a coherent brief account may be given of those intentions it appears that a few officials, above all Minister of Justice I. G. Shcheglovitov, hoped that a highly publicized trial of a Jew for ritual murder would discredit Russia's Jews, weakening the case for lifting their civil disabilities and embarrassing the left more generally. Shcheglovitov and others like him also apparently believed that any such trial would be pleasing to Nicholas II, although ironically Nicholas himself, as well as the trusted "friend" of the royal family, Rasputin, finally recognized Beilis's innocence. But Stolypin had had nothing to do with the government conspiracy to frame Beilis; a ritual murder trial was simply not his style. He was at any rate assassinated before Beilis came to trial.

The colorful trial was closely followed by the press of Europe and America. The case for the prosecution collapsed in the courtroom, exposing bribery, intimidation, and corruption, often to the laughter of the large audience. Beilis was by all accounts well liked by his neighbors and co-workers, so that his personal qualities played a different role from those of Dreyfus in his trial.

Although the jurors were mostly peasants, obviously selected for their credulity, and the judge was outrageously partial to the prosecution, Beilis was found innocent, to great jubilation in the courtroom, and subsequently in Russia at large. "Strangers embraced on the streets with shining faces and streaming eyes; Jews and gentiles congratulated each other, proud of their country and of its 'simple citizens,' gloating over the happy ending and the humiliation of the administration."[88] The trial tended to confirm right-wing visions of Jewish power, given the forces that defenders of Beilis were able to muster, whereas the left was naturally encouraged.

But whatever the hopeful signs and momentary elation, the war, which broke out in the following summer, radically altered all calculations. And incomparably worse tragedies awaited Russia's Jewish subjects.

Romanian Anti-Semitism: "The Worst in Europe?"

Romania's history, violent and confused in the eighteenth and early nineteenth centuries, continued in much the same vein until 1914, indeed in grotesque spirals into the last decade of the twentieth century. Romania's people and culture, insofar as they were known to western Europeans and Americans in the nineteenth century, were viewed condescendingly, if not contemptuously; Romanians were widely portrayed as backward, corrupt, and mendacious. It is a mark of the problematic stature of the nation that even the spelling of its name (Romania, Rumania, Roumania) has not been generally agreed upon – a less trivial matter than might at first seem the case, as will be explained in the discussion that follows.

Bismarck, whose derision for the Balkans as a whole is well known ("not worth the bones of a single Pomeranian grenadier"), remarked in 1879 that what happened to the Romanians was a matter of utter indifference to him personally. However, he recognized that developments in the area were of concern to German Jews, "whom I need to coddle, win over, and who can be very useful to me in Germany – and whom I like to pay in Rumanian [i.e., worthless] money." In the previous year he had expressed to Lord Russell of Great Britain "his aversion for the Romanians in language too violent to be placed in official record."[89]

The interest of German Jews in the area was partly economic, but it was also directed at the precarious status of Jews there. Since the Romanians were often considered to be even more anti-Semitic than the Slavs of eastern Europe, the hostility of many western Jews for Romanians, not surprisingly,

[88] Samuel, *Blood Accusation*, 250.

[89] Fritz Stern, *Gold and Iron: Bismarck, Bleichröder and the Building of the German Empire* (New York, 1977), 383.

paralleled that of Bismarck. Moritz von Goldschmidt, a friend of Bismarck's banker, Bleichröder, advocated a boycott of Romania by western Jewish business and finance, so that "these impudent men . . . would smother in the filth they call civilization."[90] At the other end of the political spectrum, Leon Trotsky wrote that "Rumania as a whole manifests itself through its Jewish question"; in a country that was corrupt and ridiculously misgoverned, "anti-Semitism has established itself as a state religion – the last cementing factor of a feudal society rotten through and through."[91]

It is a moot point whether Romanian anti-Semitism was the worst in Europe; certainly nowhere else did hatred of Jews become so prominently a part of national identity or one that so obsessed the intellectual classes. Violent outbursts against Jews, from attacks on the streets to the burning of synagogues, were regularly reported in the world press. Jewish–Gentile relations in Romania must be considered a failure in almost every regard. Yet, the large numbers of Jews who moved into the area in the course of the nineteenth century, from the Russian Pale and from Austrian Galicia, suggest that the issue may not be quite so simple. Why would Jews move in large numbers from Russia to an even more oppressive area or, indeed, from Galicia, where they did not face government persecution?

Romania suffered from crushing poverty, lack of industrial development, widespread illiteracy, and competing, usually xenophobic identities – ethnic, religious, and national. Tensions between peasants and large landowners were even worse than in Russia; land holdings were grossly unequal, and the peasantry was brutally exploited. As in the Pale of Settlement, Jews in Romania served as agents for the large landholders, and were described as alien, parasitic, and contemptuous of the non-Jewish people among whom they lived. And even more than in the Pale, such judgments were both plausible and widely accepted as accurate, even by Jewish observers. Zionists often cited Romania as an area where hatred of Jews was especially justified, the clearest example of "objective anti-Semitism" in Europe. Inside Romania Jews had few if any non-Jewish defenders of stature and integrity comparable to Prince Urussov; even Romanian moderates, almost without exception, described Jews as alien and exploitative.[92] The consensus, from conservative to liberal among Romanian nationalists, was that hostility to Jews was an integral part of Romanian national feeling. If the concept of anti-Semitism as an *Integrationsideologie* made sense anywhere, it was in Romania, as Trotsky suggested.

One historian has commented, "the history of Rumanian Jewry has always been written with more polemics than factuality."[93] The British historian R. W.

[90] Ibid., 375.

[91] Joseph Nedava, *Trotsky and the Jews* (Philadelphia, 1971), 78.

[92] Walter Laqueur, *A History of Zionism* (London, 1972), 443.

[93] Stern, *Gold and Iron*, 354.

Seton-Watson wrote one of the very few sympathetic histories of Romania in English,[94] but more typical in tone is Howard Morley Sachar's chapter, in his history of the Jews: It is a tirade, without the slightest effort at balance. He dismisses Romania as a "third-rate power." The hatred that Jews encountered there was "small, poisonous, mean-minded," "even more pathological" than Russian anti-Semitism.[95] He mentions little that might put such hatred into historical context, that might make it in the slightest degree understandable. Romanian anti-Semitism is for him simply a moral issue. Romanians were thoroughly evil people, confronting powerless and innocent Jews, whose attitudes or actions had nothing at all to do with the hatred they faced.

Sachar's treatment of Romanian anti-Semitism is yet another example of the kind of interpretation that has been questioned throughout this book, as extreme as the opposite kind of interpretation that places the blame for anti-Semitism entirely on the shoulders of the Jews. The Romanian example is revealing in a number of ways, however, since even in the 1880s there seem to have been few who believed that Jewish reform in Romania was the key to reducing anti-Semitism, and even fewer who came to the defense of the Romanians.

In the latter half of the nineteenth century Romanian national identity was still young and insecure. If it is accepted that the youth and insecurity of German national feeling helps explain why men like von Treitschke lashed out against the dangers of Jewish influence, or if the paranoia about the corruptions associated with the "foreign" Jews is one key to understanding Russian anti-Semitism, such arguments are incomparably more apt in regard to Romania. Romanian culture and language enjoyed none of the admiration and emulation that German language and culture had since the eighteenth century, nor could Romanian literary figures bask in anything like the worldwide esteem that Russian authors like Tolstoy or Dostoevsky did.

Those few who came to the defense of the Romanian national spirit believed that the Romanian people, inarticulate and defenseless in the international arena, had been demonized, their defects unfairly exaggerated; they were an easy target, and Jews had taken a leading role in that demonization. It was not a difficult task, since nearly all observers recognized serious defects of the Romanian temper; even Romanian nationalists openly discussed the ways that the many negative traits of their fellow countrymen could be remedied.[96] But that did not mean accepting the monotonously mean-spirited denigration of their homeland and its people that was spread by many prominent Jews.

94 R. W. Seton-Watson, *A History of the Roumanians: From Roman Times to the Completion of Unity* (Cambridge, U.K., 1934).

95 Howard Morley Sachar, *The Course of Modern Jewish History* (New York, 1977), 259; similar in tone is Nedava, *Trotsky and the Jews*, 78–82.

96 Cf. William O. Oldson, *A Providential Anti-Semitism: Nationalism and Polity in Nineteenth Century Romania* (Philadelphia, 1991), 120.

Prominent Jews in many countries attempted to put pressure on Romanian leaders, with a blatancy that would have been inconceivable or even dangerous in regard to Russia. The reaction of those leaders, sensitive to issues of national dignity and sovereignty, was predictably angry. A century later the reactions of Israeli politicians – leaders of a vulnerable, widely disliked country no less concerned about national dignity when international pressure was exerted on them because of their harsh treatment of minority populations – was revealingly similar.

Prince Carol, the German prince who would become the first king of Romania, described the Romanians as "the most tolerant of all Christian peoples,"[97] remarkably like the description given earlier of the Moldavian population in Kishinev. Similarly positive evaluations of the Russian peasantry, or of the Poles – also termed unusually tolerant by their defenders[98] – have been made. Given such radically opposed opinion, where does the truth lie?

Even the most superficial examination of the history of Romanian–Jewish relations in the nineteenth century reveals how utterly different that history was from the history of Jews and Gentiles in such countries as Great Britain and the United States. And even a small effort at evenhandedness reveals that Romanian anti-Semitism derived from something more than the lower moral tone of Romanians: The activities and nature of the Jews in Romania had something quite palpably to do with the hatred directed at them. A brief look at Romanian history is revealing.

The three large and competing empires (the Ottoman, Russian, and Habsburg) that surrounded the Romanian-speaking peoples traded Romanian provinces and sovereignty over Romanians in a dizzying succession from early modern times to the mid–nineteenth century. All three of them, especially the first two, preserved Jewish disabilities, in law and in custom. The history of the Romanian-speaking peoples was for most of this period that of two principalities, Moldavia and Wallachia. Their despotic princes were from the late Middle Ages until the eighteenth century vassals of the Ottoman Empire, with extensive autonomy, marked by bloody rebellions. By the early nineteenth century the principalities had become Russian protectorates while remaining technically within the Ottoman Empire. Transylvania, another area of predominantly Romanian-speaking people (but with a large and historically important Magyar enclave), remained under Hungarian rule until the end of World War I.

In 1861–1862 the two principalities were united as Romania under a Moldavian colonel, Ion Cuza. His despotic manners and corruption led to a coup d'état in 1866, when the previously-mentioned Carol, who was related to the Prussian Hohenzollerns, was chosen as his successor. A cautiously liberal constitution

[97] Stern, *Gold and Iron*, 355.
[98] Cf. Norman Davies, *The Heart of Europe: A Short History of Poland* (Oxford, 1986).

was also adopted in 1866. In 1878, with the Congress of Berlin, Romania gained international recognition as an independent country, contingent on fulfilling certain stipulations of the great powers, which included granting of civil equality to Jews in the country. In 1881 Romania was proclaimed a fully sovereign kingdom.

But these were confused and tumultuous years for the country. Romania's struggle for independence had none of the drama and heroism of German unification. Romania was the plaything of the great powers; its leaders had to rely more on supplication and guile than Bismarckian military prowess or Garibaldean heroics. And the Jewish Question, again unlike the situation in Germany or Italy in the 1860s and 1870s, was deeply intertwined into the convoluted processes of that unification.

Romanian nationalist intellectuals cultivated certain rather dubious national myths, as did all European nationalities at the time. They claimed descent from the Roman settlers in ancient Dacia. Nineteenth-century Romanians fancied themselves, as the name they chose for their new nation suggests, a Latin people, heirs to an illustrious civilization and different from the backward Slavic peoples of the region. (Those who have insisted upon alternate spellings, "Rumania" or "Roumania," have often done so disparagingly, to mock the claims of a "Roman" ancestry.) Moreover, as a Latin people, speaking a Latin-based language, the Romanians claimed special affinities with western Europe, especially with the Italians, who had themselves just completed their national unification and who showed a special sympathy for Romanian problems and aspirations. Romanian leaders referred to Rome as their "mother."[99]

Again much like other young nationalists, Romanian intellectuals were inclined to blame others for their misfortunes, to exploit the concept of the threatening outsider in galvanizing the Romanian people. The Germans or the Russians blamed the French in the early nineteenth century, and liberation from French oppression was central to German and Russian national mythology. However, in the Romanian case the myths of victimization were much more central, in no small part because they corresponded to an obvious reality for a much less powerful people brutally dominated by Turks and Russians for centuries.

Whatever the origins of their race – as problematic a concept in the Balkans as elsewhere – Romanians were overwhelmingly a peasant people, in truth profoundly isolated from western Europe for many centuries and scarcely to be distinguished from the Slavic peoples around them in literacy, economic development, or other signs of western civilization. Similarly, whether all outsiders in the new state were bad for the nation is not easy to determine. Jews were credited, as in Kishinev, with building it up while at the

[99] Oldson, *Providential Anti-Semitism*, 25.

same time were also blamed for a myriad of evils, from capitalist exploitation to prostitution, drunkenness, and revolutionary violence. Similar charges in Romania were levied against Greeks, Germans, and Magyars – but most of all against the Jews.

Romanian nationalists claimed that their lands had been flooded in the early nineteenth century by Jews with no previous connection to Romania, mostly those fleeing the new decrees in Russia that made Jews eligible for military service, although a large number also came from Galicia in pursuit of economic opportunity. As we have seen, there was a mass movement in the course of the nineteenth century of Polish Jews to the south. A very small, mostly Sephardic settlement in Moldavia and Wallachia had existed during the period of Turkish rule, but the overwhelming majority of Jews in Romania by the second half of the century were of recent origin, Yiddish-speaking and to an important extent hasidic. That they came in such numbers to Romanian territory, and continued to come well into the twentieth century, would seem to indicate that they concluded it was a better place than impoverished Galicia or despotic Russia. As in the case of post–Dreyfus Affair France or Vienna ruled by an anti-Semitic mayor, these migration patterns suggest that economic opportunity ranked higher than anti-Semitism as a mover of large numbers of people.

Jews also migrated to neighboring Hungary in the same years, but the relationships of the Magyar elite to Jewish immigrants in the nineteenth century were revealingly different from those of the Jews to the ruling orders in Romania. To begin with, the economic utility of the Jews was much less widely recognized by the Romanians. The willingness to let Jews handle commerce, so prominent a trait of the Magyar nobility, was less characteristic of the Romanian ruling class. Moldavian boyars (nobles) certainly used Jews as agents to manage their estates, but Romanian national identity, as it was being fashioned by leading Romanian intellectuals at the time, included a vision of being commercial or entrepreneurial, as were their Italian and French models. Much more than in Hungary Jews were considered to be unwelcome rivals economically – threatening rather than useful. Most Romanian nationalists claimed that if Jews were offered civil equality, the numbers coming to the country would rise precipitously. Romanians feared the implications of their country's appearing any more attractive to eastern European Jews, especially given the notoriously strong religious–nationalist identity from that area, than it already did. Many among the Romanian elite concluded that making life difficult for those Jews already in the country, legally or otherwise, was a justifiable policy. And although nearly all Romanian leaders claimed that they disapproved of violence against Jews, many of them tacitly accepted it.

The leading political force in the country, the Liberal Party, dominated by the powerful Bratianu family, one of the largest landholders in the Balkans, was explicitly committed to the cause of industrializing Romania, of supporting a native Romanian commercial and industrial class, and more generally of modernizing the country, bringing it up to western standards. The Bratianus actually claimed that they were willing to cooperate with at least part of the Jewish bourgeoisie in modernizing Romania, so long as the political power of native Romanians was not threatened and as the presence of Jews did not effectively block the formation of a native Romanian bourgeoisie.

These claims turned out to be mostly empty rhetoric. In truth the Liberal Party remained uncompromisingly anti-Semitic. The cooperation of Polish Jew and native Romanian did not work for the simple reason that the Jewish bourgeoisie refused to become Romanian and in truth *did* threaten native Romanians, who were unable to compete with Jews or other foreigners. As Prince Carol stated the matter, paralleling the views of the Slavophiles, Jews were a people whose superior industry and inferior morals allowed them to exploit and take advantage of the simple and good-natured Romanian people. It was a perspective shared by most Romanian nationalists.[100] Thus, while liberalism in Hungary and most other countries encouraged extensive cooperation with the Jews – who willingly embraced Magyar, German, or French identities – in Romania the liberal slogan was "through ourselves alone," certainly not in cooperation with Jews who insisted on retaining a different language and culture and who denigrated Romanian culture.

The slogan reflected another important reality: Romanians constituted a comfortable majority in Moldavia and Wallachia; Romanian leaders did not feel the need for Jewish allies, whereas the Magyars, a minority in their own country, did. Similarly, Jewish immigrants to Romania up to 1914 continued to show very little interest in becoming Romanian. Jews lived apart from the native population in Romania out of preference. Intermarriage was far less common in Romania than in Hungary or other areas where Jews admired and embraced non-Jewish culture. Jews in Romania had not come from an advanced, westernized area, as had the Jews who moved into Hungary; their strong sense of Jewish national identity and attendant separatism increased, if anything.

Jewish belittlement of Romanian culture particularly incensed spokesmen for Romanian nationalism. For such reasons they insisted that tests demonstrating a firm command of the Romanian language and a knowledge of Romanian history be a prerequisite for nationalization, since they were confident that the overwhelming majority of Jews in Romania could not pass such tests and were unlikely to make the effort to do so. Certainly the overwhelming majority of those who had been in Romania for as much as three generations had not made the effort, in sharp contrast to the way in which Hungarian Jews had in the course of the same years embraced Magyar language and culture.[101]

[100] Oldson, *Providential Anti-Semitism*, passim; Stern, *Iron and Gold*, 357.

[101] Oldson, *Providential Anti-Semitism*, 122–9.

In this regard, prominent figures in the Italian government expressed sympathy for the Romanian point of view. In general their advice to the Romanians was to bend over backwards to alleviate the condition of Jews in the country, but officials in Rome, including a number of high-placed Jews in the ministry of foreign affairs, accepted as accurate the charge that the hasidic Jews from Poland were a hostile, "germanizing" element, one that was likely to have a detrimental effect upon the Latin identity of Romanians.[102] The much less numerous Sephardim of the area, since they spoke Ladino, a Latin-based tongue, and had resided in the area for a longer period, were seen as more admissible. Indeed, some of them accepted, at least in public pronouncements, the government line about Jews from Poland.[103] Sephardic Jews of this area were known to harbor a special contempt for the hasidim, part of a larger distaste for Ashkenazic Jewry that they shared with Sephardim in France and other parts of Europe.

Even if Jewish immigrants to Romania had been more willing to take up a non-Jewish national identity, it would not likely have been with such a "primitive" and widely denigrated people as the Romanians. Even those many Jews who abandoned Jewish tradition in this period only rarely identified with such people – powerless, "historyless," and destined, so many argued, to be absorbed by the superior, historic peoples. In Transylvania (ruled by Hungary but containing a Romanian majority) magyarized Jews were widely known to be among the most aggressive and intolerant of magyarizers, a reputation they also had in Hungarian-ruled Slovakia. But even inside the new Romanian state, even when Jewish immigrants learned the Romanian tongue to some degree, they did not often embrace Romanian culture or accept Romanian nationality (as distinguished from demanding civil equality). The situation was summed up by a special commission of the Romanian Chamber of Deputies in 1879: "There were not, and . . . never have been, any Rumanian Jews; there were merely Jews who have been born in the Principality [of Romania], but who never have been assimilated . . . by the Rumanian nation."[104] It became almost a litany of Romanian nationalists that there "were no Romanian Jews, only Jews in Romania."

Jews in Romania moved to the principal urban areas as the century progressed. That movement became a cause for growing alarm by Romanian nationalists, since many of their largest cities (Jassy, Czernowitz, Radaut) already by the 1850s were developing Jewish majorities,[105] and it was intolerable for Romanian nationalists that in their new and vulnerable country this growing urban class, which in Italy or Germany was the backbone of the nationalist

---

[102] Ibid., 27, 93–4.

[103] Ibid., 148.

[104] Stern, *Gold and Iron*, 385.

[105] Laqueur, *Zionism*, 443.

movement, retained a foreign identity and was palpably not interested in becoming an integral part of the nation. Imagine, they asked, if such a situation were developing in Rome, London, or Paris. Would the nationalists of those countries be so complacent about their Jewish problem if their capital cities had a majority of Jews who denigrated Italian, English, or French identity?

The notion of granting civil equality to Jews thus took on a wholly different aspect in Romania than it had in Hungary in the 1860s. Whereas the Hungarian rulers saw Jewish full citizenship as a way of reinforcing their own influence and of strengthening the nation, Romanian leaders saw Jewish political influence as dangerous and divisive to the nation. While such nations as Germany, Austria, and Hungary were preparing to grant full civil equality to their Jewish citizens in the mid-1860s, Romanians bristled ever more stubbornly at the prospect.

Similarly, interest grew among Romanian leaders, as it did among leaders in Russia, in finding ways to encourage Jews to leave the country. Precisely how many Jews there were in Romania by the 1860s was a hotly disputed point. Those who were most alarmed asserted that there were over 400,000, out of a total population of around 5 million; a more likely and a more generally accepted figure was 250,000.[106] Even the lower figure suggests that the Jewish population of Romania, at 5 percent of the total, was proportionately one of the largest in Europe and had indeed grown very fast since the early part of the century.

To the charge that Jews were taking over the country, or fatally crippling its efforts to become a real nation supported by its own native bourgeoisie, Romanian nationalists added the related complaint that Jews in Romania were trying to use international connections to gain advantage inside the country. That charge, too, was hardly without foundation, although whether their efforts were purely self-interested and hostile to Romanian interests or simply defensive – in reaction to a pervasive and sometimes brutal anti-Semitism – is by its very nature impossible to determine.

Jewish exaggeration was here, as in Russia, undoubtedly a factor, but virtually all observers agreed that the situation of Jews in Romania was deplorable and, at least for a large numbers of the poorest class of Jews, getting worse as the century progressed. It was a vicious cycle, in that Jewish efforts to appeal to outside intervention and protection merely fanned anti-Semitism in Romania, whereas Romanian anti-Semitism spurred western Jews to come to the rescue of their coreligionists in Romania.

The poverty of the country tended to brutalize class and ethnic tensions. Western observers, both Jewish and non-Jewish, were almost unanimous in recognizing the "characteristic Jewish vices," the low moral tone of Jews in Romania. Wilhelm I, the German Emperor, in a letter to the father of King Carol,

---

[106] Stern, *Iron and Gold,* 354.

observed, "I know from experience what the Jews are like in those areas [Poland and the Pale] . . . and the Rumanian Jews are said to be even worse!"[107] The old saw that "each country gets the Jews it deserves" was often quoted, since western observers were also almost unanimous about the low moral tone of non-Jews in the country: The Jews in Romania and the native Romanians deserved one other. A more justifiable and less cruel formulation would have been that when poor and oppressed people are thrown together under unfavorable circumstances, it should come as no surprise that they do not get along or that they appear morally corrupt to those whose material circumstances are happier than theirs.

Even in the "honeymoon years" of Jewish–Gentile relations in western and central Europe, the 1850s through the early 1870s, the scene in Romania was tense. The self-satisfaction of such countries as Great Britain, France, and the United States, their sense of themselves as advanced and highly civilized, made it all the more tempting for them to censure the backward Romanians. "All the world was trying to instruct the Rumanians on how to behave to their Jews."[108] Typically, Carol's father advised him to recognize reality, however unfair it might seem: The support and sympathy of France was vital to Romania; Jewish money dominated the French press, and therefore the Jewish question would be kept before the French public unless Romanians made efforts to treat their Jews better. The advice was, indeed, strikingly like that given Witte, a half century later, by American Jewish leaders, when he was in America to negotiate the end of the Russo–Japanese war. Many of Romania's leaders came to a certain resignation: They could not get around the pervasive Jewish influence in the rest of Europe.

The alleged Jewish dominance of the French press was by no means the only concern of Romanian leaders. Emperor Napoleon III was deeply in debt to the Rothschilds. At the Congress of Paris in 1858 following the Crimean War, Baron James de Rothschild strongly urged Napoleon to speak up on behalf of persecuted minorities in Romania. But the most the French emperor could get from the Romanians was a promise to guarantee the political rights of Christian peoples who did not belong to the Romanian Orthodox Church. When Moldavia and Wallachia were united in the following years, Cuza seemed to be making friendly noises in regard to the Jews, and on January 1, 1864, in addressing a visiting Jewish delegation, he promised that "you will be gradually emancipated. Wherever I have been, I have liked you, and I have never discriminated against religions."[109]

Little came from these promises, and pressure from foreign Jews, especially influential financiers like the Rothschilds and Bleichröder, continued –

[107] Ibid., 388.
[108] Stern, *Iron and Gold,* 356.
[109] Sachar, *History,* 256.

with growing frustration. When representatives of the Alliance Israélite Universelle made a visit to Bucharest in 1866, Ion Bratianu also spoke soothing words, and the French delegation received a standing ovation from the Romanian Chamber of Deputies. In later contacts with Bleichröder, Bratianu indicated he was willing to consider certain measures to provide certain basic protections for Jews in Romania, although he balked at the notion of full emancipation.[110]

Bratianu seems to have been much like Plehve in dealing with foreign Jews: He had different faces for different occasions. He received the French Jews cordially, stressing how important friendly relations with France were to him, but once they had left, he termed Jewish presence in the country a "leprosy."[111] Similarly, many of the deputies could easily embrace "civilized" French Jews, while vilifying the "barbaric" Jews in their own land. The contrast between the advanced Jews of the West and the backward Jews of the East was a constant refrain by leading Romanians: "If all Jews were Rothschilds and Crémieux, then the situation would be different," but who could blame the Romanian government "if it sought to protect its people against these bloodsuckers."[112]

Many of the Romanians who spoke in such terms considered themselves liberal and modern. In the Romanian context those terms had more to do with a belief in the necessity of economic development than with civil liberties or minority rights. Romanian liberal anti-Semitism also raises an interesting point, since in most of the rest of Europe, anti-Semitism was associated with antiliberal trends, with a fear of modernization, whereas in Romania anti-Semitism was associated with ostensibly progressive forces, in certain ways comparable to the Radical shopkeepers who believed themselves progressive, against exploitation and favorable to the "little man."

Mihail Kogalniceanu (1817–1891), who was foreign minister as well as a prominent intellectual in the country, publicly expressed a hope that Jews might eventually be useful to the country, even while he referred to them habitually with the insulting Romanian term *Jidani*. Similarly, he declared himself resigned to a certain Jewish influence, for "there is no deliverance from the Jews," who were too numerous and too powerful in Europe to fend off entirely.[113] The more radical Mihai Eminescu, the national poet and a man of high visibility and influence in the country, also recognized that there might be a few useful Jews among the "hundreds of thousands of nonproductive and alien intruders," but his more potent and persistent assertion was that Jews were an "extraordinarily greedy, unscrupulous, and inhumane . . . element."[114]

[110] Stern, *Gold and Iron*, 375.

[111] Sachar, *History*, 257.

[112] Stern, *Gold and Iron*, 356.

[113] Oldson, *Providential Anti-Semitism*, 106.

[114] Ibid., 120.

Throughout the 1860s and 1870s Romania received protests by foreign governments about its treatment of Jews. Aside from the satisfaction many western governments took in assuming the high moral ground, a number of other agendas were at work in these protests. The debts owed to Jews by prominent politicians were often more than simply financial. President Ulysses S. Grant had fences to mend, given his infamous orders during the Civil War. Thus he appointed a prominent American Jew, B'nai B'rith Grand Master Benjamin F. Peixotto, as United States consul at Bucharest. He did so, significantly, in response to appeals from Simon Wolf, who represented the Union of American Hebrew Congregations, and to urgings and pressures from other prominent Jewish Americans, a number of whom were long-standing personal friends of his. As briefly referred to previously, Grant said to them that

the story of the sufferings of the Hebrews in Roumania profoundly touches every sensibility in our nature. It is one long series of outrage and wrong, and even if there is exaggeration in the accounts which have reached us, enough is evident to prove the imperative duty of all civilized nations to extend their moral aid in behalf of a people so unhappy.[115]

Bismarck had debts of many sorts to Bleichröder, whose complex role in Romanian affairs defies summary,[116] but in balance one may more accurately speak of Bismarck's using him than his pressuring the Iron Chancellor. Nevertheless, Bleichröder was "deeply involved in the effort of Jewry to mobilize European opinion against Rumanian anti-Semitism,"[117] and he was in constant contact with leading Jews in nearly every country of central and western Europe in addressing the issue. He had Bismarck's ear and conveyed to him directly the many reports of mistreatment of Jews in Romania. In turn, Bismarck repeatedly pressured Carol: Jews were, he advised, an "always more useful than dangerous class of the population"; Romania's leaders should recognize that influential Jews "in all Europe would turn . . . persecution [of Jews in Romania] into a dangerous enterprise for the [Romanian] government."[118]

The Alliance Israélite Universelle, whose officially designated task was to come to the rescue of Jews in less fortunate countries than France, competed with Bleichröder and wealthy Jews in other countries on the Romanian issue. As one historian has commented, "there was a kind of concert of European Jewry" in regard to Romania.[119] That concert, devoted to protecting helpless Jews, struck many, in Romania as elsewhere, as a conspiracy of foreign Jewish

[115] Best, *To Free a People*, 6–7.

[116] For a detailed account, see Stern, *Gold and Iron*, 351–93.

[117] Ibid., 355.

[118] Ibid., 356.

[119] Lloyd P. Gartner, "Romania, America, and World Jewry: Consul Peixotto in Bucharest, 1870–1876," *American Jewish Historical Quaterly*, vol. 58, 1968, 54; from Stern, *Gold and Iron*, 369.

interests and power. Jewish efforts in regard to Romania in the late 1870s, especially at the Congress of Berlin (1878), where Romania was forced to accept western-dictated clauses in support of Jewish civil equality, was one of many factors that helped to fuel the fires of anti-Semitism in the 1880s, when it was everywhere more important.

While the efforts of Romanian politicians no doubt aggravated the poverty and sense of helplessness of thousands of Jews in Romania, the larger issue of the implications of Jewish presence in the country remained unresolved well into the twentieth century. In 1888 the new German consul in Jassy (the major city of Moldavia) reported that

all trade was in the hands of the Jews. By hard work, frugality, economy, and tight cohesion they prevented the rise of the Rumanian traders. . . . I came to know the Jewish trader most thoroughly. Our German export trade found him an invaluable instrument and scored brilliant successes thanks to his nimbleness and inventiveness.[120]

The role of Jews, or certain numbers of them, in the countryside might also be said to have gone from bad to worse from the standpoint of Romanian nationalism and social harmony. The Jewish managers in the large estates were reputed to drive the peasants relentlessly. Some sense of the conditions of the peasants is reflected in a law passed in 1900 that stipulated "it is absolutely forbidden to take peasants' clothes" in the settlement of debts related to labor–rent on the great estates. In 1907 a revolt over peasant rents broke out, and peasant mobs stormed the towns and cities of Moldavia, often attacking Jews. Before the government gained control, approximately 20,000 people were killed, overwhelmingly peasants.[121] Romanian nationalists claimed that thousands of their starving compatriots had been massacred in order to protect ruthlessly exploitative Jews.

The combination of population growth, poverty, government pressure, rising popular anti-Semitism, and new opportunities abroad did result in large-scale Jewish emigration. In spite of all the pressure and promises, civil equality for Jews in Romania was offered to a very small number of them (about 30 a year from the 1880s to 1914).[122] From the mid-1870s to 1914, the movement of Jews out of Romania was comparable to that out of Poland, the Russia Pale, or Galicia. But the Jewish Question in Romania was no closer to solution in Romania than in Russia. For such reasons, a new solution, the Zionist, gained increasing attention.

[120] Wilhelm Ohnesseit, *Unter der Fahne schwarz-weiss-rot: Erinnerungen eines Kaiserlichen Generalkonsuls* (Berlin, 1926), 34; from Stern, *Gold and Iron*, 372.

[121] Philip Gabriel Eidelberg, *The Great Rumanian Peasant Revolt of 1907* (Leiden, 1974); Stone, *Europe Transformed*, 127–8; Mendelsohn, *Class Struggles*, 277.

[122] Oldson, *Providential Anti-Semitism*, 152.

10

The Ambiguities of "Failure" in the Belle Epoque: Germany and Austria

The Wilhelmine Period was not an intellectually boring time. (V. R. Berghahn)[1]

We are not hyphenated Jews; we are Jews with no provision, qualification or reservation. We are simply aliens, a foreign people in your midst. . . . Your spirit is alien to us; your myths, legends, habits, customs, traditions and national heritage . . . are all alien to us. (Jacob Klatzkin, German Zionist)[2]

Morality aside, the enmity against the Jews is nonsense, because it is simply impractical. Everybody I know here [in Berlin], especially the military and nobility, are eminently dependent upon the Jews and are daily becoming more so. . . . There is no other way but to hold one's tongue and be content with gradual Christianization. (Theodor Fontane)[3]

Everything profound loves a mask. (Friedrich Nietzsche)

Enough has been said about Germany and Austria to make clear how they might be considered, already by the 1880s, failures as models of harmonious Jewish–Gentile relationships. On the other hand, we have seen how the term "failure" had many degrees and can be too much colored by retrospective bitterness. Millions of German-speaking Jews and Gentiles continued to live beside one another in reasonable harmony, Jewish material success continued at an impressive rate, and Jewish–Gentile interplay counted many impressive aspects. Many of those in the German-speaking world who spoke out in criticism of the Jews were not willing to go beyond mere exhortation, urging

[1] V. R. Berghahn, *Modern Germany* (New York, 1982), 27.
[2] Jacob Klatzkin, *Krisus und Entscheidung* (Berlin, 1921).
[3] Quoted in Fritz Stern, *The Politics of Cultural Despair* (Berkeley, Calif., 1961), 182.

the Jews to improve themselves in manners and economic morality or encouraging them to become more whole-hearted in their national feelings. Antiliberal trends become stronger everywhere after 1890, and heightened tensions between Jews and non-Jews could be noted in nearly all countries. But those tensions often took on curiously unfathomable forms.

The Appearance of Zionism

Modern Jewish nationalism, or Zionism, began to spread in these years, especially in eastern Europe, but also to a lesser degree in central Europe. It may be viewed as a logical conclusion to a growing Jewish combativeness, from at least the 1880s, ranging from the groups in Russia that began to take up arms against pogromists to those in western Europe that decided finally to enter Jewish defense organizations, joining the propaganda war against those who defamed them.

The Zionist phenomenon may be considered an aspect of the failure of the liberal ideals of the earlier part of the century or of the weakening of hopes for Jewish integration into Europe's modern states, although many, probably most Zionists in fact, remained liberal in a number of fundamental ways – certainly true of Herzl. It might also be considered a corroboration, by eloquent Jewish leaders, of the charges made by anti-Semites that there was something deep in Jewish consciousness that finally could not accept absorption into a modern nationalist identity. That Zionism seemed to corroborate anti-Semitic charges is one of the reasons that many assimilated Jews reacted so angrily at first to its appearance.

Zionism, with its insistence that Jewish nationalism was more natural for Jews than becoming members of the French or German nations, undoubtedly suggested an emphatic break with prevailing modern Jewish consciousness in Europe and with existing notions of modern Jewish–Gentile interplay. Yet Zionism, like modern anti-Semitism, was not merely a reversion to premodern patterns; its antiliberalism was hedged and limited, its hostility to certain modern trends different from that of the non-Jewish conservative and reactionary right. Similarly, its attitude to traditional Judaism was ambiguous, making it possible for a few observant rabbis to become Zionists, even if the great majority angrily denounced it as heretical.

Within the new but still very broad Zionist belief in Jewish nationalism and voluntary separation from the Gentile world, Zionist thought came to constitute a universe of its own, with a remarkable range of opinion and depth of analysis. It could be broadly cultural or single-mindedly political. It could emphasize the need for a spiritual separation or for a physical separation, ultimately a move to Palestine. Zionists came from the left and the right. The kinds of people who rallied to its banners ranged from selfless, cerebral idealists to intensely practical, ambitious schemers; Herzl often railed against the "sluggishness, selfishness, or sheer poltroonery" of those to whom he looked to help him forward the Zionist cause.[4]

The fine gradations and range of opinion within Zionism were only a part of the dizzying, fiercely hostile divisions within the Jewish world as a whole by the end of the nineteenth century. The Bundists charged that "the Zionists kowtow and lick the hand of the slaughterer of the whole Jewish people, the tsarist autocracy [that has] . . . made paupers, beggars, sick, weak, and feeble wretches out of the Jews."[5] The Jews in the Marxist parties similarly denounced the Zionists as reactionaries who refused to recognize class differences as more important than those of ethnicity and who were unwilling to break with the reactionary rabbis and other supporters of the old order. The Zionists in turn charged that Marx and his Jewish followers were traitors to their people, self-haters who were acquiescing in the disappearance of Jews in modern times. All of them assailed the self-satisfied, westernized Jewish bourgeoisie, Jewish millionaires like the Rothschilds and Bleichröders most of all. Within each of these movements were yet further factions that attacked each other with no less ferocity than they attacked competing Jewish movements. Such rhetorical overkill, such stunning charges of Jew against Jew – "lackey," "traitor," "reactionary" – were only part of a colorful list, characteristic of a people among whom verbal excess had a long history. It is particularly remarkable that this kind of strident insult and reckless divisiveness assumed such deadly earnestness at the same time that a belief by non-Jews in international Jewish collaboration seems to have been spreading as never before.

Zionism was more than a disappointed reaction by naturally liberal and assimilationist Jews to Gentile hatred and rejection, as it is sometimes presented. It also grew out of ideas that came from within the Jewish world, recalling the familiar issue of whether Jewishness in the most general sense may be considered essential or existential, whether Jews are Jews by choice or by circumstance, whether modern Jewish consciousness is derived most decisively from Gentile contempt or from something deep and ineradicable in Jewish memory and identity.

Jews were no doubt rejected by Gentiles in this period, but many of those Gentiles earnestly believed that *they* and their values had been rejected by Jews, that Jews were not living up to the concessions they implicitly accepted when they gained civil emancipation. And those Gentiles, as we have seen, were not entirely mistaken. In other words, they correctly perceived that many, perhaps most, Jews had refused to become "pure" German, French, or Russian, especially as those Jews themselves began to realize what that purity finally seemed to mean. Indeed, by the turn of the century, many Jews began to understand more fully that most Gentiles expected them to "disappear," dropping all distinctively

[4] David Vital, *The Origins of Zionism* (Oxford, 1975), 327.

[5] Jehuda Reinharz, *Chaim Weizmann: The Making of a Zionist Leader* (Oxford, 1985), 52.

Jewish traits, allegiances, or habits of mind. The familiar distinction that religion was a private matter, one that was compatible with various nationalities, which satisfied many Jews in earlier years, began to appear unworkable or at least very awkward in practice.

This dialogue of the deaf between Jew and non-Jew ultimately went back to the flawed assumptions, on both sides, of civil emancipation in the first place. The honeymoon was over; divorce was being contemplated. But its costs promised to be terribly high, and the decision was being avoided – perhaps something could still be worked out. In this, Gentile–Jewish relations were not unlike a great many marriages in the everyday world: However saddening the realization that initial enthusiasms were based on faulty assumptions, would a divorce not make things even worse? And was it finally not better to put a good face on things, not to speak publicly of inner tensions and disappointments?

Zionism, in the sense of a specifically modern Jewish nationalism that looked to a separation of Jews from non-Jews, had already found eloquent if not widely accepted expression as early as the 1860s. Taking inspiration primarily from the Italians, another ancient, humiliated people, who had dramatically begun to build a modern nation-state in the 1860s, Moses Hess, a close associate and admirer of Karl Marx in the 1840s, rejected the ideal of assimilation and called for the creation of a Jewish nation-state. He wrote that "The Jews have lived and labored among the nations for almost two thousand years, but nonetheless they cannot become rooted organically within them." He saw especially little hope for harmony and understanding between Jews and Germans: "The Germans hate the religion of the Jews less than they hate their race – they hate the particular faith of the Jews less than they hate their particular noses."[6] Years before, Disraeli had written in much the same vein in his clearly autobiographical novel *Vivian Grey* (1826): The Jewish protagonist was a "seditious stranger"; between him and his schoolmates there was "no similitude": "Their blue eyes, their flaxen hair, and their white visages . . . [contrasted] with my Venetian countenance. Wherever I moved I looked around me and beheld a race different from myself. There was no sympathy between my frame and the rigid clime whither I had been brought to live."[7]

Hess's *Rome and Jerusalem* (1862), however, did not capture the imagination of his Jewish contemporaries. Similarly, Disraeli, although he may have exercised an important influence on both anti-Semitic and Zionist writers, did not follow the logic of the position in his novel – since he entered British politics – nor did his brilliant success quite support his early sense of encountering "no sympathy" wherever he looked. In the 1860s and early 1870s, at any rate, the time was not ripe for a positive reception of such racist–nationalist messages by large numbers of Jews.

---

[6] Arthur Hertzberg, *The Zionist Idea: A Historical Analysis and Reader* (New York, 1969), 119, 120.

[7] Isaiah Berlin, *Against the Current: Essays in the History of Ideas* (New York, 1979), 268–9.

It was not until two decades later that Enlightened Jews in Russia, after the pogroms of the early 1880s, also began to ponder ways in which a Jewish homeland might be established. The most famous (again, retrospectively) of these, Leon Pinsker, published in 1882 what was later elevated to the status of seminal document of Zionism, *Autoemancipation!* Written in German, it beseeched western Jews to take the lead in a modern Zionist movement, to recognize the central Zionist assertion that "the other nations, by reason of natural antagonism, will forever reject us."[8] Yet this work, too, was largely ignored by western Jews. Pinsker did win a small if zealous following among intellectual Jews in eastern Europe, especially in the mid-to-late 1880s.

Zionism did not begin to attract attention among the broad masses of Jews until the 1890s, in large part due to the remarkable efforts of Theodor Herzl. Both through his writings and his tireless activism, he became widely identified as the father-figure of modern Zionism, the George Washington of the modern state of Israel. By the turn of the century, hundreds of thousands of Jews, in their disarray and yearning for deliverance, turned to him as to a messiah. His confident assertion that the Jews were one people – not French, German, English, or Hungarian – a people who must have their own homeland, found an increasingly receptive audience.

His writings and career as activist amply illustrate what a protean phenomenon Zionism became, and Herzl's biographers have differed markedly in their evaluations of him.[9] For some his humanistic and heroic qualities override his defects. Hannah Arendt, in contrast, finally concluded that he was a "crackpot," generating an ugly, chauvinistic, and undemocratic movement.[10] Many students of his life have been struck by the odd mixture of self-assurance, emotional instability, and childishness – and, even more, by the profoundly neurotic qualities of his parents, wife, and children.

Working as a reporter and editor for the *Neue Freie Presse* in Vienna in the 1880s, Herzl could be cited as a perfect example of the highly assimilated, remarkably talented, German-speaking Jew of Austria–Hungary, one whose language of choice was German and who had a profound admiration for things German, although he was born and spent his early years in Budapest. Interestingly, although he was highly literate and widely read, he knew nothing of the work of Hess, Pinsker, or other early theorists of Zionism; there is no known causal relationship of their writings to his – nor was there any such relationship between Hess and Pinsker. All three apparently came to similar conclusions independently and "from within," so to speak, or at least from the

[8] Vital, *Origins*, 130.

[9] Alexander Bein, *Theodor Herzl* (Vienna, 1934); Amos Elon, *Herzl* (New York, 1975); Ernst Pawel, *The Labyrinth of Exile: A Life of Theodor Herzl* (New York, 1989); Stephen Beller, *Herzl* (New York, 1991).

[10] Walter Laqueur, "Hannah Arendt in Jerusalem: The Controversy Revisited," in Lyman Letgers, eds., *Western Society After the Holocaust* (Boulder, Colo., 1983), 107.

interplay of their Jewish awareness and the surrounding Gentile environment. One could not find a better example of how misguided is much traditional intellectual history in its effort to document the movement of ideas, portraying the supposed influence of one great thinker upon another, as if ideas moved like billiard balls.

One of the more unexpected aspects of this budding Jewish nationalist was his often graphically expressed contempt for his own people and his lasting admiration for the Gentile world, especially its aristocracy. His play *The New Ghetto*, written in France, where he had been sent as a reporter just before the beginning of the Dreyfus Affair, portrayed Jews as cringing, duplicitous, and wholly lacking in nobility. After visiting a synagogue in Paris, he wrote in his diary of the mix of familiarity and revulsion he felt in observing the "bold, misshapen noses, the furtive, cunning eyes" of the Jews at the services.[11] His private letters were filled with comparable venom about Jews. He reported that his travels were often spoiled by the presence of his *Stammesgenossen* ("racial comrades"). At a soirée in Berlin, he noted there were "some thirty or forty ugly little Jews and Jewesses. Not a very edifying sight."[12] On the other hand, his admiration for the European nobility, and his toleration of its defects, seemed boundless. He confided in his diary, "If there is one thing I would like to be, it is a member of the old Prussian nobility."[13] In this great admiration for the European aristocracy, and in his sense of himself as a natural aristocrat, Herzl was much like Disraeli.[14]

One scholar, echoing charges of Herzl's critics within the Zionist movement in the 1890s, has provocatively stated that Herzl "sought Jewish power in order to make Jews into Gentiles" – "disappearing," thus, even when insisting upon the impossibility of assimilating into Gentile society. That such was Herzl's unarticulated goal is not surprising, for he was so distant from his Jewish roots that what it meant to be a Jew had little meaning for him beyond the bitter experience of rejection by Gentiles. We have seen that he accepted as valid many of the attacks on Jews by Dühring. One of the reasons that he had at first embraced the ideal of assimilation was that he believed a mixing of Jews and non-Jews would "improve the Jewish race."

Set on normalizing what he perceived as a deformed Jewish people, Herzl "came close to rejecting [the value of] Jewish particularism."[15] He certainly seemed to perceive little merit to Jewishness in the forms that it had assumed by the late nineteenth century in Europe – or more precisely and revealingly,

[11] Jacques Kornberg, "Theodore Herzl: A Re-evaluation," *The Journal of Modern History*, vol. 52, no. 2, June 1980, 231.

[12] Pawel, *Exile*, 97.

[13] Herzl, *Diaries*, July 5, 1895, i, 196; from Vital, *Herzl*, 235.

[14] Cf. Berlin, *Against the Current*, 266.

[15] Kornberg, "Herzl," 227.

the forms of which he was aware. He might be termed a typical self-hating Jew, one who not only harbored anti-Semitic convictions but who shared the widespread belief that anti-Semitism was salutary, "useful to the Jewish character."[16]

But from such initial beliefs he gradually worked toward a position that denied the possibility of most Jews becoming Gentiles, and he lost hope that Gentile hatred for Jews could be remedied, at least within any realistic span of time. Consequently, he called for a separation of Jews and Gentiles. Yet, he remained to the end profoundly western European in ideals and consciousness. He not only continued to identify with the European aristocracy but also remained, for someone of his general education, astonishingly uninformed about Jewish religious tradition – and even more ignorant of the life and culture of Jews in eastern Europe, where his greatest following was eventually to be found. "He generated his highly creative approach to the Jewish question not out of immersion in the Jewish tradition but out of his vain efforts to leave it behind."[17]

Even the ideal state Herzl proposed, in his book *Judenstaat* (1896), was in most respects a modern liberal state, certainly not a religious one, or one based primarily on the traditions of the Jewish people. It could not even be termed a problem-filled blend of the premodern religious and modern liberal–democratic, as the state of Israel eventually became. In his ideal state there was to be a harmonious coexistence and mutual respect between Jews and other peoples. Consistent with European liberal ideals, religion would be relegated to a distinctly subsidiary place, lest it cause difficulties to his ideal, "a state committed to free thought."[18]

Herzl's subsequent utopian novel, *Altneuland* (Old–New Land), which appeared in 1902, revealed the same tastes: The future state of the Jews was in effect a piece of Europe, an idealized, liberal Europe, transplanted to the Middle East – a point that critics within the Zionist movement were quick to spot and denounce,[19] presaging the subsequent criticism of Arab nationalists after 1914. Both Arab nationalists and Herzl's Zionist critics lamented how oblivious he was to the presence of a large indigenous Arab population in Palestine and how blithely he assumed – again typical of the western European bourgeoisie of the day – that all peoples would gratefully accept becoming an enclave of a superior European civilization.

The hagiographic instinct in regard to Herzl, as with so many founding fathers of modern states and ideologies, from George Washington to Lenin, has been badly battered by scholars, in this age of historical revisionism. Aside from his distaste for what he understood to be Jewishness and his abiding concern for

---

[16] Ibid., 228.

[17] Carl Schorske, *Fin-de-Siècle Vienna, Politics and Culture* (New York, 1981), 146–7.

[18] Schorske, *Vienna*, 172.

[19] Cf. Reinharz, *Weizmann*, 139–40.

what Gentiles thought of Jews, much else about Herzl's tragically short life makes for uncomfortable reading if one is looking for a shining hero. His emotional dependence on his parents continued into adulthood. Like many overindulged children, he was unshakably self-centered and self-absorbed. He developed, as an adult, into a misogynist unable to reconcile sex and love; he married a spoiled, spendthrift, often hysterical daughter of the Jewish upper bourgeoisie and lived miserably ever after. She had scant understanding of and absolutely no sympathy for his life's work. She cordially detested his beloved mother, who in turn could not abide the presence of her dear son's wife. To further complicate the story, that wife was herself halakhically not Jewish, since her maternal grandmother was a Gentile.[20] In a life so full of paradoxes, one of the more strange ones is that the lineage of Herzl's wife meant that his own children might not have been acceptable to the rabbis who so influenced the definition of who was accepted into the Jewish state formed in his name a half century later. But that was finally an irrelevant consideration, since all of his children's lives ended in suicide and madness, before the creation of the state of Israel.

Although an accomplished journalist, Herzl's efforts at artistic creation, in writing plays, were consistently second-rate, which he himself finally recognized. He was completely out of sympathy with many of the artistic currents of his day; his aesthetic and moral values remained those of the Viennese nouveaux riches, which were in turn the values of his adored parents. Yet he brutally parodied those values in his plays.

Still, the more fruitful aspects of Herzl's thought and action are undeniable. And it is in the realm of action, in the astonishing willpower with which he pursued his goals, that his claim to greatness lies. He put forth in relentless, often riveting form the rationale for Jewish separation and the establishment of a Jewish homeland at a time when growing numbers of Jews were ready to hear such urgings. Herzl brought to the Zionist idea an energy, a confidence, a panache, and a visibility that had eluded its earlier partisans. He was by all accounts an imposing figure, a classic example of the charismatic leader. "He was a big, well-made man with a head like an Assyrian god's and a stately demeanor."[21] When the Russia minister, Plehve, met with him in 1903, he commented that Herzl was the first Jew he had ever met who did not "crawl." (He would soon meet another: his assassin.) Herzl proved himself able to articulate powerfully the feelings of thousands of Jews of his day, and he undoubtedly helped many Jews to have a new understanding of their condition, to assert themselves in new ways.[22]

Even these more positive qualities in Herzl were not without what appear in

---

[20] Pawel, *Exile*, 122–3.

[21] Connor Cruise O'Brien, *The Siege: The Saga of Israel and Zionism* (London, 1986), 72.

[22] Vital, *Origins*, emphasizes this point.

retrospect as darker, more ominous sides. His followers, as the years went by, mobbed him at the train stations, screaming slogans that resembled those that have been called protofascist.[23] And there is little question that his own political ideas, from their aristocratic starting point, moved in antidemocratic directions. ("The people are sentimental; the masses do not see clearly."[24] "The folk is everywhere a great child."[25]) One eminent scholar has seen a "deep kinship" between Herzl and von Schönerer, Hitler's idol,[26] but the comparison completely fails in terms of the moral stature of the two men. Herzl was personally far less driven by hatred, nor were his organizational techniques based on hatred of non-Jews. He remained to the end profoundly attached to rationalist liberalism and to the ideal of mutual respect between peoples.[27] A more appropriate term than "protofascist" for Herzl might simply be "messianic." Jewish crowds did see in him a modern messiah, and he did little to discourage such perceptions. An observer at the first congress of the Zionist movement, in Basel August 1897, wrote,

Many eyes filled with tears. . . . Herzl mounted the rostrum calmly. . . . Not the Herzl I knew, the one I had seen only the previous evening. Before us was the splendid figure of a son of kings with a deep and concentrated gaze, handsome and sad at one and the same time. It was not the elegant Herzl of Vienna, but a man of the house of David risen all of a sudden from his grave in all his legendary glory.[28]

Even to the minimal extent that Herzl connected with Jewish tradition there was still much irony. He did not conceive his role as leader of the Jewish nation in the heroic mode of nationalist leaders like Garibaldi, who organized and armed the masses for action. Rather, he played a role resembling the traditional *shtadlan*, the Jewish go-between, who worked with the Gentile powerful, trying to use the levers of Jewish finance and other behind-the-scenes contacts to gain what he wanted. But there was an important difference: In Herzl's case, it was as a proud, ostensibly self-confident go-between, not one willing to abase himself before the Gentile powerful.[29] Herzl did begin to establish contacts with Zionist groups in eastern Europe by the late 1890s, and they became increasingly important to his movement, but he had been wholly ignorant of their activities before that. He tended to value them less than his contacts with kings, sultans, princes, and dukes; they in return were often bitterly critical of him.

One of the most widespread of the myths surrounding Herzl was that he

---

[23] O'Brien, *Siege*, 73.

[24] Ibid.; from Herzl, *Diaries*, 421.

[25] Theodore Herzl, *Judenstaat* (Vienna, 1933), 14.

[26] Schorske, *Vienna*, 160.

[27] Cf. Beller, *Herzl*, 70.

[28] Vital, *Origins*, 356.

[29] Kornberg, "Herzl," 240.

experienced a sudden conversion experience to Zionism while as a reporter covering the Dreyfus Affair.[30] It was a dramatic fiction that he helped to foster, and like many myths contained elements of truth. The myth has it that he was surprised and profoundly shocked by the arrest of an innocent Jew and, even more, by the popular hatred directed at Dreyfus. Under what he himself later described as "the shattering impact of the Dreyfus trial,"[31] Herzl supposedly concluded – suddenly and ruefully – that if anti-Semitism could be so strong and utterly irrational in an enlightened country like France, then there was little hope for Jewish–Gentile harmony anywhere in Europe.

The reality was less clear-cut. Before arriving in France Herzl had already began to abandon hope for the future of Jewish assimilation. A questioning of liberal tenets was at any rate natural enough for a sensitive and proud Jew who had lived in Austria–Hungary through the 1880s. Having joined the Albia fraternity, he was shocked to find that his self-absorbed "Jewish personality" was not highly regarded by many of his fraternity brothers. An official record of the fraternity noted that Herzl "openly mocked or covertly sneered at everything his fraternity brothers hold sacred"; he, like a spoiled child, constantly "demanded special treatment." He was unpopular not only with "pure-blooded Germans"[32] but also with the other Jews in the fraternity.

He was humiliated when, contrary to his expectations, his resignation from the fraternity over a disputed matter was quickly accepted. A number of similar events added to his torment from the mid-1880s through the early 1890s. In May of 1895, only a few months after Dreyfus's conviction, Karl Lueger and his anti-Semitic Christian Social Party won the elections in Vienna by a landslide. The Dreyfus Affair may well have pushed Herzl over the edge, so to speak, but it was an edge over which he had been poised for some time.

Like nearly everyone else at the time of Dreyfus's arrest, Herzl concluded that the Jewish captain was in fact guilty of treason, though he, also like many others, was puzzled and disturbed by the case. His unease as a Jew may have been all the stronger, since he was among the group of journalists that was invited to witness Dreyfus's ritual degradation by the military in 1894. Later, in 1899, when a major part of the French left had come around to a belief in Dreyfus's innocence, Herzl tried to build upon his claims to prophecy by asserting that he had known all along that Dreyfus was innocent and that anti-Semitism had been responsible for his arrest.[33] His belief in the utility of this dramatic tale for the Zionist movement apparently overwhelmed his memory of what had actually happened.

Even as the Affair began to heat up, anti-Semitism in France was hardly the

[30] Kornberg, "Herzl," 228.
[31] Quoted in O'Brien, *Siege*, 667.
[32] Pawel, *Exile*, 67.
[33] Kornberg, "Herzl," 228.

sudden, searing revelation to Herzl that he later wished it to appear. Before the outbreak of the Affair, he was a regular at salons in Paris where anti-Semitism was rampant, and he professed to find much of value in the writings of Drumont. He wrote in his diary: "I owe Drumont much for my present freedom of conception, because he is an artist."[34] The admiration was mutual: When Herzl's *Judenstaat* appeared in 1896, it received what Herzl himself described as a "highly flattering" review in Drumont's paper.[35] Anti-Semites elsewhere also had warm praise for Zionism; the anti-Semitic deputy Ivan von Simonyi lauded Herzl to the skies and visited him often. Herzl reported that von Simonyi "had an uncanny sympathy for the Jews," even while believing that they killed Gentiles for their blood.[36]

Herzl wrote a friend that his book had earned him the "greatest of hatreds [from fellow Jews while] . . . the anti-Semites treat me fairly."[37] That "fair treatment" constituted one of the earliest examples of what would later become fairly common, that is, open agreement, even an occasional, opportunistic kind of cooperation, between Zionists and some anti-Semites, since they both agreed that Jews should get out of Europe.

Although now generally recognized as the founder of modern Zionism, Herzl had many bitter enemies within the movement. He certainly did not speak for all who were moving toward modern Jewish nationalism, nor did all of those share his peculiar opinions and remedies, beyond the fundamental beliefs that Jews were irremediably foreigners in Gentile lands and that new, modern remedies for the Jewish dilemma had to be found. There were any number of more profound and knowledgeable theorists of Zionism than Herzl. If he was the George Washington of the movement, there were also Ben Franklins, Thomas Jeffersons, James Madisons – even Benedict Arnolds. Some of them, most notably Ahad Ha-am, were little concerned with what Gentiles thought of Jews (Herzl's main concern, Ahad Ha-am charged) and were more interested in the survival of Jewish values than in Jews, as Jews, or in the establishment of a Jewish national home within the foreseeable future.[38] There were Orthodox Jews, though a distinct minority of them, who became Zionists (the *Mizrahim*), and there were socialist Zionists (*Po'alei Zion*), opponents of Herzl, who himself had a low regard for socialism. Other Zionists assumed more explicitly racist and antiliberal attitudes than he did. Zionist youth organizations often used proto-fascist language (the Jewish "community of blood," for example).[39]

[34] Schorske, *Vienna*, 157.

[35] Quoted in O'Brien, *Siege*, 667.

[36] Pawel, *Exile*, 267.

[37] Vital, *Origins*, 267.

[38] Cf. Jacques Kornberg, ed., *At the Crossroads: Essays on Ahad Ha-Am* (New York, 1983).

[39] Jehuda Reinharz, *Fatherland or Promised Land: The Dilemma of the German Jew, 1983–1914* (Ann Arbor, Mich., 1975), 151.

Some of the writings of these other Zionists appear in retrospect no less paradoxical or awkward. Max Nordau, a friend of Herzl's in Paris and a co-worker in founding the Zionist movement, like him a Hungarian-born, German-speaking journalist, was as alienated from his Jewish background as Herzl. Unlike Herzl, however, he knew a great deal about that background. In 1892 Nordau published a widely acclaimed book, *Degeneracy,* which was a sweeping indictment of modern civilization. Nordau attacked nearly all prominent European artists as "sick," from Swinburne to Wagner and Zola. His proposals for dealing with such degenerates were hardly liberal in tone and make for uncomfortable reading in an age that has seen the uses to which similar language has been put.[40]

Nordau was but one figure in a diverse and contentious Zionist movement. That movement, at any rate, marked a new Jewish scene, an emerging new image of Jews, one that raised the self-esteem of many Jews, even among those who were not themselves Zionists. The impact of Zionism on non-Jews was also mixed: While anti-Semites pointed to it as evidence that they had been right all along, other non-Jews saw Zionism as a potentially acceptable solution to the Jewish problem. Some liberal Gentiles were puzzled or even offended by Zionist ideas, while others were willing to cooperate with Zionist leaders.

In an article on anti-Semitism for the 1911 edition of the *Encyclopedia Britannica,* Lucien Wolf, a leading Jewish activist, offered some fascinating reflections on its impact. The article was written well before the great debacle of the anti-Semitic parties in the elections of 1912 in Germany. He termed the anti-Semitic movement throughout Europe "exhausted"; after all the sound and fury, it had

left no permanent mark of a constructive kind on the social and political evolution of Europe. . . . So far from injuring the Jews, it has really given Jewish racial separatism a new lease on life. Its extravagant accusations . . . have resulted in the vindication of the Jewish character. Its agitation . . . has helped to transfer Jewish solidarity from a religious to a racial basis. The bond of a common race, vitalized by a new pride in Hebrew history and spurred on to resistance by the insults of the anti-Semites, has given a new spirit and a new source of strength to Judaism at a moment when . . . the revolts against dogma were sapping its essentially religious foundations. In the whole history of Judaism, perhaps, there have been no more numerous or remarkable instances of reversions to the faith than in the period in question.[41]

Anti-Semitism and German Traditions

Herzl attracted very few German-speaking Jews; most of those living in Germany who did rally to the Zionist cause were either originally from eastern

[40] Cf. Pawel, *Exile,* 179.

[41] Reprinted in Lucien Wolf, *Essays in Jewish History* (London, 1911), 459–60.

Europe or had immediate connections with it through parents and relatives. Whatever the disappointments of German Jews with developments in Germany and Austria, most could not yet conceive of acceptable alternatives to their situations. Moreover, the vibrant, highly creative world of German-speaking Jews was in some ways in its heyday in the generation before World War I. Retrospective reflections about the failed dialogue between Germans and Jews tend to project onto the past an awareness that is both unfair and ahistorical to expect of people actually living in that period.

Still, there were revealing differences from Germany to Austria, from older liberals to newer radicals, from the social democrats to the bourgeois parties. Aside from Germans who opposed the anti-Semites, such as Mehring, Engels, Bebel, and Mommsen, even men like von Treitschke recognized a Jewish contribution or acceptable mix of Jewish and German culture while expressing a rising anxiety that many Jews themselves were not genuinely interested in mixing but were rather bent on destruction and domination. Evidence of harmonious interplay among ordinary German Jews and Gentiles is more elusive; clearly new tensions were arising, but still it goes too far to speak of a clear sense of failure at this point.

Gentile fears about the meaning of "rising" Jews were undoubtedly exaggerated if not utterly without foundation, whereas those fears at the same time had something to do with the move of many Gentile Germans to a more tribalistic identity. Other factors, particularly the rise of social democracy and the cluster of concerns around Germany's changing role in the world, almost certainly played a larger role in that evolving bourgeois–Gentile identity than did fear of Jewish incursions, but it is impossible to separate those various factors because of the way that they meshed one with the other. Gentiles could hardly miss noting how many liberal German-speaking Jews had begun to assert that a Jewish background engendered enlightenment, while a Germanic heritage was a burden, pulling in the direction of irrationality and barbarism. As historian Steven Beller has commented, "Jews . . . began to see themselves as the real bearers of the Enlightenment" in Austria and Germany.[42] The matter was stated quite openly in a speech by Solomon Ehrmann to the B'nai B'rith in Vienna in 1902. His vision of the future was not simply one in which Jews were to be an honored part; it was to be in fundamental ways a Jewish future, one in which "not only the B'nai B'rith but all of Judaism will have fulfilled its task. . . . All of mankind will have been jewified [*verjudet*, the same term used by the anti-Semites] and joined in union with the B'nai B'rith." In short, *Verjudung* meant *Aufklaerung*, jewification equaled enlightenment.[43] It was in truth a broad and humane vision, but it cannot come as a surprise that many non-Jews were wary of it.

[42] Steven Beller, *Vienna and the Jews, 1867–1938* (Cambridge, U.K., 1989), 142.
[43] Beller, *Vienna*, 143.

Even if some Jewish leaders were inclined to make invidious distinctions between Jewish and German traditions, most Jews in the German Reich by the turn of the century did not agree with the assertion by French Jews that anti-Semitism in France was a "Germanic import." They were concerned about anti-Semitism in their country, but they were not convinced that it was typically German – and certainly not that it was stronger in German-speaking areas than in the rest of Europe, especially after the Dreyfus Affair. Racism and anti-Semitism were, in the eyes of many German-speaking Jews, more accurately seen as products of reactionaries and of the mob. Hatred of Jews, they believed, was most typically to be found in eastern Europe, or in the less developed parts of the German-speaking world. The Prussian–German state, even if in the hands of Junker reactionaries, remained in the opinion of most Jews who lived in it a scarcely questioned font of justice and a bulwark of probity. They had supported the Reich at its creation, they had prospered materially in it, and they remained reticent to criticize it in a fundamental way. As Jehuda Reinharz has stated in relation to the leadership of the *Centralverein* (a German–Jewish self-defense organization, described later on), their "faith in the justice of the German state never wavered."[44]

German-speaking Jews in Austria were much less likely to have confidence in the probity of their imperial bureaucracy, yet they recognized its decided superiority to the bureaucracy in Russia, and they did not feel that its incompetence or corruption turned in systematically anti-Semitic ways. They continued to venerate Franz Joseph in a way that in fact much exceeded the feelings of German Jews for Wilhelm II, to say nothing of the attitudes of Russian Jews to Nicholas II.

There was a deeper and more elusive issue involved, one that has already been discussed in reference to German Jews' attachment to Bildung. As Beller has emphasized, this attachment was to an idealized set of North German cultural values, ones that most German-speaking Jews, whether in Berlin or Vienna, did not examine deeply. They did not, similarly, quite comprehend that even for revered figures like Lessing and Schiller, it was the "pure humanity" of Jews, linked to their oppression, that was attractive, not their Jewishness as such, a concept that Lessing and Schiller would not likely have understood, for they, too, looked to the eventual disappearance of Jewish particularity in an ideal future of common humanity.

In more practical, everyday terms, the stubborn Prussophile attitudes of Jews in Germany may appear unfathomable, in that most Jewish leaders were perfectly aware of the de facto, if strictly speaking unconstitutional, obstacles that Reich officials continued to put in the way of unconverted Jews' attaining high office in the state. Yet, those same Jews were not yet ready to abandon

<hr />

[44] Reinharz, *Fatherland*, 70.

hope that the state would be further reformed and unconstitutional practices eventually ended. The so-called *Paritätsfrage*, the equity question, was also a central concern for other minorities in Germany in the twenty to thirty years before the war, most notably for the Catholics, who similarly agitated for more equitable access to high positions in the state. That struggle, if often discouraging, did not present itself as utterly hopeless to them either.[45] A faith in progress was still deeply embedded in the consciousness of Europeans, above all middle-class Europeans.

At any rate, to concentrate on political issues misses the point that the fidelity of German-speaking Jews was not only or even predominantly to the existing German-dominated political structures. Their love affair with German language and culture, and with the associated notion of Bildung, made it painful to contemplate a break with things German. The "war" between Jews in Russia and the tsarist authorities became so serious in part because Russian language and culture did not exercise quite so powerful an appeal to most of Russia's Jews.

In what must be termed a highly Germanic respect for Prussian legal and constitutional traditions, many German Jews believed themselves actually in a *better* situation than French Jews. The Jacobin traditions that French Jews faced, the centralizing, unitary French state, were perceived, in the words of one German Jewish observer, as "French leveling without freedom."[46] The pressure to disappear, in short, appeared stronger in France than in Germany, as did the danger to property and social position – and this was most likely the most important consideration – given the political instability in France. Similarly, the plebeian democracy of the United States, with its corrupt political machines and pervasive materialism, might have held out some attractions to desperately poor eastern European Jews but not much to the prosperous and cultivated Jewish citizens of the German Reich.

Most Jews in the German Reich were not persuaded that they faced an inexorably rising tide of anti-Semitism, especially not one supported by the German state or linked to German character and forces peculiar to German history. What they *did* see was something considerably more ambiguous and shifting, ominous in some respects, hopeful in others. The reflexive pessimism of the post-Holocaust Jewish world, or even the less bitter pessimism of Herzl and the contemporary Zionists, was far from the mind-set of most German liberals before 1914. There had been a wave of anti-Semitic agitation in Germany from the mid-1870s to the early 1880s, which then receded in the mid-1880s.

---

45 Cf. Beverly Heckart, *From Bassermann to Bebel: The Grand Bloc's Quest for Reform of the Kaiserreich, 1900–1914* (New Haven, Conn., 1974).

46 Quoted in Uriel Tal, *Christians and Jews in Germany: Religion, Politics, and Ideology in the Second Reich, 1870–1914* (Ithaca, N.Y., 1975), 294–5.

Another wave gathered force in the late 1880s through the first years of the 1890s, with a high point in the elections of 1893, but it, too, receded, leaving the anti-Semitic parties more discredited and weaker than ever.

The next twenty years were similarly indecisive: In the elections of 1907 a wave of nationalist, antisocialist, and anti-Catholic sentiment resulted in the election of a new crop of anti-Semites. Yet they remained a confused and politically impotent company, accomplishing nothing concrete in the political realm with these electoral victories. And for the most part they were treated as pariahs by both the left and right. In the elections of 1912, the left won a great victory, and the anti-Semites were routed, to an extent that many observers deemed definitive. As in the French case, a persuasive case could have been made at this time in Germany for a receding rather than a rising tide of anti-Semitism or, perhaps more accurately, a despairing aggressivity on the right but a more impressive growth of opposing forces on the left, ones that were committed to protecting the rights of Jews as citizens.

For German-speaking Jews of Austria the situation was, to be sure, one that seemed to support pessimism more than was the case in the German Reich. Yet, as we will see, even there Zionism did not attract anything like a majority of German-speaking Jews before 1914, and even there pessimistic conclusions were avoided by most Jews, especially long-time residents.

The "Dormant Period" of Anti-Semitism in Germany

The Wilhelmine period (1890–1914) has gone down in most histories as a relatively dormant period insofar as political anti-Semitism is concerned. In accounting for the political weakness of German anti-Semitism at this time, in a land where it would later take on such horrifying dimensions, a number of historians have argued that anti-Semitic sentiments or beliefs, as distinguished from open political agitation against Jews, in fact grew stronger but found a "special" Germanic expression – in the realm of the spirit, away from the messy realities of open, vigorous political agitation, so characteristic of the French, British, or American scene.

A völkisch tribalism was replacing the older liberal humanitarianism among large segments of Germany's cultured middle class. That much was widely discussed and widely recognized, troubling many contemporaries in Germany, Jewish and non-Jewish. It could be argued that in France, in the United States, even in Russia, the demons of anti-Semitism were fought off in the open political arena; the result was a clearing of the air, an instructive testing of fidelities. Decent citizens were awakened, and they resolved to fight any future outbreaks of anti-Semitism. In Germany, the reasoning continues, the air was never cleared to the same degree, the issues never fought out so openly, and the resolve of the opponents of anti-Semitism to fight it never tested in the same way. The educated German continued to cultivate his "spiritual" anti-Semitism as an integral part of his awakening völkisch identity.

There was undoubtedly a decline of both liberal and anti-Semitic parties from the late Bismarckian period, a decline that continued into the Wilhelmine years. The descending fortunes of each of these parties may have worked upon the other. Since liberal parties were perceived by many right-wing Germans as parties that served Jewish interests, their weakening tended to alleviate the concern over "jewification." Similarly, since the powerful Conservative Party, in its Tivoli Program of 1892, identified itself with anti-Semitism,[47] hostility to Jews was further legitimized. The need for special parties devoted to fighting Jewish inroads was seen as less pressing. In short, the decline of the anti-Semitic parties by no means necessarily indicated a decline in anti-Semitic sentiment.

However, the anti-Semitism of the Tivoli Program was not radical. (In it the party denounced "the multifarious and obtrusive Jewish influence that decomposes our people's life"; a clause was voted down that said "we repudiate the excesses of anti-Semitism."[48]) That the latter clause was even proposed suggested that many leaders of the Conservative Party were not anti-Semitic in the radical–racial sense. A number of the party's leading figures had Jewish wives; a much larger number of them continued to be concerned about the rowdy, low-brow elements in the anti-Semitic parties of the day, which were judged to be dangerous to public order and property.[49] The vote nonetheless suggested that most of the leaders of the party were willing to exploit anti-Semitism as a political device. It was a cynical, manipulative, and "insincere" use of Jew-hatred in many instances, but in other instances German conservatives genuinely worried about the role of secular Jews, most notably in the left–liberal and social–democratic parties, in undermining conservative values.

Further reinforcing a sense that anti-Semitic parties were unnecessary, a number of powerful anti-Semitic extraparliamentary organizations appeared from the 1890s to the eve of World War I, the most important of which were the Pan-German League, the Navy League, and the Army League. They were certainly more effective in influencing the German government and its leaders than any of the anti-Semitic parties had been.[50] In George Mosse's view, such institutionalization of anti-Semitic forces was "more important than political failure [of the specifically anti-Semitic parties], and this partly explains why the so-called 'dormant' period after 1900 was only the lull before the storm."[51]

[47] Cf. Richard S. Levy, *The Downfall of the Anti-Semitic Parties in Imperial Germany* (New Haven, Conn., 1975).

[48] Ismar Schorsch, *Jewish Reactions to German Anti-Semitism, 1870–1914* (New York, 1972), 104–5.

[49] Norman Stone, *Europe Transformed, 1878–1919* (Cambridge, Mass., 1984), 182.

[50] Cf. Marilyn Shevin Coetzee, *The German Army League: Popular Nationalism in Welhelmine Germany* (Oxford, 1990).

[51] George Mosse [in review article], *The American Historical Review*, April 1965.

Still, the fact remains that the Conservative Party, the anti-Semitic pressure groups, and the anti-Semitic parties themselves were either unwilling or unable to pass a single piece of significant legislation against the Jews in Germany. Indeed, such legislation did not have a remote chance of being passed in these years. One may draw many conclusions about that failure, but one seems reasonably justified: Anti-Semitism in Germany remained inchoate, without a program of action based on an anti-Semitic consensus. The propagation of a vast amount of ultranationalistic, often anti-Semitic literature at the time does not lead inexorably to the conclusion that the German population at large accepted the material put forth in that literature.

If hostility to Jews was growing in some subterranean sense, or somehow gaining acceptance and texture in the psyches of educated Germans, it remained ostensibly a hostility of limits, one that recognized certain norms of civilized conduct, including respect for the rights of Jews both as human beings and as citizens. The various leagues did enjoy many successes, especially in pushing bills through the Reichstag that supported Germany's military growth, but the ideology of radical–tribalistic nationalism that some of its leaders embraced so fanatically was not accepted by a large part of the German population. And even among those highly nationalistic leaders, anti-Semitism was in most instances an ancillary concern, or one that was part of a larger tribalistic worldview, rather than a central or driving force as such.[52]

Indeed, it is uncertain that the consensus in Germany about humane and civilized conduct in regard to the Jews ever altered fundamentally, even after the traumas of 1914 to 1924 and in the depths of the Great Depression. What did change was the nature of the political system under which Germans lived. It was the acceptance of Nazi rule by the German people that had ominous meaning for Jews, but that acceptance can be distinguished from a fundamental change of opinion about Jews among the great mass of the population; what they were willing to let the Nazis do to the Jews is not the same thing as what they themselves would have done, left to their own devices.

Lobbying efforts by German Jews, along with the establishment of self-defense organizations that paralleled the nationalistic leagues, became ever more forthright in the generation before World War I, both inside Germany and outside, as for example in the efforts of figures like Paul Nathan to come to the aid of oppressed Jews in Russia. So, too, did the lobbying of all interest

---

[52] Cf. Coetzee, *Army League,* 11, and passim, which suggests a corrective to Eley's assertion that in the immediate prewar years "the right engineered a further feat of self-orientation no less far-reaching than the earlier one of 1878–9. It was characterized by a further ideological compromise, this time by the freshly mobilized petty bourgeoisie, and by the decisive acquisition of a genuinely popular base. . . . The nationalist panacea supplied the ideological fixative which aided the integration of previously discordant forces." Coetzee argues that the "old" and "new" right remained fragmented. The disunity she points to remained in the arena of anti-Semitism perhaps more than in nationalism.

groups.[53] Particularly after the electoral victory of the left in 1912, many liberal Jewish activists basked in a sense of accomplishment, of battles won, and of future battles to be undertaken with confidence.

Similarly, the political struggles of Jews in Germany against anti-Semitism lacked the scale and drama of those going on in the same years in France and Russia. More to the point, Jews and Gentiles in Germany did not come together so decisively in a struggle for tolerant, civilized values, nor were they challenged to do so in any comparably concrete way.

While Jewish exercise of civil rights and access to hitherto prohibited arenas of employment did not much improve in this period, neither did conditions in those areas consistently worsen. The material welfare of the Jews in Germany, at the same time, continued its remarkable, seemingly inexorable rise. Insofar as real, concrete actions were taken against Jews in Germany, they remained mostly in private, nonpolitical or semipolitical arenas, such as social clubs, fraternities, and educational establishments. These measures appear to have hit younger Jews hardest, if not in their pocketbooks, then in their sense of dignity and worth. But pocketbooks were also sometimes hit because success in many positions depended on informal social connections. In comparison, the political agitation of the 1870s and 1880s does not seem to have offended that generation of young Jews in quite the same way. There is evidence that the turn to Zionism in the 1890s on the part of a growing if still very small numbers of young German-speaking Jews was linked to experiences of rejection in fraternities and social clubs. Herzl's experience in that regard is one of the better known, but similar experiences were increasingly common in German-speaking central Europe.

Anti-Semitic Agitation in Austria: Karl Lueger

As we have seen, anti-Semitism in Austria had a significantly broader, more "progressive" appeal in the 1870s and 1880s than it did in the German Reich, but it was also cruder, more inclined to lawlessness and disrespect for the state. In the generation before World War I anti-Semitism in Austria, especially Vienna, was far from politically dormant. The social isolation of Jews was stronger in the German-speaking areas of the Austro–Hungarian Monarchy than in Germany, even if resistance to the entry by Jews into such elite areas as the military was less pervasive. Even among the secular Jewish bourgeoisie, contact with traditional Jews was more common, and the numbers of Jews of that category in Austria, especially in Vienna, were larger. The proportion of Jews to non-Jews in the educated classes was yet larger, so that even if Jews were interested in mixing with non-Jews, the opportunities were simply in the

---

[53] Cf. Marjorie Lamberti, *Jewish Activism in Imperial Germany* (New Haven, Conn., 1982), passim. Tal, *Christians and Jews*, contains relevant remarks on this point as well.

nature of things less abundant. In other areas of the Empire, particularly in Galicia, there was a very large population of traditional Jews who had no interest whatsoever in social or cultural mixing with Gentiles. Indeed, their religious leaders sternly warned against it.

It will be recalled that von Schönerer's movement suffered a sharp and humiliating decline after its initial successes of the 1880s. He was arrested, thrown into jail, and stripped of his title of nobility. Within a short time, however, political anti-Semitism found a more adept practitioner in the person of Karl Lueger, far and away the most successful anti-Semitic politician of prewar Europe.

Hitler's admiring references to Lueger have helped to place him in that cast of villains who are mentioned in any study of the roots of Nazism. As with Treitschke, the point here is by no means to rehabilitate the man but rather to present a more balanced picture.[54] Undoubtedly, some of Lueger's German-language biographers have sought to minimize the more unsavory aspects of his career. But apologetics of that sort do not justify equally unbalanced accounts from the opposite direction.

Like von Schönerer, Karl Lueger began his political career as a liberal but then turned against key liberal tenets. Both of these aspiring politicians found support among anxious, threatened elements of the population, especially students and artisans.[55] But where Lueger finally excelled was precisely where von Schönerer failed, that is, in political flexibility and in assuming an authentic Austrian tone.

Austrian–German political style has been described as "theatrical," close in tone to an Italian style, whereas the Prussian–German political style was more sober and disdainful of theatrics. The Austrian army was known to have better bandmasters than generals; its military parades were breathtaking in their pageantry, but Austria's armies lost every war from 1740 to 1918. And for all their often rancorous disagreements, Austrians of every social class and background found at least one area of common interest and enthusiasm – the arts, above all music and the theater.

More broadly, Catholic Habsburg rule has been distinguished from that of the Protestant Hohenzollerns by its baroque trappings. The Counterreformation had emphasized triumphalism; the great baroque edifices conveyed a sense of glory and power to the ordinary believer – and a need to submit to a powerful authority, expressed in terms of aesthetic grandeur. "The beauty of the forms chosen to convey the revealed truths of religion came to overshadow those truths." By the mid–nineteenth century, Austrian political cul-

[54] Cf. Richard S. Geehr, *Karl Lueger: Mayor of Fin de Siècle Vienna* (Detroit, Mich., 1990), especially Chapter 5, where the case against Lueger is taken up with unrelenting fervor; John W. Boyer, *Political Radicalism in Late Imperial Vienna: Origins of the Christian Social Movement 1848–97* (Chicago, 1981), presents a more favorable picture.

[55] Schorske, *Vienna*, 133.

ture was one of "aesthetic celebration of authority which had a large element of aesthetic enjoyment for its own sake."[56]

Unlike von Schönerer, who so admired Prussia, Lueger was comfortable with Habsburg traditions. He was a son of the Viennese common people; their virtues and vices were his. He spoke their language, both figuratively and literally – he often used the slangy speech of the common people – as the liberals before him were either unwilling or unable to do. Yet there was also something uncommon about him: Through scholarships and arduous struggle, Lueger had advanced through the elite schools in Vienna, at that time almost the exclusive preserve of the upper and upper-middle classes. He was anything but a frustrated petty bourgeois.

Der schöne Karl (handsome Charles) became a great political actor in a city where theater in the broadest sense was much esteemed. He was also a consummate modern politician, in ways that were being perfected by the political bosses of New York and Chicago at this time. Like them he accepted the people as they were, demonstrating a willingness to come to their aid in immediate, palpable ways – mingled with deception, corruption, and ruthless ambition. Lueger put together coalitions in a skillful if opportunistic way. He could hardly overlook the political potential of Jew-hatred. As Beller has put it, "Antisemitism was the common denominator with which all members of the rag-tag Christian Social coalition, renegade Liberals, Democrats, German Nationals, Clericals, artisans' leaders, could agree."[57]

Insofar as Lueger was moved by ideology, it was democratic–radical; he concentrated his attacks on privilege and sought to help the beleaguered common people. For him the exploiters and deceivers of the people were the capitalists and the liberals – which in Vienna meant overwhelmingly the Jews. Separating liberal corruption from Jewish corruption was in theory possible but in practice difficult. Lueger and his political allies did not much try.

Liberal practices were perhaps nowhere more compromised, more universally denounced as corrupt, hypocritical, and fraudulent than in Austria's capital city. Jews themselves, men as different as Karl Kraus, Friedrich Austerlitz, and Theodor Herzl, took a leading role in withering denunciations of prominent liberal Jews – as capitalists, journalists, lawyers, and religious leaders. It is revealing that the Austrian Social Democratic Party, part of a Marxist movement that officially opposed anti-Semitism and was led largely by Jews, nevertheless mixed into its anticapitalism elements that were difficult to distinguish from anti-Semitism. It is, in short, almost inconceivable that any antiliberal mass movement in Austria, even if it had found saintly leadership, would have avoided the temptations of anti-Semitic agitation.

Karl Lueger was no saint – far from it. But neither was he a monster. If the

[56] Beller, *Vienna*, 107.

[57] Ibid., 193.

historical record demands that hagiography in Herzl's regard be resisted, so the temptations to demonology in Lueger's case must also be put on hold. Both Herzl and Lueger were flawed human beings, yet neither had lost contact with a fundamental humanity and a sense of limits. In that regard, they had more in common with one another than they did with the radical racists and nationalists, non-Jewish and Jewish, of the day or after 1914.

The "capitalist corruptions" of the Jews were by no means the only issue. The Jews who came to Vienna in the course of the nineteenth century found no figure like Bismarck with whom to ally, as liberal Jews had done at least temporarily in Germany, but Viennese Jews, to return to Beller's points, nonetheless upheld a "Protestant" Weltanschauung. Thus, the much-discussed Bildung of German-speaking Jews was to a degree not consonant with the cultural traditions of either the ruling elite or the common people of Austria. Quite aside from the crude charge that Jews were alien "Semites," many members of the Jewish cultural elite of Vienna were "foreign" in regard to the modern cultural values they upheld, doubly alienated from Austrian and Viennese non-Jewish society. In spite of the ostensible desire of Jewish elites to be accepted by the Austrian upper classes, an important contingent of those elites harbored a contempt for the values of both the upper class and masses – for their laziness, hedonism, and superficiality.

The paradox is further remarkable in that a key theme of modern anti-Semitic theory was that Jews lacked spirituality. Judaism was allegedly a religion of empty ritual rather than heart-felt belief, outer action rather than inner conviction. Anti-Semites charged that Jews worshipped only money and were much prone to vulgar display and social climbing. Beller has intriguingly argued, in contrast, that from the first Jewish salons established in Vienna in the early nineteenth century – revealingly, by Jewish women from Berlin – German–Jewish elite culture resisted Catholic-Habsburg-baroque values and was instead deeply concerned with ethical issues, ones that derived ultimately from traditional Jewish religion, filtered through the Haskala and the German Romantics.

Mention has been made of Treitschke's aversion to the "jewified" German culture of Austria, of Graetz's desire to "destroy" Christianity, of Hess's opinion that Christianity was "religion of death," and of Ehrmann's conclusion that "jewification equals enlightenment." Many other Enlightened Jews saw themselves as upholders of justice, as a "light unto the nations" in a modern way. The theme was endlessly manipulated, and it found expression in nearly every country, but the relevant point is that "jewification" was actually more than an absurd fantasy of the anti-Semites. Leading German Jews in Vienna did look to a jewification of the non-Jewish world.

The word now sounds ugly because of the vicious use made of it by anti-Semites, but it was in truth a high ideal, benevolent rather than malevolent. On the other hand, it does not take much imagination to understand how alien and hypocritical such an ideal may have seemed to the average citizen in Vienna at the turn of the century, especially when, in its immediately perceptible form, jewification seemed to mean financial scandals, unfair competition, the revolver press, social exclusiveness, and capitalist exploitation. Much more appealing was the program of radical–democratic reform offered by Karl Lueger. In his very person Lueger was more attractive, more warmly accepting, than were those who composed sophisticated, Enlightened, and haughty editorials for the *Neue Freie Presse*, ones that mordantly mocked and derided the common man in Vienna and in Austria more generally.

Lueger has often been presented as a man utterly without principles. Whether or not that is fair, his lack of "sincerity," of a sternly consistent attachment to abstract ideals, extended also to his anti-Semitism. He was perfectly willing to make opportune compromises with any established power, Jews included. Even beyond his considerable political flexibility and willingness to compromise, Lueger retained an underlying respect for the old order and the Austrian establishment – the emperor, the church, the old aristocracy – however much he also introduced modern, mass democratic politics in a new key. His demagogic attacks on Jews, although popular among the lower orders, were a definite liability in terms of his efforts to impress the members of Austrian establishment, the emperor most of all, who was deeply offended by political anti-Semitism. Moreover, the Rothschilds, widely recognized as important to Austria's financial survival, let it be known that they would leave Vienna if the emperor approved Lueger's election as mayor.[58]

Lueger's attacks often took on tones of hostility to the educated, snobbish upper classes, a familiar enough theme in Chicago or New York as well. He appealed to an awakening mass electorate, which at this time, especially in Vienna, was ever more openly contemptuous of the cultured middle and upper classes. The *Spiesser* (roughly, "Philistine") in Austria, even took a certain pride in his ignorance and laziness, his *Schlamperei* (sloppiness). Under Lueger's patronage, many such people found new employment in the much-expanded bureaucracy of the city. The cultured elite was scandalized; Lueger and his followers were seen as the equivalents of the barbarians at the gates.

However, Lueger mixed into his anti-intellectual demagoguery large elements of characteristically Viennese *Gemütlichkeit*, of good-natured sociability. He and most of his followers were not racists in the way that von Schönerer was. Such a stance would have been entirely too "sincere," too abstract and theoretical for Lueger's crowd. Yet, his education allowed him to move with reasonable comfort in the cultured, sophisticated circles of the city. Indeed, he acted as a valuable mediator between social classes, answering a pressing need at this time of rapid change and disorienting shifts. In this, as in many other ways, Lueger's influence on Viennese political life was by no means only negative.

[58] Geehr, *Lueger,* 89–92.

Actors are by definition not sincere. Anti-Semitism was simply one of his many "acts." Resentment concerning Jews had a definite advantage from his standpoint, since, as noted, it tended to unite groups that had previously been hostile to one another or that had different interests. In other words, Lueger's anti-Semitism tended to act as an *Integrationsideologie* – that recurring concept. He put together a broad modern political movement in a way that anti-Semites in Germany had not been able to do. He brought together Slavs and Germans, rich and poor, racial and religious anti-Semites, left and right, an extraordinary, unprecedented entourage.

When both Schönerer and Lueger had moved away from liberalism, they agreed in attacking those aspects of it that they believed were deformed by Jewish domination. But Lueger was put off by von Schönerer's increasingly fanatical racism, his open admiration for Prussia, and his strident attacks on the Catholic Church. In a more elusive way, Lueger retained a more warmly human exterior than did von Schönerer, generating fewer determined enemies and many more supporters.

In 1893 Lueger formed the Christian Social Party.[59] This new product, Christian socialism, was incomparably more popular and more durable than von Schönerer's own efforts at a different synthesis of left and right Pan-Germanism. Similarly, Lueger's Christian socialism proved substantially more attractive to the common people than Stoecker's earlier efforts to blend Prussian–conservative, Lutheran Christianity with a humanitarian concern for the oppressed lower orders.

Lueger was able, furthermore, to pull together the conservative Catholic politicians, those *Honoratioren* who had more or less resigned themselves to marginality in the liberal 1860s and 1870s, with the so far inarticulate, fragmented, and politically weak lower orders. Both of these groups were antiliberal and increasingly alarmed about the meaning of modernity in most of its guises.[60] Lueger presented to them an opportunity to redress their grievances.

Lueger was first elected mayor of Vienna in 1895. However, Franz Joseph would not condone a mayor of the capital city of his realm who had so demagogically attacked both "his" Jews and the Hungarians. He annulled Lueger's election. It would take four more elections, with ever increasing majorities, to persuade Franz Joseph to accept Lueger's installation as mayor. (The Rothschilds' threat to leave was not carried out.)

When Lueger was finally allowed to assume office, in April 1897, he did not disappoint his supporters. For thirteen years, until his premature death from diabetes in 1910, he basked in the fervent adulation of Vienna's common people. He successfully implemented "municipal socialism," a set of reforms and projects of urban renewal that notably improved the living conditions of

---

[59] Boyer, *Political Radicalism*, 64; Schorske, *Vienna*, 131–2.

[60] Schorske, *Vienna*, 140.

Vienna's citizens. Under his direction the gas works were taken over by the city, electric street lights were introduced, the water supply improved, and schools built for the poor, all without raising taxes. These projects were often based on earlier initiatives and not so original as Lueger and his many admirers claimed, but it is difficult to deny his success in implementing them. Similarly, the middle and upper classes benefited from his "socialism," finally mollifying many of them. The improvement in the conditions of the lower orders was less substantial than Christian Social propaganda claimed but was nonetheless real.[61] And in spite of his claims to drive out liberal corruption, Christian Social corruption soon enough paralleled or even exceeded it.

Lueger was diligent in trying to help the common people. He was remarkably hard-working and personally not touched by scandal. Even at the height of his political success, he retained the common touch. He was a regular at all manner of popular festivities: In the year 1904 he attended some fourteen golden wedding anniversaries and countless other christenings and funerals; he habitually visited sickbeds, delivered speeches in beer halls, and played Tarock (a popular card game in Vienna) in the open air with the regulars. Hitler later observed: "He had a rare knowledge of men and in particular took good care not to consider people better than they are."[62] He was intent on protecting small proprietors and shopkeepers from the threats of the modern market, from the "unfair competition" they faced from large, more efficient, often Jewish concerns. For a time department stores were prohibited in Vienna. Some Jewish municipal employees lost their jobs, and Jewish peddlers were legally harassed.

Jews in Vienna were hardly passive in response – yet another example of how Jews, and not only the Rothschilds, "fought back" in this period. The overwhelmingly Jewish writers of the Jewish-owned *Neue Freie Presse* repeatedly attacked Lueger, and Vienna's Jewish banks refused him the loans he needed for his projects of urban renewal. He responded by securing funds from the Deutsche Bank of Berlin and by sometimes barring the reporters of the *Neue Freie Presse* from meetings of the city council. When challenged to a duel by a brother of the editor of that newspaper, Lueger refused, saying that such violent means were unjustified to resolve political differences – and that he detested dueling as a stupid remnant of preenlightened age.[63] The irony was heavy: A Jew acting like a member of the old military aristocracy and an anti-Semite responding in a rationalistic–humanitarian manner.

The dimensions of Lueger's struggle with the Jews of Vienna are easily exaggerated, again because of retrospective distaste for anything smacking of

---

[61] Geehr, *Lueger*, is intent on exposing the exaggerated claims of Lueger and his followers, cf. especially Chapter 4.

[62] Adolf Hitler, *Mein Kampf* (New York, 1943 [Karl Manheim trans., 1977 ed.]), 99.

[63] Geehr, *Lueger*, 86.

excuses for anti-Semitism. He had begun his political career in the company of Jewish radical–democratic reformers, men whom he openly honored to the end of his days, and throughout his life he retained Jewish friends and advisers. As one Jewish observer put it, Lueger "met with truest friendship, purest devotion, great self-abnegation from Jews." He took advice from them and dined and even slept with them.[64] His deputy mayor was half-Jewish. After the initial rebuffs from Jewish financiers, he did eventually obtain loans from some of them in support of his projects. And when Baron Albert Rothschild agreed to let the city use some of his land in the construction of a mountain spring reservoir – a project dear to Lueger's heart – the mayor praised this Rothschild as "one of the best Viennese and a true cavalier."[65]

This equivocal record in regard to Jews provided the context for his infamous quip, in response to complaints about his Jewish connections: "I say who is a Jew!" *(Wer a Jud is, bestimm i)*.[66] He could play to the Germans at one moment, to the Czechs at the next. His public face was often not his private one. Typically, he confided to the leaders of Viennese Jewry, in a special meeting with them, that "I dislike the Hungarian Jews even more than I do the Hungarians, but I am no enemy of our Viennese Jews. They are not so bad and we cannot do without them. My Viennese always want to have a good rest. The Jews are the only ones who always want to be active."[67]

George Clare's bittersweet memoir of Vienna recalls that his grandfather, Ludwig Klaar, a Jewish doctor during the years that Lueger was mayor, was appointed to high and honorific office, after many disappointments, when three members of Lueger's own Christian Social Party presented a petition in Ludwig's favor.[68] Testimonies of this sort concerning Lueger and his Christian social movement are not uncommon.

Such episodes cannot erase the cruel demagoguery, the injustice, the ugly compromises on Lueger's part. Still, it can be misleading to identify Lueger as a linear precursor to Hitler. The two in truth had much less in common than often believed.[69] In 1894 in an oration later compared to William Jennings Bryan's "Cross of Gold" speech, Lueger urged a return to Christian values, of a "religion of love, of justice and mercy in contrast to the [liberal] theory and relentless hegemony of the powerful over the weak." One observer wrote of

[64] Ibid., 137, 218.

[65] Ibid., 153.

[66] Richard S. Geehr, ed., *"I Decide Who Is a Jew": The Papers of Dr. Karl Lueger* (Washington, D.C., 1982), 322. Geehr maintains that there is no documentary source for this remark, the one that he himself uses for the title of his book. He speculates that it may be a misunderstanding or distortion of other recorded anecdotes.

[67] P. G. J. Pulzer, *The Rise of Political Anti-Semitism in Germany and Austria* (New York, 1964), 204.

[68] George Clare, *Last Waltz in Vienna: The Rise and Destruction of a Family, 1842–1942* (New York, 1980).

[69] Cf. Schorske, *Vienna*, 140 ff.

"an indescribable scene. Men stood pale with emotion and tears in their eyes; from the tribunes and galleries waved the handkerchiefs of women bent over the balustrade, cheering the speaker. Applause and cheers thundered without end."[70] Hitler approvingly noted Lueger's "royal habits": "When he held a festivity in the City Hall, it was magnificent. I never saw him in the streets of Vienna without everyone's stopping to greet him. His popularity was immense. At his funeral, two hundred thousand Viennese followed him to the cemetery. The procession lasted a whole day."[71]

Hitler and Lueger, in terms of personal values, were utterly different men, even if both used anti-Semitism and pandered to the anxieties of the lower orders. The measures that Lueger took against Jews in balance caused the great majority of them little material harm, and, interestingly, in his surviving private papers anti-Semitic statements are extremely rare.[72]

Even while Lueger was mayor, Jews continued to move into the city at a rapid rate, Jewish upward mobility continued unabated, and Jewish wealth remained impressive. The period considered the "Golden Age of Viennese Jewry" (1897–1910) coincided with the years that Lueger was mayor. The mother of the subsequently world-famous Jewish writer Elias Canetti continued to think of Vienna in this period as close to a secular paradise and much preferable to living in England. Again, if this is "failure," one needs to recognize how mixed and ambiguous that failure was.

To observe that Hitler admired Lueger and imitated him or to remark that Lueger put together the first "successful" anti-Semitic movement[73] can put too heavy a weight on this precedent, especially if he is to be seen as part of an unbroken chain or an inexorably rising tide of anti-Semitism. One needs, similarly, to ask what the "success" of Lueger's movement actually entailed.

In truth, his anti-Semitism was mostly noise. The period of his ascendancy marked an end to the honeymoon of Jewish–Gentile relations, but Lueger did not hate all Jews, especially not as a race, or in the vicious ways that radical anti-Semites did. He undoubtedly *did* want to limit their extremely rapid rise and curtail the power of the liberalism with which they were associated; he unquestionably sought to gain some control over the extraordinary economic influence of certain prominent Jews, since he believed that it threatened the "little people" of Vienna and of the rest of Austria. He exploited unjustly and

---

[70] Quoted in Geehr, *Lueger,* 86.

[71] *Hitler's Table Talk, 1941–44; His Private Conversations* (London, 1973), 147.

[72] Geehr, *"I Decide,"* 323. Many of Lueger's papers have been lost, and it is difficult to be certain how representative are those that remain. Scarcely ten pages out of over 300 in Geehr's collection of documents deal with Lueger the anti-Semite, and even in those ten pages the references to Jews consist mostly of complaints about the venality of the Jewish liberal press and its unfair attacks on Lueger.

[73] Cf. Robert Wistrich, *Socialism and the Jews: The Dialectics of Emancipation in Germany and Austria–Hungary* (East Brunswick, N.J., 1982), 111, 202.

sometimes cynically the resentments that the various successes of Jews evoked. But he never looked forward to a Vienna that would be *judenrein* (free of Jews, an expression made notorious by the Nazis). In a conversation with a prominent Austrian politician, Lueger typically confided that "anti-Semitism is a good means of agitation, in order to get ahead in politics, but once one gets up there, one doesn't need it any more, for it is a sport for the common people."[74]

The distinguished historian of Austria–Hungary, Henry Wickham Steed, observed that Lueger was a "Jew-baiter but not a Jew hater." Steed offered a new verse to a familiar refrain by observing that Lueger "in the long run rendered a service to the Jews themselves by compelling them, under pressure, to observe a circumspection of which they previously seemed incapable. The better Jews, indeed, soon recognized that Lueger had been a blessing in disguise by tempering the immoderation that is a prominent Jewish failing." Steed regretted, however, that Lueger merely replaced "Jewish–liberal corruption with Christian–social corruption."[75]

The social–democratic opponents of Lueger went one step farther than Steed: They asserted that Lueger, after all, turned out to be no more than yet another lackey of the Jews (*Judenknecht* – a common epithet of the day). The powerful Jews of Vienna had found in him a way of rendering anti-Semitic reformism impotent, of working around him – or, finally, with him, behind the scenes. With all his theatrical noise, he made it seem that there were changes, but nothing substantial changed as far as Jewish wealth and power were concerned.

The Jewish editor of a social–democratic newspaper noted sardonically that "If there is anyone to whom one can apply the word 'Jewified' it is to the Viennese mayor."[76] And some Jewish leaders, after they calmed down and after Lueger's attacks on Jews lessened, unquestionably did come to consider Lueger a lesser evil; in their eyes he acted as a restraining force on the more radical, racist anti-Semites in Vienna.[77] And he helped to defuse the more troubling threat from the left. Even some poor Jews, who almost certainly suffered more from Christian–social rule than did the rich, seem to have reasoned in that way: An anonymous and ungrammatical letter to Lueger, found in his papers, from a "good patriotic Hungarian Jew" wished the mayor good health, complimented him on his administrative talents, and observed that many Viennese Jews agreed that if men like Hermann Bielohlawek (a crude,

[74] Carvel de Bussy, ed. and trans., *Memoirs of Alexander Spitzmüller Freiherr von Harmersbach* (Boulder, Colo., 1987), 49.

[75] Henry Wickham Steed, *The Hapsburg Monarchy* (London, 1913), xxv–xxvii.

[76] *Arbeiter Zeitung,* 6 April 1900; quoted in Robert S. Wistrich, "Social Democracy, Antisemitism, and the Jews of Vienna," in Ivar Oxaal et al., eds., *Jews, Antisemitism and Culture in Vienna* (London and New York, 1987), 120.

[77] Cf. Robert Wistrich, "Karl Lueger and the Ambiguities of Viennese Antisemitism," *Jewish Social Studies,* vol. 45, Summer–Fall 1983, 251–2.

radical anti-Semite) came to power, "then woe to Israel in Vienna."[78] Indeed, Hitler himself, even while expressing admiration for Lueger as a flexible popular tribune, would later condemn the position of the Christian socials as "sham anti-Semitism."[79]

Such remarks do not address the charge that by exploiting anti-Semitism, Lueger further legitimized hatred of the Jews, with ominous long-range implications. It is a serious and telling charge, one that has also been leveled at figures like von Treitschke and Stoecker. And it is one that can by no means be dismissed: Lueger, like those two, obviously has small claim to being a hero, a moral leader of pre-1914 Europe. In order to have been such a leader he should have condemned anti-Semitism rather than exploited it. But if he had, he would not have become mayor of Vienna. And in fairness one must recognize that he did not desire for the Jews the tragedies that were to befall them in the following decades – he would have been appalled by the prospect of such tragedies. Lueger's most recent biographer alludes to Lueger's "criminal irresponsibility."[80] If that term is to be accepted, it must also be recognized that there are many degrees of criminality; Lueger's was closer to that of a reckless driver than that of a man guilty of premeditated murder. There were, it should be added, many reckless drivers in the political world of the day.

The "Unpolitical" Germans: Langbehn, Lagarde, Chamberlain

Developments in the German Reich and in its capital city, Berlin, took a revealingly different direction from those of Vienna in the generation before the war. Berlin remained a stronghold of the left–liberals and, increasingly, of the social democrats, both firm opponents of the anti-Semites. The German Reich from 1890 to 1914 had no anti-Semitic politician of Lueger's abilities and broad, popular appeal, certainly not in its capital city.

In 1890 Bismarck was dismissed by the new emperor, Wilhelm II, who then attempted to put his own stamp on German politics. The following decades witnessed an increase in international tensions, paralleled by internal tensions. But as already suggested, historians of German anti-Semitism have generally been less impressed with anti-Semitic political activism than with developments in the intellectual and cultural sphere, in the evolution of what Fritz Stern has termed the "Germanic Ideology." This ideology was "curiously idealistic, unpolitical"; it constituted "the main link between all that is venerable and great in the German past and the triumph of national socialism."[81]

---

[78] Geehr, *Lueger*, 192.

[79] Cf. *Mein Kampf*, 98 ff.

[80] Geehr, *Lueger*, 178.

[81] Fritz Stern, *The Politics of Cultural Despair* (Berkeley, Calif., 1961), 15.

Yet again the question: Have these influential propagators of the German Ideology been viewed with adequate attention to the sometimes remarkable ambiguity of their thought? A case can be made that they, like Lueger, have usually been presented in potted biographies and tendentious resumés as an aspect of alleged poisoned roots, an inexorable growth of fascism or Nazism. Inadequate attention has been devoted in many histories to those aspects of their thought that do not fit into a neat picture of their being intellectual ancestors to Nazism.

The 1890s in Germany saw an often intense interest on the part of the educated German public in writers and thinkers who may be considered in one way or another antiliberal. Feodor Dostoevsky's brooding, mystical works were translated into German in these years and gained a wide readership. Friedrich Nietzsche, relatively little noticed when he wrote his major works in the 1870s and 1880s, gradually became one of the most influential writers of the nineteenth century, if also one whose epigrammatic, often delphic writings lent themselves to radically opposed interpretations. Revealingly, he was as popular with Jewish intellectuals as with anti-Semites. Marx's writings, attacking liberalism from an entirely different perspective, also attracted much more attention by the 1890s than when he was alive. His thought, similarly characterized by pervasive obscurities, was also eventually vulgarized and misinterpreted.

Nietzsche was frequently cited in the late nineteenth and early twentieth centuries to give support to racism and anti-Semitism, neither of which he supported. Indeed, he sometimes mordantly excoriated them. Even the tendency to cite his writings in support of the anti-Christian paganism that was being propagated by men like Dühring, although more justifiable in terms of what Nietzsche actually wrote, also tendentiously twisted his rarified pronouncements. Nietzsche lent eloquent support to the attacks from many quarters in the late nineteenth century on what in ordinary language are termed "Christian virtues" – meekness, concern for the weak and downtrodden, simplicity, plebeian benevolence. He called for a return to the pre-Christian virtues of the ancient Greeks, virtues that evolved from the aristocratic values of a conquering, warrior people. Nietzsche's ideals were far from the mindless certainties of the Nazis, but Hitler and his followers were able nonetheless to persuade millions of people that Nazism was in part inspired by Nietzschean philosophy.

The Nazis similarly misrepresented the thought of a number of other important "Germanic Ideologists." Much more broadly acclaimed in the 1890s than Nietzsche's writings was a work entitled *Rembrandt als Erzieher* (*Rembrandt as Educator*), which first appeared anonymously in 1890. It was "the great literary fad of 1890," not only among the general reading public but also among the artistic elite of Germany; "no other work of the Germanic critics penetrated German culture so deeply, no other mixture of cultural despair and nationalist hope ever proved so popular." Sales of the book remained high into the 1920s.[82]

Yet the work, whose author was finally revealed to be Julius Langbehn, was a very odd one for a best-seller. It was murky and disjointed, the kind of work that perhaps only in Germany could have won so much acclaim. It has been termed a "rhapsody of irrationalism," a "wild and chaotic" book, a judgment that most modern English-speaking readers would almost certainly share.[83] Even its main theme, apparently so entrancing to his contemporaries, today appears curiously abstruse: Art, Langbehn insisted, was the only source of genuine knowledge and virtue. Reason could not compare to it in terms of genuine, deep understanding. Even religion could not offer a comparable path to real virtue. It was through a study of Rembrandt's art that Langbehn sought to develop these elusive pronouncements.

Rarely had the antiliberal, antimodern trends of the late nineteenth century received such an extreme yet lyrical expression as in Langbehn's work. For him, such expressions of modernism as "science" – which, typically, he did not bother to define – became an embodiment of all that was hateful and evil: the spiritual disorientation of the modern citizen, the impersonal cities, the superficial certainties of the middle class. All such lamentable developments could, he believed, be laid at the feet of a deceptive belief in the powers of science and technology.

It can come as no surprise that Langbehn attacked the highly urbanized, politically liberal Jews of imperial German and Austria. They conveniently symbolized for him what was objectionable about modern trends in Germany. Even so, he did not revile Jews as a race, nor did he place them into any other sort of hard-and-fast category. He made a sharp distinction between Orthodox Jews (the subjects of many of Rembrandt's paintings) and modern, secular, assimilated Jews. In striking contrast to the views of Treitschke and Stoecker, Langbehn believed that Orthodox Jews might constitute a valuable complement to the German people. He also expressed warm admiration for a number of Jews in history, most notably Spinoza and Rahel von Varnhagen.[84] This was hardly Nazism before the word.

Langbehn identified himself as a student of Paul de Lagarde, another famous antiliberal, antimodernist "Germanic" thinker, whose thought has also been typically listed in the genealogy of Nazism. Lagarde was a noted scholar and university professor, in fact a prodigiously learned one. He belonged to the same generation (b. 1827) as Treitschke (b. 1834), although he never enjoyed anything like the acclaim that Treitschke did by the 1870s. Like Treitschke,

---

[82] Stern, *Politics,* 199–200.

[83] Ibid., 132.

[84] Ibid., 181.

Lagarde described the Jews as a "misfortune" (*Unglück*), not only to Germans but also "to all European peoples." Indeed, Lagarde expressed himself in shockingly venomous terms: Jewish capitalists were "trichinae and bacilli" who should be "exterminated as quickly and thoroughly as possible."[85]

Nazi leaders used such quotations, yet placing Lagarde in a coherent anti-Semitic tradition remains problematic. Remarks made in earlier chapters about the doubtful influence of Christianity or racist theory on the development of modern anti-Semitism find a revealing example in Lagarde's writings: He had no use for Christianity and was especially caustic in his dismissal of "scientific" racism. His attacks on Jews did not borrow from Christian imagery, nor did he believe that Jewish characteristics were determined by a Semitic race.

Lagarde rejected racial anti-Semitism as a crude form of scientific materialism, which was for him, as for Langbehn, the root source of the evils of modern times. True Germanism, he insisted, was not a matter of blood but rather of spirit. He recognized the existence of a Jewish race, one that was physically different, but he believed that the spirit always would overcome something so material as body type. As he saw it, the reason that "Jews" [he meant modern secular Jews] were a "misfortune" was because of the ideas they propagated. Jews "destroy all faith and spread materialism and liberalism. . . . They are the carriers of decay and pollute every national culture."[86]

Lagarde did not support the anti-Semitic movement of the 1880s, whereas he befriended and encouraged a number of Jewish students in those years. He remarked, in regard to whether Jews should convert to Christianity, that he saw no reason for them to trade in "their coarse but warm clothing for our trashy rags."

Lagarde detested both Luther and Wagner, whom the Nazis would present as shining examples of pure Germanism. His comments on Wagner, Hitler's favorite composer, are especially revealing. After a performance of *Siegfried,* Lagarde wrote that he was "bored to extinction. Four hours of *recitativ* is intolerable. . . . I am completely cured of Wagner; of my own accord I shall not again expose myself to such suffering."[87] In complete contrast to Treitschke or Schönerer, he admired the English but not the Prussians, whom he reviled for their "reactionary monarchy and sporadic witch hunts."[88]

Both Langbehn and Lagarde had close Jewish friends. Langbehn in later years broke with many of them, but he also broke with nearly all his friends; he was, like Lagarde, an impossibly contentious man, suspicious, hypersensitive, and abrasive. *Rembrandt as Educator* deals with Jews in only a few pages, and Langbehn apparently had himself encountered few of them who personally

---

[85] Stern, *Politics,* 93.

[86] Ibid., 91.

[87] Ibid., 122.

[88] Ibid., 31.

offended him. He left very little evidence in his papers of private hatred for them; that hatred was more abstract: "The Jews" had led the Germans down the disastrous path "to science, democracy, and educated mediocrity."[89]

Langbehn and Lagarde must take a definite second place in demonstrable influence to another thinker of the day, Houston Steward Chamberlain. Interestingly, his biographer employs much the same language to describe his popularity that Langbehn's biographer uses for the year 1890: Chamberlain's most celebrated book, *The Foundations of the Twentieth Century,* was the "literary fad" of 1900.[90] It, too, went into many editions and was widely discussed, both inside Germany and out. But Chamberlain is yet another "Germanic" thinker (He was of English parentage, related to Joseph Chamberlain, but spent most of his life on the Continent.) whose ideas fit awkwardly into the notion of a rising tide of Nazi-style anti-Semitism.

Today a special odium surrounds Chamberlain's name because, unlike Lueger, Nietzsche, Lagarde, or Langbehn, he lived to see the rise of Nazism, and he accepted Nazi adulation, once he warmed to the idea of Hitler as the long-awaited savior of Germany. (He first met Hitler in 1923; he was thereafter mostly bedridden and feeble, dying in 1927.) Moreover, the intellectual connections with Nazism in his case are unquestionably more extensive than in the case of those other figures, but his ideas still merit a more careful treatment than one generally finds, for those connections are less certain than usually believed.[91]

Chamberlain's *Foundations of the Twentieth Century* (first published in 1899 but many editions followed, including an inexpensive one in 1906 that was distributed in Germany's schools) became a hugely popular book by the standards of the day. Its success was all the more remarkable because, by the standards of any day, it was a lengthy tome that made large intellectual demands on its readers. And, whatever may be said about the defects of the book, it grappled with many substantial issues. Emperor Wilhelm II read and reread it avidly; he quoted it constantly and sent copies to friends and acquaintances. To be sure, Wilhelm was not an intellectually distinguished or discriminating man, but among the many others who openly and effusively admired the book were Albert Schweitzer, Winston Churchill, George Bernard Shaw, D. H. Lawrence, and Carl Becker, the distinguished American historian. Becker wrote in a review that "one despairs of conveying any adequate idea" of the book's "intellectual mastery," "keen analysis," "brilliant originality," and "trenchant humor."[92] How could such opinions be expressed by men who would

---

[89] Ibid., 184.

[90] Geoffrey G. Field, *Evangelist of Race: The Germanic Vision of Houston Stewart Chamberlain* (New York, 1981), 226.

[91] These remarks do not hold for Field's excellent work *Evangelist,* which has much influenced the following pages.

[92] Field, *Evangelist,* 463–6.

later become staunch opponents of Nazism? Indeed, how do we deal with the alleged demonic power of anti-Semitic ideology if such men could read Chamberlain's work and not be drawn in?

Chamberlain may be seen as continuing a tradition of nineteenth-century belief in the power of racial determinants, one which was very widespread and seen in such diverse thinkers as Heine, Disraeli, Hess, Knox, Gobineau, and Dühring. In his book he tried to show, with richly arrayed historical examples, how racial determinism had operated from the distant past to the present. The racial element explained the rise and fall of civilizations, the particular genius of cultures throughout history. Like Gobineau, he was much concerned with racial mixing and the degeneration that he believed came from it.

Also like Gobineau, Chamberlain considered the Aryans to be the truly creative race in the history of western civilization. But Chamberlain's definition of race was slippery; it was certainly not a scientific one if precision and consistency are implied in that term. The notion of race seems in some passages of his work to be biological and fixed, but elsewhere it appears to be cultural and changeable.[93] Nowhere was this more obvious than in his definition of "Jew," where he seems to have simply abandoned the notion of racial determinism:

> The term Jew . . . denotes a special way of thinking and feeling. A man can very soon become a Jew without being an Israelite. . . . On the other hand, it is senseless to call an Israelite a "Jew", though his descent is beyond question, if he has succeeded in throwing off the fetters of Ezra and Nehemiah, and if the law of Moses has no place in his brain, contempt for others no place in his heart. . . . A purely humanized Jew is no longer a Jew because, by renouncing the idea of Judaism, he *ipso facto* has left that nationality. . . .[94]

Much Nazi racist jargon derived from or found corroboration in Chamberlain's pages, but doctrinaire racist anti-Semites who actually read his writings with any care must have had problems in accepting substantial parts of them. There is undoubtedly more that is anti-Semitic in Chamberlain than in Gobineau, and much more than in Treitschke. Yet a pervasive, puzzling ambiguity surrounds Chamberlain's views about the role of Jews in history and in the contemporary world, especially in his pre-1914 writings. He repeatedly denied harboring any personal animus against Jews and pointed out a rather surprising detail: His *Foundations* was dedicated to a Jewish professor under whom he had once studied. He once replied, when charged with hostility to Jews, that "I have remarkably many Jews or half-Jews for friends, to whom I am very close."[95] That was an exaggeration; his friendships with Jews were not "remarkably" numerous, close, or long lasting, yet he did have some. That he felt the need to deny his animus against Jews is itself worth noting; no such denial

[93] Field, *Evangelist,* 154, 189.

[94] Quoted in F. L. Carsten, *The Rise of Fascism* (Berkeley, Calif., 1980), 30.

[95] Field, *Evangelist,* 155.

would have been forthcoming from Dühring or Schönerer, nor would any Nazi have been likely to claim remarkably many Jewish friends.

Chamberlain explicitly rejected the assertion that Jews were necessarily enemies of Teutonic civilization, and he attacked the "revolting tendency to make the Jew the scapegoat of all the vices of the time."[96] He quipped that "a German idiot or Teutonic ass is much less congenial to me than a serious and productive artist of Jewish heritage. . . . I need only refer to Lueger and Mahler."[97] These are not, to say the least, the kinds of opinions to be later expressed by Hitler, who supposedly learned so much from a careful reading of Chamberlain.

Chamberlain's other writings had an intellectually respectable quality to them. His study of Kant was widely recognized not only as philosophically competent but also as an important contribution to the understanding of the great thinker's difficult philosophy.[98] The breadth of learning and sophistication of reasoning evident in Chamberlain's work put him in a different category than Marr, whereas his tone was unmistakably different from the venomous ranting of Dühring or the unsystematic anecdotes of Drumont.

His intellectual respectability was no doubt important in gaining for Chamberlain such enthusiastic reception by the educated classes of many countries. He was perceived as above the vulgar crowd, a cultured gentleman of considerable learning and Bildung. Yet he wrote in a style that made his writings more accessible than those of the German academic "mandarins" of the day – among whom, it should be noted, there were almost no admirers of Chamberlain's work.

Chamberlain was closely associated in the 1880s with the Wagner cult in Germany. He eventually married one of Wagner's daughters. Yet it is instructive that Wagner's audiences, especially in the beginning of his career, were heavily Jewish, as were his financial supporters. Even his favorite conductor was Jewish.[99] Key themes of the cult were a revulsion from the Philistinism of the age (associated with Jewish nouveaux riches), a stress on inwardness and subjective experience ("not Jewish"), and a belief in self-realization through art (Langbehn again).[100] Ideas of this sort, while especially strong in Germany, found eminent defenders elsewhere during these years, as for example in the socialist and noted artist William Morris in England. In the hands of Chamberlain and other German racist thinkers, however, aesthetic sensibility became inextricably linked with the Volk, with its culture, traditions, and historic religion.

These remarks are not intended to deny the tribalistic aspects, or at least implications, in Chamberlain's work. It is pervaded with negative images of

---

[96]   Ibid., 186.

[97]   Ibid., 159.

[98]   Ibid., 75, 283.

[99]   Peter Gay, *Freud, Jews, and Other Germans* (Oxford, 1978), 189 ff.

[100] Field, *Evangelist,* 54–5.

Semitic influence in history, images that often connected to those discussed by Renan, Kant, and other respectable thinkers (e.g., Semitic intolerance, vengefulness, ritualism, and sensuality). Chamberlain's biographer has persuasively argued that in spite of repeated denials, he harbored a tenacious if fluctuating animus against Jews, one that found clearest expression in private communications, especially after 1914, as his health and fortunes declined.[101]

The point made earlier about Treitschke (that he had no real program and did not support political action against Jews) holds even more for Chamberlain. He spoke of an inner, *spiritual* struggle against Jewish influence, not a physical battle against Jewish individuals or groups. The struggle was necessary in order to preserve a distinct German character. His concern was not radically different in that regard from the concerns of the Zionists, or even of non-Zionist Jews. Indeed, nationalists in many areas feared that their identity was being overwhelmed, and all urged a struggle against the forces that were undermining the true identity of their people.

An obvious danger in dwelling on the "ambiguities of failure" is that it might appear to be apologetic in design, trying to rehabilitate a discredited German tradition. That has not been the purpose of these pages. The discredit is not undeserved, but nonetheless many neglected points and distinctions need to be kept in mind. If we are to understand how it was that so many German-speaking Jews remained so unshakably attached to German culture and civilization, we need to understand the full dimensions of that ambiguity, even if it seems in retrospect that terrible portents of future disasters were there for all to see.

[101] Ibid., 90, 190.

The Ambiguous Successes: Great Britain and the United States

Does anyone seriously suppose that a great war could be undertaken by any European state . . . if the House of Rothschild and its connections set their face against it? (J. A. Hobson)

Why resent when your object is to overcome? Why bluster and fight when you may manipulate or control in secret? (Beatrice Potter Webb, on the tendency of eastern European Jews to remain silent "in the face of insult and abuse.")

In the generation before World War I, Jewish–Gentile relations in the English-speaking countries continued on a distinctly more even keel than in Russia, Germany, Austria, or France. Few contemporaries, when lamenting the failures of Jewish-Gentile relations in these years, had countries like Great Britain or the United States in mind. Tensions between Jews and non-Jews did increase in Great Britain and the United States, but political anti-Semitism never made a notable appearance in those lands; modern anti-Semitic ideology emerged in only feeble forms, and no anti-Semitic mass movement even came close to being successful. Nevertheless, attacks on Jews, especially on Jewish financiers, were made by a number of prominent British figures, and the agitation surrounding the Boer War (1899–1902) or the trial of Leo Frank in Georgia (1913–1915) had suggestive similarities to the excitements associated with the Dreyfus and Beilis Affairs. If we note the ambiguities of failure in Germany and Austria, certain ambiguities of success must be noted in Great Britain and the United States.

Jews in Great Britain in the Edwardian Period

To speak of British Jews in the Edwardian years evokes, to those who know anything about the period, the many friendships of the sybaritic King Edward VII with prominent British Jews. Intimate contacts between Jews and the British royal family, as we have seen, may be found already in the early nineteenth century. Yet, Edward VII, who became king in 1901, seemed even more likely than any of them to seek out the company of Jews. Even in Austria–Hungary, where Jews were notable for the affection they expressed for Franz Joseph, the relationship was a much more distant one. In a broader sense, Great Britain remained one of the best places in Europe for a Jew to live, and thousands more flocked to British shores from the 1880s to 1914. By the eve of the war the Jewish population of Great Britain stood at about 300,000, representing a fourfold growth in a little over three decades.[1]

Edward's Jewish friends were not universally admired. The Sassoons, Ernest Cassel, Baron Maurice de Hirsch, Edward Levy-Lawson (later Lord Burnham), Felix Semon, and the other Jews who became part of the king's inner circle were considered by some to be "loud, sophisticated and byzantine."[2] Yet, it is hard to disagree with the conclusion that "with the entry of such Jews into the highest ranks of English society, Jewish emancipation received the highest form of recognition and publicity."[3] Rufus Isaac's career carried an important symbolism: from the stock exchange in the 1880s to attorney general in 1910 to lord chief justice in 1913. That dazzling record, too, inevitably inspired a mixture of admiration, concern, and envy. According to Herzl, such a rise of the Jews, in both numbers and fame, was destined inevitably to provoke hostility – the larger the numbers or the greater the success, the greater the eventual hostility. Yet Isaac was by no means the only such brilliantly successful Jew in Great Britain in these years, and rising hostility to Jews did not become a major issue. The British case, like the American, does not offer much support for Herzl's beliefs.

The most fundamental reasons for the heightening of Jewish–Gentile tensions in these years are to be found in other areas. Great Britain's power, wealth, and sense of security began to be challenged more strongly than had been the case in the 1870s and 1880s. As one author has written, "*fin de siècle* . . . Britain was a time of self doubt. There was an increasing fear that the 'place in the sun' that had so long been hers was being shadowed by the rising powers of Germany and the United States. Doubts arose about her economic strength, her military prowess, and even the viability of the two-party system."[4]

Britain's growing sense of international insecurity led to a gradual rap-

---

[1] Gisela Lebzelter, "Anti-Semitism, a Focal Point for the British Radical Right," in Paul Kennedy and Anthony Nicholls, eds., *Nationalist and Racialist Movements in Britain and Germany before 1914* (Oxford, 1981), 90.

[2] B. Connell, *Manifest Destiny* (London, 1953), 54; Colin Holmes, *Anti-Semitism in British Society, 1876–1939* (New York, 1979), 87.

[3] Holmes, *Anti-Semitism in British Society,* 87.

[4] Richard Price, *An Imperial War and the British Working Class: Working-Class Attitudes and Reactions to the Boer War of 1899–1902* (London, 1972), 1; Elie Halévy, *Imperialism and the Rise of Labour* (London, 1951).

prochement with tsarist Russia, which meant that British statesmen grew more reticent to denounce the Russian government for its anti-Jewish policies. That reticence in turn incensed many Jews living in Great Britain. The confluence of Jewish and British interests in Liberal foreign policy that had been accepted as a given for most of the nineteenth century began to change by the turn of the century, and Jews in Great Britain who continued to agitate against tsarist Russia found that they were attacked for putting Jewish interests over British national interests.

By 1900 British liberalism, especially the principles of free trade and free immigration, came under unprecedented criticism, both from the left and the right. More than ever before, prominent British spokesmen linked Jews to what were considered the rotten fruits of liberalism: plutocratic capitalism on the one hand and revolutionary socialism on the other. Liberal universalism came under attack; racist ideas gained greater popularity and respectability.

Although shaken by the issue of Home Rule in Ireland, the British political scene remained essentially two party, Liberal and Conservative. Right-wing extraparliamentary pressure groups, such as the British Brothers' League, appeared in Britain as elsewhere, but most of them found anti-Semitism a less useful device than did their counterparts in western Europe. The Brothers' League did experiment with it, but timidly and without success. Extreme right-wing organizations in Great Britain, as elsewhere, lacked competent leader-ship and were plagued with factionalism.[5] And while conservative parties on the Continent were tempted to exploit anti-Semitic feelings as a way to bolster popular support for conservative principles, such politically opportunistic or "insincere" anti-Semitism had few parallels in Great Britain.

We have seen how newly potent the old image of the Jewish power broker had become in the decade or so before World War I: Schiff in America, Bleichröder in Germany, the Rothschilds in Austria, France, Italy, and Great Britain were widely believed to exercise great power in the councils of govern-ment. Jews working behind the scenes for selfish reasons were believed by some in Britain to be behind the Boer War (1899–1902). As that tragic con-flict developed, it so passionately divided the population of the country that it might be roughly compared in effect to the Dreyfus Affair, which was raging in France in the same period. Anti-Semitism was not a central issue in the war in South Africa, but inflammatory charges about Jewish influence in it were made by a number of prominent figures. The war, in the words of one histo-rian, "served for a time as the focus of all the fears that many Britons had about their country's future." It gave them a chance to demonstrate that they were still "the finest race on earth," and many of them rallied to the colors with an astonishing passion.[6]

[5] Holmes, *Anti-Semitism in British Society,* 92.
[6] Price, *Imperial War,* 1.

The Boer War was part of what has been termed an "orgy of imperialism"[7] around the turn of the century, one that helped intensify hostilities between Europe's major powers. A "scramble for Africa" began in the early 1890s, mostly between France and Great Britain. Italy launched its disastrous campaign in Abysinnia (1896), and there was a war scare between Great Britain and France in 1897–1898 when their forces collided in the upper Nile at Fashoda. These years marked as well America's entry into the imperialistic competition. The war with Spain in 1898 gained for the American republic new possessions in the Caribbean and the Pacific but left Spain deeply embittered over its defeat.

These conflicts engaged a mass public as never before. William Randolph Hearst's yellow press, in inflaming the American public over the alleged perfidies of Spain, must be understood as part of broader trends, in which the passions engaged in imperialistic adventures were tapped for the purpose of engendering national unity, to say nothing of selling newspapers. In Great Britain, the press of Alfred Harmsworth (later Lord Northcliffe) was similar: giant headlines, vivid, often irresponsible reporting, attention to murders, scandals, and a tendency to whip up chauvinism and xenophobia. The Spanish–American War and the Boer War are hardly conceivable without the efforts of such newspapers, just as Drumont's reporting was central to the Dreyfus Affair.

Defenders of imperialistic expansion openly argued that domestic problems would be alleviated by the acquisition of a colonial empire. Some saw imperialism as others saw anti-Semitism, that is, as an emotionally powerful ideal that would bring previously hostile factions together. Measures toward the acquisition of an empire were termed *Sammlungspolitik* in Germany, that is, a policy that would "pull together" [*sammeln*] the Catholic Center, the Conservative Party, and the National Liberals in a Reichstag majority, with the associated purpose of rallying antisocialist forces. In Great Britain proponents of imperialism linked it to larger programs of "national efficiency," which would raise tariffs, streamline government, and introduce social legislation. All of these measures, it was argued, would get the country moving again and restore its confidence in itself.

British imperialists regarded Germany with a mixture of admiration and alarm. Well into the 1890s, the German "cousins" were generally admired. The English and Germans were believed to be racially linked; Queen Victoria and Wilhelm II were closely related by blood. Yet there was a rising unease about Germany's power, especially after the accession to the imperial throne of the bumptious, saber-rattling Wilhelm. Not long after he became kaiser, he was writing confidentially to his ministers that once a powerful German navy was built, he would speak in ways that would gain the world's attention.[8] In

---

[7] Norman Stone, *Europe Transformed: 1878–1919* (Cambridge, Mass., 1984), 96.

[8] G. R. Kesteven, *The Boer War* (London, 1970), 35.

1897 Admiral Tirpitz began to build a great battle fleet, a step that in turn provoked an accelerating Anglo–German naval race, since all British politicians agreed that Tirpitz's plans directly threatened British national security.

Long-standing tensions between Great Britain and the Boer republics in South Africa flared up again in 1895, at which time Wilhelm sent a telegram to President Kruger, of the Transvaal Republic, ominously expressing his "sincere congratulations that without calling on the aid of friendly powers, you have succeeded in defending the independence of your country." His reasons for doing so were made clear in an unofficial note to one of his ministers: "We must make capital vigorously out of this affair, for eventual naval increases."[9]

The "Kruger Telegram," news of which reached London in 1896, transformed British opinion from ambivalence to hostility toward Germany. Indignant denunciations of Germany's interference in British affairs came from nearly all quarters, from the Queen to the man on the street, and were taken up with gusto by the press of Lord Northcliffe. The initial victories by the Boers over British forces in the so-called "Black Week" in December 1899 were profoundly humiliating; the delirium that greeted the most insignificant of British victories thereafter revealed a new atmosphere: The British public was not only yearning for glory but looking for easy targets to blame for the mess.

It was in reaction to an earlier foreign policy issue, the "Bulgarian Horrors," that one of the more notable expressions of anti-Semitism in Great Britain had briefly appeared. As was the case in the 1870s, it was mostly the left, both liberal and socialist, that charged Jews with playing a clandestine and nefarious role. Some socialist circles in Britain claimed that "the capitalists who bought up or hired the press both in South Africa and England, to clamour for war, [were] largely Jews and foreigners."[10] More broadly, the argument was made that thousands of young British soldiers were being sent to South Africa to die in the name of protecting the interests of Jewish capitalists.[11]

Whether British interests in South Africa were important enough to justify the war that ensued might easily be questioned, but the mineral wealth of the area, particularly after the discovery of vast lodes of gold and diamonds in the 1880s, could not be ignored, quite aside from issues of national prestige. The imperialists, led by Colonial Secretary Joseph Chamberlain, dreamed of British holdings in Africa from "Cairo to the Cape." The independent Boer republics stood in the way. Further adding to the causes of war, the so-called Uitlanders (foreigners, non-Boers), most of whom had come in search of gold, were in constant conflict with the Boers. The Uitlanders, mostly British subjects, appealed to Great Britain for protection, and that appeal connected to the earlier concerns of the British, who saw themselves as forwarding a progressive

---

[9] Kesteven, *Boer War*, 33.

[10] Holmes, *Anti-Semitism in British Society*, 30.

[11] Ibid., 13.

European civilization in Africa, putting an end to slaveholding among the Boers, and more generally striving to "elevate" the reactionary, fundamentalist Boers, to bring them into the modern world.

Jewish interests in this area, as in so many others, are not easy to define. Jews were closely associated with international finance, which often meant financing wars. The manufacture and trade of precious stones was also a Jewish specialty. Jews played a large role in the economy of South Africa, and a few of them had become fabulously wealthy by the 1880s. But in South Africa as in Great Britain, the interest of Jews in the war differed notably. The great financiers had quite different attitudes to the war than did the masses of the Jewish poor in London's East End, and Jews in South Africa, themselves split into a wealthy, mostly German Jewish elite and an eastern European, overwhelmingly Lithuanian lower class, also stood in radically different relations to the war.

At any rate, knowing how to profit from war, a skill that Jewish contractors had undoubtedly acquired in European history, is not the same as planning and causing war, or even desiring it. And such contractors represented only a tiny fraction of the Jewish population; the great majority suffered horribly in the wars of the nineteenth, to say nothing of the twentieth, century. Even many of the wealthy Jewish mine owners in South Africa lost heavily in the Boer War.

Another too easy assumption about Jews in South Africa is that they naturally supported the British cause. South African Jews had a fundamental interest in liberalism, modern civilization, a network of world trade, and thus in British dominion, but Jews and Boers got along far better than might be expected, given the reputation of the Boers as backward-looking and xenophobic.[12] The biblically based racism of the Boers against African natives did not extend to the People of the Book, a situation with parallels in the American South in the nineteenth century, where anti-Semitism was also weaker than often assumed. Just as many Russian peasants seem to have welcomed the Jewish peddler, so many Boers found Jewish merchants useful, not threatening. In all these areas, modern racist ideas had not really spread and were largely irrelevant. Boers were much less friendly to the large-scale Jewish entrepreneurs, again with suggestive parallels in the Populist movement in the United States in the 1890s. Such entrepreneurs played a key role in the development of deep-level mines in South Africa, to say nothing of the financial system that raised the capital to make such mines possible.[13] Ernest Oppen-

[12] Patrick Furlong, *Between Crown and Swastika: The Impact of the Radical Right on the Afrikaner Nationalist Movement in the Fascist Era* (Hanover, N.J., 1991), Chap. 1 and passim. Hannah Arendt's well-known description of the hatred of the Boers for the Jews clearly needs qualification. Cf. Hannah Arendt, *The Origins of Totalitarianism* (New York, 1963), 195.

[13] Cf. D. M. Schreuder, *The Scramble for South Africa, 1877–1895* (Oxford, 1980), 181 ff.; Paul Johnson, *A History of the Jews* (New York, 1987), 573.

heimer became fabulously wealthy and came to be seen as a South African Rothschild.

It was plausible to conclude that Jews supported the war because they stood to profit from a British victory, or even from a war as such, but actual evidence of such support is meager and contradictory. On the other hand, evidence that Jews, either in Great Britain or in South Africa, actively opposed the war is similarly mixed. The so-called "pro-Boers" (initially intended in Britain as an insulting epithet but then taken up proudly by the harassed and maligned opponents of the war) were a diverse group,[14] among whom, as might be expected, were Gladstonian Liberals, with whom Jews in Great Britain had long been associated.

In the midst of the war fever of 1899 a number of prominent Jewish leaders made public their support for the government. Hermann Adler, the son of Chief Rabbi Nathan Marcus Adler, and deputized by his father as "Delegate," went much beyond the hitherto accepted policy of offering prayers for the safety of British troops: He fervently defended the bellicose policies of the Conservative government of Lord Salisbury. In speaking to the North London Synagogue, Adler said that "the government of our Queen had no alternative but to resort to the fierce arbitrament of war, with the view of restoring just and righteous government to the Transvaal, and to vindicate the honour of England." Six hundred copies of the sermon were distributed to the press, and specially bound copies were sent to the Queen, the Prince of Wales, Lord Salisbury, Arthur Balfour, and Joseph Chamberlain.[15]

By this time native-born Jews were being rapidly outnumbered by the foreign born, and among those who were politically active, socialist sentiments were common. Socialists were in principle opposed to imperialism, and they interpreted wars like that in South Africa as benefiting the capitalists – including Jewish capitalists – not the working class. It was natural for socialists in Great Britain to oppose the war, in part because the political right was all too obviously trying to use imperialist passions for antisocialist, anti–trade union purposes.[16] A working-class leader complained that

the Rothschild leeches have for years hung on with distended suckers to the body politic of Europe. . . . This blood-sucking crew has been the cause of untold mischief and misery in Europe during the present century, and has piled up its prodigious wealth chiefly through fomenting wars between States which ought never to have quarreled. Wherever there is trouble in Europe, wherever rumours of war circulate . . . you may be sure that a hook-nosed Rothschild is at his games and somewhere near the region of disturbance.[17]

[14] Cf. Stephen Koss, ed., *The Pro-Boers* (Chicago, 1973).

[15] Geoffrey Alderman, *The British Community in British Politics* (Oxford, 1983), 43–4.

[16] Cf. Price, *Imperial War*.

[17] Holmes, *Anti-Semitism in British Society,* 82–3.

In 1899 J. A. Hobson, a left–liberal journalist, went to South Africa to cover the war for the *Manchester Guardian*. He and his paper had been vilified as pro-Boers and threatened by mob violence. His political convictions inclined him to suspicion of capitalists, Jewish capitalists included, but to such suspicions he added more sweeping judgments: Jews were "almost devoid of social morality," whereas their "superior, calculating intellect" allowed them to "take advantage of every weakness, folly and vice of the society" in which they live.[18] His experience, once he arrived in South Africa, was a case of suspicions confirmed: Jews seemed to be everywhere. They dominated the stock exchange to such an extent that it was officially closed on Yom Kippur. In the next year, as the conflict was still raging, he published a book, *The War in South Africa, Its Causes and Effects*. In a chapter entitled "For Whom Are We Fighting?" he charged that

recent developments of Transvaal gold-mining have thrown the economic resources of the country more and more into the hands of a small group of financiers, chiefly German in origin and Jewish by race. By superior ability, enterprise and organization these men, out-competing the slower-witted Briton, have attained a practical supremacy which no one who has visited Johannesburg is likely to question.

He concluded that "not Hamburg, not Vienna, not Frankfurt, but Johannesburg is the New Jerusalem."[19] Another journalist referred to "Jewhannesburg."[20] In Hobson's writings, as in those of many who opposed the war, Johannesburg was presented as a modern-day Babylon, corrupt and alien to the simple-living Boers. As another left-wing observer stated it: Since the discovery of gold, Johannesburg became "a hell full of Jews, financiers, greedy speculators, adventurers, prostitutes, bars, banks, gaming saloons, and every invention of the devil." In this observer's opinion, the Boers had every right to "pack off the whole crew." He asked his readers to "think for a moment, if Liverpool were to be overrun by 100,000 Chinese, smothering our civilization, and introducing their hated customs and ways – what should we do?"[21] Hobson remarked that "a very large proportion of the Transvaal farmers [Boers] are as entirely in the hands of Jewish moneylenders as is the Russian . . . or Austrian peasant."[22]

In his widely acclaimed study of imperialism, published two years later, Hobson asked if anyone could "seriously suppose that a great war could be undertaken by any European state . . . if the House of Rothschild and its connections set their face against it?"[23] He observed that "it is difficult to state the

[18] Johnson, *History*, 573; from Geoffrey Wheatcroft, *The Randlords* (London, 1985), 205.

[19] J. A. Hobson, *The War in South Africa, Its Causes and Effects*, part II (London, 1900), 189, 190.

[20] Holmes, *Anti-Semitism in British Society*, 68. The journalist in question was Robert Blatchford, editor of the *Clarion*.

[21] Koss, *Pro-Boers*, 55–6.

[22] Hobson, *War*, part II, 194.

[23] J. A. Hobson, *Imperialism: A Study* (London, 1902), 64; Johnson, *History*, 574.

truth about our doings in South Africa without seeming to appeal to the igno-
minious passion of Judenhetze [anti-Semitism]." He did distinguish between
rich and poor Jews: The latter "are everywhere to be seen [in South Africa],
actively occupied in small dealings, a rude and ignorant people, mostly fled
from despotic European rule." They were quite different from "their highly
intelligent, showy, prosperous brethren, who form the upper crust of Johannesburg society." It was the activities of the rich Jews that needed to be studied,
"if we would understand the economic and political import of the present
movements."[24]

As Hobson and many on the left in Britain saw it, capitalist greed for the
material riches of South Africa explained how Great Britain was brought to
war in that distant land. Jewish financiers, working hand-in-hand with the
owners of influential Jewish newspapers, also played an important role.
Henry Hyndman, a leading figure of the Marxist left (also the lover of one of
Marx's daughters), wrote, "It is high time that those who do not think that
Beit, Barnato, Oppenheim and Co. ought to control the destinies of Englishmen at home, and of their empire abroad, should come together and speak
their mind." Hyndman subsequently charged that the prime minister, Salisbury, was being drawn into a war by a "Jew clique" that was more powerful
than he.[25]

Most modern scholars have rejected the arguments of Hobson and the
many Marxists who argued along the same lines. The motivations of British
imperialists cannot be satisfactorily reduced to calculations of economic gain,
nor can those imperialists be considered mere tools of Jewish financiers,
whether in South Africa or in Great Britain. Prominent Jews were undoubtedly
listened to by British political leaders, but if one is to speak of personalities as
being decisive, the most important movers and shakers remained non-Jews,
men like Joseph Chamberlain, Lord Milner, or Cecil Rhodes. They required
no Jewish pressure to do the things they did, nor were they the sort to be easily
manipulated.

But Hobson's charges were both plausible and widely believed at the time,
even by those resistant to anti-Semitic arguments.[26] The belief in Jewish power,
or at least in the extensive behind-the-scenes influence of Jewish financiers
and capitalists, was solidly entrenched at this time in Great Britain as elsewhere. Such was true both on the left and on the right, and frequently by otherwise sophisticated observers. Disraeli's boasts seem to have gained ever-wider
credence.

In fairness to Hobson and his supporters, it should be noted that his arguments were hedged and provisional. The closing lines of the chapter "For

[24] Hobson, *War,* part II, 190.

[25] Holmes, *Anti-Semitism in British Society,* 69.

[26] For further examples, see Holmes, *Anti-Semitism in British Society,* 68 ff.

Whom Are We Fighting," although emphasizing that the war was being fought "in order to place a small international oligarchy of [non-British] mine-owners and speculators in power," nevertheless remarked that his evidence "gives no grounds for any final judgment on the merits of the war. This international oligarchy may be better for the country and for the world than the present or any other rule; and England may be performing a meritorious world-service in establishing it. But it is right for us to understand quite clearly what we are doing."[27]

Even if Hobson did equivocate, even if he did emphasize the importance of studying the power of rich Jews, not Jews in general, and even if he tried to dis-associate himself from Continental anti-Semitism, there were undercurrents in his writings that touched all Jews in what can only be termed anti-Semitic ways, especially insofar as he implied that Jews had certain inherent traits, ones that were destructive to the societies in which they lived.

These were not unusual opinions among the educated and liberal minded in Great Britain. Another interesting and remarkable example may be found in the writings, less than a decade earlier, of the noted and influential socialist Beatrice Potter Webb (1858–1943). Her intellectual sophistication was not inferior to that of Hobson, and she was probably more prominent than he in the intellectual world of the 1890s in Great Britain. He had read her works with interest and cited them in his own writing.[28]

She was the daughter of a wealthy industrialist and had taken an early inter-est in social problems. In 1891 her book *The Cooperative Movement in Great Britain* appeared. In 1892, at the age of forty-four, she married the Fabian Socialist Sidney Webb, forming one of the most influential partnerships in British life. (Among many other accomplishments, they played an important role in the formation of the British Labour Party and in the founding of the London School of Economics in 1895.) Her case prompts further questioning about what kind of intellectual or psychological preconditions are conducive to anti-Semitic conclusions. She was hardly an unbalanced or resentful petty bourgeois, a member of a threatened, decadent nobility, or in thrall to patho-logical fantasies. Yet many of the comments she made about the Jews of Lon-don's East End paralleled what was being said by the anti-Semites of the day.

Webb had contributed a chapter on the Jews of London's East End in the first volume of Charles Booth's celebrated *Life and Labour of the People of London*, published in 1889. This was a period in Great Britain of intense overcrowding, appalling working conditions, and often outrageous exploitation of Jewish workers, mostly by Jewish employers. In many regards, Webb's account may be described as well informed and sympathetic to the Jews she observed. She wrote a friend that in preparing the chapter, she had met Jews of all stations in

---

[27] Hobson, *War*, part II, 197.

[28] Holmes, *Anti-Semitism*, 20.

life, "and on the whole I like and respect them – I almost think I have a *true* feeling for them."[29] On the other hand, she spoke – it seemed straight out of Disraeli – of the "tenacity" with which Jews preserved the "purity of their race." She marveled at how the Jew from eastern Europe "suffers oppression and bears ridicule with imperturbable good humor," remaining silent "in the face of insult and abuse." Jews were capable of such abnegation, she concluded, as part of a larger Jewish strategy – "to overcome." "Why bluster and fight when you may manipulate and control in secret?"[30]

British politicians as different from the Webbs as Winston Churchill (who detested and mercilessly ridiculed her) nevertheless agreed that powerful Jews preferred to work behind the scenes and did so with notable success. However, in the Webbs' case there was a curious twist, not present in Hobson or Churchill: Beatrice and Sidney Webb had great admiration for those who could work quietly and effectively behind the scenes; they took pride in their own success in doing so, in being able to manipulate others without the general public knowing about it.

The extent of Beatrice Webb's ambiguously negative impressions of Jews did not end there. In explaining why the most recent Jewish arrivals in Great Britain were so different from those Jews who had long resided in the country, she described the oppression Jews faced under the tsars and noted that they were driven into "low channels of parasitic activity"; their "superior mental equipment" allowed them to outsmart and exploit "their Christian fellow-subjects." They could withstand oppression because of "the Old Testament, with its magnificent promises of universal dominion [and] . . . the Talmud, with its minute instructions as to the means of gaining it." "The pious Israelite recognizes no obligations [aside from those in the Talmud] . . . the laws and customs of the Christians are so many regulations to be [ostensibly] obeyed, evaded, and set at naught."[31]

Webb emphasized that it was the superior intellect and flexible morality of the Jews that allowed them to succeed, not only in Russia but also in the East End. Jews were "brain workers," whereas non-Jews were "manual workers." And Jews quickly put themselves into a position in which they gained control of property and money, allowing them to exploit the less cunning non-Jew. Webb described the eastern European Jews as unaffected by considerations that inhibited native small-scale capitalists, such as personal reputation and dignity, class loyalty, or traditions of honesty in a given trade. Low-quality products, ruthless competition, and exploitation of those who worked for them allowed Jews to succeed rapidly. She concluded, "in short, the foreign Jew

---

[29] Cited in Gertrude Himmelfarb, "Victorian Values, Jewish Values," *Commentary*, vol. 87, no. 2, Feb. 1989, 25.

[30] Ibid., 26.

[31] Ibid., 27.

totally ignores all social obligations."[32] In these Jewish qualities, she continued, were to be found the reasons for anti-Semitism: resentment over Jewish success, fear of Jewish power, distaste for Jewish ruthlessness.

Webb's description of the eastern European Jew was transparently like that of the "economic man," the *homo economicus* of the Classical Economists, the wholly "rational" agent who made decisions only in terms of maximizing profit. Her account of the Jewish petty capitalist also resembled the generalized capitalist of Marx, who, in his "On the Jewish Question," had written that for the "Jew" [that is, the capitalist] "money is the jealous god . . . before whom no other god may exist." Webb was determined to denounce this warped vision of humanity in favor of a broader, more generous, more socially responsible one, which would mean abandoning laissez-faire capitalism. Oddly, neither Webb nor Hobson paid much attention to the pronounced secular–socialist convictions of an important part of the immigrants from Russia.

How, then, can Webb's account be termed "sympathetic," even ambiguously? She praised Jews as attentive parents, reliable and diligent workers, charitable to their own kind. They were much less inclined to alcoholic abuse than workers of English or Irish background. Of course, much of what she admired in Jews – their discipline and secretiveness, their desire to dominate by slow and careful work – was seen in a different light by others. But Webb's purpose was not an anti-Semitic one, at least not in the sense understood at the time. She wrote without anger and was not seeking to gain political advantage at their expense or even bemoaning the power Jews might come to have one day. Thus, she could write things that, separated from their context, might seem even more hostile, more persuaded of ineradicable Jewish differences. But the context was all-important; Beatrice Webb has not been included in histories of anti-Semitism, while Treitschke, whose actual descriptions of Jews is similar to hers, has.

Even by the mid-1880s, concern about Jewish immigrants had begun to become a political issue in Great Britain. Many worried that the impoverished Jews from eastern Europe would, in their willingness to work for substandard wages, undermine the native British working class at a time of worldwide depression. Jews were described as presenting more of a danger than other immigrants because of the elaborate charities that had been established by native-born Jews: Eastern European Jews, confident that they could apply for aid or supplementary income from such institutions as the Jewish Board of Guardians, were often willing to work for less than a living wage, pushing out others who had no such charities to rely upon.[33]

This kind of friction between the native population and Jewish immigrants must finally be seen as unremarkable – a lack of friction would have been sur-

---

[32] Ibid., 29.

[33] Holmes, *Anti-Semitism in British Society,* 15.

prising. As one historian has commented, "The complaints of [non-Jewish] East End residents were not simply the crude blather of ignorant xenophobes. Some were unfounded, but others expressed legitimate grievances against the newcomers." The *Jewish Chronicle* stated that the Jews from eastern Europe represented "a state of society utterly different from that which prevails in this country." It was a familiar refrain, and editorial after editorial in the Jewish press expressed concern that these new Jews, with their profoundly religious–nationalistic attachments, would never be able – or even want – to blend into English society.[34]

Many native-born Jews in Great Britain had fought since the early nineteenth century to dispel the charge that Jews were a distinct national group, incapable of whole-hearted assimilation. Now, large numbers of Jews were arriving who seemed strongly to corroborate that hated charge. The appearance of Zionism in the 1890s made the Jewish nationalism of the new immigrants all the more upsetting to the older generation of westernized Jews. Prominent native-born Jews up to this point accepted the notion that they had reduced Gentile hostility because they had sincerely tried to become British. They genuinely believed that Jewish reform could remedy anti-Semitism, but these newcomers were not interested in reforming themselves. The hatred they would awaken would then inevitably extend to those native-born Jews who had secured a comfortable and respected position in British society.[35]

The issue of what should be done about the rising tide of Jewish immigration, debated without much passion since the mid-1880s, came to a head by the turn of the century. Adding to the concern about Jewish laborers working for substandard wages was the resentment over how Jewish immigrants were flooding the housing market, driving out native English. The *East London Advertiser* in 1898 complained that "the greatest industrial area in the capital city of Europe will be entirely populated by Yiddish-speaking aliens." Related complaints were voiced that some Jewish landlords ("unscrupulous and merciless") were buying up property and turning out long-established tenants to make room for the more easily exploited "greeners," the bewildered arrivals from eastern Europe. In addition, "Foreign Jews . . . either do not know how to use the latrine, water and other sanitary accommodations provided, or prefer their own semi-barbarous habits and use the floor of their rooms and passages to deposit their filth."

A. T. Williams, who was associated with the British Brothers' League, spoke to an angry East End crowd in January 1902: "As I walk about in your streets, I see names that have changed; I see good old names of tradesmen who have gone, and in their places are foreign names – the names of those who have

---

[34] Todd Endelman, "Native Jews and Foreign Jews in London, 1870–1914," in David Berger, ed., *The Legacy of Jewish Migration: 1881 and Its Impact* (New York, 1983), 111.

[35] Ibid., 111.

ousted Englishmen into the cold." [Loud cries of "shame" and "wipe them out."] Another speaker urged that a sign be put at the mouth of the Thames: "No rubbish to be dumped here."[36] Ahad Ha-am concluded that "the native [British] population has an unbelievable contempt for them [the eastern European Jews], and their fellow Jews are ashamed of the connection."[37]

From 1903 to 1905, when pogroms swept across Russia and the numbers of Jews seeking to escape Russia again rose dramatically, Balfour's Conservative government sponsored two successive "Aliens Bills." In principle the bills were directed at all immigrants, but it was widely recognized that they reflected a particular concern about eastern European Jews. In testimony before a royal commission established in 1903 to study the issue of immigration, the point was made time and again that national feelings among eastern European Jews were of an essentially different quality from those of western Jews and of other immigrants. It came as no surprise that the commission's report was pessimistic about the prospect of eastern European Jews becoming genuinely English in the foreseeable future.

The first bill, which failed to make it through the House of Commons in 1904, would have given the secretary of state the power to prohibit without appeal the landing of any alien who fit into the following categories: those associated with prostitution, those likely to be a charge on public funds, those convicted of a serious crime in the past five years (frequently the case with those fleeing Russia), and those "of notoriously bad character." The bill would also have given the Local Government Board the power to prevent any aliens from settling in areas already overcrowded owing to alien immigration.

The Liberal Party predictably opposed the bill, basing its opposition on Great Britain's long-established record of granting asylum to victims of persecution. Even many Conservatives found it difficult to support the bill because of its carelessness in composition. It then went to committee, and a new bill was introduced in 1905, which passed. That passage was unmistakably influenced by a series of intervening bye-elections in which Conservatives were elected by appealing to working-class fears of alien competition. But some of the Liberal objections to the older bill were satisfied.[38] Ironically, Balfour's Conservative government fell within four months, and it was left to the ensuing Liberal government to enforce the bill.

Debate on the bill in the course of 1904 and 1905 was vigorous, divisive, and revealing. Prime Minister Balfour was not quite the philo-Semite that many later believed him to be, although his attitudes to Jews defy easy catego-

---

[36] Holmes, *Anti-Semitism in British Society*, 15–17, 91.

[37] Lebzelter, "Right-wing," in Kennedy and Nicholls, 90.

[38] John A. Garrard, *The English and Immigration, 1880–1910* (Oxford, 1971), 42; Bernard Gainer, *The Alien Invasion: The Origins of the Aliens Act of 1905* (London, 1972), 146, 185, 190; Michael Joseph Cohen, *Churchill and the Jews* (Totowa, N.J., 1985), 18–19.

rization. He argued that it would not be to the advantage of "the civilization of this country that there should be an immense body of persons who, however patriotic, able and industrious, . . . [by their own choice] remained a people apart and . . . only married among themselves."[39] He also warned that if the Jewish population continued to rise, Great Britain might well follow "the evil example" of countries on the Continent with large Jewish populations by becoming anti-Semitic.[40]

Equally resisting easy categorization is the record of Winston Churchill. He was at this point in his long and varied career a member of the Liberal Party, and he depended upon the support of the sizable Jewish vote from his district in Manchester. In attacking the first bill, he accused Balfour's government of pandering to anti-Jewish prejudice; he insisted that "English working men . . . do not respond in any marked degree to the anti-semitism which has darkened recent Continental history." He added that they would not "shut out the stranger from the land because he is poor and in trouble."[41] But these sentiments did not mesh well with some that he expressed shortly afterwards in parliament. During a confused set of maneuvers, prior to the bill's being sent to committee, Churchill was accused of deliberate obstructionism. Already notorious for his intemperate outbursts and contradictory positions in parliament, he angrily replied that the Conservative government was backing away from its own bill in order to appease its "wealthy Jewish supporters," who, hidden from public view, had exerted great pressure. That remark provoked a scene, amidst cries of "monstrous, absolutely monstrous!" from a Jewish M.P., Sir Harry Samuel. Shortly thereafter, the *Jewish Chronicle* heatedly dismissed Churchill's charges that Jewish money was at work in the bill's defeat. But he did not back down: In November he again charged that "it is perfectly well known that the opposition of wealthy and influential Jews [in the Conservative Party] . . . has always prevented, and probably always will prevent, their passing such a measure into law."[42]

The passage of the revised 1905 law did not radically limit the number of Jews coming into Great Britain in the next decade. Nor did the bill significantly poison relations between British Jews and the Conservative Party. Other issues, however, did act as more significant irritants. Prominent among them was the changing attitude to tsarist Russia. A formal entente between Russia and Great Britain was arrived at in 1907, and in numerous ways leading British representatives sought to reduce tensions with Russia in the ensuing years. Such efforts ran contrary to the policy of Jewish activists like Lucien Wolf, who carried on a vigorous campaign against Russia's treatment of its Jewish subjects. With

[39] Cohen, *Churchill and the Jews,* 19.

[40] Ibid., 20.

[41] Ibid., 21.

[42] Ibid., 22–3.

increasing frequency, Wolf was publicly accused of putting Jewish over British interests. He and other British Jews were, similarly, suspected of sympathies for Germany, in part because of their many contacts with German-speaking Jews in Jewish defense issues (such contacts were notable, for example, in the Beilis Affair of 1911–1913). Wolf was even accused of accepting money from Germany's foreign office.[43]

Such charges came mostly from the right and extreme right in Britain. Leo Maxse, the editor of the *National Review,* became obsessed with the threat from Germany, and he believed that many Jews in Britain favored appeasement of the Germans. He denounced the Jewish-owned press in Britain as the "Potsdam Press," which, he charged, "knowingly or unknowingly, is wirepulled in the interests of Germany . . . largely by . . . cosmopolitan Jews who repay the excessive hospitality they enjoy here by . . . 'working for the King of Prussia.'" Other articles in the journal spoke of "Hebrew journalists at the beck and call of German diplomats."[44] Maxse's obsessions aside, there were indeed many prominent Jews in Britain of German origin who retained German contacts and who promoted the cause of Anglo–German friendship. More broadly, in the pacifist movement there were, in the words of Elie Halévy, "a disquietingly large proportion of German or German Jewish names," including Lucien Wolf, Sir John Brunner, Sir Alfred Mond, Sir Edgar Speyer, and Sir Ernest Cassel.[45]

Concurrently, many prominent non-Jewish figures, across the political spectrum, spoke up in favor of a less moralistic, more equitable attitude to Russia, implicitly critical of the emotional anti-Russian crusades of Wolf and others. One noted apologist for Russia, also a celebrated historian of the country, Sir Bernard Pares, condemned the tsarist police in the pogroms of 1906 but also noted that given the number of assassinations of police officials by Jews, the actions of the police were somewhat understandable.[46] By the eve of the war, an intensifying debate about attitudes to the Russian Empire could be followed in the pages of the British press. Such prominent figures as H. G. Wells praised Russia. To the outrage of activists like Wolf, the *London Times* introduced panegyric Russian "supplements" and played down the anti-Semitism of the government, or at least so Wolf charged. He blamed the editor-in-chief, Henry Wickam Steed, professing to be especially appalled by Wickam Steed's article, "Russia and her Jews," of June 5, 1914; it contained arguments, Wolf charged, that even overt anti-Semites had long abandoned.[47]

But the bitterness of these exchanges was finally of a different quality from

[43] Max Beloff, "Lucien Wolf and the Anglo–Russian Entente, 1907–1914," *Lucien Wolf Memorial Lecture, 1951* (London, 1951), 27.

[44] Holmes, *Anti-Semitism in British Society,* 71–2.

[45] Elie Halévy, *The Rule of Democracy, 1905–1914* (London, 1961), 409–10; Holmes, *Anti-Semitism in British Society,* 257.

[46] Beloff, *Wolf Lecture,* 27.

[47] Ibid., 34–5.

comparable exchanges on the Continent. Wickham Steed may not have presented matters as men like Wolf wanted to see them, but most Jews in Great Britain continued to recognize that their situation was fundamentally different from that of virtually all Jews on the Continent. Even Maxse denied that his journal was properly considered anti-Semitic, since he did not attack Jews as Jews; he emphasized that he had "the greatest respect" for *some* Jews. The British Brothers' League similarly denied a racial hostility to Jews. Neither denial was particularly credible, but that such denials were made so repeatedly and with such passion says something about how unacceptable anti-Semitism, at least in politics, still was in Great Britain at this time. Arnold White, in testifying before the Royal Commission in 1903, spoke of "the dreaded charge of anti-semitism [which] . . . in these days spells ruin to most people."[48]

After the outbreak of war, in spite of some explosive charges that Wolf and others remained favorable to Germany, British Jews would have reason to reaffirm their "exceptional" situation. Indeed, to offer such ample narrative of the various tensions between Jews and non-Jews in Great Britain in the Edwardian period may give an inappropriately negative impression of the actual state of the relationship. But these tensions help one to understand how Jews in Germany could look around and feel that their condition was no worse, and possibly better, than in most countries of Europe, even in the liberal model, Great Britain.

The United States: Still "Exceptional"?

The numbers of Jews finding refuge in the United States greatly exceeded those going to Great Britain, and the influx remained steady, with minor ups and downs, until 1914. Most of America's leaders continued to be receptive to immigrants, arguing that the country needed a rapidly growing population to fill its vast spaces and to work in its expanding industries. It is a sign of this continuing acceptance that by the turn of the century, a number of Jewish leaders were publicly articulating claims about American exceptionalism that went even further than those made earlier in the century. They claimed that not only was America a land of unusual freedom and toleration but also that American ideals and Jewish ideals had a deep kinship, exceeding that of any modern nation. Supreme Court Justice Louis Brandeis argued that the "fundamentals of American law, namely life, liberty, and the pursuit of happiness are all essentially Judaistic and have been taught by [Jews] for thousands of years."[49]

Rhetorical exaggerations concerning this kinship were undoubtedly made, both by Jewish and non-Jewish leaders, and the openly expressed attitudes of Jews and non-Jews to one another naturally varied according to the audience

---

[48] Holmes, *Anti-Semitism in British Society*, 72, 96, 104.

[49] Quoted in Irving Howe, *World of Our Fathers* (New York, 1976), 208.

and the occasion. A most revealing example of how a particular historical occasion could influence what was publicly expressed about Jews can be seen in American reactions to the Kishinev massacres in Russia in 1903.

The preceding two decades had seen a rising alarm in some quarters about the mass migration of Jews out of Russia, but with the news of the pogrom there was a remarkably unanimous outpouring of moral indignation against Russia's leaders, accompanied by fulsome praise for Jews as desirable citizens. Sermon after sermon, editorial after editorial, political speech after political speech praised the Jews as sober, productive, and "inoffensive" (a telling and frequently used adjective).

One editorial concluded that "the Jews of Russia are persecuted now because they talk in Russia as our forefathers talked here in 1776."[50] Other editorials expressed utter puzzlement as to why any country would want to persecute and drive out those people who "have the money, who are the money lenders and the money savers." One noted that Spain's decline began with its expulsion of the Jews.[51] The Jews of Russia, one might have concluded from these scores of editorials and sermons, were brothers under-the-skin and cultural kin to Americans.

There was important symbolism in President Theodore Roosevelt's meeting, following upon the Kishinev pogrom, with a Jewish delegation. He expressed deep sympathy for the Jewish victims in Russia and delivered a speech full of praise for Jews. The secretary of state at the time, John Hay, also commonly made pro-Jewish public statements. Both of them, like many prominent American politicians, had established intimate contacts with leading American Jews.[52]

On the other hand, many of the ruling elite in America at this time, Hay in particular, were known to make disparaging private remarks about Jews. Roosevelt was a strong believer in an Anglo–Saxon America and attacked the idea of "hyphenated" Americans. Still, it would have been unthinkable for Nicholas II or Plehve to have offered similar praise. Roosevelt emphasized with obvious pride that no major power, including Great Britain, had been so diligent as the United States in protecting the rights of Jews. He made a special point of how one of his most valiant officers in the Spanish–American War was Jewish and of how when he was chief of police in New York, many of his most valued officers were Jews.[53]

These statements of mutual admiration reached a crescendo in the celebra-

[50] Cyrus Adler, ed., *The Voice of America on Kishineff* (Philadelphia, 1904), 296; from an editorial of Hearst's *Chicago American*, May 22, 1903.

[51] Adler, *Voice of America*, 312; from an editorial of the Janesville, Wisc., *Gazette*, May 29, 1903.

[52] Cf. Gary Dean Best, *To Free A People: American Jewish Leaders and the Jewish Problem in Eastern Europe, 1890–1914* (Westport, Conn., 1982), 68 ff., and passim.

[53] The full text of the speech may be found in Henri Dagan, *L'Oppression des juifs dans l'Europe orientale* (Paris, 1903).

tions held on Thanksgiving Day 1905 to commemorate the 250th anniversary of the settlement of Jews in North America. Many non-Jewish dignitaries, including the governor of New York, addressed the various assemblages, and President Roosevelt sent a letter, noting that even in the colonial period Jews had been essential to the "upbuilding of this country." Jacob Schiff, chairing the meeting in New York, hammered home the point that Jews "are justified in the claim that this is our country." Jews throughout the world, he intoned, look "longingly and hopefully toward these shores." Other speakers recalled the tradition of the Pilgrims, who, they claimed, had come to America to assure that there would always be a shelter for the poor and persecuted.[54]

But such celebratory episodes of Jewish–Gentile relations need to be measured against less auspicious developments. By the turn of the century problems of a more profound and lasting sort for Jews began to emerge in the United States. The mostly latent hostility, the potentials of existing negative stereotypes and religious imagery, now began to connect more solidly and abundantly with objective problems, with real conflict between Jews and non-Jews. Not only were hundreds of thousands of Jews from eastern Europe moving into the country, but the earlier Jewish immigrants, the upwardly mobile and often sensationally successful German Jews, started to move as never before into the terrain of older Anglo–American elites. Newly rich Jews also began to compete with newly rich Gentiles for positions in high society, and the Gentile nouveaux riches were apparently even less inclined than the older American elites to mix socially with Jews.

A palpable, now more irritating Jewish presence began to be a more important reality in the United States, particularly on the eastern seaboard in areas of considerable Jewish density, such as in New York. Jews and Gentiles began to compete as never before for positions in boardrooms and resort hotels, factories and neighborhoods. Trade union leaders feared that the new eastern European arrivals would take the jobs of American workers and lower wages. Liberals and progressives, concerned with issues of public morality, feared political corruption, bossism, and a swelling of the ranks of the Democratic Party (three closely related phenomena in their eyes). Urban gangs and organized crime were cause for further alarm. Social conservatives pointed to the Marxists and anarchists among the immigrants, especially among the Jews and the Italians.

In America, as in Europe, those challenged by the Jews were tempted by pre-existing anti-Semitic images and fantasies, but in America there was so far relatively little about the response to Jewish–Gentile conflict that was fundamentally different from ordinary or real conflict, as found in all groups. It is difficult, in other words, to see how inherited hostile imagery about Jews

---

[54] Arthur Hertzberg, *The Jews in America: Four Centuries of an Uneasy Encounter* (New York, 1989), 185–6.

significantly intensified Gentile–Jewish conflict in the United States. Nor does it seem justified to speak of anti-Semitic ideology, linked to mass movements, as appearing at this time.

A few qualifications to those general remarks need to be registered, however. Just as many European intellectuals bemoaned the advent of a materialistic industrial society, so now American intellectuals, usually part of the older Anglo–American elites, began to express a basically aesthetic revulsion from what was happening to their country. Whereas Jefferson had known only a small number of Jews and had extended a friendly hand to them, Henry Adams, a man of roughly comparable intellectual eminence, saw large and rapidly growing numbers of them in the late nineteenth century and disliked what he saw. Among those he could scarcely ignore was the husband of his sister – a Jew had became a member of the Adams clan.

Adams, a member of a venerable American family, felt shunted aside by an emerging industrial America, the rise of new money, and mass society. Moreover, that society deeply offended his aesthetic sensibilities. He seemed at times consumed with hatred for "infernal Jewry," and that hatred was inextricably mixed into his aesthetic concerns about modernization in America. He believed that "we are in the hands of the Jews. They can do what they please with our values. . . ."[55]

However, Adams was widely considered to be a crank on this particular issue; his complaints never attracted the same attention that parallel complaints of anti-Semitic antimodernists in Europe did. His remarks on Jews were mostly private and often ambiguous ("The atmosphere [in 1914] really has become a Jew atmosphere. It is curious and evidently good for some people, but it isolates me. . . . We seem to be more Jewish every day.")[56] He did not try to bring his anti-Semitic ideas into the political arena or to transform them into action; his was not the crusading or populist anti-Semitism of a Drumont or a Krushevan, nor did it have the texture to be seen in the writings of Barrès, Treitschke, or even Pobedonostsev. Similar remarks hold for other American anti-Semitic Brahmins, such as James Russell Lowell, who saw Jewish machinations everywhere and exclaimed that the rise of the Jews to world power was driving him mad. But when he began to rant about the Jews, he was more often mocked than respectfully listened to.[57]

Other prominent Americans of Adams's and Lowell's class, such as William James or William Dean Howells, were forthright critics of anti-Semitism.[58]

---

[55] W. C. Ford, ed., *Letters of Henry Adams, 1892–1918,* vol. 2 (New York, 1938), 338, 620; from Paul R. Mendes-Flohr and Jehuda Reinharz, *The Jew in the Modern World, A Documentary History* (Oxford, 1980), 370.

[56] Ford, *Letters,* 110 ff.

[57] Grose, *Israel,* 42.

[58] Ibid., 42.

Howells warmly supported the work of aspiring Jewish authors, earning deep-felt gratitude from many of them. Even Henry James, inclined to a distant, condescending snobbery in relation to Jews, did not stoop to viciousness. On returning to the United States from England in 1904–05, he was bewildered by the changes he saw. American cities looked "alien" to him, especially New York, which he termed "New Jerusalem." Yet he was willing to grant that the emerging culture in his homeland might become "the most beautiful on the globe and the very music of humanity," even if it was profoundly different from the English culture that he and others of his class saw as originally and most genuinely American.[59]

At the end of the nineteenth century the structures of America's economy, as most of the economies of Europe, were shifting in ways that threatened as never before the welfare of those involved in small-scale production, above all small family farms in the South and West. Imagery that laid blame on the Jews for these developments, with potential connections to long-standing anti-Semitic fantasies, started to appear and to take on an uglier tone, especially following the depression that hit with unprecedented fury in 1893–1894. Unemployment rose to record levels in the cities as did bankruptcies and ruined farms in the countryside.[60]

The destitute eastern European Jews who were arriving in such unprecedented numbers were no less shocking in hygiene, manners, and religious practices to Americans than they were to western Europeans in the same years. Secretary of State Walter Quintin Gresham declared them "degraded and undesirable persons, unfitted in many respects for absorption into our body politic."[61] Undoubtedly, a larger percentage of them than Jewish immigrants in years past wanted as little as possible to do with the general American population. Nonetheless, many eastern European Jews soon merged into American society with unbounded enthusiasm. In the end, the overwhelming majority of them assimilated in one way or another, but not before a long and painful process of adjustment, on their side certainly more extensive and painful than on the side of non-Jewish Americans.

In America as elsewhere openly expressed dismay at the manners and beliefs of eastern European Jews was often more pronounced among the established Jewish population than among the Gentiles. There was as well an economic chasm between these two Jewish communities; they would remain distant from one another until the mid–twentieth century. Jews from eastern Europe often brought with them a particular distaste for rich Jews because of

---

[59] Salo Wittmayer Baron, *Steeled by Adversity: Essays and Addresses on American Life* (Philadelphia, 1971), 321.

[60] Allan Nevins, *Grover Cleveland: A Study in Courage* (New York, 1932), 649; C. Vann Woodward, *Tom Watson: Agrarian Rebel* (Savannah, Ga., 1972), 223.

[61] Grose, *Israel*, 41.

the way the Jewish upper bourgeoisie in Russia had cooperated with the authorities. To that was added an aversion on the part of the garrulous Russian Jews to the stiff manners and aura of superiority of German Jews.

German Jews in America often shared the racist views of the surrounding society, including a belief in the racial inferiority of eastern and southern Europeans. Eastern European Jews were not welcome in German–Jewish country clubs, even when they could afford them. Ironically, Jews from eastern Europe were shunned socially by German Jews in much the same way that German Jews were shunned by Anglo–American elites. Such invidious stratifications occur in all societies, but the treatment by German Jews of Russian Jews undermined the moral basis for their own indignation when they experienced exclusion at the hands of Gentile elites.

On the other hand, charities of great importance and variety were organized by German Jews to benefit the newly arriving Jews and to speed their integration into American society. As one Jewish observer put it, the German–Jewish elite did what it could to americanize the new arrivals, yet "despised them cordially."[62] Even when racism was not predominant, many Americans, Jews among them, feared an array of social evils arriving with the new immigrants.[63]

Still, among the eastern and southern European immigrants, to say nothing of those from Asia, Jews probably had the most favorable press. At the time of Kishinev, the Jews were described in a Wisconsin newspaper as a "thrifty, energetic, far-seeing race," whereas "their Slavic neighbors [are] too sodden with drink and too bestial by nature to take any thought for the morrow."[64] Twelve years earlier, in 1891, when President Benjamin Harrison had expressed his "serious concern" about the estimated one million "Hebrews" that would be coming to the United States in the next few years, he nevertheless remarked that "the Hebrew is never a beggar; he has always kept the law . . . even under severe and oppressive civil restrictions."[65]

Many American editors, even in defending the Jews, implicitly and unwittingly accepted a point made by many Russian nationalists and government officials (or, indeed, left-wingers like Hobson and Beatrice Webb): that the peasants were no match for the Jews and would inevitably come under their power. The *Commercial Gazette* of Pittsburgh, Pennsylvania, for example, in an editorial that strongly condemned the civil inequalities of the Jews in Russia, noted that "in competition with the weak and thriftless Russian peasant, the

[62] Ibid., 43.

[63] Edward J. Bristow, *Prostitution and Prejudice: The Jewish Fight Against White Slavery, 1870–1939* (Oxford, 1983), 146 ff.

[64] Adler, *Voice of America*, 314.

[65] James A. Richardson, *A Compilation of the Messages and Papers of the Presidents, 1789–1908*, vol. 9 (Washington, D.C., 1908), 188; quoted in Salo W. Baron, *The Russian Jew Under Tsars and Soviets* (New York, 1987), 49.

Jew acquires all the trade and prosperity."[66] A few years earlier, Mark Twain, in a light-spirited article that was obviously intended to praise the Jews and counter anti-Semitic charges, had written that it would be wise for Gentiles to prevent the establishment of a Jewish state: "It will not be well to let that race find out its strength. If horses knew theirs, we should not be able to ride any more." He similarly commented that in the Mississippi valley, the Jews were just like the Yankees; both were able to outsmart and exploit the poor whites and blacks. Twain wrote at some length concerning the intellectual superiority of the Jewish race to the non-Jewish. That Jews should be disliked was no surprise to him, for the Jew "is substantially a foreigner wherever he may be, and even the angels dislike a foreigner."[67]

Even more surprising was how much prominent Jewish leaders in America seemed to corroborate what Russian officials maintained about Russia's Jewish population: It was disdainful of others, religiously fanatical, and bent on domination. Isaac Mayer Wise said that it was "impossible . . . to identify ourselves with that half-civilized orthodoxy," and Emma Lazarus, whose poem was placed at the base of the Statue of Liberty, was not so sure about the huddled masses of Jews from Russia. She suggested that another place, not America, should be found for that unappealing "mass of semi-Orientals, Kabbalists, and Hassidim."[68] Walter Lippmann wrote that Jews had "many distressing personal and social habits . . . selected by a bitter history and intensified by a pharisaical theology." He believed that if American universities were to take in more than 15 percent Jews, the result would be a "disaster."[69]

Ethnic riots occurred in America in the troubled years around the turn of the century, but they were directed against Italians and Chinese, not Jews. The characteristic form of American "pogrom," lynchings of blacks, occurred with great regularity and stomach-turning brutality. Nineteen Italians were lynched in Louisiana in the 1890s, apparently because they fraternized with blacks.[70] Many of the editorial writers in 1903, on the occasion of the Kishinev pogrom, were obviously troubled by the similarities between Russia and America in regard to such violence. They were quick to dismiss as inaccurate and unfair any suggestions that the two countries suffered from similar problems, since the authorities in the United States did not encourage these actions (an assertion that certainly might be contested in terms of local authorities).

[66] Adler, *Voice of America*, 445.

[67] Mark Twain, *Concerning the Jews* (Philadelphia, 1985), 18–27. [From the March 1898 issue of *Harper's New Monthly Magazine.*]

[68] Grose, *Israel*, 32.

[69] Ronald Steel, *Walter Lippmann and the American Century* (London, 1980), 194; Johnson, *History of the Jews*, 469. Lippmann, it should be remarked, was referring to the Jewish population in general.

[70] Leonard Dinnerstein, *The Leo Frank Affair* (New York, 1968), 65.

What particularly irked many American editorial writers was that the Russian ambassador to the United States, in responding to the criticism of his country surrounding the Kishinev pogrom, had freely recognized that the lower orders in the Russian Empire, when driven to frenzy by race and religious hatred and when under the influence of alcohol, were capable of violence – "just like Americans." He observed that Americans had recently lynched blacks or attacked unpopular minorities in many parts of the country – and in numbers that significantly exceeded the number of Jews that were killed or injured at Kishinev.

The closest that Jews in America at this time experienced to riots against them was in New York City in July 1902. In this case, the Jews themselves had violently attacked a factory whose mostly Irish workers had insulted a Jewish funeral in progress. Called in to restore order, the police officers, also mostly Irish, themselves went out of control. One Jewish observer lamented shortly afterwards that "it was a thing that even a Russian, with all his dislike of our people, would have been ashamed of."[71] The Jews in this instance were provoked beyond measure, but there was no little symbolism in the episode: The old stereotype of the cowed and defenseless Jew was increasingly being challenged, replaced by an image of an active and self-respecting Jewish citizen who was unafraid to stand up and fight for his dignity. The episode also reflected real issues between two ethnic groups, the Irish, established in the city, and the Jews, who were rapidly increasing in numbers and threatening to change the character of the Lower East Side in ways that were unacceptable to the Irish. In broad outlines it paralleled the conflict in cities such as Vienna, Paris, Berlin, Kiev, and Kishinev. A key difference, again, was the relatively unimportant linkage of ideological fantasy in the United States.

While the mesh or fit of inherited Jewish manners and traditions with native American manners and traditions was extensive, it was by no means perfect. In a few regards there were deep-rooted differences, ones that began to become more visible by the late nineteenth century. Respect for heavy manual labor, in particular for working the land with one's own hands, was a central American virtue. Such respect was not a prominent part of the European Jewish tradition, both for what might be termed cultural–religious reasons[72] and for reasons having to do with history: that is, the Jews' own preference since ancient times for trade and mobile occupations, linked to the restrictions imposed on Jews in many areas concerning ownership of land. Americans who worked the land, like the peasantry of Europe, were inclined to think of their

[71] Leonard Dinnerstein, "The Funeral of Rabbi Jacob Joseph," in Gerber, ed., *Anti-Semitism in American History*, 287; Howe, *World of Our Fathers*, 124.

[72] "For a man 'who comes from yikhus' [who is of distinguished lineage] to engage in manual labor, even under the stress of economic necessity, is a calamity, for manual labor has come to symbolize the antithesis of the social ideal – a life devoted entirely to study." Mark Zborowski and Elizabeth Herzog, *Life is With People: The Culture of the Shtetl* (New York, 1969), 78.

labor as both real and honest. The work of men who sold the goods produced by others was suspect, and even more suspect were the moneylenders, bankers, and financiers.

Such perceptions and reasoning were central to European democratic radicalism and to socialism. In the United States distrust of those who manipulated money rather than doing "honest" work was one of the points of departure for the Populist movement, which gained an ardent following in the depression years of the 1890s around the themes of protecting the small farmer against the incursions of "Money Power" and the "international Gold Ring." American Populists were similar to the Christian social movements in Europe at the turn of the century; important parallels with the republicanism of the Paris shopkeepers can also be seen.[73] A debate raged for some time among American historians about how much the Populists, like the parallel movements in Europe, were anti-Semitic.

Without delving into the intricacies of the debate,[74] it is clear that a few Populist leaders attacked Jews and that the mass of increasingly impoverished small southern and western farmers during the 1890s were aroused by Populist denunciations of financiers, such as the Rothschilds, as well as other powers in the international and American economy, such as the (non-Jewish) Rockefellers and Morgans. In this area, potential for anti-Jewish feeling, and for a linkage of real conflict and ideological fantasy about Jews, had always existed; that potential now began to be realized, especially among the dirt farmers who were desperately clinging to their land but who found the market price for their produce steadily declining. For them modern times were undoubtedly threatening. As in Europe, the visibility of Jews as symbols of market forces was increasing, and for uneducated and despairing farmers the Jewish financier was an obvious, tempting target. Such farmers could easily share Henry Adams's perception: Their country was being taken over by un-American, parasitic Jews.

It is by no means clear, however, that large numbers of small farmers in America actually saw things in such terms or that many of them turned to anti-Semitic ideologists who were capable of supplying focus and coherence to their resentments. About as close as any major American writer or thinker in the late nineteenth century came to formulating a modern anti-Semitic ideology, of being an American equivalent to Marr, Drumont, or Krushevan, was Ignatius Donnelly (1831–1901), a prominent figure in the Populist movement and author of the ringing preamble of the party platform in 1892.

In the middle years of the century Donnelly had served in Minnesota as lieutenant governor, as congressman, and as member of the state legislature.

---

[73] Cf. Philip G. Nord, *Paris Shopkeepers and the Politics of Resentment* (Princeton, N.J., 1986), 488.

[74] See James Turner, "Understanding the Populists," *Journal of American History,* vol. 67, no. 2, Sept. 1978, 354–73, for balanced discussion of the problem, with ample bibliographical references.

He edited the weekly *Anti-Monopolist* in the late 1870s and the Populist *Representative* in the 1880s. His political and literary interests ranged widely, including works on Bacon and Shakespeare, but his best-known work was the novel *Caesar's Column* (1891), in which he set forth his views on the destructive role of the Jews in the modern world.

Donnelly has sometimes been dismissed as an eccentric, "the prince of cranks." Yet there was genuine content to his thought, and his attitude to Jews was more complex and even ambiguously sympathetic than brief resumes of his work might suggest. Donnelly portrayed the Jews in social Darwinistic terms: They were tough, having survived centuries of persecution; they had now become "as merciless to the Christian as the Christian had been to them."[75] However, Donnelly was not a racist, since he saw Jewish character as formed by history. He did not develop that historical perspective with the acuity of a Barrès, but it was nevertheless different from the simple racist determinism of many European anti-Semites. Donnelly was a man of some learning, and, like Barrès or Schönerer, his sympathy for the downtrodden was genuine. He worked long and hard to help the common people.[76]

In most regards the images of Jews developed in Donnelly's book were similar to those already frequently described: contempt for non-Jews, uncontrollable greed, lust for power, secretiveness, and indifference to national allegiance. But one of the images stands out in Donnelly's writings: the Jew as lecherous, lusting after Gentile women. Donnelly's Jewish villain, Prince Cabano, hungers for the Anglo–Saxon woman, Estella Washington.

It is difficult to know how widespread or widely believed such images were around the turn of the century in America, but they popped up in sometimes surprising quarters, not simply in the fictionalized imaginings of Donnelly. E. A. Ross, a prominent Progressive and highly respected sociologist, wrote in 1914 that "pleasure-loving Jewish businessmen . . . pursue Gentile girls," which "excites bitter comment."[77] In Great Britain there were similar rumblings about "Yiddish gorillas" who preyed upon Gentile women. One writer complained that "no Jew is more of a hero to his fellow tribesmen than one who can boast of having accomplished the ruin of some friendless, unprotected Christian girl." He concluded that Jews were "probably the most lecherous breed in existence."[78]

This negative stereotype, associated as it was with sexuality in an epoch of sexual repression, was almost by definition one that could not be openly discussed. Even today determining its appeal as a fantasy is difficult. Some

---

[75] Quoted in Baron, *Steeled,* 322.

[76] Cf. the perceptive and balanced discussion in Frederic Cople Jaher, *Doubters and Dissenters* (New York, 1964), 130–40; reproduced in Dinnerstein, *Anti-Semitism,* 78–86.

[77] E. A. Ross, "The Hebrew of Eastern Europe in America," *The Century Magazine,* vol. 88, Sept. 1914, 787; cf. Dinnerstein, *Frank,* 198.

[78] Lebzelter, "Right-Wing," in Kennedy and Nicholls, 93.

observers have argued that fear of Jewish sexuality explains the special vehemence and irrationality of Hitler's anti-Semitism,[79] and related fears unquestionably played an important role in Nazi propaganda against Jews.[80] Even
among Jewish observers the sexuality of Jewish males and their alleged special
attraction to non-Jewish females have been perennial topics. The longed-for
goldene shikse (golden Gentile girl) is a central theme in best-selling fiction by
American Jews[81] and appears even in such unexpected places as the life of
Chaim Weizmann, the Zionist leader and first president of Israel.[82] It played a
key role in what many consider the most important outburst of anti-Semitism
in American history before World War I.

The Leo Frank Affair

In the spring of 1913 Leo Frank, the manager and part owner of a pen-
cil factory in Atlanta, Georgia, was accused of murdering a fourteen-year-old
employee, Mary Phagan. The case developed dizzying complexities, but what
caused special excitement in the Frank case were intimations of sexual perversity on his part. (He had allegedly killed Mary when she refused to give into
demands for "perverse" sex.) Another peculiarity of the case was that a black
employee of Frank's, Jim Conley – most likely the actual murderer – testified
against Frank, and Conley's testimony was accepted against that of Frank,
which represented an almost unprecedented development in the South,
where the word of a white was almost always accepted over that of a black.

Many in the North concluded that Frank's arrest and conviction were the
result of anti-Semitic prejudice. On the other hand, many in Georgia believed
that Frank, with powerful evidence against him (Conley's testimony was only
one element of it), was using his wealth and his connections to escape the
hangman, once he had been convicted. The case became much envenomed
with the entry of Tom Watson, a popular politician in Georgia, who may be
described as the closest approximation in American history before World War
I to someone who used anti-Semitism as a political device. He charged that "a
gigantic conspiracy of Big Money" was at work to free a rich "Sodomite." He
described Frank as belonging to "the Jewish aristocracy," adding that "it was
determined by the rich Jews that no aristocrat of their race should die for the
death of a working-class Gentile."[83]

Frank's innocence was less clear at the time of the trial than many accounts

[79] Johnson, *History*, 475.

[80] Cf. Dennis E. Showalter, *Little Man, What Now? Der Stürmer in the Weimar Republic* (Hamden, Conn., 1982).

[81] Cf. Philip Roth, *Portnoy's Complaint* (New York, 1969); Mordecai Richler, *Joshua, Then and Now* (New York, 1980).

[82] Jehuda Reinharz, *Chaim Weizmann: The Making of a Zionist Leader* (Oxford, 1985), 367–72.

[83] C. Vann Woodward, *Tom Watson: Agrarian Rebel* (Savannah, Ga., 1972), 382.

have suggested. Similarly, anti-Semitism seems to have been of marginal importance in both his arrest and conviction. Many who were not anti-Semites firmly believed in Frank's guilt. More important in explaining the widespread hostility to Frank in Georgia were his northern origins, his wealth, and his position as "capitalist exploiter" in a factory with mostly impoverished southern woman as employees. His Jewishness mixed into each of these in ways that are impossible to untangle. But it seems clear that, as was the case with Dreyfus, Frank's stiff and distant personality had a great deal to do with the way his accusers jumped to conclusions. Similarly, his odd physical appearance, his strange reticences, and the contradictions of his initial remarks to the police – to say nothing of the damning and graphic testimony of Conley and others – made it easier for people to continue to believe him guilty. His trial was not quite the travesty of justice that many have believed it to be, but on the other hand, there were enough holes in the prosecution's case that Frank's guilt was not demonstrated beyond a reasonable doubt.

But the notion of innocence beyond a reasonable doubt was not one that much spoke to a large proportion of Georgia's population from 1913 to 1915, and it did not speak loudly enough to his jurors. Many were convinced that a sexual pervert, a "monster," had been caught by the police and deserved to be put to death. When Frank's lawyers launched a series of appeals, hoping to commute his sentence and ultimately to prove his innocence, "Mary's people," the common people in Georgia, saw only scheming, high-priced lawyers and Jewish money used to bribe politicians and influence newspapers.

At the last hour, after repeated and fruitless appeals to higher courts, the governor of the state, John M. Slaton, commuted Frank's death sentence, provoking outrage and violent demonstrations. Slaton received over a thousand death threats; it was widely believed that he had either given in to Jewish pressure or had been otherwise corrupted by Jewish money. The truth was that he had made a careful study of the trial and perceived many flaws in the prosecution's case that even Frank's lawyers – who were among the best legal minds in the South – had somehow missed.

Outside of Georgia, as the case gained national visibility, widespread sympathy for Frank was expressed. He received at final count close to a hundred thousand letters of sympathy in jail, and prominent figures throughout the country, including governors of other states, U.S. senators, clergymen, university presidents, and labor leaders, spoke up in his defense. Thousands of petitions in his favor, containing over a million signatures, flowed in.

But this sympathy was not enough to save Frank's life. In July 1915 at the prison farm where he was incarcerated, a convicted murderer cut Frank's throat with a kitchen knife. Only the speedy intervention of a surgeon, himself serving a life sentence for the murder of his wife, saved Frank's life.[84] Scarcely

---

[84] Golden, *A Little Girl*, 286–7.

had Frank's wounds healed when he was spirited from the prison, in a daring commando-like operation, by a group calling itself "the Knights of Mary Phagan." They took Frank to the site of Mary's grave and hung him there until he was dead. Tom Watson expressed satisfaction: "In putting the Sodomite murderer to death" the Knights had "done what the Sheriff should have done. . . . Georgia is not for sale to rich criminals."[85]

Yet, however horrifying the lynching of Leo Frank, however much it and the events surrounding it stood in flagrant violation of the ideals of American democracy, it is still a fair question whether the Frank Affair represented a victory, in a deeper sense, for the forces of anti-Semitism in the United States, or even in the South. It may be argued that the Frank Affair contributed to the articulation and dissemination of an American variety of anti-Semitic ideology, particularly as expressed by Tom Watson, but to speak of a gathering storm of anti-Semitism in the United States makes little sense. And it should not be overlooked that those agitating for Frank's death, Watson included, made no suggestion that Jews in general should be attacked or that Jews should be put under some sort of special legal control.

To be sure, there is much evidence of rising tension between Jews and Gentiles in the United States, with some sharp ups and downs, from the 1890s until the early 1950s. Watson would be followed by men like Henry Ford and Father Charles Coughlin, who attracted a following throughout the United States and who made more solid connections with mainline anti-Semitic traditions. Yet even their anti-Semitism paled in comparison with that found in Europe. It is indicative of American reality that Ford, a man whom Hitler and the Nazis lionized, finally backed away from his anti-Semitism, even openly apologized for it.[86] There is little reason to believe that he gained in popularity because of his anti-Semitism and much evidence that he distanced himself from it in part because of the popular disfavor it incurred.

In America, as in Europe, one might more accurately speak of a rising tide *against* anti-Semitism, one that paralleled, opposed, and stifled efforts of the anti-Semites to organize and to spread their ideas. Mobilization and institutionalization of forces opposed to anti-Semitism in the prewar world, especially by Jews, were in certain regards even more impressive in the United States than in Europe.[87] The Frank Affair did not play a major role in initially galvanizing these forces, since they had begun to organize a number of years before his arrest. Moreover, in the Frank Affair there was no clear-cut victory, as there was in France and Russia. The forces that came together to oppose Frank's conviction did not go on to win power in congress, as the Dreyfusards did in

[85] Ibid., 299.

[86] Cf. Albert Lee, *Henry Ford and the Jews* (New York, 1980); Michael N. Dobkowski, *The Tarnished Dream: The Basis of American Anti-Semitism* (Westport, Conn., 1979).

[87] Cf. Naomi W. Cohen, *Not Free to Desist: The American Jewish Committee, 1906–1966* (Philadelphia, 1972).

the French Chamber of Deputies, nor was there violent revolution against those who supported anti-Semitism, as in Russia.

Still, the Frank Affair touched on basic issues of American identity in a most painful way and almost demanded expressions of regret as expiation. This was, after all, the country whose president, just a decade before, had boasted that no other country in the world had done so much to protect the rights of Jews. It was, to say the least, awkward that in the same year that Mendel Beilis was freed by a jury of peasants – and was cheered as national hero by millions of ordinary Russians – a jury of middle-class Americans, in an atmosphere of mob violence, found Leo Frank guilty, and subsequently he was lynched by an organization of "respectable" citizens.

Americans from many backgrounds had abundantly expressed their indignation at the pogrom at Kishinev. They had expressed outrage over Beilis's arrest, and there had been an enormous outpouring of sympathy for Dreyfus in America. The sympathy expressed for Frank was unquestionably more broad based in the United States than the hatred for him personally; those who spoke out against anti-Semitism at this time outnumbered by far those who sought to exploit it. Those who called for a new trial were more prominent and incomparably more numerous than those agitating for his execution. If we can accept the paradoxical conclusion that the Kishinev pogrom marked a rising Jewish combativeness, it is no less paradoxically accurate to conclude that the reaction to the Frank Affair underlined the existence of a more friendly environment for Jews, in the sense that their enemies were weaker than in other countries, their friends more willing to identify openly with the struggle for toleration and decency in regard to their fellow Jewish citizens.

By the time of the Frank Affair American Jews who were long-time residents had come to appreciate more than ever before the dilemmas and ambiguities of life among the Gentiles, but they hardly concluded that the future was impossibly bleak. As influential Jews saw it, anti-Semitism had raised its ugly head in the Frank Affair, but it had been widely discredited. Jews were obliged to recognize once again what had always been obvious, that they had numerous and powerful enemies. But they also had numerous and powerful friends. Or, if that overstates the matter, Jews could take some comfort in the fact that their enemies faced even more powerful enemies – who, to be sure, were not always whole-hearted friends of the Jews.

Such twisted formulations, even more appropriate for the situation in France and Russia, are often necessary to suggest the ambiguous texture of Gentile–Jewish relationships, but the "Zionist lessons" of the Frank Affair were even less persuasive to the overwhelming majority of American Jews than were those lessons in the Dreyfus Affair for French Jews. In Russia, of course, the spread of Zionism much predated the Beilis Affair, but even there, where by the eve of World War I it had won over many more followers than in the West, it attracted only a minority of the total Jewish population. French Jews felt so confident after the victory of the Dreyfusards that a major French–Jewish journal commented, "in giving birth to the Dreyfus Affair, anti-Semitism had died."[88] Lucien Wolfe, it will be recalled, had reached similar conclusions in his article for the *Encyclopedia Britannica.* Much the same can be said for the attitudes of Jews in the rest of western and most of central Europe, where, as a leading scholar has stated, "relative security and well-being characterized the middle classes, and [where] the differences which had rent apart nations like France seemed to have ended in compromise."[89] Some Jewish observers, in utter contrast to Herzl, went as far as to argue that the Dreyfus Affair had ultimately had a positive effect, in that anti-Semitism had been fatally exposed: It was not directed really or exclusively at Jews but rather at tolerance, at humane, modern values more generally,[90] and thus all people of good will had an interest in combating it.

Even in Atlanta, where the Jewish community was deeply shaken by the Frank Affair and where Jewish leaders long opposed efforts to rehabilitate Frank because of the hostility such efforts might revive, Jews continued to move into the city in numbers no less impressive than before the Frank Affair. The Jewish population of Atlanta more than doubled by the end of World War II and quadrupled by 1968.[91] In the long run, the economic opportunities in the city outweighed any reputation it had for being anti-Semitic. Similarly, a leading historian of French Jewry has remarked on how little the Dreyfus Affair seemed to affect native French Jews in the long run. Rather than abandoning their belief in assimilation, they "remained practically unchanged, and the most important anti-Semitic crisis of nineteenth-century France appeared as only a ripple in the smooth course of Jewish life in that country."[92] We have seen as well how Jews continued to move into Vienna in great numbers while Lueger was mayor.

The world before 1914 was still a basically hopeful one, whatever the brooding of intellectual and artistic elites. But that world was soon to change drastically. Even as Leo Frank was being lynched, hundreds of thousands of young men were falling in senseless slaughter across the Atlantic. The cataclysmic and brutal decade between 1914 and 1924 would transform, as nothing so far had, the relations of Jews and Gentiles, in both Europe and America. Those events would also transform the way that subsequent generations viewed the decades immediately preceding the Great War.

---

[88] "La nouvelle revision," *Univers Israelite,* June 22, 1906. Quoted in Paula E. Hyman, "The French Jewish Community from Emancipation to the Dreyfus Affair," in Norman L. Kleeblatt, ed., *The Dreyfus Affair: Art, Truth, Justice* (Berkeley, Calif., 1987), 22.

[89] George L. Mosse, *Toward the Final Solution: A History of European Racism* (New York, 1980), 168.

[90] Marrus, *Assimilation,* 280.

[91] Hertzberg, *Atlanta,* 217.

[92] Marrus, *Assimilation,* 282.

PART FOUR

A DECADE OF WAR
AND REVOLUTION,
1914–1924

THE DECADE OF WAR and revolution between 1914 and 1924 stands out as one of the major watersheds in European history. From the smoking ruins of those years emerged a transformed and much diminished Europe. It was a twentieth-century world that was in far-ranging ways different from the world of the nineteenth century. The political map of Europe was fundamentally altered; most of the prewar empires collapsed, their territories taken over by revolutionary and nationalist successor states. In sheer destructiveness, in lives lost, material goods destroyed, and social relations poisoned, these years had few if any parallels in European history. One would have to go to the Thirty Years' War of the seventeenth century or to the Black Death of the late Middle Ages to find something equally vast and horrifying in death and destruction. If the proposition is accepted that "bad times" in the Gentile world find expression in even worse times for the Jews living in that world – a proposition central to explaining the appearance of modern anti-Semitism in the Great Depression of 1873–1891 – then the decade of war and revolution could be expected to be catastrophic for the Jews.

And it was. Indeed, the Holocaust itself may be said to have evolved directly if not inexorably out of the catastrophes of 1914–1924; the mass murder of Jews during World War II is at any rate scarcely comprehensible without giving that decade careful study. If the various "rising tide" arguments that find the origins and inexorable momentum of the Holocaust in late nineteenth century are not persuasive, a more compelling argument along those lines may be traced to 1914–1924. Even without the culminating horror of 1938–1944, developments in the decade following 1914 were the most adverse for Jews of any in European history up to that date. Many of the dark portents of the prewar years, the tribalism and the ideologies of irrationalism, moved from the margins to nearer the center stage of European civilization. The conscience and sensibilities of that civilization were profoundly brutalized by a decade of war, revolution, and civil war. The ideals of both Christianity and the Enlight-

387

enment were shaken; confidence in the future, in progress, in human solidarity dwindled.

The entry of "mass man" as an active agent in European society, however nebulous and problematic the concept, found often nightmarish expressions between 1914 and 1924, as did the linkage of mass society to mass production: The machine gun, in its ability to mow down row upon row of advancing soldiers – the mass production of death – may be seen as an appropriate symbol of new realities. Concentration camps made an appearance at this time as well (though they had precedents in the Boer War). The mobilization of the masses through such devices as the yellow and government-controlled press, new antiliberal parties, and the armies that recruited and indoctrinated nearly unparalleled numbers, went much beyond what had been achieved in the generation before the war. The careers of Hitler, Stalin, and Mussolini were, in the words of Alan Bullock, "possible only in the new world created by the breakdown of the old order."[1]

Much of the ambiguous hopefulness about the future of the relations between Gentile and Jew in the Belle Epoque now vanished, and Jews became visible in ways that made them much more vulnerable to the furies of frustrated, resentful, and traumatized elements of the population. If Jews had seemed to certain observers to benefit from the misfortunes of non-Jews in the late nineteenth century, they now seemed to derive even greater benefit from even greater misfortunes. They were perceived as war profiteers and ruthless revolutionaries, unpatriotic slackers and treacherous back-stabbers. In the chaos that emerged from war and civil war in eastern Europe, pogroms erupted of a dimension that far transcended what had happened before the war. George Mosse has commented, "The First World War and its aftermath revitalized racism in all its forms, whether National Socialist, conservative, or merely nationalist, whether as the science or the mystery of race. . . . By 1914 . . . it looked as if [racism] had run its stormy course. . . . War and revolution propelled racism into a more durable and awesome practice."[2]

Jews were prominent in the revolutionary parties that took over, permanently in Russia, temporarily in other areas of central and eastern Europe, and that were perceived as threats in most of the rest of Europe. Jews were also highly visible in the new German republic, not only on the left but also in center and right-center parties, nourishing visions of a Jewish takeover there, too. "Judeo–bolshevism," a new word applied to a perceived new reality – Jews in power in a major nation – massively reinforced prewar visions of Jews as alien destroyers. The kinds of anxieties and fears that had affected primarily the lower-middle class prior to the war spread to ever-widening elements of the population, since ever-greater numbers felt threatened by Jews and what they

---

[1] Alan Bullock, *Hitler and Stalin: Parallel Lives* (New York, 1992), 3.

[2] George Mosse, *Toward the Final Solution: A History of European Racism* (New York, 1978), 168.

were believed to represent, by a new dimension of the rise of the Jews, and by Jews who were in truth in positions of unprecedented political power and authority, both in Russia and in the West. Revealingly, Leo Maxse, the editor of the *National Review,* who had expressed suspicions of Jews but still defended Dreyfus, now came to believe wholeheartedly in what he termed "the evil machinations of world Jewry." He concluded that "the international Jew rules the roost."[3]

[3] Gisela Lebzelter, "Anti-Semitism, a Focal Point for the British Radical Right," in Paul Kennedy and Anthony Nicholls, eds., *Nationalist and Racialist Movements in Britain and Germany before 1914* (Oxford, 1981).

=12=

World War I

Ich kenne keine Parteien mehr. Ich kenne nur noch
Deutsche. [I no longer recognize any parties. I recognize only Germans.] (Wilhelm II)

Wir lieben unser Heimat, wenngleich man uns nicht
liebt. [We love our homeland, even if we are not
loved.] (Sept 24, 1916. From the diary of Julius
Marx)[1]

I long for the holy, redeeming war. (Heinrich Class)[2]

The guns of August, and September, and October,
the guns of fifty-two blood-drenched months,
destroyed morale, destroyed a generation, destroyed
Europe. Everything afterward seems provisional. . . .
(Hugh Kenner, *The Pound Era* [1971])

The Mood of August 1914

World War I began with astonishing enthusiasm and confidence in victory on all sides. The opening stages were also characterized by a mystical
spirit of common cause and self-sacrifice, one that many observers remembered with yearning in the bitter years of disillusionment that followed. It is
tempting to speculate that if the war had been the brief and glorious campaign that nearly all expected it to be, Jews and non-Jews in many countries
might have been able to forge a more lasting sense of unity and fraternity.
Even if there had been, necessarily, dramatic losers as well as dramatic winners
in a decisive contest of six to eight weeks – as in 1866 and 1870 – it is hard to

---

[1] Julius Marx, *Kriegs-Tagebuch eines Juden* (Zurich, 1939), 129; from Eva G. Reichmann, "Der
Bewusstseinwandel der deutschen Juden," in Werner E. Mosse, ed., *Deutsches Judentum in Krieg
und Revolution, 1916–23* (Tübingen, 1971), 514.

[2] Quoted in Norman Stone, *Europe Transformed: 1878–1919* (Cambridge, Mass., 1984), 152.

believe that it would have produced anywhere near the rancor among the losers that followed the more than four years of senseless destruction. Indeed, among the victorious powers Jewish–Gentile relations were in some regards improved by the long struggle in common. At least relations between Jew and non-Jew in those countries did not suffer anything like the catastrophic worsening that prevailed in the defeated powers.

The enthusiasm for war in August 1914 was by no means confined to the nationalist right or to those nations that were known to be militaristic. Germany and France, Great Britain and Russia, right and left, rich and poor, and Jews as well as non-Jews were powerfully drawn into it. The Zionist leader Chaim Weizmann, living in England, bitterly commented that "in 1914 the Jewish intellectuals in Germany were the most arrogant and bellicose of all Prussians."[3] For many Germans the war seemed to offer an uncanny sense of release, of an escape from the ordinary, from the much lamented sense of sterility and *Verdrossenheit* (peevishness) of the immediate prewar years. Shining vistas of heroism and self-sacrifice now opened up. There were many who, like the English poet Rupert Brook, could be described as "a golden-haired Apollo, magnificently unprepared for the long littleness of life."[4] Seeking adventurous release in the battlefield, they and others found death or mutilation in staggering numbers.

Enthusiasm in Germany was palpably linked to the belief that a German victory would mark the definitive triumph of the German spirit, as the French had triumphed in the eighteenth and early nineteenth centuries. For those who accepted Treitschke's vision of Germany's transcendent mission, who saw meaning in history through the triumph of German ideals, this was the moment of truth. The rancorous exchanges since the 1880s about whether the attachment to German ideals of German Jews was pure enough found a riveting focus: Would German Jews risk death for their country?

Many young German Jews welcomed the chance to prove their often questioned patriotism. Even those who had been active in Jewish self-defense activities before 1914, those who had ample reason to feel bitter about the inequities of the German state and of German society, now celebrated, in nearly messianic terms, what they believed was an imminent German victory. Germany's triumph was to be a great turning point in history, one that would, in prevailing over tsarist Russia, institute a reign of justice and equality.[5]

Relations between liberal–assimilationist Jews and Zionists in Germany had become especially envenomed by June 1914, but the war seemed to change

---

[3] Mosse, *Judentum*, 30, quoting the memoirs of Viscount d'Albernon, *An Ambassador of Peace*, vol. 1 (London, 1929), 236.

[4] Robert Wohl, *The Generation of 1914* (Cambridge, Mass., 1979), 87. See also Dan S. White, *Lost Comrades: Socialists and the Front Generation, 1918–1945*, Chap. 2 (Cambridge, Mass., 1992).

[5] Werner Jochman, "Die Ausbreitung des Antisemitismus," in Mosse, *Judentum*, 410.

everything, almost as if a magic wand had been waved; there was little difference in the attitudes of liberals and Zionists to war in August 1914. Ernst Simon wrote that Jews in Germany accepted the war as an "unbelievable experience, an intoxicating happiness which enabled them to forget their complicated egos and to be able to participate in the fate of the fatherland with millions of others." The Zionist Martin Buber, who later gained fame as a philosopher, ardently defended the invasion of Belgium and the violation of its neutrality. Thereafter he stubbornly defended Germany's conduct of the war. Even Kurt Blumenfeld, among the most radical of the young Zionists in Germany before the war, declared that "every man saw the war as his personal mission because the future of humanity depended upon Germany's victory." Some Zionists who had already emigrated to Palestine made the arduous voyage back in order to join battle on Germany's side.[6]

Do these astonishing examples of famous individuals provide an accurate impression of the whole of German Jewry? There was undoubtedly some ostentatious overcompensation in individual cases, the overachieving Jacob in yet a new form, but is it reasonable to expect that German Jews, whose cultural traditions did not emphasize military virtue, were really as unanimously, blindly, and lastingly in favor of war as the rest of the nation? Even before the furor over Treitschke's articles, many Jews took pride in distancing themselves from the state worship and militarism of non-Jewish Germans.

In a speech to the Reichstag in the early days of the war, the deputy Ludwig Haas openly acknowledged that German Jews might have felt less "joy in war" and may have been less characterized by a "readiness to fight" than non-Jews, but the centuries-long oppression of Jews by Gentiles was the explanation – he did not, in other words, present the matter in terms of superior Jewish morality. However, as the war continued, a number of prominent Jews stated with pride that German words like *Volk* and *Staat* did not stir in them the deep feelings that they did in non-Jewish Germans. Other Jewish leaders, especially as the war began to bog down and the casualties mount, not only recognized but also proudly emphasized that modern Jews were not a warlike people and that Jews instinctively favored international understanding and a negotiated peace, not victory at all costs.[7]

There is at any rate little debate among historians about the remarkably pervasive intoxication with war in August 1914. Even the socialists, whose resolutions, through the Socialist International, had threatened a general strike in the event of "imperialist" war, were not immune to the paroxysm of patriotic fervor that swept across Europe. The leaders of the German Social Democratic Party, whom Wilhelm II had earlier maligned as the "fatherland-less fellows,"

[6] Jehuda Reinharz, *Fatherland or Promised Land: The Dilemma of the German Jew, 1893–1914* (Ann Arbor, Mich., 1975), 222–3 ff.

[7] Eva G. Reichmann, "Der Bewusstseinswandel der deutschen Juden," in Mosse, *Judentum*, 517 ff.

quickly fell into line. The Social Democratic parliamentary delegation voted unanimously for war credits, and the Social Democratic Party enthusiastically joined into the official *Burgfrieden* (civil peace), the end of party strife in Germany. One Social Democratic leader, in later defending his violation of previously firm commitments against war, remarked that he and his party comrades had voted for war credits in order to avoid being beaten to death by their followers on the steps of the Reichstag.[8] Opponents of the war in other countries later gave similar accounts: A French anarchosyndicalist reported, "On August 2, disgusted and morally reduced to dust, I left in a cattle-car jammed with men who were bellowing 'to Berlin! to Berlin!'"[9]

The divisive anti-Semitic parties were expected to blend into the national community; the Burgfrieden meant that the petty strife of the prewar scene was no longer to be tolerated by the state. The German authorities moved against the anti-Semitic parties and censored their newspapers,[10] although such action was not at first necessary – many prewar anti-Semites suddenly embraced Jews as brothers-in-arms. H. S. Chamberlain remarked that German Jews were no longer visible "as 'Jews,' for they are doing their duty as Germans."[11] A number of patriotic Jews were given prominent attention by the government, most notably Ernst Lissauer, who composed the wildly popular refrains of the *Hassgesang Gegen England* (Hate-Song against England). The Kaiser decorated him with the Order of the Red Eagle.[12]

Jews now began to breach the last bastion of Junker privilege, the Prussian officer corps.[13] In retrospect, however, that apparent success may have generated an ominous resentment in that corps, especially among those younger officers who were uncomfortable with this incursion of "alien elements." The rise of the Jews, under the overwhelming pressures of war, now began to touch more directly a class that had so far been relatively little alarmed by it. By the end of the war, in the bitterness of defeat, many more young officers would join the ranks of the radical anti-Semites than had been the case in the 1880s.

In France, too, Jews and non-Jews rallied with unparalleled unanimity to the defense of *la patrie en danger*, the fatherland in danger. Here too the bitter political squabbling of the immediate prewar years suddenly ceased. The socialist leader Jean Jaurès, active during the summer of 1914 in protests against the threat of war, was assassinated by a nationalist fanatic just before the declarations of war were issued. But had Jaurès lived it is doubtful that

---

[8] Joseph A. Berlau, *The German Social Democratic Party, 1914–1921* (New York, 1949), 73.

[9] Edouard Dolléans, *Histoire du mouvement ouvrier, 1871–1920* (Paris, 1953), 221.

[10] Geoffrey Field, *Evangelist of Race: The Germanic Vision of Houston Stewart Chamberlain* (New York, 1981), 379.

[11] Jochman, "Ausbreitung," in Mosse, *Judentum*, 411.

[12] Saul Friedländer, "Die Politische Veränderung der Kriegszeit und ihre Auswirkungen auf die Judenfrage," in Mosse, *Judentum*, 30.

[13] Field, *Envangelist of Race*, 378.

matters would have developed differently. Once German troops began to crash into the north of France, antiwar agitation became unthinkable.

The end of party strife in France took on the form of the *Union sacrée,* or Sacred Union. Prominent socialists, including many Jews who had been attracted to socialist activism by the Dreyfus Affair, now entered the government of national defense, breaking the prewar taboo of socialist participation in bourgeois governments.

Even in Russia the opening weeks of the conflict saw what in retrospect appears an unbelievable reconciliation of prewar enemies. According to one story circulated abroad, the notorious anti-Semite Purishkevich "visited a synagogue, kissed the scroll of the law, and amidst copious tears, embraced the rabbi."[14] Even some revolutionary socialists spoke up for the defense of Mother Russia against the German threat. In the Duma the Jewish deputy N. M. Friedman declared that "the Jews are marching to the battlefield shoulder to shoulder with all the peoples of Russia; there are no forces that can tear the Jews away from their fatherland, to which they are bound by ties centuries old."[15] In contrast, one historian has concluded that "Russian Jews prayed for the tsar's defeat"; he refers to the numerous memoirists who, out of the public eye, wrote of the continued hatred by the Jewish masses for the tsar. One described how Jews "eagerly await the defeat of Russia in the war. . . . Germany and Austria . . . are not considered our enemies."[16]

In Great Britain the *Jewish Chronicle,* which had previously maintained a hard line in regard to Russia as a prospective ally in war, declared, "England has been all she could be to the Jews; Jews will now be all they can be to England." And statistics supported that promise: The number of British Jews who served in the armed forces was 41,500, about 14 percent of the total Jewish population, compared with a participation rate among the general population of 11.5 percent.[17]

These enthusiasms lasted for a remarkably long time in many countries. Even when it began to appear, by the end of 1914, that the initial confidence in dramatic victory was not justified and that a costly war of stalemate was beginning, fidelity to the nation at war held firm.

The Expansion of Germany into Russia

The quickest disillusionment came in Russia, where the deepest divisions had existed before 1914 and where Jews were notorious for their aversion to military service. The most important factor, however, in spreading disillusion

---

[14] Salo W. Baron, *The Russian Jew under Tsars and Soviets* (New York, 1987), 157.

[15] Louis Greenberg, *The Jews of Russia: The Struggle for Emancipation,* vol. 2 (New Haven, Conn., 1965), 95.

[16] Joseph Nedava, *Trotsky and the Jews* (Philadelphia, 1972), 24.

[17] Geoffrey Alderman, *The Jewish Community in British Politics* (Oxford, 1983), 88.

was that Russia lost badly to Germany in the early months of the war. The victory of German forces at Tannenberg, under the leadership of generals Ludendorff and Hindenburg, has been described as one of the most dazzling in the history of warfare. Similarly, tsarist Russia was, as the most backward of the major powers, less able to mobilize its forces, whether troops and weapons or opinions and enthusiasms.

Much of the fighting on the eastern front occurred in the Polish provinces and in the Pale of Settlement, with disastrous implications for all inhabitants. When the Russian armies were forced to retreat, Grand Duke Sergei, the Russian commander-in-chief, announced that Jews could not be trusted to remain faithful to Russia when the Germans took over; the Jewish population was to be moved back into Russia. The tsarist government doubted the loyalty of most of the population on its western frontier, Poles even more than Jews, and had good reason to do so. In retreating, the Russian armies drove nearly a million people from their homes.

The rapid advance of the German forces prevented even greater excesses, but perhaps a half million Jews were driven before the retreating Russian troops, many dying of exposure. A typhus epidemic added thousands to the toll. It is not often realized that the death toll from 1914 to 1919 in this area was comparable to that during World War II. Calculations based on the territory later incorporated into the Polish republic reveal that a prewar population of 30.9 million had fallen by 4.6 million by 1919, representing a nearly 15 percent drop. The toll for the same area between 1939 and 1945, including over 3 million Jews systematically murdered by the Nazis, was approximately 18 percent.[18]

Arnold Margolin, fresh from the Beilis case, wearily commented on the changes brought about by the war:

> In place of the calumny about using Christian blood . . . we were now accused of a lack of patriotism, of defeatist views, of sympathizing with the enemy and similar sins. . . . Denunciation by any good-for-nothing would be sufficient for a death sentence. On this ground there could not help thriving luxuriantly all manner of blackmail, extortion of money from the Jews on pain of denunciation as spies, profiteers, etc.[19]

The approximately 300,000 Jewish recruits in the tsarist armies were subject to suspicion and petty harassment. It was a formula for disaster – only one of a great many in the Russian military. Recruits were sent into battle without ammunition, adequate clothing, or sufficient food.

Although representatives of the tsar at first made promises of better conditions for Jews and other minorities once the war had been won, the measures taken by the authorities from the beginning of the war put such promises into

---

[18] Norman Davies, *The Heart of Europe: A Short History of Poland* (Oxford, 1987), 112–13.

[19] Arnold D. Margolin, *The Jews of Eastern Europe* (New York, 1926), 236.

doubt. Jewish leaders spoke of a "willingness to offer sacrifices for the Russian mother country,"[20] and no doubt some Jews were caught up in the general enthusiasm, but there was simply too much bitterness over what had happened in the past for Jewish loyalty to be very widespread or lasting. Given the more than 6 million Jews in Russia and the differences between many of them, there was of course a wide variety of responses to the idea of national defense, but there is little question that a large part of the Jewish population in Russia had no stomach for it.

At the same time, in the eyes of many Russian Jews, Germany remained a land of progressive, humane civilization and the rule of law. Even if Germany was also tainted with anti-Semitism – what country was not? – many Russian Jews considered the German variety of Jew-hatred a less pervasive and certainly less brutal sort. It was an explicit policy of the German and Austro–Hungarian governments to appeal to the subject minorities in Russia, Jews prominent among them, and to stir up suspicion on the part of the Russian authorities about the fidelity of those minorities. German officials were able to enlist the enthusiastic assistance of many prominent German Jews in that task.

Subsequent German history has made it nearly unbearable for many readers to learn of the extent to which Russian Jews in 1914 looked to Germany with favor and hope. The notorious brutalities of German troops on the eastern front in World War II and the earlier actions of "the Huns" in the "rape of Belgium" in World War I (in fact much exaggerated by Entente propaganda) make it now painful to learn how often Russian Jews actually greeted German armies as liberators during World War I. The sister of Menachem Begin recalled that before 1914 her father was very much pro-German and that when the Germans arrived in Poland during the war, "They treated the Jews marvelously. . . . They gave each child sweets and biscuits. These were different Germans, a different period."[21]

General Erich Ludendorff, allied with Hitler in the 1920s, was known in 1915 and 1916 for his concerted efforts to win over Russia's Jews. As soon as German armies had overrun Russian Poland, he summarily repealed existing anti-Jewish legislation. He went so far as to dedicate synagogues and issue proclamations – "in the choicest Yiddish" – of German–Jewish friendship to his "dear Jews."[22] Jewish leaders in Poland had easy access to him; he and his staff attended and enthusiastically applauded performances of the then vibrant Yiddish theater. Whatever their faults, German military men were much preferable, as far as many Jews were concerned, to the Russian generals and their soldiers.

Ludendorff's efforts were part of a well-conceived anti-Russian policy and had little to do with genuine sympathy for the Jews of Russia. Moreover, the

[20] Baron, *Russian Jew,* 157.

[21] Eric Silver, *Begin* (London, 1948), 5, 9; Paul Johnson, *A History of the Jews* (New York, 1987), 423–5.

[22] Howard Morley Sachar, *The Course of Modern Jewish History* (New York, 1977), 297.

evidence does not indicate that fraternization of German soldier and Ostjude had many beneficial long-term results for the latter. Ordinary German soldiers were often revolted by the poverty, the filth, and the alien ways of the Jewish masses they encountered. Even journalists who were opposed to anti-Semitism reported that they were flooded with anti-Semitic letters and articles from soldiers on the eastern front.[23] Similarly, the evidence is that the tens of thousands of Jewish workers in Poland who volunteered for service in the war industries of Germany were not well received by the civilian population inside Germany, not only because of their unfamiliar appearance but also because of the attachments of large numbers of them to revolutionary socialism.[24]

The Beginning of Disillusionment in the West

Athough discipline and enthusiasm held for a remarkably long time in the major industrialized powers of the West, waging total warfare over many years extracted its price; mobilizing the entire economy for war production soon touched nearly every citizen. More to the point, some citizens were touched to a much greater extent than others, with ultimately disastrous effects on the sense of community that developed at the outbreak of war.

It was at the front, of course, that the most horrendous price was paid. Single battles saw hundreds of thousands of young men massacred and large areas turned into moon landscapes. The battles of 1916, particularly at the Somme and Verdun, by far exceeded in senseless death and destruction anything known in the annals of warfare. Those clashes, which were finally indecisive in military terms, induced even some of the most patriotic to question how much longer a war of this sort could continue.

The millions who fell at the front in 1916 (3 million casualties in that year, half of which were fatalities) resulted in ever more energetic recruitment and in growing suspicions about those who were able to avoid service at the front. In Germany, governmental agencies were swamped with complaints from citizens that Jews, using money and connections, avoided the most dangerous assignments.[25] In Great Britain, the large number of recent Jewish immigrants from Russia attracted growing suspicion. By 1916 the *Jewish Chronicle* recognized a "major problem" in the unwillingness of many Jews of Russian origin to enlist for frontline service. The Zionist leader Vladimir Jabotinsky complained that the Russian–Jewish community in Great Britain was astonishingly blind to what was happening in the world around it. Jewish immigrants preferred to "entertain their girl friends and play billiards."[26] In the following year

[23] Field, *Evangelist of Race,* 386.

[24] Friedländer, "Politische Veränderung," in Mosse, *Judentum,* 35.

[25] Werner Angress, "Juden in politischen Leben der Revolutionszeit," in Mosse, *Judentum,* 231.

[26] Vladimir Jabotinsky, *The Story of the Jewish Legion* (New York, 1945), 62; Colin Holmes, *Anti-Semitism in British Society, 1876–1939* (New York, 1979), 127.

serious rioting and looting of Jewish stores occurred in Leeds and London's East End. A police official, in explaining the disturbances, pointed to

the large number of alien Russian Jews of military age . . . who can be constantly seen promenading about our principal streets and the various pleasure resorts. . . . Members of the Christian population have been heard to ask why these men are not serving in the Army as the husbands, brothers, and sons of the Christian population have had to do.[27]

In July 1917 a law was passed that threatened to deport unnaturalized Jews who refused to volunteer for duty at the front; their earlier excuse that they would not risk their lives to preserve a regime that had so oppressed them no longer held after the fall of the tsar. Deportations actually began in September, but the Bolshevik Revolution in November soon halted them. The bill received the full support of Jewish leaders in Great Britain.[28]

German propagandists made much of what they termed the "pogroms" in Britain. But potentially serious anti-Jewish developments were occurring in Germany, too. In October 1916 the war minister announced that he would began an inquiry, subsequently termed the "Jew count" (*Judenzählung*), to determine how many Jews had avoided military service. He insisted that the inquiry was being initiated not to discredit Jews but rather in response to widespread complaints and rumors; he implied that the inquiry would serve to disprove anti-Semitic charges. Whatever the real motives behind this measure, singling Jews out in this way was humiliating to them. But the Judenzählung proved to be a popular measure among the general German population.[29]

The results were not released until after the end of the war, allowing suspicions to spread that the findings actually confirmed the charges of the anti-Semites and that the government was afraid to release them. Unauthorized summaries of them were distributed by anti-Semitic organizations. The actual statistics gathered are mired in complexities that cannot be pursued here, but studies by scholars since World War I have tended to put into doubt charges that German Jews avoided frontline service.[30] Some have denounced the charges against the Jews as utterly without foundation: "Men whose grandfathers had spoken Yiddish, which had no words for war, went on in 1914–18 to amass over 31,500 Iron Crosses."[31] The death rates of all groups at the front were staggering, and the deaths of young men of Jewish extraction were not notably different from those of Catholic or Protestant background.

---

[27] Holmes, *Anti-Semitism in British Society*, 131.

[28] Alderman, *Jewish Community*, 89.

[29] Jochmann, "Ausbreitung," in Mosse, *Judentum*, 425–6.

[30] Werner Angress, "Das deutsche Militär und die Juden im Ersten Weltkrieg," *Militärgeschichtliche Mittelungen*, vol. 19 (1976), 77–146.

[31] Johnson, *History*, 408. The claims about Yiddish's lack of a word for war are typical of the fatuousness that sometimes characterizes discussions of this matter. Yiddish has words for war of both Germanic and Hebrew origin.

As we have seen, the relationship of German Jews to their state, society, and culture before the war was profoundly different from that of Russian Jews to their state, society, and culture. German Jews had historically not gone to the extremes of Jews in Russia to avoid military service, but nonetheless there is no getting around the observation already made that militarism, blind obedience to the state, and death in violent conflict were not cultivated virtues among German Jews as a whole. In an article that became notorious, entitled "Hear O Israel!" written before the war, Walther Rathenau had remarked to his fellow Jews that

Your east Mediterranean appearance is not very well appreciated by the northern tribes. You should therefore be the more careful not to walk about in a loose manner, and thus become the laughing stock of a race brought up in a strictly military fashion. As soon as you have recognized your unathletic build, your narrow shoulders, your clumsy feet, your sloppy, roundish shape, you will resolve to dedicate a few generations to the renewal of your outer appearance.[32]

The stereotypes that Rathenau drew upon were cruel and unjust but still widely accepted, by Jew and non-Jew alike. They paralleled those made by Herzl and, indeed, others not tainted by Herzl's peculiar variety of hostility to fellow Jews. If we may speak of a *mentalité collective* about Jews prior to 1914, that they typically had an "unmilitary bearing" is a good example. Other perceptions blended into a composite picture of Jews at the time. Since German Jews on the average were notably richer and better educated than the rest of the population, they undoubtedly had greater resources, material and intellectual, if they wanted to avoid frontline service.

And undoubtedly many did, as did other parts of the population, especially after 1916. The widespread suspicions were plausible, whatever the elusive exact truth. Individual Jews who fit negative stereotypes were especially noticed by those who found psychological satisfaction in such stereotypes, whereas those Jews who did not fit were not "seen." As an example of how such stereotypes were nourished, Kurt Tucholsky, a journalist who became one of the most hated Jews in Germany – if also one of the most widely read on the left – wrote after the war:

During the three and a half years of war I hid wherever, however I could. I regret that I did not have the courage, like the great Karl Liebknecht, to refuse military service. For that I am ashamed. So I did what was generally done: I used any means in order not to be shot or to shoot at anyone – and sometimes these were the worst kinds of means. There was no trickery, no bribery, no matter how punishable, that I would have avoided. Many others did the same.[33]

---

[32] Excerpts in Paul R. Mendes-Flohr and Jehuda Reinharz, eds., *The Jew in the Modern World, A Documentary History* (Oxford, 1980), 232.

[33] Field, *Evangelist of Race*, 387.

Doubts about the military inclinations of Jews may have been stronger in Germany than elsewhere in western Europe, but they were widely expressed in other countries. Many were willing to recognize, as one observer stated, that "in the war Jews took part in great numbers as Englishmen, Frenchmen, Americans, and so forth," but they were inclined to doubt the meaning of that participation. That observer continued:

I remember how after arriving in London I was struck by the enormous number of Jews in officer's uniforms on its streets. True, later during my tours of the English front, I did not meet even one. This does not mean that they were not there at all. I even heard of some who were decorated. Yet, the overwhelming majority did not serve at the front, and that [was the case] in all armies.[34]

The Judenzählung, linked to the huge losses in the field in 1916, may be said to have marked the definitive end of "civil peace" in Germany. By early 1917 prewar political divisions had revived in the form of vehemently held differences in the Reichstag about the war. In that year the emergence of "two Germanies" was widely remarked upon, a split in German political opinion, with roots in the prewar years, that would be fundamental to the establishment of the Weimar Republic in 1919. In July 1917 a left–center coalition in the Reichstag, composed of the SPD, the Center Party, and the Progressives, supported a resolution in favor of a negotiated peace. Shortly before that Hindenburg and Ludendorff had persuaded the Kaiser to dismiss the chancellor, Bethmann Hollweg, and replace him with a nonentity. The de facto rule by the military became even more evident. The peace resolution of the Reichstag had no real effect on the government.

On the left, principled opposition to the war was at first limited to very small groups. They denounced the "treachery" of socialist leaders to the principles of revolutionary socialism and to the antiwar resolutions of the International. But even after revolution broke out in Russia in early 1917 and a majority in the new Duma declared itself in favor of a negotiated peace, the deep divisions of the left throughout Europe crippled its resistance to the war.

The Russian social democrats, especially Lenin's Bolsheviks, had been among the earliest in denouncing the concept of national defense under capitalism. From the beginning Lenin called for "revolutionary defeatism"; only proletarian socialist revolution could assure a lasting peace. But in the first year of the war, Lenin attracted almost no following. Rosa Luxemburg was instrumental in the formation of a revolutionary Marxist antiwar group in Germany in late 1915, again with a minuscule following. Her Jewish and foreign origin did not go unnoticed by those in power, nor did the prominence of

---

[34] Roman Dmowksi, *Polityka Polska i Odbudowanie Panstwa*, vol. 1 (Hanover, 1947), 227–33; excerpted in Richard S. Levy, *Antisemitism in the Modern World, An Anthology of Texts* (Lexington, Mass., 1991), 185. The author of this passage was the leader of the right-wing, anti-Semitic National Democratic Party in Poland.

Jews around her, Lenin, and the antiwar factions of other countries. Karl Liebknecht, son of the party founder, Wilhelm Liebknecht, was also active in the antiwar agitation, and it is indicative of how such activity was perceived that he, too, was widely but incorrectly believed to be Jewish.

The prewar undertones of Jewish–Gentile conflict within the SPD between Luxemburg and Kautsky had, by the time of the war, become more open. Luxemburg's dwindling friendships within the party had become more exclusively Jewish, whereas her contempt for the (mostly non-Jewish) leaders of the party became more open and vitriolic. Her references to the leadership were often laced with characteristically Jewish phrases: The leaders were the "shabbesgoyim of the bourgeoisie."[35] For many right-wing Germans, Luxemburg became the most detested of all revolutionaries, the personification of the destructive Jewish alien.

There also continued to be a number of superpatriotic hardliners among German Jews. They spoke out in favor of the annexations of French and Russian territories that were now demanded by the German right, and they, too, supported a war of total victory, rejecting any idea of a compromise peace. These hardliners were especially to be found among the prewar *Kaiserjuden* (Albert Ballin, for example). The center of gravity of Jewish opinion, however, moved toward support of a negotiated peace, especially by early 1917. Aside from the previously mentioned parliamentary initiative, influential newspapers, such as the Jewish-owned *Frankfurter Zeitung* and *Berliner Tageblatt*, spoke up against annexations and in favor of a peace of reconciliation. Their editorials provoked a fierce denunciation from the right – such weak-kneed and treasonous stuff, it was proclaimed, was to be expected from the Jew-press.[36]

By this time there were yet other, if more paradoxical, reasons for German xenophobes to direct their suspicion at Jews. Jews had been, since early modern times, important in the financing and provisioning of warfare; lending money for such purposes was one of the original sources of the fortunes built up by the Rothschilds.[37] The financial demands of World War I far transcended those of earlier wars, where the funds of a single Jewish financier could be decisive, but the role of Jewish economic interests was also important in World War I, and individual Jewish entrepreneurs in Germany reaped huge profits from it. More visibly, individual Jews emerged as centrally important in the government's often heavy-handed organization of the war effort.

The war years witnessed an acceleration of modernizing trends everywhere but above all in Germany, where the exigencies of total war were finally felt with the greatest severity, resulting in rapid industrial concentration in such

[35] Angress, "Juden in politschen Leben," in Mosse, *Judentum,* 228.

[36] Friedländer, "politischen Veränderung," in Mosse, *Judentum,* 41–2.

[37] Cf. Werner E. Mosse, *Jews in German Economy: The German–Jewish Economic Elite, 1820–1935* (Oxford, 1987).

key sectors as metal and chemical. Many elements of the independent Mittel-stand, already under steady economic pressure before 1914, found that their services were not much needed in a war economy; many were pushed into bankruptcy. Industrial workers, on the other hand, since they were of decisive importance in war production, gained a new importance and recognition from the state.

German authorities had not made plans for a long war, and, as the prewar anxieties about encirclement reflected, Germany was not self-sufficient in food or a number of strategic materials. Organization of the economy for total war fell largely under the direction of the general staff of the military. Indeed, Ludendorff came to be, as deputy chief of staff, the de facto ruler of Germany (The chief of staff, Paul von Hindenburg, was largely a figurehead.); he straightforwardly termed the measures taken "war socialism." The German state, under the direction of the military, eventually intervened in the economy and society of Germany more than was the case in any other belligerent power.

In these regards Walther Rathenau came to play an extremely significant role. He was a well-known figure before 1914, a prolific writer and an immensely successful industrialist, but one who envisaged a world that would transcend capitalism and socialism. Perhaps even more notorious than his remarks about how Jews' lacked military bearing was an article he had written for the *Neue Freie Presse* in 1909, in which he had stated that some 300 men guided the destiny of Europe. These men, according to Rathenau, knew one another and picked their successors from their own circles. He had made the remark as a general observation, and he did not describe the 300 as all Jews. Nevertheless, he was critical of the role of Jews as financial oligarchs, and anti-Semites trumpeted the article as an admission by a Jewish magnate of the power of the Jews.

Rathenau was called upon to organize the Raw Materials Section of the army in the early stages of the conflict, and the measures he took led to extensive state control over strategic raw materials. His office usually favored large concerns over small ones, out of considerations of productivity and efficiency. It was either not feasible or not conceivable for Rathenau to control the exorbitant profits made by many industrialists, and a disproportionate number of those industrialists were Jews. (They represented about 10 percent of the total, whereas Jews were only 1 percent of the population.) Of course 90 percent of the firms favored by the Raw Materials Section were non-Jewish, a point often ignored in subsequent denunciations of Jewish war profiteering.

Rathenau's activities, and those of the other Jews whom he chose to work under him, might have won for them the status of permanently enshrined national heroes had Germany won the war within a year or two. Indeed, initially he was praised by the ruling elite as effusively as was Lissauer, the composer of the *Hate-Song Against England*. But his activities in the context of a humiliating defeat after years of unspeakable hardship for the German people were seen differently. The accusation arose that while pure-blooded Germans were fighting and dying at the front, Jews were making huge profits. Theodor Fritsch, a leading figure among the radical anti-Semites, related the experiences of a manufacturer who, Fritsch claimed (he was perfectly capable of making up such stories), had gone to Berlin to negotiate some military contracts:

> To his amazement, he met in the offices not the high officers and military officials he expected but rather Hebrews – and more Hebrews. Finally, he pushed his way to the authoritative department. There, in a large hall, at a diplomat's desk surrounded by others of his tribe, sat Mr. Walther Rathenau arranging things. . . . And it was no suprise that Jewish firms almost always received preference.[38]

Ludendorff, in bitter retirement after the war, spoke in his memoirs of Germans "fighting for their freedom, with weapons in hand, while Jews did business and betrayed."[39] H. S. Chamberlain, who had praised Jews in August 1914 for acting "like Germans," before long was writing as follows:

> I learned today from a man who is especially well placed to observe these things . . . that the Jews are completely intoxicated by their success in Germany – first from the millions they have gained through the war, then because of the praise showered on them in all official quarters, and thirdly from the protection they and their machinations enjoy from the censor. Thus, already they are beginning to lose their heads and to reach a degree of insolence which may allow us to hope for a flood-tide of reaction. May God grant it![40]

Resentments of a similar sort were widely reported from Austria–Hungary. The capitalist class in Budapest, close to 90 percent Jewish, was according to one Jewish observer "singularly gross in profiteering"; Oszkar Jaszi was appalled by the contrast between the luxury of the Budapest business world and the misery of the war front. He circulated a questionnaire, asking leaders of Budapest's intelligentsia whether there was now a "Jewish problem" in Hungary (which Hungarian leaders had so often denied prior to 1914). He received a decisively positive reply.[41] It is revealing, however, that the aged emperor, Franz Joseph, retained his belief that Jews were "brave and patriotic men [who] happily risk their life for emperor and fatherland." When it was proposed to send Jewish refugees from the front to camps in Moravia, he replied "If Vienna has no more room for refugees, I shall make Schönbrunn [the imperial residence] available for my Jewish subjects."[42]

[38] Paul Lehmann, ed., *Neue Wege: Aus Theodor Fritschs Lebensarbeit* (Leipzig, 1922), 351–59; excerpted in Levy, *Antisemitism*, 195.

[39] Erich Ludendorff, *Kriegsführung und Politik* (Berlin, 1923); Friedländer, "politische Veränderung," in Mosse, *Judentum*, 37.

[40] Field, *Evangelist of Race*, 382.

[41] William O. McCagg, Jr., *A History of Habsburg Jews* (Bloomington, Ind., 1989), 105.

[42] Nikolaus Vielmetti, ed., *Das Oestereichische Judentum* (Vienna and Munich, 1974), 118; Arthur J. May, *The Passing of the Habsburg Monarchy, 1914–1918*, 2 vols. (Philadelphia, 1968), 1:311; Richard S. Geehr, *Karl Lueger, Mayor of Fin de Siècle Vienna* (Detroit, Mich., 1990), 364.

The Burgfrieden had introduced new industrial relationships. The representatives of the workers, the social–democratic politicians and the trade union leaders, prewar pariahs, now met with cabinet members, generals, and industrial magnates; their opinion in regard to needs of the workers was given a consideration that had not existed prior to 1914. As the war became more desperate, the material conditions of nearly all classes of society worsened in an absolute sense, but those of workers involved in war production improved relative to many other classes. Their incomes rose (again, only relatively; in absolute terms they fell), and they were allocated coupons to buy rationed foodstuffs because they engaged in heavy physical labor for the war effort.[43]

From the standpoint of rationalizing the war effort, Rathenau's favoring of large, modern firms and the more general reallocation of scarce resources to workers in the war industries made sense, but that is not the way the measures were perceived by many of those hit hardest by them. Food became scarce: By 1916 even those with ration coupons were reduced to an average caloric intake of 1,350 (normal: 2,000);[44] the winter of 1916–1917 was especially bleak, going down in German history as the "turnip winter."

Such grim developments provoked increasingly desperate social conflict. As members of the Mittelstand saw their material situation decline in regard to workers, ideologies of resentment grew in appeal, as did the long-standing fears of the more traditional classes that Germany was becoming dominated by large, impersonal units of production and socialistically inclined proletarians. The tens of thousands of Jewish factory workers, recruited from the occupied territories, were even more resented. Native German workers, interestingly, seemed to elect representatives to prominent leadership posts frequently from the ranks of Jews. This Jewish–proletarian alliance had roots in the prewar world, but it now further fed anti-Semitic fantasies of Jewish control of the world of labor.

Powerful industrial and landed groups that previously avoided the crudest forms of anti-Semitism were now more tempted to use emotionally laden charges against Jews as a device to mobilize popular frustrations against a negotiated peace or internal reforms.[45] One cannot help but be impressed with the far-ranging ways in which fears and resentments were finding focus in anti-Semitism: Jews as shirkers at the front; Jews as weak-kneed parliamentarians and pacifist press lords; Jews as capitalists making money from the war; Jews as all-powerful and self-serving bureaucrats in the government; Jews as treacherous revolutionaries; even Jews as rank-and-file workers who were especially prone to destructive radicalism. The old anti-Semitic refrain – "the Jew is everywhere" – gained unparalleled plausibility in Germany and began to attract a larger part of the population than ever before.

[43] Cf. Gerald Feldman, *Army, Industry, and Labor in Germany, 1914–1918* (Princeton, N.J., 1968).

[44] Hajo Holborn, *A History of Modern Germany, 1840–1945* (Princeton, N.J., 1969), 460.

[45] Field, *Evangelist of Race*, 308.

The Peace Settlement

The ultimate victory of France and Great Britain alleviated to some degree the bitterness and social tensions within their respective societies. They retained contact with foreign supplies of food, whereas the Germans faced an ever more crippling blockade. Still, the war years were also traumatic for the English and French, especially the latter. France's rich and industrially important northern territories were occupied from 1914 to 1918 and massively bombarded. France finally lost a greater proportion of its male population at the front than did Germany. On the other hand, civilian control of the military prevailed in both France and Great Britain, and in neither country was the tendency to point an accusing finger at Jews as strong as in Germany, Austria–Hungary, and Russia.

David Lloyd George, who took over as prime minister in December 1916, had headed the Ministry of Munitions, which handled tasks roughly comparable to those of Rathenau's Raw Materials Section; the extent to which Lloyd George's ministry assumed control of Great Britain's economy was at any rate remarkable – a "one-man Welsh revolution,"[46] in the words of historian George Dangerfield. In this role, Lloyd George did not avoid hostility and popular resentment, but they were of a different quality from those finally faced by Rathenau. Similarly, at the most desperate stage of the war for France, after the failure of the Nivelle Offensive in the spring of 1917, which provoked mutinies among the French soldiers, it was Georges Clemenceau, a former Dreyfusard, who oversaw a brutal repression of all "defeatists" in France. If anything, Jews and Gentiles in France were drawn more closely together in these hours of national crisis. No doubt, not everyone saw things that way at the time. In Great Britain the *Jewish World* commented, in response to an anti-Semitic exchange in the columns of the *London Times,* that Jews faced "the beginning of a new and evil era. . . . We cannot say any more that there is no anti-Semitism in this country that loved the Bible above everything."[47]

It was in the areas where the Jewish population was most concentrated that anti-Semitism was the most intense between late 1918 and 1920. From the beginning of the war the Jews of Austrian Galicia experienced a particularly unhappy fate: first, from the hostility of invading Russian generals and troops, thereafter from the repeated offensives and counteroffensives of Russian and Austro–German armies, catching the bewildered Jews of the area in between. In the course of the war, very large numbers of Jews moved out of Galicia (estimates range as high as 400,000, half the Jewish population of the province), swelling the urban areas and refugee camps of the Austro–Hungarian Empire.

The Polish overlords and neighbors of the Jews in Galicia had hardly been

---

[46] George Dangerfield, *The Strange Death of Liberal England* (London, 1935), 19.

[47] Johnson, *History,* 457.

free of anti-Semitism before the war, but the empire's constitution protected Jews, and mutually beneficial political arrangements had been worked out, encouraging a degree of Polish toleration. These fell apart under the hammer blows of war, and the non-Jewish population began to blame the Jews, natural targets given their central role in local commerce, for the shortages, high prices, and generally catastrophic economic conditions of the time.

The first steps in the formation of an independent Polish state were received cautiously, even suspiciously, by Galician Jews, who had reason to feel gratitude and attachment to Franz Joseph and his empire; contending Polish and Ruthenian activists charged the Jews with disloyalty to the new state. "Poland was reborn in Galicia in 1918–1919 to pogrom music."[48] Much the same can be said for developments in the Slovakian areas to the south, formerly dominated by Hungary, soon to be incorporated into the new Czechoslovak state. Jews there were regarded, not without reason, as pro-Magyar and anti-Slovak. When the first steps in establishing the new state were taken, there were episodes of anti-Semitic violence, not really on the scale of the Galician pogroms but serious enough.[49]

To the east, in the chaos and moral anarchy of the Russian civil war, conditions were far worse and for a longer period. The Red Army of the new Bolshevik regime faced not only the reactionary Whites but also anarchist forces and the rag-tag armies of various nationalities that hoped to gain independence. Again, Jews were often caught in between, blamed for allegiance to one side or the other or simply plundered because they were there, weak and vulnerable. The troops themselves were driven to the edge of desperation; many became little more than marauding bands. The White armies were particularly prone to anti-Semitism, since they believed the Soviet regime was ruled by Jews and assumed that Jews, even traditional ones, were sympathetic to the Bolsheviks. Such beliefs became all the stronger when a pro-Bolshevik soviet regime took over in Budapest in March 1919 led by a communist council of people's commissars that was in fact composed entirely of Jews.

The entry of the United States, in the spring of 1917, gradually tipped the balance in favor of France and Great Britain. American intervention was not immediately decisive, but the promise of thousands of American troops meant that France and Great Britain could more easily reject the idea of a negotiated peace with Germany and instead push on for a total victory. That victory was finally achieved in the autumn of 1918 after internal upheavals in Germany brought to the fore those who were willing to negotiate a peace.

For the anti-Semitic right in German-speaking central Europe, America's alliance with the French and the English meshed into a by now well-established image of Jewish-controlled powers that were conspiring to destroy Ger-

---

[48] McCagg, *History of Habsburg Jews,* 203.

[49] Ibid., 204.

many. The prewar assertion by men like Treitschke, Langbehn, and Chamberlain that the English and the Americans were shallow, commercial minded, and materialistic – Jewish in spirit – was now made even more adamantly. Chamberlain, in a letter to Wilhelm II, wrote that "England has fallen totally into the hands of the Jews and the Americans. . . . This war . . . is in the deepest sense the war of Jewry [*Judentum*] and its near relative, Americanism, for the control of the world."[50]

In January 1918 President Wilson set down his Fourteen Points, which represented in part an effort to regain the propaganda initiative from the Bolshevik regime. The Bolsheviks had published the tsarist government's secret prewar treaties, revealing the expansionist or revanchist goals of France and her allies and weakening their claims to be waging a defensive war of high principle, of democracy against militaristic and imperialistic aggression. Wilson's Fourteen Points promised a just and lasting peace, based on open diplomacy, reduction of armaments, freedom of trade, and self-determination of peoples. Wilson also looked to a "general association of peoples" that would oversee world order after the war was won. The American president became wildly popular in much of Europe. Even the socialists, when answering the oft-posed question of that period, "Wilson or Lenin?" chose Wilson by a large majority. When the Germans agreed to an armistice, they thought that it would be in accordance with Wilson's Fourteen Points. They were tragically mistaken.

The Paris Peace conference that gathered in early 1919 oversaw the redrawing of the map of most of Europe and large parts of the rest of the world. The Jewish Question was on the agenda at Paris, one of a large number of nettlesome issues, seemingly impossible to resolve in a way that would be just to all concerned. The German right quickly labeled it a "Jewish peace," not only because they believed it vindictive, which it unquestionably was, but because they were persuaded that it meant even greater Jewish power in the postwar world.

Again, their fantasy world found much in the real world to nourish it. Even many of those who were not notably anti-Semitic viewed the peace settlement as part of a titanic struggle between German and Anglo–American values. Germans saw themselves as an idealist, disciplined, self-sacrificing people facing peoples devoted to shallow liberalism and egotism. Those Germans who had put their faith in Wilson's points believed themselves cynically betrayed. In their eyes, the final "dictated peace" (*Diktat*) was an act of unspeakable perfidy.

Even discounting such predictable reactions, in practice Wilsonian ideals clashed with one another and were simply impossible to implement in many instances. A major problem was that large areas of Europe were so mixed in population that national self-determination could not be introduced in any workable fashion. A related dilemma of the points was that if they had been

---

[50] Field, *Evangelist of Race,* 384.

applied with strict consistency, the result would have been to establish a new German nation that was larger and potentially more powerful than before 1914, since the German-speaking populations of the Austrian half of the monarchy would be added to a new self-determined Germany. With the collapse of the Austro–Hungarian Empire, the old question of the *kleindeutsch* or *grossdeutsch* German state was again posed. But the idea of a new, "large-German" state, even if democratic in constitution, was absolutely unacceptable to France and Great Britain. They were determined both to punish and permanently weaken Germany, to prevent it from once again becoming the troublemaker that they believed it had been before 1914. The Wilsonian principle of self-determination came to be applied only insofar as it did not undermine the punitive war aims and general interests of the victorious powers. And in those situations that were inherently difficult to arbitrate, Germans were not given the benefit of the doubt.

Linked to such considerations was the problem of constructing militarily and economically viable individual states out of the collapse of the Austro–Hungarian Empire. Czechoslovakia, in order to be economically and militarily viable, needed the western areas of Bohemia and Moravia (often referred to as the Sudetenland), which contained a large German-speaking population, one that was not enthusiastic about being a minority in the new Czechoslovak state. Similarly, Hungary, as a defeated power, was not able to make effective claims on those areas that were in their majority Magyar speaking but that Czechoslovakia and Romania appropriated.

The "agreement" finally imposed on Germany, known as the Treaty of Versailles, went much beyond what might have been reasonably expected of an effort to weaken Germany's trouble-making potential. But to speak of what might have been reasonably expected misses by a wide mark the atmosphere of Europe at the end of the war. The popular mood was ugly and vindictive; slogans such as "Make Germany pay!" and "Hang the Kaiser!" were to be heard everywhere among the victorious powers. Even if Europe's politicians, recognizing the dangers of a vindictive peace, had been inclined to moderation – which most were not – popular pressures pushed in a contrary direction.

Some French leaders were determined to dismantle the German Reich into smaller, separate states, but when that proved impracticable, a truncated Germany was agreed upon. The new German state lost not only Alsace–Lorraine to France but also large stretches of Prussian lands to Poland, establishing an awkward intrusion, the "Polish Corridor" to the sea, for the new and otherwise land-locked state of Poland. A number of smaller adjustments favoring Germany's neighbors only added to the sense of impotent outrage in Germany.

The worst outrage in the eyes of many Germans was the huge reparation payments with which they were saddled. They were similarly forced to acknowledge guilt for starting the war in 1914. Germany's military power was to be radically curbed; the revered general staff was dissolved, the navy sharply reduced – submarines prohibited – and the army limited to 100,000 volunteers. Most Germans concluded that these measures were designed not only to punish but to humiliate and ultimately destroy their country.

Enormous debate emerged at the time and for many years afterward about the wisdom and justice of these draconian arrangements. Those German leaders who eventually agreed to work within the terms of the treaty did so not because they accepted them as reasonable but because they finally saw no realistic alternative. Among those realists was Rathenau, further encouraging the belief that he was involved in a Jewish conspiracy to ruin Germany. The policy of regretful–realistic "fulfillment" (*Erfüllung*) of the terms of the treaty so incensed the German right that many of its leaders called for violent resistance. That option was rejected by most of the nation as promising only greater suffering for an already prostrate, half-starved people. Soon the fantastic charge of a "stab in the back" of the German armed forces by craven or treasonous politicians would be taken up by the radical right. For the parties of the left, on the other hand, the ultimate absurdity was that they, the supporters of the peace resolution of 1917 – who had no responsibility for starting the war – were now forced to assume the responsibility for signing the detested *Diktat*.

The Germans were hardly the only people to feel cheated by the peace treaties, or to blame Jews for them. The Hungarians lost a much larger proportion of their prewar territory than did the Germans. They could not claim that all of their lost lands were ethnically Magyar, but large portions of them undoubtedly were. Being on the losing side was only one of the disadvantages suffered by the Hungarians: The soviet republic that was established in Hungary from the early spring to the late summer of 1919 fatally weakened the country both in terms of negotiating with the victorious powers and of protecting its territory from invasion. The weakness of Hungary in defeat made possible the temporary victory of a communist takeover; no other political tendency was willing to assume responsibility. That the soon notorious communist dictator of Hungary, Bela Kun, and all the commissars of the short-lived soviet republic were Jews helped to bring about a sharp change in the climate of opinion in Hungary. From being a country whose elites recognized the usefulness of Jews, it became one in which Jews were widely seen as destroyers. The virulence of Magyar anti-Semitism soon came to rival that in other parts of east–central Europe.

Austria was also reduced to a fragment of its former self, encompassing only the German-speaking alpine provinces of the old empire. The rump state of Austria was flatly denied the option of an *Anschluss,* unification with Germany, which apparently most German-speaking Austrians favored at this point. The new country was even forbidden to call itself "German Austria," so fearful were the victorious powers of the notion of Germans unifying.

Italian representatives to the peace conference denounced *la vittoria mutilata,* the mutilated victory, since their country was denied some of the territories bordering on Austria that had been promised during the war. These resentments would constitute a key propaganda theme of Mussolini's fascist movement.

Most of the new countries to emerge from the collapse of the Russian and Austro–Hungarian empires had sizable Jewish populations, and the new leaders of these countries were required by the Allies to accept so-called minority clauses. The clauses, attached to the various treaties establishing the new countries, not only stipulated that civil equality be given to minorities, long an issue in Romania, but also that minorities had the right to use their own languages in official relations with the state, such as courts of law. Furthermore, the state was obliged to support separate primary schools for the minorities in their own languages.

The manner in which the minority clauses were imposed lent itself to a belief in international Jewish power. The minorities in question, Jews in particular but also large numbers of Germans and Magyars, worried about their fate in the new nations. The dominant nationalities in the new countries, on the other hand, angrily objected that sovereign states could not accept or long tolerate impositions and prescriptions from outsiders. Many of the leaders of the new nations saw the minority clauses as providing a way for the Jews to be able to continue in their prewar economic prevalence – or even to exercise a behind-the-scenes domination of the new countries – whereas Jews saw the clauses as absolutely necessary protection, as did other minorities.

The underlying problem, similar to the more general problem associated with national self-determination, was that the minority clauses sought to solve things that were not really soluble, at least if a "solution" meant leaving all conflicting claimants reasonably satisfied. Antagonistic national claims in the context of a modern nation-state were even more irreconcilable than they had been under the old multinational empires, especially when the nationalisms involved tended to be new and lacking in confidence (Romanian, Yugoslav) or long suffering (Polish, Jewish). All of them, Jewish nationalists included, were inclined to xenophobia and self-righteous posturing; their experience with liberal–democratic practices and pluralistic toleration was limited, and for most of them the very notion of compromise was considered treasonous.

American and British Jews at the Peace Conference played a key role in the formulation of the terms of the minority clauses. As one author put it, "such distinguished Jewish spokesmen as Louis Marshall, Stephen Wise, and Julian Mack . . . laid siege to the Allied plenipotentiaries" and were "in continual contact with President Wilson and Colonel House."[51] Another scholar has observed that the British activist Lucien Wolf had established an "intimate relationship" with Jacques Bigart, the secretary of the Alliance Israelite Universelle, and "essentially fused the policies of Anglo–French Jewry during and after the First World War. The Quai d'Orsay considered Wolf to be a man of

---

[51] Sachar, *Course of Modern Jewish History*, 354.

utmost importance. John Headlam-Morley, treaty draftsman for the British peace delegation, called Wolf the effective author of the Minority Treaties imposed on the Succession States in 1919."[52]

Most of the representatives of the new nations considered the American and British Jews to be their enemies. In the eyes of those representatives, the minority clauses imposed or perpetuated autonomous enclaves of foreign peoples on them of a sort that would not have been acceptable to Wilson or any other major American politician in their own country, or by the leaders of the other Allied countries. The apparent double standard was defended by the Allies with the argument that one could not compare the situation in these new, backward countries with that of modern states like the United States, Great Britain, or France.

But even from the standpoint of American, British, and French Jews the situation was awkward. The usual position of modern Jews had been, since the time of the French Revolution, that being a Jew had to do with religious belief, not nationhood; now Jewish nationality was being recognized and incorporated into official treaties – so far had the influence of Zionist perspectives come since Herzl first presented them to an often hostile or incredulous world.

Fantasies about Jewish power aside, Jewish lobbying at Paris was unquestionably effective; Jewish leaders had the ear of many influential politicians. That Jewish leaders in the victorious states were so active in demanding minority treaties is hardly surprising, given the anti-Semitism of leading politicians in states like Poland and Romania. But far from having established an international conspiracy, Jews were now, perhaps even more than before 1914, terribly divided among themselves. The American Jews were able to work out common goals in regard to the minority clauses, but only after acrimonious internal controversy and mostly because they agreed at least on one thing: The Jews in the new states needed help from outside. Jewish minorities in each of the new countries could appeal to no other nation-state, as could the German or the Magyar minorities, to look after their interests. Well-placed Jews in America, Great Britain, and France believed that they had an obligation, now even more than before the war, to defend Jews in eastern and central Europe, even if those well-placed Jews also differed vehemently among themselves about the notion of Jewish nationalism as such.

If the goals of Jews in the Allied countries were understandable, it is also not difficult to understand that the leaders of the new nations did not want their economies in the hands of "foreigners" (which undeniably many Germans, Magyars, and Jews considered themselves to be in relation to the new states). The issue was much like that already discussed in regard to Romania: The leaders of the new nations wanted to develop their own national middle

---

[52] Eugene C. Black, *The Social Politics of Anglo-Jewry, 1880–1920* (Oxford, 1988), 34.

class, and they did not want that class to be predominantly Jewish, especially if
the Jews in question did not speak the national language or identify with the
national culture. Jews also understandably tried to hold on to the social and
economic positions they had established in countries like Poland and Czechoslovakia. In some ideal world the leaders of the new nations might have
worked things out with the minority peoples in their midst, but such a world
did not exist after the war any more than before. As economic conditions
worsened in the 1930s, relations between national leaders and minorities
worsened disastrously.

One might conclude that the victory of the liberal–democratic powers, the
United States at their head, should have been "good for the Jews." But on
examination, that conclusion may be doubted. In spite of the success of American and British Jews at the peace conference in getting minority clauses
inserted in the peace treaties, the situation of Jews in most countries of
east–central Europe in the interwar years turned out to be even more precarious than prior to World War I. Even after the disruptions of the immediate
postwar period had settled down, Jewish fortunes continued to be uncertain, in
many instances seemingly hopeless. Large numbers of Jews came to the conclusion that the situation under the Austro–Hungarian Empire had been much
more auspicious for them than the situation in most of the successor states.
Some Jews even concluded that the long-reviled tsarist regime was preferable to
the new state of Poland in its treatment of Jews, especially after 1929.

The Balfour Declaration
and the Palestinian Mandate

The Peace Conference dealt with many issues, including carving up the
defunct Turkish Empire, which had profound implications for the Jewish
Question in Europe, in that it opened up a possible fulfillment of the Zionist
dream, the establishment of a national home for Jews in Palestine. The story
of the genesis of the Balfour Declaration, in which Great Britain officially
favored the establishment of such a home under British protection, is an
improbable, even astonishing one. Some have presented the Balfour Declaration and the eventual establishment of a modern Jewish state as a modern miracle; others have seen the emergence and survival of the state of Israel as evidence of how the power of Jews, operating in the corridors of power in
Europe and America, has been able to achieve things that defy all probability
– and justice.

A key area of scholary difference concerns the motivation of Great Britain in
issuing the Balfour Declaration in the first place. Was it in the interest of the
country to do so, or was some form of British altruism – a genuine sympathy for
the plight of Jews – more important? Did the purported philo-Semitism of leading British politicians, based on a peculiar biblical romanticism, play a decisive

role in their support for Jewish aspirations? And did that same philo-Semitism account for their blindness to the injustices done to the Arabs of the area?

We have seen how Chaim Weizmann, like many Jews in Europe, considered the English to be the "best Gentiles." One historian has commented that Weizmann "always accepted the British at their own valuation, as tolerant and fair-minded, loving freedom and justice."[53] The character of leading British politicians, and their mystical religious beliefs, unquestionably played some role in the fulfillment of Zionist goals, but we have also seen that the attitudes of leaders like Balfour and Churchill to Jews and Zionism before World War I were an impenetrable mix of admiration and aversion, of idealistic sentiment and transparent self-interest. Much the same holds for the British decision to support the establishment of a Jewish homeland: Had there not been a fusion of sympathy for Zionist aspirations with hard-headed calculations of national self-interest, a Jewish homeland under a British protectorate certainly would not have come into existence. If the establishment of a Jewish national home in Palestine had been widely perceived as contrary to those interests – as indeed in retrospect many British leaders came to believe it was – the philo-Semitism or religious sentimentalism of individual leaders would have counted for little. Also decisive were a number of broad historical developments, above all the collapse of the Turkish Empire, linked to the sultan's ill-fated decision to support Germany in the war, resulting ultimately in a British conquest of Palestine.

Whatever the exact role of British national interest and broad historical development, Weizmann knew how to take advantage of the opportunities open to him. His success in gaining access to leading British statesmen and his skill in making the case for a Jewish homeland were crucial. On the other hand, the widely accepted tale that the Balfour Declaration was a reward for Weizmann's contributions as a chemist to the war effort must be dismissed as not only implausible but demonstrably false, as Weizmann himself later emphasized.[54] Weizmann's scientific contributions, in synthesizing acetone (important in producing explosives), helped him gain access to leading officials, but it was his ceaseless lobbying for his cause that counted the most.

He encountered a number of Jewish allies among those statesmen, such as the Liberal M.P. Herbert Samuel, but also vehement Jewish opponents of Zionism, such as Lucien Wolf and Edwin Montagu (who in 1909 had been the first British Jew to win a cabinet post). Both of them considered Zionism an unfortunate, reactionary development and a threat to the status of western Jews. Among non-Jews, Churchill, Lloyd George, and of course Balfour were among Weizmann's most important supporters. Others, such as Herbert Asquith, mixed their skepticism about a Jewish homeland with disdain for

---

[53] Johnson, *History,* 425.

[54] Chaim Weizmann, *Trial and Error* (London, 1949), 155; cf. Cohen, *Churchill and the Jews,* 53.

Jews, finding private amusement in watching how bitterly Jews themselves quarreled over the question.

Lord Kitchener, the war minister, and the only British minister who had extensive firsthand experience in the Middle East, believed that a British presence in Palestine would be of no value whatsoever to the empire. Lord Grey, the foreign minister, admitted that he felt a "strong sentimental attachment" to the notion of a Jewish homeland, but he perceived a myriad of insurmountable obstacles. Asquith declared himself "not attracted to this proposed addition to our responsibilities."[55] Lord Robert Cecil found Weizmann's arguments "extraordinarily impressive . . . [in spite of] his rather repellent and even sordid exterior."[56]

One argument especially impressed most ministers: The power of international Jewry. Weizmann did not much use it – or believe in it – but neither did he openly dismiss it, since a belief in Jewish power was useful to his cause. Churchill and others argued that Jewish financial clout and the control of the news media by Jews were compelling reasons to have them on Great Britain's side. Churchill was particularly concerned to rally American Jews. Other British leaders worried about the reaction of the indigenous Arab population in Palestine, and those who knew something about that population warned that British support for a Jewish national home in Palestine risked permanently alienating the Arab world, with disturbing long-term implications for British national interest.

During the war, British concern about the role that Germany might play in the Middle East, especially if some sort of compromise peace were eventually negotiated, prompted many British politicians to look favorably upon the idea of a British-sponsored Jewish homeland in Palestine as part of a general policy to secure the lines of communication with India and points east of the empire. These leaders also favored a British presence in Mesopotamia (later Iraq) and in the Arabian peninsula. Egypt was of course already under British control.[57] Thus, both by land and by sea routes vital to the empire would be secured.

The opinions and positions of Lord Balfour may stand as symbolic of the nuances of the issue. Balfour's government had introduced the Aliens Bill in 1904; one of the reasons he had early on expressed an interest in Zionism was that it offered a way of limiting further immigration of Jews to Great Britain. Such concerns were not necessarily anti-Semitic, nor were they divorced from broader, humanitarian ones. In 1906 when plans to settle Jews in East Africa were being considered, Balfour wrote to Israel Zwangwill that "my anxiety is simply to find some means by which the present dreadful state in which so

[55] Johnson, *History*, 426–7.

[56] Ronard Saunders, *The High Walls of Jerusalem: A History of the Balfour Declaration and the Birth of the British Mandate for Palestine* (New York, 1984), 313–14; Johnson, *History*, 427.

[57] Cf. David Fromkin, *A Peace to End All Peace: The Fall of the Ottoman Empire and the Creation of the Modern Middle East* (New York, 1989), 276–83.

large a proportion of the Jewish race find themselves in may be brought to an end."[58] Balfour doubted that most Jews could or would become genuinely English, and he did not much care for those of his Jewish acquaintances who were pursuing that elusive goal. He admired Jews like Weizmann because of their obvious talents but also because they had no illusions about being or ever becoming English. In a highly revealing conversation with Weizmann in December 1914, Balfour referred to his friendly contacts with Cosima Wagner and observed that he was "in agreement with the cultural antisemites, insofar as we believe that Germans of the Mosaic faith are an undesirable, demoralizing phenomenon." He added, however, that "we totally disagree with Wagner and Chamberlain as to the diagnosis and the prognosis."[59] (Weizmann was hostile to German Jews, and Balfour's words were probably less offensive to him than might be assumed.)

Balfour was an enigmatic personality, impressing many of those he met as cynical and remote. In spite of his distaste for the great masses of eastern Jewry, he considered the Jews a "gifted race," and he spoke of an "immeasurable debt" owed to them by Christianity.[60] Many scholars have concluded that he, more than any other British politicians, was moved by religious sentiment and a related doctrinaire attachment to Zionist ideals.[61] However much that was the case, he was a man who, once having committed himself, pursued a project with an iron will, proving to be Weizmann's most important Gentile convert to the Zionist cause.

Weizmann won over a number of British leaders, not the least of whom was the prime minister in 1917, Lloyd George, whose religious mysticism, too, mixed in elusive ways with his Zionist sympathies.[62] Just after the turn of the century, he had worked as a lawyer for Herzl, when Jewish settlement in the Sinai Peninsula or in East Africa was being considered. Although Lloyd George had earlier denounced the power of the English Rothschilds, he was markedly more sympathetic to Zionism than Asquith was, whom he replaced as prime minister in late 1916. Weizmann later wrote that the new prime minister once confided to him an instinctive sympathy for the Jews as a small nationality because of his own Welsh background.[63]

In early 1917 it was as if events conspired to favor the Zionist cause: The armies of the British Empire began the conquest of Palestine, the tsarist regime crumbled, and Germany's resumption of unrestricted submarine warfare brought the Americans into the war. American support was extremely

---

[58] Marmor, *The Diplomatic Negotiations*, 201–2; Cohen, *Churchill and the Jews*, 28.

[59] Connor Cruise O'Brien, *The Siege: The Saga of Israel and Zionism* (London, 1986), 122.

[60] L. Stein, *The Balfour Declaration* (London, 1961), 152; Walter Laqueur, *A History of Zionism* (London, 1972), 188.

[61] Stein, *Balfour Declaration*, 158; Laqueur, *Zionism*, 189.

[62] Cf. Fromkin, *Peace to End All Peace*, 263–75.

[63] Sanders, *High Walls of Jerusalem*, 69, 131; Johnson, *History*, 427.

important, although up to this point the U.S. State Department had strongly opposed Zionist goals. Indeed, leading State Department professionals came to resent bitterly what they considered a Jewish power so great that it was able to contravene completely the established role of the State Department. A most striking case in point was the meeting in Washington, D.C., in May 1917 between Balfour and Justice Brandeis. Although he was close to President Wilson, Brandeis had no official authority to speak on foreign relations. Nevertheless, he communicated to Balfour a strong American support for the ideas of Zionism. Historian David Grose has commented that "as an illustration of back-channel diplomacy at its most effective, the Balfour–Brandeis meeting was exceptional. A Foreign Minister seeking understanding on a delicate political issue turned not to his official opposite number, the Secretary of State, or even to the other foreign policy advisers known to be close to the president."[64] Of course Balfour had every right, even obligation, to seek out spokesmen for American Jewry on such an issue. What is remarkable is that State Department officials, including the secretary of state, were totally ignored.

President Wilson's own anti-Semitic background did not prevent his becoming close not only to Brandeis but also to Rabbi Stephen Wise, and both men exercised a strong influence on the American president on the issue of a Jewish homeland. On the other hand, his intimate adviser in the White House, Colonel House, advised Wilson against supporting it. He noted that "the Jews from every tribe have descended in force, and they seem determined to break in with a jimmy if they are not let in."[65]

The catalyst for an official British declaration in favor of a Jewish homeland in Palestine, after much hesitation, was a rumor that the Germans might make such a declaration. Both Balfour and Wilson were alarmed by the possibility of a German initiative to gain worldwide Jewish support, one that would rally influential Jews to the cause of the Central Powers. Thus, again in Grose's words, "without bothering to clear it with anyone, the President of the United States joined in a foreign policy initiative that would shape the course of world affairs for the rest of the century. And his Secretary of State still knew nothing about it."[66]

Only two months later did Secretary of State Lansing communicate formally with the president, advising against support of the Balfour Declaration. He offered three reasons: The United States was not at war with Turkey and should avoid the appearance of carving up the Turkish Empire; American Jews were deeply divided on the subject, and nothing was to be gained in supporting one side or the other; and "many Christian sects and individuals would undoubtedly resent turning the Holy Land over to the absolute control of the race credited with the death of Christ."[67]

[64] Peter Grose, *Israel in the Mind of America* (New York, 1983), 64.
[65] Ibid., 68.
[66] Ibid., 69.
[67] Ibid., 69–70.

These arguments – from a State Department that would continue to show a lack of sympathy for Jewish concerns during the following three decades of unparalleled danger for Jews – did not prevail, though they help explain why leading Jews did what they could to isolate Lansing. The official declaration made by the British government, in the form of a letter from Balfour, as foreign secretary, to Lord Rothschild, the head of the Jewish community in Great Britain, reflected in its vague, hedged language some of the most important objections to Zionism. In his own draft proposals, Weizmann had stipulated that Palestine as a whole should be recognized as the national home of the Jews, that Jews should have unrestricted rights of immigration to it, and that within their national home Jews should have substantial autonomy. To his horror and mortification, none of these points were accepted. His disappointment was all the more bitter because, as he later stated, "there cannot be the slightest doubt that without outside interference – *entirely from Jews!* – [our] . . . draft would have been accepted . . . as we submitted it."[68]

Weizmann was especially indignant over the emotional opposition within the British cabinet of Edwin Montegu, but other powerful Jewish voices in opposition had been raised, including those of the presidents of the Board of Deputies and the Anglo–Jewish Association. In a letter published in the *London Times* on May 24, 1917, the presidents predicted that a Jewish homeland in Palestine would be a "calamity." It would be a dangerous violation of the principle of equal rights if Jews in Palestine were to get special political privileges and economic preferences. Prophetically, the letter warned that the result would be endless, bitter warfare with the Arabs of the region.[69]

The relevant paragraph of Balfour's letter to Lord Rothschild, dated November 2, 1917, read as follows:

His Majesty's Government view with favour the establishment in Palestine of a national home for the Jewish people, and will use their best endeavours to facilitate the achievement of this object, it being clearly understood that nothing should be done which may prejudice the civil and religious rights of existing non-Jewish communities in Palestine, or the rights and political status enjoyed by Jews in any other country.

The wording skirted most of the key issues, only "favoring" the establishment of "a" Jewish national home (thus not excluding others), not firmly committing Great Britain to establishing one or protecting it once established. No mention was made of any Jewish organization, Zionist or not, that would be in charge of the national home, nor were any promises made in regard to Jewish autonomy in the homeland or special privileges for Jews there. The issue of unlimited Jewish immigration was not explicitly addressed, although the words about nothing being done that might "prejudice the rights of existing

---

[68] Weizmann, *Trial and Error*, 257; Johnson, *History*, 430.
[69] Laqueur, *Zionism*, 193–4.

non-Jewish communities in Palestine" implied that unlimited immigration would not be acceptable.

However distant from Weizmann's full Zionist program of the time, the Balfour Declaration must finally be considered an extraordinary accomplishment, and Weizmann, swallowing his initial disappointment, came to recognize it as such. The term "window of opportunity" has nowhere been more appropriate, for a declaration of this sort could never have been made before a short period in 1917, and certainly at no time afterward. Wilsonian principles were ignored: The overwhelming Arab majority in Palestine at the end of the war (Jews constituted at most a quarter of the population.) was simply not to be given the same consideration as the Czech majority or the Polish majority in their respective lands. As Paul Johnson has remarked, "if the Arabs as a whole had been properly organized diplomatically during the war – if the Palestinian Arabs had been organized at all – there is not the slightest doubt that the Declaration would never had been issued."[70] Throughout the ensuing interwar period, the British steadily backed away from even the vague commitments of the Balfour Declaration.

The arguments in favor of a Jewish homeland were nevertheless widely persuasive at the time, ranging from the humanitarian to the historical and romantic–religious. Balfour and Lloyd George prided themselves in righting a long-standing injustice to the Jews and in helping to solve a seemingly insoluble problem in Europe. Again, as was so often the case during the Peace Conference, the problems ostensibly solved, the injustices righted, merely created other problems and introduced new injustices. And in this regard as in the general European settlement, when there were impossible dilemmas to be dealt with, someone had to get the short end. In Palestine it was the Arabs; in Europe it was the Germans and Magyars. And there would be in both cases eventually a heavy price to pay.

Zionist leaders were close to the corridors of power in Great Britain, formed friendships with influential politicians, and argued their points effectively, whereas the concerns and claims of the Arabs were simply not presented with anything like a comparable persuasiveness. Even many European anti-Semites supported Zionism. Insofar as there were contacts with Arab leadership during and after the war, they were tenuous and unsatisfactory. A planned Arab insurrection against the Turks, negotiated with Sherif Hussain of Mecca, never took place. As Lloyd George testily stated the matter, "the Arabs of Palestine, who might have been helpful to us in many ways, were quiescent and cowering."[71] Of course, there was no Jewish insurrection either; the first steps in the establishment of the modern state of Israel had more in common with Herzl's reliance on contact with the Gentile powerful than with Garibaldian

[70] Johnson, *History,* 430.
[71] Laqueur, *Zionism,* 190.

heroics. Jews in Palestine eventually showed themselves to be capable warriors, to say the least, but the most dazzling demonstrations of that capability were to come only after World War II.

A declaration by the British foreign minister in favor of a Jewish national home did not automatically make such a home acceptable to the rest of the world. In late 1917 most countries were distracted by more pressing issues. News of the Balfour Declaration shared headlines on November 8 with the announcement of the Bolshevik victory in Petrograd. In the midst of raging war and revolution, the declaration simply did not get the scrutiny it deserved. It was at any rate a political document of the British government, not a legal one based on international consensus, appropriate deliberation, and due process.

The vagueness of the declaration also accounts for the degree to which it was not much discussed. The French were particularly distracted at this time, in that they were losing their Russian ally and about to face another concentrated onslaught of the German army; they understandably did not devote much attention or energy to the Middle East. Still, French officials refused to recognize the Balfour Declaration and were decidedly hostile to the idea of a British protectorate of Palestine. Asquith's government had conducted secret negotiations with the French in early 1916, agreeing to a partition of the Middle East into French and British zones, placing Palestine under an Anglo–French condominium, without any commitment to the Jews. The Italians, too, were hostile to the idea of a British protectorate and looked to some sort of international control in Palestine.

These differences and many related ones had to be addressed at the Paris Peace Conference, and the story is all-too familiar: the play of conflicting promises and diplomatic agreements, contradictory principles, power politics, and backroom wheeling and dealing, leaving many bitterly disappointed. But it is not clear whether alternate settlements would have been more broadly satisfactory, or more just, since what was just, even with the best of wills, was impossible to derive uncontrovertibly from the welter of competing claims. Weizmann and other Zionist lobbyists were again extremely active, and again, as with the Balfour Declaration, only partially successful. He tried to persuade the Allies to use the term "historical right" in regard to the Jewish claim to settle in Palestine, but the final language spoke only of a "historical connection."[72] It was, again, an issue of profound implications that would be endlessly debated in subsequent decades.

The British were able to secure a mandate, supported by the League of Nations, over both Palestine and Mesopotamia, whereas the French were given mandates over Syria and Lebanon. But the Palestinian Mandate was

---

[72] See the discussion of the issue in John Quigley, *Palestine and Israel: A Challenge to Justice* (Durham, 1990).

from the beginning a headache for the British, who particularly resisted the prospect of an unimpeded movement of Jews into the region. The opposition of the Arab majority, as predicted, became the central issue in the new Jewish homeland. What the European powers or Great Britain had to say about the future of Palestine was not considered binding by the Arabs of the region, who had not been consulted – indeed, who felt cynically misused and betrayed, not unlike the Germans in reaction to the Versailles Treaty. They soon began to mobilize in violent opposition to Jewish settlement, which they saw as a form of European imperialism.

They also began to pick up some of the baggage of modern European anti-Semitism. Already by early 1919 Arab leaflets were comparing Jews to poisonous snakes. No nation, it was asserted in them, had ever welcomed or long tolerated Jews, and the Palestinian Arabs would fight to prevent Europeans from solving their problems at the expense of the Arabs – dumping unwanted Jews from Europe into Palestine.[73] These words uncomfortably recalled Herzl's own searing and widely quoted remarks that "we move where we are not persecuted; our appearance then leads to persecution. This is a fact and is bound to remain a fact everywhere."

Many in the British military administration of the region sympathized with the Arab majority. They also viewed the Jews as "refuse" from Europe, economic parasites and communist revolutionaries. However, in response to the furor, Balfour stated, in terms that only further infuriated the Arab world, that "zionism, right or wrong, good or bad, is rooted in age-long traditions and in present needs and future hopes of far profounder import than the desires of 700,000 Arabs."[74] His position, while lasting in its influence, was in the long run worn down by a contrary spirit, reflected in Churchill's comments in 1919 that "the Palestine venture is the most difficult to withdraw from and the one which certainly will never yield any profit of a material kind." He was not much persuaded of the moral legitimacy of the enterprise either: He commented caustically that "we are pledged to introduce [the Jews] into Palestine, and . . . [they] take it for granted that the local population will be cleared out to suit their convenience."[75]

As suggested in the Preface, it would be grotesque to argue that the hostility of the Arabs, this "anti-Semitism" by "Semites," was mysterious, having to do only with their own psychic problems and not at all with Jewish actions. One might argue that the Arabs made many mistakes, had poor leadership, and showed many moral flaws. That they picked up some of the crudest anti-Semitic myths developed in Christendom is hardly to their credit. But an irreducible reality remains: They were not treated with fairness, and their resent-

---

[73] Laqueur, *Zionism,* 239.

[74] Ibid., 239.

[75] Cohen, *Churchill and the Jews,* 62–3.

ments were understandable, indeed predictable. To recognize that does not preclude sympathy for the Jewish cause, which was also tragic, and would become much more so. Tragedy, after all, entails the clash of two just causes.

For all its troubling, portentous imperfections, this Jewish homeland was a beginning, a first substantive step toward something that seemed an utter impossibility to most observers before 1914. A new stage of Jewish history had begun, with untold implications for the relations of Jew and non-Jew in Europe and America. But it was only a beginning, one with many harrowing chapters to come, and even by the last decade of the twentieth century it could not be said that a secure, "normal" state, a genuine haven for the Jews had been achieved – certainly not one that was recognized by the great majority of its neighbors or even by the majority of the world's population. At the same time, another bold experiment, which might be described as an utterly contrasting attempt to resolve the Jewish Question, had begun in Russia.

=13

Jews and Revolution
(1917–1934)

The revolutionary flame which has burned beneath the surface of world history is now blazing up for the first time in a Jewish genius: Leo Trotsky! It is blazing with a god-like force that shames every earlier revolutionary craving and consciousness.[1]

The Trotskys make the revolutions; the Bernsteins pay the bills. (Jacob Maze, chief rabbi of Moscow)[2]

This mystic and mysterious race has been chosen for the supreme manifestation, both of the divine and the diabolical. . . . [Jews have been] the mainspring of every subversive movement during the nineteenth century. . . . [They have now] gripped the Russian people by the hair of their heads and have become practically the undisputed masters of that enormous empire. (Winston Churchill)[3]

The emancipation of the Jews is one of the finest achievements of our Revolution. By granting to the Jews the same rights as to Russians, we have erased from our conscience a shameful and bloody stain. (Maxim Gorky)[4]

---

[1] Quoted in William O. McCagg, Jr, *Jewish Nobles and Geniuses in Modern Hungary* (New York, 1972), 207.

[2] Quoted in S. M. Melamed, "St. Paul and Leon Trotsky," *Reflex*, no. 5, Nov. 1927, 8; Joseph Nedava, *Trotsky and the Jews* (Philadelphia, 1971), 167.

[3] Quoted in Gisela C. Lebzelter, "Anti-Semitism – a Focal Point for the British Radical Right," in Paul Kennedy and Anthony Nicolls, eds., *Nationalist and Racialist Movements in Great Britain and Germany before 1914* (Oxford, 1981), 100.

[4] Quoted in Reuben Ainsztein, "Jewish Tragedy and Heroism in Soviet War Literature," *Jewish Social Studies*, vol. 23, 1961, 68; Salo W. Baron, *Russian Jew under Tsars and Soviets* (New York, 1987), 181.

The Jew as Revolutionary: Fantasy and Reality

The horrors of revolution from 1917 to 1921 were in some areas even more devastating than those of war; the connections of Jews and socialist revolution were more visible than ever before and the anti-Semitic potential greater. The perception that revolutionaries were predominantly Jewish and that Jews were particularly vicious as revolutionaries spread now from minds like those of Nicholas II – limited, paranoiac, almost pitiful – to those of a different cut, such as Woodrow Wilson and Winston Churchill. It was no longer only scandal sheets like *La Libre Parole* or the *Bessarebetz* that identified radical revolution with Jews; now that identification was made by newspapers like the *London Times,* the *Chicago Tribune,* or the *Christian Science Monitor,* all of which had enjoyed a reputation for sobriety on Jewish issues and at least relative fairness.

Many of those who had been inclined to a hesitant or inconsistent anti-Semitism before the war, such as Wilhelm II, now embraced more extreme opinions. Wilhelm's attitude to "the threat of international Jewry" was influenced by reports like those of Walther von Kaiserlingk, the German admiralty's chief of operations, who had visited Petrograd in the winter of 1917–18: He described the new government as run by Jews in the interests of Jews; it was "insanity in power," and it presented a mortal threat not only to Germany but to the civilized world. Wilhelm agreed that the Russian people had been "turned over to the vengeance of the Jews, who are connected with all the Jews of the world."[5]

In addressing the issue of Jews and revolution, the precise meaning of the word "Jew" takes on particularly crucial significance. If one defines Jew narrowly, as applying to those who adhere to traditional ritual and belief, then there were not many Jewish revolutionaries, and no Bolsheviks. If one accepts broader definitions, such as the traditional one (anyone with a Jewish mother), then the issue of the "revolutionary Jew" becomes a live one. It becomes even more an issue when Jews are defined in the broadest ways (as certainly occurred in this period): "non-Jewish Jews," half-Jews (with a Gentile mother but Jewish father), Jewish converts to Christianity, Jewish atheists, and even "jewified" if unconverted Gentiles who were closely associated with Jews by marriage or personal friendships.

Even accepting such all-encompassing definitions, however, it is beyond serious controversy that the overwhelming majority of Jews in Europe were not revolutionaries in the sense of favoring violent upheaval and that even among secular Jews in Russia only a minority actively identified with the Bolshevik Party before the autumn of 1917. Of course, only a minority of Great Russians, too, identified with bolshevism, and the same may be said of Poles, Byelo–Russians, Georgians, Armenians, or any of the other nationalities that finally came to be ruled by the Bolsheviks.

[5] Richard Pipes, *The Russian Revolution* (1990), 585, 586.

The issue of Jews and revolution, especially between 1917 and the outbreak of World War II, became hopelessly entangled with anti-Semitic accusations and Jewish defensiveness and apologetics. Given the often low intellectual quality of attempts to link Jews and revolution – to say nothing of the malevolent intent of most of those claiming the link – a natural inclination has been to deny it, to ridicule it, or to maintain that it has been grossly exaggerated. It has undoubtedly been exaggerated, but there was a more substantial reality, feeding the exaggerations, than has been generally recognized.

Not many Jews, even traditional ones, mourned the fall of the tsar. And for a while at least, many Jews were ready to conclude, if hesitantly, that the Bolsheviks were the lesser of two evils. On the other hand, large numbers of Jews were alert to the grave dangers of a social revolution, and before too long many of them came to the conclusion that as far as Jews were concerned, the Bolsheviks were even worse than the tsars. It is a conclusion that in retrospect is difficult to avoid in relation to practically any group that one wants to consider, industrial workers included, the presumed beneficiaries of the Bolshevik takeover.

We have seen how, even in western countries where Jews experienced less oppression, an active and highly visible minority of them, especially young, secularized Jewish intellectuals in the generation before the war, were powerfully attracted to socialist ideas. Jews such as Hess, Marx, Lassalle, Bernstein, Otto Bauer, Luxemburg, Martov, Trotsky, and Léon Blum played a major role in formulating, refining, and propagating those ideas. Non-Jews (Engels, Kautsky, Bebel, Plekhanov, Lenin, Guesde, Jaurès) were also important, in many regards more important than Jews, but considering that the Jewish population of Europe was approximately 2 percent of the total, the Jewish participation in socialism, revolutionary and democratic, was remarkably large.

The conditions of war intensified the attractiveness of revolutionary socialism for many Jews. To recognize that fact does not entail giving credence to the accusation made by anti-Semites – as well as by Churchill and, earlier, Disraeli – that Jews were "always" behind modern revolutionary upheaval. Gentiles were perfectly capable of making revolution without Jewish inspiration, whether in Russia, where the Decembrists and the earliest Narodniks had almost no Jewish members, or elsewhere. The French Revolution, the model for all modern revolutions, was led entirely by native French. It might be more accurate to suggest that Gentiles taught the Jews about revolution, and the Jews, being late-comers but quick studies, learned the lesson extremely well.

Both Jewish and non-Jewish socialists in the late nineteenth century saw great merit in the idealism and radicalism of a moral elite of Jews. Just as the non-Jew, Friedrich Engels, had praised Jews for their contribution to the socialist movement, so V. I. Lenin, in a speech in Zurich in 1905, observed that "the Jews furnished a particularly high percentage . . . of leaders of the revolutionary movement. . . . It should be noted to the credit of the Jews, they furnish a relatively high percentage of internationalists."[6] On another occasion Lenin, in lamenting the low moral and intellectual level of his compatriots, remarked to Maxim Gorky that "an intelligent Russian is almost always a Jew or someone with Jewish blood in his veins."[7] Léon Blum, who after his participation in the Dreyfus Affair went on to become a prominent figure in the French socialist movement, "gloried in the messianic role of the Jews as social revolutionaries."[8] Although he was one of the most perceptive critics of Bolshevik theory in the debates within his own party in 1919 and 1920 concerning whether it should join the new Communist International,[9] he had earlier written that "the collective impulse" of the Jews "leads them towards revolution; their critical powers . . . drive them to destroy every idea, every traditional form which does not agree with the facts or cannot be justified by reason." Revolutionary socialism, he asserted, was a modern form of "the ancient spirit of the [Jewish] race." Justice was a central idea of Judaism, just as love and charity were central to Christianity.[10]

Large numbers of similar testimonies by influential socialists could be added. On the other hand, an equally impressive list of contrary testimony, insisting on the naturally conservative inclinations of Jews, could also be produced. The message that Jews were natural conservatives was one that Herzl tried to bring to Plehve in his meeting with him in 1903. The natural conservatism of Jews is a plausible notion, since in the West they were by 1914 predominantly middle and upper-middle class. Even in Russia, most Jews, linked as they were to commerce, trade, and private property, by personal interest were not attracted to socialism, especially not to extreme varieties of it that called for violent revolution and socialization of the means of production. Arnold D. Margolin, one of Beilis's lawyers, emphasized that in Paris and Berlin, where "the most influential anti-Bolshevist newspapers and magazines" were published, "the majority of their contributors are Russian Jews." Indeed, "the number of Jews among the active anti-Bolshevist groups is much larger than in the ranks of the Bolshevist Government."[11]

Trotsky, for one, agreed. He observed that Jews as a whole were not worth much to the cause of revolution, for they tenaciously resisted proletarianization. Even when pushed into desperate poverty, Jews stubbornly retained a

[6] Hyman Lumer, ed., "Lecture on the 1905 Revolution," *Lenin on the Jewish Question* (New York, 1974) 134.

[7] Maxime Gorki, *Lénine et le paysan russe* (Paris, 1924), 83–4; from Pipes, *Russian Revolution*, 352.

[8] Paul Johnson, *A History of the Jews* (New York, 1987), 458.

[9] Cf. Albert S. Lindemann, *The 'Red Years': European Socialism vs. Bolshevism* (Berkeley, Calif., 1974), 220 ff.

[10] Léon Blum, *Nouvelles conversations de Goethe avec Eckermann* (Paris, 1901); from Robert S. Wistrich, *Revolutionary Jews from Marx to Trotsky* (London, 1976), 83. Johnson, *History of the Jews*, 458. Walter Laqueur, "The Revolutionaries," in Douglas Villiers, ed., *Next Year in Jerusalem: Jews in the Twentieth Century* (London, 1976), 80–1.

[11] Arnold D. Margolin, *The Jews of Eastern Europe* (New York, 1924), 78–9.

"petty-bourgeois consciousness," which for Trotsky was the most contemptible of all forms of consciousness. For him, as for many young revolutionary socialists, "bourgeois" and "cowardly" were nearly synonymous, as were "liberal" and "hypocrite." That the capitalist class in eastern Europe was predominantly Jewish and that many prominent figures in the liberal Kadet (Constitutional Democratic) Party were Jewish resulted in an almost unavoidably anti-Jewish tenor to many of Trotsky's pronouncements.[12] Like Herzl or Marx, Trotsky believed that Jews had handled money for so long that their souls were almost irremediably warped.[13] But Trotsky had no use for Zionism, either; he dismissed Herzl as a "repulsive figure."[14] Even when describing the alienated minority of Jewish intellectuals, Trotsky was harsh: They were fickle, untrustworthy pursuers of fashion, "semiforeigners, not totally assimilated; they adhere to any new critical, revolutionary, or semirevolutionary tendency in politics, in art, and in literature."[15]

Most Russian Jews were pulled unwillingly, even uncomprehendingly, into the vortex of revolution and ensuing civil war from 1917 to 1921, observers rather than actors. But others, especially many who had felt blocked in their dreams of a career or who had suffered daily under the irrationality and inefficiency of the tsarist regime, were only too understandably moved by a desire for violent revenge. Some of those revolutionaries, especially when driven into the moral anarchy of civil war, proved themselves capable of breath-taking ruthlessness. The defenders of the old regime, or those who in other ways opposed the revolutionary left, were no less ruthless. As the revolution developed, it was often a question of kill or be killed. There was, however, one important difference from earlier confrontations: Jews after 1917, along with other groups that had been formerly at the receiving end of tsarist oppression, had a more ample chance to turn upon their oppressors. They also died in incomparably greater numbers than ever before, whether in battle or as victims of pogroms or because of the hunger, disease, and disastrous material conditions that accompanied the breakdown of central authority.

For many observers the Bolsheviks became the embodiment of the Jewish revolutionaries, but Lenin and his followers were only one of many revolutionary groups in Russia in 1917. Moreover, the proportion of Jews in Bolshevik ranks was smaller than in virtually all others. The other major faction of the Russian Marxists, the Mensheviks, by this time a separate party, counted a distinctly larger proportion of Jews. It is also apparently true, as implausible as it may seem, that there were more Jews in leadership positions of the terrorist

---

[12] Cf. Robert S. Wistrich, *Socialism and the Jews: The Dilemmas of Assimilation in Germany and Austria-Hungary* (East Brunswick, N.J., 1982), 54–60.

[13] Nedava, *Trotsky and the Jews,* 123.

[14] Johnson, *History of the Jews,* 451.

[15] Nedava, *Trotsky and the Jews,* 136.

and peasant-based Socialist Revolutionary Party than at the head of the Bolshevik Party.[16]

The Jews in all of these revolutionary socialist parties stood apart in a number of ways from the great mass of the tsar's Jewish subjects. These revolutionaries, except for those in the Bund, were Russian speaking and had lived mostly outside of the Pale of Settlement; even those who lived in the Pale usually led privileged or otherwise atypical existences in it. Trotsky, for example, was the son of a nonbelieving, non–Yiddish-speaking, and illiterate Jewish peasant, or *kulak*, a description that could be applied to less than 1 percent of Russia's Jews by 1914. Trotsky's hostility to other Jews was not uncommon among Jewish revolutionaries; almost all had rejected Jewish belief and custom, and they saw the rabbis as collaborators with the officials of the tsar. The absorption of Jews into the larger nationalities seemed to them natural and desirable, a progressive development.

There were occasional revolutionary Jews who retained traditional beliefs, one of the most bizarre being I. N. Steinberg, an Orthodox Jew but also a member of the Socialist Revolutionary Party, who served in the second Bolshevik government from December 1917 to March 1918. He continued to observe kashrut, Sabbath, and the obligations to daily prayer, surrounded by aggressive atheists, the Gentiles among whom gave a new meaning to *shabbes goy* by carrying his briefcase to Saturday meetings.[17] The leaders of the specifically Jewish organizations, such as the Bund and the Labor Zionists (Poale Zion), did not of course share Trotsky's peculiar distaste for Jews, but the antagonism of the Bund to many aspects of traditional Judaism was notorious.

Before the war, Jewish issues had popped up repeatedly in the fiery and intricate controversies of the Russian Marxists. The aspirations of the leaders of the Bund to establish separate Jewish institutions had prompted Lenin and other prominent Marxists to force them out of the nascent Russian Social Democratic Workers Party (R.S.D.W.P.). Like most Marxists at the time, Lenin did not accept that the Jews were a legitimate nationality; he believed that they should work within the main party and blend into the surrounding peoples.

The conflicts thereafter between Bolsheviks and Mensheviks were not over Jewish issues per se, but the large number of Jews in the Menshevik faction did not pass unnoticed. At the 1907 London Conference of the R.S.D.W.P., Stalin offered the delegates a typically coarse witticism: He observed that the Mensheviks formed a Jewish faction, whereas the Bolsheviks were a truly Russian faction of the Social Democrats; it might be a good idea, then, for the Bolsheviks to organize "a pogrom within the party."[18]

[16] Bertram D. Wolfe, *Three Who Made a Revolution* (New York, 1964), 185; Nedava, *Trotsky and the Jews,* and others make the same point.

[17] Nedava, *Trotsky and the Jews,* 102.

[18] Josef Stalin, *Sochineniia,* vol. 2 (Moscow, 1946–1952), 20–1; Nedava, *Trotsky and the Jews,* 171.

These remarks shocked some at the conference – Russia had recently witnessed wave after wave of murderous pogroms – but it was not only men like Stalin, known for his crudity, who uttered such anti-Jewish remarks. At the same conference, Rosa Luxemburg, justifiably renowned for the refinement of her intellect, caustically attacked one of the leaders of the Bund, Abramovich "and his ilk"; they were, she charged, "among those who speculate with the rising and falling prices of sugar." The Bundist delegates were so incensed by her slur that they refused to let her continue speaking. The offending words were finally erased from the stenographic account of the congress.[19]

Leonard Schapiro, a pioneering historian of Russian social democracy, has argued that behind the Menshevik–Bolshevik schism was indeed a Jewish–Gentile issue, in that Lenin's extreme elitism, his disdain for formal majorities, and his belief in the "leading role" of the party in relation to the proletariat, reflected a Great Russian mind-set; tsarist autocracy and suspiciousness had sunk deep into the Russian soul over the centuries, even in the case of those opposed to tsarism. On the other hand, the ideas of the Menshevik leader, Julius Martov, and of other leading Jewish Mensheviks were more consistent with international standards of Marxist socialism.[20]

Recognizing that there were fewer Jews in the Bolshevik faction than in the Menshevik, or even that Bolshevism was not a typically Jewish ideology, does not mean that the issue of the role of Jews in Bolshevism is settled, for there were still many Jewish Bolsheviks, especially at the very top of the party. And there were even more in the dreaded Cheka, or secret police, where the Jewish revolutionary became visible in a terrifying form. In both party and Cheka there were also a remarkably large number of other non-Russians, however "typically Russian" Lenin's theories may have been.

Determining the exact number of Jews in the leading ranks of the party and the secret police is nearly impossible, in large part because of the difficulty of deciding who was Jewish. Simple numbers or percentages fail to address the key issues of visibility and qualitative importance; Jews as prominent party leaders were undoubtedly much more numerous than in the rank-and-file. Even in the case of the party's central committee, citing the absolute numbers of Jews, or their percentage of the whole, fails to recognize certain key if intangible factors: the assertiveness and often dazzling verbal skills of Jewish Bolsheviks, their energy, and their strength of conviction.

Any effort to compose a list of the most important Bolsheviks must be unavoidably subjective, but it seems beyond serious debate that in the first twenty years of the Bolshevik Party the top ten to twenty leaders included close

[19] N. Mikhalevich, *Zikhrones fun a Yiddishen Sotsialist,* vol. 1 (Warsaw, 1929), 150; Nedava, *Trotsky and the Jews,* 146–7.

[20] Leonard Schapiro, "The Role of Jews in the Russian Revolutionary Movement," *The Slavonic and East European Review,* December 1961, 167; Nedava, *Trotsky and the Jews,* 148.

to a majority of Jews. Of the seven "major figures" listed in *The Makers of the Russian Revolution,* four are of Jewish origin, and of the fifty-odd others included in the list, Jews constitute approximately a third, Jews and non-Russians close to a majority.[21]

Trotsky's name (originally Lev Davidovich Bronstein) would of course head any list of Jewish Bolsheviks and alone might count for more than all the others. His case will be more amply considered later on. Grigori Yevseyevich Zinoviev (Radomyslsky), the son of a Jewish dairy farmer, was known as Lenin's closest associate in the party during the war years and a key figure in its central committee. Among Zinoviev's many highly visible posts were president of the Communist International and chairman of the Petrograd Soviet. He was a celebrated orator: The four-hour speech he delivered in German at the Congress of Halle in Germany in October 1920 was considered by friend and foe alike to be a tour de force of pro-Communist rhetoric, almost demonic in effectiveness.[22]

Lev Borisovich Kamenev (Rosenfeld), long closely associated with Zinoviev, also held a string of important positions: He was in charge of *Pravda,* the party newspaper, a member of the party's Central Committee, and chairman of the Second Congress of Soviets in November 1917, which formally ratified the revolutionary seizure of power. He also became chairman of the Moscow Soviet and was briefly titular head of the Soviet state. He, like Zinoviev, was recognized as one of Lenin's closest associates in the party. Kamenev's mother was non-Jewish, and he was formally a Christian. That he was born in Moscow, the son of a Jewish railway worker, is further indication of his status as a non-Jewish Jew, for his father's occupation was as rare for Jews as that of Trotsky's father. But Kamenev had married a Jew – interestingly, Trotsky's sister, Olga.

Adolf Yoffe was also a member of the party's Central Committee in the autumn of 1917. He had joined the party when Trotsky did, in August of that year. He served as chair of the Revolutionary Military Committee of the Petrograd Soviet. Trotsky also sat on the committee, indeed dominated it in the crucial period when the committee directed the seizure of power in early November. Yoffe then headed the Soviet diplomatic delegation in negotiating the Brest–Litovsk Treaty with Germany, and after that became Soviet ambassador to Germany in 1918. He was thus much in the public eye, both in Russia and abroad – notoriously so after it was discovered that he was supporting German revolutionaries, with propaganda materials and large sums of money, activities that resulted in his expulsion from the country.

Yoffe was one of Trotsky's few close friends in the party and also one of Stalin's staunchest and earliest enemies, but, again, he was an unusual Jew: He was of Karaite origin, that is, born into an ancient dissident Jewish sect

---

[21] Georges Haupt and Jean-Jacques Marie, *Makers of the Russian Revolution* (Ithaca, N.Y., 1971).

[22] Lindemann, *'Red Years,'* 253–4.

that did not recognize the Talmud. A few thousand of its followers survived in the Caucasus area. Karaites were ethnically distinct from the Jews in the rest of the empire. They did not speak Yiddish and indeed insisted that they were not "Jews," certainly not Semites. Interestingly, the tsarist regime recognized this distinctness and did not apply anti-Jewish legislation to them. Karaites lived mostly outside the centers of Jewish population in the Pale; Yoffe was born in the Crimea. Still, for such a man to be the new regime's leading diplomat, when the diplomats of most other countries were chosen from the older ruling elites, was symbolic of how different Soviet Russia was from the regime of the tsars.

At a notch down in visibility was Yakov Mikhailovich Sverdlov. Described as "very Jewish-looking,"[23] he was another early associate of Lenin and stalwart of the Central Committee. He became secretary and main organizer of the Bolshevik Party in 1917 and 1918 and served as head of state after Kamenev relinquished that position. Sverdlov was born in Nizhny–Novgorod, outside the Pale, and attended state schools, but he soon became involved in revolutionary activities. His premature death in 1919 was widely recognized as especially damaging to the party; Lenin remarked that it would take several men to do the work he did, although as party secretary Stalin would finally make much more of the post than had Sverdlov. There was at any rate no little symbolism in the fact that a Jew was both the head of the state and the secretary of the ruling party. Percentages of Jews in state positions or in the party do not capture that adequately.

In approximately the same second-level category was Moisei Solomonovich Uritsky, notorious as the chief of the Cheka in Petrograd, where the Red Terror raged with special brutality. For anti-Semites he became the personification of "Jewish terror against the Russian people."[24] Unlike most other Jewish Bolsheviks, Uritsky was born into an Orthodox family inside the Pale. His mother had even hoped he would become a rabbi. Instead, he became involved in revolutionary violence at an early age. By 1917 he was closely associated with Trotsky and, like Yoffe, only joined the Bolsheviks in the summer of 1917. However deserved his reputation for harshness, he was actually known in the party as a moderate among the Chekists. He was certainly less fanatical than Zinoviev, whose pervasive cruelty and vindictiveness toward alleged counterrevolutionaries prompted Uritsky at one point to lodge an official complaint.[25]

To the list of leading and highly visible Jewish Bolsheviks could be added such names as Grigory Sokolnikov (one-time editor of *Pravda* and leader of the delegation that finally signed the Brest–Litovsk Treaty with Germany after Yoffe adamantly refused to have his name associated with such a "disgraceful"

---

[23] Haupt and Marie, *Makers of the Russian Revolution*, 81.

[24] Nedava, *Trotsky and the Jews*, 157.

[25] Roy Medvedev, *Let History Judge: The Origins and Consequences of Stalinism* (New York, 1989), 138.

treaty) or Karl Radek, who became unusually well known in the West because of the "political salon" he maintained while in prison in Germany in 1919; many leading politicians visited him there. He, too, was described as highly Jewish in physical attributes and manner.

A list of prominent non-Jews in the party would begin with Lenin, whose name outweighs the others, although in the first year or so of the revolution, Trotsky's fame rivaled his. Yet his status as a non-Jew and "real Russian" is not as clear as subsequent Soviet propaganda tried to make it. His grandfather on his mother's side was Jewish, though a convert to Christianity and married to a woman of German origin. On Lenin's father's side were Kalmyk and Swedish forebears. Lenin the non-Jew, in other words, was Jewish enough to have fallen under the shadow of doubt in Nazi Germany or to have been accepted in the state of Israel. He was of course widely believed to be a Jew, although he was Great Russian in a cultural sense and of mixed origin in other regards.[26]

Stalin, who was a Georgian (his real name was Josef Dzhugashvili) and who always spoke Russian with an accent, became widely visible only after 1921. Whether he would have made a top-ten list before that is doubtful, although he did serve in the first Bolshevik government, as commissar of nationalities.[27]

Nikolai Ivanovich Bukharin, the son of Moscow elementary school teachers, was widely considered, after Lenin, to be the most able theorist in the party. He held as well many important and visible posts in the party and in government. Lenin often differed with Bukharin, on a few occasions vehemently, but he retained an intellectual respect and personal affection for him to the end of his life.[28] Bukharin, too, became more prominent in the 1920s but is a stronger candidate for the top-ten in the years of the revolution than is Stalin.

Other non-Jews might be mentioned but almost certainly do not quite measure up to Trotsky, Zinoviev, Kamenev, Yoffe, Sverdlov, Uritsky, or Radek in visibility, inside Russia and abroad, especially not in the crucial years from 1917 to 1921. Among them were Alexander Shlyapnikov (a leader of the Bolshevik Petrograd organization during the revolution and commissar of labor in the first Soviet government), Mikhail Tomsky (a Politburo member and prominent in the trade union movement), and Aleksei Rykov (commissar for home affairs and then deputy chairman of the Council of Peoples' Commissars). Shlyapnikov and Tomsky had proletarian backgrounds, actually exceptional in the higher ranks of the party – Lenin was a member of the nobility – and even more exceptional among Jewish Bolsheviks. Each, however, also had unusual

---

[26] Dmitri Volkogonov, *Lenin, a New Biography* (New York, 1994), 1–11.

[27] Revealingly, in 1915 Lenin could not even remember Stalin's last name, and John Reed's famous account of the revolution, *Ten Days That Shook the World*, does not mention Stalin once (which later resulted in the book's being banned in the Soviet Union); Medvedev, *Let History Judge*, 35, 48. On the international level, too, Stalin was unknown; he apparently did not even attend the first three meetings of the Communist International (1919, 1920, 1921).

[28] Stephen F. Cohen, *Bukharin and the Bolshevik Revolution* (New York, 1973), 81.

and revealing backgrounds. Shlyapnikov, for example, came from a family of Old Believers, a group that had historically been persecuted under the tsars even more brutally than were Jews.

Mikhail Kalinin, who filled the largely ceremonial post of president of the Soviet Union, is another revealing case. He was a man of limited education and mental horizons, seen as a symbol of the proletarianized peasantry, but his concern for Jewish welfare was so strong and apparently sincere that Jewish Bolsheviks considered him "more Jewish than the Jews." In a much-noted episode, he broke down crying and was unable to finish a speech in which he was describing the killing of Jews in the pogroms of the civil war.[29]

Kalinin's case suggests another category, the jewified non-Jew, to use the language of the anti-Semites. The term, freed of its ugly connotations, might be used to underline an often overlooked point: Even in Russia there were some non-Jews, whether Bolsheviks or not, who respected Jews, praised them abundantly, imitated them, cared about their welfare, and established intimate friendships or romantic liaisons with them. Lenin was of course considered jewified, if not exactly Jewish, by anti-Semites. As noted, he openly and repeatedly praised the role of the Jews in the revolutionary movement; he was one of the most adamant and consistent in the party in his denunciations of pogroms and anti-Semitism more generally.[30] After the revolution, he backed away from his earlier resistance to Jewish nationalism, accepting that under Soviet rule Jewish nationality might be legitimate. On his death bed, Lenin spoke fondly of the Jewish Menshevik Julius Martov, for whom he had always retained a special personal affection in spite of their fierce ideological differences.

An even more remarkable case was Felix Dzerzhinsky, the head of the Cheka, a "non-Jewish Jew" in a different sense. (The destruction of his statue in front of the KGB building in Moscow in August 1991, after the ill-fated putsch by party conservatives, was widely seen as symbolic of the destruction of a hated past of secret police domination.) In origin a member of the Polish gentry, he had learned Yiddish as a young man in Vilna and had established close friendships with many Jews in the revolutionary circles of the town. He had several romances with Jews and finally married one.

The backgrounds and personal contacts of non-Jews such as Lenin, Kalinin, and Dzerzhinsky help explain how it was that so many observers believed the Bolsheviks were mostly Jews or were in some way under Jewish tutelage. The various refinements of Jewishness – traditional Jew, reform Jew, cultural Jew, half-Jew, non-Jewish Jew, self-hating Jew, Karaite, jewified Gentile – did not have much meaning to most of those who were in a life-and-death struggle with the Bolsheviks and who of course were not used to seeing Jews in any

---

[29] D. Charney, *A Yortsendlik Aza, 1914–1924* (New York, 1943), 251; Nedava, *Trotsky and the Jews*, 213.

[30] Cf. Lumer, *Lenin on the Jewish Question*, 135–6.

position of political authority in Russia; to see them in such numbers spoke for some radical undermining of a previously accepted order. The leaders of the anti-Bolshevik White armies were convinced that they were fighting Jews and other foreigners (Georgians, Armenians, Lithuanians, Poles) – but mostly and most importantly Jews – who had somehow seized control of Mother Russia. To most of the Whites the differences between the various revolutionary factions were of little importance; they all appeared alien, foreign in inspiration, jewified, and destructive. Indeed, for many on the right even the liberal Kadets were viewed as westernized and jewified.

Such exaggeration was hardly limited to the White armies. One book published in the West, *The Causes of World Unrest,* presented a list of fifty members of the Bolshevik government and declared that 95 percent of them were Jews, a common conclusion, as was the notion that the Bolsheviks were murderously destructive. Churchill, in discussing the leading role of Jews in the Bolshevik Party, observed that "this amazing race has created another system of morality and philosophy, this one saturated with as much hatred as Christianity was with love."[31] The noted Catholic author and parliamentary deputy Hilaire Belloc, who had favored the Dreyfusards and denounced Beilis's trial, in 1919 wrote *The Jews,* claiming that Bolshevik outrages had created real anti-Semitism in Britain for the first time. His assertion that Jewish Bolsheviks had spread anti-Semitism more widely than ever before was taken up by many others. It would find echoes even at the end of the twentieth century, most notably in the efforts of German historian Ernst Nolte to explain the Holocaust as stemming from Hitler's fear of the Bolsheviks' "Asiatic deeds." Destruction of the Jews by the Nazis was from this perspective to be considered a preventive measure, ultimately one of self-defense.[32]

As early as November 1917 Belloc's friend and intellectual colleague, C. K. Chesterton, had sternly warned the Jews in Great Britain who were sympathetic to the revolution that "if they continue to . . . [incite] people against the soldiers and their wives and widows, they will learn for the first time what anti-Semitism really means."[33] (At this time, the Bolsheviks, having just assumed power, were trying to spread revolutionary defeatism to the West and had begun negotiations to sign a separate peace with Germany.)

In France, observers of nearly all political stripes were even more appalled than the British by the prospect of a separate peace between Germany and Soviet Russia. Anti-Semitism, well entrenched on the right, revived in the rest of the political spectrum, undermining what had been achieved through the patriotic unity of August 1914. The older charges that Jews were unpatriotic

---

[31] Johnson, *History of the Jews,* 457.

[32] Ernst Nolte, *Der europäische Bürgerkrieg, 1917–1945: Nationalsozialismus und Bolschewismus* (Frankfurt, 1987).

[33] Johnson, *History of Jews,* 456; from *The Jewish Chronicle,* Nov. 2, 1917.

or part of a capitalist conspiracy now refocused on the Jew as a social subversive, "taking orders from Moscow."

These anti-Bolshevik passions raged even after the defeat of Germany in the following year, as fear of the spread of revolution from Russia gripped much of the Continent. In the elections of the autumn of 1919, the French right, allied as the *Bloc national* and in many areas grouping all parties except the socialists (SFIO), plastered the walls and kiosks of France with the image of an unshaven revolutionary, demonic and Jewish-looking, a bloody knife between his teeth. The right's campaign was devastatingly effective against the SFIO, whose leaders had made the unwise decision to reject all electoral alliances and identify boldly with the party's prewar revolutionary tradition.

Fear of Jewish radicals and revolutionaries added significantly to a change of opinion in favor of restricting immigration in the United States. Attorney General Mitchell Palmer referred to the "Trozky doctrine" of spreading revolution to the world, "Trozky" himself being "a disreputable alien . . . this lowest of all types known to New York City." In the United States, too, an effort was made to show that the overwhelming majority of the leaders of Soviet Russia were Jews. Jacob Schiff was allegedly involved in the decision to overthrow the tsar,[34] a charge, as we have seen, that had more than a little plausibility since he had fed large amounts of money to revolutionaries in Russia and openly boasted about his role in combating the tsar.[35]

As revolutionary unrest spread to central Europe in late 1918 and 1919, apprehensions – and anti-Semitic fantasies – were further fueled. The Jewish-led Hungarian Soviet regime played an important role. Jews were less numerous in the German Communist Party than in the Hungarian, but they were still important and, again, highly visible. The party's first two leaders, Rosa Luxemburg and, after her murder in January 1919 at the hands of a right-wing paramilitary organization, Paul Levi, were of Jewish origin. Even in France and Italy, with their small and overwhelmingly bourgeois Jewish populations, the emerging Communist parties counted a number of Jews in leadership positions. The main claim to authority of Boris Souvarine, of Russian–Jewish origin, in the French party, was support from Moscow; he had little experience in the party or popularity with its rank-and-file. Thus, even within the various and often violently contending factions of the nascent Communist parties of the West, "foreign Jews, taking orders from Moscow" became a hot issue. It remained mostly taboo in socialist ranks to refer openly to Moscow's

[34] A. Mitchell Palmer, "The Case Against the Reds," *Forum*, Feb. 1920; Leon Poliakov, *History of Anti-Semitism, Suicidal Europe, 1870–1933* (Oxford, 1985), 231–2; Johnson, *History of the Jews*, 459.

[35] For further details, see Zosa Szajkowski, *Jews, Wars, and Communism: The Attitude of American Jews to World War I, The Russian Revolutions of 1917, and Communism (1914–1945)*, vol. 1 (New York, 1972).

agents as Jewish, but the implication was often there that such foreign Jews were destroying western socialism.

News from Russia through the ensuing chaotic years of revolution and civil war was confused and unreliable. Reports of Bolshevik atrocities were sometimes wildly exaggerated, but the truth of terror and counterterror between the Reds and Whites was horrible enough. In western Europe it was feared that such fratricide would spread out of Russia. Even most of those socialists who chose to join the Communist International in 1919 and 1920 argued that revolution in the West would not be as bloody and dictatorial as it was in Russia.[36]

The Bolsheviks justified their assumption of power in backward, underdeveloped Russia on the prediction that proletarian revolution would spread from Russia to the rest of Europe. In retrospect, it is easy to see that the likelihood of world Communist revolution in those years was not great, but that was not the way it appeared to many at the time. A Communist coup was attempted in Berlin in January 1919 (the Spartacus Uprising, when Rosa Luxemburg was killed), and in the course of that tumultuous year in Germany pro-Bolshevik revolutionaries took over, however briefly and confusedly, in Munich. In France a general strike was launched in the spring of 1920, and in the autumn of that year there were massive factory occupations in the industrial north of Italy. Perhaps most worrisome to the western powers, the Red Army, headed by Trotsky, launched an offensive against Poland in the summer of 1920 that was touted as the beginning of a triumphant advance of the Red Army into western Europe. The revolutionary proletariat, it was proclaimed from Moscow, would rise up to welcome the liberating armies of revolutionary Russia. These and similar violent challenges to existing authority all proved abortive or ephemeral. Most were drowned in blood. But they added fuel to the raging fears and fantasies of the time.

Russian Jews in Revolution: From March to November

Although Jews had every reason to hope for the fall of the tsarist regime, they had almost nothing directly to do with the revolutionary events in Petrograd of March 1917. Rather, by 1916 the tsar had so discredited himself that a broad consensus emerged that he had to go. It is revealing that the radical–populist anti-Semite Purishkevich joined forces with members of the court nobility to murder Rasputin, the holy-man "friend" of Nicholas and Alexandra, revered by them for his ability to stop the bleeding of their hemophiliac son and heir to the throne.[37] It is also revealing that by May 1918 Purishkevich offered grudging support to the Soviet regime, even after spending

---

[36] Cf. Lindemann, 'Red Years.'

[37] Alex de Jonge, *The Life and Times of Grigorii Rasputin* (New York, 1982), 302–7, 317–23.

time in its prisons. The Soviets could at least provide order, he believed, and were preferable to the anarchy that threatened the country.[38]

The revolution in March grew out of bread riots in the capital, Petrograd, led mostly by hungry housewives, not self-conscious socialist revolutionaries. Soldiers refused to repress the rioters or to deal with other aspects of civilian restiveness, and that unwillingness then developed to actual mutiny. The Provisional Government that tried thereafter to exercise power faced massive problems. Its authority was challenged by various soviet organizations. The Soviet of Workers' and Soldiers' Deputies was soon established in Petrograd, building on the precedents of the 1905 revolution. The proliferating revolutionary soviets (the word simply means "councils" in Russian) enjoyed a broader popular support than did the Provisional Government, which was made up of former deputies to the last and highly unrepresentative Duma. But the Petrograd Soviet was initially willing to let the Provisional Government assume the daily tasks of governing.

One of the first measures taken by the Provisional Government was a decree conferring complete civil equality upon Russia's Jews. That action was hailed as long overdue by the Russian press; even *Novoe Vremia*, which, as a semiofficial organ before 1917, had often published anti-Semitic material, applauded the move and commented that "nothing evoked more hatred against the former government on the part of Russian society than the persecution of minority groups and religions."[39]

Many of Russia's Jews were jubilant at the news. In some Jewish homes, Passover was celebrated that year with the reading of the decree instead of the traditional Haggada.[40] Plans were quickly made by Jewish activists for an all-Russian Jewish congress. The excited appeal that went out for it proclaimed that whereas elsewhere Jews had received civil equality, only now, in revolutionary Russia, were they also going to receive recognition of their separate nationality *within* another nation.[41] Nothing finally came of this congress, since the Bolshevik Revolution, and then civil war, got in the way.

In Russia, perhaps even more than elsewhere, civil equality for Jews, to say nothing of an official recognition of Jewish nationality, opened up a Pandora's box. The concerns voiced so often before the war – that the Jews, if made equal under the law to non-Jews, would take over Russia – continued to have potent reverberations after 1917, especially after the Bolshevik Revolution in November. Significantly, even in Great Britain, Henry Wickham Steed later wrote that the events of 1917 represented a massive victory for "the Jews": "The joy of Jewry at these events [civil emancipation and then the Bolshevik

[38] Pipes, *Russian Revolution*, 556n.

[39] Louis Greenberg, *The Jews in Russia*, vol. 2 (New Haven, Conn., 1951), 109–10.

[40] Greenberg, *Jews in Russia*, vol. 2, 110.

[41] Baron, *Russian Jew*, 168–9.

takeover] was not merely the joy of triumph over an oppressor; it was also gladness at the downfall of hostile religious and semi-religious institutions." He added that "potent international financial interests were at work in favour of the immediate recognition of the Bolsheviks."[42]

The state of Jewish–Gentile relations by late 1917 was incomparably more envenomed, more filled with mutual fear and suspicion, than it might have been had the tsar granted civil equality to the Jews in, say, 1900, when he and others drew back, claiming that emancipation of the Jews would only awaken much worse anti-Semitism in the general population. Now the tsarist bureaucracy was dissolving; the outsiders were becoming the insiders. Jews who had faced pervasive discrimination and persecution suddenly found government positions opened to them while closed to the older privileged classes, who were overwhelmingly of Great Russian background. That Jews, among the most highly educated and urbanized of Russia's population, should benefit dramatically is not surprising, but that rapid change in fortunes entailed a backlash – jealousies, apprehension, and a perception of a "Jewish takeover."

In balance, the initial benefits for some Jews were outweighed by the tragic misfortunes to the great majority of them caught in the middle of revolution and civil war. It is possible that the Jews, given their previous degree of oppression, gained more and suffered less than the rest of the population in a time of unparalleled hardships for all of the people of the Russian empire. Even that convoluted speculation risks giving an inaccurate impression, for in many areas Jews were violently attacked from all sides of the political spectrum: from the right as revolutionaries (or sympathizers with the revolution) and from the left as capitalists and exploiters.

Still, after 1917, especially after November 1917, there was in Europe a most remarkable change in the status quo: Large numbers of individual Jews assumed, for the first time in modern history, a major role in the government of non-Jewish peoples. Such was the case not only in Russia but in other areas, most notably Hungary and Germany. At first, there were no Jews in the shifting cabinets of the Russian Provisional Government, at least in part because those Jews who were qualified feared their presence might discredit the new government.[43] Even the Council of People's Commissars of November, responsible to the Soviets and composed entirely of Bolsheviks, numbered only one Jew, Leon Trotsky, although that soon changed.

The near-universal jubilation at the fall of tsarism did not last long. The new Provisional Government soon found itself confronted with a series of urgent crises, conflicting claims, and pressing demands, many of which were ultimately irreconcilable. No doubt the most important of them was whether

---

[42] Henry Wickham Steed, *Through Thirty Years – 1892–1922: A Personal Narrative*, vol. 2 (New York, 1924), 391; Nedava, *Trotsky and the Jews*, 140, 256.

[43] Margolin, *Jews of Eastern Europe*, 8.

Russia should continue the war. In retrospect at least, the new government's decision to honor Russia's alliance with France and Great Britain and to launch another offensive in the spring of 1917 seems to have been a mistaken one, making possible the ensuing victory of the Bolsheviks.

It is common to speak of the many mistakes made by the Provisional Government, but it may well be that no party, or coalition of parties, could have effectively ruled Russia in the spring and summer of 1917. Certainly the Bolshevik Party could not have done so initially, since at that time, in stark contrast to the legends it subsequently nurtured, it was scarcely more than a sect, with little popular following and weak, disoriented cadres. Part of the secret of the eventual Bolshevik victory was the party's initial marginality; Lenin and his lieutenants could stand on the sidelines while the other parties exhausted and discredited themselves. By the late summer of 1917 many who had at first paid little attention to the Bolsheviks began to take them seriously, if only out of frustration with the poor showing of the Provisional Government.

The rapid transformation of the Bolshevik Party from being regarded as a near lunatic fringe to one that enjoyed majority support in the soviets of the capital is a remarkable story. However crucial the role of the decision by the Provisional Government to continue the war, the talents of Bolsheviks in the techniques of rallying, or at least neutralizing, key elements of the working class and soldiery, in the context of a chaotic disintegration of all authority, cannot be ignored. Even more crucial was the Bolsheviks' ruthlessness in retaining power once it had been seized.

Indeed, the feat of holding onto power in the months and years after November 1917 was finally more impressive than seizing it. At any rate, "seizure of power" is a misleading term, and Bolshevik "rule" was at first not so much the establishment of a new kind of authority as the recognition of the collapse of authority. To that degree, the Bolsheviks, although formally believers in a strong, centralized state under a proletarian dictatorship, resembled anarchists more than Marxists. Rather than resolving the conflicting demands of the Russian people, the Bolsheviks began by acceding to them all – indeed, encouraging them – in a way that the Provisional Government refused to do: to the peasants, land; to the soldiers, peace; to the workers, control of production; to the minorities, promises of autonomy or independence; to all of Russia's suffering population, promises of bread. Whatever the adroit efforts of Lenin or Trotsky to reconcile these opportunistic promises with Marxist theory, they remained opportunistic promises. They were not reconcilable with Marxism or indeed with any other revolutionary theories, except possibly anarchism. The simple truth is that Bolshevik promises were a means to power.

Beyond the tortured reasoning of Russian Marxist theories lay one proposition that did make some sense: The seizure of power by the Bolsheviks in industrially backward Russia was only the first step on the way to world revolution. Russia would provide a spark that would ignite proletarian uprisings in more advanced areas, most importantly German-speaking central Europe, and the victory of communist revolution there would assure its spread to the rest of the world. In a related way, revolution in Russia would break the chain of world imperialism, making economic survival impossible for the western capitalist powers.

The implication of this idea of the spread of revolution to Russia's neighbors, and eventually to the world, closely resembled a fantasy of the anti-Semites: That the Jews, in the guise of proletarian revolutionaries, sought to rule the world. But even those who did not perceive the Bolsheviks as a front for a worldwide Jewish conspiracy were alarmed by the idea of ever-widening social revolution. Soon many of them began to take measures to snuff out the nascent revolutionary regime in Russia.

Before dealing with the hostility of the capitalist world in general, the Bolsheviks had more immediate problems. Peace had to be made with Germany, and enemies inside the former Russian Empire had to be fought. Peace negotiations with Germany extended through late 1917 and into early 1918; the peace eventually signed was not so much negotiated as dictated by the Germans. With their utterly commanding military position, the German generals felt no need to agree to any of the demands of Russia's new rulers and simply ordered their troops to advance further when those leaders tried to negotiate favorable terms. In the final treaty, signed at Brest–Litovsk in March 1918, much of European Russia was handed over to German control.

Most Bolshevik leaders opposed the treaty, but Lenin believed that no other choice was possible if the Bolsheviks were to retain power. He was almost certainly correct. The same ruthless realism characterized Lenin's reactions to the threats to Bolshevik power inside the country. Having released the genie of rebellion and having encouraged the disintegration of all existing state forms of repression (army, police, courts, bureaucracy), he had to build a new state, new repressive agencies, almost from scratch. It was a laborious and extremely messy process, some of the abominable details of which are only now coming to light.

The Red Terror – a Jewish Terror?

The task of establishing political legitimacy and new agencies of repression was all the more herculean because the Bolsheviks had never come close to enjoying majority support in the country as a whole, in spite of their fleeting and often contrived majorities in some of the urban soviets, especially those of large industrial cities such as Petrograd and Moscow. Whatever support the Bolsheviks did enjoy in the country at large was mercurial and based on vague or false perceptions. The winning slogans, "all power to the soviets!" or "land, bread, and peace!" obscured what was really happening: The Bolshevik Party was establishing itself, behind the cover of soviet democracy, as a single-party, minority dictatorship, determined to crush all challenges to its authority. Many of the revolutionary workers, soldiers, and sailors who supported the Bolsheviks in the late summer and autumn of 1917 against the Provisional Government assumed that the new government would represent all revolutionary socialists, not just a faction of them. In the vote to the Constituent Assembly in the autumn of 1917, the only national election that came close to the liberal–democratic ideal of universal manhood suffrage, the Bolsheviks won only about a quarter of the vote. In that election Jewish voters apparently cast the majority of their votes for the Zionists and the nonsocialist parties, mostly the Kadets.[44]

Lenin had categorically refused to ally with other parties, though he did briefly relent, from December 1917 to March 1918, by bringing the left of the Socialist Revolutionary Party into the Council of People's Commissars. The notion that the majority as expressed in parliamentary elections had a legitimate claim to rule the nation was not in any event something that Leninist theory recognized. The Bolsheviks claimed to speak for the oppressed, even if the oppressed did not immediately recognize the role the Bolshevik Party was to play. Similarly, Lenin and his followers, as professional revolutionaries who "knew better," believed themselves to be the representatives of historical progress, on the right side of history, against the forces of reaction inside Russia and in the world. Such claims were easily translated into justifications for systematic terror against the enemies of the new regime. Those enemies, similarly, began almost immediately to use violence and terror against the Bolsheviks, providing Lenin and his lieutenants with the excuse that terror was necessary as a response, in defense of the revolution.

The Bolsheviks ruled as an unapologetic minority dictatorship. In such a rule the secret police became an indispensable weapon. One of the first steps taken after the formation of the Council of People's Commissars in November was to establish the Cheka. The man who came forward to head it, with Lenin's enthusiastic approval, was Felix Dzerzhinsky. He was already an experienced activist, one who had spent many years in prison and in exile. He had only just been released from a five-year prison term with the general amnesties for political prisoners in March 1917. As head of the new secret police, his devotion to the revolutionary cause was "so intense," in the words of Isaac Deutscher, "that it made him a fanatic who would shrink from no act of terror so long as he was convinced that it was necessary for the cause." At the same time he was "incorruptible, selfless, and intrepid – a soul of deep poetic sensibility, constantly stirred to compassion for the weak and suffering."[45] Another

---

[44] Margolin, *Jews of Eastern Europe*, 13. Margolin maintains that support for the Bolsheviks came overwhelmingly from non-Jewish workers.

[45] Isaac Deutscher, *The Prophet Unarmed* (Oxford, 1959), 85.

historian has commented that Dzerzhinsky "subordinated all accepted ethical principles to whatever cause he was serving. Lenin's word, the Party's command, these were his only laws."[46] But the appallingly cruel measures taken by the Cheka tormented him; the "objective needs" of the revolution to protect itself were "in permanent conflict with Dzerzhinsky's emotional, romantic temperament, with his inborn compassion, which he could never banish, and which induced agonies of remorse for the bloody deeds committed by his Cheka."[47]

In a New Year's celebration, December 31, 1918, after many drinks, Dzerzhinsky beseeched Lenin and other party leaders to shoot him on the spot: "I have spilt so much blood that I no longer have any right to live. You must shoot me now."[48] On a later occasion he lamented that "only saints or scoundrels" could survive in secret police work, "but now the saints are running away from me and I am left with the scoundrels."[49]

This Dostoevskian character, known to contemporaries as the "saint of the revolution," had, as noted, many close relationships with Jews and was widely believed by anti-Semites to be himself Jewish. His youthful activities with the Jewish Bund and with the Polish social democrats put him into close contact with the alienated Jewish intelligentsia of Poland. They composed an overwhelming majority of the top leaders of social democracy – more so than in the Russian social democrats, even more than in the Menshevik faction of the movement.

Dzerzhinsky's close affiliations with Jews continued in the Cheka, notably and notoriously with Uritsky, the head of the Cheka in Petrograd. In some areas, for example, the Ukraine, the Cheka leadership was overwhelmingly Jewish. By early 1919 Cheka organizations in Kiev were 75 percent Jewish, in a city where less than a decade earlier Jews had been officially forbidden to reside, except under special dispensation, and constituted about 1 percent of the total population. According to the testimony of a Cheka officer who later defected to the Whites, in the autumn of 1918–1919 the Chekists in Kiev went on a rampage of random violence, rape, and looting, led by a Jewish "riffraff [that was] incapable of other work, cut off from the Jewish community, although careful to spare fellow Jews."[50] Dzerzhinsky had initially instructed his lieutenants in the Cheka to avoid taking Jewish hostages, perhaps because of his sympathies for Jews but more likely because he recognized that Jewish hostages would carry little weight as far as the mostly anti-Semitic opponents of the Bolshevik regime were concerned. After the first few years, however,

---

46 George Leggett, *The Cheka, Lenin's Political Police* (Oxford, 1981), 251.

47 Ibid., 252.

48 Ibid.; *In tsvei revoluties.*

49 Deutscher, *Prophet Unarmed*, 109; Leggett, *Cheka*, 266.

50 Pipes, *Russian Revolution*, 824.

Jewish "bourgeois" hostages were taken with increasing frequency by the Bolsheviks.[51]

The pattern of employing non-Slavic ethnic minorities in the Cheka was duplicated in many other areas of Russia. George Leggett, the most recent and authoritative historian of the Russian secret police, speculates that the use of outsiders may have been a conscious policy, since such "detached elements could be better trusted not to sympathise with the repressed local population."[52] Of course, in the Ukrainian case that population had the reputation of being especially anti-Semitic, further diminishing the potential sympathies of Jewish Chekists in dealing with it.

Aside from such speculations, the reasons for the Jewish overrepresentation in the Cheka appear fairly obvious. Given the high proportion of Jews in the revolutionary movement and their generally higher educational levels, it is not surprising that many of them turned to intelligence activity, at least to its upper ranks. (Lower-level Cheka functionaries, those most directly involved in the actual arrests, tortures, and killings, were known to be less educated; some were even illiterate.)[53] Party activists had had much direct experience with the tsarist secret police, or Okhrana, and the Okhrana had frequent recourse to Jewish spies, double agents, and agents provocateurs. That some of those men would, after the revolution, go to work for the Cheka was only natural. It is instructive that the high percentage of Jews in the secret police continued well into the 1930s, when the proportion of Jews gradually diminished in most other areas of the Soviet and party cadres.

Work with the Cheka offered other attractions. Its agents were normally exempt from military service, yet they enjoyed the same privileges in regard to food rations as did those in the military, no small consideration in times of desperate scarcities. Top Cheka officials were among the narrow elite that was entitled to motor cars and other perquisites. And there was simply the matter of prestige and power: "Cheka personnel regarded themselves as a class apart, the very incarnation of the Party's will, with a power of life or death over lesser mortals."[54] Comparisons to the secret police in Nazi Germany have tempted many observers, as has the suggestion that the Nazis learned from, even copied, the Bolsheviks in this as in other regards.[55] Whether or not these suggestions have any merit, the extent to which both Cheka and Gestapo leaders prided themselves in being an elite corps, characterized by unyielding toughness – unmoved by sympathy for their often innocent victims and willing to carry out the most stomach-turning atrocities in the name of an ideal – is striking.

[51] Ibid., 824n.
[52] Leggett, *Cheka,* 263.
[53] Ibid., 265.
[54] Ibid.
[55] Cf. Pipes, *Russian Revolution,* 827, 832 ff.

The overrepresentation of Jews in secret police work led to grumbling inside the party. In a Politburo meeting in April 1919 Trotsky commented that "the Latvians and Jews constituted a vast percentage of those employed in the Cheka," and he noted that the lack of those groups in combat units at the front, where people were dying for the revolution, was causing a "strong chauvinist agitation." He recommended that measures be introduced to assure that "there will be a more even distribution of all nationalities between the front and rear."[56]

Such concerns were characteristic of Trotsky. When he later discovered that Jews in the Red Army were highly overrepresented in office jobs, away from the front, he immediately ordered many of them to dangerous combat zones. He was similarly much concerned by the evidence that Jews were filling up the white-collar jobs in the new government, instead of joining the factory proletariat.[57] We have seen how in the West denunciations of Jews as slackers and war profiteers were widespread by 1916, as was the belief that Jews were both psychologically and physically unsuited for combat. In Russia, the stereotype of the Jew as physically weak and unenthusiastic about military service was even more pervasive. In the internationally famous novel of Mikhail Sholokhov, *And Quiet Flows the Don,* there is a passage describing how during the civil war, the commander of a machine-gun detachment discovers, to his astonishment, that one of his recruits is Jewish – and a woman. He remarks, "Well, the Jews have a certain reputation. And I know many workers believe it to be true – you see, I am a worker, too – that the Jews do all the ordering and never go under fire themselves."[58]

Trotsky's concern that the non-Jewish masses might perceive the Jews as privileged in the new regime was widely shared in the party. Partly in response to such concerns, a special commission to deal with Jewish issues was created under the Commissariat of Nationalities. This *Yevseksiia* (Jewish Section), led by Jews, was assigned the task of bringing the Jewish population into harmony with the principles of communism. It was a tall order, given the predominance of petty commerce among Jews. Thirty-five percent of them were by this time branded as *lishentsy* (deprived, as a propertied class, of all political rights under Soviet democracy), whereas only 6 percent of the non-Jewish population fell into that category. The leaders of the Yevseksiia attacked Jewish religion with special ferocity, arguing that unless Judaism was forthrightly denounced as a tool of reactionary forces, the masses would not understand the regime's attacks on Christianity. (This was a period when some 32 bishops, 1,560 priests, and 7,000 monks and nuns had been killed by revolutionaries.)

---

[56] Leggett, *Cheka,* 262.

[57] Isaac Deutscher, *The Non-Jewish Jew* (London, 1968), 70.

[58] Mikhail Sholokhov, *And Quiet Flows the Don* (Moscow, 1968 [first Russian edition, 1928]), 536; Nedava, *Trotsky and the Jews,* 253–4.

The head of the government-supported Russian Society of Atheists was a Jew, Emilian Yaroslavsky.[59]

For those ordinary Jews who retained attachments to the traditions of their ancestors, the Yevseksiia loomed as a form of the Red Terror; it came to be feared scarcely less than the Cheka, for the leaders of the Yevseksiia, too, tended to spin out of control, to lose a sense of reality and humanity. And, like the officials of the tsar, its leaders often expressed frustration at the stubborn tenacity of the Jews, their passive yet effective resistance to being "reformed." The Yevseksiia's program undoubtedly came down to the destruction of a separate Jewish life in Russia, as had been the program of some tsarist ministers.

The worst excesses of the Red Terror occurred after the attempts on Lenin's life. On January 1, 1918, a *Pravda* article warned: "Let them [the bourgeoisie] remember: for every one of our heads they will answer with a hundred of theirs. . . . If they endeavour to destroy the people's leaders, they will themselves be mercilessly destroyed."[60] Lenin escaped injury this time, although the Swiss socialist Fritz Platten, who was with him, was wounded. The next assassination attempt was more nearly successful: On August 30, 1918, after a speech that ended with the words, "with us there is only one way, victory or death," Lenin was seriously wounded by revolver shots from the gun of a young Jewish woman, Fanya Kaplan. She had already been sentenced to life imprisonment in 1906 in Kiev for participation in a terrorist act. By 1918 she was associated with the Socialist Revolutionary Party, but she denied having acted as the agent of any party; it was an entirely individual action, she maintained, against a man she believed had betrayed the revolution. After a speedy investigation, she was executed by the Cheka and all traces of her body destroyed.[61]

Uritsky was assassinated on the same day by a Jewish student, Leonid Kanegisser, in revenge for the execution of a close friend of his by the Cheka. He, too, claimed to work alone, but because of his associations with the Socialist Revolutionary Party and with the Mikhailovsky Academy (where a plot against the regime had been hatched in which his friend was involved), his act and that of Kaplan were regarded as part of a larger conspiracy. Kanegiesser was also immediately executed, and the Communist and Soviet press clamored for wider revenge. The organ of the Red Army, *Krasnaya Gazeta,* wrote in words that were by no means atypical: "Without mercy, without sparing, we will kill our enemies in scores of hundreds. Let them be thousands, let them drown themselves in their own blood. For the blood of Lenin and Uritsky . . . let there be floods of blood of the bourgeois – more blood, as much as possible."[62]

---

[59] Baron, *Russian Jew,* 176; Nedava, *Trotsky and the Jews,* 105–7.

[60] Leggett, *Cheka,* 106.

[61] Volkogonov, *Lenin,* 219–29 (which includes new material from the archives).

[62] Leggett, *Cheka,* 108.

The number of Jews involved in the terror and counterterror of this period is striking. In the decade or so immediately before 1914 many tsarist officials, including the highest ministers of the tsar, had been killed by Jewish assassins. Aside from Kaplan and Kanegiesser, Jacob Blumkin, again a Jewish member of the Socialist Revolutionary Party, assassinated Count Mirbach, the German ambassador to Moscow, on July 6, 1918, in hopes of stirring up the war again between Germany and Russia.[63] Before 1917, the large number of Jewish assassins could be plausibly attributed to the anti-Semitic oppression of the tsarist regime. But such explanations fall short in the case of assassins like Kaplan, Kanegiesser, and Blumkin. These many Jewish terrorists helped to nurture, even when they killed Jewish Chekists, the belief that Jews, especially once they had broken from the confines of their traditional faith, turned naturally to fanaticism and anarchic destructiveness.

An even more important institution than the Cheka in defending the revolution was the Red Army, and, again, Jews played a key role in its leadership. To be more precise, it was above all one Jew, Trotsky, although Jewish commissars attached to Red Army units were essential to its operations, and Jewish soldiers in some areas constituted an important presence in it. Such was especially the case in Byelo–Russia and the Ukraine, where pogroms remained a constant threat. Many Jews joined the Red Army as a means of survival.

Trotsky fascinated a broad public inside and outside Russia. In Hungary, a Jewish observer who was in fact hostile to the Bolsheviks nonetheless wrote: "The revolutionary flame which has burned beneath the surface of world history is now blazing up for the first time in a Jewish genius: Leo Trotsky! It is blazing with a god-like force that shames every earlier revolutionary craving and consciousness."[64] However, if a case can be made for Dzerzhinsky as a jewified Gentile, an even stronger case can be made for Trotsky as "gentilized" Jew, who generally preferred the company of Gentiles and eventually married one. He was prone to denials of his Jewishness (Asked point-blank by a member of the Bund whether he considered himself a Jew or a Russian, Trotsky emphatically replied "neither, I am a social democrat!"). In his autobiography he made much of the influence of non-Jews on him, beginning with the handyman on his father's farm. Anti-Semitism, which was of course all around him, did not scar his psyche, at least not in the same way that it did so many young Jews in the late nineteenth and early twentieth century. By his own testimony he did not sense hostility to him as a Jew by the Gentiles he came to know, whether in his native village or in the russified Lutheran school he later attended in cosmopolitan Odessa.

Trotsky's positive experiences with the non-Jewish world were paralleled by negative ones with Jews. He was little attracted to, and was mostly repelled by,

[63] Nedava, *Trotsky and the Jews*, 157.
[64] McCagg, *Jewish Geniuses*, 207.

the Jewishness and Judaism he encountered as a boy and young adolescent. For him achieving a cultured and civilized status meant abandoning not only the Ukrainian peasant dialect and culture of his childhood but also Yiddish and all its cultural associations. "Abandon" is not quite the proper word in the latter case, since Yiddish was not spoken in his home, and he appears to have been unable to understand it when he later came into close contact with Yiddish speakers. The Russian language, the language of Tolstoy, Dostoevsky, and Chekhov, was the one he enthusiastically chose as his own, much as Jews elsewhere chose German, Magyar, French, or English as the languages of high culture. He remained throughout his life a stickler for correct speech and a decorum in dress and manner that implicitly rejected much of the lifestyle of the common people.

Trotsky did not ignore or deny the importance of Jewish issues, but his attention to them lacked the focus and the obsessiveness seen in many Jewish activists of the day. The pride he took in being admired by non-Jews, or even being mistaken for one, was only too obvious. He recounted in his autobiography how a Cossack who had served with him in the Red Army had been captured and then taunted by his captors for having fought under the command of a Jew. The Cossack indignantly insisted that Trotsky was not a Jew; he was "a fighter . . . ours . . . a Russian! . . . It is Lenin who is a Communist Jew."[65] Trotsky similarly cited with transparent pride a short story by Isaac Babel, in which a Russian soldier defended the leader of the Red Army against charges of working for the Jews. The soldier insisted that Trotsky, Lenin, and other Bolshevik leaders worked "like Niggers" for the Russian common people.[66]

Trotsky recounted these stories because they flattered him, but he was perfectly aware that his Jewish origins were a source of suspicion and hatred by large numbers of the common people in the Russian Empire. He repeatedly observed how Lenin, as a Great Russian, was somehow more genuinely at one with the people than he was. When Lenin first suggested to him that he take the position of commissar of home affairs [interior], Trotsky refused, saying that the enemies of the new regime would exploit his Jewish origin. However, he then accepted the position of commissar of defense, where he was finally far more visible – admired, feared, and hated – than he might have been as commissar for home affairs.

Jewish or gentilized, Trotsky was a man of unusual talents. The neoconservative writer Paul Johnson has provocatively described Trotsky as the "executive agent" of the revolution, while Lenin was merely "the architect of the *Putsch*" of November 1917.[67] According to Johnson,

---

[65] Leon Trotsky, *My Life: An Attempt at an Autobiography* (New York, 1930), 360–1.

[66] Nedava, *Trotsky and the Jews*, 260.

[67] Johnson, *History of the Jews*, 450.

Trotsky taught Lenin the significance of workers' soviets and how to exploit them. It was Trotsky who personally organized and led the armed uprising which actually overthrew the Provisional Government and placed the Bolsheviks in power. It was Trotsky who created . . . the Red Army, and who ensured the physical survival of the new Communist regime during the Civil War. . . .[68]

Trotsky's paramount role in the revolution cannot be denied; Johnson's views, even if exaggerated, underline how powerful and durable has been the mystique around Trotsky's name. He was second to Lenin, but a strong second, a point that Lenin himself freely recognized. One must pause to take in the significance of it all: That a man born of Jewish parents in the Russian Empire should become not only an accomplished revolutionary propagandist but also a man of action, of breath-taking personal bravery, an orator wildly popular with the industrial working class, and a brilliant military leader. There was no Jew in modern times, at least until the creation of the state of Israel, to rival him.

If one accepts that anti-Semitism was most potently driven by anxiety and fear, as distinguished from contempt, then the extent to which Trotsky became a source of preoccupation for anti-Semites is significant. Here, too, Johnson's words are suggestive: He writes of Trotsky's "demonic" power – the same term, revealingly, used repeatedly by others in referring to Zinoviev's oratory or Uritsky's ruthlessness. Trotsky's boundless self-confidence, his notorious arrogance, and sense of superiority were other traits often associated with Jews. Fantasies there were about Trotsky and other Bolsheviks, but there were also realities around which the fantasies grew.

Stalin and Trotsky

Even though Stalin was capable of crude jokes about Jews, he also spoke out against anti-Semitism throughout his career. To this day scholars differ as to the importance of anti-Semitism and related Jewish issues in Stalin's victory over Trotsky. There is little question that Stalin and some of his supporters resorted to anti-Semitic innuendoes against Trotsky in the mid-1920s. Whether they were of decisive importance, however, may be doubted, for Stalin was a formidable opponent, one who might have defeated even a non-Jew with Trotsky's many talents.

At first it seemed that Trotsky held all the good cards, that after Lenin's series of strokes, beginning in early 1922 and ending in his death in January 1924, Trotsky was the heir apparent, the only Bolshevik leader who came close to being Lenin's peer. But this initial strength, or appearance of it, may finally have been Trotsky's greatest weakness. He was not popular with most party leaders in part because he had made no effort to conceal his sense of superiority to them. Since they so feared Trotsky and what his leadership of the party

---

[68] Ibid., 451.

might mean for their own futures, Zinoviev, Kamenev, and Stalin came together in the so-called Triumvirate, with Stalin the junior member and Zinoviev the senior one.

Since Zinoviev and Kamenev were themselves of Jewish origin, the Triumvirate did not resort to anti-Jewish innuendoes in the beginning of the power struggle. Moreover, at this point, some of Trotsky's most prominent supporters, such as Yevgenii Preobrazhensky, were non-Jews. Much more at issue than Jewishness in the recriminations that marked the beginnings of the struggle for power was Trotsky's pre-1917, non-Bolshevik record, especially his sometimes vituperative conflicts with Lenin. Trotsky had, for example, once described Lenin as a "professional exploiter of every kind of backwardness in the Russian working class," and he had added that "the whole edifice of Leninism at present is built upon lying and falsification."[69]

The records of Zinoviev and Kamenev in the crucial days of early November 1917 constituted their most obvious weaknesses. Both had violated party discipline and had publicly denounced, in a nonparty paper, the party's plans to take power, earning Lenin's fury and his demand that they be expelled from the party, though he later retracted it. Trotsky linked this faint heartedness to the more general danger of a complacent party bureaucracy, a danger that Lenin, too, had warned against in the last years of his life.

The Triumvirate's fear of Trotsky blended into a larger concern in the party that Trotsky had Bonapartist aspirations. Bolshevik leaders were careful students of the French Revolution. They claimed to recognize certain laws of revolutionary development, suggesting that in Russia, as in France after 1794, a thermidorian stage, and then a Bonapartist one, were to be expected. The New Economic Policy, introduced in early 1921, which drew back from the War Communism of the preceding years and allowed a limited amount of private enterprise, was widely considered to be thermidorian in tendency. The concern that a strong man might soon make a bid for power was openly discussed in the party. Of all those who might betray the revolution, the outsider, Trotsky, with his military position, insatiable ego, sovereign disdain for other party leaders, and overbearing manners seemed the most likely candidate.

Speculations that he was destined to be Russia's Napoleon outraged Trotsky. That he so readily relinquished his military offices in early 1925, as the power struggle intensified, may be partly explained by his concern to demonstrate beyond doubt that he was not a Bonaparte, that his attachment to revolutionary principles was unshakable. Therein lurked yet another potentially anti-Jewish theme. Trotsky put forth the theory, to which the term "Permanent Revolution" became associated, that the Soviet state could not long survive without revolution in the West. Therefore, every effort was to be made to

[69] Robert F. Tucker, *Stalin as Revolutionary: A Study in History and Personality* (New York, 1973), 349–54.

speed revolution along in Europe, whereas Soviet Russia had to be prepared to take advantage of the inevitable next wave of revolution. Stalin, and the party's right wing more generally, came to be identified with the slogan "Socialism in One Country," which meant that the new Soviet state could and should begin building socialism on its own, without necessarily being aided in the near future by more advanced industrial countries.

This bare summary of the two positions does not do justice to their many subtleties, but it should be sufficient to suggest the symbolism involved: The stance of the party right wing could appeal to Great Russian nationalism, whereas that of Trotsky and the left implied that Russia could not arrive at the promised land of socialism without help from more advanced countries. Similarly, Permanent Revolution could be perceived as a cosmopolitan ideology, one that appealed to the rootless and countryless – in short, the Jews. Socialism in One Country promised a reprieve from the years of revolutionary crisis and constant warfare, while Permanent Revolution implied yet many more years of struggle and sacrifice. To a population as exhausted as that of the Soviet republics in the early 1920s, Stalin's moderate position had an understandably wider appeal, whereas that of Trotsky – easily dismissed as a fanatical and destructive Jew – understandably less.

Stalin's personality, too, suggested modesty, realism, and moderation, as contrasted to Trotsky, who was perceived as an adventurer, a brilliant gambler. Trotsky's traits were appropriate to the years 1917 to 1921, but he seemed somehow out of his element in times of peace and hum-drum reconstruction, when the revolutionary mystique had disappeared. Similarly, Stalin, as the junior partner in the Triumvirate, ostensibly reserved and self-effacing, was consistently underestimated by those around him, perhaps by Trotsky most of all. In this personal realm, too, it is possible to detect subliminal themes of Gentile and Jew. Trotsky was uncompromising and ferocious in polemic; Stalin, the unassuming, hardworking party secretary, repeatedly played the role of mediator, of simple and faithful representative of the party's will, making many friendships and clients, which his job as party secretary facilitated. Trotsky's "colossal arrogance and an inability or unwillingness to show any human kindness or to be attentive to people, the absence of that charm which always surrounded Lenin, condemned [him] . . . to a certain loneliness." (These are the words of Anatoly Vasilievich Lunarcharsky, the first commissar for education and, at least for a while, a close personal friend of Trotsky's. That qualifying "at least for a while" might be applied to large number of those who worked closely with Trotsky but who were finally repelled by his personal traits.[70])

Stalin seemed willing to recognize Trotsky's value to the party; he in fact resisted calls to oust him. The gray and unambitious party secretary thus

---

[70] Anatoly Vasilievich Lunacharsky, *Revolutionary Silhouettes* (London, 1967), 62.

impressed many in the party as the man most to be trusted with power. Zinoviev, who was even more ferocious in polemic than Trotsky, seemed likely to be corrupted by power. Zinoviev's widely lamented deceitfulness also did not help his cause; "he was a man who won little true sympathy from anyone."[71]

Trotsky further weakened his position by joining in the chorus of hero worship for the party's deceased leader. He recognized, in a way wholly untypical of him in other regards, how Lenin had been right, and he wrong, especially in issues pertaining to the organization and leading role of the party. In the debates before the war, Trotsky had denounced Lenin's concept of the party as highly dangerous; it would lead to a "dictatorship *over* the proletariat." Such a party would be especially dangerous, Trotsky added, when led by a man with Lenin's "malicious and repulsive suspiciousness."[72] In short, Trotsky's all-too-eloquent pen before 1917, his penchant not only to defeat ideological opponents but to demolish and humiliate them caused him much embarrassment when the party was reminded of what he had once said about Lenin.

Even after 1917 Lenin had made remarks about Trotsky that proved no less awkward if Trotsky was to become Lenin's successor. One of the mildest in tone, but also one of the most damaging, was in a casual conversation to Maxim Gorky: Lenin observed that Trotsky was "not one of us. With us but not of us."[73] In angrier moments, Lenin had branded Trotsky's behavior as "bureaucratic, unsoviet, unsocialist, incorrect, and politically harmful."[74] And in a less polemical mood, on his death bed, composing his famous "Testament," Lenin warned about Trotsky's "excessive self-confidence" and his "disposition to be too much attracted to the administrative aspect of affairs."[75]

Trotsky was aware of the traits that alienated so many from him, though he seemed unable to change. "In my inner life . . .", he wrote in his autobiography, "individuals occupied a lesser place than books and ideas. . . . For a long time people passed through my mind like random shadows. . . . I frequently trod on the toes of personal prejudice, friendly favoritism, or vanity. Stalin carefully picked up the men whose toes had been trodden upon."[76]

Trotsky did not mention the extent to which tactlessness, arrogance, unshakable self-confidence, rigid moralism, and fanatical idealism fit into anti-Semitic stereotypes. Of course, a swaggering self-confidence and a sense of persevering against all odds characterized nearly all Bolsheviks, Lenin most of all. Yet, by all accounts, the special quality of Trotsky's arrogance stood out. Again, Trotsky acknowledged what others complained about: that he lacked

[71] Medvedev, *Let History Judge*, 140.

[72] Nedava, *Trotsky and the Jews*, 149.

[73] Maxim Gorky, *Days with Lenin* (New York, 1932), 57; Nedava, *Trotsky and the Jews*, 6.

[74] Tucker, *Stalin*, 349–54.

[75] Ibid., 270.

[76] Trotsky, *My Life*, 59, 442; Nedava, *Trotsky and the Jews*, 168–9.

deeply emotional, experiential bonds to the Russian masses, or to any national or ethnic group.[77] One of his biographers has termed him "the wandering Jew – in modern garb."[78]

With Trotsky out of the competition, Stalin turned his attention to his former allies, Zinoviev and Kamenev, feeling freer at the same time to resort to anti-Jewish themes. By that time (1926), in addition, there was a clearer alignment of prominent Jewish Communists on the left of the party, in what was called the United Opposition, whereas Jews on the party's right, supporting Stalin and his new ally, Bukharin, were less common. That alignment made Stalin's job all the easier and the temptation to play a subtle anti-Semitic game all the more irresistible. At the 1927 Comintern Congress in Moscow, Karl Radek reportedly asked some delegates a riddle: "What is the difference between Moses and Stalin?" The answer: "Moses took the Jews out of Egypt; Stalin takes them out of the Communist Party."[79]

The game remained subtle at the highest levels of the party, although it could be played crudely away from the center of power, at the local levels of the party and state, where sneering references were made to "petty bourgeois elements" and where Jewish party members found themselves isolated or removed from responsible posts. At times there were ugly episodes, in which the insulting term *zhidy* was used.[80] But the official stance against anti-Semitism was constantly reiterated by leading party organs; Stalin denounced it as "an extreme form of race chauvinism, . . . a dangerous survival of cannibalism." He assured Jews throughout the world that "according to the laws of the USSR, active anti-Semites are punished with death."[81]

To some observers Stalin's anti-Semitism became unmistakable only after 1928. It then grew until, by the Moscow Show Trials of the mid-1930s, it approached that of the Nazis. But not all scholars have agreed with those evaluations. Significantly, the preceding remarks of Stalin's date from January 1931, and for many Jews, even anti-Communist ones, the Soviet Union retained a reputation through the 1930s as the least anti-Semitic of the great powers. As one of them wrote, "We are accustomed to look at the Soviet Union as our sole consolation as far as anti-Semitism is concerned. . . . All those who have been to the Soviet Union, Jews and Gentiles alike, have brought back the word that there is no anti-Semitism in the life of the country."[82]

In evaluating what now seems an astonishing blindness, one must remember what these observers were comparing the Soviet Union to, how rampant

---

[77] Nedava, *Trotsky and the Jews*, 134–5.

[78] Ibid., 169.

[79] Ibid., 268.

[80] Ibid., 174–6.

[81] Ibid., 171–2.

[82] Ibid., 186.

anti-Semitism was in the interwar years, especially in the 1930s, even in the liberal democracies. Moreover, to many Jews after 1933, the Soviet Union had a peculiar status: It was the worst enemy of their worst enemy, Nazi Germany. The issue was not so simple as "my enemy's enemy is my friend," but even those who were not blind to the faults of the Soviet regime seemed to feel that the Soviet Union and the Communist movement allied with it throughout the world stood as the most unshakable bulwark against Nazism and anti-Semitism.

Determining Stalin's real attitude to Jews is difficult. Not only did he repeatedly speak out against anti-Semitism but both his son and daughter married Jews, and several of his closest and most devoted lieutenants from the late 1920s through the 1930s were of Jewish origin, for example, Lazar Moiseyevich Kaganovich, Maxim Litvinov, and the notorious head of the secret police, Genrikh Yagoda. There were not so many Jews allied with Stalin on the party's right as there were allied with Trotsky on the left, but the importance of men like Kaganovich, Litvinov, and Yagoda makes it hard to believe that Stalin harbored a categorical hatred of all Jews, as a race, in the way that Hitler did. Scholars as knowledgeable and as diverse in political opinion as Isaac Deutscher and Robert Conquest have denied that anything as crude and dogmatic as Nazi-style anti-Semitism motivated Stalin.[83] It may be enough simply to note that Stalin was a man of towering hatreds, corrosive suspicions, and impenetrable duplicity. He saw enemies everywhere, and it just so happened that many of his enemies – virtually all of his major enemies – were Jews, above all, *the* enemy, Trotsky.

Jews in the party were often verbally adroit, polylingual, and broadly educated – all qualities that Stalin lacked. To observe, as his daughter Svetlana has, that Stalin "did not like Jews," does not tell us much, since he "did not like" any group: His hatreds and suspicions knew no limits; even party members from his native Georgia were not exempt. Whether he hated Jews with a special intensity or quality is not clear.[84]

As he grew older, Stalin's general paranoia seemed to grow worse; as his power grew, it seemed to corrupt him as power has so many others in history. Even if not anti-Semitic in the "sincere" way that Hitler or Himmler were, Stalin was perfectly willing to exploit the anti-Semitism of the popular masses. It should not be forgotten that he was ruthless to all those he perceived as opponents; millions upon millions of non-Jewish citizens of the Soviet Union perished for having fallen under the suspicion of opposing him in one way or another.

The most blatant examples of Stalin's exploitation of anti-Semitism come in

[83] Isaac Deutscher, *Stalin: A Political Biography* (New York, 1968), 605; Robert Conquest, *The Great Terror: Stalin's Purge of the Thirties* (New York, 1968), 76; Nedava, *Trotsky and the Jews*, 267.

[84] The most insistent case is made by the Russian journalist Arkady Vaksberg, *Stalin Against the Jews* (New York, 1994).

the years immediately before his death in 1953, with the new round of purges in eastern Europe and the so-called "Doctors' Plot" in the Soviet Union, and are thus beyond the scope of these pages, but there was certainly enough in the Purge Trials of the 1936–1938 period to awaken fears that Stalin was somehow taking a page from Hitler's book. A large proportion of the hundreds charged in public trials with crimes against the state were of Jewish origin, a point the prosecutors called attention to by the kinds of questions they asked Jewish defendants and by consistently putting in parentheses the Jewish names of many of the accused (e.g., "Kamenev [Rosenfelt]"). The crimes, too, were often "Jewish crimes": treason, espionage, sabotage, clandestine international connections, economic corruption, assassination. Nearly all confessed their guilt; a few, such as Karl Radek, cooperated enthusiastically in admitting the most unlikely crimes.

Even in these Kafkaesque proceedings, the prosecutors made use of innuendo and allusion, avoiding open, explicit charges against Jews as Jews. Moreover, insofar as the Show Trials may be seen as a purging of the Bolshevik Old Guard and a making way for a new generation of Communists, many Jews were necessarily included in those purged, since there were so many Jews in the Old Guard. Nearly all of those who had worked with Lenin from the turn of the century to his death were purged in the 1930s; non-Jews fared no better than Jews. Of those very few Old Bolsheviks who survived the 1930s, both Jews and non-Jews can be found. Litvinov, for example, although dismissed as foreign minister in May 1939, on the eve of the Nazi–Soviet Pact, then served as ambassador to the United States until 1943 and survived to 1951. Kaganovich lived to 1991, an unrepentant Stalinist to the end. Similarly, there were some Jews among the new generation of Stalinist henchmen, particularly in the secret police. In 1937 *Pravda* published a list of 407 officials of the secret police who had been decorated; 42 of the names were recognizably Jewish.[85]

It has been claimed that the actual proportion of Jews in top party and state positions in the 1930s did not notably drop from the 1920s.[86] However, "visible" Jewish leaders, comparable to Trotsky, Zinoviev, or Uritsky, diminished in numbers and would continue to do so in subsequent years, so that by the mid–twentieth century there were almost no Jews among the highest officials in the Soviet Union. Undoubtedly, too, the effort to recruit a new leadership from among the working class, "real proletarians," resulted in fewer Jewish leaders because there were not as many Jews in the working class.

Even if one accepts that there were anti-Semitic undertones to Stalin's rise to power in the 1920s and, even more, to his establishment of a totalitarian dictatorship in the 1930s, for Jews Stalin never came to rival Hitler as their enemy.

---

[85] Baron, *Russian Jew*, 170.
[86] Arno Mayer, *Why Did the Heavens Not Darken?* (New York, 1989), 62–3.

To state the obvious, Jews were never purged explicitly as Jews in the Soviet Union, and millions of them survived the worst years of Stalin's terror – cowed, frightened, terrified, no doubt, as was most of the population, but never openly and systematically selected for death merely because of their racial–religious origins. A Jew who was a Soviet citizen had an incomparably greater chance of surviving the years 1938 to 1948 than a Jewish citizen of the overwhelming majority of other states in continental Europe where the Nazis ruled.

PART FIVE

THE FASCIST ERA:
EUROPE BETWEEN
THE WARS

THE YEARS BETWEEN 1919 and 1945 have been described as the fascist era.[1] In those years fascism seemed to many a genuinely new movement, building upon but also breaking out of nineteenth-century patterns. To many it also appeared the voice of the future, a perception that gathered force and plausibility by the mid-to-late 1930s. There are problems associated with the concept of a fascist era, not the least of which is the meaning of the term fascism itself. The debate about it will be examined briefly in the pages that follow, but from the standpoint of the relations of Jews and Gentiles, the years of fascist ascendancy are easily recognized as a time of crisis and tragic failure. Tribalism and resentment, often pushed to violent fury, characterized virtually all parties and movements that have been designated as fascist; "the enemy" played a key role in the fascists' ability to mobilize their followers, and the Jew was usually seen as prominent among the enemies that fascists faced.

Yet anti-Semitism was not quite so pervasive, powerful, or universal among fascists as many assume. It is not widely recognized, for example, that hatred of Jews played almost no role in the early years of the pioneer, model fascist movement in Italy. Native-born Italian Jews themselves were attracted in large numbers to Mussolini's banners. In other fascist movements, too (in Holland, Finland, Spain, Bulgaria), anti-Semitism was not of major importance. And in some of the countries where it played a major role (Hungary, Romania) fascist leaders nonetheless distanced themselves from the extreme racism of the Nazis.[2]

Narrow resentment, too, was not quite so pervasive among fascists as is often assumed. In the words of one scholar, "Many of its creators and followers

---

[1] Ernst Nolte, *Three Faces of Fascism: Action Française, Italian Fascism, National Socialism* (New York, 1966), 3 ff.; similar perspectives can be found in Stuart Woolf, ed., *European Fascism* (London, 1968), and George L. Mosse, "Fascism and the Intellectuals," in Stuart Woolf, ed., *The Nature of Fascism* (London, 1969).

[2] Cf. Michael Arthur Ledeen, *Universal Fascism: The Theory and Practice of the Fascist International, 1928–1936* (New York, 1972), especially Chapter 4, "The Fascist International."

were men of generous idealism and lofty aspiration from whom violence was limited to displays of verbal flamboyance."[3] The lofty idealists tended to depart from fascist ranks by the 1930s or to lose touch with their youthful idealism, but even then a modicum of decency occasionally persisted – as many Jews, fleeing from Nazi tyranny, were to discover when they were aided and protected by officials in Italy and Spain. Even as late as 1933, the British fascist leader Sir Oswald Mosley wrote that "fascism is in no sense anti-Semitic. . . . [It] was never known in Fascist Italy, and Mussolini has often expressed himself in this sense. The attacks on Jews in Germany do not rest on any Fascist principle but are a manifestation of an inherent quality in the German character."[4] In Italy young dissident fascists expressed disappointment with the existing fascist regime; they complained that "fascism had not provided a spiritual unity, a coherence of vision, which could offer the Italian people a feeling of cohesion and creative strength and so enable them once again to civilize the world."[5] Such fascists believed that Italy needed to continue its civilizing mission to the West: Roman Law, Roman Catholicism, and the Renaissance emerged out of Italian genius; fascism should tap that genius and continue the civilizing mission. These young idealists did not achieve their vision, but that they, too, used the term "fascist" to describe themselves is another indication of how much the term meant different things to different people and of how its meaning shifted significantly over time.

The fascist era was imprinted by the catastrophic decade of war and revolution. Fear and hatred of Communism were major factors in Fascism's appeal, but fascists typically expressed contempt for the goals of the European left as a whole, encompassing the liberals, democratic socialists, and communists. Anxiety about what a proletarian dictatorship would mean rallied broad strata of the general population but especially property owners, both large and small. Similarly, fears about loss of status and jobs in the newly established liberal–democratic states rallied white-collar workers, civil employees, and military men.

Such relatively palpable concerns played a major role, but they were inextricably mixed with more elusive issues. Those who were serious about their religion worried not only about the militant atheism of the revolutionary left but also the milder secularism of many liberal democrats. Other elements of the general population were alarmed by what seemed to them a massive imposition of alien values by those newly in power, linked to a pervasive denigration of hallowed tradition and familiar ways of doing things.

The generation before 1914 had witnessed similar anxieties, but they

---

[3] Nathanael Greene, *Fascism, An Anthology* (New York, 1968), i.

[4] Moseley's remarks appeared in the *Jewish Economic Forum*, July 28, 1933; cited in Meir Michaelis, *Mussolini and the Jews: German-Italian Relations and the Jewish Question in Italy, 1922–1945* (Oxford, 1978), 61.

[5] Ledeen, *Universal Fascism*, xv.

underwent a quantum leap in emotional power during the interwar years. Shock after shock – defeat, revolution, inflation, depression – left many feeling stunned, rudderless, and yearning for stability. Such yearnings did not translate directly or quickly into support for men like Adolf Hitler, who were also distrusted for their radical views. More appealing at first were Field Marshal von Hindenburg or Admiral Horthy of Hungary, who were traditionalists in most regards, including their attitudes to Jews, and also distrustful of the new fascist movements in their lands.

Jews in these years were irresistible targets, but even though anti-Semitism after World War I was unquestionably more serious than it had been before the war, many of the cautions expressed in previous chapters still hold. The inchoate resentments and yearnings of the postwar period were not pulled together into an effective Integrationsideologie; attacks on Jews were loudly acclaimed in some quarters, but extreme forms of political and racial anti-Semitism came nowhere near winning majority support. Quite the contrary: Hitler found it necessary to tone down his attacks on Jews, as well as on the church and on capitalism, in hopes of gaining wider support.

The initial successes of Fascism were not based primarily on hatred of Jews. In the Nazi case, ultimate victory may be described as occurring in spite of the radical anti-Semitism of Hitler and some of his lieutenants, whereas in Italy Jews took a leadership role in the fascist movement, and Italian Jewish voters supported Mussolini's movement. In speaking of fascist successes we have only two real examples, Italy and Germany. Elsewhere fascist movements, whether strongly anti-Semitic or not, notably failed to gain broad support and remained remote from power, with a few brief exceptions that were dependent upon Nazi patronage once Germany had taken over much of Europe.

Many scholars have thus come to question an earlier commonly accepted generalization, that anti-Semitism was the ultimate driving force of fascist movements, especially of Nazism. There is much evidence that exploiting hatred of Jews was nowhere near as effective in gaining popular support as some of the first impressionistic and less empirical studies of Fascism maintained. The scholarly doubts about the centrality of anti-Semitism, however, by no means lead to the conclusion that anti-Semitism was unimportant. If a pronounced hatred for Jews and a willingness to act on that hatred were not prevalent among the broad population, those passions certainly were present among leading Nazis and among significant numbers of Nazi rank-and-file, as well as among other parts of the population. And since such men eventually came to have almost limitless power to express their hatreds, what the majority believed was not decisive. Similarly, if hatred for Jews was not openly expressed or felt by large numbers of people, milder or more diffuse forms of negative feelings about Jews were widespread, as was indifference to their fate. It may not be accurate to include this wide spectrum of vague opinions about Jews under the jolting rubric "anti-Semitism," but the eventual mass murder of Jews could not have been accomplished without the indifference and milder forms of contempt on the part of the general population.

Images of Mussolini and Hitler, especially the latter, have become so much a part of commercialized kitsch-history that attempting to see them afresh as real human beings entails many risks. Similarly, Hitler and Nazism have become convenient as measures of absolute, demonic evil; to attempt to discover the human or, indeed, the ordinary or banal in them – which is an unavoidable aspect of placing them in historical perspective – is likely to be resented. Some observers have been inclined to mystify the Nazi experience and, in a related way, to define the Holocaust in religious terms – outside history and beyond human understanding. That will not be the position presented in these pages.

=14=

Fascism and Anti-Semitism

Nothing will ever make me believe that biologically pure races can be shown to exist today. . . . National pride has no need of the delirium of race.[1]
(Mussolini)

Fascism does not require that Jewry should renounce its religious traditions, its ritual usages, its national memories, or its racial peculiarities. Fascism only requires that the Jews should recognize the national ideals of Italy. . . . Wherever I have detected the faintest trace of anti-Semitic discrimination in the life of the State, I have at once suppressed it.[2]
(Mussolini)

[Mussolini] is a man of great genius, a spiritual heir of the prophets of Israel. We Jews . . . remain struck with admiration by the noble figure of Il Duce, powerful, gifted with amazing – I would almost say divine – qualities. No, the true Jew does not follow fascism . . . out of opportunism. . . . The true Jew considers fascism as a providential phenomenon, meant to take him back to God and his forefathers. (Rabbi Gino Bolaffi of Turin, May 20, 1934)[3]

Hitler was a gramophone with just seven tunes, and once he had finished playing them he started all over again. (Mussolini, after his first meeting with Hitler in 1934)[4]

---

[1] Quoted in Alexander Stille, *Benevolence and Betrayal: Five Italian Jewish Families under Fascism* (New York, 1991), 48.

[2] Quoted in Meir Michaelis, *Mussolini and the Jews: German–Italian Relations and the Jewish Question in Italy, 1922–1945* (Oxford, 1978), 83.

[3] Stille, *Benevolence and Betrayal*, 53.

[4] Ibid., 54–5.

It would mean the end of European civilization if
this country of murderers and pederasts [Nazi Ger-
many] were to overrun Europe. Hitler is . . . a horrible sexual degenerate and a dangerous fool. . . .
National Socialism . . . is savage barbarism. . . . Murder and killing, loot and pillage and blackmail are
all it can produce.[5] (Mussolini, after the Night of the
Long Knives, June 1934, and the effort of Austrian
Nazis to take over their country in the following
month)

Defining Fascism

Fascism is one of those terms – anti-Semitism is another – that is widely
used and assumed to have at least a core of meaning, but critics have argued
that it is so empty of consistent meaning and full of contradictions that it is of
no use, indeed is an obstacle to understanding.[6] It is undeniably true that the
tendency to categorize a heterogeneous collection of people and movements
as "fascist" has obscured their often large and revealing differences. As is the
case with many of those who have written about anti-Semitism, those who have
written about Fascism have often done so with a crusading, polemical purpose,
and they are thus inclined to denounce any perspective that lacks black-and-
white distinctions as aiding the enemy, apologizing for or giving ammunition
to anti-Semites or fascists.[7]

Some observers have considered fascism to be a peculiar kind of sickness,
or drunkenness, an irrational ideology without firm connection to material
reality, again with obvious similarities to theories about anti-Semitism. This
view has been typical not only of those who have approached the subject with
a polemical purpose but also of those who could not accept fascism as an
authentic expression of Italian or German traditions (e.g., Benedetto Croce or
Friedrich Meinecke).[8] As a scholarly critic of this view has stated it, Fascism
allegedly had "neither a vitality of its own, nor an ideology, nor mass support,
and was nothing more than a terroristic dictatorship of a demagogue and of a
class."[9] He and others have insisted, in contrast, that Fascism was as much a

[5] E. R. von Starhemberg, *Between Hitler and Mussolini* (London and New York, 1942), 169–71;
quoted in Michaelis, *Mussolini and the Jews*, 75.

[6] Cf. Gilbert Allardyce, "What Fascism is Not: Thoughts on the Deflation of a Concept," *American
Historical Review*, vol. 84, no. 2, April 1979, 367–98.

[7] For an able overview of this problem, with references to the relevant literature, see Ian Kershaw,
The Nazi Dictatorship: Problems and Perspectives of Interpretation (Baltimore, Md., 1985), 35–6.

[8] Cf. Denis Mack Smith, *Italy, A Modern History* (Ann Arbor, Mich., 1959), 411.

[9] Emilio Gentile, "Fascism in Italian Historiography: In Search of an Individual Historical Identity," *Journal of Contemporary History*, vol. 21, no. 2, April 1986, 180.

reflection of broad, significant forces in history as were liberalism, conservatism, or socialism.[10]

Hoary issues of historical understanding arise, most of which go too far afield to be considered here,[11] although a few will be further explored in the Conclusions. The main concern of this chapter will be to explore the relatively little known relationship of Italian Fascism to Jews and anti-Semitism, to trace the tangled evolution of Fascism out of Italian socialism, and to evaluate the relationship of Italian Fascism to German Nazism.

Definitions of various modern ideologies have often been encumbered by the assumption that a perfect definition of them exists and can be discovered. Scholars have consistently failed to uncover these elusive essences for the simple reason that they do not exist. Modern ideological terms, far from deriving from platonic ideals, have typically been coined in a haphazard, even contradictory manner. They have then acquired richer, more consistent meaning through growing usage over time, but many have remained exasperatingly untidy.

When "fascist" was first applied to Mussolini and his followers in 1919, the term had many associations or connotations that are now unfamiliar. Before 1914 it had been used in regard to collectivities of one sort or another, usually on the left, especially organizations of the common people. "National socialist," a term also used in vague ways before World War I, might have been more appropriate, since Mussolini and others in his entourage emphasized the centrality of the modern nation and denigrated the internationalism of Marxist socialism. But Mussolini mocked efforts to pin him down with an ideological label, encouraging some commentators to insist that the fascist phenomenon of the interwar years does not deserve to be considered an "ism" at all. Rather than being a formal ideology in the way that socialism is, Fascism was little more than a mood, a trend, an opportunistic hodgepodge.

What the term Fascism meant, even to its proponents, was undoubtedly ever-changing, amebalike. From country to country and from year to year it gradually assumed forms that only distantly resembled the original parent. To be sure, all modern ideologies have assumed various shapes in history and have overlapped one another in sometimes perplexing ways, but that process was particularly characteristic of Fascism. Alongside the familiar negative adjectives applied to it (irrationalist, resentful, reactionary, tribalist, violent), others that are no less appropriate might also be used (idealistic, altruistic, forward looking, youthful, dynamic, innovative), especially for the early 1920s.

---

[10] Prominent in this school is Renzo de Felice, who was charged with trying to defend Fascism when he called for a less moralizing approach to studying it. See his *Storia degli ebrei italiani sotto il fascismo* (Milan, 1961). De Felice is himself of Jewish background.

[11] For a readable overview, with ample bibliographical notes, see Thomas Childers and Jane Caplan, eds., *Reevaluating the Third Reich* (New York and London, 1993).

Even the familiar generalization that fascists defined themselves in terms of what they were against rather than what they were in favor of is not particularly helpful, since this holds for most movements in their early stages. The evils of capitalism, for example, were more amply and precisely described by socialists than were the dimensions of the future socialist state.

What has been called Fascism overlapped and is easily confused with other phenomena of the time. Following World War I, violent repression of the left, for example, was undertaken by a number of rulers who considered themselves antifascist. Admiral Horthy, who oversaw the bloody destruction of the Hungarian Soviet regime in 1919 and who blamed "communist Jews" for the horrors of that regime, was not, by his own lights, a fascist. Joseph Pilsudski in Poland established in 1926 what he termed a "moral dictatorship," necessary to the "cleansing" of his country from the ravages of parliamentary democracy, but he, too, did not embrace the term fascist. He was recognized by many Jews in Poland as friendly, a term that must be seen as relative in a country where most parties avoided appearing pro-Jewish, while many were openly anti-Semitic. Even Pilsudski's successors, who moved more decisively than he had in the direction of authoritarian, one-party rule, were not fascists in any but the most slipshod of senses. In much of eastern and southern Europe, monarchs, generals, or other strongmen suppressed the left, usually denouncing the role of Jews in it, abolished the freedom of the press or undermined parliamentary rule, without qualifying as fascists, whether in their own minds or in the minds of most of their contemporaries.

The Origins of Fascism: Mussolini, from Socialist Revolutionary to Il Duce

What, then, distinguished Mussolini from such traditional authoritarians and anti-communists? For one thing, he was recognized as having "new ideas," a judgment that was to an important degree retrospective; his ideas were more widely recognized as novel once he had securely installed himself in power. Relatively few recognized the extent of his difference from traditional authoritarians when he first began to attract attention at the end of the war. Mussolini himself had no definite sense of where he was heading or how unique his movement would finally be. This amorphous quality in the beginning is a point of no small significance in evaluating both Mussolini and Hitler, since the issue of how much these men later operated according to clearly worked-out plans has been much debated by historians, as has the related issue of how much their personal genius was able to overcome impersonal forces (their "triumph of the will" over obdurate structural realities).

Mussolini did stand out from the military men and monarchs of eastern and southern Europe in some obvious regards. While they usually had intimate connections with the older ruling elites, he was much more of an outsider. Born to a working-class family in the Romagna, he had been a prominent figure in the prewar socialist party (PSI) in Italy, leading its revolutionary, violently anti-imperialist and antinationalist left wing. But even in the PSI he was considered an outsider, distrusted by many of the older party leaders.

He began to break distinctly out of the mold of a left–socialist agitator in late 1914 and early 1915, when he rejected the PSI's passive policy of "no support, no sabotage" (*nè aderire nè sabotare*) of the war. He urged that Italy abandon its German–Austrian allies and join the side of the Entente. Even then, his break was not particularly remarkable, since many revolutionary socialists who had been antiwar before 1914 suddenly rallied to their countries' banners. Mussolini's initial intention was to win over his party to a prowar, pro-Entente policy, rather than to break with socialist ideals.

The leaders of the PSI, in expelling him, charged him with selling out to the nationalist bourgeoisie and betraying the working class. That charge would become more plausible in a few years, but at this point Mussolini seems to have struggled with socialist principles more than is often realized. He was no mere toady, following the dictates of those who offered him the most money. Men who must be counted as principled – a remarkable number of Jews among them – were attracted to Mussolini's banners in this earlier period.[12] He took risks and impressed many with his idealism and energy.

The Marxist interpretation of Fascism, which would be widely influential in the following years, dates from these initial charges that Mussolini was in the pay of the bourgeoisie. Mussolini's motives were not only more inscrutable than Marxists maintained; the support he won was also not so easily described. Some elements of the nationalist bourgeoisie did support him – again, a fair number of Jews among them – but others did not. And within the property-owning classes there were important differences: The rural landowners, for example, were more enthusiastic about the Fascists than were the leaders of heavy industry. Small landholders and owners of small businesses formed yet another distinct constituency. Class identities or interests, while playing a role, were simply not decisive.

According to historian Meir Michaelis, Mussolini's Jewish contacts in 1914–1915 played an important role "in the conversion of the future Duce to intervention and nationalism."[13] Among them were Giuseppe Pontremoli, Ermanno Jarach, Elio Jona, and Cesare Sarfatti (husband of Margherita, Mussolini's mistress, to be discussed later on), figures who are not easily passed off as spokesmen for capitalist interests in Italy, however broadly capitalist is defined (rural, industrial, or petty bourgeois).[14]

---

[12] Among the many works that illustrate this point, see Philip V. Canistraro and Brian R. Sullivan, *Il Duce's Other Woman: The Untold Story of Margherita Sarfatti, Mussolini's Jewish Mistress, and How She Helped Him Come to Power* (New York, 1993).

[13] Michaelis, *Mussolini and the Jews*, 11.

[14] Cannistraro and Sullivan, *Il Duce's Other Woman*, 116 ff.

But these were contacts with wealthy elites, whereas eventually Mussolini's stature had more to do with the popular enthusiasm he was able to generate. The enthusiasm among elements of the lower-middle class for Mussolini has led some historians to suggest that fascism might best be categorized as an expression of a rising (rather than declining) lower-middle class, as indeed might anti-Semitism, as has been suggested already, in the case of the German Mittelstand. But if anti-Semitism was a notable aspect of lower-middle class mentality in Germany, it was not in Italy. Appeals to racial hatred played no role in Mussolini's initial pronouncements after his break with the socialist party. Anti-Semitism was simply not a significant issue in Italian politics at this point, nor did it become one when the war turned in ever more disastrous directions for Italy. The Bolshevik takeover in Russia occurred when Italy had suffered humiliating defeats and when Italian nationalists were more tempted by scapegoating than ever before, yet Jews in Italy were not singled out. Indeed, Mussolini's initial reaction to the news of the Bolshevik victory in Russia was admiring; "Jewish Bolsheviks" were not a concern of his.

To be sure, Mussolini harbored a number of racial stereotypes about Jews, and his subsequent remarks about the Bolshevik Revolution grew distinctly less supportive, shifting about in almost comical ways. Before long he was describing bolshevism as an "unholy alliance of Hindenburg and the synagogue." That description reflected a widespread belief in the Entente that Lenin, brought to Russia by the Germans in early 1917, remained in their pay. Mussolini apparently also came to believe that Lenin, whose real name he gave as "Ceorbaum," was Jewish.[15] This bizarre alliance of the Jews and the German High Command was confirmed, for those whose minds worked in that way, when the Bolsheviks unilaterally signed a peace with Germany, leaving France, Great Britain, and Italy in the lurch. By March of 1919 Mussolini's pronouncements again shifted: He concluded that the Bolshevik Revolution was not the result of a German and Jewish alliance; it was Jewish alone, part of a worldwide conspiracy "against the Aryan race" by Jewish bankers like the Rothschilds, Schiffs, and Warburgs (in Mussolini's unique spelling, "Rotschild, Schyff, and Warnbert").[16]

He soon shifted from that position, too, ostensibly because his Jewish supporters complained. He described as false the widespread belief – his own belief just a few months previously – that bolshevism was Jewish (*"non è, come si crede, un fenomeno ebraico"*). On the contrary, it was leading to the ruin of Jews in eastern Europe, and he predicted that the Bolshevik takeover would be followed by a ferocious anti-Semitic wave in Russia (*"sarà seguito da un pogrom di proporzioni inaudite"*).[17] Mussolini's Jewish contacts had apparently also

[15] Benito Mussolini, *Opera Omnia*, vol. 10 (Florence, 1951–1963), 41–3, 110, 111–13, 137–9, 202; Michaelis, *Mussolini and the Jews*, 12.

[16] Michaelis, *Mussolini and the Jews*, 12–13.

[17] de Felice, *Storia*, 82.

expressed a concern that linking Jews and Germans might awaken anti-Semitism in Italy, and so he added that "anti-Semitism is foreign to the Italian people." He warned the Zionists in Italy, however, that they should be careful not to stir up anti-Semitism in "the only country where it has never existed." Again, it is likely that this warning reflected the opinion of Jews in Mussolini's entourage, many of whom were fiercely anti-Zionist. Most Italian nationalists were suspicious of Zionism, especially after the Balfour Declaration, since they perceived a conflict of interests in Palestine between Italy and Great Britain.

One searches in vain for some underlying consistency in Mussolini's pronouncements about the Jews in these years. It is obvious that he spoke in different ways to different audiences, usually to suit immediate and shifting agendas. But it may be said with some confidence that Mussolini had no particular emotional attachment to Jewish issues. His zigzagging pronouncements about the role of Jews mostly reflected his perception of their power, in Italy and in the world, linked to a perception that attacks on Jews would be politically unwise in Italy. His remarks to the Austrian ambassador to Italy a decade later (in 1932) are revealing: "I have no love for the Jews, but they have great influence everywhere. It is better to leave them alone. Hitler's anti-Semitism has already brought him more enemies than is necessary."[18]

Mussolini's willingness to believe in Jewish conspiracies was different in quality from that of radical anti-Semites. He did not accept theories of rigid racial determinism. More to the point, he did not demonize Jews or view them as unified in opinion and goals, no matter which country they were in. His attitudes differed as well from those anti-Semites who recognized and even befriended a few "exceptional" Jews, while denouncing the great majority of them, for Mussolini's experiences with Jews went much beyond recognition of a few exceptional ones. He knew many of them, sought their advice, and indeed was personally very close to quite a few.

Given a mind as inconstant and coarse as Mussolini's, these distinctions may seem overfine. By 1938, he would turn against the Jews in Italy, even against those who had been his earliest and most ardent supporters. But in the first part of his life things were certainly different. Mussolini had love affairs with a number of Jewish women. Angelica Balabanova, born in Russia and prominent in both the Italian socialist movement and the Socialist International, was a tutor in socialist theory and lover to Mussolini before the war. She was a woman of no great physical beauty but was widely recognized, by Mussolini among others, for her intellect, idealism, and generosity of spirit. Mussolini fathered a child by Fernanda Ostovoski, another Russian Jew, whom he had met some time before the birth of his daughter, Edde (by his wife, Rachele).[19] Margherita Sarfatti, Mussolini's mistress from 1913 until the early

[18] von Staremberg, *Between Hitler and Mussolini*, 93; quoted in Michaelis, *Mussolini and the Jews*, 31.
[19] Cannistraro and Sullivan, *Il Duce's Other Woman*, 97–8.

1930s, was more beautiful than Balabanova but also, in Mussolini's own words (once their relationship had cooled), "guileful, greedy, and even sordid."[20] She wrote an official biography of Mussolini and was a close adviser to him during the crucial early years of the Fascist movement – "the uncrowned queen of Italy."[21]

Mussolini had other close contacts with Jews in the prewar socialist movement, both in Italy and in the International. Such familiarity did not preclude fantasies about Jews in general but must have made the kinds of outlandish visions typical of German and Russian racial anti-Semites more difficult to maintain. We have of course seen that having a series of Jewish wives did not prevent Wilhelm Marr from becoming an anti-Semite (though not one who harbored wild fantasies about Jews). The sexuality of the Jewish female, at any rate, assumed different and mostly less threatening dimensions in the minds of non-Jews than that of the Jewish male. Anti-Semitic charges dealing with sex were mostly directed at Jewish males.

Once Mussolini had broken with the socialists and launched the Fascist movement, his contacts with Jews were perhaps even more extensive. In the *fasci di combattimento,* precursor to the Fascist Party, there were five Jews, and in the violent clashes from 1919 to 1922 between anti-Fascist and Fascist forces, three Jewish Fascists fell, becoming *martiri fascisti,* celebrated in the ceremonies of the Fascist movement. Well over 200 Jews participated in Mussolini's March on Rome in 1922.[22] The notion of Jews being prominent among the founding members of Hitler's National Socialist German Workers Party or among the celebrated fallen martyrs to the Nazi cause is so unlikely as to be grotesque.[23]

Why were so many Jews attracted to Fascism? The answer in part is that Jews were attracted for the same reasons as other Italians, but we must remember that Mussolini's following was at first small; even when he took over as prime minister in late 1922, Italians who voted Fascist were still a distinct minority of the total population. Widespread popular support for Fascism did not develop until the late 1920s, and how genuine or extensive that support was cannot be easily ascertained. Nevertheless, there is little question that Mussolini began to attract much greater attention at the end of the war than he had during it, from both Jews and non-Jews, and that the quality of that attention was indeed "different."

---

[20] L. Rafanelli, *Una donna e Mussolini* (Milan, 1946), 50–1; Michaelis, *Mussolini and the Jews,* 11.

[21] Cannistraro and Sullivan, *Il Duce's Other Woman,* 243.

[22] de Felice, *Storia,* 85.

[23] However, it is true that in Germany a significant number of Jewish soldiers joined the Freikorps. Even the *Fahnenträger* (flagbearer) of the Schlageter company was a Jew (Schlageter became a hero for the Nazis after he was killed by the French in 1923). Later Jewish veteran groups would stand on the right on most issues, and a few Jewish right-wing figures indicated that they accepted all of the Nazi program except for its radical anti-Semitism; Werner Angress, "Juden in politischen Leben der Revolutionszeit," in Werner E. Mosse, ed., *Deutsches Judentum in Krieg und Revolution, 1916–23* (Tübingen, 1971), 301.

The force of Mussolini's personality in a broader sense cannot be ignored. If Max Weber's overused adjective "charismatic" may be applied to any modern political leader, it must be to *il Duce* (the leader). Many Italians were attracted by his willingness to act, his apparently unshakable self-confidence, his coarse certainties. He vowed "to make history, not endure it," and quipped that "to live is not to contemplate but to act."[24] The antipositivist revolt against the neat certainties of nineteenth-century liberal civilization found a forceful partisan in this man, who openly spoke of the force of myth, of dark powers and irrational drives that move people in ways that material interest could not. A remarkable cult of personality eventually developed around him, spawning such slogans as "Mussolini is always right!" His style of nationalism was arrogant and boisterous; it was not linked to liberalism or a belief in gradualism and reasoned compromise. In this regard, he had much in common with the Bolsheviks. Like Lenin or Trotsky, Mussolini spoke in intransigent, often militaristic terms. Like Lenin, he mocked the "softs," yet was capable of great flexibility in the pursuit of power.

It was not Mussolini's ideology, then, so much as his personality that counted, and, similarly, fascism became known less for its program than for its style. Mussolini volunteered for the front and was gravely wounded there. Recuperating from his wounds, he established a newspaper, *Il Popolo d'Italia,* which pushed a strident and irredentist nationalism. He made a major effort to attract returning veterans by denouncing the great powers' mistreatment of Italy at the Paris Peace Conference and by describing Italy as an abused and exploited "proletarian nation." The program of the *fasci di combattimento* offered a peculiar mix of irredentist nationalism and social radicalism. Prominent among those in attendance at the first meeting of the fasci in Milan in March 1919 were the *arditi,* returning veteran commando units, whose black uniforms became those of the new movement. Also prominent were right-wing university students and members of prewar syndicalist organizations, non-Marxist socialists who advocated direct revolutionary action – strikes and violent deeds – against the established order. All factions at this meeting detested the PSI, though often for different reasons, and the PSI now denounced Mussolini as an arch-renegade.

Italy was in tumult between 1919 and 1921, *il bienno rosso* (the red two years), but the state was in many regards paralyzed. A new electoral law introduced proportional representation and removed the remaining restrictions on male suffrage, adding many younger and illiterate voters. The single-member constituencies were replaced by larger ones, with lists of candidates from each party. These changes gave a tremendous boost to the only organized mass parties at the end of the war, the PSI and the *Partito Popolare* (the Populist Party, akin to the Christian social parties in central Europe). In the national elections of November

---

[24] Paul Johnson, *Modern Times: A History of the World from the 1920s to the 1990s* (London, 1992), 96; Mussolini, *Opera Omnia,* vol. 3, 206, v 67.

1919, votes for the PSI doubled as compared with prewar figures, and its parliamentary representation tripled, making it, with 156 seats out of 508 total, the largest in the parliament. The *popolari*, in second place, drew heavily from rural regions and the South. A center–left coalition based on these two parties might have been capable of major reforms in Italy. In Germany, a roughly comparable coalition (of Social Democratic Party and Center Party) was the core of the Weimar coalition, but Catholic–Socialist differences were more unbridgeable in Italy; the leaders of the *popolari* could not conceive of working with the godless atheists of the PSI, and the Socialists, similarly, reviled Catholic leaders as purveyors of superstition and as lackeys of the capitalist class.

The result was parliamentary deadlock in a country whose population, especially its lower classes, had never had much respect for parliament anyway. To the alarm of the propertied, wave after wave of strikes rolled over the north of the country, while in both North and South peasants seized land. Socialist orators loudly predicted social revolution. A culminating confrontation occurred in September 1920 when factories were occupied in a number of major industrial centers; socialist leaders openly debated the issue of moving to a revolutionary takeover of the state.

The prime minister at this point was Giovanni Giolitti, the crafty politician of prewar fame, bent with age but back in power one last time. He was convinced that the leaders of the PSI were incapable of taking revolutionary action, and he judged it better to avoid provocation: Give them enough rope and they would be exposed as empty braggarts. But this policy, which was undoubtedly based on an accurate perception of the socialists and had worked for Giolitti in prewar confrontations with revolutionaries of the left, had a dangerous side effect. Property owners were inclined to panic, to conclude that the state was not protecting them, and they naturally looked for a savior.

In the Blackshirts was a force both willing and capable of repressing socialist agitators. From early 1919 they had engaged in street brawls with socialists, had attacked socialist party offices, destroyed party printing presses, and administered doses of castor oil to prominent socialist and trade union leaders. Mussolini began to receive money from wealthy, anxious property owners – and weapons from elements of the Italian military. Thousands of small property owners applauded the Blackshirts. Mussolini's stance as a man of action exercised attraction for many who found the chaotic postwar situation unbearable.

The campaign of terror against the Italian "bolsheviks" grew steadily in scope. Even where the organized working class was strongest, as for example in Bologna, whose legally elected city council was heavily socialist, relatively small bands of Fascist toughs were able to establish a de facto authority. In many instances, the police and the older authorities gave covert support to the Blackshirts.

Mussolini was able to parley this burgeoning support among the propertied classes into support for his becoming prime minister in 1922. However, there was nothing particularly decisive about Mussolini's victory at this time, and the grip of the Fascists on the country remained uncertain until the later 1920s. A crucial development at the time of the March on Rome was the Italian monarch's support; Mussolini would almost certainly not have become prime minister without it. That support in turn bolstered support for Mussolini in other parts of the population, including the police and military.

Italy's Jews were especially ardent in their devotion to the monarchy and thus inclined at this point to support Mussolini. Before examining the further evolution of Fascism in Italy, that peculiar devotion of Italian Jews requires further scrutiny, for it is revealing in a number of ways.

The Jews of Italy

It might be said that in no other modern nation was the situation of Jews less in need of "normalization" (in the Zionist sense) than in Italy from the late nineteenth century to the 1930s. Italian Jews had lived for many centuries under the heavy hand of the Catholic Church in a country close to 100 percent Catholic. Nonetheless, virtually all observers agree that the Italian people of all classes in modern times were singularly lacking in hatred for Jews. One Italian Jew of a prominent family recalled that in school "there was absolutely no difference between us and non-Jews except that we left class during the hour of religion. In history class they taught that the Jews killed Christ. But we just accepted it."[25] So apparently (and almost unbelievably) did the non-Jews, without deriving notable anti-Semitic conclusions. Again, the fundamental role of "religion" in the genesis of modern anti-Semitism must be questioned.

The rise of the Jews in a material sense was particularly rapid and palpable in modern Italian history, whereas a degrading poverty remained the lot of the great mass of non-Jewish Italians. But expressions of hatred for Jews linked to envy or class conflict were also remarkably rare in Italy. As one Jewish observer has remarked, "The desire to climb socially, shared at that time by all the Jews of western Europe, was probably resented less in Italy than elsewhere."[26] Jews were nowhere more prominent politically than in Italy, which was the first country in Europe to have a Jewish prime minister (Disraeli being a Christian). In the cultural sphere, too, Jews in Italy excelled; in art and music their accomplishments, at least in the opinion of one Jewish observer, were "unparalleled by any other European Jewish community."[27] Yet anti-Semitism of a political or cultural slant was similarly almost nonexistent in Italy. As with Hungary and the United States, a rapid rise of the Jews cannot be cited as a development that inevitably provokes anti-Semitism.

[25] Stille, *Benevolence and Betrayal*, 45.
[26] Dan Vittorio Segrè, "My Mother's Conversion," *Commentary*, vol. 83, no. 2, Feb. 1987, 28.
[27] Segrè, "Mother's Conversion," 28.

Italy and France had approximately the same population (ca. 45 million) at the turn of the century, but France had long been unified and was recognized as a major power; Italy had long suffered the humiliations of disunity, only completing its unification in the second half of the nineteenth century, and even then far from satisfactorily in the eyes of most Italian nationalists. After 1870, Italy was counted in the second rank of European powers. Much of the country, especially its South, was scarcely distinguishable from an underdeveloped, non-European country, although in the North were dynamic industrial centers, similar to the advanced regions in France and the rest of Europe.

The political and racial anti-Semitism in the 1880s had no counterpart in Italy. That may seem particularly surprising in that the most successful of Europe's anti-Semitic movements was just across the border in Austria, and one of the most anti-Semitic countries of Europe, Romania, was embraced by Italy's leaders as a sister Latin state. Italy was the country where the term "ghetto" originated. It was also a country of widespread illiteracy and superstition, with severe dislocations associated with the shift to a modern industrial economy.

What made Italy such a relatively benevolent environment for Jews, free of major outbreaks of hostility to Jews? The size of the Jewish community is an element of the explanation, but hardly sufficient, since France, too, had a small Jewish community. More important was the nature of the Italian Jewish community and, relatedly, the nature of Italian national identity. Jews constituted a slightly smaller proportion of the population of Italy in the nineteenth century than of France, that is, about one-tenth of one percent by the end of the century. Italian Jews were more evenly dispersed in the general population than were French Jews, although very few were to be found south of Rome. The observation that French Jews were overwhelmed by the sheer numbers of Gentiles holds even more for the even less dense Jewish communities of Italy. Most Italian Jews mixed freely in non-Jewish society and typically had numerous non-Jewish friends. Italian Jewish families were, to be sure, close-knit, as were non-Jewish families in Italy, and intermarriage was less common than in France. Still, the social situation of Italian Jews was qualitatively different from that of Jews in eastern Europe, where most lived among large numbers of other Jews, often in an almost entirely Jewish environment. In dress, manners, and physical appearance, Jews in Italy by the end of the century were indistinguishable from the non-Jewish population.

Italian Jews spoke Italian rather than Yiddish or any other peculiarly Jewish dialect. In this as in other ways Italian Jews resembled the Sephardic Jews of France and were in fact largely of Sephardic origin. They were not perceived as "foreign"; most were incontestably long-term residents, ones who did not feel the need to make the kinds of distinctions that were common in France or Germany ("French of Jewish religion" or "Jews by race but not religion"). They were simply Italians, and they had few worries that their religion or their race disqualified them from being genuine members of the Italian nation. Since Italy was not flooded with eastern European immigrants, Italian Jews did not have to deal with those embarrassing cousins to anything like the same degree that German, British, or American Jews did.

Sephardic Jews had everywhere in Europe a better reputation among non-Jews than the Ashkenazic, even among anti-Semites like Houston Stewart Chamberlain. An Italian racist author, Giulio Cogni, who praised the fair-haired Nordic race, nonetheless emphasized the superiority of the Italian Sephardic Jew over the German Ashkenazic. "The hatred and expulsion of the Jews in the North originated chiefly from the fact that the two races, all too different, . . . never merged, . . ." whereas Sephardic Jews and Italians did.[28]

By the second half of the nineteenth century, Italian Jews had begun to participate actively in the public life of the cities and towns in which they lived, becoming mayors or local officials with remarkable frequency. They were overwhelmingly urban and less restricted to certain economic roles than in most other European countries. In the course of the century many acquired land, in some cases large amounts of it. More generally, they entered the prosperous *borghesia*, the Italian urban middle class, in large numbers. By the turn of the century the Jewish lower class in Italy was very small, mostly to be found in the older ghetto areas of Rome. In the northern provinces, Jews typically moved into stylish neighborhoods without notable resistance or resentment from their neighbors.

The racism that spread in northern Europe did not much appeal to Italians, a people too obviously the product of repeated invasions, foreign settlements, and racial mix over millennia. Although there were tall, blond, blue-eyed Italians in the northern part of the country, Italian identity was Mediterranean, as was Jewish; both Italians and Jews similarly conceived of themselves as ancient, civilized peoples. The claims of northern European racists to be "pure Aryans" were the source not only of bemusement by Italian intellectuals but resentment by ordinary Italians, who chafed under the presumption of racial superiority by other Europeans. As a young man, Mussolini had experienced German racial arrogance in the Trentino and retained bitter memories of it. Before the war, he denounced Pan-Germanism as reactionary and "an insult to the Latin race."[29] One of many sources of tension between Mussolini and Hitler was the fact that Chamberlain, one of Hitler's supposed intellectual inspirations, had described the Italians as degenerate because of excessive racial interbreeding.[30]

By the early twentieth century, there was no population of Jews in Europe that was more fully integrated into a modern nation-state than the Jews of

---

[28] Giulio Cogni, *Il rassismo* (Milan, 1937), 157–9. Quoted in Michaelis, *Mussolini and the Jews*, 116.

[29] Mussolini, *Opera Omnia*, vol. 33, 153–213; Michaelis, *Mussolini and the Jews*, 10.

[30] Michaelis, *Mussolini and the Jews*, 35–6.

Italy. In terms of acceptance by the ruling elite, there was no country of the world, including Hungary, Great Britain, or the United States, in which Jews encountered a more favorable environment. Jews had been especially ardent German nationalists, but the rise of racism in the German-speaking world came as a bitter rebuff, diminishing the confidence of German–Jewish nationalists. French Jews were shaken by the Dreyfus Affair. Even English Jews faced a crisis of confidence during the Boer War and the subsequent debates around the Aliens Act.

Few if any crises had comparable effects upon Italian nationalist Jews. Italian Jews enthusiastically identified with the new Italian state, and even more than the Jews of France, the Jews of Italy were important to the establishment, success, and survival of that state. Unified Italy was a monarchy, not a republic, but by all accounts the devotion of Italian Jews to the royal house of Piedmont-Sardinia was even more ardent than their devotion to Italian nationalism. That house had early in the century sponsored Jewish emancipation and had then played a prominent role in the unification of Italy. The kings of Piedmont-Sardinia were often compared to the kings of Prussia, but Italian royalty accepted their Jewish subjects to a much greater degree, not only ennobling a number of them but mixing socially with them more extensively than did the royalty of Prussia. Italian Jews were even chosen for the sensitive and symbolically significant post of tutors to the royal family.[31]

The extent to which Italian Jews entered the highest ranks of the military was without real parallel. "It was common for 'good' Turinese Jewish families to send their children to military academies to prepare them for the army or the navy."[32] Jews were often honored guests at the weddings, funerals, and other important ceremonies of the highest ranks of the Piedmontese nobility, including the royal family. Even in the case of the Jewish entourage of Edward VII, there was not such an extensive mixing of Jews, nobility, and the royal family.

Italian politicians, too, had many Jewish contacts. Jews in other countries had of course established close contact with men like Bismarck, Gambetta, Churchill, or Wilson, but the Jewish contacts of Count Camillo Cavour, who played a role in Italian unification comparable to that of Bismarck in German unification, were more pervasive. In the words of Cecil Roth,

At every turn . . . Cavour found Jewish sympathy and help. It was from the Rothschilds of Paris that the Piedmontese treasury received its main support during this fateful period [1851]. . . . His confidential secretary and faithful lieutenant was Isaac Artom, one of the most significant figures of the *Risorgimento*. His official organ, *Opinione,* was directed by Giacomo Dina, for many years his literary spokesman and advocate.[33]

---

[31] Cecil Roth, *The History of the Jews of Italy* (Philadelphia, 1946), 479.

[32] Stille, *Benevolence and Betrayal,* 29.

[33] Roth, *History,* 468–9.

Jews entered all of the upper levels of the Italian state, in those areas usually considered last bastions of privilege, the senate, the diplomatic corps, the cabinet, and the military. In 1910 Luigi Luzzatti, a Jew from Venice, became prime minister. Sidney Sonnino, whose father was Jewish, had been prime minister earlier in that same year. He was one of the most important Italian politicians of the period, holding many cabinet posts.[34] By the early twentieth century, Italian Jews had become part of the political establishment. Yet even those who attacked that establishment almost never mixed anti-Semitic themes into their attacks. In nearly all other areas of prestige and power, from industry to education and the arts, the numbers of Jews were utterly out of proportion to their one-tenth of one percent of the total population. By 1930, for example, fully 8 percent of university professors in Italy were Jews, thus some eighty times over-represented.[35]

If Dreyfus was a typical member of the French Jewish bourgeoisie in his profound patriotism, his unquestioning respect for the military, and his generally right-wing views, there were many such typical members of the Italian Jewish borghesia. Dan Vittorio Segrè, writing in 1987, observed that in reading "the correspondence of . . . members of my family that found its way into the nationalistic press of the time, I feel a deep embarrassment at the cloying banalities, the forced romanticism, and the spiritual emptiness."[36] And if Judaism played a small and declining role in the lives of French Jews in competition with the religion of French patriotism, such was the case even more in Italy. As Carla Ovazza, daughter of a prominent Jewish Italian nationalist (and Fascist) recalled, "We followed the formal, material traditions of religion, but there was no moral substance to it. My father never once explained a passage of the Bible to me or said a kiddush [blessing]. . . . We knew no Hebrew. There were some religious Jews, but they tended to be poorer, closer to the roots."[37] Segrè remembered of his father that "no one could accuse him of consciously breaking Jewish law, since no one had taught it to him."[38]

Italy's declaration of war in 1915 – the "radiant days of May" in Mussolini's words – was greeted by the Italian Jewish bourgeoisie with enthusiasm, unlike much of the rest of the nation. These sons of privileged backgrounds volunteered for the front in record numbers; more than a thousand Italian Jews won medals of valor, and Jews were prominent among those who won Italy's very highest military honor, the Gold Medal (including seventeen-year-old

[34] Luigi Villari, 'Luigi Luzzatti," in H. Bolitho, ed., *Twelve Jews* (London, 1934), 123–5; Michaelis, *Mussolini and the Jews*, 5–6.

[35] Roth, *History*, 480.

[36] Segrè, "Mother's Conversion," 33.

[37] Stille, *Benevolence and Betrayal*, 26.

[38] Segrè, "Mother's Conversion," 30.

Roberto Sarfatti, the son of Mussolini's mistress). By the end of the war, eleven Jewish generals had commanded Italian troops.[39]

It should not be difficult to understand, then, how the humiliation of Italy in World War I and then at the Paris Peace Conference, was received by many Italian Jews as particularly *their* humiliation. The wave of lower-class unrest that swept across Italy at the end of the war threatened the propertied Jewish bourgeoisie no less than it threatened other privileged orders. The desire to put an end to the postwar chaos was easily as strong among Italian Jews as it was in other quarters. Similarly, among the veterans returning from the front were thousands of Jews, among them a large number of officers and decorated war heroes. They and other veterans encountered hostility on the streets if they wore their uniforms or medals. They were outraged to hear the leaders of the PSI denounce the war as a sham, the product of capitalism. As one Italian Jew recalled,

My father felt deeply wounded; he became convinced, like many other landowners of the time, that nothing could stop the 'Bolshevik hydra' except a new, strong, patriotic regime, capable of forcing draft dodgers to recognize the contribution of blood and suffering that the veterans had given the country. . . . More out of anger than ideology, he enrolled himself in the Fascist party, which was gaining strength and credibility with the help of enraged war veterans like himself and with the covert support of the police and the army.[40]

Since the right wing and the military in most countries of Europe typically had a low regard for Jews, it is difficult to get used to the notion that in Italy the militaristic right wing had a disproportionately large numbers of Jews in its leading ranks and that, further, the non-Jewish officer corps was determined to defend the Jews in its ranks against attacks from civilians. Similarly, since Jews were elsewhere charged with being agents of revolution and disorder, it takes some effort to appreciate the extent to which Jews in Italy were widely and accurately recognized by those in power as being mostly on the side of the established order. Looking back on the year 1922, Vittorio Foa spoke in terms that were typical of the Italian Jewish bourgeoisie:

You would see crowds of workers protesting, and fascist rallies, and continual strikes; there was a sense of impending violence. I was at that point in favor of fascism and Mussolini. . . . At bottom, I was a little simpleminded. I had the impression that Mussolini would straighten things out and end this time of uncertainty and violence.[41]

As another wealthy Italian Jew commented, "the fact that there was no more freedom of the press or freedom of ideas didn't matter a bit. . . . We were all fascist and all our friends were fascist. You just took it for granted."[42]

[39] Roth, *History,* 488.

[40] Dan Vittorio Segrè, *Memoirs of a Fortunate Jew: An Italian Story* (Bethesda, Md., 1987), 7.

[41] Stille, *Benevolence and Betrayal,* 96.

[42] Ibid., 40.

The Italian Model of Fascism

Many others, inside Italy and in the rest of Europe and America, were also "a little simpleminded" in regard to Italian Fascism. Because we now appreciate how disastrously the Italian Fascist experiment finally turned out, we too easily assume that its ignoble and tragic end should have been obvious to contemporaries from the beginning. But opinion everywhere in Europe and America tended toward sympathy for the Italian Fascists in the late 1920s and early 1930s. Tourists returning from Italy were full of praise for the new regime ("The trains run on time!"). Conservatives were especially prone to praise Mussolini, but many centrist liberal democrats were willing to entertain the notion that Fascism, if not appropriate for their own countries, might be just what the Italians needed to counter their unsettled politics and undisciplined nature.

Winston Churchill, one of the earliest and most intransigent opponents of Nazism, was nonetheless decidedly soft on Italian Fascism well into the early 1930s.[43] In a visit to Italy in 1927, he greeted Mussolini with the words, "If I had been Italian, I am sure that I should have been wholeheartedly with you from start to finish in your triumphant struggle against the bestial appetites and passions of Leninism."[44] Jews in liberal–democratic countries, although usually leery of Fascism, were not immune to the temptation to accept Mussolini as "good for the Italians." Hermann Otto Kahn, a German–Jewish banker in the United States, was an especially ardent admirer of Mussolini.[45]

Restoring order and destroying the socialist/communist threat were no doubt Mussolini's most important selling points. His followers often used brutal means, but the Italian Fascists were no more violent, and often less so, than the right wing in other countries. Many on the right and center saw nothing particularly alarming about Fascist methods; conservatives often described violent repression as a lesser evil, compared with what could be expected from the revolutionary left if it ever gained the upper hand.

Many observers were impressed as the 1920s progressed that Mussolini was dealing effectively with a range of other problems, with the "unfinished tasks" of Italian unification. Making the Italians more reliable and hardworking, more a modern, industrial people, may be viewed as part of the overall agenda of establishing order, but Mussolini tackled another large and related problem: the distance between the elite that ran the Italian state and the general population.

For all the heroics of Garibaldi at midcentury, it could not be said that the Italian common people had won, or even much participated in, the struggle

---

[43] A. J. P. Taylor, *English History 1914–1945* (London, 1937), 317.

[44] Quoted in Richard Griffiths, *Fellow Travellers of the Right: British Enthusiasts for Nazi Germany, 1933–9* (London, 1980), 14.

[45] Michaelis, *Mussolini and the Jews*, 33.

for a unified state. That victory had been "managed" by the crafty Cavour, who played off the great powers to Italy's advantage. After unification, similarly, the lower orders were not even given the vote until the eve of World War I. During the late nineteenth century, the highly unrepresentative parliament was run by corrupt political machines. Italy's government might charitably have been termed liberal–parliamentary in this period, but it was not a democracy, if that word is understood to mean a significant degree of popular participation in government.

Mussolini was more than a prime minister selected by a political elite; he was, or became, a popular leader in a way that could not be said of prewar leaders like Giolitti or Sonnino. And whatever the despotic tendencies of the Fascists, they did bring new elements of the population into active, even if not genuinely liberal–democratic political participation. We have seen already, in examining the origins of popular anti-Semitism in Germany, how morally ambiguous the concept of popular participation can be, whatever the axioms of liberal–democratic faith about the voice of the people.

Mussolini could make plausible claims to healing other major rifts in Italian society, most notably that between the state and the Catholic Church, which had vexed the country since the time of unification. In 1929 Mussolini negotiated the Lateran Accords, advancing the cause of national unity by making it possible for sincere Catholics to feel at one with both the Italian people and state.[46]

Perhaps most important of all, Mussolini worked to remedy the sense of inferiority that many Italians felt in regard to other nations. As one scholar has put it, "nearly all of Italy's troubles have stemmed from the inferiority complex of its people."[47] An Italian Jew recalled of her uncle, who was a prominent Fascist: "He thought Mussolini would be the savior of Italy, that he would bring dignity to Italy, that it would become one of the leading nations of Europe. No one would spit at us, the way England used to. He hated England."[48]

The hundreds of thousands of new recruits to Fascist banners between 1920 and 1922 shifted the movement's initial center of balance. From being predominantly urban, it became predominantly rural; from being ambiguously left wing, it became ambiguously right wing; from representing social change, it came to represent reaction – though always ambiguously, differing from overtly reactionary regimes.

Given this lasting ambiguity, it is tempting to focus on Mussolini's personality as the real key to defining fascism – as his own celebrated quip, "I am fascism," suggested. There is something to be said in favor of such a focus, but the limits of his personal role are also clear: The evidence does not support

---

[46] Alan Cassels, *Fascist Italy* (Arlington Heights, Ill., 1985), 62.

[47] Ibid., 62.

[48] Stille, *Benevolence and Betrayal*, 65.

the contention that Mussolini planned or even foresaw the shifts that characterized his movement from 1919 to 1922. Hitler later reported that Mussolini had confided to him that "at the moment he undertook the struggle against Bolshevism, he didn't know exactly where he was going."[49] He was not in firm control of what Fascism became. There were many competing factions, some that did not even accept his leadership.[50] He almost certainly would have preferred a more leftist orientation, perhaps even to a reconciliation with the socialists. In August 1921 he signed a pact of nonviolence with them, only to have it rejected by the local Fascist bosses, resulting in his temporary resignation. The Fascist program initially adopted in March of 1919 had been remarkably left wing: It had demanded the vote for women, heavy taxes on capital, worker control of factories, confiscation of church lands, and a redistribution of those lands to the landless peasantry. But by November 1921, when the growing Fascist movement assumed the form of a political party, the *Partito nazionale fascista*, it described itself as "decidedly antisocialist" and in favor of the free market. And while pledging itself to serve the masses it also promised to "flog them when they make mistakes." Again, it is obvious that these shifts were not the work of Mussolini alone and certainly were not planned by him.

The propaganda image of *Il Duce* as a man of unwavering will was deceptive; the Leader was in truth continually led – or pushed – in directions he had not himself chosen. Giacinto Serrati, who had worked closely with Mussolini in the PSI before the war, quipped: "He is a rabbit – a phenomenal rabbit: He roars. Observers who do not know him mistake him for a lion."[51] Fascism by late 1921, before the March on Rome, was still very much in the making. The power of contending groups within the party surged and waned in the ensuing years. Italo Balbo, officer of the Alpine troops and *ras* (party boss) of Ferrara, led the veterans of the front, the more brutal, nihilistic face of fascism in this period. Michele Bianchi spoke for the prewar syndicalists and more generally for the social revolutionary wing of the party, the one with which Mussolini himself was at first associated. Cesare De Vecchi was a traditionalist and a monarchist, typical of those who rallied to fascism out of disgust with parliamentary democracy but also, ironically, the kind of man that Mussolini, in his earlier years, had most energetically attacked. These were strange bedfellows, and they constituted anything but a stable alliance under a forceful and clearheaded leader.

Mussolini became ever more adept at playing factions off against one another, of testing the wind by seeming to favor one faction over another.

[49] *Hitler's Table Talk, 1941–44: His Private Conversations* (London, 1973), 267.

[50] Cf. MacGregor Knox, "Conquest, Foreign and Domestic, in Fascist Italy and Nazi Germany," *Journal of Modern History*, vol. 56, no. 1, March 1984, 28 ff.

[51] Cassels, *Italy*, 55.

Such devices are used by all rulers, even in democracies, but he used them with a brazenness that was remarkable. The point is worth emphasizing because it helps explain his ultimate (1938) move against the Jews: It was not really because he had always hated them, or had long secretly planned to attack them, but rather because he came to doubt their power, given what had happened to them by that time in Germany. Relatedly, he concluded that the previously benign attitudes to Jews in Fascist Italy were inconsistent with the struggle of newly allied Germany and Italy against liberal democracy. Interestingly, direct pressure from Nazi Germany evidently played no role in this move.[52]

Immediately after the March on Rome, Mussolini ruled in a way that continued to reassure many of those who feared the violent, social revolutionary aspects of fascism. The gangsterish qualities of the squadristi had finally begun to worry many of those who first applauded the suppression of the left, and Mussolini took measures to control them. He dressed in a respectable, bourgeois fashion. He spoke up for international reconciliation, and in his cabinet were centrists and traditional right-wing figures, only a minority of whom were members of the Fascist Party. (Aldo Finzi, an early Jewish supporter of Mussolini, became undersecretary of the interior.[53]) The first years of Fascist rule in Italy, in short, did not much resemble the ruthless and sweeping changes in Germany from early 1933 to mid-1934.

By 1924 Mussolini succeeded in winning 374 seats (out of 535) for his coalition slate in elections that were not models of liberal–democratic procedure but were not yet farces either. Mussolini took other measures of normalization, including the incorporation of the squadristi into the regular state militia, though they now swore allegiance to him personally rather than to the king or the state. In the same year he survived his greatest crisis, in the so-called Matteotti Affair. Giacomo Matteotti, a prominent socialist and eloquent critic of the Fascists, was murdered by thugs on the payroll of one of Mussolini's lieutenants. How much Mussolini actually approved of the murder, or even knew of it beforehand, remains uncertain, but it grew into a major scandal. Doubts revived among the more socially conservative Fascists about whether Mussolini could control the criminal element among his followers. Mussolini himself appeared disoriented, indecisive, and irritable. Many predicted that he would not last.

But he did, emerging from the crisis convinced that he needed more power if he and the movement were to continue to rule. In a series of decrees he transformed Italy from a parliamentary democracy, however flawed, into a one-party, self-styled "totalitarian" state. (The term *totalitario* was taken up by

---

[52] Michaelis, *Mussolini and the Jews,* explores at some length the reasons that Mussolini finally moved in explicitly anti-Semitic directions in 1938.

[53] Stille, *Benevolence and Betrayal,* 46.

Mussolini and by his critics.) By 1926 all parties except the Fascist Party were outlawed, and leading antifascist figures were arrested. Yet another important stage of Fascist "becoming" had been reached, but this totalitarianism was actually limited in comparison to that developing in Russia, or later in Germany. The king, the military, the church, and the senate remained independent of Fascist control. Still, Mussolini was much more powerful than any previous ruler of modern Italy, and he did seem to be forging an original manner of rule.

How popular was this new direction? Hostility to the Fascists among those who had been associated with the socialist and communist movements naturally remained, as it did with a small stratum of western-style liberal intellectuals, but admiration for Mussolini reached its high point in the late 1920s. Even those who were repelled by the dictatorial aspects of his regime still believed that Mussolini had prevented Italy from collapsing into the chaos and brutality that Russia had suffered. The issue of "choosing between two evils" was absolutely central to the age of Fascism, in Italy as elsewhere.

The Establishment of the Weimar Republic

Fascism as an alternative to liberal democracy took on growing attractions in many countries, especially among those elements of the population that had not benefited from liberal democracy in the first place. In most of these lands the image of Jews had deteriorated badly in the course of the war. That deterioration was one aspect of a generally disastrous fragmentation and radicalization of Germany's political community as the country's military situation worsened and defeat loomed in 1918. Already deeply split before 1914 and only fleetingly unified in the opening days of the conflict, Germany collapsed into revolution and near civil war in the autumn of 1918. As noted, from late 1918 through the early 1920s, it seemed to many Germans that Jews were "everywhere."

From the humiliation and fratricide of 1918 and 1919 a republican form of government, the Weimar Republic, emerged uncertainly, replacing the Imperial Reich of 1871–1918. The coalition of Social Democratic, Center, and left–liberal (Progressive) parties that had supported a Reichstag resolution in favor of a negotiated peace in 1917 now provided the political foundation for what was called the Weimar Coalition. This coalition introduced many progressive measures, among them universal suffrage (male and female), proportional representation, and elaborate protections of individual liberties. The Weimar Republic was widely acclaimed as a model of liberal democracy, but it also had many bitter enemies, both on the right and the left. For the followers of the new Communist Party (KPD), it was no more than a bourgeois republic, and they looked to its violent overthrow. Many on the right denounced it as a *Judenrepublik*, a "Jew republic." Right-wingers yearned for a return to the old order or to some more authoritarian, more authentically German form of government, not one they believed imposed upon them by the French, English, and Americans, with the Jews pulling the strings.

Having signed the detested Versailles peace treaty, the leaders of the new republic started under heavy disadvantages. They were forced to quell violent revolts on both the left and the right, in the Spartacus Uprising of January 1919 and then the Kapp Putsch of March 1920 (brought down with the help of a remarkably successful general strike after the army refused to repress the putschists). The leaders of the republic survived these initial years but did not gain widespread or deep-felt popularity. Many of those who finally decided to support the new republic did so without enthusiasm, earning the epithet of *Vernunftrepublikaner,* "republicans in their reason" – not in their hearts. Much of the military, judiciary, and police forces remained hostile, as did the government bureaucracies. There was a republican constitution and a new, left–center government coalition, but the cadres of the former regime were not renovated. German officialdom remained attached to the old order and all too obviously yearned for its return, leading many historians to speak of a "failed revolution."

The alleged failure of the revolution of 1918–1919 in Germany also derived from the initial measures taken once the Kaiser had abdicated. The provisional government headed by Prince Max of Baden soon relinquished control to the Council of People's Commissars, a six-member body of social democrats headed by the leader of the SPD, Friedrich Ebert. Ambiguously representing the workers' and soldiers' councils that had sprung up everywhere, the Council was quite different from the Bolshevik-led Council of People's Commissars in Russia. Ebert was a moderate social democrat, determined not to repeat the mistakes of Kerensky in Russia. When challenged by the revolutionary left, he turned for support to the generals and to the *Freikorps* organizations, staffed by veterans and others who were mobilized by the prospect of communist revolution.

The Freikorps played a role in Germany much like that of the Blackshirts in Italy, but with some important differences. They repressed the revolutionary left yet acted under the authority of Ebert's government, even while openly expressing contempt for him and his party. There were a number of charismatic Freikorps leaders, but as yet none comparable to Mussolini. Hitler remained an obscure corporal at this point (1919). Ebert successfully pressed for national elections and a constituent assembly, thus accomplishing what moderates failed to do in Russia. Thereafter the Freikorps were disbanded, although many of their members eventually moved into kindred organizations, most prominent of which was the Nazi SA (*Sturmabteilung,* storm troop), or Brownshirts. Although in these regards successful, Ebert himself was far from a charismatic leader. He later became president of the Weimar Republic but failed to gain much heartfelt popularity among the population at large.

Anti-Semites found much to feed their hatred in the new republic. Jews assumed a number of leading positions in it. Three of the Council of People's Commissars were Jewish. The Weimar constitution was written by a Jew, Hugo Preuss, and in the various ministries and subministries of the first governments were many Jews, often socialists. The commission that was set up to study the causes of Germany's collapse had a number of Jewish members, further nurturing visions on the right that German Jews were collaborating with foreign Jews in saddling Germany with guilt for the war.[54]

The newly founded left–center Democratic Party won a heavy majority of the votes of the Jewish bourgeoisie and had many Jews in its leadership.[55] Allied with the SPD and Center parties in the Weimar Coalition, it played a key role in the creation and preservation of the republic, winning nearly 19 percent of the vote in the elections of early 1919. However, by the June elections of 1920 that figure had dropped to 8.3 percent, and by 1924 to 5.7 percent.[56] Walther Rathenau became a prominent figure in the Democratic Party. Long the focus of towering hatred by anti-Semites, he now stood out all the more. From his commanding position in organizing the war economy, he became foreign minister. Right-wing demonstrators chanted slogans calling for the death of this "Goddam Jew-Pig" (*Schlägt tot den Walther Rathenau, die gottverdammte Judensau!*). In 1922, he was assassinated by a right-wing fanatic.

Both Germans and Italians began the immediate postwar years under a parliamentary regime that lacked legitimacy in the eyes of broad strata of the population and was reviled by both extreme right and left. Both countries stumbled from crisis to crisis. The year 1923 saw a particularly disastrous turn of events in Germany, when France moved troops into the Ruhr, pressuring Germany to pay reparations, which set off guerrilla warfare and rampant inflation, provoking renewed attempts by both radical right and left to seize power.

Hitler's Early Career; the Genesis of His Anti-Semitism

It was at this time, in the so-called Beer Hall Putsch of November 1923, that Adolf Hitler first came into wide visibility, increasingly identified as a "German Mussolini." (The term was first used by a National Socialist leader in November 1922.[57]) Hitler was, even more than Mussolini, an outsider, a man of the common people who had seen frontline service and who had no connections to prewar parties or other established authorities. Like Mussolini,

---

[54] Saul Friedländer, "Die Politische Veränderung der Kriegszeit und ihre Auswirkungen auf die Judenfrage," in Mosse, *Judentum*, 56–7.

[55] Ibid., 57.

[56] Ibid; see also tables in Alan Bullock, *Hitler and Stalin: Parallel Lives* (New York, 1992), 982–3.

[57] Werner Maser, *Die Frühgeschichte der NSDAP: Hitlers Weg bis 1924* (Frankfurt and Bonn, 1965), 356.

Hitler denounced the old parties, the wornout ideologies, and seemed to win followers more for his raw energy and self-assurance than for the exact details of his program. Both men attracted a fractious and violent following that many believed impossible to organize around a workable program of action.

Hitler repeatedly expressed his admiration for Mussolini. As late as 1942 he observed in a private conversation, "I have a deep friendship for this extraordinary man,"[58] and in the early 1920s he openly stated his intention to follow the Italian Fascist model. In 1942 he also remarked, "Don't suppose that events in Italy had no influence on us. The Brownshirt would probably not have existed without the Blackshirt. The March on Rome . . . was one of the turning points in history."[59] Given Hitler's contempt for non-Germans, that he continued to admire Mussolini and Italian Fascism is remarkable.

This German Mussolini in fact differed from his Italian idol in some telling ways. Mussolini was only six years older (b. 1883, Hitler b. 1889) but had been in public life far longer. He had been a major figure in the PSI in the years immediately preceding World War I, when Hitler was an obscure vagabond. Both Hitler and Mussolini were more sophisticated and better read than many accounts lead one to believe, but Mussolini's intellect was the more open, trained, and flexible of the two. As a young man, he had enjoyed daily contact with first-rate intellectuals. His patrician Jewish mistress, Margherita Sarfatti, prided herself in polishing his prose and manners, a task that his previous Jewish mistress, Angelica Balabanova, had also worked on. Hitler, in contrast, remained intellectually and socially isolated, an autodidact with many rough edges, contemptuous of the university trained. Hitler's class origins were petty bourgeois rather than working class; he harbored a sense of superiority to manual laborers.[60] In other ways, too, Mussolini appears more normal. He had wide-ranging social contacts and friendships and pursued many love affairs. He married, had children, and obtained regular employment as a journalist and party activist. Hitler, on the other hand, was a loner, with few friends, apparently no intimate contact before 1919 with women outside his family, working at odd jobs and selling his art work. He was prickly, brooding, and inflexible.

But the most remarkable difference was Hitler's attitude to Jews. In spite of recognizing Mussolini and Italian fascism as models, he seemed to avoid discussion of the role of Jews in the Italian movement.[61] If one accepts that anti-

---

[58] *Hitler's Table Talk*, 267.

[59] Ibid., 10.

[60] Cf. Adolf Hitler, *Mein Kampf* (New York, 1943), 167–9 [Karl Manheim trans., 1971 ed.].

[61] The issue of the role of Jews in Fascism and in modern Italian history is not even mentioned in *Mein Kampf*, in *Hitler's Secret Book* (New York, 1962), in *Hitler's Table Talk*, in Hermann Rauschning's *The Voice of Destruction* (New York, 1940), in Otto Wagener's *Hitler – Memoirs of a Confidant* (New Haven, Conn., 1985), or in Eberhard Jäckel, ed., *Hitler: Sämtliche Aufzeichnungen, 1905–1924* (Stuttgart, 1980) – covering thousands of pages of his speeches, writings, and informal conversations, in which he pontificates endlessly on nearly every subject under the sun.

Semitism was absolutely central to Nazism, an assertion that Hitler himself often made, then it is extremely curious that the movement he repeatedly recognized as his model was not anti-Semitic. Hitler asserted that Jews inevitably undermine or corrupt any enterprise with which they have contact. Yet they were undeniably of great importance in the personal life of the man whom Hitler most admired in the world and in the movement he described as his inspiration.

It is hard to believe that Hitler was unaware of the role of Jews in Italian Fascism. Time and again those who met him were impressed with the range and detail of his historical knowledge. They may have been taken in to some degree, but still it seems unlikely that he would have missed such a point, since he was especially alert to the role of Jews in all countries. Moreover, Fascist leaders, from Mussolini on down, repeatedly criticized Nazi anti-Semitism and tried to dissuade Hitler and his lieutenants from taking such a hard line in regard to the Jews, often pointing to the beneficial role of Jews in modern Italian history.[62] Fascist leaders in other countries, too, criticized Nazi racism; Hitler and other Nazi leaders were undoubtedly aware of those criticisms.[63]

When encountering criticism of this sort, Hitler typically remained aloof, letting his lieutenants speak for him. Some of them actually seemed to accept that Italian Jews were different from German Jews, an acknowledgment that one might extrapolate from Hitler's rare comments on the issue.[64] As we will see, this aspect of Hitler's rule – his calculated aloofness, one that allowed him to avoid awkward subjects and divert potential hostility to his lieutenants – was an important one, central to his continued popularity and also to the tangled issue of his exact role in the murder of Europe's Jews.

The genesis of Hitler's anti-Semitism in actual experiences with Jews is in some regards not so mysterious as is sometimes maintained. We lack for Hitler, before 1919, the ample public record that has been traced for Mussolini, but we do have a fair amount of information, if sometimes of questionable reliability, from those who knew Hitler before then, as well as from Hitler himself (particularly unreliable, it must be said). There is suggestive and plausible evidence in these accounts of how Hitler's hatred of Jews evolved, from his early manhood until 1924 (that is, from the time he left home in 1907 at age eighteen until he wrote *Mein Kampf* at age thirty-five). The more fundamental

---

[62] This tangled issue is elaborately investigated in Michaelis, *Mussolini and the Jews,* passim.

[63] Cf. Michael Ledeen, *Universal Fascism* (New York, 1972), esp. 104 ff; Michaelis, *Mussolini and the Jews,* esp. Chapters 2 and 3.

[64] When the Italian ambassador in early 1933 tried to dissuade Hitler from anti-Jewish actions, Hitler reportedly told him, in a heated exchange, that "no one understands this problem better than I do . . . and I know how dangerous the Jews in Germany are." The qualifying "in Germany" cannot bear much weight, however, since Hitler time and again spoke of "world Jewry" and rarely if ever explicitly recognized that Jews differed significantly from country to country. Robert Wistrich, "Hitler vs. Mussolini," *Wiener Library Bulletin,* vol. 18, no. 4, Oct. 1964, 50; cited in Robert Wistrich, *Hitler's Apocalypse: Jews and the Nazi Legacy* (New York, 1985), 71–2.

issue, however, lies deeper than individual experiences and has to do with Hitler's character. His life experiences provide much suggestive information, but nonetheless others had experiences similar to his without becoming radical anti-Semites. It is reasonably clear that some people, from the earliest stages of childhood, are psychologically rigid, less open or inclined to toleration than others. Education, or environmental factors in a more general sense, can influence such inclinations, but the essentially mysterious inclinations remain, often resistant to education.

Almost all the evidence we have about Hitler indicates that he was from an early age remarkably rigid – "self-willed and resistant to the discipline of regular work," in the words of his most celebrated biographer.[65] His boyhood friend, August Kubizek, in a memoir covering the years 1904 to 1908 (when Hitler was fifteen to nineteen years old) described those traits amply and, for the most part, credibly.[66] Their friendship was based on a mutual passion for music and theater; it seems to have lasted as long as it did because of Kubizek's conciliatory nature. Transparently concerned to make his friendship with Hitler understandable and thus often dwelling on his friend's more admirable traits, Kubizek nonetheless frequently drops remarks such as the following: "Hitler was exceedingly violent and high-strung. Quite trivial things, such as a few thoughtless words, could produce in him outbursts of temper which I thought were quite out of proportion to the significance of the matter."[67]

What a genuinely liberal education might have accomplished in altering Hitler's personal traits is a moot point, for he did not have the benefit of such an education. He was not, at least not in the crucial years between 15 and 25, put into an environment where he was encouraged to listen with an open mind to diverse points of view and to be prepared to change his opinion about things. Similarly, he experienced little comparable to the extended period of intellectual tutoring that Mussolini did while working with the Italian Socialists. Hitler never learned intellectual discipline, the need to persist with a topic, to study its various angles and not be content with first impressions or facile explanations. The years he might have spent at a university learning from others and acquiring a measure of intellectual discipline were spent mostly in isolated self-education and daydreaming. He claimed to be a voracious reader, but he brought to his reading the same headstrong and dilettan-

---

[65] Bullock, *Hitler and Stalin*, 8.

[66] Werner Maser, *Hitler: Legend, Myth, and Reality* (New York, 1973), warns, however, that "Kubizek's memoirs are a medley of truth and fiction in which the latter predominates," 356, n. 17; see also Maser, *Frühgeschichte*, 61, where he notes that Kubizek began his memoirs before the war in cooperation with Nazi Party officials in order to document the origins of Hitler's later greatness and to confirm things written in *Mein Kampf*. Maser's own reliability has been put into question by a number of historians. See, for example, Anton Joachimsthaler, *Korrektur einer Biographie: Adolf Hitler, 1908–1920* (Munich, 1989).

[67] August Kubizek, *Young Hitler: The Story of Our Friendship*, E. V. Anderson, trans. (London, 1954), 10.

tish qualities that were apparent in the rest of his life (and it is unlikely that he in fact devoted serious study to many of the books he claimed to have read; much of his knowledge was picked up from the popular press, which he did read assiduously). More and more as he matured he read only to gather information that would confirm his set beliefs; less and less was he able to "learn" in the sense of broadening his vistas. He had a lively intellect, verbal agility, and, at least in some regards, an awesome memory for details. He was able to dazzle many, whatever their educational background, but his intellectual vistas remained much the same. Revealingly, he told Kubizek, who questioned how adequate his friend's education could be based on reading alone: "Of course, *you* need teachers, I can see that. But for me they are superfluous."[68]

His shows of temper when encountering opposing viewpoints were legendary, if also sometimes transparently staged. But with women he was infallibly courteous, even gallant – "an Austrian charmer." As one of his biographers has remarked, "When women were present his harsh voice became soft and caressing so that many who had expected to find a boorish vulgarian came away charmed and delighted." The women who worked for him as secretaries and typists have testified that he was unfailingly kind, even when their errors might have given cause for anger on his part.[69] He also showed respect to his social superiors, at least in direct encounters with them, even while attacking the upper class in his speeches. His charm was put to good effect in such contacts, too, especially in fund-raising for his movement.

Countless testimonies have been made concerning the force and attractions of his personality in a broader sense, both when he addressed large audiences and when mixing in narrower circles.[70] Typical was the reaction of Otto Wagener, a prominent Nazi official, when first meeting Hitler in 1929: "From the first moment, his eyes caught and held me. They were clear and large, trained on me calmly and with self-assurance. His gaze came not from the pupil but from a much deeper source – I felt as if it came from the infinite."[71] Wagener, who was not an unsophisticated or inexperienced observer, was also impressed, indeed overwhelmed, by Hitler's command of factual data, the organization of his ideas, and the clarity with which he could present them.

Hitler's bigotry and inflexibility may have been influenced by his family background, but the evidence in that regard is inconclusive. His parents were not anti-Semitic, both by his testimony and that of others. His father, a customs official and loyal servant of Franz Joseph, was remote, overbearing, and selfish, but the emperor, as we have seen, made abundantly clear his regard for the Jews under his rule; his officials, if not immune from harboring anti-Semitic

---

[68] Ibid., 136.

[69] Cf. Maser, *Hitler*, 201.

[70] One of the more remarkable of these is Albert Speer, *Inside the Third Reich* (New York, 1970).

[71] Wagener, *Hitler*, 3.

beliefs, were also not likely to proclaim them loudly. Hitler claimed that he had not even heard the word "Jew" at home. Others testified that his father was cosmopolitan and free thinking. Hitler's anti-Semitism seems more plausibly part of a rebellion from his father than something he learned at home.

Hitler's broader environment, however, is another question. Until he left for Vienna, he lived in areas, most lengthily in Linz, known as Schönerer strongholds. A few of his favorite teachers were anti-Semitic. At least one of his instructors was Jewish, about whom he has curiously little to say in *Mein Kampf*. The teacher for whom he had the greatest contempt was Father Schwarz, a Catholic priest. He wrote in addition that "At the *Realschule* [roughly, high school], I did meet one Jewish boy, who was treated by all of us with caution. . . . Various experiences had led us to doubt his discretion and we did not particularly trust him; but neither I or the others had any thoughts on the matter."[72] In fact, there were a fair number of Jews in the school. In 1902, in his class there were six Jews, five Protestants, and twenty-eight Catholics.[73] The Jewish population of Linz, too, was larger than he indicates ("There were few Jews in Linz."[74]), although we have almost no evidence about his contacts with Jews in the city.

There is one important exception: The Hitler family doctor was Jewish, and one experience does stand out as potentially fraught with implications for Hitler's attitudes to Jews. In 1907 his mother, Klara, died of breast cancer. By the time her illness became serious, Hitler had already left home for Vienna to attend school. He returned to nurse his mother through her dying days. *Mein Kampf* only briefly refers to Klara's "long and painful illness." Hitler wrote that "it was a dreadful blow. . . . I had honored my father, but my mother I had loved."[75] Much else in these laconic lines is transparently doctored to fit the image of himself that Hitler was trying to construct in 1924–1925, but most accounts, Kubizek's included, agree that he was shattered by his mother's death. The doctor, Eduard Bloch, later wrote that "In all my career, I have never seen anyone so prostrate with grief as Adolf Hitler." When first informed of Klara's illness, Hitler was inconsolable: "His long, sallow face was contorted. Tears flowed from his eyes. Did his mother, he asked, have no chance? Only then did I recognize the magnitude of the attachment that existed between mother and son."[76]

Mein Kampf does not even mention Dr. Bloch – a remarkable lapse – but it is only natural to speculate that Hitler retained bitter feelings about Bloch and

---

[72] *Mein Kampf*, 51.

[73] Maser, *Hitlers*, 165.

[74] *Mein Kampf*, 52.

[75] Ibid., 18.

[76] John Toland, *Adolf Hitler* (New York, 1976), 29, 36; Dr. Edward Bloch, "My Patient Hitler," *Collier's*, March 15 and 22, 1942.

that his hatred for Jews may be traced back to this terrible trauma. Bloch's bill was high, representing about 10 percent of Klara's estate, and the treatment he prescribed caused her much suffering. (It involved the application of iodoform to the cancerous area, where one breast had been surgically removed – a task to which young Hitler personally attended.) A number of historians have speculated imaginatively but not persuasively about the impact of this episode.[77] It is certainly plausible that Hitler blamed Dr. Bloch. Kubizek recounted that Hitler's temper once again flared up: "Incurable! What do they mean by that?" he screamed. "Not that the malady is incurable but that the doctors aren't capable of curing it. My mother isn't even old . . . but as soon as the doctors can't do anything, they call it incurable."[78]

However, Dr. Bloch was, according to Kubizek, "very popular . . . known in the town as 'the poor people's doctor,' an excellent physician and a man of great kindness, who sacrificed for his patients."[79] Bloch's own testimony was that young Hitler, in paying a formal visit to him after Klara's death, grasped his hand and, looking directly at him, vowed "I shall be grateful to you forever." A year later Hitler sent Bloch a cordial New Year's greeting and signed it "your ever grateful Adolf Hitler." Hitler later made gifts of his watercolors to Bloch,[80] and Bloch believed that Hitler allowed him to leave Austria in 1938, unharmed, because of this lasting gratitude.[81] There is no record of Hitler ever expressing hatred for him.

Whether or not Hitler's anti-Semitism had some connection with this episode, historians have been almost unanimous in concluding that his subsequent years in Vienna were crucial to developing that hatred. He returned to the capital city after his mother's death and remained there for six years, until early 1914. Karl Lueger was at the peak of his popularity when Hitler arrived. An avid newspaper reader, Hitler explored the anti-Semitic press of the day. A devoted admirer of Richard Wagner, he was almost certainly familiar with Wagner's anti-Semitism. Kubizek's memoirs report that Hitler was already a follower of Schönerer. Kubizek also described how Hitler refused to speak to one of Kubizek's acquaintances, who had promised to try to find Hitler work as a newspaper writer. Hitler shouted, "You idiot! Didn't you see that he is a Jew?"[82]

Yet Hitler's hostility to Jews at this point may have been less adamant or doctrinaire than this testimony suggests. In *Mein Kampf* he writes of his "greatest

[77] Cf. Rudolph Binion, *Hitler Among the Germans* (New York, 1976); R. G. L. Waite, *The Psychopathic God* (New York, 1977), 138 ff; Toland, *Hitler*, 63.

[78] Kubizek, *Young Hitler*, 80.

[79] Ibid., 81.

[80] Maser, *Hitler*, 55, 358, n. 49.

[81] Toland, *Hitler*, 37, 63.

[82] Kubizek, *Young Hitler*, 186.

inner soul struggles" during these years. Anti-Semitism had previously seemed to him "so monstrous, the accusations so boundless, that, tormented by the fear of doing injustice, I . . . became anxious and uncertain."[83] It was only gradually, and after much reading and reflection,[84] that he came to the "greatest transformation of all." By his own not very plausible account it was the interplay of concrete experience and cold reason that pushed him – hesitant and unwilling – toward uncompromising Jew-hatred. He began to notice Jews on the streets. He "suddenly encountered an apparition in a black caftan and black hairlocks"; he noted the "foreign face" and the "generally unheroic appearance." The Inner City "swarmed with a people which even outwardly had lost all resemblance to Germans." Their filth was unbearable. "You often knew it with your eyes closed. . . . I often grew sick to my stomach from the smell of these caftan wearers." Curiosity and aversion gradually turned into anger and fury:

Was there any form of filth or profligacy, particularly in cultural life, without at least one Jew in it? If you cut even cautiously into such an abscess, you found, like a maggot in a rotting body, dazzled by the sudden light – a little Jew [*Jüdlein*]! . . . This [jewified culture] was pestilence, spiritual pestilence, worse than the Black Death of olden times, and the people were being infected with it![85]

These loathings, however, were almost certainly read back into Hitler's Vienna experience, or at least made more definite and dramatic in retrospect. The "inner soul struggles" seem to have lasted through the war years. What particularly clouds the issue is that Hitler's prewar and wartime experiences with Jews, at least those we know about, were not so negative as the above passages suggest. Indeed, it is tempting to conclude that Hitler's positive encounters with Jews heavily outweighed the negative and that the warm feelings he repeatedly expressed to Bloch were not exceptional.

It would have been impossible to have passed these years in Vienna without daily encountering Jews in great numbers, especially in the neighborhoods that Hitler frequented. Kubizek's testimony about Hitler's refusal to accept a job from a Jew notwithstanding, Hitler had friendly contacts with Jews, as did Kubizek. Such contacts were entirely natural given their interests in art, where Jews were much in evidence. Hitler "zealously read" the *Neue Freie Presse*, remarking that he was "amazed at what [it] offered [its] readers and the objec-

---

[83] *Mein Kampf,* 55–6.

[84] Most accounts of the origins of Hitler's anti-Semitism attribute a large influence to Lanz von Liebenfels, a cultish theorist of blond, Aryan superiority. Whereas other Nazis, for example, Himmler, clearly were influenced by von Liebenfels, the evidence in Hitler's case is tenuous. Cf. Maser, *Hitler,* 167–8: "If, as seems possible, Hitler came across Lanz's pamphlets during his time in Vienna, his development as an anti-Semite can have been little affected by them. After the Wehrmacht's occupation of Austria he prohibited their publication."

[85] *Mein Kampf,* 56–8. Mannheim translates *Jüdlein* as "kike."

tivity of individual articles."[86] Hitler's companion Reinhold Hanisch later wrote that many of Hitler's favorite actors and opera singers were Jewish, an observation that Kubizek also made. Hanisch did not recall Hitler expressing the kind of hostility to Jews that he expressed to Kubizek. There is a plausible explanation: Hanisch was selling Hitler's artwork to mostly Jewish art dealers.[87] In the boardinghouse where Hitler lived for some time after separating from Kubizek, he had at least two Jewish acquaintances, one a locksmith named Robinson and another a part-time art dealer from Hungary, Josef Neumann. Hitler later referred to Neumann as a man that he "highly esteemed" and who was "very decent" (Neumann had given him a winter overcoat in time of need.). Hitler began selling directly to Jewish art dealers after he had broken with Hanisch, grateful to them because they would take chances on a fledgling artist like him.[88]

There is some uncertainty in these reports and much that we never will know about Hitler's contacts with Jews, but it is a reasonable conclusion that those he encountered represented the range of human types, good and bad, "alien" and "German looking" that one would expect to find in a city as large as Vienna, with its diverse Jewish population. The parallels with his reactions to Vienna itself are suggestive: He was uneasy with the number of foreigners there, but he was also attracted to and excited by much of the culture of the metropolis. He did not yearn to return to the provinces, even if they were more purely German.

Hitler had many opportunities to form positive or balanced opinions about Jews, to appreciate their diversity in a way that ran counter to his later uncompromising attitude to them. To cite yet another example of hardly marginal importance, it was his Jewish senior officer, First Lieutenant Hugo Guttmann, who initiated and personally presented Hitler's award of the Iron Cross, First Class "for personal bravery and general merit."[89] Again, those who knew him at the front did not remember him as an anti-Semite. He was "an odd character," who lived "in his own world, . . ." as one of them recalled. He lectured the other recruits on the evils of smoking, and he did not join in their talk of women.[90] One of them did remember Hitler saying that "if all Jews were no more intelligent than Stein [their telephone operator], then there wouldn't be any trouble."[91] But it seems a reasonable conclusion that

---

[86] Ibid., 53.

[87] Cf. Maser, *Hitler,* 49. The reliability of Hanisch is also doubtful. "It was he [Hanisch] who was responsible for the dissemination of tendentious stories which were taken up, not only by journalists, but also by biographers and historians."

[88] Toland, *Hitler,* 61.

[89] Maser, *Hitler,* 88; Toland, *Hitler,* 94.

[90] Toland, *Hitler,* 83–5.

[91] Ibid., 90.

the "granite foundation" of his worldview, as he would later term anti-Semitism, was still not yet firmly in place.

The key issue is not whether the Jews Hitler encountered were unpleasant or alien, since some undoubtedly were. His character is the key issue, how he filtered his experience, especially retrospectively. That character, already stiff and overbearing before leaving for Vienna, became all the more so in the city. His repeated failure to be admitted to the schools of art and architecture to which he applied was a terrible blow to his ego. A young man of such already overweening self-confidence and vanity needed to find an explanation. He later made comments to the effect that the number of Jews in the art and architecture schools was the reason he was rejected, but, again, that seems almost certainly a retrospective judgment; at the time he was more inclined to blame bureaucrats and stuffed-shirt academics without making the charge specifically against Jews.

But one point deserves emphasis: It is simply not true that Hitler had no or very few direct contacts with Jews before 1919. Even in his case, we can speak of an interplay of fantasy and reality, although fantasy played a far more important role: "The Jew" as fantasy, as Satan, eventually came to be a central part of his Weltanschauung ("To him the Jew represents the very principle of evil."[92]), causing him to suppress his knowledge of Jews that did not correspond to that vision, while seizing every example of those that seemed to. Many of those who knew Hitler at firsthand, from Kubizek to those in his immediate entourage in the 1930s, such as Hermann Rauschning, remarked on the extent to which he was a bundle of hostilities: "He was at odds with the world. Wherever he looked, he saw injustice, hate, and enmity. Nothing was free of his criticism; nothing found favor in his eyes."[93] Another commented that "He seemed always to feel the need of something to hate."[94]

"The Jew" eminently satisfied that need, although he had many other, often overlapping hatreds – Czechs, Gypsies, lawyers, journalists, socialists, aristocrats, priests, to mention a few. In this regard *Mein Kampf* is revealing in ways that Hitler did not intend. In it he speaks of how the masses are best organized by hatred. He insists, even more revealingly, that those masses could hate only one thing at a time. A leader of the masses had to simplify and exaggerate, to provide that clear and simple object of hatred. Later he openly derided the notion that "the masses can be satisfied with ideological concepts. . . . The only stable emotion is hatred." The common people respond to power and confident assertiveness; they shy away from complexity, uncertainty, tolerance.[95] In speaking of the masses, Hitler seemed to be revealing his own psychodynamics, his own sense of what was true.

---

[92] Rauschning, *Voice of Destruction,* 233.

[93] Kubizek, *Young Hitler,* 109.

[94] Rauschning, *Voice of Destruction,* 85.

[95] Ian Kershaw, *Hitler* (London and New York, 1991), 51.

In private Hitler did occasionally recognize that key concepts of Nazism, such as race, were more complicated than party leaders presented them. He privately mocked figures like Rosenberg and Himmler for their simplemindedness. He was a talented mimic and delighted in caricaturing them in the long evenings at Berchtesgaden.[96] He resisted changing the party program not because he disagreed with those who found it inconsistent and dated but rather because he believed that the masses should not be confused by such changes.

It is tempting to conclude that the crudity of Hitler's anti-Semitism had something to do with this desire to avoid complexity, as well as with his perception that the Jews were relatively vulnerable. Attacks on the Catholic Church or on capitalists might have had dangerous repercussions: There were many Catholic Germans, and the capitalists were essential to national strength, to say nothing of financing the party at crucial points. He was understandably more reticent to attack either of them with the same unrestrained language that he used in regard to the Jews. But he harbored, nonetheless, a profound hatred for the church; he clearly intended to "annihilate" it, too, when the time was right. His hatred for the capitalist bourgeoisie may have been less intense, but it seems likely that he had dark projects in mind for many of them as well.

Hitler's endless monologues, during which he often spoke about how "useful" anti-Semitism was to him, persuaded some observers that his hatred of Jews was not genuine, that he was simply another in the long line of insincere anti-Semites who used anti-Semitism to stir up the masses without themselves much believing in it. When Rauschning asked Hitler if he intended to "destroy the Jew," Hitler replied,

No. We should then have to invent him. It is essential to have a tangible enemy, not merely an abstract one. . . . Jews have been ready to help me in my political struggle. At the outset of our movement some Jews actually gave financial assistance. If I had but held out my little finger I would have had the whole lot crowding around me.[97]

The impression that Hitler was using anti-Semitism as a propaganda device was further enhanced by those occasions in which he made relatively conciliatory remarks about Jews, as he tended to do in the late 1920s and early 1930s. Ironically, Ludendorff, who had done much to win over the Jewish masses under his control in World War I, publicly charged Hitler with betraying the anti-Semitic cause after 1928 – a charge that Hitler scarcely resisted, responding

---

[96] "Hitler made fun of his closest associates with striking frequency." Himmler, according to Hitler, wrote "nonsense," Rosenberg "stuff nobody can understand." Speer, *Inside the Third Reich*, 94, 96.

[97] Rauschning, *Voice of Destruction*, 237. Some national–conservative Jewish groups openly expressed "ambivalence" rather than hostility to Hitler's accession to power, as did some Orthodox Jewish leaders. Cf. Uwe Dietrich Adam, *Judenpolitik im dritten Reich* (Dusseldorf, 1971), 26.

"that law-abiding Jews had little to fear from his movement"[98] or that he had no intention of limiting the rights of Jews living in Germany (*dass er nicht dafuer sei, die Rechte der in Deutschland lebenden Juden zu beschneiden*).[99] Such remarks now appear to be utterly mendacious and transparently calculated for tactical reasons, especially to attract a wider following to the Nazi Party. But at the time, many believed that Hitler himself was not a radical anti-Semite and that he did not approve of rowdy attacks on Jews by some of his followers.

Even privately Hitler made remarks that appeared inconsistent with radical anti-Semitism. Such was most notably the case when he was talking to women admirers, or the wives of his lieutenants, a number of whom tried to persuade him to tone down his attacks or at least to recognize the exceptional Jews in Germany, the genuine patriots. Among those women were Henriette von Schirach, wife of the leader of the Hitler Youth, and Ilse Braun, sister of Hitler's mistress, Eva Braun. He remarked to Ilse that every German was entitled to his own pet Jew, but unfortunately there weren't enough good Jews to go around (She worked as a receptionist for a Jewish doctor whom she admired.).[100] He worshipped the tall, blonde, and extremely beautiful Helene Hanfstängl, an American of German descent who had a number of Jewish friends in the artistic world. Both she and her husband tried to persuade Hitler that his position in regard to Jews was too categorical. As late as December 1941, in his "table talk," he stated, in an entirely private interview, not to make points as a public orator:

I'm convinced that there are Jews in Germany who've behaved correctly – in the sense that they've invariably refrained from doing injury to the German idea. It's difficult to estimate how many there are, but what I also know is that none of them has entered into conflict with his co-racialists in order to defend the German idea against them. . . . Probably many Jews are not aware of the destructive power they represent.[101]

Further complicating his public stance, Hitler, in *Mein Kampf* and in many speeches, emphasized the need for "rational anti-Semitism," as distinguished from Jew-hatred driven purely by emotion. The term remained murky, but he seemed to be suggesting that irrational outbursts, the pogroms typical of eastern Europeans, were ineffective; in order to deal effectively with the wily Jew – which eastern Europeans had failed to do – it was necessary to develop a carefully conceived, "rational" program. Hitler often remarked that even his German Volk failed to understand precisely why Jews were dangerous. Germans

---

[98] Erich Ludendorff, *Weltkrieg droht auf deutschem Boden* (Munich, 1930), 19–20; Michaelis, *Mussolini and the Jews*, 49.

[99] Adam, *Judenpolitik im dritten Reich*, 26.

[100] Maser, *Hitler*, 201–2.

[101] *Hitler's Table Talk*, 140.

were sometimes repelled by individual Jews, he noted, but this was an emotional or superficial reaction, one that did not usually extend to those German Jews who had assimilated. For Hitler the assimilated Jew was even more dangerous because his destructive work was less obvious.[102]

If competing images of the Jew continued to contend with one another in Hitler's psyche while he was a young man, the hostile images seem to have won at the end of World War I, especially in terms of what he stated publicly. The beginning of the war had come to him as a deliverance, giving meaning to his life: "I sank down on my knees to thank Heaven for the favor of having been permitted to live in such a time."[103] Earlier in the year, ironically, he had been arrested for evading military service in the Austrian army; he was ordered to report for duty at Linz, but he was finally declared "unfit for combatant and auxiliary duties on grounds of physical weakness"[104] – matters that, not surprisingly, he failed to mention in *Mein Kampf.* In August nonetheless he volunteered for service in the German army, and all evidence indicates that he was a courageous soldier. After years of sacrifice, Germany's defeat was an unbearable blow to him. He later wrote that while in the hospital, recovering from a gas attack that had temporarily blinded him, he heard the news of Germany's defeat:

Again, everything went black before my eyes; I tottered and groped my way back into the dormitory, threw myself on my bunk, and dug my burning head into my blanket and pillow. Since the day when I had stood by my mother's grave I had not wept. . . . Only now did I see how all personal suffering vanishes in comparison with the misfortune of the fatherland.[105]

It may have been at this stage of massive psychological vulnerability that Hitler began to channel his already extraordinary capacity for hatred more uncompromisingly toward the Jews. The preceding passage is followed by one of the more ranting tirades of *Mein Kampf;* he emphasizes how much a frustrated hatred raged in him during these days. He was above all infuriated, as he lay recovering in the hospital, by the antiwar sailors who "arrived in trucks and proclaimed the revolution; a few Jewish youths were the 'leaders' in this struggle. . . . None of them had been to the front. . . . Now they raised the red flag of revolution."[106]

In the following months, back in Munich, he watched revolutionary events in the city, first led by the socialist (and Jew) Kurt Eisner and then the short-lived rule by German-style soviets, led almost entirely by Jewish revolutionaries. The

---

[102] Cf. Maser, *Hitler,* 115–6.

[103] *Mein Kampf,* 161.

[104] Quoted in Bullock, *Hitler and Stalin,* 44.

[105] *Mein Kampf,* 294.

[106] Ibid., 202–3.

Munich soviet dictatorship was itself inspired by the soviet regime in Hungary, again led by Jews. Atrocity stories about these soviet dictatorships, and even more about Bolshevik rule in Russia, began to spread widely in Germany. It is not difficult to imagine how a man of Hitler's experience and character could seize this psychologically satisfying vision, "the Jew," as the cause of Germany's disasters – and vow to fight to his dying breath against the spreading Jewish plague.

Hitler gained one of his first and most important recognitions as an agitator and orator when attending a course organized for demobilizing soldiers in 1919, he eloquently attacked a speaker who had tried to defend the Jews.[107] How completely he believed his own propaganda at this point is impossible to know, but he concluded that "the thing I had always presumed from pure feeling without knowing it was now corroborated: I could speak."[108] Once he had taken this public stance, he was of course attacked in return by Jews and other opponents of anti-Semitism. Hitler was now irrevocably engaged; his stubbornness and pride added force to his categorical pronouncements against the Jews.

The familiar question arises again: Was Hitler referring to a fantasy Jew, wholly unrelated to real experience? Most Jews were not communists or socialists, nor were most "destructive" in the way Hitler understood the word, but on the other hand, it is also true that nearly everywhere Hitler looked at the end of the war, there were Jews who corresponded to anti-Semitic imagery. It was certainly fantastic to believe that revolution in Munich, Budapest, or Moscow was part of a worldwide Jewish conspiracy or to conclude that the work of Jews like Eisner, Kun, or Trotsky derived from their race. Nonetheless, there was a reality of a sort, one that men as previously friendly to Jews as Churchill accepted as valid. Hitler's reaction was more extreme but had much in common with the reactions of large numbers of established politicians, intellectuals, or academics in the immediate postwar period.[109] At this very time Lord Milner, British secretary of state for war, circulated a letter calling for intervention in Russia, which contained the following:

We must not lose sight of the fact that this movement [Bolshevism] is engineered and managed by astute Jews, many of them criminals, and nearly every commissar in Russia is a Jew. . . . Meetings of protest against intervention are composed of alien Jews, . . . and in constituencies where there is a large Jewish vote, it has invariably gone to the extreme Socialist candidate.[110]

[107] Ibid., 215.

[108] Ibid., 215–16.

[109] For an in-depth exploration of this issue, see Griffiths, *Fellow Travellers of the Right*.

[110] Quoted in Gisela C. Lebzelter, *Political Anti-Semitism in England, 1918–1939* (Oxford, 1978), 18.

What was most remarkable about Hitler was not his willingness to make sweeping generalizations about Jews but rather the stubbornness, the monomania, the ferocity with which he pushed from his consciousness all contrary evidence: The Jewish spirit, he intoned, "has been there from the beginning, and there is no Jew, not a single one, who does not personify it."[111] Men like Treitschke and Hobson came to their beliefs about Jews through an intricate interplay of perception and preconception; they freely recognized Jewish diversity and exceptions to the negative images they forwarded. In Hitler's case this interplay is of special interest, for it seems to have been closest to the theoretical model that has been repeatedly questioned in previous chapters. For him the human diversity of Jews – the Dr. Blochs, the Neumanns, and the Guttmanns of his life – seems to have finally exercised no restraining role on the emotionally gratifying fantasies about the malevolent Jewish race that he began to embrace so energetically and dogmatically in 1919. This sharp and enduring disjunction between actual experience and psychological construct in Hitler was actually not typical of all anti-Semites, in Germany or elsewhere, and his all-too-famous example has encouraged the tendency to overgeneralize about others.

Was the nature of Hitler's hatred such that the murder of *all* Jews was a logical conclusion – the only logical conclusion? An extensive historical literature has been devoted to the question of the relationship of ideology and action in this instance.[112] On one side, the Intentionalists have argued that the Holocaust was contained in Hitler's speeches and writings in the immediate postwar years; all the zigzags thereafter were nothing more than tactical devices on the way to that goal. On the other side, the Functionalists have proposed a more complicated dynamic, suggesting that the systematic killing of Jews emerged less from dogmatic ideology and long-range planning than unforeseen situations; Hitler's exact plans for the Jews took shape only gradually, emerging out of the dilemmas and opportunities that presented themselves to him and to other Nazi leaders. The Functionalists have not denied Hitler's towering rage in regard to Jews, or indeed that of an important part of the German population, but they have tried to put the concrete expressions of that rage into a more plausible and textured explanatory framework. Unlike some academic debates, this one has been mostly fruitful; a consensus, one that borrows from both positions, appears to be emerging. But to understand the nature of that consensus one must first explore the evolution of the Nazi Party in the 1920s and early 1930s.

---

[111] Quoted in Ernst Nolte, *Three Faces of Fascism* (New York, 1966), 332 (from Dietrich Eckart's *Der Bolschewismus von Moses bis Lenin. Zwiegespräch zwischen Adolf Hitler und mir* [Munich, 1924]).

[112] Two of the most readable studies, with ample bibliographies, are Childers and Caplan, eds., *Reevaluating the Third Reich,* and Peter Hayes, ed., *Lessons and Legacies: The Meaning of the Holocaust in a Changing World* (Evanston, Ill., 1991).

Hitler and the Nazi Party

At approximately the same time that Hitler discovered he could "speak," he also began to make contact with right-wing political activists, first with a small band that called itself the German Workers Party in 1919. He rapidly rose to prominence in it, or in the renamed National Socialist German Workers Party (*Nazionalsocialistische Deutsche Arbeiterpartei*, NSDAP). Much of the anti-Semitic propaganda that he had imbibed in Vienna was now brought into sharper focus. He found not only intellectual stimulation but also emotional sustenance in a curious figure, Dietrich Eckart, a man to whom he dedicated the second volume of *Mein Kampf*. Hitler later suggestively described Eckart as his "fatherly friend." Even in his last years, Hitler repeatedly referred to this friend in reverential terms; whenever the Führer spoke of Eckart, tears came to his eyes, according to his secretary.[113]

Given a man as emotionally isolated as Hitler was by 1919, this evidence deserves careful attention. There were very few men with whom he shared such closeness, and Eckart's intellectual influence may have been all the greater because of it. This father-substitute's death in December 1923 made him a more convenient figure for Hitler to venerate than other theorists with whom he had to deal in the flesh. Eckart was a typical Bohemian crank and a second-rate poet; what it was about his personality that so attracted Hitler is anything but clear, but it does seem that Eckart nourished both Hitler's anti-Semitism and his anticapitalism, one that distinguished between creative and destructive capital, the first being Aryan and the second Jewish.

Tracing such intellectual influences is risky, however, since Hitler mixed with many other right-wing thinkers and activists at this time. It is curious that Eckart's anti-Semitism was not crudely biological, as Nazi doctrine came to be. His attacks on Jews were primarily spiritual or "religious," in that he denigrated Jews as materialists, people who did not believe in an afterlife. Since they recognized no souls in themselves, they sought to deny the spirituality of others. More broadly, he believed in a Manichaean struggle within all individuals and nations; the materialistic, Jewish element had to be overcome but could never be entirely eliminated. Indeed, Eckart believed that some element of "Jewishness" was necessary for a nation to survive, and he did not agree with the more biologically inclined Alfred Rosenberg that Jews should be driven from German life entirely. He also asserted that Jews who converted to Christianity should be respected.[114]

These ideas were much like those of such prewar thinkers as Lagarde, Langbehn, and Mommsen – indeed, are not "Nazi" in the sense normally

---

[113] Albert Zoller, *Hitler Privat – Erlebnisbericht seiner Geheimsekretärin* (Düsseldorf, 1949), 119; Nolte, *Three Faces of Fascism*, 329.

[114] Barbara Miller Lane and Leila J. Rupp, eds., *Nazi Ideology Before 1933, a Documentation* (London, 1978), xiv, 17.

understood. Most of Hitler's own statements about Jews at this time actually seem closer to Rosenberg than Eckart, and it is again intriguing that Hitler so revered Eckart but mocked Rosenberg as simpleminded. Alongside Hitler's lasting veneration of Mussolini, who explicitly rejected biological racism and anti-Semitism, this veneration of Eckart fits awkwardly in any effort to trace the intellectual origins of Hitler's uncompromising hatred of Jews.

The nature of Hitler's emotional life in these years is also difficult to decipher. Without venturing into the swampland of psychohistory, a reasonably plausible picture, one that offers insight into his actions once he gained power, can be constructed. The evidence that the death of his mother was traumatic for young Hitler rings true because there was no one else to whom he could show – or at least did show – whatever warmth or tenderness was in him. She was herself aware of that: On her deathbed she pulled Kubizek to her side and whispered: "Gustl, go on being a good friend to my son when I am no longer here. He has no one else." After her death, Kubizek commented, "Not only had he now lost both his parents, but with his mother he had lost the only creature on earth on whom he had concentrated his love, and who loved him in return."[115]

Tender emotions in such a man as Hitler? These are uncomfortable, some would say repellent and dangerous, notions. Few figures in history deserve demonization more than Hitler, but if the goal is genuinely to understand one must put aside the familiar one-dimensional portraits. They betray in their dogmatism something psychologically related to Hitler's own coarse certainties – he did not want to hear opposing evidence. Even the most negative conception of Hitler must entertain the proposition that he had "human" qualities and was not simply and in all regards an unfeeling brute from the moment of his birth.

It makes sense, in other words, to conceptualize his brutal adult personality as the result of a process. Even after the death of his mother, after the years of humiliation and growing psychological isolation in Vienna, after the searing experiences of the front, after the disillusionment of the failed Putsch in 1923, when he was near suicide, Hitler was still to some degree capable of tender emotions. When his niece, Geli Raubal, killed herself in 1931 for reasons that still remain unclear – probably because of a spat with Hitler or jealousy over another woman – Hitler was again close to utter despair. She was the "love of his life." He reflected:

It is true that I have overcome the urge to physically possess a woman. But the value placed on the loving hand of a female being who was close to my heart, and how much the constant solicitude she shed on me meant to me – that I am learning only now. . . . [Geli's] cheerful laughter always gave me deep pleasure, her harmless chatter filled me with joy. Even when she sat quietly by my side working a

115 Kubizek, *Young Hitler,* 86, 87.

crossword puzzle, I was enveloped in a feeling of well-being that has now given way to a chilly sense of loneliness. . . . Now everything has been taken from me. Now I am altogether free, inwardly and outwardly.

A few years earlier he had exclaimed,

How very much I too would love to have a family, children – children! Oh, God, you know how much I love children. . . . What can be more beautiful than the beaming eyes of a child who has been made happy by some insignificant little gift, a seashell, a block of wood, a pebble! And how happy parents become through such happiness![116]

It would be easy enough to pass these remarks off as cynical play-acting, since Hitler was so adept at that. Yet the evidence of his affection for Geli, or the delight he took in the children of his lieutenants, spontaneously playing hours on end with them, is abundant.[117] There is also ample evidence of his further emotional distancing from others after 1931, of his "inward and outward freedom." Astonishingly – and chillingly – he requested to be present at Geli's autopsy, observing the surgeon's tools rip into the flesh of the love of his life. His "freedom," his distancing from normal human feelings, continued to grow.

In the notorious "Night of the Long Knives" in the summer of 1934, Hitler felt it necessary to approve a bloody purge, the execution of some of his oldest and closest comrades-in-arms, further enhancing his sense of being chosen for superhuman tasks, ones that did not permit normal human feelings. The strain, nevertheless, was obvious: He aged so rapidly in the eight years between Geli's death and the outbreak of World War II that many close to him suspected he was suffering from syphilis or some other degenerative disease (which indeed may have also been the case; his symptoms were much those of Parkinson's Disease).[118] He was plagued by an array of health problems, and he began to resort to drugs and dubious medications in a way that almost certainly made things worse. He brooded increasingly over what he believed was his impending death and spoke of his mission – to do things that only he could do, in the short time left him.

The temptation to portray Hitler as without normal human emotions is paralleled by another: to deny that he was moved by idealism or altruism or to assert that it was only the search for power that explains his actions. Again, there is ample evidence that in his strange way Hitler was both altruistic and idealistic, with the obvious qualifier that what one person considers lofty ideals will be considered monstrous by another. Hitler was, like many revolutionaries – Trotsky is an obvious example – more attached to "the people" in the

[116] Wagener, *Hitler,* 222, 33.

[117] Cf. Speer, *Inside the Third Reich,* Ernst Hanfstängl, *Hitler: The Missing Years* (London, 1957).

[118] Cf. Maser, "The Ailing Father," in *Hitler.*

abstract than in any concrete way, but he does seem to have felt indignation over their sufferings, an indignation that he was able to convey with great effectiveness to the crowds that flocked to his speeches.

A related question is how Hitler and his movement became more than a band of fringe rabble-rousers, for there were scores of right-wing, revanchist, ultranationalistic, and anti-Semitic groups in Germany at the end of the war. In attempting to explain Hitler's rise, the Marxist interpretation was for many years pressed with even greater energy than in the case of Mussolini's rise – but even less persuasively. The German economy, or "capitalism," was "in crisis," but scholars have increasingly revealed as inadequate the notion that Hitler and his NSDAP were tools of the capitalists or that the capitalists were especially attracted to anti-Semitism as a device to rally the masses against the threat from the left.[119]

Some owners of industry did come to see Hitler and his party as preferable to the parties of the Weimar coalition. A smaller number of capitalists embraced radical racist ideas, but most preferred other parties of the right and right–center, judging them more reliable in protecting property and profits.[120] Similarly, the leaders of German industry were mostly unsympathetic to radical anti-Semitism, whether in 1919 or 1939.[121] In his "table talk" Hitler repeatedly expressed contempt for the "sniveling" of German businessmen. Some of them had expressed concern over the harshness of Nazi policies toward the Jews; those "same Jews," he declared, had stabbed Germany in the back, and "our softhearted bourgeoisie now sheds tears when we ship them off somewhere to the east!"[122]

After 1929, larger numbers of industrialists took an interest in Hitler and his even more rapidly growing party, but so did many other elements of the established powers in Germany; all misjudged the nature and power of Nazism. Ironically, some business leaders did assume a stance that conformed to Marxist theory in believing that they could manipulate the Nazis, but they were as mistaken as those who believed that the capitalists *did* manipulate the Nazis. The responsibility of the capitalists for making Hitler's success possible must be evaluated in light of the much more extensive funds channeled by businessmen into the parties of the right and right–center, without making those parties successful. Money was no doubt important, but it was not all-powerful.

To observe that Hitler was not a tool of the capitalists is not the same as to suggest that he did try to attract them. It is necessary, at any rate, to distinguish different stages of Nazi development; the ragtag anticapitalist party of 1919–1920

[119] Cf. Sarah Gordon, *Hitler, Germans and the "Jewish Question"* (Princeton, N.J., 1984), 50 ff.

[120] Cf. Ian Kershaw, *The Nazi Dictatorship: Problems and Perspectives of Interpretation* (London, 1989), 42 ff.

[121] Kershaw, *Nazi Dictatorship*, 57.

[122] *Hitler's Table Talk*, 107, 134, 397.

had been transformed by the late 1920s. The difference was not in actual program but in the more moderate tenor of Hitler's speeches and other public announcements. The extent to which industrialists and bankers eventually began to look with interest at the NSDAP was influenced by the extent to which Hitler toned down his radical rhetoric.

And that is a crucial point: After 1925 Hitler succeeded in persuading growing numbers of Germans that he was a statesman, standing above the quarrels of his lieutenants, even that he was committed to peace and reconciliation between classes and nations. The process developed in intricate ways even after Hitler took power in early 1933. Many ordinary Germans refused to believe that the excesses of his followers reflected Hitler's own intentions; "if the Führer only knew!" was heard in many areas. Actually, Hitler, like Mussolini, stood over a party that continued to be rife with factionalism; his lieutenants had their own, often conflicting agendas. His control of the NSDAP was by no means so total or even autocratic as was often believed. Hans Mommsen has provocatively described Hitler as a "weak dictator," who characteristically hesitated and procrastinated endlessly, fearing any action that might diminish his personal popularity or alienate one of the party's factions.[123]

Perhaps even more than was the case with the Italian Fascist Party, the NSDAP embraced factions with strikingly different programs, reflecting different regions of the country, social classes, and religions. In Bavaria, where there was a Catholic, monarchist, and peasant majority, Nazism looked different than it did in large cities like Berlin or highly industrialized areas like the Ruhr. The Bavarians were more inclined to antimodernism, crude racism, and categorical antisocialism, whereas in Berlin and the Ruhr the more progressive and generally more intellectual Nazi recruiters borrowed much of the Marxist rhetoric of the Communist and Social Democratic parties. The gangsterish faction of the Italian Fascists had a rough equivalent in the Brownshirts. Its leaders were social revolutionaries in a different sense than was the progressive wing of the party. Rather than trying to recruit workers away from the Marxists, Brownshirt leaders drew more characteristically from former military men, the lower-middle class, and the urban riffraff. For them "revolution" was less theoretical and more like simple plunder. It meant taking the wealth from those who had it, especially Jews, or taking over the jobs of the older elites. The Brownshirt leader Ernst Röhm was a notorious homosexual who used his party connections to scour the countryside in search of handsome young men of similar tastes. He and those around him had a withering contempt for bourgeois respectability and barely more positive feelings about other members of the NSDAP, especially the respectable citizens, military officers, university professors, and white-collar workers who joined the party as it became more successful. A further element of the Nazi movement, small at

---

[123] Hans Mommsen, *From Weimar to Auschwitz* (Princeton, N.J., 1991), especially Chapter 8.

first but growing until it came to challenge all centers of power in Germany, was the elitist SS (*Schutzstaffel*), led by Heinrich Himmler, one of the more fanatically racist of Nazi leaders.

Hitler's "weakness" as dictator derived from more than a concern not to tarnish his popular image. Even more than Mussolini, he skillfully manipulated the factions of his party. He characteristically gave his lieutenants ambiguous, even contradictory encouragement and then waited to see how they managed. He would wait until a situation had festered, or until his lieutenants implored him to intervene, before coming down on one side or another. Hitler had been repeatedly informed of Röhm's homosexual activities, for example, and of how those activities were damaging the reputation of the Nazi movement. But he long hesitated to take action. In early 1931 he told Otto Wagener, one of those who had complained to him about Röhm and who was at this point being dismissed as Brownshirt chief of staff, "The [appropriate] situation will have to arise [for my intervention]. . . . If I do it, I will be expected to proceed against Röhm and expel him. Surely your first advice is better: to do nothing. In politics, that is generally a medicine that is always effective."[124]

As was the case with Mussolini and Lenin, Hitler's genius, his claim to greatness as a politician, had much to do with his ability to keep these various factions within a single party, all loyal to him. His lieutenants thoroughly detested one another and were constantly scheming to enhance their power relative to that of others in the party. Hitler's genius also extended to his ability to sway the great mass of the population that did not actually join his party, or any party. It was, indeed, his uncanny ability to rally those masses that persuaded some of his more independent-minded lieutenants that he was the longed-for Leader.

But the meaning of Hitler's victory in January 1933 is not quite so simple as sometimes asserted. His assumption of power in Germany certainly can be conceptualized as symbolic of a culminating failure of the experiment in Gentile–Jewish relations that was launched in the nineteenth century, and of course, has been accepted as such in the dates and conceptualization of this book. But beyond the symbolism are some rarely appreciated enigmas, to be pursued in the final chapter.

[124] Wagener, *Hitler*, 106.

Epilogue and Conclusions

Seen as a whole, Hitler was not petty bourgeois at all, nor was he Catholic, or even German. His most essential characteristics . . . were . . . unique, shaped by his own . . . talents, by certain fateful events of his life . . . and by certain strokes of good fortune . . . for no matter how gifted and ruthless he was, he might well have been stopped, and more than once he almost was.[1]

It was the experience of power which finally turned Hitler into an irreconcilable fanatic. It took me most of 1933 to realize that the demon had entered into him. Even then many of us did not believe that the point of no return had been reached. We thought the impetus of the movement could be braked, the direction altered, even reversed.[2]

It is impossible to believe there could be a god, given such evil. And such evil had a human face – he [Adolf Eichmann] was not a devil but a human being.[3]

Epilogue: Nazi Germany, 1933–1945

German history and German forms of anti-Semitism have played a paramount, often defining role in these pages; evaluating the extent to which our post-Holocaust awareness has distorted perceptions of anti-Semitism has been central. Similarly, it has been repeatedly asked if German history, and European history more generally, can be properly viewed as moving inexorably,

---

[1] Percy Ernst Schramm, *Hitler: The Man and the Military Leader* (London, 1972), 125; from Werner Maser, *Hitler: Legend, Myth, Reality* (New York, 1971), 185.

[2] Ernst Hanfstaengl, *Unheard Witness* (New York, 1957), 224–5.

[3] Quoted in Diane Cole, "Nissenson's Tree of Life," *Present Tense,* vol. 13, no. 1, Autumn 1985, 59.

owing to essential or genetic flaws, toward mass murder. This Epilogue tries to offer only an interpretive overview of the Third Reich, but certain aspects of Nazi rule need to be underlined, since they connect in highly revealing ways with the long-range history of anti-Semitism, both in Germany and elsewhere.

I have tried to illustrate how many observers ascribe to anti-Semitism more centrality, more historical influence, a wider acceptance by the general population than the evidence for such a view will support. Simply put, a tradition of hatred for Jews in the German case, although obviously part of the story, is inadequate to explain the brutalities of the concentration camps and the horror of mechanized mass murder; many other aspects of German history and the nature of the Third Reich need to be examined, as indeed must aspects of human nature. A tradition of obedience to political authority, for example, was crucial – a tradition that paradoxically in the past had been mostly favorable to Jews. German thoroughness and efficiency, similarly, had been mostly admired by Jews, especially as those qualities applied to the operations of the Prussian state and bureaucracy. These and other previously admired German traits became horrifying when put in the service of Hitler's monstrous personal manias, but it is highly problematic to describe them as inherently rather than potentially evil, or as part of a uniquely poisoned German tradition. Even the failures of Germany's liberals are not quite so patent as many believe; German liberalism, if history had turned in different directions, might well have been seen as no less valid than the versions in France and the Anglo–Saxon democracies. Germany's defeat in World War I, with the ensuing catastrophes – revolution, inflation, depression – further discredited and crippled liberalism in Germany, but all of these developments are, again, not directly related to a tradition of anti-Semitism in Germany, however much they eventually played a role in the Jewish catastrophe.

In studying German history, I have been more impressed with the indeterminacy of events than with the power of an anti-Semitic tradition or "Germanic ideology" to shape or determine them. Similarly, it seems to me that the evidence for a planned murder of all Jews before the eve of World War II is unpersuasive, particularly given the pervasive chaos of Nazi decision making. Some of those who argue that such a plan existed seem more motivated by indignation than evidence – by a desire to make the charge of premeditated, first-degree murder stick, as it were. It is important to look carefully at some of the crucial stages of the history of the Third Reich in order to appreciate how, even after Hitler became chancellor, many different paths remained open.

As I noted in the Preface, there is a style of writing about the Holocaust and the anti-Semitism that preceded it, especially in older or popular works, such as Dawidowicz's, but forcefully revived in Goldhagen's and also present in Gilbert's, that anyone exploring the literature can hardly miss: angry, declamatory, dwelling upon outraged descriptions of anti-Semitic hatred while avoiding analysis or explanation of it, leaving it as mysterious and unrelated to Jewish action. Moreover, that writing tends toward what has been termed "foreshadowing" (an assertion that future events, in particular the implications of pre-Nazi anti-Semitism, were or should have been obvious to contemporaries).[4] Similarly, some Jewish leaders have expressed fears about the "desacralization of unspeakable suffering" that a scholarly study of the Holocaust, or any study by those who had not themselves directly experienced its horrors, might entail. Others have suggested definite "limits of representation,"[5] the inadequacy of the normal tools of understanding and communication when applied to the Nazis' mass murder of Jews. Against such positions, a number of scholars have warned of the subtle, often unappreciated dangers of claiming "Jewish proprietorship."[6] Among those dangers is to repel or at least puzzle non-Jewish observers and, more seriously, to nourish efforts to deny there was a mass murder of Jews.

The Holocaust deniers have no following among serious scholars, and their claims to have discovered the truth behind the smoke screen of Jewish proprietorship are transparently bogus to anyone familiar with the field.[7] Their agenda appears puzzling in some regards, but one goal is transparent enough: to discredit and denigrate Jews. A few Jewish leaders facilitate that goal by the dogmatic and simplistic tenor of their assertions, by the sometimes heavy-handed admonitions that accompany fund-raising efforts, and by the more general tendency to brand as moral lapses rather than intellectual errors any observations about Nazism or the Holocaust, or indeed anti-Semitism, with which they disagree. Of course, the notion of Jewish suffering as "sacred," placing it in a religious/mystical rather than secular/rationalist arena, implicitly removes it from history and normal historical inquiry, again offering an attractive target for the enemies of Jews, who can plausibly pose as proponents of telling the truth in opposition to Jewish efforts to suppress or somehow mystify it.

This study is not about the Holocaust, but certain aspects of that tragedy necessarily connect to my main concerns, particularly in dealing with historical determinants. Although I have often been concerned to counter a too simple determinism, I am also persuaded that the Holocaust should not be conceptualized as accidental, or as a complete aberration from the main themes of German history – or indeed just another example of the blood lust that is in the human species. Describing the violent Jew-hatred of the Third Reich as a product of totalitarianism, rather than the history of German anti-Semitism – and especially Hitler's anti-Semitism – also strikes me as problematic, although it, like the argument of "accidental" Nazism, poses some interesting and

[4] Michel André Bernstein, *Foregone Conclusions: Against Apocalyptic History* (Berkeley and Los Angeles, 1994).

[5] See Saul Friedlander, ed., *Probing the Limits of Representation* (Cambridge, Mass., 1992).

[6] Michael Marrus, *The Holocaust in History* (Toronto, 1987), 202.

[7] Cf. Deborah Lipstadt, *Denying the Holocaust: The Growing Assault on Truth and Memory* (New York, 1993).

potentially productive questions. The genuine challenge for the historian is to strike an appropriate balance, one that recognizes the reality of national character and intellectual traditions without crudely simplifying them or ascribing overly deterministic qualities to them. The flaws of the totalitarian argument, too, can be recognized without rejecting it as worthless or morally suspect.

The role of national character and national traditions may be revealingly compared in regard to Nazi Germany and Fascist Italy. There is little question that German and Italian national traditions were starkly different in the years under consideration, especially in regard to Jews. It is difficult to imagine a turn of events in Italy that would have resulted in a program by Italians to murder Jews systematically, as the Nazis did. Even when the Italian Fascist regime took up an anti-Semitic agenda, it had little of the inhuman efficiency, the disciplined singlemindedness, the revolting and pervasive brutality of the German case – and many ordinary Italians, including Fascists, offered covert aid to persecuted Jews. Even in Poland or Romania, where anti-Semitism was more a central issue of nationalist identity than in Germany, mass murder was less likely, if for no other reason than the relatively backward situation in those countries, economically, socially, and politically. That backwardness cannot be considered a moral virtue, even if it meant a less effective or efficient anti-Semitism. Similarly, that the Germans were relatively advanced economically was neither a moral virtue or defect, even if the implications of German industrialization and modernization were far more doleful for the Jews who fell under German rule.

The shadow of the Holocaust and its chilling effect on the way history has been written and understood are to be felt in many ways, both obvious and subtle. One prominent example is the tendency to believe that a result as massive and monstrous as the Final Solution must have had, as a cause, a hatred just as monstrous and massive. That cause is then "found" in German history, German national character, and German intellectual traditions. One may certainly find a monstrous hatred in certain elements of the German population, and most pertinently in Hitler himself, but that does not justify the conclusion that all Germans, or even most, harbored a hatred of similarly unbridled dimensions. Comparable reasoning may be encountered in those who, searching for an explanation of any number of what are considered contemporary calamities (sexist, racist, homophobic, or ecological), find appropriately massive causes in the Judeo–Christian tradition of western civilization.

The issue is not whether relevant causes can be found but whether the investigator is blind to all but what he or she sets out to "discover" – which, again, appears to be an all-too-obvious aspect of Goldhagen's work. Such singleminded evaluations, like those of a criminal prosecutor, often do, to be sure, turn up provocative information, and the debate around them has sometimes changed the nature of historical understanding, but nonetheless the large dangers of such singlemindedness remain. Drumont did expose some Jewish scoundrels, but that does not legitimate the rest of what he did. That he was initially applauded by some decent men, Jean Jaurès, for example, suggests further how muddied the issue can become (as does, indeed, the evidence that Jaurès, however decent, still harbored prejudices and preconceptions about Jews).

Much of the scholarly debate about understanding the Holocaust has become too fine-spun to allow even a summary here. The arcane nature of that debate, sometimes burdened by academic jargon, also feeds the pseudopopulist claims of the Holocaust deniers.[8] My main concern in this book, at any rate, is not with the Nazi period but with the sixty or so years before 1933 and with how instincts similar to those influencing interpretations of Nazism have played a role in the way that modern anti-Semitism is approached: It can only be "described, not understood" (Rosten); non-Jews somehow lack the credentials to appreciate the suffering it has caused; if you haven't experienced it, you cannot understand it.[9] For some of those who reason in this way, it is not only morally abhorrent to attempt to enter the mental and emotional worlds of leading Nazis but equally so to invite readers to try to understand the minds and spirits of such men as Treitschke, Vogelsang, or Lueger, who did not call for violence against Jews, or even demand that their civil liberties be curtailed.

Lucy Dawidowicz has written that sympathetic understanding is necessary in order to write "genuine" Jewish history. Non-Jews – as well as "self-hating" Jews (her main target) – lack the required emotional closeness, the mystical "love of Israel" (*ahavat yisrael*). Yet, in her approach to German history, the need for this kind of intellectual preparation is implicitly denied or turned upside down: In order to write "genuine" German history, she seems to think, hatred and resentment rather than sympathy or love constitute the appropriate state of mind. She makes precious little effort to understand the motivations of nineteenth-century nationalistic Germans; they are simply contemptible "other people." To ask the question, "Might I or those with whom I identify have been capable of similar thoughts and actions?" is, again, implicitly relegated to a

---

8 Recent volumes that pursue these matters, with ample bibliographical references, include Marrus, *Holocaust in History* [the best short introduction]; Friedlander, *Probing the Limits of Representation* [where some of the jargon and murky reasoning can be found]; Peter Baldwin, ed., *Reworking the Past: Hitler, the Holocaust, and the Historians' Debate* (Boston, 1990); Peter Hayes, ed., *Lessons and Legacies: The Meaning of the Holocaust in a Changing World* (Evanston, Ill., 1991); Thomas Childers and Jane Caplan, eds., *Reevaluating the Third Reich* (New York, 1993).

9 Jacob Katz has commented, "Gentile historians know a good deal more about non-Jewish societies than about the Jews. So alien is the internal Jewish milieu to most of them that even the sufferings caused by anti-Semitism are hardly ever portrayed in a realistic or convincing manner"; in "Misreadings of Anti-Semitism," *Commentary*, vol. 76, no. 1, July 1983, 39. Walter Laqueur, similarly, has commented that "it is a matter of interest and regret that few non-Jews have given attention to the history and sources of anti-Semitism"; *Commentary*, vol. 44, July 1967, 84.

morally suspect status. Similarly, Sachar's treatment of the Romanians is little more than a screed, without the slightest effort at balance. These are two extreme but by no means isolated examples, and the remarkable reception of Goldhagen's even more unbalanced history suggests that the problem is not simply something of the past.

Insofar as the purported uniqueness of the Nazi period or the Holocaust comes down to this kind of reasoning – and it is often difficult to make out what is actually meant by the term "uniqueness" – I cannot accept it as a valid or useful distinction, for I do not find the Germans uniquely contemptible, however appalling large numbers of them were. It has been a key assertion of these pages that although no historian can be free of love or hatred, a determined effort to understand and confront the opposing tugs of those two passions must be made, for one of them alone typically does not lead to "genuine history" but to skewed, tendentious versions of it, conducive to self-righteousness and new cycles of misunderstanding and hatred.

The Germans and the Nazis were human beings, and the history they made can be understood by human beings just as other human history is understood. For all the labyrinthine complications introduced into the discussions of understanding the Holocaust, that simple axiom remains the one to which I return. "Sympathy," although a tricky concept, should not be categorically withheld from any human group, even if it is exploited for repellent purposes. It is no doubt painful to face the implications of accepting Hitler or Eichmann as "human," in some sense "like us." Sorrow or revulsion at being part of a flawed humanity is not an unfamiliar reaction in studying other appalling chapters of human history – the African slave trade, the treatment of Native Americans, the slaughter in the trenches of the First World War, the Soviet Gulag. All of these were in their own way unique, and all have mysterious, haunting aspects to them, especially for those who identify them as happening to their ancestors. Some Jewish leaders worry that to recognize these other chapters trivializes the Holocaust, draining it of its peculiar horror. That is, again, a point of view that is to some extent understandable but, I believe, profoundly mistaken.

The familiar, analytically impoverished narratives of events between 1933 and 1945 to be found in countless history bestsellers, general texts, newsreels, and television specials typically carry with them a heavy cargo of unexamined assumptions, judgments, and messages. Many important things are lost in the process, prominent among them a sense of the indeterminacy of events as experienced at the time, the uncertainties of the actors, the paths not taken. Again, it is more often a matter of style or packaging than factual errors or misrepresentations. In such accounts, for example, the *Machtergreifung*, the Nazi "seizure of power" in early 1933 is narrated with drama and power: Reichstag fire, Hitlerian oratory, hysterical crowds, torchlight rallies, storm trooper violence against Jews. As popular entertainment it is hard to find recent history that is more fascinatingly horrific. But a number of inaccurate messages are purveyed, among them that the Nazis were diabolically clever and awesomely disciplined under Hitler's charismatic and Machiavellian leadership and that the German population was in its great majority swept away by Nazi propaganda.

This kind of popular entertainment ironically accepts important elements of the image that Goebbels's Propaganda Ministry itself sought to purvey. Scholars have increasingly come to understand how little the Machtergreifung was a "seizure" of power. It was in truth a confused and fumbling affair, in which plain luck and initiatives by non-Nazis were absolutely crucial.[10] Machtergreifung was a Nazi propaganda term; it served to mask a number of important details that detracted from the image that the Nazis sought to present of Hitler and the NSDAP. As one of the most able of the historians of Nazism, Ian Kershaw has observed: "In bringing Hitler to power, chance events and conservative miscalculation played a larger role than any actions of the Nazi leader himself."[11]

The large role of chance in the developments of late 1932 and early 1933 makes it difficult to consider them an inevitable, or even a highly likely result of the flow of German history. One can easily imagine any number of choices by leading protagonists that would have resulted in a different set of developments. Even the notion that Hitler's charismatic leadership, especially his will to power, was the decisive factor is difficult to accept without important qualifications, since time after time in late 1932 and early 1933 crucial developments did not reflect his initiative but that of others. Even what many have considered Hitler's inspired opportunism often came not from him but from others, frequently non-Nazis. As we have seen, from early manhood on Hitler was personally lazy and intellectually undisciplined, unwilling to deal with the often tedious details that had to be considered in order to translate his extravagant and irresponsible rhetoric into practical policies. He usually left the working out of such details to subordinates.

Hitler's proclaimed path to power after the failure of the Putsch in 1923 was by popular mandate at the polls. His success in that regard was at first not impressive. By the May 1928 Reichstag elections the NSDAP had won only 2.6 percent of the vote, although party membership had grown from 27,000 to 108,000 between 1925 and 1928.[12] It was only after the Depression hit that the NSDAP's popular vote skyrocketed. By July 1932, with 230 seats in the Reichstag, the party became Germany's largest. The meaning of that rapid growth is, however, uncertain. Undoubtedly many Germans were in a mood to

---

[10] A recent and persuasive exploration of this theme is Henry Ashby Turner's *Hitler's Thirty Days to Power* (New York, 1996).

[11] Kershaw, *Hitler*, 38.

[12] Hans Mommsen, *Weimar to Auschwitz* (New York, 1992), 147.

try radical solutions; they were frightened and indignant. Millions of them blamed the Weimar Republic, the free-market economy, and other liberal institutions. But whether these many Germans, in casting a vote for the NSDAP, actually embraced – even understood – Nazism is doubtful. And can we confidently conclude that anti-Semitic feelings, the alleged basis of Nazi popularity, suddenly jumped from around 3 percent to around 40 percent within a year or two?

What it meant to be a Nazi, even for the well informed, remained uncertain. The party's many factions, the contradictory promises made by its leaders, the sloganeering, and the extremely rapid growth resulted in an NSDAP by 1933 that presented substantially different faces to different people. Partly for such reasons, votes for the NSDAP and membership in it were volatile; people joined the party and then left it or voted for it and then for another party in ways that hardly spoke of firm commitment. Indeed, even after Hitler became chancellor, hundreds of thousands left the Nazi Party, as hundreds of thousands were simultaneously joining it.[13] It is instructive that the votes for the Nazis slumped in November 1932, from 37 percent of the total to 33 percent, causing many to believe that the beginning of the end for Hitler and his party had been reached. It seemed that the rapid growth was little more than a flash in the pan – the most that could be accomplished by crude demagogy in troubled times – but now the contradictory promises were coming back to haunt the Nazis.

It is further instructive that Hitler and his lieutenants were themselves deeply alarmed by the drop in votes. *They* did not believe in their inevitable victory. The party's coffers were empty, after a series of all-out electoral campaigns. Morale was low in the party rank-and-file, and party officials were exhausted, while the party's factionalism was growing worse, threatening to destroy it. (The parallels with Russia are both striking and instructive: Trotsky and Lenin, too, argued that the opportunities of the autumn of 1917 were unique; unless the Bolshevik Party – also wracked by factionalism and enjoying a highly volatile support by a minority of the population that only dimly understood the Bolshevik program – seized the reins of power in early November, proletarian revolution might never succeed in Russia. The logic of Russian history, too, can hardly be seen as moving inexorably toward a Bolshevik seizure of power.)

Large elements of the German population, most notably the Catholics and the organized working class, the main supporters of the Catholic Center Party and the SPD, remained resistant to Nazi propaganda. Close to two-thirds of the German electorate had voted for non-Nazi parties through November 1932. Even the March 1, 1933, elections, which cannot be described as free,

---

[13] Mommsen, *Weimar to Auschwitz*, 150. Out of 239,000 members joining before Sept. 1930, only 44 percent were still in the party by 1935; some 1.5 million had left the party.

gave the Nazis less than a majority (43.9 percent), although with the 8 percent of the vote won by the right-wing Nationalists, Hitler could count on a bare majority supporting him in the Reichstag. Once the KPD, representing 12 percent of the vote, was outlawed, his majority became more comfortable.

It is reasonable to conclude that a majority of German voters had lost whatever commitment to liberal democracy they may have once had and were in an ugly mood, since the large vote for the Communists, even if anti-Nazi, was no less intensely anti-Weimar. The non-Nazi votes on the right, too, often reflected authoritarian sentiments as well as anti-Semitism and xenophobic nationalism. Even among voters for the Center Party there was undoubtedly much anti-Semitism and xenophobia. Many new voters (young, first-time voters and previous nonvoters) voted Nazi, and so did those who were expressing an inchoate sense of frustration and protest rather than clear identification with any party program. At any rate, the Nazis never gained a clear majority in free elections; the support they did win was soft, and many of the ballots cast for the NSDAP represented panicked conservatism rather than an informed preference for Nazism. Again, Hitler and his advisers were perfectly aware of this large body of essentially uncommitted voters, and his caution in the early years of his rule must be understood in terms of his all-consuming preoccupation with retaining and enhancing his popularity, a preoccupation that in many regards lasted until the outbreak of World War II and even beyond.

The nature of Hitler's accession to power is frequently misunderstood. He was never "elected" chancellor, as is often stated, if only because chancellors were not elected under the Weimar constitution. He, like chancellors before him, was appointed to the post by President Hindenburg, who until January 1933 had refused to believe that "corporal" Hitler was competent to fill such a high position. But Hindenburg, 86 years old in 1933 and increasingly feeble, finally agreed with those advisers who argued that in coalition with conservatives, Hitler and his party could be controlled, since the Nazis had no experience in the exercise of governmental power. Most of all, the NSDAP seemed to those conservatives a bulwark against the Communists, whose ranks had also grown rapidly, to the point that the KPD enjoyed approximately as much popular support as the Bolshevik Party had in Russia in the late summer of 1917.

That the Bolsheviks had come to power with a distinct minority of the population behind them, and then had ruthlessly used that power to establish a terrorist dictatorship, haunted many in Germany as elsewhere. This Bolshevik model undoubtedly played an important role in German politics in this time of extreme crisis. Comparisons between 1917 and 1933 are further revealing in that fundamental misperceptions were widespread concerning what either Bolshevik or Nazi rule might entail. In 1917 the slogan "All power to the soviets!" was by no means understood to mean all power to the Bolshevik Party. Similarly, many Germans had little sense of what Hitler's Nazi/conservative cabinet would produce. Both Bolsheviks and Nazis benefited from the division and floundering of more democratic forces. Both also benefited from a sense that as rapidly growing outsider parties they ought to be given a chance, since the mainline parties seemed unable to rule.

Those in Russia or in Germany who reasoned that things could not be worse learned soon enough that things could be *much* worse, but only after the Bolsheviks and Nazis had fashioned one-party dictatorships that rendered opposition dangerous if not suicidal. Whether or not one accepts the theoretical trappings associated with the concept of totalitarianism, Nazi rule may be seen as departing in substantial ways not only from liberal democracy but also from the Prussian-dominated Reich of 1871 to 1919. Again, one does not have to accept the apologetically inspired notion that Nazism was a total aberration from German history, a mysterious madness, to agree that in 1933 a genie had been in some sense released. Options for opponents of Nazism narrowed rapidly. For those in the Nazi movement many restraints, especially moral restraints, fell away, whereas ambitions and appetites, often of the crudest sort, were awakened. A peculiar kind of anarchy began to spread in Germany, what Hans Mommsen has termed "a chain-reaction of anti-humanitarian impulses."[14]

This anarchic situation needs to be kept in mind in considering one aspect of Arendt's theorizing that seems puzzling if not absurd when initially encountered: The mass murder of Jews under Nazi auspices, she argued, emerged out of the logic of the totalitarian system, its insatiable appetite for mass death and terror, *not* the power of anti-Semitic ideology.[15] The murder under Soviet rule of millions of Russians was an expression of the Russian form of that system and not really of Russian history or what might be termed a Russian parallel to anti-Semitism, class hatred. In countries where there was more popular anti-Semitism than in Germany, the existing regimes oppressed the Jews but did not organize mass murder. That occurred only when those countries were taken over by Nazi totalitarianism.

However retrospectively revealing the parallels between Germany and Russia, for most people in the 1930s the differences between the situations in the two countries seemed more important than the similarities. The Bolsheviks broke promises and violated legality at every turn, rapidly losing most of the limited support they initially enjoyed. They held on to power through terror. Between 1917 and 1921 tens of thousands died in Russia as a direct result of measures taken by the Cheka, while hundreds of thousands, finally millions, perished in less direct ways (imprisonment, starvation, homelessness, or disease in battles between Red and White armies). In contrast, Hitler came to power in a legal manner and operated in ways that gave an appearance of respecting constitutional restraints. He and his lieutenants could plausibly

---

[14] Mommsen, *From Weimar to Auschwitz*, 184.
[15] See the discussion of Arendt in ibid., 262.

boast, by the end of 1933, that the Nazi revolution was actually a humane one; it had cost the lives of fewer people than any revolution in history, several hundred at most – whereas the Bolshevik Party and the Cheka, in the hands of fanatical Jews, had heartlessly murdered millions.

Bloodshed in Germany remained relatively minor until the eve of World War II, whereas repeated waves of mass murder rolled over Soviet Russia. In 1917 Lenin came to power in a poor, illiterate, industrially backward country devastated by war and revolution; the first years of Bolshevik rule seemed only to worsen Russia's backwardness, poverty, and economic isolation. In contrast, Hitler became the leader of a country that although weakened by depression enjoyed one of the highest rates of literacy in the world and was one of the richest and most industrially advanced. Under Nazi rule Germany's economy revived. The Bolsheviks destroyed the existing Russian state, murdered the tsar and his family, and killed or forced into exile thousands of the members of the old ruling elites. By 1921 Russia's social structures were profoundly transformed as compared with 1914, its economy in utter shambles, its people homeless and starving. The Nazis, on the other hand, were invited by the older elites to share governmental responsibility. There was thereafter no dramatic showdown between those elites and the Nazis. The Nazi *Gleichschaltung* ("bringing into line," roughly equivalent to "revolution") did not alter social and economic relationships in immediate ways. Various Nazi organizations gradually infiltrated established German institutions, but the changes in social and economic relationships before the war years were incomparably less important than in Russia. Although the Nazis assumed a number of leading positions in the German state, conservative elites continued to predominate in most of the governmental bureaucracies. The upper echelons of the military and business, too, remained mostly unchanged. The same elites, in other words, that had persisted throughout the Weimar years, after the "failed revolution" of 1918–1919, also remained in place throughout most of the 1930s.

Hitler became incomparably more popular than Lenin or any other Bolshevik. It is indeed likely that Hitler enjoyed a broader, more fervent popularity by the mid-1930s than any politician in the world, since the economies of most countries continued to flounder and internal divisions became more serious, even in the liberal democracies. Although the hope by German conservatives that the experience of power would expose Hitler as incompetent proved unjustified, many believed throughout most of the 1930s that Hitler had indeed moved away from his earlier radicalism. Moreover, these conservative hopes were not entirely without fulfillment, for, in Mommsen's words, "seldom has any party been so unprepared for political power as was the NSDAP on January 1933,"[16] and without the continuing cooperation of con-

16 Ibid., 151.

servative cadres in the various agencies of government, a cooperation that Hitler cultivated,[17] he almost certainly would not have survived as chancellor for more than a short time. His assiduous courting of those elites, and his failure to replace the overwhelming majority of them with Nazis, was the cause of much grumbling and disappointment among the "old fighters" of the Nazi movement, who also spoke of a failed revolution, as had the German left after 1918.

This Nazi–conservative cooperation made for a reasonably efficient, day-to-day operation of the German government. And because the drift and frustrations of the Weimar years appeared to be over, Hitler was able to persuade growing numbers of his compatriots that he was a politician of genuine stature, a stern yet benign leader who was administering the strong medicine that Germany needed to restore its internal health and its international position. Many former opponents lapsed into silence; others were not only neutralized by Hitler's successes and the wild popularity he came to enjoy but themselves began to admire him. Even in other countries, where skepticism about Hitler naturally remained stronger, many prominent politicians were ready to tolerate him on the basis of his accomplishments, his popularity, and his exceedingly effective anticommunism.

In the months immediately following his appointment as chancellor, Hitler succeeded in outlawing all parties but the NSDAP and in winning Reichstag support for the Enabling Act, which allowed him to rule by decree for the following two years. Yet, even with these steps, Hitler's power remained limited. We have seen how Mussolini never succeeded in eliminating the king, the church, or elements of the older establishment. Similarly, although Hitler gathered power more rapidly and completely than Mussolini had, he still felt the need to give the impression that he was respecting the constitution. He faced a number of powerful restraining forces, chief among them President Hindenburg and the Prussian Junker elite, concentrated in the chiefs of staff of the Reichswehr. That elite remained skeptical of Nazism, particularly its social radicalism.

Hitler's freedom of action was complicated in another, more paradoxical way. The anarchy unleashed in early 1933, although undoubtedly a byproduct of his actions, allowed for developments that escaped his control or even threatened his authority.[18] The most immediately obvious threat was from the Brownshirts under Ernst Röhm's leadership. Hermann Göring's various ministries also took off in directions not under Hitler's close control, as did the Gauleiters (local Nazi Party bosses). Such developments implicitly went contrary to Hitler's alliance with the conservative elites. It is clear in retrospect

---

[17] Hitler "did not always support radicalizing tendencies in the regime." Ibid., 184.

[18] Cf. Hans Mommsen, "Reflections on the Position of Hitler and Göring in the Third Reich," in Childers and Caplan, *Reevaluating the Third Reich*, 86–97.

that he had reason to repeat the familiar refrain: "I can handle my enemies; it's my friends that worry me."

Hitler proved capable of "handling" his friends – even when it meant murdering them – while events seemed to play into his hands time and again in ways that almost certainly shaped his policies. The Reichstag fire of February 23, 1933, for example, long thought to have been set by the Nazis in order to provide a pretext for repressing the Communists, actually caught Hitler and his closest advisers by surprise. Believing that it had been set by the Communists as part of a revolutionary counteroffensive, Hitler was at first on the edge of panic, but he regained his composure and moved to repress and outlaw the German Communist Party. Revealingly, the emergency decrees, establishing the legal foundations for that action, were not formulated by Hitler but by an equally panicked Nationalist official in the Prussian Ministry of Interior.

Conservative nationalists were no less motivated by fear of communism than were the Nazis and were no less willing to take constitutional shortcuts in putting down the Communist menace. Indeed, there was a broad concern at this time, something like a popular mandate, to "do something" about the rapidly growing KPD, which was believed to be planning its own seizure of power. Hitler's strong-arm tactics, like those of Mussolini in Italy in the early 1920s, could easily be rationalized as necessary to preserve the country from Communist terror and actually save millions of lives

As Führer of the newly proclaimed Third Reich, Hitler understood that his followers expected something more than torch-light rallies and inspiring ceremonies. He had to offer them, especially the old fighters, something yet to prevent the more radical of them from alienating other parts of the population. These competing agendas were not easily reconciled. Violence against the Communists was one thing, attacks on property another, and Hitler understood that attacks on Jewish property would tarnish his popularity in many quarters and cause further economic dislocation. The boycott of Jewish stores, forwarded by the party's radicals, was a complete failure. Most German consumers continued to frequent the Jewish stores that they had previously favored. Hitler also knew that the violent attacks by the Brownshirts offended most respectable Germans, much as the criminal element of Blackshirts in Italy a decade before finally had come to alarm many middle-class Italians. Hitler, like Mussolini, was aware that he had to reassure that class in order to remain in power.

The issue of the "second revolution" became a major headache for Hitler by the summer of 1933, but he repeatedly postponed making a decision about it. Röhm demanded that Jewish jobs and property be taken over by Nazi old fighters, and if Hitler had had a free hand, he might have acceded to those demands, but his economic advisers were unanimously against the Brownshirt claims. Other Nazi leaders both feared and detested Röhm; they repeatedly urged Hitler to repress the Brownshirts. Military leaders were outraged by

Röhm's claims that the Brownshirts should take over the military function of the Third Reich. It seemed possible that the Reichswehr would stage a preventative takeover if Hitler refused to do something about Röhm. But still Hitler procrastinated.

Procrastination in formulating a definite policy in regard to the Jews was even more obvious in Hitler's first year in power. A general planning body had been set up in the Nazi Party in 1930, under Gregor Strasser, who complained that the NSDAP did not know what it would do if it ever actually gained power. Thereafter plans were worked out in some areas, such as agriculture and law, but revealingly no planning of any sort was even attempted in regard to the Jewish question.[19] When Jews were arrested or violently attacked in the first months of 1933, it was not usually as Jews but as communists, socialists, or other prominent anti-Nazis. There was simply no consistent or clearly articulated anti-Jewish program. Hitler's familiar rhetorical flights, his dire warnings to the Jews of what they could expect from him, were notable for their rarity in the first months of his rule. There were individual anti-Jewish actions by various Nazi contingents, ambiguous pronouncements by Hitler and other Nazis, and much confusion. Brownshirt leaders bullied Jews on the streets and pushed for a boycott of Jewish shops, but the Brownshirts failed to win consistent public support from Hitler. As one observer quipped at this time: "[Hitler] rants much less. He has stopped breathing fire at the Jews and can make a speech nowadays lasting four hours without mentioning the word 'Jew.'"[20]

Was Hitler's reticence in this regard merely part of an elaborate ruse, as the Intentionalists have argued? Or was he unwilling to make a definite decision on a matter that did not yet require it? Intentionalists and Functionalists agree that it was in his interest to cultivate a statesmanlike image and to enhance his reputation as a moderate on the Jewish issue. But the Functionalists have asked why Hitler should have been programmatically clear and precise in regard to the Jews, when in every other aspect of his political activity he was inclined to vagueness and opportunism and to putting off decisions until they were absolutely necessary. Functionalists point to the ample evidence that such figures as Himmler and Göring seriously entertained, throughout the 1930s and even into the first stages of World War II, a number of "solutions to the Jewish problem" that did not entail mass murder: at first, internal persecution and forced emigration, then deportation to Madagascar, and finally resettlement in the East. Presumably, if he had decided on mass murder, Hitler would have given some indications before the war of his ultimate intentions to men like Himmler or Göring, which he almost certainly did not.

---

[19] Karl A. Schleunes, "Retracing the Twisted Road: Nazi Policies Toward German Jews, 1933–39," in François Furet, ed., *Unanswered Questions* (New York, 1989), 54–8.

[20] Toland, *Hitler*, 416; from Hermann Eich, *The Unloved Germans* (New York, 1965), 92.

Few scholars, of whichever school, have questioned the intensity of Hitler's anti-Semitism. Few have doubted that he intended to harm the Jews in some major way – to isolate them, humiliate them, or strip them of influence, property, and position. The more difficult issue remains, however, whether he was intent on systematic murder from the beginning or whether his ideas about the nature of the harm to be done to the Jews evolved and gained precision as his power grew, his physical and mental health deteriorated, and new opportunities suggested the possibility of measures that had not been considered in the preceding years. Again, there is little question that the logic of Hitler's inflamed rhetoric implied some sort of extreme solution, but political rhetoric and practical policy are different matters. Few observers, even among Jews, took his rhetoric seriously at first, and he himself, as we have seen, occasionally made comments that seemed to counter or qualify his rhetorical flights.

Even the "moderate" solutions that Hitler's henchmen contemplated were cruel, madly utopian, and morally outrageous. But given the spotty nature of the evidence, to say nothing of the difficulty of knowing what is going on in any person's mind – let alone one as cluttered as Hitler's – there will necessarily remain a degree of honest doubt about his exact role. The Nazi system of rule contained an ever-radicalizing dynamism that almost inevitably ensnared Jews in it, whatever Hitler's intentions. They were among the most vulnerable of Germany's citizens; their wealth and position in Germany's economy and society awakened the appetites of various competing Nazi agencies. But recognizing Jewish vulnerability is not the same as agreeing that attacks on them were carefully planned and coordinated.

As noted, the reason that some of the more intransigent Intentionalists (e.g., Dawidowicz or Robert Wistrich) insist on the charge of planned genocide seems to be their aversion to any position that even implicitly softens the charge of murder in the first degree. That aversion is understandable, but what is easily overlooked is that the Functionalist argument makes a more subtle and in some ways more credible indictment of Hitler. Moreover, it points to the participation of a larger part of the German population than does Intentionalism. The Functionalist perspective suggests how many elements of German society finally became actively involved in the complex and far-reaching efforts necessary to accomplish mass murder. This did not occur simply because the overwhelming majority of Germans "were behind their Führer," or because they were only following orders, but for much more intricate and plausible reasons.

There were many practical reasons to hesitate in early 1933 as far as concrete measures against the Jews were concerned, and Hitler was above all a savvy politician. To begin with, Jews in Germany and elsewhere were not quite so defenseless as some accounts suggest. More important, they did not appear so to Hitler and his advisers. Hitler believed in Jewish power and was reticent to challenge it head-on. Nazi leaders entertained outlandish fantasies about international Jewry, but they were not misinformed in their belief that public opinion in Great Britain, France, and the United States opposed persecution of the Jews in Germany. The issues were not unfamiliar: In the prewar years, it was believed that Tsar Nicholas II had lost his "war" against Jacob Schiff and "international Jewry" in considerable part because of the international obloquy earned by Russia's anti-Jewish policies. That defeat, which of course became catastrophic by 1919, was duly noted and much commented upon in Germany as elsewhere.

Hitler was almost certainly even more impressed with what had happened to one of his heroes, Henry Ford. In *Mein Kampf* Hitler had written that in the New World "only a single great man," Henry Ford, had been able to stand up against the Jews, "to their fury."[21] In the early 1920s Ford had launched a campaign against the Jews in his paper, *The Dearborn Independent;* articles from it were eagerly translated into German by the Nazis. But Ford then apparently concluded that the "fury" of the Jews was indeed formidable, for a boycott of his products loomed, as well as lawsuits. He finally backed down, offering a formal apology to the Jews, even publicly burning some of his anti-Semitic works.[22] As the American humorist Will Rogers quipped: "Henry Ford used to have it in for the Jewish people – until he saw them all in Chevrolets."

Ford's capitulation to the economic power of the Jews, a power that appeared especially impressive when it could rally liberal opinion, can hardly have been unnoticed by the Nazis, and a showdown with "international Jewry" was not something that Hitler or his closest advisors could comfortably entertain in early 1933. They understood that unifying Germany and getting the country back on its feet economically were central to gaining wider support from the German people. Similarly, a boycott of Jewish enterprises in Germany in 1933 would have been economically disruptive and would have entailed the risk of a retaliatory international boycott of German goods at a time when Germany was concerned to expand its foreign trade and strengthen its foreign credits.

The parallels with Plehve at the time of the Kishinev pogrom are suggestive: He tried to reassure various foreign observers because he feared the economic implications for Russia if he appeared to condone anti-Jewish rioting. Plehve lost his war with the Jews in the most direct sense; he was assassinated by a Jew not long after the Kishinev pogrom. The propaganda war surrounding the events in Kishinev, and the inclination of both sides to misrepresentation and exaggeration, assumed even greater dimensions in the pogroms that followed the revolution of 1905.

After World War I, the temptation of some Jews to exaggerate, or even make up atrocity stories, later exposed as false, had inured a number of observers to

---

[21] Adolf Hitler, *Mein Kampf,* 639.

[22] The story is covered in Albert Lee, *Henry Ford and the Jews* (New York, 1980).

the charges of "wailing Jews," observers who in most instances were little inclined to sympathize with Jewish concerns anyway. Hitler played upon that discredit by charging the world Jewish press with making up atrocity stories about Nazi Germany (and most Germans believed, with greater justification, that anti-German atrocity stories from 1914 to 1919 had indeed been made up). Jewish leaders in Germany acceded to Nazi pressure and signed a statement denying that atrocities against Jews in Germany had occurred.

There was much parrying and bluster, both from the Nazis and from their opponents in the rest of the world, as boycotts on both sides were threatened. The result was an international standoff, both sides finally backing away from a confrontation. But beyond all the posturing, a key point should not be lost: The boycott of Jewish stores in Germany fizzled. It lasted a day or two – "a symbolic victory" was the hollow claim. Thereafter the issue of boycotting Jewish stores dropped from center stage.

The failure of the boycott aggravated Hitler's problem with the Brownshirts, whose complaints grew that they had nothing to show for their devotion to the cause. Hitler's violent showdown with Röhm and the SA might easily be described as the most crucial event in the internal history of the Third Reich. It is difficult to believe that Hitler would have survived for long without that much-postponed confrontation. Not only were most of his own lieutenants and the leaders of the military eager to destroy Röhm, but also a large part of respectable opinion hoped that Hitler would deal with these lawless hooligans the way that he had already dealt with the Communists. A further complicating but crucial factor was the aged President Hindenburg, whose health was visibly declining. Hitler wanted to combine the office of president and chancellor upon Hindenburg's death, but army leaders made it clear that they would not support that move unless he did something about the Brownshirt threat.

The destruction of the SA leadership was undertaken by Himmler's SS, in the so-called Night of the Long Knives, June 30, 1934. The ruthlessness of this purge made a powerful impression in Germany. By putting a number of the leading old fighters to death, Hitler gave a sobering example to other potential opponents of what might await them. Congratulations came in from all over Germany: President Hindenburg, the chiefs of staff, business and community leaders – all lauded the purge. Again it was widely believed that by decisive action Hitler had prevented a bloody civil war in Germany; he had done to the Brownshirts, as with the Communists, what they had planned to do to others.

The Night of the Long Knives was not planned by Hitler. Its actual implementation, which did require careful planning, was also the work of others – indeed, Hitler was led to it by others in ways he may never have fully appreciated (Himmler fed him false information, for example, about Röhm's plans.). But after these bloody events, Hitler's emotional distancing became even more pronounced, as did his sense of being chosen to perform tasks that others would shrink from. Hitler became increasingly unwilling to listen to remarks that were even implicitly critical of his policies. He more and more divorced himself from contact with leading governmental figures, avoiding "any attempt to confront his ideological dream-world with political and social reality."[23]

A number of Jews returned to Germany after June 1934, since it appeared that the most powerful faction of anti-Semites in the Nazi movement had been crushed and that the regime was settling down. Indeed, some suspected that Hitler was quietly abandoning the Jewish issue; rather than being a unifying force, anti-Semitism continued to be divisive, and Hitler wanted most of all to be popular. Revealingly, Leni Riefenstahl's famous propaganda film, "Triumph of the Will" (1935), contained not a single anti-Semitic reference, a puzzling lapse if hatred of Jews had been considered a useful device in attracting broader sympathy for the Nazi movement, and even more puzzling if anti-Semitism is considered central to Nazism.

President Hindenburg died on August 2, 1934, and Hitler, assuming the office of president, orchestrated an elaborate ceremony that included an oath of personal fidelity to him. A plebiscite was held to determine support for the merging of the offices of chancellor and president, which won 86.6 percent of the vote. For many Germans the state had long held a special position, standing above social conflicts and responsible for resolving them. In its more extreme forms this "state worship" had elevated the state to the role of a divine force, accomplishing God's purpose in history. For growing numbers of Germans, "the Führer's will," now that he was not only head of the government and popular acclaimed leader but also head of the state, become synonymous with legality.

The Jewish issue remained unsolved, and Hitler moved cautiously toward measures that might be broadly acceptable, especially to his conservative allies. Dissatisfaction by conservatives with the role of Jews in German life had undoubtedly intensified in the Weimar years. Even outside the ranks of the conservatives, many Germans were not opposed to the idea of rectifying what they believed to be the unnaturally large numbers of Jews in leading positions of Germany's state, economy, and culture. But Hitler continued to refrain from making any major pronouncements about the Jewish issue throughout 1934 and the first half of 1935. The measures that he did finally take, were again revealingly spur-of-the-moment, anything but the product of long-range planning.

His intended agenda at the Nuremberg party rally in September 1935, to which he had invited the Reichstag and the diplomatic corps, had been a declaration outlining Germany's foreign policy goals, but he was dissuaded from doing so by Baron von Neurath, his foreign minister, who considered the

---

[23] Mommsen, *Weimar to Auschwitz*, 238.

moment inauspicious.[24] He thus faced a potentially embarrassing contretemps – so many dignitaries and nothing of major importance to say to them. He decided to use the occasion to announce what amounted to a compromise between radicals in the party, who had been pressing anew for anti-Jewish actions, and officials in the Ministry of Interior, who had been urging that attacks on Jewish business be expressly prohibited and a clear position be taken against confiscating Jewish property.

Hitler himself had repeatedly emphasized that the removal of Jews from German life should be done "rationally" and legally. Other leading Nazis made statements that supported what might be termed Gentile Zionism. Göring, widely regarded as the number two man in the Nazi Reich, had informed an Italian journalist in May 1932 that Jews would have to be removed from leading positions in Germany's state and society, but "the decent Jewish merchant who is willing to stay in Germany as an alien protected under the law will be allowed to pursue his business undisturbed."[25] In early 1933, Arthur Ruppin, a prominent Zionist, in a meeting with Professor Hans F. K. Günther, a leading theorist of race, was assured that the Jews were not considered inferior to the Aryans but simply "different"; a "fair solution" to the Jewish problem had to be found. Ruppin found the Nazi professor extremely friendly.[26]

In this as in so many other arenas, an exact Nazi position was impossible to determine. One could quote the venomously anti-Semitic Julius Streicher on the one hand and Göring or Günther on the other. Hitler's own pronouncements alternated similarly. The turn of events at the Nuremberg rally seems to have finally pressured him to make a clear policy statement. In an all-night session he went over various drafts of proposed legislation that he had abruptly demanded be composed by experts from the Ministry of Interior. Hitler then let it be known that he had accepted the most moderate of the drafts that were presented to him, adding that this would be his "last word on the Jewish question." In his speech to the rally – the first time he had devoted a major public speech to the Jewish question since he became chancellor[27] – he struck a statesmanlike tone. He asserted that public pressure had been growing to do something about the Jewish issue, and he held out the possibility "through a once-and-for-all secular solution, of perhaps creating a basis on which the German people might be able to find a tolerable relationship with the Jewish people."[28] In subsequent speeches he urged the party to maintain legality and discipline.

---

[24] Ibid., 229.

[25] Schleunes, "Retracing the Twisted Road," in Furet, *Unanswered Questions*, 58.

[26] Arthur Ruppin, *Chapters of My Life*, vol. 3 (Tel Aviv, 1968), 223; Tom Segev, *The Seventh Million: The Israelis and the Holocaust* (New York, 1993), 19.

[27] Ian Kershaw, *The 'Hitler Myth': Image and Reality in the Third Reich* (New York, 1989), 235.

[28] Ibid., 236.

The Nuremberg Laws that were formally introduced in the following months established legal differences between Jews and non-Jews in Germany. Even so, the exact implications of excluding Jews from Reich citizenship were unclear. Jews lost the right to vote, but that right by the autumn of 1935 no longer meant much to anyone in Germany. The Nuremberg Laws' definition of who was a Jew turned out to be more lenient than party radicals had demanded. In other regards, the various elements of the Laws were a confused jumble, all too obviously patched together under pressure.

It is revealing that Streicher, the most notorious anti-Semite in the party, was not even consulted about the laws – he learned about them in the press – causing him considerable irritation.[29] When the text of the laws was made public there was an angry response from the radicals in the NSDAP.[30] Implementing and attempting to iron out the many contradictions of the laws also entailed endless complications, in particular because the definition of Jewishness in them seemed to touch many more German citizens than the long-recognized figure of about a half-million. The Aryan credentials of several million were put into doubt because they had Jewish ancestors or relatives of one sort or another.[31] The Nuremberg Laws threatened to become a Pandora's box; many in the government and in society at large expressed concern.

But insofar as the laws appeared to emphasize a clearly delineated legal approach, some Jewish leaders were relieved: If Nazi policy was simply to treat Jews as resident noncitizens, as Göring had maintained, that was hardly good news, but at least Jews could live with such a policy. It did not entail driving them from the country or stripping them of their property, as the radicals had been demanding. Life under the Nuremberg Laws, some concluded, would not be all that different from life in Germany before Jews had been granted full civil equality, and Jews had in fact prospered then.

In speaking to a reporter from the United Press Hitler emphasized that the struggle against communism was one of the main reasons for introducing the laws: "Nearly all Bolshevist agitators . . . and agents of Bolshevism" in Germany were Jews, he stated. Moreover, during the Weimar years Jews had "flooded the intellectual professions," exercising "everywhere a disintegrating effect." Thus the laws were designed not to be disruptive but to enhance social peace in Germany. Popular anti-Semitism in Germany, he maintained, was declining now that Jews were protected through a "clear and clean separation between the two races."[32]

Intentionalists have interpreted the Nuremberg Laws as part of an insidious

---

[29] Randall L. Bytwerk, *Julius Streicher* (New York, 1983), 36.

[30] Mommsen, *From Weimar to Auschwitz*, 231.

[31] Cf. Raphael Patai, *The Jewish Mind* (New York, 1977), 281–2.

[32] Norman H. Baynes, ed., *The Speeches of Adolf Hitler*, vol. 1 (London, 1942), 733–4; Robert Wistrich, *Hitler's Apocalypse: Jews and the Nazi Legacy* (New York, 1985), 70.

general plan, a subtly calculated step in a preconceived policy of progressively tightening the noose around the neck of Germany's Jews. The reassuring remarks that Hitler made were merely "a shrewd tactical move,"[33] waiting for the next opportunity to apply ever harsher measures toward the ultimate or final solution. This view is plausible, since it is incontestable that Hitler was capable of any deception in achieving his goals, and he had emphasized that the Jewish issue would only be solved by a crafty, long-range struggle. Still, most of the evidence indicates a lack of detailed planning almost everywhere in the Third Reich, and the Nuremberg Laws were no exception. One must also wonder if dealing with the Jews was in fact Hitler's highest priority, his constantly most prized and carefully planned project, for after the passage of the laws, he again refrained from public commentary on Jewish issues for well over a year.

If the Jewish question was not the highest or all-consuming priority for him, what were his genuine first priorities? Hitler's own often-stated goals could be summarized as two: to establish Germany as a racially pure, unified *Volksgemein-schaft* (people's community) and to assure *Lebensraum* (living space) for the future needs of the German Volk. But could Lebensraum be achieved without war? A Volksgemeinschaft unquestionably entailed destroying the "Marxists" (the SPD and KPD); less clearly it meant depriving both liberals and conservatives of the political freedom they had previously exercised. But what did it mean as far as the Jews were concerned?

Many were willing to believe that the Nuremberg Laws answered that question, since it excluded Jews from the German community. Regulatory measures of this sort, they argued, did not much differ from what was being done, or had been done, in other countries with large Jewish populations, such as Poland, Hungary, and Romania. Even Great Britain and the United States, in passing measures that were transparently designed to prevent further immigration of eastern European Jews, had demonstrated their concern to limit the numbers of Jews in their countries. There is little reason to believe that after September 1935 large numbers of German citizens were pressuring the regime for more radical or violent actions against Jews. There is also little evidence, to be sure, that many Germans were deeply opposed to the anti-Jewish measures so far introduced. Indifference to the fate of Jews in Germany rather than active, militant hatred of them seems to have been characteristic of German public opinion in these years. Avoidance rather than principled, courageous resistance, similarly, was the preferred stance of the great majority. Only a small minority – which of course could still mean thousands – actively pressed for more far-reaching anti-Semitic measures. Many Germans simply withdrew from political involvement in the liberal–democratic sense. Impressed with Hitler's many accomplishments by late 1935, and inclined to

---

[33] Wistrich, *Hitler's Apocalypse*, 70.

respect the authorities, they gratefully concluded that the Führer knew best what should be done.

Hitler did all in his power to strengthen this bonding of the German population to him as its leader. And that meant continuing to appear moderate and statesmanlike. In the following year, 1936, there were further reasons for Nazi Germany to present a reassuring face to the world and to minimize evidence of racial strife inside the country. The Olympic Games were scheduled to take place in Berlin in the summer, and there would be many foreign visitors. Anti-Semitic rhetoric in the press was toned down, and other expressions of anti-Jewish sentiment were discouraged.

The summer of 1936 may be considered the acme of the Nazi "golden years." The economy had revived to a gratifying degree, and in March Hitler had accomplished his most astonishing foreign policy coup. Violating agreements that Weimar leaders had freely made at Locarno, Hitler remilitarized the Rhineland. France was in the midst of an internal crisis and unwilling to get into another unilateral intervention after the disastrous occupation of the Ruhr in 1923. French leaders protested the remilitarization but finally took no military action to prevent it. Promptly building fortifications on the Franco–German border, Germany became much less vulnerable to invasion from France. Once France lost its option to invade Germany with ease, it also lost its attractiveness as an ally for countries to Germany's east. In just a few months, then, diplomatic relations were fundamentally transformed. Nazi Germany had already begun breaking out of the limits imposed by the Versailles Treaty, rearming itself and leaving the League of Nations. Under Hitler's leadership, by 1936 the country regained its sense of full sovereignty and earned a new place of respect among nations.

Hitler's popularity soared. And success after intoxicating success followed, chief among them being the unification or *Anschluss* with Austria in March of 1938 and the Munich Agreements of September 1938 that authorized Germany to take over the Sudetenland, the German-speaking western areas of Czechoslovakia. With those victories, the overwhelming majority of the German Volk had been brought into the Third Reich. By late 1938 many Germans revered Hitler as a near god, and even those conservatives in the government and military who retained reservations about him had to grant that he had accomplished things they never believed possible. And while the Nazi Party or other prominent Nazi officials never enjoyed anything like the popularity that Hitler personally did, nazification of the German population, especially the young, advanced in many ways.

The Anschluss and the incorporation of the Sudetenland brought around 300,000 more Jews into the Third Reich, approximately doubling the Jewish population. It also added a notably more anti-Semitic non-Jewish population than was true of pre-1938 Germany. The Anschluss was marked by widespread anti-Jewish violence in Vienna. It similarly marked a new stage of radicalization in Nazi Jewish policy after a period of relative calm between September 1935 and March of 1938.

The nationwide explosion of violence against Jews in November 1938, in a pogrom known as *Reichskristallnacht,* or "Night of the Broken Glass," when mobs attacked Jews, broke the windows of Jewish shops, and burned synagogues, would seem to have demonstrated beyond serious question how much the entire German population was filled with hatred for Jews. The official line of Goebbels's Propaganda Ministry was that this pogrom reflected a spontaneous outburst of popular indignation over the assassination of a Nazi official in Paris by a young Polish Jew. But the spontaneity of and popular support for Kristallnacht is doubtful. It was planned and orchestrated by Goebbels in conjunction with anti-Semitic radicals in the Nazi movement, in most areas the work of Brownshirt thugs, with varying degrees of complicity by the police and other authorities. In some places elements of the general population did join in, whereas elsewhere the rioters were opposed by ordinary citizens. Most Germans observed passively, taking no overt action one way or the other, although many were clearly appalled by the lawlessness and by the damage to life and property.[34]

To describe this pogrom as planned may overstate things, however, since many in the government and the Nazi hierarchy were unaware of Goebbels's machinations and denounced them once they were revealed. Göring and Himmler, who detested Goebbels, were outraged by the economic damage of the rioting. Hitler's exact role in approving, or failing to veto, plans for the riot remains uncertain. Again it appears that there was a chaotic competition of various agencies for control over Jewish policy, and Hitler avoided indicating unequivocal support for one or the other. Karl Schleunes has succinctly described the riots as "a product of the lack of coordination which marked Jewish planning in Jewish policy and the result of a last-ditch effort by the radicals to wrest control over this policy."[35] Goebbels, who had suffered a number of setbacks and humiliations, apparently hoped to regain favor in Hitler's eyes with this initiative. Hitler must have somehow allowed Goebbels to believe that he would welcome expressions of popular indignation, but on the other hand the Führer in the past had consistently deprecated this kind of rioting. Afterward Hitler studiously avoided critical comment, though he implicitly censured Goebbels by turning Jewish policy over to Himmler, a firm proponent of the "rational" approach, and to Göring, whose main interest in Germany's Jewish population seemed to be to plunder its riches, not attack it violently.

The Night of Broken Glass represented a sharp escalation of pressure on Germany's Jews. Nonetheless, Jewish deaths, and the arrests of Jews and their incarceration in concentration camps, remained small in number compared

---

[34] Kershaw, '*Hitler Myth*', 238–42.

[35] Quoted in Kershaw, *Dictatorship*, 94–5.

with what would later develop; violent, widespread persecution had not yet become mass murder. Indeed, Nazi policy at this point appears still to have been concentrated on forcing as many Jews out of Germany as possible and on expropriating the wealth of those that remained.

When, then, was the decision to murder the Jews made? There is by now a very large literature on the subject,[36] in which many refined points are pursued, but it is clear that the war, which finally closed Germany's borders, narrowing and then eliminating the possibility of emigration (though it was still possible until the fall of 1941), changed the options of those formulating Jewish policy. The ensuing victories over Poland brought under German control a large population of Jews, creating yet new dilemmas for Jewish policy and ostensibly altering the feasibility of the solutions that had been previously planned. The introduction of a "final solution" was near.

It is difficult to ignore the abundant evidence that these changing situations, which again could hardly have been anticipated by Nazi leaders, led to fundamentally new plans. It may even be the case, however implausible it first seems, that no single order from Hitler authorizing the Final Solution was ever issued. Instead, it may have been that a growing escalation of relatively random violence against Jews – of course growing logically out of Nazi ideology – especially after war with Soviet Russia began, finally merged into an ever-more explicit program of mass murder. But the exact point at which it was decided to kill all Jews under Nazi rule, given the chaotic way in which policy was formulated and decisions made in the Third Reich, may remain impossible to state with confidence.

Hitler must have condoned this process of accelerating violence. It is plausible and in many instances supported by documentary evidence that various ad hoc initiatives and detailed plans – precisely when and how the killing was to be done – were the work of men like Himmler and Heydrich, or others dealing directly with the Jewish population, but Hitler's general responsibility is beyond serious question. His hatred for Jews, linked to his enormous prestige and authority, provided energy, direction, and rationalization for genocide. The Nazi system itself no doubt generated violence, and Jews were not the only people to be murdered by the millions, but that system, too, is ultimately hard to visualize without Hitler's inspiration and direction. The Holocaust would not have occurred without World War II, but again responsibility for that war ultimately must be linked to Hitler and the system he oversaw.

Hitler's long-standing but ever-increasing psychological isolation, his declining health by the late 1930s, his premonitions of premature death, his rising fury and vindictiveness in reaction to Germany's military situation once the

---

[36] For one of the most carefully documented studies that amply documents the chaotic bureaucratic rivalries of the Third Reich, see Richard Breitman, *The Architect of Genocide: Himmler and the Final Solution* (New York, 1991).

defeats began, and his belief that there were "world-historical" tasks that only he could accomplish are also plausibly key factors, but there is a danger in insisting too much upon Hitler's responsibility, for he found many "willing executioners" – Goldhagen's phrase has unquestionably a kernel of truth – men whose ideas from the early 1920s paralleled and then evermore mimicked his, seeking to gain his favor by acts consistent with what were believed to be his wishes. And many were ready to kill Jews with or without Hitler's sanction. Whether men like Himmler, Heydrich, Göring, or Goebbels would have, on their own initiatives and without inspiration from Hitler, actually proceeded to systematic mass murder remains an open question. Goebbels had had a Jewish lover[37] and Göring a number of Jewish friends;[38] neither of them seemed, at least before the mid-1930s, to believe in the kind of crudely doctrinaire racism that became more or less official. Below them in the Nazi hierarchy were tens of thousands who were in the sway of complex motivations – ambition, hatred, opportunism, cowardice – who formulated the specific policies and carried out the orders. And beyond those active cadres were the millions of Germans who turned their faces, again for complex reasons – fear, conformity, inertia, ignorance, and indifference as well as hatred of Jews. We may certainly speak of moral failings, but those failings were not always the result of specifically or intensely anti-Semitic sentiments.

Moral judgments about what various individuals, Jews and non-Jews, did in these horrifying years must be made with circumspection. The moral responsibility of Nazi leaders is relatively easy to establish and not to be minimized. Such responsibility is hardly to be compared to the guilt, if that is the word, of those in the ghettos and concentration camps who did shameful things in order to survive. Nor, again, are those responsibilities much like that of German citizens who avoided confrontation with the authorities. But whether referring to concentration camp inmate or ordinary citizen, those who have not faced such choices obviously need to be extremely cautious in making judgments. Imagining oneself into such situations and answering the question "what would I have done?" – either as concentration camp inmate or ordinary citizen – is more than most people are able to do confidently and honestly, although the question nonetheless needs to be confronted, the effort made.

Historians have commonly dealt with other kinds of "extreme situations," such as the experience under fire in the battlefields of World War I or in the torture chambers of the Cheka, that have also been described as placing their survivors in a unique world of experience, impossible to convey to others. As with these examples, to situate the "concentration camp universe" entirely beyond the ken of those who were not in it raises unsettling questions. Some

---

37 Helmut Heiber, *Goebbels* (New York, 1972); Rober Manvell and Heinrich Fraenkel, *Dr. Goebbels* (London, 1968).

38 See Bent Blütnikow, "Göring's Jewish Friend," *Commentary*, vol. 94, no. 3, Sept. 1992, 50–3.

Holocaust survivors are patently not infallible witnesses, since, as was also the case with the survivors of the pogroms from 1903 to 1921, they contradict one another and "remember" things that can be proved not to have happened. There is no necessary surprise or even shame to be associated with such inconsistencies: The memory plays tricks on us, a common problem with eyewitnesses in other arenas, especially when observation is under the pressure of powerful emotions. Victims are not automatically reliable observers or saints.

There remains much that is enigmatic about events between 1933 and 1945, to be sure, but one conclusion emerges with reasonable clarity: The Holocaust did not simply represent a logical culmination to German history or the will of the German people as a whole or in its majority. Support for Hitler did not derive primarily from his anti-Semitism. There was nothing like a plebiscite on the Holocaust or even on the relatively moderate measures introduced by the Nuremberg Laws, and some evidence suggests that in free elections even those laws might not have won majority support from the German people. The decision to move to mass murder was kept a secret, after all, because those in charge believed that the majority of Germans would not support such a solution. The noted philosopher Karl Jaspers, an anti-Nazi with a Jewish wife and hardly known for apologetic stances in regard to Germany's guilt, wrote Hannah Arendt after the war that "Most Germans, 99.9%, did not commit such murders, not even in their thoughts."[39] Jaspers undoubtedly overstated the case – he certainly saw things differently than Goldhagen does – but it still remains unlikely that most Germans committed murders or actively desired them.

One of many paradoxes about the Final Solution is that Streicher was kept in the dark about it, just as he had been about the composition of the Nuremberg Laws. He was condemned to death by the Nuremberg war crimes tribunal for his thoughts and writings, not for actually participating in mass murder. Eichmann, who escaped the Nuremberg tribunal, was deeply involved in the mass murder of Jews, and although it is impossible to be certain what his thoughts actually were, Arendt has made a provocative and troubling case that this "banal" bureaucrat was not an anti-Semite before the Nazi years and did not harbor any particular hatred for those he helped to murder.[40] Similar observations have been made about the lack of an anti-Semitic past in other leading Nazis, including those with more direct responsibility for the killing process.[41]

This bewildering disparity between anti-Semitic belief and anti-Jewish action, extending back into the nineteenth century, has been another theme

---

[39] Lotte Kohler and Hans Saner, eds., *Hannah Arendt, Karl Jaspers: Correspondence, 1926–1969* (New York, 1992), 75 [letter of March 19, 1947].

[40] Hannah Arendt, *Eichmann in Jerusalem: An Essay on the Banality of Evil* (New York, 1963).

[41] Cf. Gitta Sereny, *Into That Darkness* (New York, 1983) [a study of Franz Stangl, Commandant of Sobibor and Treblinka].

of this book, one perhaps now more widely recognized in the case of the Holocaust than in various manifestations of anti-Semitism preceding it. The argument in these pages has not been that anti-Semitic thought and action have no discernible relation to one another but rather that the relationship is far more tangled than usually appreciated. On the other hand, it is simply not the case that the relationship between anti-Semitic thought and action in the 1930s and 1940s defies rational explanation, for one can construct a reasonably coherent and plausible explanation of how the Holocaust emerged out of the cauldron of the Third Reich and German history, as I hope has been done in this chapter, at least in general outline.

The rhetoric about the incomprehensibility of the Holocaust often derives from arcane definitions of "comprehension" and should not be allowed to obscure the fact that historians have made substantial progress in presenting the Holocaust in understandable form. We now *do* understand it better than we did in the years immediately following Word War II. Michael Marrus has made a persuasive case that scholarly sophistication in the field of the history of the Holocaust is, by the early 1990s, actually richer than in many long-established historical fields.[42] It is at any rate not possible to make a hard-and-fast distinction between "remembering" and "understanding," since those who "remember" have in truth their own understanding – one that some of them seem to believe must be accepted by others without question. That will not happen, and indeed should not happen.

Conclusions

Who has made us Jews different from other people? Who has allowed us to suffer so terribly up to now? It is God that has made us as we are, but it is God, too, who will raise us up again. . . . Who knows, it might even be our religion from which the world and all peoples learn good, and for that reason only do we have to suffer now. We can never become just Netherlanders, or just English, or the representatives of any country for that matter; we will always remain Jews, and we want to, too.[43]

When and how will Esau's tears be dried, the fears and resentments of non-Jews fade and at last disappear? Even after the Holocaust, will hatred of Jews ever vanish, the Jewish problem finally be solved? The question has been asked endlessly, to the point of caricature. These pages have suggested that the answer may be even more elusive than generally recognized – far more so than current programs of education about Jewish life might assume ("If non-Jews only learn the truth about Jews, anti-Semitism will disappear."). The pervasive belief in the nineteenth century that Jewish "reform" would cause non-Jews to

---

[42] Michael Marrus, "'Good History' and Teaching the Holocaust," *Perspectives: American Historical Association Newsletter,* vol. 31, no. 5, May/June 1993, 1–12.

[43] Anne Frank, *Anne Frank: The Diary of a Young Girl* (New York, 1953), 186–7.

cease hating Jews proved to be naive, if not completely without foundation; it has been replaced with the no-less-imperfect but equally confident assertion that anti-Semitism has nothing whatsoever to do with Jewish behavior or the nature of real Jews. These pages have offered evidence that contradicts that assertion, recognizing nonetheless that non-Jewish fantasies do play a significant role in anti-Semitism and that remedies for the hatreds that Jews encounter are not easily achieved, for the simple reason that those fantasies are often integral parts of the larger identity of non-Jews.

Since the aversion of Gentile to Jew, and Jew to Gentile, is so deeply embedded in their respective traditions, the two groups are unlikely, without fundamental changes in their identities, to arrive at a lasting harmony in the foreseeable future, certainly not in every country, probably not in most. The potential for new explosions of hatred will remain, sparked by "bad times" – economic difficulties, wars, revolutions, natural disasters, or pandemic disease. So long as most Jews retain an identity with a substantial connection to Jewish tradition, and so long as the rest of the world has some sense of that identity and its related history, anti-Semitism will endure, much as embers of a fire, ready to flare up again when fanned.

The rise of the Jews in modern times, while the most fundamental cause of modern racial and political anti-Semitism, should not be conceptualized in the same way as "bad times." Although a Jewish rise, as is the case with the rise of other groups or nations, has not surprisingly provoked apprehension and hostility from those who feel threatened, it need not necessarily have had that impact. The experiences of "rising" Jews in Hungary, Italy, Great Britain, and the United States suggest how other factors can play a decisive role – how, indeed, under favorable circumstances a Jewish rise can not only be accepted but also applauded by those among whom Jews live, though hardly without significant ambiguities.

The argument of these pages has certainly not been that nothing can be done to combat anti-Semitism or that the situation of Jews in all countries or societies at all times is "essentially" the same. I have tried to demonstrate the extraordinary and little-appreciated range of attitudes to Jews in modern Europe and America as well as the range of possibilities in achieving relative harmony. But even in the lands of "sweet exile," such as the United States, significant if often shifting parts of the population have remained unfriendly to Jews; the potential for an explosion remains. Although there is evidence of a substantial decline in hostility among traditional elites in the United States, there is also evidence of increasing hostility among other elements of the population, especially African–Americans, though certainly less than dramatic episodes or sensationalistic press reports might lead one to conclude. The declining level of anti-Semitism among Americans of European ancestry seems to be linked not only to their currently more tolerant, less ethnocentric attitudes but also to a diminishing sense, on their part, of Jewish difference – a sense that is based on accurate perceptions, since large numbers of Jews in America no longer identify with or even understand the Jewish consciousness of their forebears. The hostility of African–Americans, similarly, has something to do with their belief that Jews are no better than other whites in their racial attitudes, possibly worse – certainly nowhere near so blameless as many Jews contend. Other non-European peoples of Christian background, a growing part of the population in the United States, may also be potentially more anti-Semitic than those of European origins, although the relatively firm stand that Christian leaders have recently been taking against anti-Semitism seems to speak against the possibility of Christianity being a brood-chamber of anti-Semitism among these people in the immediate future.

Christianity, even before the late twentieth century, must be considered one source but only one source of hostility to Jews, and since Christian traditions are so many-sided, the charge of the "ultimate" responsibility of Christian religion for modern anti-Semitism is uncomfortably vague; when things become that ultimate, responsibility has little meaning. One might as well charge the Jews, as Voltaire did, with being ultimately responsible for Christian bigotry, since they brought intolerant monotheism to the world. The Japanese have shown a pronounced affinity for fantastic images about Jews, without much aid from Christian traditions.[44] And of course other non-Christians, Moslems most prominently, have taken up the banners, as it were, of the centuries-old Christian crusade against the Jews. Images of Jews outside of Europe and America today are often unfavorable and may develop into more coherently anti-Jewish attitudes. If that happens, it will likely be because countries that previously suffered under European imperialism consider Israel an imperialist creation or that Jews are "too powerful" in the United States. Christian images of the Jews will not be the principal issue. (Even the rise of the Jews shares to some degree this problem of being an overly general ultimate cause; as I have emphasized, other factors must be taken into consideration, and rising Jews are by no means inevitably hated.)

The notion of Esau's tears has many further complications, for if one may accurately speak of Esau's tears being dried in Europe and the United States in the period since the Holocaust, it has been ostensibly at a large price, one that many Jews are finding profoundly troubling, since the process of Jewish–Gentile reconciliation seems to point toward large-scale intermarriage and the disappearance of Jews as a meaningfully separate group. Since the 1980s but especially in the 1990s, journals of Jewish opinion, whether traditional or secular humanistic, have been full of broodings and lamentations about what

---

[44] The most useful recent discussion of this tangled issue is in David G. Goodman and Masanori Miyazawa, *Jews in the Japanese Mind: The History and Uses of a Cultural Stereotype* (New York, 1995).

some Jews have termed the "bloodless Holocaust" of intermarriage and assimilation,[45] or what others consider the "curse" of friendship that is replacing the older curse of enmity.[46] The language used is both striking and strange: Rabbi Shlomo Riskin, in a weekly column for the *Jerusalem Post,* has contrasted the "candy-coated poison" of Gentile friendliness with the bitter poison of anti-Semitism. He states that it is an "open question" which of the two poisons has been worse for the Jewish people, although it is obvious that he considers friendliness the greater present danger because it is more insidious.[47] At the far other end of Jewish opinion in most regards, Alan Dershowitz, Harvard Law School Professor and famous trial lawyer, has spoken of Jews in America being "seduced," as distinguished from their being "raped" in other times and places.[48]

Non-Jews may be bewildered to discover that their friendly attitudes are considered a covert curse – indeed, that some Jewish leaders consider friendly Gentiles to be insidiously clever seducers. There is even worse or more puzzling news: Friendly Gentiles are being compared to those who give poison to children or even to Nazi murderers. (Surely "bloodless Holocaust" must qualify as one of the most obnoxious of the many careless and offensive uses of the term Holocaust.) It is unlikely that most Jews would defend the kind of language that figures like Riskin and Dershowitz have used, but these quotations are by no means unusual among the various and sundry remarks made by Jewish leaders in the past few decades about intermarriage. Given such enigmatic Jewish attitudes, efforts to understand anti-Semitism, to dry Esau's tears, may appear ultimately futile – Sisyphean: Jews are anxious about being hated but also anxious about the implications of not being hated; they attempt to combat Jew-hatred but appear to believe that Jewishness inevitably and somehow mystically provokes hostility (Jews are hated not for any definable reason but "just because they are Jews."). They lament that Jews who try to "reform" find only intensified anti-Semitism, although the country with the largest population of Jews in the world – and also the most "reformed" – has seen a substantial decline in anti-Semitism. This disconcerting jumble of opinions about anti-Semitism may help explain those strangely inconsistent theoretical efforts to explain its nature that have so often been critiqued in this book; ultimately the uncertainties about what it means, or should mean, to be a Jew are the real cause.

Anti-Semitism and its history in modern times are admittedly so tangled

---

[45] The term has been used by Rabbi Herschel Schachter of Yeshiva University, among others; see Michael D'Antonio, "Jewish Husbands, Christian Wives (and Vice Versa)," *Present Tense,* vol. 13, no. 3, Autumn 1985, 6.

[46] Charles E. Silberman, *A Certain People: American Jews and Their Lives Today* (New York, 1985), 165.

[47] Shlomo Riskin, "Poisons that strike at the heart," *The Jerusalem Post,* International Edition [week ending] Sept. 8, 1990, 23.

[48] Alan Dershowitz, *Chutzpah* (New York, 1991), 353–4.

that theoretical perplexities are to be expected, but nonetheless it seems clear that many Jews exhibit an all-too common human failing: They actually do not *want* to understand their past – or at least those aspects of their past that have to do with the hatred directed at them, since understanding may threaten other elements of their complex and often contradictory identities. Avoidances of this sort, not actually wanting to understand, are familiar enough: Non-Jews avoid uncomfortable evidence of their treatment of Jews in history; it would hardly be surprising if avoidances, different in quality yet in some regards revealingly similar, are to be found among Jews. Germans, of course, have a great deal to feel uncomfortable about, and there has been much discussion among them about the need to "master" their horrific past. The clumsy term *Vergangenheitsbewältigung* (mastering the past) parallels the psychoanalytic notion that uncovering and courageously facing unpleasant aspects of one's personal past, rather than covering them up or conjuring up implausible myths about them, is the way to psychological health (or "mastery of self"). Whatever the problems with that notion – it is not at all clear that a rapist–murderer, taking responsibility for his crime, then becomes psychologically healthy – Germans are not the only people with uncomfortable pasts, nor have they been unique in their avoidances, although precisely *what* Germans are trying to avoid is believed by many Jews to be unique in some mystical sense. That belief in the absolute uniqueness of Jewish suffering under Nazi tyranny is not shared, or at least not understood, by those who consider the suffering of their own people in history to be equal to if not greater than Jewish suffering. The unseemly clamor in late twentieth century for the status of victim – and especially the greatest victim – is disheartening, with ruinous implications for all the groups involved.

At the end of the twentieth century mastering the ugly American past of slavery and all it came to imply must qualify as a particularly pressing and imposing task for most Americans. In this regard, "most Americans" refers to Jewish Americans, for Jews unquestionably did trade in slaves, own slaves, exploit blacks, and harbor racist attitudes to them, just as many Jews shared the widespread racist attitudes to Slavic and Romanian "historyless peoples." And those Jews who resist the notion of being held responsible for things that happened in the past, that only small numbers of Jews had anything to do with – or at least with which they themselves individually had nothing to do – are engaging in much the same kind of reasoning of those non-Jews who say that they have no responsibility for things that were done by their forefathers to Jews. At any rate, Jews cannot take collective pride in their famous scientists, artists, and humanitarians but then declare that Jewish villains and scoundrels must be considered as individuals, having collectively nothing at all to do with other Jews or Jewish identity.

There is unquestionably much to master in terms of Jewish–Gentile relations in American history. The response to Jewish refugees from Germany by

American authorities and the public, for example, is an ugly chapter of that history, almost unbearable in retrospect, if also not quite so sinister or indefensible as some have presented it. The story works in various and complex ways, of course, since Jewish Americans also allegedly did not do "enough" to rescue the Jews of Europe.

From such charges emerges another tangled question: Should we expect people who are part of a victimized group, or who define themselves as powerless, to do any "mastering?" As noted in the Preface, Black History Month is not much concerned with mastering uncomfortable realities – except those that *others* are uncomfortable about. The different ways that the study of the past is approached, what "mastery" is supposed to mean, are often quite revealing. Many Jews, like many African–Americans, are inclined to assume, often no doubt without really thinking the matter through, that their status as powerless victims means that they have nothing morally unpleasant about themselves to master – and suggestions that they might are made only by anti-Semites and Jewish self-haters, part of the old "blame the victim" syndrome.

The evidence presented in these pages does not support such comfortable assumptions. It has indicated how Jewish action in the real world has had something quite relevant to do with hatred of Jews. Anti-Semitism, as an ideology or a fantasy, has been neither so mysterious nor so potent a historical force, whether in Germany or in other countries, as many believe. Rather, hatred of Jews, as the case with other hatreds, exhibits a parasitic nature; it feeds on frictions, jealousies, misfortunes, and calamities in the material world, but without them, it shrivels to relative unimportance, waiting, as it were, for new opportunities.[49]

Even in the Third Reich it was not so much the mysterious, intoxicating power of anti-Semitic ideology for all Germans as the chaotic dynamics of that regime itself, in the context of economic depression and an unstable world of competing nation-states, that best explains the complicated set of initiatives and often competing agendas that finally led toward mass murder. To be sure, anti-Semitic ideology, and German history itself, set up a likely scenario of who was to be attacked first or most, much as Marxism set up likely scenarios for the mass murders under the Bolsheviks. But in both anti-Semitism and Marxism, the power of ideology alone does not offer an adequate explanation; it needs to be firmly linked to developments in the material world, particularly to the world of politics, national culture, and the actions of political leaders.

The evidence is much more persuasive that in individual rather than collective cases – Hitler and Himmler being obvious cases in point – anti-Semitic fantasy, the belief in demonic Jewish power, may have exercised an irrational, powerfully intoxicating, and decisive effect, but that is not the same as an

---

[49] Albert S. Lindemann, *The Jew Accused: Three Anti-Semitic Affairs (Dreyfus, Beilis, Frank), 1894–1915* (New York, 1991), 276 ff.

entire society or civilization collectively embracing such beliefs, and even in the cases of Hitler or Himmler one needs to look at much more than anti-Semitic fantasy in arriving at a credible and adequately textured explanation of the genesis and implementation of the Final Solution.

Again, the most obvious material factor to take into consideration in trying to account for the growth of modern anti-Semitism – though not of course its deepest origins – is the rise of the Jews. It was not a fantasy but rather a perfectly real, measurable, and understandable development. Other developments in the real world, wars, depressions, and revolutions, tended to make that rise more noticeable and unacceptable to some non-Jews, supplying life and energy to inherited fantasies about Jews. It is far too simple to say that the rise of Jews in Germany, and particularly in the Weimar Republic, "explains" the triumph of Nazism, but it verges on the absurd to insist that the presence, activities, or nature of Jews in Germany had nothing whatsoever to do with the success of the Nazis.

The absolute numbers of Jews, whether Jews are rising or not in other regards, also needs to be taken into account. It is simply untrue that the number of Jews in a given area is irrelevant to the Jew-hatred in that area. I have tried to counter the simplistic conclusion that anti-Semitism inevitably rises as the number of Jews rises, but nonetheless the number of Jews ranks high among the many factors that one must take into consideration; there are few if any examples of areas where the Jewish population rose above 5 percent that did not also see a significant expression of anti-Semitism. The countries of "happy exile" all had small Jewish populations, 2 percent or less. When the Jewish population nears 10 percent, as in Poland, Romania, and the Pale of Settlement, the likelihood of severe anti-Semitism is high. The often-used examples of anti-Semitism in Japan or postwar Poland, where the Jewish populations are extremely small, to demonstrate that numbers mean nothing, do not in fact prove much: In both cases, anti-Semites charge *foreign* Jews – in particular powerful American Jews – with evil designs in regard to Japanese and Polish interests. Such charges cannot sustain examination, but they have some relationship to fact, however remote. The more interesting and revealing question is why modern Poles or Japanese feel the need to blame Jews rather than face problems mostly of their own creation or at least palpably the result of developments over which Jews have no control.

The nature of the Jewish population, whatever its numbers, in a given country is also important in influencing that country's attitude to Jews. One particularly clear demonstration of that point is in the history of neighboring Hungary and Romania, where the relative numbers of Jews, as well as the rate of their growth, were roughly the same. In Hungary Jews enthusiastically took up Magyar language and culture and came to be recognized by ruling elites as beneficial to their country's economic health and national power. In Romania, Jews resisted becoming Romanian and mostly ignored or even denigrated

Romanian culture and history. Jews in Hungary were in various ways western-ized and modernized, whereas Jews in Romania were more often hasidic and traditional–nationalistic. The acceptance of Jews by Magyar elites and the rejection of Jews by Romanian elites had something quite directly to do with the actual nature of Jews in each country, not simply fantasies about Jews, or the virtue of Hungarians and the vice of Romanians. Anti-Semitic fantasy played a role in both countries, but it gained a much wider belief where Jews were plausibly seen as hostile and alien. The nature of Hungarian and Roman-ian non-Jews is an even more important consideration than the nature of the Jews in each country; Hungarians found Jews useful in ways that Romanians did not. Jews in Germany were unquestionably "state preserving" – if not quite so vital to German national interests as were Jews in Hungary – but Germans were finally more attracted to modern racial theory than were Hungarians.

One of the most easily refuted beliefs about anti-Semites in the period from the late nineteenth century to the 1930s is that they did not know Jews or had little contact with them, relying entirely on inherited fantasies about them. Marr, Wagner, Lagarde, and Chamberlain – even Stalin and Hitler – had extensive, firsthand contact with Jews. I have found no major figure who corre-sponds to the widely accepted generalization that anti-Semites do not know Jews or have no real contact with them. It is true that these anti-Semites knew only certain kinds of Jews and that their visions were partial, incomplete, and distorted, but that is not a particularly persuasive objection; it would be diffi-cult to determine what is a "complete" vision of Jews or who might qualify as having such a vision. The crucial point that these partial visions were used in the service of a fantasy hostile to most Jews must not be overlooked. But, again, the fantasy had some sort of connection with real Jews; the nature of that connection, the interplay of fantasy and reality, is the interesting if also difficult question. Hitler is a particularly suggestive but not necessarily typical case, in that his contact with Jews seems to have been overwhelmingly positive, but that contact was unable to counteract his emotional needs and, especially at first, his political opportunities, which were powerfully satisfied by an anti-Semitic fantasy.

The term "partial visions" could be revealingly turned in another direction, in that most non-Jews, including most anti-Semites, recognized differences between various kinds of Jews. The actual diversity of Jews – indeed, their perennial and passionate divisiveness on nearly every imaginable issue – sug-gest that these "partial visions" were in some sense appropriate. When Jews were perceived as useful, not harmful, the favorable aspects of a many-faceted Jewish imagery were more amply tapped; where Jews were seen as harmful, the unfavorable aspects were tapped. But both parts remained available. The old saw: "Is it good for the Jews?" has a revealing counterpart: "Is it good for the Gentiles?" Even Lueger openly recognized that sometimes Jews were good for the Gentiles. Indeed, Eckart, Hitler's revered companion of the early 1920s, did so to an even more extensive and theoretical degree. Supposed philo-Semites, men such as Churchill or Balfour, in truth much resembled men known as anti-Semites; whether purportedly anti-Semitic or philo-Semitic, these figures continued to harbor shifting, ambiguous images of Jews, some who were in their eyes beneficial, others who were harmful. They expressed friendship or hostility according to the context. Even men who have gone down as prominent heroes in modern Jewish history, such as Emile Zola, Balfour, Churchill, or Thomas Masaryk, made comments about Jews that if expressed today would cause a scandal and be denounced as blatantly racist.

Provinciality in Jewish history, concentrating on a single country or a narrow span of time, can lead to unjustified conclusions. Many common assumptions or facile generalizations, similarly, are put into question by a close look at the history of Jews in relatively little known areas. More importantly, comparing the Jewish experience in countries as different as the United States, Russia, Romania, Italy, and Germany provides the kind of broad context in which human realities can be appropriately compared with one another, rather than holding individual countries up to an abstract standard of perfect justice, liberality, or toleration. Churchill once quipped that democracy was a terrible form of government, except in comparison to all the others. Anti-Semitism in the United States might similarly be termed "terrible" – and *seem* terrible in the light of certain experiences or when certain kinds of narratives are composed, but it appears decidedly less terrible when compared to most of the other examples in the real world over time.

Hatred for Jews has arisen nearly everywhere that Jews have settled, and those historians who have set out determined to uncover evidence of anti-Semitism have had little trouble in finding it. But this single-minded quest has sometimes entailed giving little attention to contrary evidence. Similarly, the tendency to dramatize or elaborately narrate instances of anti-Semitism in order to expose and denounce it risks legitimatizing the assertion that there was "essentially" little difference in Gentile–Jewish relations from one country to the other. From that assertion emerges a series of others: that "the Jew" is always hated, that Gentiles are all alike in some genetic sense, that "eternal" anti-Semitism is always the same, that even in liberal–democratic countries Jew-hatred has been and remains a major problem. I hope these pages have illustrated that such efforts are not only misleading but are also finally "bad for the Jews," even if one accepts, as I do, that hatred of Jews is both endemic and tenacious, a potential danger in most countries – appropriately termed "the longest hatred" – and thus never to be taken lightly. But vigilance and paranoia must be distinguished from one another, since paranoia in this instance can actually intensify the ill it is supposed to be combating. The line between the two, to be sure, is often damnably difficult to draw.

Comparative history over a long period, too, may shed some light on the knotty issue of the uniqueness of the Holocaust. I have been at pains to show

how the notion of historical uniqueness, whether in the United States' "exceptionalism" or Germany's *Sonderweg*, sometimes reveals the provinciality and misperceptions of national historians. Virtually all countries consider themselves "special," but the meaning of specialness emerges with sufficient clarity only in comparison. As one writer has stated it, "uniqueness, too, is relational, hence subject to an inherent relativism. This is the very foundation of the comparative method in history and the social sciences."[50] Comparing Jewish suffering in the Holocaust to the suffering of the kulaks in collectivization helps to make both comprehensible. Again, I am at a loss to see how such a comparison *necessarily* diminishes or trivializes Jewish suffering.

The indignation many Jews felt when the pope, during World War II, refused to speak out against the specific Nazi program of mass murder of Jews, contenting himself instead with banalities about the evils of war or of human cruelty, is understandable. Similar problems, kindred banalities, have undoubtedly arisen in the various discussions of the uniqueness of the Holocaust. But many of those who insist upon the absolute uniqueness of the Holocaust fail to perceive the possible ramifications of their position. If the Holocaust was utterly unique and incomprehensible – a demonic and cosmic explosion unrelated to "normal" historical forces – then there is really nothing to be done about preventing a recurrence of it, except perhaps to pray that the inscrutable forces in the universe will not unleash another such "incomparable" tragedy. With such preconceptions, a study of the Holocaust can aspire to be little more than a religious ritual of grief, awe, and remembrance, comparable to Easter in commemorating another cosmic and utterly incomparable event, the crucifixion.

Not recognizing comparative quality and texture in expressions of anti-Jewish sentiment has been an obvious problem in American historiography, but it is in some regards an even greater problem in countries where anti-Semitism has been more significant. Because of the tragedies of German history, figures such as Treitschke or Vogelsang have not usually been accorded an adequately nuanced and dispassionate hearing. One does not have to be driven by apologetic motives to recognize that such men, although hardly paragons, were still governed by principles that made it unlikely that they would have supported collective injustice done to Jews, let alone mass murder. Figures who were more explicitly and actively anti-Semitic, such as Marr, Lueger, or Chamberlain, have often been the subject of stubbornly prosecutorial treatments, ones that fail, ostensibly out of aversion to the possibility of mitigating their historical guilt in even the slightest degree, to give appropriate recognition to the many sides of their characters and the paradoxes of their positions over time.

Picquart was an anti-Semite who had no use for Dreyfus and his family but

---

[50] Andrei S. Markovits, "Coping with the Past: The West German Labor Movement and the Left," in Baldwin, *Reworking the Past,* 263.

who nonetheless risked his career and perhaps his life in order to see that the injustice done to Dreyfus was remedied. That victory of high principle over low hatred was by no means so unusual for men of the political right as many assume. The equally remarkable support of the even more openly anti-Semitic Shulgin for Beilis is another of many examples. However one finally judges the thought of intellectuals like Treitschke or Chamberlain, there remains a substantial leap from pre-1914 anti-Semitic thought to post–World War I mass murder. There were of course connections, some important, but they need to be examined carefully and dispassionately, as free as possible of the mentality that is interested only in "guilty or not guilty," black and white.

I have tried to show how specific historical events, such as the pogroms in Russia, the great anti-Semitic affairs, and even the Holocaust, have been less conditioned by mythic projections about Jews than widely believed and have been more the result of various historical contingencies, even of miscalculation and chance. Personality is an important contingency, whether the personal idiosyncrasies of victims like Dreyfus and Beilis, on the one hand, or movers and shakers like Trotsky and Hitler, on the other. The key role of personality has been frequently emphasized in this study, but this unfashionable emphasis is fundamentally different from that of such nineteenth-century historians as Thomas Carlyle, who argued that the individual genius of Great Men was the motor of historical development and thus the appropriate main focus for historians. Moreover, I have made what may at first appear to be opposing points on this issue: The intellectual influence of men like Marr, or even Chamberlain, has been overemphasized in many accounts, I believe, whereas the crucial role of personality in specific historical situations, such as the Dreyfus Affair and the Holocaust, has been often overlooked.

The attention I have devoted to these now faddishly denigrated Dead White Males has to do with my concern about how tendentiously they have been treated in many studies of anti-Semitism, but I have also tried to show how their influence as theorists and propagandists was less axiomatic than many of those studies suggest and how important were impersonal forces. Similarly, I have not accepted the proposition that historical imagination is incompatible with moral aversion. I recognize that dangerous confusions may arise, but I still believe, to put the matter in its starkest form, that it is possible to feel sympathy, or at least a sense of tragedy, for the murderer as he ascends the gallows – even when one approves of the death penalty for murderers. Recognizing the banality of a man like Eichmann, or his reliance on orders from superiors, does not necessarily lead to the conclusion that he should not have been punished. (What the appropriate penalty should have been is a more difficult question, since there was no conceivable punishment in his case that would have come close to fitting his crime.)

My position has been that it is precisely those moral weaknesses that we recognize as conceivable in ourselves, as ordinary, normal, or "banal," that deserve the closest and most serious scrutiny; morally outraged descriptions of what others – "those evil people" – did may be psychologically satisfying but do not take us very far in understanding how to prevent or deal with such evil. I consider the ability to confront dangerous confusions and morally perplexing situations without losing one's bearings in self-righteousness to be one mark of a civilized human being. The temptation to denounce moral uncertainties takes us in the direction of fanaticism.

Neoconservatives have emphasized, in opposition to the usually leftist social historians, the crucial role of ideology in history. The neoconservative label is a tattered and problematic one, applied to historians as diverse in other regards as Lucy Dawidowicz and Ernst Nolte, but they both have expressed a belief in the role of abstract systems of thought as the prime movers in history, a belief defended as well by anti-Semitic theorists such as Lagarde and Eckart. Throughout this book I have voiced reservations about the "essentialist" drift of such positions, which posit "the Jew" or "the Semite" – or "the German" – as tenacious essences that exercise a pervasive influence in history. The primary role of anti-Semitic ideology in the Third Reich is entirely plausible. But a careful examination of the historical record puts that plausible assertion into serious doubt, or at least suggests the need for major qualifications. Hitler often expressed irritation that the general German population was so slow to understand the Jewish danger – at least, as he believed it should be understood. The same qualifications might be offered about the great anti-Semitic affairs or the Russian pogroms; in each the plausible role of anti-Semitic ideology or Jew-hatred among the general population becomes less certain and far less simple upon closer examination.

Although I have been critical of the notion that the abstract productions of intellectuals may be considered the prime movers in history, I believe it impossible to write a coherent modern history in which men of action (also often intellectuals, or at least men with ideas) – Herzl, Lueger, Lenin, Trotsky, Stalin, or Hitler – are not a central concern: "No Hitler, No Holocaust" is only the most striking of slogans that might be cited; "No Lenin, no Bolshevik Revolution" is another. And there would almost certainly not have been a Dreyfus or Beilis affair if the personalities of Alfred Dreyfus and Mendel Beilis had been different. Contemplating the extraordinary historical significance of the Holocaust, and recognizing that it might not – almost certainly would not – have occurred without Hitler, justifies paying careful attention to Hitler's personality. The same holds for the Bolshevik Revolution and the personalities of Lenin and Trotsky. Indeed, however important Bolshevik ideology, I am persuaded that understanding those personalities is finally far more important; Marxist ideology, like anti-Semitic ideology, suggested many potential lines of development but it did not rigidly determine any single one.

There were, on the other hand, definite limits to the power of great men. "No Hitler, no Holocaust" has an obvious counterpart in "no anti-Semitism, no

Holocaust." Quite aside from the discussion about Hitler's being a "weak dicta-tor," his goals were finally thwarted. Trotsky, however impressive a personality, was perhaps an even greater failure, to a large degree because his ideas about the nature of historical reality were no less flawed than Hitler's. Bolshevik ide-ology has been said to exercise much the same kind of intoxicating effect as that other profoundly flawed modern ideology, anti-Semitism; it certainly could be charged with greater death and destruction, but finally both ideology and personality must be carefully evaluated within a nexus of other historical factors.

The ineffably tangled issue of the survival of anti-Semitism cannot be sepa-rated from the no less ineffably tangled issue of the survival of the Jews. If Jews, in environments of toleration and equitable treatment, are "committing suicide" in ever rising numbers, what does that say about the attractions and benefits of Jewish separateness, of a specifically Jewish consciousness? Might one conclude that it has been oppression that has been most effective in assur-ing Jewish separateness and solidarity, rather than the attractions of Jewishness in some inherent positive sense, so that once oppression disappears most Jews no longer much care about being Jewish – or, stated more precisely, lose sight of what it once meant? It is intriguing that the Jewish settlement of Kaifeng, in China, which dated back to the Middle Ages, disappeared by the nineteenth century, not apparently because of persecution but because of a lack of it.

An unavoidable question arises, one that cannot be separated from the issue of the origin of anti-Semitism: What is the utility or meaning of Jewish survival in modern times to a modern, secular consciousness? From a tradi-tional religious standpoint, justifications for Jewish survival are obvious and coherent, but a solid majority of Jews in the world today, in Europe, in the United States, and even in Israel, are not religious in the traditional sense. Indeed, a significant proportion of the formally religious are in truth only marginally so, or are religious in a way that is difficult to distinguish from what is normally understood as culture or ethnicity.

For non-Jews, even those who are explicitly Christian, age-old justifications for Jewish survival retain almost no meaning, beyond the ranks of a minority of fundamentalists. If being a Jew is a purely secular matter, an issue of ethnic-ity or nationality, how can Jewish survival be considered any more important than, say, the survival of the Wends, Byelo–Russians, Chechens, or Croats? In the context of a multicultural society such as the United States, why should a Jewish ethnicity or cultural style resist blending and "disappearing" any more or any longer than the cultural styles of the Germans, Swedes, or Irish? Inter-marriage and assimilation have occurred and are occurring in most other communities, but do prominent Armenian–American or Japanese–American leaders publicly address the issues with such terms as "bloodless Holocaust" and "candy-coated poison?"

There may be consistent and reasonable answers to these questions. If so, it would be useful for them to be more widely articulated by non-religious Jewish leaders, who need to explain why so many non-religious Jews seem to believe that their case is fundamentally different, not merely another example of the change and adaptation that work upon all human communities. As Deborah Lipstadt has remarked, "to survive in order simply to survive risks turning our tradition into nothing more than ethnic chauvinism."[51]

These questions have suggestive connections to the issue of the superiority of the Judeo–Christian tradition and, even more broadly, the values of western civilization. One's attitude to that issue has implications for the way that the history of Jewish–Gentile relations is understood. Fewer and fewer people nowadays believe in the superiority of western civilization; growing numbers of those who live both in and outside that civilization consider the West to be pernicious, indeed inferior to the cultures of "primitive" peoples, as they used to be called, and enduringly alien to the ancient civilizations of Asia. It is certainly a fair question if modern Americans, in a self-proclaimed multicultural society, can continue to believe that the peoples of the world who do not believe in the God of the Bible are morally inferior. And if that belief is not tenable, is it justified to make claims for the monotheism and associated morality that the Jews believe they have brought to the world? Why indeed should Judaism or Christianity survive? Those questions, however awkward, cannot be avoided in pondering the issue of the survival of anti-Semitism.

There are suggestive parallels between the arguments of the anti-Semites, who see the Jews as destructive – the very opposite of Jewish self-image and of much evidence – and the arguments of those critics who see western civilization as destructive – the very opposite of its own self-image, and also much evidence. There are further suggestive similarities to the Jewish sense of superiority (including certain kinds of perfectly measurable Jewish superiority) and the envy/hatred it has engendered, on the one hand, and the western sense of superiority (including its own kinds of measurable superiority), which has also provoked hatred and envy, on the other.

Jews in modern times have been notably liberal in orientation. Modern Jews, as distinguished from those religiously orthodox who reject or denounce the freedom and individualism associated with modern times, have favored openness and liberty, have believed that liberal societies are ones in which Jews will prosper. Israel, it is no accident, is a liberal democracy, if also one exhibiting some notable aberrations from liberal norms, mostly the result of compromises with Orthodox Judaism but also because of the hostility of its Arab neighbors. Most Jews in modern nation-states have actively participated in the surrounding non-Jewish societies, have willingly sent their children to public schools, and have been active politically. But Jewish "suicide" in modern societies has begun to put that liberal faith to question, with unforeseeable consequences.

---

[51] Deborah Lipstadt, "Why Be Jewish?" *Moment,* vol. 18, no. 4, Aug. 1993, 14.

An underlying premise of this work, too, has been liberal, in the sense that it has expressed a belief in the value of open, free, and mutually beneficial inquiry, one that paradoxically has been weakly represented in many studies of modern Jewish history or Gentile–Jewish relations more generally. The turn to ethnocentrism that has affected Jews as well as other ethnic groups in the United States and elsewhere is perfectly understandable, but like many other perfectly understandable phenomena it carries within it potent dangers, in particular those next-door neighbors to ethnic identity, tribalism and bigotry. I admittedly do not know what a workable balance is between identity and community, but it is clear to me that community inevitably demands some loss of identity and that identity pushed unthinkingly and uncompromisingly transforms into tribalism.

People who want to be part of the same society require a common language, in both the literal and figurative senses; they must hold values that are not so widely separated that every action is fraught with misunderstanding and danger. Cultural variety can be and has been enriching – but only when the will to mutual enrichment and respect exists. The range of shared values must be adequate to permit, among ordinary, flawed citizens, a substantial degree of mutual comprehension. Hasidic Jews and Black Muslims are simply not going to join in a celebration of multiculturalism; they are too committed to a belief in the superiority of their own ways – and the evil of others. The ultraleft utopianism implicit in the notion that "all people will get along if only they know each other" points toward tragedy. Of course a country as large as the United States can easily survive with small numbers of fringe separatist groups like the hasidim, Black Muslims, Mennonites, or Jehovah's Witnesses, but if the governing or hegemonial culture lacks shared values of adequate attractiveness, if its leaders lack the will to understand, compromise, and share cultural diversity, then it is likely to come to grief – true not only for the United States but also other countries, including (and especially) Israel.

In the Preface I remarked that I would be putting forth for consideration a number of problematic or controversial perspectives in the conviction that they have not yet received the kind of ample and fair hearing they deserve. A reviewer of my previous book commented that one of its main achievements was not to reveal events in all their clarity but in all their ambiguity. I would be content to receive a similar review of these pages. While I do not think of history as incomprehensible, I am time and again impressed with how easily simplistic versions of it – ones that typically serve emotional need rather than a desire for genuine understanding – gain wide credence. My inspiration, if that is the word, is captured in the deceptively simple words of a famous Jew, Baruch Spinoza: "With regard to human affairs, not to laugh, not to cry, not to become indignant, but to understand."

Index

Abramovich, 429
Abwehrverein, 150, 152
Abysinnia, 358
Académie Française, 222
acculturation, 208, 281, 286–7. *See also* assimilation; historic peoples
acetone, 414
Adams, Henry, 374
Adams, John, 257
Adler, Hermann, 361
Adler, Nathan Marcus, 361
Adler, Victor, 159, 177, 179, 201
adoption, 73
aesthetic anti-Semitism, 222, 353, 374. *See also* modern anti-Semitism
aestheticism (in baroque triumphalism), 338–9
affairs, anti-Semitic. *See* Beilis, Dreyfus, Frank, Tiszaeszlár
Africa (African): Arabs' views of, 72, 79; DuBois's views, 78; increasing European contact with, 79–80; Gobineau's views, 88–9; Broca's views, 94; Marx's references to, 164–5; "scramble for Africa," 358. *See also* Boer War; racism
African-Americans. *See* blacks
Ahad Ha'am, 85, 329, 368
ahavat yisrael, 509
Ahriman, 166
Albia fraternity, 328
Alexander II, 63, 64, 67, 305
Alexander III, 63, 68–9, 70, 279
Alexander, Edward, xvii
Alexandria, 27–9, 283
Aliens Bills, 368–70
Allgemeine Zeitung des Judentums, 135
Alliance Israélite Universelle: believed cover for Jewish Syndicate, 212; warning to Jews about "arrogance," 215; Brafman's charges of Russian contacts, 279; believed instigator of Revolution of 1905, 303; role in Romanian affairs, 316, 317–18; role in Paris Peace Conference, 411–12
Alsace, 47, 48, 209
Alsace-Lorraine, 409
Altneuland, 325

ame ha'aretz, 31
America. *See* United States
Americanization: feared in France, 213; in Boulangist political methods, 216; condemned by European intellectuals, 260; seen as Jewish by Chamberlain, 408. *See also* assimilation; modernism
American Political Tradition, 259
anarchism (anarchist): Proudhon's thought, 166; reaction to WW I, 394; anarchist armies in Russian civil war, 407; Bolshevik resemblance to, 439
anarchosyndicalism, 394
And Quiet Flows the Don, 444
Anglo-American culture, 258, 259
Anglo-German naval race, 358–9
Anglo-Jewish Association, 418
Anglophobia, 239
Anglo-Saxon, 90, 247, 254, 372, 380
Anschluss, 409, 410, 526–7
Anthropological Society of Paris, 94
anticlericalism, 55–6, 214, 236
anti-Dreyfusards, 219, 231, 233, 236. *See also* Dreyfus Affair
Anti-Dühring, 160–1
antiliberalism, 98–9, 126, 347–54. *See also* antimodernism; belle époque; Fascism; liberalism; modernism; Nazism
antimodernism, 197–200, 347–54. *See also* antiliberalism; modernism
Anti-Monopolist, 380
Antioch, 33–5
Anti-Semites' Petition, 147
anti-Semitism. *See* modern anti-Semitism
"anti-Semitism of reason." *See* "rational" anti-Semitism
Antisemitism: The Longest Hatred, x
Anti-Socialist Laws, 143
apikoyros, 53
Arab (Arabs): racism in, 72, 79–80; as Semites, 86n, 87, "Jews on horseback," 90; seen as kin to Jews by Istóczy, 269; misunderstood by Herzl, 325; in Palestine, 414, 415, 418–19, 421
Arbeterbund. See Bund
arditi, 469

547

Arendt, Hannah, 77, 200–1, 276, 514, 530. *See also* totalitarianism
Arendt Thesis, 276
Arianism (cf. Aryan), 34
aristocracy (aristocrat, aristocratic): in Austria-Hungary, 188, 190; in Toussenel's theories, 221–2; British aristocracy and Jews, 241, 254; Watson's charges of a "Jewish aristocracy," 381. *See also* Junker
Aristotle, 72
Artom, Isaac, 474
army. *See* military
Army League, 335
arondator, 66
artel, 168
Article VI (of American Constitution), 256–7
Aryan: related to biblical chosenness, 6; Greek views of, 72; evolution of term, 85–9; as part of *Gemeinschaft*, 112; "organic" connections to Volk, 117; Marr's use of, 129; use by Berlin Movement, 147; in regard to Böckel, 155; "impeccable" Aryan appearance, 173; Aryan spirit freed from the Jewish spirit, 196; Aryan Paragraph in Linz Program, 202; in Pan-German agitation, 203; application to Toussenel's thought, 222; in Chamberlain's thought, 352; use by Mussolini, 466; "pure" Aryanism rejected by Italians, 473; Aryan capitalism, 498; Aryans not superior but "different," 523; as defined in Nuremberg Laws, 524
Ashkenazim (Ashkenazic): in France, 45–6, 47; eastern and western Ashkenazim, 51; Sephardic discrimination against, 75; in Britain, 244; in Romania, 311, 313; seen as "too different" from Nordic races, 473. *See also Ostjude*; Sephardim
"Asiatic deeds," 434
Asquith, Herbert, 414–15, 416, 420
assassination(s): of Alexander II, 68; effort by Lekert, 290; of Stolypin 305; of Plehve, 326; of Bolshevik leaders, 445–6; of Rathenau, 483; setting off *Reichskristallnacht*, 527
Assembly of Jewish Notables, 48
assimilation: in France, 208; in U.S., 258, 375; in Hungary, 267; in Russia, 281; in Germany, 319; in Herzl's thought, 324, 328; in Italy, 473–4; as seen by Hitler, 495. *See also* acculturation; Christianization; "disappearing"; emancipation; intermarriage; self-hatred; separatism; Zionism
Assumptionists, 219–20, 228
Atlanta (Georgia), 381, 385
Aufklärung, 331–2. *See also* Enlightenment
Ausgleich, 186, 191, 197
Austerlitz, Friedrich, 179, 182, 193, 195
Austria (Austrians), 60, 337–47, 409, 410
Austro-Hungarian Empire: overview, 182–205, 337–47; collapse in 1918, 409; new Austrian state, 410. *See also* Franz Joseph; Hungary; Vienna
Autoemancipation!, 323

Babel, Isaac, 447
Baden, 149
Balabanova, Angelica, 467, 484
Balbo, Italo, 479
Balfour Declaration, 413–20
Balfour, Lord, 247: on Aliens Bill, 368–9; on Jewish homeland, 415–16; meeting with Brandeis, 417; pride in righting injustices against Jews, 419; defends Jewish rights over Arab resentments, 421
Ballin, Alfred, 402
Balzac, Honoré de, 206, 221
Bamberger, Ludwig, 140
banking (bank, bankers). *See* financiers
barbarism (barbarian), 71
Baron, Salo Wittmayer, 11, 15, 17
baroque, 338–9
Barrès, Maurice, 222–3, 260
bastard. *See mamzer*
Bauer, Otto, 180–1
Bavaria, 502
Bebel, August, 172, 179
Becker, Carl, 351
Beer Hall Putsch, 483
Begin, Menachem, 397
Beilis Affair, 305–6
Bela Kun, 410
Belgium, 393
belle époque, 273–8
Beller, Stephen, 331, 332, 339, 340
Belloc, Hilaire, 434
Benda, Julien, 91, 210
Benedikt, Moritz, 193
ben Varga, Solomon, 22
Berchtesgarten, 493
Berghahn, V. R., 319
Berlin: Jewish brashness in, 119, 138; Jewish role in press, 139; anti-Semitism, 147; elections of 1881, 148; trends in prewar period, 347; Spartacus Uprising in, 436; Nazi activity in, 502; Olympic Games in, 526
Berlin Electors, 150
Berliner Tageblatt, 116, 402
Berlin, Isaiah, 247–8
Berlin Movement, 147, 169
Bernanos, Georges, 224
Bernstein, Eduard, 25, 121, 125, 159, 178
"Bernsteins" ("who pay the bills"), 423
Besitzstand, 191
Bessarabia, 64
Bessarebetz, 293
best-sellers (anti-Semitic): Marr, 127; Drumont, 223; Langbehn, 348–9; Chamberlain, 351
Bethmann Hollweg, 401
Bettauer, Hugo, 134n
Bialyk, 297
Bialystok, 65
Bianchi, Michele, 479
"Big Money," 381. *See also* capitalism; financiers
Biedermeier, 185

Bielohlawek, Hermann, 346–7
Bielsk, 284
biennio rosso, 469
Bigart, Jacques, 411
Bildung, 52, 161–2, 332, 333, 340
Birmingham, Stephen, 120n
Bismarck, Otto von: relations to liberalism,
    110; and Junkers, 112; and *Kulturkampf*,
    122–5; move to right, 126; and Stoecker,
    145; disassociates himself from anti-Semites,
    148; and Lassalle, 164; relations to Romania,
    306–7, 317; dismissed as chancellor, 273,
    347
Black Death, 37
Black History Month, xi
Black Hundreds, 7, 284, 300–1
blacks: Jews and slave trade, xx; as victims, 10;
    and "subordinate cultures," 18; Negro blood
    in pharoahs, 78; Arab views of, 79; Gob-
    ineau's views of, 88–9; Broca's views of, 94;
    Lassalle compared to, 164; described as "sav-
    ages," 261; lynchings of, 377–8; Conley, 381;
    recent anti-Semitism of, 532–3
Blackshirts (Italian fascists), 470, 482, 484
Black Week, 359
"blaming the Jews," xviii, 103, 308. *See also*
    victim
"blaming the victim." *See* victim
Bleichröder, Gerson: letter to, 103; as *Kaiser-
    jude*,114; reputed richest man in Germany,
    115; Bismarck's banker, 125; contacts with
    Bratianu, 316; relations with Bismarck in
    Romanian affairs, 317
Bloc national, 435
Bloch, Eduard, 488–9
blood (as related to race), 74–8
"bloodless Holocaust," 534
Blood Libel, 36, 128, 281, 305–6, 329
Blumenfeld, Kurt, 393
Blumkin, Jacob, 446
Blum, Léon, 222, 426
B'nai Brith, 317, 331
Board of Deputies, 418
Böckel, Otto, 126, 152–6, 174
Boers, 359–60, 362
Boer War, 275, 357–64, 388
Bohemia, 192
Bohemia-Moravia, 267, 409. *See also* Sudeten-
    land
Bolaffi, Gino, 461
Bologna, 470
Bolshevism (Bolshevik Party, Bolshevik): Lenin
    welcomes Jews in Party, 181; opposition to
    WWI, 401; in Russian civil war, 407; publica-
    tion of secret treaties, 408; role of Jews in,
    427–33; Party assumes control of Russia,
    438–48; fear of Bolshevik model in Nazi
    appeal, 513–15; compared in appeal to
    Nazism, 543. *See also* Bolshevik Revolution;
    Lenin; social democrat; Trotsky
Bolshevik Revolution: ends deportation of
    Russian Jews from Britain, 399; seen as

"insanity in power," 424; overview, 438–48.
    See also Russian Revolution
Booth, Charles, 364
Börne, Ludwig, 127, 141
bonapartist, 212, 449. *See also* Napoleon
borghesia, 473, 475–6. *See also* bourgeoisie;
    Bürgertum; middle class; *Mittelstand*
Borowitz, Eugene, 74
bossism (political bosses), 178, 339, 373, 479.
    See also Gauleiters
Boulanger (Boulangist), 215–19, 222
"bourgeoisification," 178
bourgeoisie (bourgeois): less hostile to Jews,
    41; gentility of, 52; passivity of German
    bourgeoisie, 105; development of positive
    self-image, 120; in Austria-Hungary, 187–9,
    267; in Britain, 242; in Italy, 473, 475–6. *See
    also borghesia*; *Bürgertum*; middle class;
    Mittelstand
boycotts, 153, 407, 517, 520, 521
boyar, 311
Brahmins, 374. *See also* elites
Brafman, Jacob, 279–80
Brandeis, Louis, 261, 371–2, 417
Braun, Eva, 494
Braun, Ilse, 494
Bredin, Jean-Denis, 67n
Brest-Litovsk, 431–2, 440, 466
Bright, John, 250
bris, 55
Britain (British): Cicero advises against slaves
    from Britain, 72; early capitalism in, 119;
    overview, 238–51, 355–371; enthusiasm for
    war, 1914, 395; goals in Balfour Declaration,
    413–14
British Brothers' League, 357, 367–8
Broca, Paul, 94–5
Brogan, D. W., 214
Bronstein, Lev Davidovich (Trotsky), 430
Brook, Rupert, 392
Brothers' League, 357
Brownshirts: and *Freikorps*, 482; Hitler's
    remarks on, 484; interested in plunder, 502;
    in contending factions, 516–7; tensions with
    Hitler, 521–2; role in *Reichskristallnacht*,
    527. *See also* Night of the Long Knives;
    Röhm
Buber, Martin, 62, 393
Budapest, 188, 189, 264, 404, 407. *See also*
    Austro-Hungarian Empire; Hungary;
    Magyar
Bucharest, 66, 317
Bukharin, Nikolai Ivanovich, 432, 452
Bukovina, 184–5
Bulgaria, 249, 250, 359
Bulgarian Horrors, 359
Bullock, Alan, 388
Bund, Jewish (Arbeterbund): positive view of
    exile, 8; remarkable in history of socialism,
    168–9; Lenin's attacks on, 181; on Day of

Bund *(Continued)*
    Atonement, 279; in "pimp pogrom," 284;
    attacks on Zionists, 321; Yiddish-speaking,
    428; outrage over Luxemburg's slur, 429;
    Dzerzhinsky's contacts with, 442
bureaucratization, 178
Bürgertum, 52, 117. *See also borghesia;* bour-
    geoisie; middle class; *Mittelstand*
Burgfrieden, 394, 405
butchers, 225–6. *See also shehita,* ritual
    murder

Cabano, Prince, 380
Caesar's Column, 380
Caillaux, Joseph, 206
Canaan (Canaanites), 49, 72
Candolle, Alphonse de, 93
Canetti, Elias, 345
capitalism (capitalist): favorable to Jews,
    114–15; and civility, 119; Jew and capitalist
    equated by Marx, 163; Nazism as "death rat-
    tle" of capitalism; 177; as seen by Vogelsang,
    199–200; as seen by Toussenel, 221; Jewish
    capitalists attacked in Britain, 251; corrup-
    tion in Austria, 339–40; attacked by de
    Lagarde, 350; charged with role in Boer
    War, 359–64; impact in pre-WW I U.S., 375,
    379; issue in Frank trial, 381–2; Hitler's
    views of capitalists, 493; Aryan vs. Jewish cap-
    italism, 498; capitalists as supporters of
    Nazis, 501–2. *See also* decadence; degenera-
    tion; financiers; Great Depression; industri-
    alization; liberalism; modernism
Caprivi, von, 273
Carol, Prince, 309, 312, 317
Carlyle, Thomas, 541
Carvallo, Jules, 95
Cathari, 37
Catholic Church (Catholicism, Catholics),
    122–4, 134, 149, 155, 167; position of
    Church in Austria-Hungary, 196–7; clergy as
    educators in Austria-Hungary, 189; resent-
    ment of Jewish journalists in Austria-Hun-
    gary, 195; antimodernism, 200; reaction to
    Ferry Laws, 214, 219–20; investors in *Union
    générale,* 215; in U.S., 258–9; in Poland, 265;
    in Hungary, 265–6; hopes for equity in Ger-
    many, 333; Habsburg baroque, 338–9; Eng-
    lish Catholic intellectuals attack Bolshevik
    Revolution, 434; Italian Catholics and
    Jews, 471; Lateran Accords with Mussolini,
    478; Hitler's attitude to, 493; resistance to
    Nazism, 512. *See also* Center Party; Chris-
    tianity; Christian socialism; Jesuits;
    Kulturkampf; Partito Popolari, pope; religion;
    Rome
Caucasian, 90
Causes of World Unrest, 434
cavalier, 204. *See also* noble
Cavour, Count Camillo, 474, 478
Cecil, Lord Robert, 415
Center Party, 123–4, 401, 512, 513

Centralverein, 332
Ceorbaum, 466
Chamberlain, Houston Stewart: praises Dis-
    raeli, 77; derides political anti-Semites,
    148–9; overview of his work, 351–4; lauds
    Jewish patriotism, 394; denounces Jewish
    "insolence" during war, 404; sees England in
    the hands of Jews, 408; attitude to
    Sephardim, 473; describes Italians as degen-
    erate, 473
Chamberlain, Joseph, 359
charismatic leaders, 469, 482, 483–4, 487, 503
charity (charities), 376. *See also tsedaka*
Chartists, 245
Cheka, 429, 431, 433, 441–7. *See also* secret
    police
Chesterton, C. K., 434
chief rabbi of Moscow, 423
China (Chinese), 72, 377, 543
Chmielnicki, Bogdan, 59–60, 295
chosenness, 107, 161, 135–6. *See also* Aryan;
    Esau; Jacob; separatism
Christ. *See* Jesus
Christian anti-Semitism: opening remarks,
    xv–xvii, xxi, 29–39, in Stoecker, 142–7; in
    Vogelsang, 182, 198–200; rejected by
    Lagarde, 350; concluding remarks, 533. *See
    also* Catholic; Christian socialism; ideology;
    modern anti-Semitism; religion
Christianity, 444. *See also* Catholic; religion
Christianization, 319. *See also* assimilation; "dis-
    appearing"
Christian socialism, 145, 176, 198–200, 337–47,
    469–70
Christian Social Party (Austria), 176, 342
Christian Social Workers' Party (Germany),
    143, 148, 342
Church Fathers, 33
Churchill, Randolph, 246
Churchill, Winston: admirer of Chamberlain,
    351; critic of B. Webb, 365; on Aliens Bill,
    369; believer in Jewish power, 303, 415; criti-
    cal of Palestinian Mandate, 421; sees "Jewish
    race" as "mainspring" of revolution, "satu-
    rated with hatred," 423, 434; favorable to
    Fascism, 477
Chrysostom, John, 33–6
Cicero, 72
circumcision, 55
civil equality. *See emancipation*
civilizing mission, 192–3, 247, 458. *See also*
    French Revolution; "historic peoples;" Mani-
    fest Destiny
civil war (Russia), 407, 427
Civil War (U.S.), 262–3
Clare, George, 344
Class, Heinrich, 391
"classical anti-Semitism," 26–9
Classical Economists, 366
classical liberalism, 98. *See also* liberalism
Clemenceau, Georges, 406
Cobbett, William, 201, 245

Cogni, Giulio, 473
Cohen, Hermann, 136, 140
Comintern. *See* Communist International
Commercial Gazette, 376
Commissariat of Nationalities, 444. *See also* Stalin
Communism. *See* Bolshevik; Lenin; Marx; revolution; social democrat
Communist International, 426, 430, 436, 452
Communist Party of Germany (KPD), 435, 481–3, 513, 517
Compromise of 1867. *See Ausgleich*
concentration camp, 388, 529
Congress Poland, 60, 61, 64, 288. *See also* Poland
Congress of Basel, 327
Congress of Berlin, 310
Congress of Halle, 430
Congress of Paris, 315
Congress of Vienna, 60
Coningsby, 76–7
Conley, Jim, 381, 382
Conquest, Robert, 453
Conservative Party (of Britain), 243, 247–8, 250, 369. *See also* Disraeli
Conservative Party (of Germany), 151, 335
conservative movements (and anti-Semitism), 151, 234, 426
"conservative revolutionaries," 277. *See also* Chamberlain, H.; Lagarde; Langbehn
conspiracies (conspiracy theories): as seen by Austerlitz, 195; charges against "money men," 275; charges by Watson, 381; Rathenau's 300 powerful men, 403; behind Versailles Treaty, 410, 411; Mussolini's beliefs about Jewish power, 467; behind Weimar Republic, 483. *See also* financiers; Rothschilds; Syndicate.
Constantine, 34
Constituent Assembly (Russian), 441
Constitutional Convention (American), 256–7
Constitutional Democratic (Kadet) Party, 427, 434, 441
conversion (Jewish converts to Christianity), 73, 75, 210. *See also* meshumed
Cooperative Movement in Great Britain, 364
cooperatives, 154–5
corporatism, 197–9
Cossack, 447. *See also* Chmielnicki
Coughlin, Father, 385
Council of People's Commissars, 438, 441, 482, 483
counter-hegemony. *See* hegemony
Counterreformation, 338
"creationism," xiii
Crèvecoeur, St.-Jean de, 238
Croce, Benedetto, 462
Croix, 220
Crucifixion, 258, 540. *See also* deicide; Jesus; Saint Paul
crusades, 37

"cult of Ostjuden," 62
"cultural despair," 276
cultural pluralism. *See* pluralism
Cuza, Ion, 309, 315
Czechoslovakia (Czech), 191, 192, 195, 407, 409, 526

Darwin, Charles (Darwinian, Darwinism), 83, 95. *See also* social Darwinism
Das Judentum in der Musik, 89
Dangerfield, George, 406
Daudet, Léon, 227–8
Davydov, 299
Dawidowicz, Lucy, ix–xi, 509, 519, 542
Dearborn Independent, 520
"death of liberalism," 277. *See also* antiliberalism; liberalism
"death rattle of capitalism," 177
decadence, 130–1, 234–5, 273. *See also* degeneration
de Crèvecoeur, St.-Jean, 238
"deep consciousness," 277
Defense League against Anti-Semitism, 150
Degas, Edgar, 224
Degeneracy, 330
degeneration, 89, 130–1, 330, 352. *See also* "ferment of decomposition"
deicide, 30, 35–7, 88, 258, 471
Deists, English, 41
de Lagarde, Paul, 349–51
Democratic Party (of Germany), 483
democratic radicalism, 201–5, 339, 379. *See also* Christian socialism; populism; Radical Party
de Morès, Marquis. *See* Morès, Marquis de
department stores, 115, 217–18, 343
Depression (1929), 511–12. *See also* Great Depression
Derby, Lord, 77
Der schöne Karl, 339
Dershowitz, Alan, 534
Der Sieg des Judenthums über das Germanenthum, 127
Desecration of the Host, 36, 128
destructiveness ("destructive mission" of Jews): charged by Marr, 128–30; by Treitschke, 137–9, 141; by Stoecker, 143–4; by Dühring, 161; seen in R. Luxemburg, 179, 402; in Austria-Hungary, 196; charge in Drumont's writings, 206; as seen by Caillaux, 206; as seen by French Catholics, 214; as seen by Parisian shopkeepers, 217, 219; in the United States, 255; as seen by Russian anti-Semites, 280–1; by Donnelly, 380; Jews as revolutionaries, 388–9, 410; Balfour's view of Jews as "demoralizing," 416; Churchill's view of "Jewish race" as "saturated with hatred," 434; Jewish assassins, 445–6; Trotsky as destructive Jew, 450; in views of Hitler, 490, 494–5, 524. *See also* Bolshevik; capitalist; classical anti-Semitism; deicide; financier; press; revolution

Deuteronomy, 72
Deutsche Bank of Berlin, 343
Deutscher, Isaac, 171, 441, 453
deutscher Kulturbereich, 107
De Vecchi, Cesare, 479
Diaspora. *See* Galut.
Dickens, Charles, xvi, 92, 93
"dictated peace," 408
Diderot, Dennis, 40
Die Gartenlaube, 120–1
Die Juden, die Könige unserer Zeit, 153
Different Races of Mankind, 80–1
Diktat, 408
Dina, Giacomo, 474
"disappearing": 253; Magyar fears of, 266; issue
    in Zionism, 321–2, 324; current concerns,
    533–4; Jewish survival, 543–4. *See also* assimi-
    lation; Zionism
Disraeli, Benjamin: role of his novels, xvi; use
    of "race," 76–8, 90–2; influence on Marr,
    131; compared to Vogelsang, 199; critic of
    liberalism, 240; and Gladstone, 243, 245–6;
    position in British politics, 247–50; *Vivian
    Grey*, 322
d'Israeli, Isaac, 43
dissenting churches, 245
dissenting minority, 255
Dmowski, Roman, 401n
Doctors' Plot, 454
Dollaronkel, 259
Donnelly, Ignatius, 379–80
"Dormant Period" of anti-Semitism (Germany),
    334–7
Dostoevsky, Feodor, 348
draft (military), 62, 476, 495. *See also* military
Dreyfus, Alfred, 25, 219, 230, 231–2
Dreyfus, Mathieu, 233, 236
Dreyfus Affair, 219, 222, 229, 230–7, 328, 395
Dreyfusards, 231, 233, 235–6
Drumont, Edouard: denounces Jews "vomited"
    from ghettos, 206; as best-selling author,
    223–6; duels arising from articles in his
    paper, 228; Jewish patriotism seen as oppor-
    tunistic, 260, 293; influence on Herzl, 329;
    compared to Goldhagen, 508–9
Dual Monarchy, 186–7. *See also* Austro-Hungar-
    ian Empire
Dubnov, Simon, 67n, 287, 292, 298
DuBois, W. E. B., 78
Dubrovin, 304
Duce. See Mussolini
dueling, 205, 228–30, 343
Dühring, Eugen, 160–1
Duma, 304, 395
Durkheim, Emile, 210, 276
Dvinsk, 284
Dzerzhinsky, Felix, 433, 441–2
Dzhugashvili, Josef (Stalin), 432. *See also*
    Stalin
Eastern Policy, 249
East London Advertiser, 367
Ebert, Friedrich, 482

Eckart, Dietrich, 28, 498–9, 538–9
écrasez l'infâme!, 42
Edomites, 4
education. *See* schools
Edward VII (Edwardian), 273, 355–6
Egypt (Egyptians), 27–9, 49
Ehrmann, Solomon, 331
Eichmann, Adolf, 505, 530
Eiffel Tower, 217
Eisner, Kurt, 495–6
Eliot, George, 227
elitism (elitist, elites): bourgeois-liberal elitism,
    98; role of German elites, 105; in Austrian
    liberalism; 186; elites' fear of new money,
    213; Jewish Grand Dukes, 241; British elites,
    242; Jewish elites' denigration of U.S., 257;
    U.S. elites' reaction to Jews, 373, 374. *See also*
    aristocracy; Brahmins; Junker; mandarins;
    nobles
emancipation (Jewish): discussion before
    French Revolution, 43–4; in French Revolu-
    tion 44–8; as seen by Stoecker, 144; in
    Britain, 242, 244–5, 246–7; in Russia, 282,
    423, 437; in Romania, 314, 315–16, 318; as
    issue in Zionism, 322
emigration. *See* immigration; population
    growth
Eminescu, Mihai, 316
Enabling Act, 516
encirclement, 274
Encyclopedia Britannica, 330
Endelman, Todd, 43
Engels, Friedrich, 159, 160, 164, 180, 215
England. *See* Britain
"England for the English!", 251
English-speaking countries, 355
Enlightenment, 40–4, 160, 167, 257, 331–2. *See
    also* humanism; liberalism
Erfüllung, 410
Esau (Esau's Tears), ix, 3–7, 8, 75, 531, 533
Essay on the Inequality of Races, 88–9
"essentialism," 73, 74, 75, 88–9, 542
ethnic insecurity, 191–2
ethnocentrism, 71
événements, 11
exceptionalism, 239, 251–3, 255, 539–40. *See
    also* Sonderweg
Exile. *See* Galut
"extreme situations," 529

factory occupations, 436, 470
Fagin, 92, 93
Fahrradler, 123
"failed revolution," 482
"fantasy" (and "reality" in anti-Semitism):
    opening remarks, xv–xvi; modern anti-Semi-
    tes' hatred based on "real" factors, 23; fan-
    tasy in "inner-ring" anti-Semites, 26; mix of
    fantasy and reality in "classical anti-Semi-
    tism," 29; anti-Semitic beliefs linked to Jew-
    ish claims to power, 91; in literary examples,
    93–4; consensus about Jews being cause of

anti-Semitism, 125; in Marr, 128; in Treitschke, 134, 135–6; in Bauer, 181; in Austria-Hungary, 190, 195 (Kraus); in interpreting modern times, 200; in Schönerer's attitudes to Jews, 201; in regard to activities of Alliance Israélite Universelle, 212, 280; in Toussenel's thought, 222; in Barrès's thought, 222; in Drumont's thought, 224–5.; small role of fantasy in the United States, 255; in Hungary, 265; in Istóczy's experiences, 270; concluding remarks to Part Two, 271 269; in Russia, 280–1, 292, 303–4; in Romania, 307–8, 309; in U.S. in pre-WWI period, 373–4, 375, 378; about Jewish "unmilitary bearing," 400–1; in regard to Paris Peace Conference, 408; in Arab resentments, 421–2; about Jews as revolutionaries, 424–36; about Jews avoiding front-line service in Red Army, 444; in Jews as assassins, 446; about "demonic" power of revolutionary Jews, 448; in Hitler's anti-Semitism, 492, 496–7; concluding remarks, 532, 536, 537–8. *See also* ideology; modern anti-Semitism

fardaitscht, 184

fasci di combattimento, 468, 469

Fascism (fascist): resentment of Paris Peace settlement, 410–11, 469; role of anti-Semitism in early movement, 458, 459; general traits of the "fascist era," 457–60; definition of, 462–4; origins, 464–71; Marxist interpretation of, 465–6; attraction of Jews to, 468–76; favorable image in democracies, 477–8; initial left-wing tendencies, 479. *See also* antiliberalism; Italy; Mussolini, Nazism; proto-Fascism; proto-Nazism

Fashoda, 358

Fast, Howard, 7

Felice, Renzo de, 463n

feminism (feminists), 10

"ferment of decomposition," 103, 135, 247, 349–51

Ferry Laws, 214, 219

"fighting back": rejected in *Leidensgeschichte*, 17; related to Jewish "conspiracies," 275; Jewish terrorist squads, 284; in pogroms of 1903, 291; 297–8; in Romania, 317–18; against Lueger, 343; in New York riot, 378. *See also* rise of the Jews; Schiff; Zionism

"final solution," xiii, 136, 508, 528. *See also* Holocaust

financiers: German-Jewish, 115; in South Africa, 363; as seen by American Populists, 379; role in financing WW I, 402–4; Rathenau's criticisms of Jewish financial oligarchs, 403; believed to play a role in Russian Revolution, 435, 438, 466; admirers of Mussolini, 477. *See also* Bleichröder; Oppenheimer, E.; Rathenau; Rothschilds; Schiff

Finzi, Aldo, 480

First Amendment (to American Constitution), 256–7

Foa, Vittorio, 476

Fontane, Theodor, 319

Forckenbeck, Maximilian von, 150

Ford, Henry, 383, 520

foreshadowing, 507

Foundations of the Twentieth Century, 351–2

Founding Fathers, xi, 253, 256–7

"founding years." *See Gründerjahre*

Fourier, Charles, 167, 221

Fourteen Points, 408

France: overview, 206–37; reaction to Balfour Declaration, 420; Communist Party in, 435; general strike in 1920, 436. *See also* Dreyfus Affair; Enlightenment; French Revolution; Paris; socialism

France juive, 223

Frank, Anne, 531

Frankfurt am Main, 149

Frankfurter Zeitung, 402

Frank, Leo, 381–5

Franklin, Benjamin, 257

Franz Joseph: 187–8, 342, 404

Frederick, Harold, 279

Freeman, E. A., 250

free market, 82–3. *See also* capitalism; industrialization; liberalism

Freikorps, 468n, 482

French Communist Party (PCF), 435

French Revolution, 44–8, 425, 449

French Socialist Party. *See* SFIO

Freud, Amalia, 53

Freud, Sigmund (Freudian), 14, 53, 74, 257, 259, 277

Freytag, Gustave, 93

Friedberg, Emil von, 123

Friedberg, Heinrich von, 123

Friedental, Karl Rudolf, 125

Friedjung, Heinrich, 201

Friedman, N. M., 395

Fritsch, Theodor, 404

"fulfillment," 410

Functionalists, 497, 518, 519

fundamentalism, 220. *See also* hasid; ultra-Orthodox

Galen, 74

Galicia (Galician): inhabitants lacking in manners, 53; movement of Jews out of, 60, 69; after partitions, 62; percentage of Jews in, 63; Bauer's reference to, 181; population statistics, poverty, 184–5; Yiddish language and, 191–2; traditional Jewry in, 338; movement of Galician Jews into Hungary, Romania, 268, 307, 311; fate in WW I, 406–7

Galilee (Galilean), 31

Galton, Sir Francis, 92

Galut (Exile), xviii, 6, 8, 13, 15, 238–9, 252

galut metuka, 239

Gambetta, Léon, 211, 214, 229

Gartenlaube, 120–1

"gathering storm" (of anti-Semitism) 227–30, 383. *See also* "rising tide"

Gattungswesen, 163
Gauleiters, 516
Gay, Peter, 40, 172–3
Geldjuden, 125, 259. *See also* capitalists;
  financiers
Gelehrtengeschichte, 18
Gemeinschaft, 112
Gemütlichkeit, 341
general strike, 436, 482
generational conflict, 276–7
George, David Lloyd. *See* Lloyd George,
  David
Georgia (part of Russian Empire), 432, 453
Georgia (U.S. state), 381
Gerlach, Helmut von, 148
German Workers Party, 498
Gesellschaft, 112
German Communist Party. *See* KPD
Germania, 123
Germany (German, Germanic): German set-
  tlers in Russia, 59; Germany as threatening
  other states, 82; appeal of romanticism to
  Germans, 84; the German problem, 104–7;
  German-speakers in Austria-Hungary,
  183–4, 190–3, 197; Jewish-German "advance
  guard," 195–6; Pan-Germanism, 202–5;
  Franklin's worry about "germanization,"
  184, 257; Germans in U.S., 262; Germans in
  Hungary, 267; as viewed by Hess, 322; in
  Wilhelmine period, 330–7; "unpolitical"
  Germans and "Germanic ideology," 347–54;
  German Jews in U.S., 376; enthusiasm for
  WW I, 392–3; Russian Jewish attitudes to,
  395–8; modernizing trends strong during
  WW I, 402–5; treatment at Paris Peace Con-
  ference, 408–10; concluding remarks, 505ff;
  German and Italian national character com-
  pared, 508. *See also Hochdeutsch:* Holocaust;
  Nazism; Pan-Germanism; proto-Nazism;
  Volksgeist
Gestapo, 443
ghetto, 472
"ghetto traits," 174
Gibbon, Edward, 40
Gide, André, 215
Gilbert, Martin, 16
Giolitti, Giovanni, 470
Gladstone, William, 243, 245–6, 248–9, 250
Gleichschaltung, 515
Glogau, Otto, 103, 120–2
Gobineau, Count Arthur de, 87–8, 92, 160
Goebbels, Joseph, 511, 527, 529
"Going to the People," 67
Gold Medal (Italian military honor), 475–6
Golden Age of Security, 273
Golden Age of Viennese Jewry, 345
goldene shikse, 381
Golden, Harry, 11
"golden years" (of Nazi rule), 526
Goldhagen, Daniel J., x, xiv, 39, 508, 510, 529
Goldschmidt, Moritz von, 307
Gomel, 298, 304

Göring, Hermann, 516, 518, 523, 527, 529
Gorky, Maxim, 423, 426, 451
Gospels, 30–1
Goy (Goyim), 5, 7, 28, 54, 73. *See also* Other
  Nations
goyim nakhes, 54
goyishe kop, 178
Graetz, Heinrich, 90, 91, 139–42
Grand Dukes (Anglo-Jewish), 241
Grand Rabbi (of France), 229–30
grands boulevards, 217
Grant, Ulysses S., 262–3, 317
Great Britain. *See* Britain
Great Depression (1873–1894): compared to
  later depression, 100–1, 156; in Germany,
  106; in Hessenland, 153–4; in France, 207;
  easing after early 1890s, 274; in U.S., 375.
  See also capitalism; industrialization
Great Sanhedrin, 49–50
Greece (Greek, Greeks), 27–9, 71–2, 72, 74, 80
Gregory the Great, 37
Gresham, Walter Quinton, 375
Grey, Lord, 415
Grose, Peter, 417
grossdeutsch, 409. *See also kleindeutsch*
Gründerjahre, 118–20
Guesde, Jules, 175
Günther, Hans F. K., 523
Guttmann, Hugo, 491
Gypsy, 82, 95

Haas, Ludwig, 393
Habsburg Empire, Monarchy (Habsburgs),
  183–205, 338–9. *See also* Austria; Austro-
  Hungarian Empire; Budapest; Franz-Joseph;
  Hungary, Vienna
Haggada, 437
halakha, 49, 73
Halévy, Daniel, 210
"half-Jews," 32
Ham, 72
Händler, 259, 403–4
Handlin, Oscar, xx
Hanfstängl, Helene, 494
"Hang the Kaiser!", 409
Hanisch, Reinhold, 491n
"happy Galut," 238, 252
Harden, Maximilian, 138
Harmsworth, Alfred, 358
Harrison, Benjamin, 376
hasidism (hasid, hasidic), 22, 53–4, 56, 140,
  184, 311, 377. *See also* ultra-Orthodox
Haskala, 42–3
Hassgesang gegen England, 394
Hay, John, 372
Headlam-Morley, John, 412
"healthy invalid," 187
"Hear, O Israel!", 400
Hearst, William Randolph, 358
Hebrew Bible. *See* Old Testament
"Hebrews" (in reference to modern Jews),
  376, 404

hegemony, 56–7. *See also* assimilation; junkerization

Heine, Heinrich, 90, 91, 127, 141

Helden, 259, 403–4

Herder, Johann Gottfried von, 84–5, 117, 140, 266

Hereditary Genius, 92–3

Herzl, Theodor: on positive role of anti-Semitism, 125; reaction to Dühring, 160; meeting with Plehve, 297; belief in Jewish financial power, 303; rails against Jewish defects, 320–1; overview of life, 323–30; compared to Lueger, 340; Lloyd George his lawyer, 416; sees Jews as provoking persecution, 421; sees Jews as natural conservatives, 426; seen as "repulsive" by Trotsky, 427

Hess, Moses, 90–1, 141, 322–3

Hesse (Hessenland), 153–4

Heydrich, Reinhard, 528

Higham, John, 253n

High German, 54

Hillel, 33

Himmler, Heinrich: mocked by Hitler, 493; head of SS, 503; in planning for Holocaust, 518; in Night of Long Knives, 521–2; opposed to *Reichskristallnacht*, 527; role in Holocaust, 528

Hindenburg, General Paul von: victory at Tannenberg, 396; persuades kaiser to dismiss chancellor, 401; figurehead for Ludendorff, 403; broad appeal after WW I, 459; appointment of Hitler as chancellor, 513; declining health, 521; death, 522

Hippocrates, 74

Hirsch, Baron de, 282

"historic" (and "historyless") peoples, 180–1, 183, 266, 313, 407

History of the Jews, 139–40

Hitler, Adolf: as historic personality, xx–xxi; description of Jew as "exact opposite" of German, 4; as failing to stop rise of Jews, 22; borrows from Egyptian tales, 28; "eyes opened" in Vienna, 182; on Lueger, 343, 345, 347; relation to Nietzsche, 348; sexual fears of, 381; alleged fear of "asiatic deeds," 434; derided by Mussolini, 461–2; obscure corporal in 1919, 482; as "German Mussolini," 483–4; genesis and evolution of his anti-Semitism, 484–6, 487–500; character traits, family background, 486–9; as leader of Nazi Party, 498–503; and Geli Raubal, 499–500; declining health, 500–1; as "weak dictator," 502–3; his "uniqueness" and corruption by power, 505; as ruler of Germany, 505ff.

Hitler, Klara, 488–9, 499

Hitler's Willing Executioners, xii

Hobson, J. A., 355, 362–4

Hochdeutsch, 54

hoffähig, 187

Hofstadter, Richard, 259

Hohenzollern, 111, 338

Holocaust: recent interest, ix–xiv; issue of Jewish responsibility, 10; as part of God's plan, 15; issue of causality, 16; in Intentialist-Functionalist debate, 497; deniers, 507, 509; incomprehensibility of, 507, 509–10, 530–1; decision to kill Jews, 528; as culmination of German history, 530. *See also* Final Solution; Goldhagen; Hitler; Third Reich

Home Rule (in Ireland), 250, 357

homo economicus, 366

homosexuals, 503

honeymoon years, 57, 179–80, 315, 322

Honoratioren, 153, 276, 342. *See also* elites, notables

Hook, Sidney, 5

Horthy, Admiral, 459, 464

Hôtel Talleyrand, 212

Howells, William Dean, 374–5

House, Colonel, 411, 417

Hughes, H. Stuart, 24

Hugo, Victor, 92, 224

Huguenot, 130

humanism (humanistic, humanitarian), 81, 169, 197, 200–2. *See also* Enlightenment; liberalism; universalism

humors (bodily fluids), 74

Hungary: ritual murder trial, 203; as "new Jerusalem," 238; overview, 263–71; Magyar enclave in Romania, 309; pro-Magyar Jews, 407; treatment at Paris Peace Conference, 409, 410; soviet republic in, 410, 435. *See also* Austro-Hungarian Empire; Budapest; "historic" peoples; Magyar

Hussain, Sherif, 419

Hyndman, Henry, 363

Ibn Khaldun, 72

"ideologies of revenge," 14

ideology (as independent, self-generating force): in Chrysostom, 35; in German ideologists of anti-Semitism, 126–57; Schönerer's lack of familiarity with anti-Semitic ideology, 203; French ideologists of anti-Semitism, 221–7; decline of anti-Semitic ideology in France, 234; compared to material determinants, 235; interplay with other factors, 239; failure to develop in Britain, 250; power of anti-Semitic ideology in Wilhelmine period, 336; influence of Chamberlain's book, 351–2; anti-Semitic ideology vs. totalitarianism, 514; concluding remarks, 536–7, 542, 543. *See also* fantasy; *Integrationsideologie*; modern anti-Semitism; "rising tide"

il bienno rosso, 469

Il Duce. *See* Mussolini

Il Popolo d'Italia, 469

"immigrant gifts," 252

immigration: to France, 235; to English-speaking lands, 239–40; to Britain, 244, 250–1; to the United States, 252–4; Founding Fathers' hostility to, 257. *See also* Ostjuden; population

immiseration, 175
imperialism, 83, 358, 362–3, 421, 440
Indo-European, 85
industrial workers. *See* proletariat
industrialization: in Russia, 65–7, 70, 282–4;
    German Jews benefit from, 115; described
    by Marr as fundamental problem, 127; as
    seen by Marxists, 159; as seen by Saint-
    Simon, 167–8; "second industrial revolu-
    tion," 274–5. *See also* capitalism; financiers;
    Great Depression; modernism
"Infamous Decrees," 50
Inner City (of Vienna), 490
Inquisition, 75
insincere anti-Semitism, 224, 335, 341, 345–6,
    357, 493–4
integral nationalism (France), 207, 333
Integrationsideologie (unifying power of anti-
    Semitism): in Berlin Movement, 147; in
    France, 219, 222; in Romania, 307; in
    Lueger's following, 339, 342; imperialism
    serving as, 358; in WW I, 405; continued
    ineffectiveness after WW I, 459; anti-Semi-
    tism divisive rather than unifying, 522. *See
    also* ideology; *Sammlungspolitik*
Intentionalists, 497, 518, 519, 524–5
intermarriage, 247, 472, 534, 543. *See also*
    assimilation; "disappearing"
International Peace Conference (The Hague),
    301
Iran, 85
Ireland (Irish), 240, 243, 261, 262, 357, 378
Irish Home Rule, 250, 357
Iron Cross, 491
Isaac, 4
Isaacs, Rufus, 356
Israel (Israeli), 309, 326. *See also* Arab; Jacob;
    Palestine
Istóczy, Győző, 269–70
Italy (Italian): sympathies for Romania, 311,
    313; inspiration to Hess, 323; Austrian simi-
    larities, 338; war in Abysinnia, 358; riots
    against Italian immigrants, 377; reaction to
    Paris Peace Conference, 410–11; opposition
    to Balfour Declaration, 420; factory occupa-
    tions, 1920, 470; Jews in, 471–6; Fascism as
    solving long-standing problems, 477–8; Ital-
    ian and German national character com-
    pared, 508
Ivanhoe, 93

Jabotinsky, Vladimir, 398
J'accuse!, 232
Jacksonian, 201
Jacob, 3–7, 73, 75
Jacobinism (jacobin), 180, 201, 240, 333
James, Henry, 375
James, William, 374
Japan (Japanese), 72, 302, 533, 537
Japheth, 72
Jaspers, Karl, 530
Jaszi, Oszkar, 404

Jaurès, Jean, 25, 158, 224–5, 233, 236–7, 394–5
Jefferson, Thomas (Jeffersonian), 257, 259,
    374
Jerome (Saint), 37
Jerusalem, 238
Jerusalem Post, 534
Jesuits, 60, 75, 122
Jesus, 30–1, 33, 87, 471. *See also* Christianity;
    deicide
"Jew Count" (*Judenzählung*), 399
"Jewhannesburg," 362
"jewification": seen as part of Jewish drive to
    power, 15; influence of Jews in western civi-
    lization, 19; anti-Semites seek to undo jewifi-
    cation, 22; as seen by Marr, 127, 128; in Aus-
    tria-Hungary, 188–9, 196, 199; as seen by
    Vogelsang, 202; as seen by Schönerer; in the
    United States, 254; used in positive sense,
    331–2; in Wilhelmine period, 335; in Jewish
    "spirituality" in Austria, 340–1; applied to
    Lueger, 346; applied to Kalinin, Lenin,
    433; in eyes of Whites, conservatives, 434;
    Hitler's vision of, 490. *See also* assimilation;
    deicide; destructiveness; Enlightenment;
    "ferment of decomposition;" rise of the
    Jews; *Verjudung*
Jewish anti-Semitism. *See* self-hatred
Jewish Chronicle, 251, 367, 369, 395, 398
Jewish Encyclopedia, 244
Jewish Naturalization Bill, 43–4
Jewish self-hatred. *See* self-hatred.
Jewish Syndicate. *See* Syndicate.
Jewish World, 406
Jews (book by Belloc), 434
Jews, Kings of the Epoch, 221
Jidani, 316
Johannesburg, 362
Johnson, Paul, 15n, 21, 158, 419, 447–8
Joseph II, 43, 188
journalism (journals, journalists). *See* press
"judaizing" heresies, 33–4
"Judapest," 189
Juden, die Könige unserer Zeit, 153
Judenhetze, 363
Judenknecht, 346
judenrein, 346
Judenrepublik, 481–2
Judenspiegel, 129
Judenstaat, 325, 329
Judenzählung, 399. *See also* fantasy; military;
    Trotsky
"Judeo-Bolshevism," 388
Julian the Apostate, 34
Junker(s): as dangerous class, 103; Bismarck's
    devotion to, 110–14; threatened by Polish
    nationalism, 122; attacked by Böckel, 155;
    Lassalle's contacts with, 164; Schönerer's
    admiration for, 204; Herzl's admiration for,
    324; Jews entering officer corps, 394. *See also*
    aristocracy; elites; military
"junkerization," 117, 133, 274
Justice, 251

Kabbalah, ix
Kaddish, 209
Kadet Party, 427, 434, 441
Kaganovich, Lazar Moiseyevich, 453, 454
kahillot, 280
Kahn, Hermann Otto, 477
Kahn, Zadoc, 229–30
Kaifeng, 543
Kaiserjuden, 114, 241, 402
Kaiserlingk, Walther von, 424
Kalinin, Mikhail, 433
Kaisertreu, 187
Kamenev, Lev Borisovich, 430, 449, 452
Kamenev, Olga, 430
Kanegisser, Leonid, 445
Kant, Immanuel, 80–1, 353
Kaplan, Fanya, 445
Kapp Putsch, 482
Karaite, 430–1
kashrut (kosher), 44, 55, 65, 226
Katz, Jacob, 87, 509n
Kautsky, Karl, 170, 172, 175, 178–9, 196
Kenner, Hugh, 391
Kershaw, Ian, 511
KGB, 433. *See also* Cheka; secret police
khristos (Christ), 30. *See also* Jesus
Kiev, 61, 301, 305–6, 442
kike, 164, 165
Kishinev, 64, 290–300, 372, 378, 520
Kitchener, Lord, 415
Klaar, Ludwig, 344
Klatzkin, Jacob, 319
kleindeutsch, 192, 409
kleptomania, 217
Knights of Mary Phagan, 383
Knox, Robert, 87–8, 95
Koestler, Arthur, 18, 20
Kogalniceanu, Mihail, 316
kohanim, 73, 75
kosher. *See* kashrut
koyech, 75
KPD (*Kommunistische Partei Deutschlands*, German Communist Party), 435, 481–3, 513, 517
Kraus, Karl, 138, 195
Krautjunker, 114
Krasnaya Gazeta, 445
Kreuzzeitung, 122
Kruger Telegram, 359
Krushevan, Pavolachi, 293–6, 298
Kubizek, August, 486n, 487, 488–9, 490–1, 499
kulak, 428. *See also* peasant
Kulturkampf, 122–3, 197, 214
Kulturvölker, 180

La Croix, 220
Ladino, 313
Lafargue, Paul, 165
La France juive, 223
Lagarde, Paul de, 349–51
La Lanterne, 214
La Libre parole, 226–7, 229, 232

Lamsdorf, Count Vladimir Nikolaevich, 303
Länder, 114
Langbehn, Julius, 261, 349, 350
Langmuir, Gavin, xii
Lansing, Secretary of State, 417, 418
Lanterne, 214
la patrie en danger, 395
La Race Sémitique, 227
Lassalle, Ferdinand, 164, 165, 172
Lassen, Christian, 86
Lateran Accords, 478
Latvia(ns), 444
La Villette, 225–6
la vittoria mulata, 410
Lawrence, D. H., 351
lawyers, 285–6
Lazare, Bernard, 210
Lazarus, Emma, 254, 377
"leading role" (of revolutionary party), 429, 441. *See also* Leninism; Marxism; *stikhinost'*
League to Combat Anti-Semitism, 205
League of Nations, 420–1
League of Patriots, 237
League of the Rights of Man, 237
Lebensraum, 525
lechery (as anti-Semitic charge), 380, 468
Leeds, 399
Leggett, George, 443
Legoyt, Alfred, 95
Lehrs, Samuel, 93
Leidensgeschichte, 15, 16, 17, 18, 60, 62
Lekert, Hirsh, 290
Lenin, Vladimir Ilyich (Leninist, Leninism): partnership with Trotsky, 160; opposition to Bund, 181; theories about proletariat, 283; opposition to war, 401; praises Jews as revolutionaries, 425; rejects independent Jewish workers' party, 428; extreme elitism seen as Russian trait, 429; Jewish ancestors, 432; as "jewified," 433; his ruthless realism, 440; attempts on his life, 445; seen as Jew by Cossack, 447; verbal duels with Trotsky, 449, 451; Mussolini's views of, 466; Lenin and Mussolini compared, 469. *See also* Bolshevik Revolution; Bolshevism; Marxism; social democrat
leprosy, 28
Lessing, Gotthold, 332
Levi, Hermann, 94
Levi, Paul, 435
liberalism (liberal, liberals): in modernization of Judaism, 55, 56–7; Russia's "liberal" experiment, 64–7; "classical" liberalism, 98; in new German state, 107–11; in *Kulturkampf*, 122–5; Marr's experiences with, 129; in Treitschke, 132, 133, 134, 135; timidity in opposing anti-Semitism, 149–50, 151; move of socialism toward, 162; liberal preferences of most German Jews, 169; differences with socialism, 175–6; in Austria-Hungary, 186–90, 339; as criticized by Catholic anti-modernists, 197–200; in English-speaking

liberalism *(Continued)*
lands, 240; English liberalism as model to
the world, 243; in Hungary, 264 (Jewish),
267 (non-Jewish); liberal beliefs shaken
after 1890, 275; "death of liberalism," 277;
meaning in Romania, 316; in Zionism, 320,
324; as corrupt in Austria, 339; in Berlin,
347; in German ideologies, 347–54; changes
in British liberalism, 357; in Russian Revolution, 427; failures of liberalism feed fascism,
481–3; liberalism and modern Jews, 544. *See
also* antiliberalism; Enlightenment; humanism; modernism
Liberal Party (British), 243, 245, 248, 250,
368–9
Liberal Party (Romanian), 311–12, 316
Liberal Unionist secession, 250
Libre Parole, 226–7, 229, 232
Liebknecht, Karl, 400, 402
Liebknecht, Wilhelm, 172
Life and Labour of the People of London, 364
Life of Jesus, 87
Lifton, Robert J., xi
Lillienthal, Max, 238
"limits of representation," 507
lineage. *See yikhus*
limpieza de sangre, 75
Lincoln, Abraham, 262
Linz, 488
Linz Program, 202
Lippmann, Walter, 377
Lipstadt, Deborah, 544
liquor trade, 185, 289–90
lishentsy, 444
Lissauer, Ernst, 394
Lithuania (Lithuanian), 65, 360
"little man," 213, 217, 316, 343, 345. *See also
Mittelstand*
Litvinov, Maxim, 453, 454
Lloyd George, David, 406, 416, 419
Lodz, 64
London, 241, 244, 364, 367–8, 399
London Conference of the RSDWP, 428–9
London Times, 190, 370, 406, 418. *See also* press;
Wickham Steed
longue durée, 11
Longest Hatred, x
Lorraine, 209
Lost in America, 279
Lothair, 249
Louis XVI, 43
Lourdes, 220
"love of Israel" (*ahavat yisrael*), 509
Lowell, James Russell, 374
lower middle class. *See Mittelstand*
loyal opposition, 243
Ludendorff, General Erich von: at Tannen-
berg, 396; efforts to win over Jewish popula-
tion, 397–8; has chancellor dismissed, 401;
de facto ruler of Germany, 403; accuses Jews
of profiting from war, 404; denounces Hitler
for betraying anti-Semitic cause, 493–4

Lueger, Karl: sign of weakening liberalism in
Austria, 176; admired by Hitler, 182; and
Christian Social Party, 203; Jews move into
Vienna while he is mayor, 235; possible
effect on Krushevan, 294; impact of his election on Herzl, 328; career overall, 337–47;
as viewed by Chamberlain, 353
Lunacharsky, Anatoly Vasilievich, 450
Luther, Martin (Lutheran, Lutheranism),
38–9, 108–9, 122, 198
Luxemburg, Rosa, 178–80, 401–2, 429, 435
Luzzatti, Luigi, 475
lycée, 210–11. *See also* schools
lynching, 377, 383–4. *See also* mob; pogrom;
riot

Macaulay, 245, 247
machine gun, 388
Machtergreifung, 510–14
Mack, Julian, 411
Madagascar, 518
"Make Germany pay!", 409
Magyar, 186, 265–6, 309, 407. *See also* Hungary
Maharal, 73
Mahler, Gustav, 353
Makers of the Russian Revolution, 430
Malon, Benoit, 224
mamzer, 73
Manchester, 369
Manchester Guardian, 362
mandarins, 118, 353. *See also* Brahmins; elites
mandates (of League of Nations), 420–1
Manetho, 27–8
Manifest Destiny, 107
Man on Horseback, 216
March on Rome, 468, 471, 480
Margolin, Arnold, 396, 426
Maria-Theresa, 267
Marr, Wilhelm, 126–31
Marrus, Michael, 24–6, 531
Marshall, Louis, 411
martiri fascisti, 468
Martov, Julius, 160, 429, 433
Marx, Herschel (Heinrich), 162
Marx, Julius, 391
Marx, Karl (Marxism, Marxist): interpretation
of Mittelstand, 117; on Jewish background,
159–60; theories in *Anti-Dühring*, 161; theo-
ries about Jews, 162–6, 366; Marxists and
Böckel, 174–5; Marxist theories of national-
ism (Bauer), 180–1; Marx compared to
Vogelsang, 199; Marxism in Russia, 283; atti-
tude to Zionism, 321; Marx compared to
Nietzsche; interpretation of imperialism,
363; Marxist theory and Bolshevism, 439–40;
interpretation of Fascism, 465–6, 501. *See
also* Bolshevism; Lenin; social democrat
Marx, Laura, 165
"Mary's People," 382
maskilim, 43
masses (mass society, mass politics): Treitschke's
revulsion from, 137; yellow journalism, 358;

Adams' revulsion from, 374; Hitler's view of masses, 492. *See also* Americanization; mob; modernism; press; proletariat; rise of the masses; United States
Matteotti Affair, 480
matzo, 36
Maurras, Charles, 228
Max of Baden, Prince, 482
Maxse, Leo, 370, 389
Mayer, Armand, 229–30
Mayer, Arthur, 206
Mayer, Eugène, 214
Mayhew, Henry, 244
May Laws, 69, 287–9, 293
Maze, Jacob, 423
Mehring, Franz: describes Jewish brashness in Berlin, 119; on Treitschke, 136, 138; sees Jews as "intoxicated," 139; speaks of Jewish friendships, 159; radical among social democrats, 178; abrasiveness, 179; sees Jews as awe-inspiring, 193
Meinecke, 462
Mein Kampf, 485, 488–90, 492, 495, 498
Mendelssohn, Moses, 13–14, 44
mentalité, 240, 400
Menshevik, 427, 428, 429. *See also* Bolshevism; Marxism; social democrat
merchants, xx, 61, 64, 167. *See also* capitalists
Merchants of the First Guild, 64, 287
Merchant of Venice, xvi
Mercier, General, 237
meshchane, 61
meshumed, 53–4, 75
messiah (messianic), ix, 31, 32, 327, 426
mestechki, 51
Metternich, 188
Metz Society of Arts and Sciences, 46
Michaelis, Meir, 465
middle class, 41, 117, 189, 242. *See also borghesia;* bourgeoisie; *Bürgertum; Mittelstand*
Mill, John Stuart, 180
military (militarism): Jews in French army 209; Boulanger's reforms of, 216; alleged Jewish traitors in, 226; duel over military honor, 229; seen as fair to Jews, 231; new mass armies, 275; Austrian, 338; Jews in armies of WW I, 394–401; Jews charged with avoiding front-line service in Red Army, 444; Italian Jews, 474, 475–6; Hitler's experiences with, 495. *See also Judenzählung;* Junker
millionaires, 241. *See also* Bleichröder; financiers; rise of the Jews; robber barons; Rothschilds
Milner, Lord, 496
Minelli, Paolo, 273
Ministry of Munition, 406
minority clauses of Paris Peace Conference, 411–12
Mirbach, Count, 446
Mirsky, Prince, 283
Mischkultur, 137

Mississippi, 377
Mithraism, 31
mitnagdim, 54
Mittelstand: in Germany, 116–17; attracted to Stoecker, 145; in Austria-Hungary, 189, 194–5, 201; in France (petite bourgeoisie), 213, 225, 226; in Britain (lower middle class), 241–2; pressure on during WW I, 403, 405; Trotsky sees Jews as stubbornly petty bourgeois, 426–7; proclivity to fascist sympathies, 466
Mizrahim, 329
mob, 233, 276, 383–4. *See also* lynching; mass; pogroms; riots
modern anti-Semitism (racial, political): definition, 97–101. *See also* aesthetic anti-Semitism; antimodernism; "classical anti-Semitism"; Christian anti-Semitism; modernism; objective anti-Semitism; racism; "rational" anti-Semitism; rise of the Jews
modernism (modernity, modernization): role of Jews in, 19–20; in Russia, 57, 64–7; rejected by pope, 97; threat to *Mittelstand,* 117–18; in Marr, 127; in Saint-Simon, 167–8; in Austria-Hungary, 187–9, 200; in Boulanger's political methods, 216–17; in France generally, 237; British and Jews as modernizers, 238; fear of modernism in Russia, 281; western investment in Russia, 290–1; unusual definition in Romania; fear of modernism in Austria, 342; attacked in Germanic ideologies, 347–54; Adams's fear of, 374; WW I as modern, 402–4, 405. *See also* Americanization; capitalism; industrialization; liberalism; modern anti-Semitism; rise of the Jews
Moghilev, 64
Moldavia (Moldavian), 293, 309, 311, 315, 318
Mommsen, Hans, 502, 514, 515–16
Mommsen, Theodor, 103, 134–5, 140, 150, 247, 255
monarchism, 211, 474, 479. *See also* Habsburg Monarchy
"money men," 275. *See also* capitalists; financiers; Rothschilds
Montagu, Edwin, 418
Montagu, Herbert, 414
Mon vieux Paris, 225
Moor, 165
Moravia, 192, 409
Morès, Marquis de, 225–6, 229–30
Morris, William, 353
Moscow Show Trials, 452, 454
Moses, 19, 452
Mosley, Sir Oswald, 458
Mosse, George, 335, 388
Mother Russia, 395, 433
moyekh, 75
mujik, 294
Munich, 436, 495–6
Munich Agreements, 526
municipal socialism, 342–3

Mussolini, Benito: and mutilated victory, 410–11; rejects notion of pure races, 461; attitudes to Jews, 461, 465–8; mocks efforts to define Fascism, 463; salient personal traits, 464–5; warnings to Zionists, 467; experience of racism in Trentino, 473; seen as savior by Italian Jews, 476, 478; lack of clear goals in beginning, 478–9; as solving long-standing Italian problems, 478–9; Hitler's admiration for, 484
Mussolini, Edde, 467
Mussolini, Rachele, 467
mutilated victory, 410–11
mysticism, 83–4, 95, 276
mystique, 237
myth. *See* fantasy; ideology

Namier, Louis, 11, 238
Napoleon I, 48–50, 216
Napoleon III, 216, 315
narodnik, 67, 283
Nathan, Paul, 302, 336
National Anti-Semitic Party (Hungary), 270
National Assembly (in French Revolution), 45, 46
nationalism, 81–2, 83, 180–1. *See also* integral nationalism; Marxism; Pan-Germanism; Slavophile; tribalism; WW I; xenophobia; Zionism
National Liberal Party, 55, 124, 126, 152, 176
National Review, 389
national self-determination. *See* self-determination
"national socialist," 463
National Socialist German Workers Party (NSDAP). *See* Nazism
naturalization, 257
Naumann, Friedrich, 143
naval race (Anglo-German), 359
Navy League, 335
Nazism (Nazi Party, Nazis): Jewish cooperation with, 9; German people victims of, 10; Treitschke's alleged influence on, 133; dismissed as "death rattle," 177; acceptance by German people, 336; and Nietzsche, 348; and Chamberlain, 352; issue of sexual fears, 381; beginnings, 498–503; overview after 1933, 510ff. *See also* Hitler; proto-Nazism
nè aderire nè sabotare, 465
Negro. *See* Africa; blacks; nigger; racism
neoconservatism (neoconservatives), 15, 542
Neue Freie Presse: seen as powerful, 193; controlled by Jews, 194; viewed by Kraus, 195; on Schönerer, 203, 205; Herzl reporter for, 323; opposition to Lueger, 341, 343; article written by Rathenau, 403; Hitler's esteem for, 490–1. *See also* press
Neumann, Josef, 491
Neurat, Baron von, 522–3
Neusner, Jacob, 18
New Economic Policy, 449
New Ghetto, 324

"New Jerusalem," 375
"new right" (in France), 222, 234
New Testament, 258. *See also* Gospels; Paul
New York, 375, 378
Nicholas I, 56, 61–2, 63, 280
Nicholas II, 63, 279, 287, 288, 301–5, 436
niddah, 55
Nietzsche, Friedrich, 184, 319, 348
"nigger," 164, 165, 447. *See also* Africa; black; racism
Night of the Broken Glass, 527
Night of the Long Knives, 500, 517, 521–2
Nivelle Offensive, 406
Noachide Laws, 49, 151
Noah, 49, 72
Nobel Prize, 21, 205
nobility (nobles), 192, 267, 324. *See also* aristocracy; cavalier; elites; Junker
Nolte, Ernst, 434, 542
"non-Jewish Jew," 430, 433, 441–2. *See also* "jewification"; Dzerzhinsky
Nordau, Max, 7, 330
Nordbahn Railway lines, 205
Nordic race, 473. *See also* Aryan
Northcliffe, Lord, 358, 359
"no support, no sabotage," 465
notable (notables), 98, 216, 237, 276
Nothnagel, Hermann, 205
Notre Jeunesse, 236
nouveaux riches, 119, 194. *See also* capitalists
Novoe Vremia, 437
Nuremberg Laws, 522–5
Nuremberg war crimes tribunal, 530
obshchina, 168
"objective anti-Semitism," xviii, 307. *See also* fantasy; ideology; modern anti-Semitism
Odessa, 64, 66
officers (military). *See* military
Okhrana, 443. *See also* secret police
"old fighters," 516, 517–18
Old Testament, 4, 6, 7, 258, 365. *See also* Esau; Jacob; religion
Oliver Twist, xvi, 92, 93
Olympic Games (Berlin), 526
"On the Jewish Question," 163, 366
Oppenheimer, Ernest, 360–1
Oppenheimer, Franz, 58
Opportunist party (France), 211, 212, 216, 218, 219
Order No. 11, 262–3
Order of the Red Eagle, 394
Orthodox (Judaism): interpretation of history, 15; hostility to Napoleon's Sanhedrin, 49–50; move toward Reform, 54–5; ritual observance and modern industry, 65; pro-toracist notions, 72–4, 75; relations with Catholics, 123; *halakhic* view of non-Jews, 150–1; French Jews' rejection of, 210; Orthodox rabbis' cooperation with tsarist authorities, 286; in relation to Zionism, 329; in Galicia, 338; as viewed by Langbehn, 349; as seen by German Jews in U.S., 376–7;

Orthodox revolutionary, Steinberg, 428. *See also* Old Testament; *Ostjuden*; separatism; ultra-Orthodox
Orthodoxy (Russian, Greek), 59
Ostjuden: premodern conditions of, 51–2; in Russian Empire, 57–67, 279 ff. ; attacked by Glagau, 120; attacked by Treitschke, 138; Marx's view of, 164; attitudes to socialism, 168–9; R. Luxemburg's attitudes to, 180; Bauer's attitudes to, 181; attitudes to German culture, 184; in France, 209–10, 218, 250–1; in the United States, 252–4, 375–6, 377; in Hungary, 265, 268; in South Africa, 360, 363; in Britain, 361, 364–5, 365–6, 366–8; German soldiers' reactions to, 398; Hitler's encounters with, 490. *See also* Galicia; Pale of Settlement; Poland; population growth; rise of the Jews
Ostovoski, Fernanda, 467
Other Nations (*Goyim*), 7, 13–14, 31
Ottoman Empire. *See* Turkey
Our Mutual Friend, 93
Ovazza, Carla, 475
Oxford, 249, 250

paganism (pagan), 29–30. *See also* Nietzsche
Pale of Settlement, 60–4, 307, 396, 428
Palestine (Palestinian), xxi, 238, 325, 416, 418, 420. *See also* Arab; Balfour; Balfour Declaration; Turkish Empire
Palestinian Mandate (of League of Nations), 420–1
Pall Mall Gazette, 246
Palmer, Attorney General Mitchell, 435
Panama Scandal, 226–7
Pan-Germanism, 202–5, 473. *See also* German; nationalism; Schönerer
Pan-German League, 335
Paris, 208, 209–10, 211, 217, 223–5, 264
Paris Peace Conference (1919), 408ff., 420, 469
Paritätsfrage, 333
Parkinson's disease, 500
parliament (parliamentarism), 242–3. *See also* Constituent Assembly; National Assembly; Reichstag; Third Republic; Weimar Republic
partitions (of Poland), 60
Partito nazionale fascista, 479
Partito Popolare, 469
party of movement (France), 211, 228–9
party of order (France), 211, 228–9
Passover, 27–8, 36, 38, 437
Patai, Raphael, 5, 75
"patriarch of anti-Semitism," 127
patrie, 260
patrie en danger, 394
patriotism. *See* Burgfrieden; nationalism; WW I; *Union sacrée*
Paul (Saint), 30–1, 32–3
peace resolution (of Reichstag), 401, 410
peace settlement (WW I), 406–13
peasantry (peasants): in Pale of Settlement, 61; hired by Jews, 63; dealings with Jewish

arondators, 66; in pogroms of 1881, 68–9; and Böckel, 152–5; socialist attitudes to, 174–5; in Austria-Hungary, 189; in France, 214, 220, 235; in Russia, 281, 282, 285, 287, 292, 294, 376; in Romania, 307, 318
peddlers, 218, 261, 343
Péguy, Charles, 210, 227, 236–7
Peixotto, Benjamin, 317
Pentateuch, 44
People of Plenty, 255
Permanent Revolution, 449–50
personality (role in history), xx–xxi, 231–2, 233; 536, 541–2
Petrograd, 436–7
Petrograd Soviet, 430, 437. *See also* soviet.
"petty bourgeois elements," 452
petty (petite) bourgeoisie. *See Mittelstand*
Phagan, Mary, 381
Pharisees, 31–3
philo-Semitism: among liberal reformers, 52; in Poland, 59; in Marr, 127; in Engels, 159; in social democratic movement, 159, 177; literary evidence, 227; in Péguy, 236; in America, 259; in Prince Urussov, 299; in leading British politicians, 413–16
philosophes, 43
Piarist fathers, 189
Picquart, Georges, 233, 236, 541
Piedmont-Sardinia, 474
Pilgrims, 373
Pilsudski, Josef, 464
pimp, 66
"pimp pogrom," 284–5
Pinsker, Leon, 323
Pius IX, 198
Place de la Concorde, 212
Platten, Fritz, 445
Plehve, Vlacheslav, 296–7, 326, 520
pluralism, 252, 254–5
Po'alei Zion, 329, 428
Pobedonotsev, Konstantin, 282
pogroms: in 1881, 67–9; in 1903–6, 283–4, 284–5, 290–300; in U.S., 378; after WW I, 388; in Britain, 399; Stalin suggests a "pogrom" in the party, 428–9; *Reichskristallnacht*, 527. *See also* lynching; mobs; riots
Poincaré, Raymond, 234
Poland (Poles): Jewish migration in early modern times, 59; special problem for tsarist authorities, 62; "inexhaustible cradle" (of Jews), 138; percentage of Poles in Habsburg Empire, 191; May Laws and, 288; site of WWI battles, 396; German occupation of, 397; increase in anti-Semitism after 1914, 406–7; Red Army marches on, 436; Dzerzhinsky's background in, 442; as example of anti-Semitism without Jews, 537. *See also* Congress Poland; Galicia; *Ostjuden*; partitions; Polish Corridor
Polish Corridor, 409
political anti-Semitism. *See* modern anti-Semitism

"politics in a new key," 204. *See also* modernism
politique, 236
pope, 122, 198, 540
popolari, 469–70
population (growth, decline, comparative statistics): as aspect of rise of Jews, 21–2: comparative Jewish populations, 57–8; Pale, 60, 63–4; Germany, 106; Jewish ownerships of banks, 115; Vienna, 188; Budapest, 189, 264; Austria-Hungary, 191–2; France, 208, 211 (Paris); Britain, 241, 244, 251, 356; Hungary, 263–4, 267; Russia, 280–1, 287–8; Romania, 314, 318; Atlanta, 385; Jews in British military, 395; population decline in Poland, 396; Jews in Russian military, 396–7; casualties at the front, 398; war-time movement out of Galicia, 406; in Italy, 472. *See also* immigration; rise of the Jews
populism: in Russia, 67–8; move to Marxism, 283; Lueger, 339; in U.S., 379–80, in Italy, 469–70. *See also* Christian socialism; democratic radicalism; Fascism; "little man;" peasant; socialism
Posen, 60, 62, 120, 122
Potter, David, 255
Pound Era, 391
powerlessness, 17–18
Pravda, 430, 431, 445, 454
Preobrazhensky, Yevgenii, 449
press: liberal press in hands of Jews, 115–16; campaign against Jews, 120–3, oversensitivity of Jewish press,138–9, 144; Jewish press and Crash of 1873, 193–4; Jewish press in eyes of Vogelsang, 199; Catholic press in France, 220; anti-Semitic press in France, 226; popular press in belle époque, 275; Jewish control of in U.S, 302; seen as power in Romania, 315; Hearst press, 358; Lord Northcliffe, 358; favorable to Jews in U.S., 372, 376–7; Jewish press favorable to negotiated peace, 402; Russian press hails civil equality for Jews, 437; Jewish press allegedly makes up Nazi atrocity stories, 520–1. *See also* Drumont; *Neue Freie Presse*
Preuss, Hugo, 483
Preussische Jahrbücher, 132
"prince of the cranks," 380
Pritchard, J. C., 92
privilege, 201
"pro-Boers," 361–2
Progressive Party (German), 55, 125, 126, 148, 152; 401. *See also* liberalism
proletariat (proletarian, proletarianization): Jewish proletariat, 65; and P. Singer, 172; in Austria-Hungary, 189; in France, 217–18, 219; de Morès and, 225–6; in Russia, 282–4; importance in war economy, 403, 405; Jewish-proletarian alliance, 405; as presumed beneficiaries of Bolshevik Revolution, 425; proletarian revolution, 436, 439–40; rising numbers of proletarians among Soviet

leaders, 454; Italy as "proletarian" nation, 469 *See also* industrialization; Lassalle; Lenin; Marx; mass
Promissory Oaths Act of 1871, 247
Prophet Armed, 171
prophetic tradition, 171
prostitution (prostitutes), 64, 66, 93, 284, 368
Protektion, 185
Protestantism (Protestant), 59, 149–50, 155, 166, 258, 338. *See also* Luther
proto-Fascism, 216, 327, 329–30
proto-Nazism: opening remarks, xiv; in Treitschke, 132–3; in Stoecker, 142–3, 145–6; in Böckel, 155–7; in von Schönerer, 204–5; in de Morès, 225–6; in Germanic ideologies, 348–54
Proudhon, Pierre-Joseph, 166–7
Provisional Government (Russian), 437–9
Prussia (Prussian): and Polish partitions, 60; and German unification, 110–11, 113–14; as *Fahrradler*, 123; misgivings about Prussian leadership, 134; 154; admired by Schönerer, 204; compared to French military, 230; Prussophilia of German Jews, 154, 332, 333; hated by de Lagarde, 350. *See also* Bismarck; Germany; Hohenzollern; Junker; *Rechtsstaat*
PSI (*Partito Socialista Italiano*), 465, 469–70, 476, 484
psogos, 34–5
Pulzer, Peter, 119
Purge Trials, 452, 454
Purishkevich, 395, 436–7
Puritans, 258
Pushkin, 79
Putsch. *See* Beer Hall Putsch; Kapp Putsch

Queiroz, Eça de, 138
quietism, 7, 17. *See also Leidensgeschichte*
Raaben, von, 296
race (racism, racist): general discussion of, 70–96; Marxism and, 160–1; Jewish "racial solidarity" in Austria-Hungary, 190; Catholic opposition to, 198; in Schönerer, 201–5; "race" as used by French Jews, 210; appeal to the French, 218–19; in Drumont's thought, 225; "four races" of British nation, 243; racism in Britain, 247; racism in U.S., 261–2, 376; Jewish racism in Hungary, 266; concluding remarks on the issue to Part Two, 271; Russian peasants' lack of racism, 292; Krushevan's use of the concept of race, 293; in Hess, 322; in Herzl, 324; in L. Wolf, 330; as seen by German Jews, 332; rejected by Lagarde, 350; in Chamberlain, 352–3; racism in American German Jews, 376; Twain's view of Jewish race, 377; racism revived after WW I, 388; negligible racism in Italy, 473. *See also* Disraeli; Hess; Hitler; modern anti-Semitism; Nazism
Races of Mankind, 95
Race Sémitique, 227

racial anti-Semitism. *See* modern anti-Semitism; race
Radek, Karl, 179, 432, 452, 454
"radiant days of May," 475
Radical Party (France), 216, 217–18, 230, 236
Radomyslsky (Zinoviev), 430
railroads, 119, 194, 205, 217, 221
rape, 291
"rational" anti-Semitism, 156, 494–5, 523, 527
ras, 479
Rasputin, 305, 436
Rathenau, Walther, 400, 402–4, 410, 483
Raubal, Geli, 499–500
Rauschning, Hermann, 492, 493
Ravitch, Norman, 30
Raw Materials Section, 403–4, 406
rebbe, 184
Rebecca, 3, 4, 6 (mother of Esau and Jacob); 93 (character in *Ivanhoe*)
Rechtsstaat, 113, 134, 154
Red Army, 407, 436, 444, 446
Red Terror, 436, 440–8. *See also* Cheka
Reformation, 38–9
Reform Judaism, 54–5, 123, 258, 261
Reformjuden, 125
Reformvereine, 202
Reichsfeinde, 111
Reichskristallnacht, 527
Reichsrat, 186
Reichstag, 110, 126, 149
Reichstag fire, 517
Reichswehr, 513, 518. *See also* Hindenburg; Junker; military; Prussia
Reinach, Solomon, 210
Reinharz, Jehuda, 332
religion: (its role, power in history): introductory remarks, xv–xvii; biblical imagery, 6; in eyes of Enlightened thinkers, 41, 65; in German political life, 122–4; as "diseased," 130, 161; ambiguous role among Hessian peasants, 155; as interpreted by Dühring, Marx, 161; religions in Austria-Hungary, 184; role in Britain, U.S., and Hungary compared, 239; in America, 258; concluding remarks on the issue to Part Two, 270; Catholic religion and anti-Semitism in Italy, 471; concluding remarks, 533. *See also* Catholicism; Christianity; fantasy; modern anti-Semitism; Orthodox Judaism; Protestantism; Reform Judaism; Russian Orthodoxy; ultra-Orthodox
religious anti-Semitism. *See* modern anti-Semitism; religion
Rembrandt als Erzieher, 348–9, 350
Renan, Ernst, 87–8, 92, 227
Renaissance, 89
reparations, 409–10
Representative, 380
Revisionism, 178
revolution (revolutionary, revolutionaries): in Russia, 67–70; revolutionary right, 222; Jews as revolutionaries, 284, 285, 388, 398, 401–2, 423–55; revolution in West, 436, 449–50,

470; "failed revolution" in Germany, 481–2; as seen by Brownshirts, 502; as *Gleichschaltung,* 515; "second revolution" in Germany, 517; Jews seen as revolutionaries by Hitler, 524. *See also biennio rosso;* Bolshevik Revolution; Bolshevism; destructiveness; French Revolution; Lenin; Marx; Permanent Revolution; Revolution of 1905; Russian Revolution; social democrats; Trotsky
"revolutionary defeatism," 401
Revolution of 1905, 302–5
"revolver press," 194. *See also* press.
rhetor, 34
Rhineland (remilitarization), 526
Riah, Solomon, 93
Rieffenstahl, Leni, 522
Riesser, Gabriel, 129, 132
"right belief" vs. "right action," 109, 340
"right to rule," 215, 272
riot (riots, rioting), 67–9, 377–8, 398–9. *See also* Kishinev; pogrom
rise of the Jews: introductory remarks, xix–xx, 20–3; origins in Poland, 60; in Germany, 104, 106, 114–16, 132; in Austria-Hungary, 187–90, 197; in France, 206–13, 215; Zola's concern about, 232; Dreyfusard attitude to, 235; in U.S., 254, 374; in Hungary, 263–5; concluding remarks on the issue to Part Two, 271–2; in Russia, 279–82; as seen in Russo-Japanese War, 302–4; as aspect of Zionism, 330; in Wilhelmine Germany, 331, 337; in Vienna, 345; in German officer corps, 394; in new political power after 1917, 438; in Italy, 471–3; concluding remarks, 532, 533, 537–8. *See also* "fighting back"; population growth; Zionism
rise of the masses, 276–7. *See also* mob
"rising tide" (of anti-Semitism): opening remarks, xiv; moderation of prewar anti-Semitism, 156–7; confusion of German anti-Semites, 333, 334; in regard to Lueger, 348; in U.S., 383; after 1914, 387; concluding remarks, 506–7. *See also* "gathering storm"; proto-Nazism
Riskin, Shlomo, 534
Ritter, Gerhart, 108
ritual murder, 36, 203, 224, 270, 281, 305
ritual slaughter (*shehita*), 226
robber barons, 194
Robinson (locksmith friend of Hitler), 491
Rogers, Will, 520
Röhm, Ernst, 502, 503, 517–18, 521. *See also* Brownshirts; Night of the Long Knives
Romania (Romanian), 119, 263, 292, 306–18
romanticism (romantic), 83–4. *See also* antiliberalism; antimodernism; belle époque; Germany
Rome and Jerusalem, 322
Rome (Romans, Roman Empire), 4–5, 30–3, 34, 72, 80, 310, 468. *See also* Catholic; Fascism; Italy; pope
Roosevelt, Franklin Delano, 262

Roosevelt, Theodore, 372–3
Rosenberg, Alfred, 493, 498
Rosenfeld (Kamenev), 430
Ross, E. A., 380
Roth, Cecil, 474
Roth, Philip, 16
Rothschilds: Lionel, 77, 246; Meyer Carl, 103; legendary wealth, 115; invited to Vienna by Metternich, 188; as symbol of concentrated wealth, 201; hated by left-wing Jews, 202; financial empire, 212; banquet for Gambetta, 214; and Union générale, 215; works in France denouncing them, 221; Drumont's accusation of bribery, 225; among English millionaires, 241; Nathan, 246, 247; visit by Gladstone, 248; efforts to isolate Russia, 302; Baron James, 315; debts owed by Napoleon III, 315; threaten to leave Vienna if Lueger elected, 341; Baron Albert, 344; seen as powerful by Hobson, 355; attacked by working-class leader, 361; Balfour Declaration to Lord Rothschild, 418; aided Cavour, 474. *See also* conspiracies; financiers; Syndicate
Roumania. *See* Romania
RSDWP. *See* Russian Social Democratic Workers Party
Rubenstein ("friend" of Wagner), 94
Rudolf, Crown Prince of Austria-Hungary, 205
Ruhr, 483, 526
Rumania. *See* Romania
Ruppin, Arthur, 523
Russia (Russian): overview, 56–70, 279–306; reactions to war in 1914, 395–7; Trotsky's esteem of Russian culture, 447; "logic" of Russian history compared to German, 512. *See also Ostjuden;* Pale of Settlement; Russian Revolution; social democrat
Russian Orthodoxy, 59
Russian Social Democratic Workers Party, 428. *See also* Bolshevism; Marxism; Mensheviks; social democrats
Russian Revolution, 436–9. *See also* Bolshevik Revolution
russification, 58
Russo-Japanese War, 275, 302
Ruthenia (Ruthenian), 183, 191, 407

SA (*Stumabteilung*). *See* Brownshirts
Sachar, Howard Morley, 308, 510
Sacred Union, 395
Sadducees, 31, 33
Second Congress of Soviets, 430
"saint of the revolution" (Dzerzhinsky), 442
Saint Paul. *See* Paul
Saint-Simon, 167–8
Salisbury, Lord, 361, 363
Sammlungspolitik, 358. *See also Integrationsideologie*
Samuel, Sir Harry, 369
Samuel, Herbert, 414

Sanhedrin. *See* Great Sanhedrin
Sanscrit, 85–6
Sarfatti, Cesare, 465
Sarfatti, Margherita, 465, 467–8, 476, 484
Sarfatti, Roberto, 476
Satmar Rebbe, 22
scandals, 213–15, 226–7, 263. *See also* financiers; *Gründerjahre;* stock market
Schapiro, Leonard, 429
Schiff, Jacob H., 302–3, 373, 435, 520
Schiller, 332
Schirach, Henriette von, 494
Schlageter, 468n
Schlamperei, 185, 341
Schlegel, Friedrich von, 85–6
Schmidt, Karl, 293, 296
Schönerer, Georg Ritter von, 200–5, 488, 489
schools (schooling), 189, 210–11, 214, 275, 285
Schorske, Carl, 204
Schutzstaffel (SS), 503, 521
Schwartz, Father, 488
Schweitzer, Albert, 351
science, 79–80, 85–6, 94, 349–51
Scott, Sir Walter, 93
"scramble for Africa," 358
Second Empire, 211
"second industrial revolution," 274–5
"second revolution" (in Nazi Germany), 517–18
secret police, 284, 429, 443, 454
secularism. *See* Enlightenment; humanism
Segrè, Dan Vittorio, 475, 476
self-determination of peoples, 408–9, 411. *See also* nationalism
self-hatred ("self-hating Jews"): charge against Spinoza, Koestler, 20; common in West, 91; in Marx, 165–6; in R. Luxemburg, 179; Zionist theme, 234–5; charge against Marxists, 321; in Herzl, 324–5; in Trotsky, 444, 446–7; charge by Dawidowicz, 509
self-made men, 261
Semitism (Semite, *Semitentum*): compared to religious terminology, 6; linguistic origins, 23, 85–90; used by Marr, 129; used by Treitschke, 131; in Böckel, 155; Semitic appearance,173; in Austria-Hungary, 190–1, 196; in Schönerer's thought, 203; application to Toussenel's thought, 222; Barrès's use of, 223; Drumont's use of, 225, 260; *La Race Sémitique*, 227; in reference to Disraeli, 249; in Istóczy's proto-Zionism, 269; in Austria, 340; in Chamberlain, 354; Karaites not Semites, 431. *See also* Aryan; modern anti-Semitism; race
separatism (Jewish): as viewed by Spinoza, Koestler, 20; viewed by French revolutionaries, 47; liberal criticism of, 134–5; as viewed by Fourier, 167; as viewed by Lenin, 181; as viewed by Lazare, 210; in the U.S., 253–4, 257, 375; in Russia, 281; in Herzl's thought, 324–5; in Galicia, 338; issue in British discussion of *Ostjuden*, 367, 368; in Anne Frank,

531; concluding remarks, 532, 533, 543. *See also* Orthodox Judaism; *Ostjuden*; Pale of Settlement, particularism; Romania; tribalism; xenophobia
Sephardim (Sephardic): in France, 45–6, 47; preoccupation with lineage, 75; seen as more cultured, 137–8; in Britain, 244; in U.S., 256; in Romania, 311, 313; in Italy, 472. *See also* Ashkenazim
Sergei, Grand Duke, 396
Serrati, Giacinto, 479
Seton-Watson, R. W., 307–8
Seven Canaanite Nations, 49
sexism, 10
sexuality, 380–1, 468
SFIO (Section Française d'Internationale Ouvrière), 435. *See also* Jaurès, *Union sacrée*; socialism
sha'atnez, 65
shabbesgoy, 428
"shabbesgoyim of the bourgeoisie," 402
Shakespeare, xvi
Shaw, G. B., 158, 351
Shcheglovitov, I. G., 305
shehita, 226
Shem, 72, 166
sheytl, 52
shikse, 381
Shlyapnikov, Alexander, 432–3
shock troops, 266
shohet, 270
Sholem Aleichem, 3, 5, 257
Sholokhov, Mikail, 444
shopkeepers: threatened by department stores, 115; Marxist attitude to, 170; in Vienna, 189; in Paris, 217–18; attitudes to Drumont, 225; and conservative movement in France, 234. *See also* "little man;" *Mittelstand*
Show Trials (Moscow), 452, 454
shtadlan, 327
shtetl: in adjustment to modernism; 13; denigrated in West, 51; compared to villages, 61; Trotsky's view of 62–3; contrasted to big cities, 118n, 119; values conducive to socialism, 168; "a paradise full of saints," 279
Shulgin, V. V., 289, 541
Sidonia, 76–7
Sieg des Judenthums über das Germanenthum, 127
Siegfried, 350
Simon, Ernst, 393
Simonyi, Istvan von, 329
Sinai, 73
Singer, Isaac Bashevis, 8, 279
Singer, Paul, 159, 171–2, 177, 179
Slaton, John M., 382
slavery (slaves), xx, 80, 81, 261–2. *See also* "white slavery" (prostitution)
Slav (Slavs, Slavic): and Herder, 84; seen as inferior, 112–13; blend as Jews do not, 130; in Habsburg Empire, 183, 184, 191, 195–6
Slavophiles, 281. *See also* nationalism

Slovakia. *See* "historyless" peoples
Smith, Goldwyn, 249–50
smuggling, 289–90
social Darwinism: relation to Darwin's theories, 82–3; in relation to Jews, 92–3, 95; in Marr 130; in Bebel's words, 173; and French Jews' "destiny," 215; in Donnelly's work, 380. *See also* modern anti-Semitism; race
social democrats: in Germany, 134, 143, 147–8, 152, 169–74, 177–80, 273–4, 276, 393–4, 482, 512; in Austria, 175–7, 196, 203, 339; in Russia, 181, 428–9; attitude to Lueger, 346; in Poland, 442. *See also* Bolsheviks; Russian Social Democratic Workers Party; socialism; SPD
socialism (socialists): Jewish attraction to, 14; overview, 158–180; French socialist victories in 1893, 230; Jaurès, 233; and Zionists, 329; municipal socialism in Vienna, 342–3; and WW I, 393–4; French socialists and Bloc national, 435; Italian Socialist Party (PSI), 465, 469–70. *See also* anarchism; Marxism; SFIO; social democrats
"socialism of fools," 175, 223
Socialism in One Country, 450
Socialist International, 393–4
social question, 143. *See also* capitalism; Christian socialism; industrialization; liberalism; modernism; socialism
Socialist Revolutionary Party (Russia), 427–8, 441, 445, 446
Society of Atheists (Russia), 445
Sodomite, 381
Sokolnikov, Grigory, 431–2
Soll und Haben, 93
Solomons, Ikey, 93
Sombart, Werner, 259
Somme, 398
Sonderweg, 104, 157, 244, 252, 334–7. *See also* exceptionalism
Sonnino, Sidney, 475
South Africa, 239–40, 242, 359–64
Souvarine, Boris, 435
soviet(s), 435–7, 438–9, 440–1, 495–6. *See also* Bolshevik Revolution; Communist International; Hungary; revolution
soznanie, 283
Spain (Spanish), 75, 358, 372
Spanish-American War, 358, 372
Spartacus Uprising, 436, 482
SPD (*Sozialdemokratische Partei Deutschlands*): denounced by Wilhelm II, 134; seen as main problem by Stoecker, 143; supported working masses, 147–8; attitudes to Jews, 152, 169–74, 175–80; emerges from outlawed status, 273; parliamentary delegates support negotiated peace, 401. *See also* social democrats
"special path," 104. *See also* exceptionalism; *Sonderweg*
species being, 163
Speer, Albert, 493n

Spiesser, 341
Spinoza, Baruch, 20, 41, 545
spirituality (alleged Jewish lack of), 340, 498.
    See also Luther; Protestant; "right belief"
squadristi, 480
SS. *See Schutzstaffel*
"stab in the back," 410
Stadt ohne Juden, 135n
Stahl, Julius, 125
Stalin, Josef: condemns Bauer's ideas, 181; sug-
    gests a "pogrom" in the party, 428–9; stature
    in party before 1921, 432; his alleged anti-
    Semitism, 448–9, 452–5; power struggle,
    448–53
standard of living debate, 200
State Department (U.S.), 417–18
"state worship," 241, 522. *See also* Prussia;
    Rechtsstaat; Treitschke
Statue of Liberty, 254, 377
Steed. *See* Wickham Steed
Stein (Jew known to Hitler at front), 491
Steinberg, I. N., 428
Steiner, George, 20n
Stern, Fritz, 276, 347
Sternhell, Zeev, 215
stikhinost', 283
stock market, 119, 120–1, 144, 194, 215, 362.
    See also capitalists; financiers; Great Depres-
    sion
Stoecker, Adolf, 142–7, 198, 342
Stolypin, Peter, 304, 305
Storm troops, 482. *See also* Brownshirts
Strasser, Gregor, 518
Streicher, Julius, 523, 524, 530
Strousberg, Hirsch, 119
Sturmabteilung, 482
subterranean anti-Semitism. *See* "Dormant
    Period"; underground existence
Sudetenland, 409, 526. *See also* Bohemia,
    Moravia
suffering servant of the Lord, 8, 9
survival (of Jews). *See* assimilation; "bloodless
    Holocaust"; "disappearing"; intermarriage
Suttner, Bertha von, 205
Sverdlov, Yakov Mikhailovich, 431
Svetlana (Stalin's daughter), 453
"sweet exile," 239, 532–3
Syllabus of Errors, 97, 198
syndicalism, 479. *See also* anarchosyndicalism
Syndicate (Jewish), 212, 224, 231. *See also*
    Alliance Israélite Universelle; conspiracies;
    financiers
synoptic Gospels, 30–1
Széchenyi, István, 268

"table talk," 494, 501
Talmud: injunction to kill best Gentiles, 36;
    separatism from idolators, 38; criticized by
    Enlightenment, 42; caused "degeneration"
    of Jews, 43; ignored by Mendelssohn, 44;
    wickedness of Jews partially due to, 46; pro-
    toracism in, 72–3; and Noachian Laws,

151–2; references in Toussenel, 221; Jeffer-
    son's attitude toward, 257; referred to by B.
    Webb, 365; and Karaites, 430–1
Tannenberg, 396
technocratic modernism, 167–8
Temporary Laws, 69
terrorism, 284, 290, 301, 436. *See also* assassina-
    tion; Black Hundreds; Cheka; pogroms; Red
    Terror
"terrorist squads," 284
"Testament" (Lenin's), 451
Tevye, 3
Thanksgiving Day (1905), 373
The Jews, 434
thermidorian, 449
The Times (of London). *See London Times*
Third Reich, 506–31. *See also* Nazism
Third Republic, 206, 211–12, 214, 219, 226–7,
    230
Three hundred men, 403
Three Hundred Years of Jewish Life in America,
    xx
Tirpitz, Admiral, 359
Tiszaeszlár Affair, 270
Tivoli Program, 335
Tolstoy, 166
totalitarianism, 480–1, 507–8, 514
totalitario, 480–1
Tory Democrats, 199, 249
Toussenel, Alphonse de, 221–2
Transvaal Republik, 359, 362
Transylvania, 309, 313
Treaty of Brest-Litovsk. *See* Brest-Litovsk
Treaty of Versailles, 409–10, 482. *See also* Paris
    Peace Conference
Treitschke, Heinrich von, 126, 131–142, 145,
    146, 184, 250
Trentino, 473
trials: Dreyfus, 231–7; Tiszeszlár, 270; Beilis,
    305–6; Frank, 381–5. *See also* Show Trials
tribalism (tribalistic), 71, 334–7. *See also* mod-
    ern anti-Semitism; nationalism; racism; sepa-
    ratism; xenophobia
triumphalism, 338–9
Triumph of the Will, 522
Triumvirate, 449
Trier, 162–3
Trollope, Frances, 259
"Trozky doctrine," 435
Trotsky, Leon: memories of childhood, 58,
    62–3; partnership with Lenin, 160; as mod-
    ern prophet, 171; contempt for U.S., 257;
    on Romania, 307; described as "revolution-
    ary genius," 423, 446; sees Jews as unrevolu-
    tionary, 426–7; unusual background, 428;
    "major figure" in Russian Revolution, 430;
    denounced by Palmer, 435; leads attack on
    Warsaw, 436; in first Bolshevik government,
    438; criticizes overrepresentation of Jews in
    Cheka, 444; role in Red Army, revolution,
    446–8; power struggle with Stalin, 448–53; as
    "failed" historical personality, 543

tsedaka, 112, 168, 376, 426
Tucholsky, Kurt, 400
Tugan-Baranowsky, Professor, 282n
Turkey (Turks, Turkish Empire), 249, 267, 309, 413, 414, 417
"turnip winter," 405
Twain, Mark, 377
typhus, 396

Uitlanders, 359–60
ukaz, 68
Ukraine (Ukrainian), 183, 191, 442, 443
ultra-Orthodox, 15, 24
underground existence (of anti-Semitism), 234. *See also* "Dormant Period"
Unglück, 350
Uniate, 183
Union générale, 215
Union of American Hebrew Congregations, 317
Union of the Russian People, 300–1, 304
Union sacrée, 395
"uniqueness" (of Holocaust), 510, 540. *See also* exceptionalism; *Sonderweg*
unitary nationalism. *See* integral nationalism
United Opposition, 452
United States: "all nations" become "one race," 238; overview, 251–63; in eyes of German Jews, 333; in pre–WWI period, 371–85; intervention in WW I, 407–8. *See also* Americanization; "bloodless Holocaust"
universalism: contrasted to tribalism, 71; in Kant, 81; in Herder, 84; in Renan, 87; in nineteenth-century Jews, 91; in socialism, 160, 169; rejection in belle époque, 277. *See also* Enlightenment; humanism; liberalism; tribalism
"unpolitical" Germans, 347–54
unsociability (Jewish). *See* separatism
Uritsky, Moisei Solomonovich, 431, 442, 445
Urussov, Prince, 288–9, 294, 296–7, 298–300, 304
Ustrugov, 293, 296
Utilitarians, 248

Valens, 34
Valentinian, 34
vaterlandlose Gesellen, 134
Vecchi, Cesare De, 479
Verbürgerlichung, 178
Verdrossenheit, 392
Verdun, 398
Verelendung, 175
Vergangenheitsbewältigung, 535
Verjudung (*verjudet*), 184, 331. *See also* "jewification"
Vermauschlung, 138
Vernunftrepublikaner, 482
Versailles, Treaty of, 409–10, 482. *See also* Paris Peace Conference
victim (victimization, blaming the victim), 9–10, 15, 530, 535–6

Victoria (Queen), 77, 243, 246, 273, 358
Vienna: Hitler in, 182, 489–91; Rothschilds invited to 188; dominated by Jews, 189–90; Jews move into even under anti-Semitic mayor, 235; Lueger and, 337–47. *See also* Austro-Hungarian Empire
Vietnam (Vietnamese), 72
Vilna, 290
Vivian Grey, 322
Vogelsang, Baron Karl von, 182, 198–200
Volk, 201
völkisch, 334. *See also* tribalism
Volksgeist, 84–5, 117, 140
Volksgemeinschaft, 525
Volkseele, 140
Voltaire, 12, 42
Wagener, Otto, 487, 503
Wagner, Cosima, 416
Wagner, Richard (Wagnerian): and Jewish artists, 89; his experiences with Jews, 93–4; Jews "came to us" too soon, 126; compared to Marr, 127–8; Jews interested in art only to make money, 260; ridiculed by de Lagarde, 350; Chamberlain's relationship to, 353; Hitler's admiration for, 489
Waldeck-Rousseau, 236
Wales (Welsh), 406, 416
Wallachia, 309, 311, 313, 315
"wandering Jew," 452
Wandervögel, 277
War Against the Jews, ix–x
War and Peace, 166
War Communism, 449
War in South Africa: Its Causes and Effects, 362
war (Jewish interest in): Boer War, 360–3; Jewish role in financing WW I, 402–3; "war socialism," 403. *See also* military; WW I
Warsaw, 264, 284
Washington, Estelle, 380
Washington, George, 256
"water-Pollack Jew," 164, 165
Watson, Tom, 381, 383
"weak dictator," 502, 503
Webb, Beatrice Potter, 355, 364–6
Webb, Sidney, 364, 365
Weber, Eugen, 213
Weber, Max, 103, 143
Weimar coalition, 470, 481
Weimar Republic, 401, 470, 481–3
Weizmann, Chaim, 243, 244, 381, 392, 414–19, 420
West Prussia, 122
Whig (Whigs), 240
White, Arnold, 247, 281, 303
"white man's burden," 247. *See also* civilizing mission
Whites (White armies), 407, 434, 436
"white slavery" (prostitution), 66
Why the Jews?, 20
Wickham Steed, Henry, ix, 190, 193–4, 346, 370, 437–8

Wilhelm I, 125, 314–15
Wilhelm II (Wilhelmian, Wilhelmine): put stamp on era, 273, 347; not a "boring" period, 319; as "Dormant Period" of anti-Semitism, 334–7; period of "Germanic ideology," 347–51; close relation to Victoria, 358; Wilhelm's saber-rattling, 358–9; Wilhelm's words on outbreak of WW I, 391, 393; Wilhelm decorates Lissauer, 394; Wilhelm becomes more anti-Semitic after WW I, 424
Williams, A. T., 367–8
Wilson, Woodrow, 408, 411, 417
Windthorst, Ludwig, 123
Wise, Isaac Mayer, 261–2, 377
Wise, Stephan, 411, 417
Wisse, Ruth, xvii 21
Wistrich, Robert, x, 519
witchcraft, 240–1
Witte, Count, 302, 304
Wolf, Lucien: remarks on "obnoxiousness" of French Jews, 215; meeting with Plehve, 297; efforts against tsarist Russia, 302; article in *Encyclopedia Britannica*, 330, 385; anger at British alliance with Russia, 369–70; role in Paris Peace Conference, 411–12; opposition to Balfour Declaration, 414
Wolf, Simon, 302, 317
working class. *See* proletariat
World War I, 391–422. *See also Burgfrieden; nationalism; patrie en danger; Union sacrée*
"worse-is-better" syndrome, 175
"wretched refuse," 254, 255, 421. *See also Ostjuden*
Wunderrabbiner, 56

xenophobia, 201–2, 217–18, 221, 231, 251. *See also* nationalism; separatism; tribalism
Yagoda, Genrikh, 453
Yankee, 259, 377
Yaroslavsky, Emilian, 445
yellow press, 226. *See also* press
yevrei, 301
Yevseksiia, 444, 445

Yiddish: seen as "barbarous mishmash," 54; distinctions between Jew and non-Jew, 75; *yiddishkayt*, 117–18; Graetz's view of, 140; Marx's mocking of Yiddish accent, 164; as divisive, 181; not recognized as official language in Austria-Hungary, 183, 191–2; Lazarus's attitude toward, 254; Yiddishism in American speech, 254, 261; Luddendorff's proclamations in, 397; alleged lack of word for "war," 399n; and Karaites, 431; Dzerzhinky's knowledge of, 433; Trotsky's attitude toward, 447
yiddishkayt, 118
yikhus, 72, 261, 378n
Yoffe, Adolf, 430–1
Yom Kippur, 209, 362
Zaks's match works, 284
zhidy, 301, 452
Zhitomir, 289
Zinoviev, Grigori Yevseyevich, 430, 431, 449, 451, 452
Zionism (Zionist): diaspora Jews as "objectively detestable," xviii, 9; Jews corrupted by power, 7–8; view of Other Nations as "sick," 14; hostility to Yiddish, 54; similarities of Arabs and Jews, 87; similarities to Treitschke, 136; Bauer's attitudes toward, 181; in interpreting the Dreyfus Affair, 234–5; in Brandeis, 260–1; in Istóczy's thought, 269; attitude toward Romanian anti-Semitism, 307; in Germany, 319–20, 330–1, 337; main lines of development, 320–30; resented by British Jews, 367; "Zionist lessons" in prewar anti-Semitic affairs, 384–5; Zionists' enthusiasm for war, 393; Jabotinsky's complaint about Jewish immigrants, 398; Zionist perspectives reflected in Paris Peace Conference, 412; Balfour Declaration, 413–22; denounced by Mussolini, 467; "Zionism" of Nazis, 523. *See also* assimilation; "disappearing"; "fighting back"; nationalism; rise of the Jews
Zohar, ix
Zola, Emile, 215, 232
Zwangwill, Israel, 415–16